THE BRITISH TRADE UNION DIRECTORY

Other recent current affairs and economics titles from Longman Group UK Limited include the following:

Political and Economic Encylopaedia of the Pacific, edited by Gerald Segal (1990)

Religion in Politics: A World Guide, edited by Stuart Mews (1990)

World Directory of Minorities, compiled by the Minority Rights Group (1990)

Elections since 1945: A Worldwide Reference Compendium, general editor Ian Gorvin (1989)

CPA World Directory of Old Age, compiled by the Centre for Policy on Ageing (1989)

Trade Unions of the World, 1989-90 (2nd edition, 1989)

Western European Political Parties: A Comprehensive Guide, edited by Francis Jacobs (1989)

Reuters Glossary: International Economic & Financial Terms, edited by the Senior Staff of Reuters Limited (1989)

Political Parties of the World (3rd edition), edited by Alan J. Day (1988)

Women's Movements of the World, edited by Sally Shreir (1988)

Revolutionary and Dissident Movements: An International Guide, edited by Henry W. Degenhardt (1988)

Privatization, The UK Experience and International Trends, edited by Robert Fraser (1988)

The World Financial System, compiled by Robert Fraser (1988)

The Radical Right, A World Directory, compiled by Ciarán Ó Maoláin (1987)

THE BRITISH TRADE UNION DIRECTORY

Edited and compiled by
WOLODYMYR MAKSYMIW

Contributors: Jack Eaton and Colin Gill

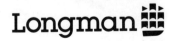

THE BRITISH TRADE UNION DIRECTORY

Published by Longman Group UK Limited, Westgate House,
The High, Harlow, Essex, CM20 1YR, United Kingdom.
Telephone (0279) 442601
Telex 81491 Padlog
Facsimile (0279) 444501

ISBN 0-582-04740-4

British Library Cataloguing in Publication Data

Maksymiw, Wolodymyr
1. Great Britain. Trade Unions
I. Title II. Eaton, Jack III. Gill, Colin, *1945-*
331.88'0941

ISBN 0-582-04740-4

Printed and bound in Great Britain by
Biddles Ltd, Guildford and King's Lynn

CONTENTS

PREFACE

The British Trade Union Directory has been compiled with the intention of providing up-to-date primary information on trade unions. Considerable effort has gone into offering readers not only reliable empirical data but also providing a qualitative analysis of the role of trade unions in the 1980s. The book aims therefore to be comprehensive in its coverage and includes entries for all TUC affiliated unions and the major non-TUC unions up to the time of the 1989 TUC Congress.

It is perhaps worth at this stage outlining in summary the key changes which have affected British trade unions after a decade of Conservative government. Since winning the 1979 general election, the political and industrial map of Britain has undergone quite radical change. The Conservatives' pledge to "curb the power of trade unions" has manifested itself in important legal and economic initiatives. Clearly, however, the key transformation brought about by the government has been in fostering the "entrepreneurial culture", which is at variance with the traditional values of British trade unions.

Dramatic changes have taken place in the labour market. The run-down of the manufacturing industry resulted in a rapid rise in unemployment and major losses to a traditional sector of trade union membership. Greater emphasis has been given to the service sector of the economy, but, because of its fragmented nature and greater reliance on casual labour, it traditionally has not been a successful source of trade union recruitment and organisation. Such changes partly signal a demise in the political influence which unions previously enjoyed. In addition, extensive changes in employment legislation, the introduction of new technologies and more complex patterns of employment have jointly resulted in creating a very different climate in which trade unions have had to operate in the 1980s.

However, it may be suggested that as the 1980s draws to a close there has been a rekindling of interest in trade unions. In 1989, for the first time this decade, a number of major unions recorded a rise in union membership. Furthermore, the summer of 1989 saw a re-emergence of union industrial action on a scale which led some commentators to call it a "summer of discontent".

The extent to which the tide in union affairs may have turned will, of course, be judged by future events. It is a maxim of the trade union movement that it learns from experience. This book contributes to the choices made about future strategy by providing a record of the collective experience of the trade union movement in Britain over the last decade of Conservative government. While the past does not determine the future, it would be reckless to proceed oblivious of the lessons which can be learnt. It is hoped that this book can contribute in some way to that learning process.

Acknowledgements are due to the many union officials, certification officers, colleagues and friends who provided information and offered advice. All tables and membership figures for TUC-affiliated unions are derived from TUC Annual Reports. Except where otherwise stated, non-TUC affiliated unions supplied their own membership figures. Special thanks are owed to Barbara Henderson for her patience and dedication in reading the entire manuscript several times as well as her encouragement and support.

Wolodymyr Maksymiw   *December 1989*

London Exchanges

From 6th May 1990 all London telephone codes will be altered.

Simply look through the numbers listed below, to find the first three digits of the present telephone number.

The new code is printed beside these first three digits. For example, 01-434 0000 will become 071-434 0000 and 01-666 0000 will become 081-666 0000.

In the 081 area, to call another number in the 081 area just dial the last seven digits.

To call a number in the 071 areas, dial the 071 code first.

In the 071 area, it will be the same procedure: just the seven-digit number for a call within the 071 area, or 081 first if calling a number in the 081 area.

When calling from outside the new areas, dial 071 or 081 as appropriate, instead of the current 01 code.

If you have any trouble finding a number on the table call the BT enquiries number **free**:

0800 800 873

1st 3 digits of your no.	Your new code	1st 3 digits of your no.	Your new code	1st 3 digits of your no.	Your new code	1st 3 digits of your no.	Your new code	1st 3 digits of your no.	Your new code	1st 3 digits of your no.	Your new code	1st 3 digits of your no.	Your new code	1st 3 digits of your no.	Your new code	1st 3 digits of your no.	Your new code
200	081	238	071	272	071	312	081	351	071	386	071	432	071	468	081	504	081
202	081	239	071	273	071	313	081	352	071	387	071	433	071	469	081	505	081
203	081	240	071	274	071	314	081	353	071	388	071	434	071	470	081	506	081
204	081	241	071	276	071	316	081	354	071	389	071	435	071	471	081	507	081
205	081	242	071	277	071	317	081	355	071	390	081	436	071	472	081	508	081
206	081	243	071	278	071	318	081	356	071	391	081	437	071	473	071	509	081
207	081	244	071	279	071	319	081	357	071	392	081	438	071	474	071	511	071
208	081	245	071	280	071	320	071	358	071	393	081	439	071	475	081	512	071
209	081	246	071	281	071	321	071	359	071	394	081	440	081	476	071	514	081
210	071	247	071	283	071	322	071	360	081	397	081	441	081	478	081	515	071
214	071	248	071	284	071	323	071	361	081	398	081	442	081	480	071	517	081
215	071	249	071	286	071	324	071	363	081	399	081	443	081	481	071	518	081
217	071	250	071	287	071	325	071	364	081	400	071	444	081	482	071	519	081
218	071	251	071	288	071	326	071	365	081	401	071	445	081	483	071	520	081
219	071	252	071	289	071	327	071	366	081	402	071	446	081	484	071	521	081
220	071	253	071	290	081	328	071	367	081	403	071	447	081	485	071	523	081
221	071	254	071	291	081	329	071	368	081	404	071	448	081	486	071	524	081
222	071	255	071	293	081	330	081	370	071	405	071	449	081	487	071	526	081
223	071	256	071	294	081	332	081	371	071	406	071	450	081	488	071	527	081
224	071	257	071	295	081	335	081	372	071	407	071	451	081	489	071	529	081
225	071	258	071	297	081	336	081	373	071	408	071	452	081	490	071	530	081
226	071	259	071	298	081	337	081	374	071	409	071	453	081	491	071	531	081
227	071	260	071	299	081	339	081	375	071	420	081	455	081	492	071	532	081
228	071	261	071	300	081	340	081	376	071	421	081	456	081	493	071	533	081
229	071	262	071	301	081	341	081	377	071	422	081	458	081	494	071	534	081
230	071	263	071	302	081	342	081	378	071	423	081	459	081	495	071	535	081
231	071	265	071	303	081	343	081	379	071	424	081	460	081	496	071	536	071
232	071	266	071	304	081	345	081	380	071	426	081	461	081	497	071	537	071
233	071	267	071	305	081	346	081	381	071	427	081	462	081	498	071	538	081
234	071	268	071	308	081	347	081	382	071	428	081	463	081	499	071	539	081
235	071	269	071	309	081	348	081	383	071	429	081	464	081	500	081	540	081
236	071	270	071	310	081	349	081	384	071	430	071	466	081	501	081	541	081
237	071	271	071	311	081	350	071	385	071	431	071	467	081	502	081	542	081

1st 3 digits of your no.	Your new code	1st 3 digits of your no.	Your new code	1st 3 digits of your no.	Your new code	1st 3 digits of your no.	Your new code	1st 3 digits of your no.	Your new code	1st 3 digits of your no.	Your new code	1st 3 digits of your no.	Your new code	1st 3 digits of your no.	Your new code	1st 3 digits of your no.	Your new code
543	081	586	071	636	071	679	081	731	071	778	081	839	071	888	081	944	081
544	081	587	071	637	071	680	081	732	071	780	081	840	081	889	081	946	081
545	081	588	071	638	071	681	081	733	071	783	081	841	081	890	081	947	081
546	081	589	071	639	071	682	081	734	071	785	081	842	081	891	081	948	081
547	081	590	081	640	081	683	081	735	071	786	081	843	081	892	081	949	081
549	081	591	081	641	081	684	081	736	071	788	081	844	081	893	081	950	081
550	081	592	081	642	081	685	081	737	071	789	081	845	081	894	081	951	081
551	081	593	081	643	081	686	081	738	071	790	071	846	081	897	081	952	081
552	081	594	081	644	081	687	081	739	071	791	071	847	081	898	081	953	081
553	081	595	081	645	081	688	081	740	081	792	071	848	081	900	081	954	081
554	081	597	081	646	081	689	081	741	081	793	071	850	081	902	081	958	081
555	081	598	081	647	081	690	081	742	081	794	071	851	081	903	081	959	081
556	081	599	081	648	081	691	081	743	081	796	071	852	081	904	081	960	081
558	081	600	071	650	081	692	081	744	081	798	071	853	081	905	081	961	081
559	081	601	071	651	081	693	081	745	081	799	071	854	081	906	081	963	081
560	081	602	071	653	081	694	081	746	081	800	081	855	081	907	081	964	081
561	081	603	071	654	081	695	081	747	081	801	081	856	081	908	081	965	081
562	081	604	071	655	081	697	081	748	081	802	081	857	081	909	081	968	081
563	081	605	071	656	081	698	081	749	081	803	081	858	081	920	071	969	081
564	081	606	071	657	081	699	081	750	081	804	081	859	081	921	071	974	081
566	081	607	071	658	081	700	071	751	081	805	081	861	081	922	071	976	071
567	081	608	071	659	081	701	071	752	081	806	081	863	081	923	071	977	081
568	081	609	071	660	081	702	071	754	081	807	081	864	081	924	071	978	071
569	081	618	071	661	081	703	071	755	081	808	081	866	081	925	071	979	081
570	081	620	071	663	081	704	071	756	081	809	081	868	081	927	071	980	081
571	081	621	071	664	081	706	071	758	081	820	071	869	081	928	071	981	081
572	081	622	071	665	081	707	071	759	081	821	071	870	081	929	071	983	081
573	081	623	071	666	081	708	071	760	081	822	071	871	081	930	071	984	081
574	081	624	071	667	081	709	071	761	081	823	071	874	081	931	071	985	081
575	081	625	071	668	081	720	071	763	081	824	071	875	081	932	071	986	081
576	081	626	071	669	081	721	071	764	081	826	071	876	081	933	071	987	071
577	081	627	071	670	081	722	071	766	081	828	071	877	081	934	071	988	081
578	081	628	071	671	081	723	071	767	081	829	071	878	081	935	071	989	081
579	081	629	071	672	081	724	071	768	081	831	071	879	081	936	071	991	081
580	071	630	071	673	081	725	071	769	081	832	071	881	081	937	071	992	081
581	071	631	071	674	081	726	071	770	081	833	071	882	081	938	071	993	081
582	071	632	071	675	081	727	071	771	081	834	071	883	081	940	081	994	081
583	071	633	071	676	081	728	071	773	081	835	071	884	081	941	081	995	081
584	071	634	071	677	081	729	071	776	081	836	071	885	081	942	081	997	081
585	071	635	071	678	081	730	071	777	081	837	071	886	081	943	081	998	081

Printed by kind permission of
British Telecommunications plc
Registered Office: 81 Newgate Street, London EC1A 7AJ
Registered in England No. 1800000.

TUC
TRADES UNION CONGRESS

Address: Congress House, Great Russell Street, London WC1B 3LS

Telephone: 01-636 3040

Telex: 268 328 TUC G

Fax: 01-636 0632

Principal officers
General Secretary: Norman Willis
Deputy General Secretary: John Monks
Assistant General Secretaries: Roy Jackson; David Lea, OBE

Heads of departments
Economic: Bill Callaghan
Equal Rights: Kay Carberry
Finance: Colin Page
International: Mike Walsh
Management Services and Administration: Mike Jones
Organisation and Industrial Relations: Brendan Barber
Social Insurance and Industrial Welfare: Peter Jacques
Trade Union Education: Alan Grant

Journal: TUC Bulletin (monthly)

Membership

Current membership (1987)
Male: 5,935,252
Female: 2,861,940
Total: 8,797,192

Membership trends

	1979	1983	1987	change 1979-83	1983-87
Men	8,625,627	7,720,161	5,935,252	−10%	−23%
Women	3,546,881	2,361,983	2,861,940	−33%	21%
Total	12,172,508	10,082,144	8,797,192	−17%	−13%

General Council committees
Finance and General Purposes;
Economic;
Education and Training;
Social Insurance and Industrial Welfare;
Equal Rights;
Trade Union Education;
European Strategy;
Employment Policy and Organisation.

Industrial committees
Construction;
Energy;
Financial Services;
Health Services;
Hotel, Catering, and Tourism;
Local Government;
Printing;
Steel;
Textile, Clothing, and Footwear;
Transport;
Distribution, Food, Drink, Tobacco, and Agriculture.

Joint committees
Arts, Entertainment, and Sports Advisory;
Media Working Group;
Race Relations Advisory;
Public Enterprise;
Public Services;
Trade Councils' Joint Consultative;
Women's.

Regional education offices

Scotland: Larry Cairns, 16 Woodlands Terrace, Glasgow G3 6ED
Telephone: 041-332 2045

Northern: Tom Cook, Swinbourne House, Swinburne Street, Gateshead NE8 1AX
Telephone: 091-490 0048

Yorkshire and Humberside: Malcolm Ball, 1 Navigation Road, Chantry Bridge,
Wakefield WF1 5PQ
Telephone: 0924 375836

North-West: Arthur Johnstone, Baird House, 41 Merton Road, Bootle,
Merseyside L20 7AP
Telephone: 051-933 4403

South-East: Steve Grinter, Congress House, Great Russell Street, London WC1B 3LS
Telephone: 01-636 4030

South-West: David Gover, 1 Henbury Road, Westbury-on-Trym, Bristol BS9 3HH
Telephone: 0272 501989

Wales: Joe Hannaway, 1 Cathedral Road, Cardiff CF1 9SD
Telephone: 0222 27449

Northern Ireland; Frank Bunting, 3 Wellington Park, Belfast BT9 6DJ
Telephone: 0232 681726

West Midlands: Pat Hughes, 10 Pershore Street, Birmingham B5 4RU
Telephone: 021-666 6179

East Midlands and East Anglia: David Marshall, 61 Derby Road,
Nottingham NG1 5BA
Telephone: 0602 472483

Regional councils

Northern: Bob Howard (Secretary), TUC Northern Regional Office, Swinburne House,
Swinburne Street, Gateshead NE6 1AX
Telephone: 091-490 0033

Tom Burlison (Chair), GMBATU, Thorne House, 77-87 West Road,
Newcastle-upon-Tyne
Telephone: 091-273 2321

Yorkshire and Humberside: Paul Jagger (Secretary), Leeds Trade Council Club,
Savile Mount, Leeds LS7 3HU
Telephone: 0532 622872

Reg French (Chair), NUPE, Blackgates House, Bradford Road, Tingley,
Wakefield WF3 1SD
Telephone: 0532 537654

North-West: Alan Manning (Secretary), Baird House, 41 Merton Road, Bootle,
Merseyside L20 7AP
Telephone: 051-933 6067

Ernie Baxendale (Chair), NALGO, 3-5 St Johns Street, Manchester M3 4DL
Telephone: 061-832 5625

West Midlands: Sir David Perris (Secretary), 10 Pershore Street, Birmingham B5 4JD
Telephone: 021-622 2050

Sid Platt (Chair), NALGO, 7th Floor, Centre City, 7 Hill Street, Birmingham B5 4JD
Telephone: 021-643 6084

East Midlands: Christine Wood (Secretary), 61 Derby Road, Nottingham NG1 5BA
Telephone: 0602 472444

Nick Wright (Chair), NUPE, 6 Sherwood Rise, Nottingham NG7 5BA
Telephone: 0602 603522

East Anglia: Ivor Jordan (Secretary), 119 Newmarket Road, Cambridge CB5 8HA
Telephone: 0223 66795

John Cannell (Chair), 22 St Georges Drive, Caister-on-Sea, Great Yarmouth, Norfolk
Telephone: 0493 720185

South-East: Ron Edwards (Secretary), Congress House, Great Russell Street,
London WC1B 3LS
Telephone: 01-636 4030

Andrew Jack (Chair), NALGO Metropolitan, 17 Highfield Road, London NW11 9PF
Telephone: 01-458 9211

South-West: Phil Gregory (Secretary), 1 Hennbury Road, Westbury-on-Trym,
Bristol BS9 3HH
Telephone: 0272 506425

Albert Bennett (Chair), 107 Cotehele Avenue, Keyham, Plymouth, Devon
Telephone: 0752 51574

Wales: David Jenkins (Secretary), Transport House, 1 Cathedral Road,
Cardiff CF1 9SD
Telephone: 0222 372345

Elwyn Morgan (Chair), c/o Wales TUC, Transport House, 1 Cathedral Road, Cardiff
CF1 9SD
Telephone: 0222 372345

Commonwealth Trade Union Council (CTUC)
Congress House, Great Russell Street, London WC1B 3LS
Telephone: 01-631 0728 or 636 4030 ext. 290
Fax: 01-436 0301
Telex: 266006 CTUC G

Northern Ireland Committee (ICTU)
NI Officer: Terry Carlin
Assistant to NI Officer: Tom Gillen

Address: 3 Wellington Park, Belfast BT9 6DJ
Telephone: 0232-681726

International affiliations
The TUC is affiliated to the International Confederation of Free Trade Unions
(ICFTU), the European Trade Union Confederation (ETUC), the European Trade
Union Institute (ETUI), the Trade Union Advisory Committee (TUAC) of the
Organisation for Economic Co-operation and Development (OECD), and the
Commonwealth Trade Union Council (CTUC). The addresses of these organisations are
as follows:

International Confederation of Free Trade Unions (ICFTU), Rue Montagne aux Herbes
Potagères 37-41, 1000 Bruxelles, Belgium
Telephone: 010-322 217 8085
Telex: 26785 ICFTU B

European Trade Union Confederation (ETUC), Rue Montagne aux Herbes Potagères 37, 1000 Bruxelles, Belgium
Telephone: 010-322 218 3100
Telex: 62241 ETUC B
Fax: 010-322 218 3566

European Trade Union Institute (ETUI), Boulevard de l'Impératrice 66, 1000 Bruxelles, Belgium
Telephone: 010-322 512 3070

Trade Union Advisory Committee (TUAC) of the Organisation for Economic Co-operation and Development (OECD), 26 Avenue de la Grande-Armée, F-75017 Paris 17e, France
Telephone: 010-331 4267 7780
Fax: 010-331 4754 9828

General
The TUC, which originated in 1868, is the oldest trade union confederation in the world. In January 1989 it consisted of 79 affiliated unions ranging from the tiny Sheffield Wool Shear Workers' Union with 17 members, to the TGWU with over 1.3 million. Its affiliated unions negotiate terms and conditions of work for between 60 to 70 per cent of the total working population. The unions affiliated to the TUC, unlike in many other countries, are not organised along tidy industrial lines, but instead are haphazardly distributed across occupations and industries.

The TUC is primarily a policy-making rather than an executive body; it is a federal body which enables affiliated unions to develop common policies, to regulate inter-union relations, and to benefit from the other services the TUC provides.

Over the years, the total affiliated TUC membership has fluctuated considerably, reaching an all-time peak membership of over 12.1m in 1979 (see "Membership trends"). Since 1979, total membership has witnessed a substantial decline, falling by 28 per cent over the period 1979-87. Figures released at the time of publication reveal that in 1988, TUC membership has continued to decline (see "Appendix 1").

Changes in the number of TUC affiliates

1979: 109
1980: 108
1981: 105
1982: 102
1983: 98
1984: 91
1985: 88
1986: 87
1987: 80

Since the mid-1980s, the pace of mergers and amalgamations between unions has quickened. In 1979 there was a total of 109 unions affiliated to the TUC. This figure had dropped to 102 by 1982 and reached 80 in 1987, representing a drop of 29 in the number of TUC affiliates. A summary of the main union mergers and affiliations since 1982 is set out in "Appendix 2".

In 1987, the 80 affiliated unions represented a total affiliated membership of 8,797,192. The majority of union members are concentrated in the 20 leading unions (see *Table 1*).

Table 1: TWENTY LARGEST TUC UNIONS BY MEMBERSHIP 1979 AND 1987

Union	Total Membership 1979	Union	Total Membership 1987
TGWU	2,086,281	TGWU	1,348,712
AUEW[1]	1,499,534	AEU	815,072
GMWU[2]	967,153	GMB	803,319
NALGO	753,226	NALGO	758,780
NUPE	691,770	MSF	653,000
ASTMS[3]	496,109	NUPE	650,930
USDAW	470,017	USDAW	387,207
EETPU[4]	420,000	EETPU	329,914
UCATT	347,777	UCATT	255,883
NUM	253,142	COHSE	207,841
NUT	248,896	UCW	197,758
CPSA	223,884	SOGAT	193,838
COHSE	212,930	NUT	178,294
UPW[5]	203,452	BIFU	165,839
SOGAT[6]	205,784	NCU	151,407
NUR	180,000	CPSA	149,484
BIFU	132,374	NGA	124,638
POEU[7]	125,723	NASUWT	120,544
NAS/UWT[8]	122,058	NUCPS	118,740
NGA[9]	111,541	NUR	117,594
Total Membership of 20 Largest TUC Affiliated Unions	9,751,651		7,728,794
Total TUC Affiliated Membership	12,172,508		8,797,192

[1] includes all four sections; now AEU
[2] now GMB
[3] now merged with TASS to form MSF
[4] the EETPU was expelled from the TUC at the 1988 Congress
[5] now UCW
[6] now SOGAT '82
[7] now NCU
[8] now NASUWT
[9] now NGA 1982

As *Table 1* shows, there has been very little overall change in composition of the 20 largest unions in the last eight years. The TGWU is still by far the largest union leading its nearest rival, the AEU, by over half a million members. With the notable decline of the NUM and the addition of the NUCPS, there has been remarkably little change in the composition of the leading 20 unions. But whereas in 1979, these unions accounted for some 80 per cent of total TUC membership, in 1987, they accounted for over 88 per cent.

In recent years the orientation of the TUC has altered from being dominated by male, manual workers employed in private sector manufacturing, extracting or heavy engineering industry, to white collar workers, increasingly employed in the expanding service sector of the economy. Women too are becoming more important in trade union recruitment as they are drawn into the labour market. As indicated in "Membership trends", there has been a significant recent increase in female membership rising over 20 per cent between 1983 and 1987.

Table 2 illustrates the leading 20 unions by size and indicates the relative proportion of male and female members.

Table 2: TWENTY LARGEST UNIONS — MALE AND FEMALE MEMBERSHIP, 1987

Union	Total	Male	% Male	Female	% Female
TGWU	1,348,712	1,125,927	83.48%	222,785	16.52%
AEU	815,072	715,072	87.73%	100,000	12.27%
GMB	803,319	551,802	68.69%	251,517	31.31%
NALGO	758,780	384,702	50.70%	374,078	49.30%
MSF	653,000	527,000	80.70%	126,000	19.30%
NUPE	650,930	216,977	33.33%	433,953	66.67%
USDAW	387,207	150,329	38.82%	236,878	61.18%
EETPU	329,914	N/A	N/A	N/A	N/A
UCATT	255,883	253,087	98.91%	2,796	1.09%
COHSE	207,841	44,042	21.19%	163,799	78.81%
UCW	197,758	149,334	75.51%	48,424	24.49%
SOGAT	193,838	137,037	70.70%	56,801	29.30%
NUT	178,294	53,488	30.00%	124,806	70.00%
BIFU	165,839	76,753	46.28%	89,086	53.72%
NCU	151,407	121,618	80.33%	29,789	19.67%
CPSA	149,484	44,837	29.99%	104,646	70.00%
NGA	124,638	117,387	94.18%	7,251	5.82%
NASUWT	120,544	65,144	54.04%	55,400	45.96%
NUCPS	118,740	78,368	66.00%	40,372	34.00%
NUR	117,594	111,635	94.93%	5,959	5.07%

As *Table 2* shows, most of these unions serve a largely male membership. However, six of the 20 unions have a higher proportion of female members — NUPE, USDAW, COHSE, NUT, CPSA and BIFU. NALGO is the only union with an almost equal balance between its male and female members.

If indeed it is the growth of female members which is going to represent the membership recruitment potential for the foreseeable future, unions such as NUPE, NALGO, and USDAW are probably in a stronger position than unions such as the AEU, TGWU, MSF and GMB; although certain unions, such as the GMB and the TGWU with its "Link-up" campaign, have explicitly targeted women in their recent recruitment campaigns.

The decline in membership, brought about by labour market factors, anti-union legislation, restructuring of the economy, the introduction of new technology across a wide range of industries and enterprises, and the trends towards more flexibility in enterprises, has plunged the TUC into crisis. An urgent problem facing the TUC as it enters the 1990s is how to arrest the decline in membership which has taken place during the 1980s.

It was against this background that the 1987 Congress set up the Special Review Body with wide-ranging powers to tackle not only the problem posed by the single-union, no-strike agreements, and the maverick actions of the EETPU (see **EETPU**), but also how the decline in union membership could be arrested and to examine the role and function of the TUC itself.

History

The TUC came into being in 1868, when the Manchester and Salford Trades Council convened the first of a series of annual meetings of trade unionists at the Mechanics' Institute, David Street, Manchester.[1] The meeting was held for four days from June 2-6, 1868, and was attended by 34 delegates representing, it was claimed, 118,367 members. There had been earlier attempts to form a national forum of trade unionists, notably the Grand National Consolidated Trade Union of the 1830s and the Association of United Trades for the Protection of Labour of 1845. The early TUC leaders were by no means committed to a revolutionary philosophy. They were cautious, craft-orientated, and concerned to secure trade unionism within a liberal capitalist society whose fundamental values they did not challenge. Indeed, prominent trade union leaders identified themselves with the Liberals, and there were even secret deals with Liberal Party politicians and employers. As Vic Allen noted: "They accepted their conventions and, with undying gratitude, their patronage, and they sought and accepted responsible, respectable advice. The willingness to accept advice was a willingness to conform."[2] The early years of the TUC were characterised by the perceived need to gain favourable legislation on trade union affairs.

The growth of "new unionism" amongst unskilled workers in the 1880s and 1890s led to a wave of new affiliations to the TUC, and these newly affiliated unions brought with them more aggressive socialist based policies which were also shared by many younger craft unionists. Despite the resistance of the older generation of TUC leaders changes were forced upon them. In 1889 the General Federation of Trade Unions was established by Congress in order to provide a much more co-ordinated approach to industrial action, and in its early days it assumed a greater importance than the TUC itself. However, only a minority of unions joined it, and in time it deteriorated into no more than a defensive mutual insurance for unions — particularly the smaller ones. The GFTU still exists today, and its principal function is to provide research and educational facilities for its affiliates and make representations to government departments on matters of importance to its collection of smaller trade unions.

In 1900 the Labour Representation Committee was also set up, which converted itself into the Labour Party in 1906. The creation of a separate wing of the trade union movement meant that the TUC itself was not involved in direct parliamentary lobbying. The activities of the TUC and the Labour Party were co-ordinated by a joint board, consisting of representatives of the parliamentary committee (set up in 1871 to effect the political lobbying of the TUC), the GFTU, and the Labour Representation Committee.

In 1920 the TUC underwent a major reform following the experiences of the railway strike the previous year. The parliamentary committee was replaced by the General Council elected from affiliated unions which were divided into 17 trade groups, with an additional group for women's representation. The General Council was seen as a co-ordinating centre for the whole trade union movement, providing a more dynamic means of pursuing trade union objectives generally. It consisted of 32 members, with nominations for elections to each trade group on the General Council confined to unions on each group, but voting for seats to be taken up by the whole affiliated membership.

This system of General Council representation lasted until 1981 when Congress finally approved changes and abandoned the increasingly archaic trade group structure of election (see "General Council"). The powers of the General Council were further extended in 1924 and 1928, and embodied in Rules 11, 12, and 13.

Relations with affiliated unions

Relations with affiliated unions are largely governed by Rules 11, 12, and 13 of the TUC constitution. Rule 11 pledges affiliated unions to keep the General Council informed of any major dispute in which they may become engaged, either with employers or amongst themselves. If a peaceful settlement appears likely the General Council cannot intervene, unless requested to do so, but in the event of a major breakdown in negotiations it may give advice to the unions involved. If the advice is accepted and a strike or lock-out results then the General Council "shall forthwith take steps to organise on behalf of the organisation or organisations concerned all such moral and material support as the circumstances of the dispute may appear to justify."[3] Thus the TUC has the powers of co-ordination but it does not threaten the autonomy of its affiliated unions.

The contradictory nature of Rule 11 was exposed during the 1926 General Strike, the first and only occasion when the powers of the TUC to lead industrial action on behalf of the whole trade union movement were tested. While the General Council was able to conduct the General Strike it had no power to effect an agreement to end the miners' dispute. In 1971 the TUC came close to sanctioning strike action against the Industrial Relations Bill, and came within a few days of a general stoppage over the imprisoned dock workers in 1972. It is difficult to imagine circumstances that would place the TUC in a position to call a general strike.

The employment legislation of the 1980s has also played its part in downgrading the TUC's ability to call a general strike, as any such action or calls for it could be considered unlawful under provisions which in effect prohibit sympathy or secondary strike action. Even in the face of a blatant attack on the right to belong to a trade union, as happened when the government prohibited trade unions at GCHQ in 1984, the TUC was unable to mount any effective campaign in support of what might be considered as a fundamental right. In announcing "GCHQ Day" the TUC was at pains to impress that this was not a call for industrial action and "cannot constitute a call for general strike action", for fear that it might be seen as being outside the framework of the law.

Rule 12 gives the General Council its main powers to deal with inter-union disputes by insisting on the submission of all such conflicts to the TUC disputes committee, holding in reserve the threat of suspension or disaffiliation to secure respect for its recommendations. Rule 12 was adopted in 1924 together with a number of "main principles" governing "trade union practice" in order to avoid inter-union competition for members; these were extended and improved at the 1939 Bridlington Congress. The "Bridlington Principles" urge unions to agree on spheres of influence, recognition of cards, conditions of transfer, etc.; to find out whether applicants for membership are, or have been, members of another union, and not to accept them if they are in arrears, "under discipline", or involved in a dispute; and to refrain from recruiting amongst a grade of workers in an establishment where another union already organises or has negotiating rights for the majority. The disputes committee acts initially in a conciliatory manner, but if it is unable to effect an agreement it will make an award. If the party to a dispute fails to carry into effect the award then the matter is eventually dealt with under Rule 13 which covers the conduct of affiliated organisations.

In 1985 Rule 12 was revised following a single-union agreement between the EETPU and Hitachi. Although sole negotiating rights had never been prohibited unions were required to take account of the interests of other unions when attempting to negotiate exclusivity of representation. The revision meant that single-union agreements were effectively restricted to green-field sites where no prior union recognition existed. But Ford's decision to locate a new plant at Dundee in March 1988, while the Special Review Body was in session, demonstrated the difficulty of defining a green-field site.

The Special Review Body, composed of 21 General Council members, reported its findings in *Meeting the Challenge* to the 1988 Congress which formally adopted the report. The recommendations included: extending the role of the TUC in regulating inter-union relations by establishing a code of conduct whereby any union contemplating a single-union agreement is asked to notify the TUC for approval and guidance which enables the TUC to ensure that other interested unions are aware of the deal; and an explicit prohibition of no-strike agreements: "unions, when making recognition agreements, must not make agreements which specifically remove, or are designed to remove, the democratic lawful rights of a trade union to take industrial action in advance of recruitment of membership and without consulting them. If faced with an employer insisting on such procedures the union should consult the TUC."

Whether these recommendations will solve the problem of inter-union disputes, particularly those concerned with single-union/no-strike agreements which have thrown the TUC relations with its affiliates into turmoil, remains to be seen.

Rule 13 empowers the General Council to investigate the conduct of any affiliated organisation if it is considered "that the activities of such organisation may be detrimental to the interests of the trade union movement or contrary to the declared principles or delcared policy of the Congress"[4] and, if necessary, to suspend its membership until the matter has been considered fully at the next Congress. Failure to comply with an award made under Rule 12 eventually leads to consideration under Rule 13. The final sanction of expulsion is reserved for Congress itself.

This power was used to expel the Electrical Trade Union in 1961 after the serious malpractices of the union's communist leadership had been exposed by the courts, and also in 1972 against a number of unions who failed to deregister in accordance with Congress policy towards the Industrial Relations Act. The expulsion of the EETPU in 1988 was also under Rule 13. Currently the TUC is also deliberating the future of BALPA under Rule 13 after its alleged involvement with a breakaway cabin crew currently organised by the TGWU (see **BALPA**).

Relations with government

The TUC's involvement with government really developed during the Second World War. Shortly after the start of the war the Prime Minister directed all government departments to consult with the TUC before taking any action on matters likely to effect workers' interests. The TUC's involvement was reinforced by the appointment of Ernest Bevin as Minister of Labour and National Service in 1940. In subsequent years the complex structure of councils, boards, and committees which was created to advise the government on industrial policy was mainly of a tripartite character, with the TUC treated as an equal partner with the central employers' organisations.

In 1963 the TUC joined the most important body on which it is represented, the National Economic Development Council, which dealt with long-term planning objectives including the economy, industrial matters, and industrial relations. The NEDC has in membership six representatives each from government, trade unions, and employers, and seven independents from state banks and major state industries. In 1976 the NEDC machinery was developed further by the setting up of 37 sector working parties (SWPs) to cover various branches of the economy. The NEDC used to meet 10 times a year and the expanded system was seen by the TUC as a major arm of government. However, whilst these SWPs were originally seen as a means of implementing the Labour government's so-called "industrial strategy", in practice they lacked any authority to control the activities of major multinational corporations within their ambit, and at company level there was a total failure to implement the practice of planning agreements as envisaged by the 1975 Industry Act.

Following the 1978-9 "Winter of Discontent", and the subsequent election of the Thatcher government, the TUC found that its reliance over the years on an increasingly bureaucratic, inward-looking strategy which was wholly committed to the conventional lobbying system in the corridors of Whitehall was shown to be a failure. During the 1970s the TUC appeared to be building up an "empire" and to be exercising more power because of its acceptance into the power structure of government, but this was no more than a façade. The harsh economic and political climate, engendered by the pursuit of monetarist policies by a government hostile to the very existence of trade unionism, could not be overcome solely by relying on the involvement of the TUC in the trappings of the decision-making apparatus of government.

During the 1980s the TUC has been increasingly ignored by the Thatcher government, and it has searched without success for a new role. The TUC did decide to withdraw from the NEDC in protest at the government ban on trade union membership at GCHQ in 1984, but the protest was short-lived and it returned to the NEDC before the end of the year. Later on, the government itself decided to downgrade the NEDC, by announcing major changes to its structure and also reducing the frequency of the meeting from 10 times a year to four. Now, instead of focusing on subjects such as macroeconomic policy, unemployment, inflation, and pay determination, the emphasis is on supply-side issues such as skill shortages and small businesses.

TUC representation is still present on various government agencies (quangos) such as the Health and Safety Commission, the Equal Opportunities Commission, and the Commission for Racial Equality. But the decision taken at the 1988 Congress to withdraw from the government's new Employment Training Scheme for the long-term unemployed contributed further to the erosion of the TUC's involvement in government.

Congress
Congress itself consists of around 1,200 delegates and meets annually on the first Monday in September for five days, invariably at either Brighton or Blackpool. Its functions are to consider the work of the General Council over the previous 12 months, and to elect the General Council for the following year. The proceedings of Congress have frequently been criticised for being little more than a television show-piece dominated by the General Secretaries of the major unions, and the debates, which are concerned mainly with government policy, have not kept up with the pace of the decline in the union's political influence in the 1980s. This criticism is at last being considered seriously by the Special Review Body as part of its wide-ranging remit to examine and make recommendations on the future role and direction of the TUC (see "TUC in the 1990s").

It is extremely rare for General Council policies to be overturned by Congress; it occurred in 1971 on the issue of deregulation under the Industrial Relations Act; in 1982 when the General Council wished to postpone the issue of automatic representation; and more recently in 1988, when delegates voted to support an unconditional phase-out of nuclear power over a period of 15 years.

The existing arrangements for Congress are currently being examined by the Special Review Body. It is proposed that the Annual Meeting of Congress, which costs more than a £1m a year, should be scrapped and replaced with one which would meet less frequently. Equivalent organisations such as the AFL-CIO in the US holds a Biennial Congress, and the West German DGB holds a Conference only once every four years. Also under consideration is how the business of Congress should be conducted. It is proposed that unions should be allowed to submit only one motion; this would not only cut down the number of debates but also allow genuine differences — which are at present glossed over by composited motions — to emerge.

General Council

The governing body of the TUC between Annual Congresses is the 48-member General Council. It is the voice of the TUC and is charged with pursuing the aims of Congress, encouraging common action between its affiliated unions, giving assistance with organisation, managing and investing TUC funds, and adjusting differences between member unions. It may wish to consult more widely by calling a special congress, as it did at Wembley in 1982 to discuss the TUC's position on employment legislation, but this is a rare occurrence.

Until 1981 the composition of the General Council remained unchanged. All affiliated unions were grouped into 18 trade groups roughly delineating an industry or sector, and allocated a certain number of seats. Only unions within each trade group were able to nominate candidates for seats within the group but if a seat was contested then all affiliated unions were entitled to vote. Once elected to the General Council the person became a representative of the trade group and not a particular trade union, free to take decisions independent of their union's policy, thereby unrestrained by mandate from the union rank and file. There were also five seats reserved for women.

This system of General Council representation remained unaltered for 50 years but increasingly it was under pressure to change. It had become an archaic, inappropriate, and unwieldy method of determining the composition of the General Council, inadequately representing technical, clerical, and professional workers and open to criticism about patronage by the block votes of the large unions. Further, the trade group arrangement reflected the idea of a gradual transition towards industrial unionism, always an ideal, but hopelessly unrealistic in the face of technological change and multinational capital.

At the 1981 Congress a motion advocating a radical restructuring of the TUC, to provide for a system which would give automatic representation on the General Council to all unions with more than 100,000 members, was passed with a majority of 1.3m votes. The decision was immediately seen as a victory for the right, and left-led unions such as the TGWU solidly opposed the plan largely because it would bring on to the General Council representatives from medium-sized unions. At the 1982 Congress, despite pleas from Len Murray, the then TUC General Secretary, to allow more time to consider the issue, a vote amending the original composite motion and pushing through proposals for automatic representation on the General Council for smaller unions from 1983 onwards was passed. Congress voted by a narrow majority to go ahead and reform the General Council.

The General Council is now composed of three sections which are partly appointed and partly elected. In Section A unions with more than 100,000 members have the automatic right to appoint a member to the Council. The number of seats they have is on a sliding scale up to 1.5m members, which entitles a union to five seats. In 1987 large unions appointed 31 General Council members. Section B consists of 11 members elected by ballot among unions with less than 100,000 members; Section C comprises six seats reserved for women, elected by a ballot of all unions, both large and small.

When, in 1982, Congress agreed to change the system of General Council representation from one organised around occupational trade groupings to one known as "automacity", it carried with it a provision for review after five years. The Special Review Body had in any case already been charged with reconsidering the composition and role of the General Council. The 1989 Congress is expected to consider plans for far-reaching changes in General Council membership, reducing the representation of small unions and doubling the number of women's seats.

General Council committee structure

The majority of the work of the General Council is conducted through its standing committees which are supported by TUC Industry Committees and Joint Committees. The most important of the General Council committees is Finance and General Purposes. Others include Economic, Education and Training, Social Insurance and Industrial Welfare, Equal Rights, Trade Union Education, European Strategy, and Employment Policy and Organisation. All these committees are composed exclusively of members of the General Council and the incumbents of the chairs of such committees enjoy considerable status.

There are 11 Industry Committees: Construction; Energy; Financial Services; Health; Hotel, Catering, and Tourism; Local Government; Printing; Steel; Textile Clothing and Footwear; Transport; and Distribution, Food, Drink, Tobacco, and Agriculture. The Financial Committee and the Distribution, Food, Drink, Tobacco, and Agriculture Committee were set up only recently, in response to the changing priorities in the economy, as was the Energy Committee which used to be known as Fuel and Power.

There are also a number of Joint Committees: Arts Entertainment and Sports Advisory; Media Working Group; Race Relations Advisory; Public Enterprise; Public Services; Trade Councils' Joint Consultative; and Women's.

All committees are served by the TUC "civil service" which consists of a group of research workers, often graduates, who develop considerable expertise in their own particular fields.

During the 1980s the influence of the TUC *vis à vis* government has waned dramatically. A great deal of the work of TUC committees involves correspondence and meetings. Yet despite its changed relationship with government it continues to devote the majority of its time and resources to providing detailed lobby papers for ministers who do not read them. Some senior General Secretaries, such as John Edmonds of the GMB, are critical of this misdirection of TUC resources. It is expected that the committee structure will be discussed at the 1989 Congress, in line with a possible shift in direction towards a greater concentration on the areas of recruitment, organisation, and publicity as proposed by the Special Review Body.

Regional machinery

The TUC is a highly centralised organisation in that its regional organisation has always been sparse and under-serviced. In 1973 the TUC reorganised its regional machinery into eight regional TUC councils on which full-time officials from various trade unions sit alongside representatives of the county associations of trades councils, which hold 25 per cent of the seats. In 1979 the TUC appointed its first series of full-time regional secretaries, and since then there have been other appointments including research officers. But the fact remains that the TUC regional organisation remains primitive.

TUC regional councils now provide for increased involvement for women. It was reported to the 1987 Congress that TUC regional councils had agreed to adopt new model rules designed to increase the involvement of women in the work of regional councils through an increase in the size of union delegations. Unions were urged to include a woman in their delegations; the creation of a special seat for a woman on the Executive Committees of regional councils from union nominations was also suggested.

The Special Review Body report drew attention to the long-standing role that TUC regional councils have traditionally played in industrial relations. It acknowledged that regional councils were under-utilised and suggested that they would be in a good position to advise and provide the TUC and affiliated unions with more specialist knowledge about local markets and the prospects for future employment growth. This would also be compatible with the ideas put forward in a recent government White Paper which suggested that regional aid could be more effectively targeted, especially when some regional councils are represented on the regional bodies concerned with distributing financial support. The Special Review Body suggested a pilot project to examine how best to tap regional council expertise. The pilot might identify areas of possible union recruitment and recognition strategies.

Trades councils

The number of trades councils functioning in England and Wales in July 1988 was 377. Trades councils meet monthly and consist of representatives of local trade union branches, lodges, or chapels. Their function is to assist in improving trade union organisation in their locality and to nominate trade union representatives on a variety of local committees and institutions (e.g. educational establishments and some local tribunals). Trades councils are deeply embedded in the history of the British trade union movement and provided common links between trade unions long before the TUC itself.

There has always been an uneasy relationship between the TUC and trades councils. On the one hand the TUC needs them as a means of establishing direct contact with the trade union movement and to ascertain reactions to particular issues. On the other hand the TUC has frequently found that such contacts provide embarrassing evidence of local dissent and left-wing activity which it sees as a possible threat to its own authority. The conflict is less acute today than it was in the heyday of the trades councils in the nineteenth century and during the 1930s; yet even today they are regarded with some suspicion by the TUC establishment. The issue of individual trades council affiliation to Congress led to the split between the TUC and the Scottish TUC in 1897 and this issue is still one which separates the two organisations today (see **STUC**).

The Trades Councils' Joint Consultative Committee (TCJCC) is composed of members appointed by General Council and nine representatives elected regionally by trades councils in England and Wales in an annual postal ballot. In 1987, following a review of trades councils organisation, the TCJCC issued a report entitled *Trades Councils: An Effective Local Voice for Trade Unionism,* which explored ways of breathing new life into trades councils and indicated how they could be of most benefit to the trade union movement.

The TCJCC decided that what was required was an extensive and sustained campaign to encourage local branches to affiliate to the trades council. This would also involve the TCJCC meeting national representatives of affiliated unions to enlist their support. As a result of the check-off system and the fact that now few branches actually handle money, unions are being canvassed on their views regarding suitable means of paying affiliation fees. The TCJCC hopes that these measures will begin to strengthen trades council work.

But their exact status still remains a concern to the TUC establishment. Trades councils are not regarded by the trade union movement as independent bodies competent to make local decisions which may conflict with regional or national trade union policy, and trades council representatives remain subject to the rules and policies of the unions that affiliate to them. Individual union sovereignty remains the trades councils' dilemma. This dilemma, along with the weak regional structure of the TUC, merely serves to emphasise that the TUC is a national organisation which devolves little power to its regions.

Women

In 1987 women accounted for approximately 33 per cent of the total membership affiliated to the TUC.[6] Details of the unions with the highest female membership are summarised in *Table 2* (see "General"). Since the Second World War women workers have provided the largest recruitment source for trade unions, mainly from the growth in local and national government departments, the National Health Service, and office work.[7] At present the TUC General Council reserves five seats for women workers' representatives, but the Special Review Body is considering plans to increase this number to 11. Norman Willis has made it clear that the opportunities offered by the review of the General Council structure must be seized and that major steps ought to be taken to deal with women's under-representation within the TUC.

Each year the TUC holds a Women's Conference. This was set up in 1931 when it was realised that women's special needs were frequently neglected by the trade union movement. The rationale for having a separate Conference is that it can act as a forum to debate issues which might otherwise not get any airing in a mixed forum. Resolutions are passed on to the General Council of the TUC which is not bound to take any notice of them and frequently does not.

The TUC has a Women's Committee which consists of 24 members: 14 representing the General Council and 10 representing the affiliated unions. In 1987 the TUC decided to organise a Women's Action Day every year to take place on International Women's Day (March 8), with the week around International Women's Day to be designated Women's Action Week. During that week the unions, trades councils, and regional councils would be encouraged to organise events at any time during the week as appropriate to their own circumstances.

In July 1987 the TUC took a very positive step to ascertain the progress that had been made since 1984 in implementing the TUC Charter: *Equality for Women Within Trade Unions*. Thirty-three trade unions responded to the questionnaire, representing 6.5 million members, including more than two million women workers. The survey found that whilst there had been many positive developments and a recognition amongst all unions of the need to remove barriers to women's involvement, women were often still not able to play an equal role. There was a clear contrast between those unions which had adopted a positive action programme to involve women in activity and those which had not.

One useful role of the TUC Women's Committee is its monitoring of developments on equal pay for equal work of equal value. In August 1987 the TUC published a revised version of its well-reviewed pamphlet *Equal Pay for Work of Equal Value Guidelines*, together with an awareness-raising leaflet on equal pay aimed at women workers. On an international level the TUC also has women's representatives on the Women's Committee of the International Confederation of Free Trade Unions (ICFTU), and the Women's Committee of the European Trade Union Confederation (ETUC). Such representation will become increasingly important as the European Community moves towards the setting up of a single market in 1992 (see "The European Community and 1992").

There is a general consensus that women will increasingly play a larger part in future trade union recruitment strategies. Women are poised to become 50 per cent of the labour force but their representation in the senior trade union positions is woefully inadequate.[8]

International links
British trade unions maintain formal connections with a variety of international organisations. The TUC itself is currently affiliated to three major bodies: the International Confederation of Free Trade Unions (ICFTU); the European Trade Union Confederation (ETUC); and the Trade Union Advisory Committee of the Organisation

for Economic Co-operation and Development (TUAC/OECD). One of the TUC's largest expenditure items is accounted for by its international affiliations, which in 1987 totalled £947,631 out of a total yearly expenditure of £6,627,603.[9]

The TUC International Committee consisted in the Congress year 1987/88 of 23 General Council members; next to the Finance and General Purposes Committee, and the Economic Committee, it is the third most powerful institution in the TUC. It is not particularly accountable and some claim that the links between the TUC's International Department and the Foreign Office are stronger than those with the International Department of the Labour Party.

The European Community and 1992

Despite the long established endeavours of the International Department such work has had little impact on the life of the ordinary TUC affiliated membership. It can also be said, along with the Labour Party itself, that the TUC has had an ambivalent stance towards the European Community. Recently, however, with the approach of 1992 and the creation of a single market, both the political and industrial wings of the labour movement have undergone a fundamental reappraisal of their attitude towards the Community.[10] Important developments have taken place in rectifying this position by the publication of a report presented to the 1988 Congress entitled *Maximising the Benefits, Minimising the Costs.*

The report identified the past doubts expressed by the UK movement towards Europe but suggested that through the creation of the single market in 1992 there are likely to be many benefits to British workers. Health and safety, women's rights, and better conditions for part-time workers are all areas in which European workers enjoy more favourable benefits than their British counterparts. The advantages of embracing Europe were further reinforced when the President of the European Commission, Jacques Delors, addressed the 1988 TUC Congress and emphasised the importance of a "social dimension", or Social Charter.

The Community Charter of Fundamental Social Rights is a framework of principles, largely drawn up by the office of the EC Social Affairs Commissioner, Vasso Papandreou. It draws on the long-standing Treaty of Rome clauses, such as Article 48 (freedom of movement), and on interpretations of the Single European Act which provides for integration in 1992.

The Charter now contains objectives on: the right to freedom of movement; employment and remuneration; the improvement of living and working conditions; the right to social protection; the right to freedom of association and collective bargaining; the right to information, consultation, and participation for workers; health and safety; the protection of women and adolescents; the treatment of elderly people, and people with disabilities.

So far the Charter is only in draft form and has yet to find its way into Community legislation. All this would be of academic concern if the British government could continue to veto social proposals accepted by the other 11 countries on the grounds that only certain issues within the Single European Act could be passed via the qualified majority vote procedure (which removes Britain's right to veto). Fortunately for the TUC the authors of the draft Social Charter base many of its principles on clauses in the Single European Act. This means that majority voting would be adequate to put them into legislative effect. The Single European Act clauses include the harmonisation of laws, improvement of the working environment, development of dialogue between management and labour at a European level, and economic and social cohesion. A great deal depends on how these broad aims are interpreted.

Other possible legislation rising from the creation of a single European market includes the proposed European Company Statute, which provides for union rights to information and representation on top management bodies. Many European officials envisage that this too will gradually be seen as requiring majority voting only. All this means that 1992 offers real hope for the British trade union movement and the TUC will be forced to emerge from its traditional insular mentality and play a full part in the Europe of the 1990s and beyond.

A composite motion by USDAW to the 1989 TUC Congress, which was almost certain to be passed, advocated that the TUC should set up a permanent lobbying office in Brussels from 1990 onwards, staffed by a full-time officer with responsibility for monitoring European Commission policy. The motion recognised the "urgent need" for UK unions to increase their co-operation with other European trade unions. The problems of influencing, let alone exerting control over the internationally competitive firm, can no longer be restricted to the national level. This motion is a step towards the search for new forms of organisation.

The TUC in the 1990s
The all-time peak membership of the TUC was reached in 1979, when 12,172,508 people belonged to 109 separate affiliated unions representing around 50 per cent of the labour force. By the end of 1987 the number of TUC-affiliated unions stood at 79, and membership had fallen to 8,797,192 million, a fall of 3,375,316 on the 1979 total. Nearly half the membership gained through the 1970s had been lost in the recession of 1980-81. In 1986 trade union density (the percentage of the occupied labour force belonging to trade unions), including membership of non-TUC affiliated unions, stood at around 45 per cent.

The labour market factors which were so important in assisting the growth of TUC-affiliated membership during the 1970s have all disappeared. Unions face a government which is keen to foster individualism rather than collectivism, has embarked on a programme of anti-union legislation, and has made it clear that it does not favour collective bargaining as the norm for conflict resolution. At the same time, employers are much more reluctant to recognise trade unions than they were in the 1970s; indeed, an increasing number of employers are terminating their agreements with trade unions. Whereas unemployment had little effect on trade union membership when it was below one million in the 1970s, once it passed the million mark it led to a massive decline in trade union membership. Having been growing in size until about 1978 the proportion of the work-force in establishments of 500 or more employees fell from 54 per cent in 1978 to 48 per cent in 1982, while the proportion of enterprises of 10,000 or more employees fell from 35 per cent to 30 per cent over the same period. This trend towards smaller enterprises is due in part to the increasing importance of new technology and will add to the problems that the TUC and its affiliated unions will have to face in the years ahead.

The geographical distribution of trade union members in the 1980s is concentrated in multi-industry unions, heavy industry, and the highly-unionised public sector. Apart from the South-East — which accounts for the bulk of UK jobs — most union members are still found in the industrial heartlands, which are bearing the brunt of company closures and redundancies. Union density is high in traditional areas like Wales (64%) or the North (67%), but low in areas where there are a large number of new jobs — the South-East (41%) and East Anglia (20%).

Against this background of trade union membership decline the TUC Special Review Body, composed of 21 General Council members, reported its findings in its first report, *Meeting the Challenge*, to the 1988 Congress which formally adopted the report. The report proposed a number of suggestions which were aimed not only at representing the image of trade unionism in a more favourable light to the public at large, but also at using the TUC's resources much more effectively in the drive to increase the appeal of union membership generally. These included: improving contacts with employers' organisations on industrial relations issues; making greater use of local/regional resources, and setting up a pilot scheme on labour market intelligence and union membership; creating a new role for the TUC in co-ordinating union services to its members, including legal and financial services which many unions are now beginning to provide for their membership; and promoting trade unionism through better public relations and targetting certain groups such as women and the young for special recruitment campaigns. The recommendations of the Special Review Body were in response to the wider organisational and membership issues and were subject to a second review report which was expected to be published in August 1989.

What hope does the TUC and its affiliated trade unions have of stemming the retreat of the 1980s? Do the 1990s hold out any prospect of a more favourable climate for trade unionism in Britain? Optimists in the trade union movement point out that the areas of non-unionism which have expanded rapidly throughout the 1980s are among part-time workers, foreign-owned multinational companies, high-technology industries, and in the services sector of the economy, and that these will eventually be unionised just as the previously non-union car industry was in the 1930s and 1940s. Optimists would also point out that there is some evidence that the decline in trade union membership was being gradually arrested by mid-1987. Several unions reported that they had their first increases in membership for nine years: NALGO and the GMB both increased by 7,000; UCATT by just under 7,000; USDAW by 5,200; in addition both the AEU and the EETPU — whose co-operation with employers did not protect them from decline — claimed that their membership had "bottomed out" at the beginning of 1987.

Such optimism, however, flies in the face of all the major changes that have taken place in the labour market since 1979. The seeds of fundamental change in the labour market have already been sown and there appears to be scant hope for the unions of any major breakthroughs in the future. Whilst the initial recommendations of the Special Review Body are eminently sensible, it is doubtful whether many of these will be relevant to the magnitude of change that is required if trade unions are to flourish in the 1990s. The most important priority is to establish closer and more substantial links with the broad mass of the membership, and not simply to rely on a more centralised TUC function at Congress House. This will involve mounting a major public relations drive to sell the idea of trade unionism to the general public and to coordinate the unions' research and information efforts on a much larger scale. In the past the public relations efforts of trade unions have been uncoordinated and patchy, and a great deal of vital information on the economy and society which has been produced by the unions has never reached the general public.

A major economic objective of trade unions must be not only to ensure that industry becomes productive and efficient, but also to make sure that the benefits arising from increases in productivity are not used solely for rewarding shareholders but are used in the rebuilding of public infrastructure and industrial progress generally.

It is significant that the current TUC policy review is taking place at the same time as the policy review within the Labour Party. As Geoffrey Goodman and Richard Clements argue:[11]

There are those who argue that, for either the Labour Party or the trade unions to succeed in the future, there must be a widening division between them. That is a silly argument which fails to recognise the fact that the organic relationship between them is inescapable. The unions need the Labour Party because industrial syndicalism has never had and never will have a future in a democratic society. The Labour Party needs the unions because a mature democracy cannot be fully achieved without a broader economic democracy. The relationship between the two bodies has always been most successful when their courses are parallel rather than integrated.

Ideas which a decade ago would have been unthinkable are being considered to arrest union membership decline. One such idea, borrowed from the AFL-CIO in the US is to offer employees associate membership, under which they receive union benefits such as financial services, including low-cost credit card, at attractive rates which are not dependent on the union being recognised by the employing company. Such a scheme has an advantage for the union concerned in that it establishes a union base within a non-union company, and a union link with non-union employees. Another idea being considered by the unions is the notion of family membership. The basis of such an idea is that the head of a family — often working in an established industry with a strong union base — takes out membership which, like associate membership of organisations such as the Automobile Association, covers spouses and children, who are likely to work in part-time or temporary jobs or in the services sector, where unionisation is difficult. In that way, when they move from job to job in work where unions find it difficult to have links, they can retain their membership and the unions can retain their membership link.

The GMB, the union in the TUC which arguably has shown the most vision in producing solutions for the trade union movement in the 1990s, is even seeking to move away from "check-off" arrangements. The GMB argues that it is only a matter of time before either employers are no longer prepared to sustain trade unionism through the check-off, or the arrangement is legislated out of existence by the government. The GMB believes that it makes more sense both in financial and membership terms for individual employees to pay their subscriptions by bankers' order. In any case, the GMB often loses members through the check-off method as they move from unionised to non-union employers.

There is not a great deal that is new in these ideas. Much early union history is steeped in the self-help tradition: homes for the retired, educational establishments (such as Ruskin College, Oxford), unemployment insurance, funeral benefits, co-operative shops, etc. Converting these ideas into the form of a modern "mail-order type club" selling life insurance, unit trusts, mortgages, holiday benefits, and so on is merely a repackaging of an old idea and not an entirely new function for trade unions. The demand for high-quality services at a reasonable price is enormous, and a union's mailing list used in this way adds value to its membership.

British trade unions are now facing their greatest crisis of this century and if the present TUC policy review fails to produce workable solutions to the present crisis then the future of British trade unionism looks bleak indeed. In view of the decline of its membership, the shift in political consensus, and the declining influence of the TUC on government, the need to restore a belief that the TUC can present policies which go beyond narrow, sectional interests and provide an alternative and credible social vision is paramount.

Far-reaching changes affecting trade unionism are on the horizon for the 1990s. The developments in the Soviet Union of *glasnost* and *perestroika,* the emergence of a Solidarity-led government in Poland, and open elections in Hungary, are of much greater significance for Europe than the narrow confines of the single European market and 1992. Political affiliation and socialist ideals have always had strong roots throughout the history of the British trade union movement. The TUC now has the chance to play a part in shaping the European labour agenda in the 1990s and beyond.

Notes

1. One of the best works on the History of the TUC is V.L. Allen, *The Sociology of Industrial Relations,* Longman, 1971.

2. V.L. Allen, ibid., p. 153

3. *TUC Rules and Standing Orders,* Rule 11, paragraph (d).

4. ibid., Rule 13, paragraph (a).

5. Robert Taylor, "Mrs Thatcher's impact on the TUC", *Contemporary Records,* Vol. 2, Summer 1989. Frank Longstreth, "From corporatism to dualism? Thatcherism and the climacteric of British trade unions in the 1980s", *Political Studies,* Vol. 36, September 1988.

6. *TUC Report 1988.* (Only as reported to the TUC — many unions do not break up their membership totals between males and females.)

7. Jenny Beale, *Getting it Together: Women as Trade Unionists,* Pluto Press, 1982. Chris Aldred, *Women at Work,* Pan Books, 1981. Judith Hunt and Shelley Adams, "Women, work, and trade union organisation", *WEA Studies for Trade Unionists,* 6, no. 21, 1980. *Labour Research,* April 1986 and September 1988.

8. Edmund Heery and John Kelly, "Do Female Representatives Make a Difference? Women Full-Time Officials", *Work, Employment and Society,* 2, no. 4, December 1988.

9. *TUC Report 1988,* p. 686.

10. Paul Teague, "The British TUC and the European Community", *Millennium,* Vol. 18, Spring 1989.

11. *Financial Times,* March 7, 1988, p. 15.

APPENDIX 1

TUC Membership: 1988

Amalgamated Association of Beamers, Twisters, and Drawers (Hand and Machine)	470
Amalgamated Engineering Union	793,610
Amalgamated Society of Textile Workers and Kindred Trades	2,512
Associated Society of Locomotive Engineers and Firemen	19,065
Association of Cinematograph, Television, and Allied Technicians	29,301
Association of First Division Civil Servants	9,353
Association of University Teachers	32,581
Bakers, Food, and Allied Workers' Union	34,032
Banking, Insurance and Finance Union	168,408
British Actors' Equity Association	40,388
British Air Line Pilots' Association	4,340
British Association of Colliery Management	9,684
Broadcasting and Entertainment Trades' Alliance	29,169
Card Setting Machine Tenters' Society	92
Ceramic and Allied Trades Union	31,308
Civil and Public Services Association	143,062
Communication Managers' Association	19,103
Confederation of Health Service Employees	218,321
Educational Institute of Scotland	44,451
Engineering and Fastener Trade Union	400
Engineers' and Managers' Associations	40,649
Film Artistes' Association	2,094
Fire Brigades Union	45,683
Furniture, Timber, and Allied Trades Union	46,096
GMB	864,021

General Union of Associations of Loom Overlookers	1,101
Health Visitors' Association	16,091
Hospital Consultants and Specialists Association	2,362
Inland Revenue Staff Federation	53,523
Institution of Professional Civil Servants	90,341
Iron and Steel Trades Confederation	66,000
Manufacturing, Science, and Finance	653,000
Military and Orchestral Musical Instrument Makers' Trade Society	35
Musicians' Union	39,598
National and Local Government Officers' Association	754,701
National Association of Colliery Overmen, Deputies and Shotfirers	8,635
National Association of Co-operative Officials	4,474
National Association of Licensed House Managers	11,851
National Association of Probation Officers	6,447
National Association of Schoolmasters/Union of Women Teachers	117,610
National Association of Teachers in Further and Higher Education	81,752
National Communications Union	154,410
National Graphical Association (1982)	125,016
National League of the Blind and Disabled	2,784
National Union of Civil and Public Servants	118,394
National Union of Domestic Appliances and General Operatives	3,100
National Union of the Footwear, Leather, and Allied Trades	33,097
National Union of Hosiery and Knitwear Workers	43,526
National Union of Insurance Workers	17,517
National Union of Journalists	32,206
National Union of Lock and Metal Workers	5,295
National Union of Marine, Aviation, and Shipping Transport Officers	19,345
National Union of Mineworkers	77,316
National Union of Public Employees	635,070
National Union of Railwaymen	110,256
National Union of Scalemakers	882
National Union of Seamen	21,575
National Union of Tailors and Garment Workers	75,908
National Union of Teachers	171,990
Northern Carpet Trades' Union	862
Power Loom Carpet Weavers' and Textile Workers' Union	3,200
Prison Officers' Association	23,699
Rossendale Union of Boot, Shoe, and Slipper Operatives	2,591
Scottish Prison Officers' Association	3,589
Scottish Union of Power-Loom Overlookers	65
Sheffield Wool Shear Workers' Union	27
Society of Graphical and Allied Trades '82	183,213
Society of Shuttlemakers	31
Society of Telecom Executives	29,040
Transport and General Workers' Union	1,312,853
Transport Salaried Staffs' Association	37,340
Union of Communication Workers	197,616
Union of Construction, Allied Trades, and Technicians	250,042
Union of Shop, Distributive, and Allied Workers	396,724
United Road Transport Union	20,681
Wire Workers' Union	5,139
Writers' Guild of Great Britain	1,678
Yorkshire Association of Power-Loom Overlookers	537

Total 8,652,318

APPENDIX 2

MAIN UNION MERGERS AND AFFILIATIONS SINCE 1982*

Former Union Name(s)	Current Position	Date of Merger
National Union of Dyers, Bleachers, and Textile Workers	To TGWU	March 1982
National Graphical Association, and the Society of Lithographic Artists, Designers, Engravers, and Process Workers	Merged to form NGA 1982	March 1982
National Union of Agricultural and Allied Workers	To TGWU	April 1982
Amalgamated Society of Journeymen, Felt Hatters, and Allied Workers of Great Britain	To NUTGW	October 1982
Amalgamated Felt Hat Trimmers, Wool Formers, and Allied Workers Association	To NUTGW	October 1982
Society of Graphical and Allied Trades 1975, and the National Society of Operative Printers' Assistants	Merged to form SOGAT '82	July 1982
Association of Government Supervisors and Radio Officers	To IPCS (now IPMS)	December 1982
General and Municipal Workers Union, and the Amalgamated Society of Boilermakers, Shipwrights, Blacksmiths, and Structural Workers	Merged to form the General Municipal Boilermakers and Allied Trades' Union (GMBATU, now GMB)	December 1982
British Roll Turners' Trade Society	To AUEW Engineering Section (now AEU)	April 1983
National Society of Brushmakers and General Workers	To FTAT	October 1983
National Union of Sheet Metal Workers, Coppersmiths, Heating, and Domestic Engineers	To AUEW-TASS (now MSF)	December 1983
Association of Broadcasting and Allied Staffs, and the National Association of Theatrical and Kine Employees	To Entertainment Trades Alliance, ETA (now BETA)	February 1984
Sheffield Sawmakers' Protection Society	To TGWU	May 1984
AUEW Foundry Section and AUEW Construction Section	To AUEW Engineering Foundry and Construction Section (now AEU)	October 1984
Association of Patternmakers and Allied Craftsmen	To AUEW-TASS (now MSF)	December 1984
National Union of Blast-furnacemen, Ore Miners, Coke Workers, and Kindred Trades	To ISTC	April 1985
Radio and Electronics Officers' Union	To Merchant Navy and Airline Officers Association (now NUMAST)	June 1985
Association of Lecturers in Scottish Central Institutions	To EIS	September 1985

National Society of Metal Mechanics	To AUEW-TASS (now MSF)	November 1985
NUM (Nottingham Area), NUM South Derbyshire Area), and the Colliery Trades and Allied Workers' Association	Merged to form UDM	December 1985
Tobacco Workers' Union	To AUEW-TASS (now MSF)	June 1986
Amalgamated Union of Asphalt Workers	To TGWU	December 1987
Society of Civil and Public Servants, and the Civil Service Union	Merged to form NUCPS	December 1987
AUEW-TASS and ASTMS	Merged to form MSF	January 1988
Association of Lecturers in Colleges of Education in Scotland	To EIS	March 1988
Greater London Staff Association	To GMBATU (now GMB)	September 1988
GMBATU and APEX	Merged to form GMB	January 1989
Imperial Group Staff Association	To MSF	March 1989
Association of Scottish Local Government Directors of Personnel	To FUMPO	April 1989
Northern Rock Building Society Staff Association	To BIFU	May 1989
Association of British Professional Divers	To EETPU	May 1989
Ministry of Defence Staff Association	To EETPU	July 1989
Springfields Foremans Association	To EETPU	August 1989

*This table only covers changes in unions included in this Directory. Changes may include either a merger with another union or a transfer of engagements to another union.

STUC
SCOTTISH TRADES UNION CONGRESS

Head Office: Middleton House, 16 Woodlands Terrace, Glasgow G3 6FD

Telephone: 041-332 4946

Fax: 041-332 3878

Principal officers
General Secretary: Campbell Christie
Deputy General Secretary: Bill Spiers

Associated journal: Scottish Trade Union Review (monthly).
Pete Smith (Editor), *Scottish Trade Union Review,* Trade Union Research Unit
(Scotland), Glasgow College, Cowcaddens Road, Glasgow G3

General

The STUC, with an affiliated membership of 900,000, is the authoritative voice of the trade union movement in Scotland. Its public standing and positive media profile within Scotland are high, and it is an authority such that even the Conservative Secretary of State for Scotland has to listen, and occasionally act on its advice.

It is financially, organisationally, and politically autonomous of the TUC, with which, however, it enjoys good relations.

In the recent past it has played a major role in Scottish public life, campaigning in defence of existing industries, for effective regional policy, in defence of the NHS, and against the Poll Tax, amongst other issues. Its policies are determined at its Annual Congress, held in April, and are executed by a General Council elected by that Congress and by a small full-time staff. There are currently 25 elected members of the General Council. The full-time staff consists of the General Secretary, Deputy General Secretary, and five Assistant Secretaries.

In addition to the Annual Congress there is an Annual Youth Conference which elects a Youth Committee to represent the views of young workers, and an Annual Women's Conference which elects a Women's Committee to perform a similar role in respect of women workers. In these respects the STUC differs completely from the TUC.

It also differs from the TUC in that trades councils, the local campaigning trade union bodies which were in fact responsible for creating the TUC and STUC in the first place, play an active part in the STUC's democracy. They elect delegates who take part in debates at the Annual Congress and a General Council seat is reserved for a trades council nominee. The secretary of the Aberdeen trades council, Ron Webster, was a recent President of the STUC.

Further reference

Keith Aitken, "Speaking for Scotland", *Marxism Today,* April 1988.

WALES TUC
(CYNGOR UNDEBAU LLAFUR CYMRU)

Head Office: Transport House, 1 Cathedral Road, Cardiff CF1 9SD

Telephone: 0222-372345

General Secretary: David J. Jenkins

General

The Wales TUC operates within a small budget, mainly comprising an annual grant from the TUC. It consists of those trade unions affiliated to the TUC that have members in Wales and trades councils and county associations of trades councils in Wales recognised by the TUC. The General Council of the Wales TUC has 49 members elected by the unions represented at the Annual Conference of the Wales TUC on a trade group basis. Unions are entitled to be represented at the Annual Conference by one delegate and by one additional delegate for every 2,000 members or fraction thereof in Wales. Trades councils are also represented.

Since its establishment in 1974 the Wales TUC has taken several initiatives to enable it to respond more effectively to the changing demands of the unions and labour force in the Welsh economy. Above all, this means directing resources and activities outward with a view to improving the public perception and awareness of the Wales TUC. Examples of this policy in action include the work of its Women's Advisory Committee on health and safety, equal opportunities, and public services; close links with the Wales Co-operative Centre, including meetings with HK (a white collar union of the Aarhus region of Denmark) and regular attendance of Wales TUC representatives at meetings of the steering committee of Wales Pensioners, the Wales branch of the British Pensioners' Trade Union Action Association. The Wales TUC is opposed to current plans to build and commission a new generation of PWR nuclear reactors, at least until there has been established the following: a hazardous waste executive of authoritative people from outside the nuclear industry to provide leadership in storage and disposal of nuclear waste; mandatory public inquiries into all nuclear accidents involving any significant radiation risk to the public or to workers; a strengthened role of the Health and Safety Commission and secure funding for an expanded Nuclear Installations Inspectorate; and UK nuclear plants to be included in a compulsory international inspections regime.

ACTT
ASSOCIATION OF CINEMATOGRAPH, TELEVISION AND ALLIED TECHNICIANS

TUC affiliated

Head Office: 111 Wardour Street, London W1V 4AY

Telephone: 01-437 8506

Fax: 01-437 8268

Principal officers
General Secretary: Alan Sapper
Deputy General Secretary: Roy Lockett
Finance Officer : G.Miniatakis
Membership Officer: Linda Loakes
Organiser: Bob Hamilton
Organiser: Jack O'Connor
Organiser:Ken Roberts
Organiser: Brian Shemmings
Organiser: Noel Harris
Organiser: Jenny Woodley

Union journal: Film and Television Technician (monthly)

Membership

Current membership (1987)
Male: 21,255
Female: 7,425
Total: 28,680

Membership trends

	1975	1979	1981	1983	1987	change 1975-87	change 1983-87
Men	15,819	17,613	16,003	17,646	21,255	34%	20%
Women	2,871	4,099	4,018	4,914	7,425	159%	51%
Total	18,690	21,712	20,021	22,560	28,680	53%	27%

General

The union organises employees in the technical side of film production including: directors, producers, writers, camera staff such as boom operators, autocue operators, sound can and sound maintenance workers, and clapper loaders; as well as grades in animation, editorial, and special effects. It also recruits in broadcasting, television, and allied industries.

ACTT is a craft union which, in the past, derived much of its strength from its ability to control the supply of labour. So effective were its closed shop agreements that most film companies found it convenient to fill vacancies directly through the union's own employment office or, more accurately, employment agency. The union supplied members who were registered with it as being currently unemployed. If there were no members available for the vacancies, the union recruited them itself. But due to new technological changes and a more hostile industrial environment, the union has run into a number of serious problems which cast doubts on the union's ability to remain an effective bargaining force.

History

According to Gus MacDonald, the ACTT was founded in the 1930s to combat "cowboy" employers in the film business. It was created by a core of leftists including film-makers such as Sidney Cole, Ralph Bond, and Ivor Montagu. On the brink of collapse during the 1930s, it was saved by Sidney Bernstein (the founder of Granada TV), then a cinema tycoon.

Organisation

The union is undergoing a period of transition and it is difficult to provide an accurate account of its organisation. When contacted, the union did not volunteer information to clarify the situation.

The General Council is entrusted with the administration of the business of the union between conferences. The 1988 Conference agreed to replace the Annual Conference with one held every two years.

Towards the end of 1986 the union invited Reg Race, a former Labour MP, to examine the internal structure of ACTT, its organisation and deployment of officers, and draw up a report detailing proposals for reform. The chief proposals of the report were that the union should appoint four regional officers and a senior administrative officer. These changes were to be implemented immediately and their effects were to be monitored before tackling any Head Office restructuring. The union decided to delay implementing the reform measures in full and chose to introduce the plan in two stages. The first stage was to follow the report's recommendations and make the necessary appointments, but the restructuring of Head Office, which it was believed would entail cutting the union's Head Office staff, would form stage two which would not be implemented until 1990.

Recent issues
Inquiry into restrictive practices
Major changes in broadcasting were signalled by the Prime Minister, Mrs Thatcher, in September 1987 when she declared that TV companies were the "last bastion of restrictive practices". Following that statement the Home Office announced that it was to increase competition in independent broadcasting by introducing competitive tendering and awarding licences based strictly on commercial considerations (subject to basic quality assurances) rather than on quality assessment.

In 1989 ACTT was cleared by the Monopolies and Mergers Commission inquiry into restrictive practices (see *Labour Practices in TV and Film Making*, CM66, HMSO, 1989). The Commission accepted the submission prepared by ACTT, *Responding To Change*, and concluded that whilst many restrictive practices had existed in the past, the situation had changed radically over the two years prior to the inquiry and the indications were that this would continue.

TV-am dispute
The push towards the end of 1987 by Tyne Tees Television to break with national agreements negotiated through the ITV Association was the first important sign that the mood of employers had changed. But it was TV-am, the new independent company set up to broadcast breakfast television, and not party to the national agreements, that was to herald the downturn in the influence of the ACTT.

In November 1987 a dispute broke out at TV-am which threatened to become as bitter and divisive in the broadcasting industry as the dispute at Wapping had been in the newspaper printing industry. TV-am was all along pushing for a showdown with the union. The company itself was suffering quite badly in the ratings, and at one point was near to collapse. Reducing its manning levels, costs, and increasing labour flexibility were crucial to its recovery plans. But to introduce these measures it had to confront the ACTT.

Management had asked technicians, who were members of ACTT, to provide them with assurances that there would be no disruptions in the run-up to the Christmas period. The technicians refused to give these assurances and on November 24, 1987 management locked out all 229 technicians. Management at TV-am had wanted to get union agreement to a package of 10 changes in working practices which involved a considerable degree of work flexibility. Talks between management and the ACTT failed to make any progress and on February 17, 1988 all 229 ACTT technicians employed by TV-am were sacked. Rather than escalate the dispute by asking BETA and NUJ members, who had consistently refused to take industrial action in support of ACTT members, to provide cover the company brought in non-union technicians from the growing freelance cable and satellite sector.

An industrial tribunal supported the action taken by TV-am management when it ruled that the technicians had not been unfairly dismissed; although the union lodged an appeal and continued to picket the studios for a further 20 months, most of the dismissed technicians have now found employment elsewhere. An attempt by the ACTT to get compensation for the dismissed workers was informally agreed in June 1989 when the company offered £800,000 in compensation if the union agreed to recommend its acceptance to the members, thereby officially ending the dispute. But at the last minute management withdrew the offer; at the time of publication the dispute was still awaiting a settlement.Management must obviously feel confident of their case to have withdrawn the offer of compensation and allow the matter to go to a formal appeal.

Merger proposals
The 1988 Conference, in response to widespread changes in independent television working practices and the threat to joint national bargaining, supported a merger between the ACTT and BETA. Traditionally there had been hostility between the two unions and previous motions calling for a merger had been rejected. Although the mood of the membership had now changed pockets of strong resistance remained. The ITV section, the strongest and most influential section in the ACTT, was not happy about the proposed merger because of the status implications of joining a "general workers' union".

External relations
In 1986 49 per cent of ACTT members turned out for the political fund ballot.Fifty-nine per cent (7,149 votes) were in favour and 41 per cent (5,043 votes) were against. In addition to the Labour Party the ACTT is affiliated to Amnesty International, NCCL, CND, and the Campaign for Press and Broadcasting Freedom.

Policy and recent events
During the 1960s the ACTT had skilfully used the agreements it had negotiated to make its membership into one of the best paid group of workers, comparable even to the élite in the printing industry. It was also active in the Labour Party and played its role in the TUC and the wider trade union movement. However, the buoyancy of the 1960s and 1970s gave way to radical changes in the 1980s. With the advent of new technologies, such as electronic news gathering and satellite broadcasting, and the government's determination to "inject competition" into the broadcasting industry (as indicated in the 1988 White Paper, *Broadcasting in the 90s: Competition, Choice and Quality*), pressure mounted on the ACTT, as well as the other unions in broadcasting, to give way on national agreements and adopt local level bargaining. The ACTT found itself increasingly on the defensive. Relying on the strategies of the 1960s became less applicable to the problems of the 1980s.

In February 1989 the independent TV companies announced an end to national pay bargaining. However, all four unions, ACTT, BETA, NUJ, and the EETPU were acting in accord, and tabled a joint counter-proposal for a single national agreement to be set up to cover terms and conditions. The agreement would provide for a minimum working week, minimum holidays, termination of employment, sickness, and dispute procedures, as well as minimum annual pay increases. Two independent companies, Tyne Tees and TWS, have already pulled out of national agreements.

As part of its strategy to deal with the pressure from other employers regarding their assault on national bargaining, the ACTT decided to seek merger talks with its rival BETA. Although the decision had the support of Conference, the large and influential ITV group within the ACTT was against the BETA merger. At shop floor level the two unions did not get on and this was exacerbated at the TV-am dispute in which BETA and NUJ members consistently refused to take industrial action in support of ACTT. Furthermore, the ITV members of the ACTT considered themselves to be the élite of the broadcasting world, and joining, as they saw it, a general workers' union like BETA, held no appeal for them.

The leaders of the ITV section, which included the former chair of ACTT's ITV division Peter Bould, organised a breakaway group. The ACTT disciplined the three leaders of the group, barring them from holding any union office for five years and eventually dismissing them from the union. Yet despite the ACTT's attempts to preserve unity, a breakaway union, the *Television and Film Production Employees' Association* (TFPEA), was formed. The breakaway union was formally listed in February 1989 and was given its certificate of independence from the Certification Officer in July 1989. Although its membership is small and confined mainly to the North, at the time of publication Yorkshire Television was considering recognising the new union for collective bargaining purposes. The breakaway is an irony, as the other major unions in broadcasting are more united than they have ever been. The TFPEA, like most breakaway unions, is likely to find that after an initial honeymoon period, it will face difficulties in maintaining its momentum.

One of the criticisms made by the ITV breakaway group was that the ACTT leadership spent too much time playing politics around the world at the union's expense, rather than dealing with the perhaps more mundane, but important issues, of looking after their members' interests at home. The ACTT revealed during the 1987 Conference, that it did indeed have some financial difficulties, and moreover, it conceded its lack of effectiveness when it called in Reg Race, the former Labour MP, to investigate the organisation and administration of the union.

The merger talks with BETA are still progressing and this looks like the best chance for the ACTT to bring the problems it faces to an end. The merger will unite the workers in the broadcasting industry, and with the NUJ indicating its interest in joining the new union, should the talks prove successful the broadcasting industry will have the majority of its workers organised by one union. Given the pressure from employers to introduce greater cost-cutting exercises and still further undermine union bargaining power (see *NUJ, BETA),* a single union voice would give workers a better chance of coping with what are obviously going to be stormy times in the broadcasting industry.

Further references

Gus MacDonald, "Television's high technology warfare", *New Statesman,* September 14, 1979.

Jeremy Bugler, "TV's industrial relations minefield", *New Statesman,* August 25, 1978.

P. Seglow, *Trade Unionism in TV: A Case Study of the Development of White Collar Militancy,* Saxon House, 1978.

Alan Sapper, "Opening the box — the unions inside television", in P. Beharrel and G. Philo (eds.), *Trade Unions and the Media,* Macmillan, 1977.

A. Jacobs, *Film and Electronic Technologies in the Production of Television News,* Ph.D. Thesis, University of Southampton, 1983.

J. Clark, et al., "New technology, industrial relations, and divisions within the work-force", *Industrial Relations Journal,* 15, no. 3, 1984.

Clive Hutt, "Industrial relations on breakfast-time television", *Industrial Relations Journal,* 18, no. 2, 1987.

AEU
AMALGAMATED ENGINEERING UNION

TUC affiliated

Head Office: 110 Peckham Road, London SE15 5EL

Telephone: 01-703 4231

Telex: AEW001 265871 MONREF G

Telecom Gold: 79: AEW001

Fax: 01-703 7862

Principal national officers
President: Bill Jordan
General Secretary: Gavin H. Laird, CBE
Assistant General Secretary: T. Butler
Assistant Secretary: J. A. Crystal

Executive Councils:
Division 1: J. Airlie
Division 2: C. Dawber
Division 3: W. J. Purvis
Division 4: K. G. Cure, OBE
Division 5: W. B. Morgan
Division 6: J. P. Weakley
Division 7: J. R. Whyman

ENGINEERING SECTION

National organisers:
J. Byrne
P. McCoy
C. Moore
H. Hewitt-Dutton
J. N. Laffey
D. J. Graham
E. T. Hepple

Regional officers:
Division 1:
H. McLevy, AEU House, 145/146 West Regent Street, Glasgow G2 4RZ.
Telephone: 041-248 7131

Division 2:
J. Bowers, AEU House, 46/48 Mount Pleasant, Liverpool L3 5SE
Telephone: 051-709 9561

Division 3:
H. Wilkinson, 66 Duke Street, Darlington DL3 7AN
Telephone: 0325-65791

Division 4:
J. Dougherty, AEU House, 43 Crescent, Salford M5 4PE
Telephone: 061-736 5206/7

Division 5:
W. R. Pritchard, AEU House, Furnival Gate, Sheffield S1 3HE
Telephone: 0742-736 79041/2/3

Division 6:
M. P. Burke, 8 St Paul's Road, Bristol BS8 1LU
Telephone: 0272-39321

Division 7:
J. W. Bracher, 20 Durand Gardens, London SW9 0PP
Telephone: 01-587 1831

FOUNDRY SECTION

Head office: AEU House, First Floor, 43 Crescent, Salford M5 4PE
Telephone: 061-736 5206
Telecom Gold: 79 AEW 022

National Secretary: N. J. Harris
Assistant National Secretary: A. G. Lloyd
National Organiser: B. Salt

Foundry Committee:
National Officer (Area A): Vacant
National Officer (Area B): G. P. Burns
National Officer (Area C): J. Shaw
National Officer (Area D): W. Baker

Divisional organisers:
District 1:
A. Down, 11 Grahams Road, Falkirk FK1 1LD
Telephone: 0324-24459

District 2:
J. Gauthier, AEU House, High Street, Gateshead NE8 1JB
Telephone: 0632-770403

District 3:
L. Crossley, AEU House, Furnival Gate, Sheffield S1 3HE
Telephone: 0742-738729

District 4:
K. W. Smith, AEU Foundry Section, First Floor, 71 Vaughan Way, Leicester LE1 4SG
Telephone: 0553-24100

District 5:
D. O'Flynn, AEU House, 588 Rainham Road South, Dagenham, Essex RM10 7RA
Telephone: 01-593 4893

District 6:
W. Chapman, 4 Southview Close, Shoreham-by-Sea, West Sussex BN4 6LJ
Telephone: 0273-591300

District 7:
G. Tomlinson, AEU House, 43 Crescent, Salford M5 4PE
Telephone: 061-736 2465

District 8:
A. J. Harvey, AEU Foundry Section, 67 Old Meeting Street, West Bromwich B70 9SS
Telephone: 021-553 2026/3876

District 9:
W. Law, AEU Foundry Section, 67 Old Meeting Street, West Bromwich B70 9SS
Telephone: 021-553 2026/3876

CONSTRUCTION SECTION

Head Office: 110 Peckham Road, London SE15 5EL
Telephone: 01-703 4231
Telecom Gold: 79 AEW 003

National Secretary: J. Baldwin, OBE
National Officer: G. Garbett

Divisional organisers:
London Division:
D. Wheaton, 588 Rainham Road South, Dagenham, Essex RM10 7RA
Telephone: 01-592 7700

South Wales and South-Western Division:
P. Jones, 8 St Pauls Road, Clifton, Bristol BS8 1LU
Telephone: 0272-732634

Midland Division:
K. Antell and D. Croft, 218 Mansfield Road, Nottingham NG5 2BU
Telephone: 0602-621181

North-West Division:
S. E. Howard, AEU House, 48 Mount Pleasant, Liverpool LS3 5SD
Telephone: 051-709 4888

North-East Division:
G. Douglas, AEU House, Furnival Gate, Sheffield S1 3HE
Telephone: 0742-25453

T. Gaynor and T. Woods, AEU House, 190 Borough Road, Middlesbrough, Cleveland TS1 2EH
Telephone: 0642-242383

Scottish Division:
T. Lafferty, 83 Crown Street, Aberdeen AB1 2EX
Telephone: 0224-595454

R. Sneddon, 145 Morrison Street, Edinburgh EH3 8AL
Telephone: 031-228 3194

T. MacLean and J. Connolly, AEU House, 7 Incle Street, Paisley PA1 1HJ
Telephone: 041-889 8228

Union journal and publications: AEU Journal (monthly, free to all members, circulation around 79,000).

The union's publications list includes the following booklets: *The Union That Leads; Health and Safety; Shop Steward's Booklet; Equal Pay for Work of Equal Value;New Technology — Access Points; Financial Services Package; Nuclear Power and Defence Policy.*
The AEU is a keen supporter of education and regularly sends members on TUC-sponsored courses. The union also supplements the TUC's educational programme and provides schools for specific sections which the TUC cannot supply, such as full-time officials, branch secretaries, convenors and senior stewards in selected industries, women and youth, supervisory staff and technical branch members. While the union's expenditure on education has risen since 1981 (when it spent £97,884, compared with £99,408 in 1985), in real terms it has declined.

Membership figures

Current membership (1987)

Male: 715,072
Female: 100,000
Total: 815,072

Membership trends

	1975	1979	1981	1983	1987	change 1975-87	1983-87
Total	1,287,535	1,298,580	1,104,425	1,005,087	815,072	−37%	−19%

Foundry section and construction section membership figures have been aggregated with the engineers. The AEU has only recently made separate male and female membership figures available.

General
In 1987 the AEU was the second largest union in Britain. The union is comprised of the following sections: engineers, foundry workers, and construction workers, along with the small roll turning section. All these sections are now united by a single rule book, the *Fourteenth AEU Rules Revision Meeting.*

The union has grown from a number of amalgamations in 1851, 1920, 1969-70, and 1984, which finally saw the adoption of a single rule book, albeit with the loss of the white-collar section TASS. Traditionally to the right in the trade union movement, the AEU suffered a serious set-back when the protracted merger discussions with the EETPU broke down (see "Recent events", *AEU/EETPU merger*). The merger would not only have enhanced the right's political position in the union movement but would also have enabled the AEU to maintain its status as Britain's second largest union. It seems likely that in the not too distant future the AEU will have to surrender that position to its rival the GMB which has been far more astute in its management of the overall decline in union membership (see **GMB**).

History

Trade unionism in the engineering industry can be traced back to the emergence of the industry in its post-industrial revolution form at the end of the eighteenth century and beginning of the nineteenth century. At first machinery was built mainly by millwrights who often combined the functions of engineer, mechanic, drafter/designer, and civil engineer in one person. As industrialisation developed, the skills of the millwrights were at a premium and their wages rose well above the rates for skilled workers. The introduction of self-active tools reduced the power of the millwrights, and the development of the factory system led to the trade union organisation becoming established among relatively unskilled engineers.

By the time the Combination Acts were repealed in 1824/25 successful friendly societies existed in many of the engineering trades which became increasingly differentiated as the division of labour progressed. Various societies (many of which did not survive) were formed in the years prior to and just following the repeal of the Combination Acts covering smiths, millwrights, iron and brassfounders, mechanics, engineers, and machinists. Since these trades protection societies were generally confined to one or two trades within a specific locality and limited membership to those who had served an apprenticeship, funds were too low to permit any continuity. The strongest union to be formed in that period was the *Journeymen Steam Engine and Machine Makers' and Millwrights' Friendly Society* (known as the *Old Mechanics)* which was founded in 1826 in Manchester by John White, the first secretary. White championed the new union enthusiastically in Manchester, Bolton, Stockport, and Oldham under very difficult circumstances, frequently having to change his lodgings to evade police detection. By 1838 the *Old Mechanics* had nearly 3,000 members. Its nearest rival was the *Steam Engine Makers' Society* formed in 1824, with only 525 members in 14 branches by 1836.

By 1849 a United Trades Association of the "Five Trades of Mechanisms" had been formed in Manchester bringing together millwrights, engineers, iron moulders, smiths, and mechanics. Although this body was short-lived the attempts by the employers in the north to introduce the Quittance Paper in 1844 led to the formation of a stronger federation known as the *Mechanics' Protective Society of Great Britain and Ireland.* As Jeffreys writes: "The purpose of this society was not in any way to rival or compete with the existing trade unions among engineers, but to act as a defensive alliance between the different societies, so that if one trade was attacked all the trades in that workshop would strike. The Old Mechanics co-operated in building this society."

It was clear that further amalgamation in the engineering trades was necessary following a number of strikes and the arrest and trial for conspiracy of the leaders of the *Old Mechanics* in 1847. In 1850 the executive of the *Old Mechanics* decided to invite the executive councils of the engineers', smiths', millwrights', moulders' and boilermakers' societies to elect deputations to meet and discuss amalgamation.

The first amalgamation
When the *Amalgamated Society of Engineers, Machinists, Smiths, Millwrights and Patternmakers* was launched in 1851 the membership was only 5,000 — less than half of the component societies and smaller than the *Old Mechanics* of a year earlier. Vigorous campaigning by the new union brought the membership up to nearly 11,000 by the end of the year as reluctant branches and societies joined the amalgamation.

At its birth the amalgamated society had one paid official, William Allan, the General Secretary, and became known generally as the *Amalgamated Society of Engineers*. The ASE had from the start a high rate of contributions and a generous scale of benefits. Whilst its district committees were permitted a high degree of autonomy, most of the funds were centralised at its London headquarters. The General Secretary was supervised by an Executive Council elected from the branches in the metropolitan area. Many of the characteristics of the "new model" union were borrowed from the *Old Mechanics* and were later hailed by the Webbs as a landmark in the history of trade unionism. Its high contributions and exclusiveness meant that its model of organisation could be copied only by craft unions.

A few months after its foundation the ASE became involved in a desperate struggle with the employers in Lancashire and London, who locked out their trades people when they refused to accept an increase in the number of unskilled workers in shops. The 1852 lock-out over dilution was a defeat for the ASE largely because its trade protection fund rapidly proved unable to support ASE members out of work and also because of the clever way in which the employers manipulated public opinion in their favour. The employers forced their men to sign the document and the membership of the union slumped far below the figure of the previous year.

During the 1850s the union gradually recovered and won recognition from a number of employers. Its unity was fostered because members in Scotland and Lancashire were prepared to submerge their regional loyalties and accept leadership from London. Fortunately for the union, the employers' organisation disintegrated, except for moribund local associations.

Jeffreys noted that the attempts to crush the ASE out of existence had ended in a paper victory for the employers but it was their organisation that disappeared while the society gained greater strength than ever. By December 1866 membership of the ASE stood at 33,067 and the union's branches numbered 305.

By 1866 the ASE had largely escaped the pitched battles in the early 1860s that characterised other trades, and the employers realised that the steadily growing amalgamated unions posed a serious challenge to their authority on the industrial front. Allan attempted patiently to display unionism as respectable and efficient, although the general public was usually ill-informed about the issues behind the disputes and too readily blamed the workers. Following the murder of a non-unionist in Sheffield in 1866 the employers seized the initiative to demand an investigation with the aim of indicting trade unionism as a whole.

In the same year another blow was struck at trade unionism following the decision of the Lord Chief Justice in the case of *Hornsby* v. *Close,* in which the boilermakers were suing a branch secretary for withdrawal of funds. The Lord Chief Justice ruled that trade unions were in restraint of trade and therefore constituted illegal conspiracies which in turn made them ineligible for registration under the Friendly Societies Act. The trade union funds lay unprotected from the wiles of dishonest members. A Royal Commission was set up in 1867 and the efforts of the ASE were directed towards political and parliamentary action.

Allan played a major part in the proceedings of the Royal Commission, together with Applegarth of the carpenters. The final report of the Commission in 1869 did not give the employers any grounds for suppressing trade unions. The 1871 Trade Union Act gave the trade unions protection for their funds, and the parliamentary lobbying to repeal the Criminal Law Amendment Act was carried out by the newly formed TUC, which later acted in concert with the Conference of Amalgamated Trades in which Allan was a powerful influence. Allan died in 1874 and John Burnett, the hero of the rank and file Nine Hour Movement, was elected General Secretary to succeed him. When Burnett assumed the office the membership of the ASE had reached 43,150.

Burnett's period as General Secretary was characterised by the strains on the union's structure and organisation posed by the increasing size and diversity of the industry. Burnett preferred to change neither policy nor methods, and the possible changes that could have been made — widening or restricting membership, centralisation or decentralisation, an aggressive or conciliatory policy towards the employers — remained largely unconsidered until the reorganisation of the ASE in 1892.

The ASE used its strength skilfully against concerted attacks by the employers and successfully defended the nine-hour day. Periodic fluctuations in wages arising from changes in trade took place, but the district committees managed to achieve substantial increases in wages in the 1880s. By 1891 ASE membership had reached 71,221 and it had 509 branches. Compared with other unions, which often appeared and lasted for a short time only, the ASE maintained its continuity and stability. Burnett resigned in 1886 to take up a newly created post of Labour Correspondent of the Board of Trade and was succeeded as General Secretary by Robert Austin.

By 1890 it was clear that the ASE needed a radical reorganisation. Its conservatism in policy, its growing unwieldiness, and the rigidity and exclusiveness of its structure combined to weaken the role it could play in the wider labour movement. The ASE was top-heavy and there were inadequate links between the leadership and the branches, while the General Secretary was overwhelmed by administrative work.

A movement for reform grew up around Tom Mann and John Burns, who strongly attacked the conservatism and lack of fight of the old trade union. Mann had joined the ASE in 1881 but left in 1887 to act as travelling spokesman for the Social Democratic Federation. In 1889 he was elected President of the dockers' union following his organisation of the 1889 dock strike. He remained active in the ASE and ran for election as General Secretary when Austin died in 1891, but was defeated by a narrow margin by John Anderson. The impact of Mann's campaign was reflected in the reforms adopted at the Leeds Delegate Meeting of 1892.

The ASE rule book still contained provisions which had been inherited from the *Old Mechanics,* and sweeping changes were made. The Local Executive Council of London members working at the trade was replaced by an Executive Council of full-time officials elected in eight divisions. Six full-time organising district delegates were to be elected and the central district committees were to be abolished. The number of paid officials thus increased from four (General Secretary and Assistant General Secretaries) to 17. Two new sections of membership were created and membership was widened slightly. A superannuation reserve was set up to free the ASE's resources for more militant action. The Executive Council was empowered to consult the membership on raising funds to engage in national politics.

During the 1890s the employers managed to build up an effective counter-organisation and in 1898, after a 30-week lock-out in response to the ASE's demand for a 48-hour week, the notorious "terms of settlement" were imposed which gave the employers the right to introduce any changes in working conditions at the commencement of any dispute (the "status quo" provisions) in federated firms. Despite this defeat the ASE continued to grow, largely by skilful use of the central negotiating machinery and guerrilla tactics in the districts. At the outbreak of the First World War in

1914 ASE membership stood at 174,253.

The period leading up to 1914 was marked by growing hostility between the members and the leadership as resentment about the "terms of settlement" and the lack of policies to deal with the effects of new technology and new methods of organisation built up. A reform movement under Tom Mann's leadership, together with the increasing influence of shop stewards, emphasised direct industrial action at the expense of parliamentary representation (the Executive Committee (EC) had been active in the launching of the Labour Representation Committee and the membership had rejected proposals for a political levy on behalf of the Labour Party).

At the 1912 Delegate Meeting the rift between the executive and the membership came out into the open. It was decided to reduce the EC to seven members, that an independent chairman should be elected directly by the membership, that the entire EC should come up for election in 1913, and that the ranks of the ASE should be open to unskilled workers. The executive opposed these changes, balloted the membership using a one-sided circular and received their support. The Delegate Conference was recalled to invite the EC to retract its decisions but it refused to do so. Executive Council members locked themselves in at their new headquarters in Peckham Road and refused admission to the provisional Executive Council newly appointed by the delegates. After an undignified skirmish the old EC was ejected into the street, and after legal proceedings the old executive lost its case, giving way after six months in office to the newly elected Executive Council with J. T. Brownlie as the first independent Chairman.

The First World War and the second amalgamation
During the First World War wage rates were established at national rather than district level with direct contact between the Executive and the War Cabinet. A notable feature of the war years was the growth in the shop stewards movement, with a number of major strikes, particularly on the Clyde. The stewards' power grew rapidly in the struggles to defend workers from the attempts of the government and employers to increase production and minimise wage increases while the cost of living and manufacturers' profits grew rapidly. The links on the shop floor between the different unions were strengthened by joint committees, and in 1917 the amalgamation committee joined the national shop stewards movement. All this served to emphasise that further amalgamation was both possible and necessary. During 1918, following instructions from the Delegate Meeting, the executive of the ASE started negotiations which resulted in 17 societies balloting their members on amalgamation in May 1919. The membership of the ASE cast 92 per cent of the vote in favour of amalgamation. Other societies having the requisite percentage of vote and majorities were the Steam Engine Makers' Society, the United Machine Workers' Association, the United Kingdom Society of Amalgamated Smiths and Strikers, the Associated Brassfounders, Turners, Fitters and Coppersmiths' Society, and the North of England Brass Turners, Fitters and Finishers' Society.

Subsequent voting added three more societies to the number in favour, the East of Scotland Brass Founders' Society, the Amalgamated Instrument Makers' Association, and the Amalgamated Society of General Toolmakers, Engineers and Machinists.

Of the societies that voted and failed to obtain a 50 per cent poll the most important were the United Pattern Makers' Association and the Electrical Trades Union. As in 1851 the boilermakers again declined to take part, as did the iron founders. The Amalgamated Engineering Union came into existence on July 1, 1920 with J. T. Brownlie as President and Tom Mann as General Secretary. The AEU rules were based on those of the old ASE, but they made an important attempt to overcome the longstanding problem of the powers of the executive *vis-à-vis* the membership. In place of the Delegate Meeting, a National Committee consisting of two representatives of each divisional committee was to meet annually to receive a report from the Executive Council and to give guidance as to future policy. Every fourth year the National Committee was empowered to consider suggestions and decide any alterations to the rules. Thus for the first time the union was able to make policy decisions other than by changing the rules. Day to day running of the union was to continue in the hands of the Executive Council but members would have the right to appeal against its decision at a final appeal court of 15 members elected by the divisions. The rights of shop stewards were extended through shop stewards' quarterly meetings to be held in each district, and they were given representation on district committees. The amalgamation meant that the total membership of the AEU was over 450,000 members.

The period of optimism which followed the second amalgamation proved to be short-lived. The severe depression of 1921-2 enabled the federated employers to turn demands for overall wage increases into a negotiated reduction of wages. Under threat of national lock-out the AEU suffered its first major defeat, and had to concede most of the gains made during the war. The lock-out lasted for 13 weeks over the issue of enforced overtime, and the AEU had to settle on terms similar to those of 1898. The York Memorandum was reaffirmed, with the right to enforce overtime working as an additional prerogative of management.

The 1922 defeat again brought into question the narrow basis of the union's membership. In 1914 skilled workers outnumbered unskilled by three to one; by the early 1920s the ratio was almost one to one as technological change forced the pace of reform especially with the increasing use of mass production techniques. The National Committee in 1922 amended the AEU rules slightly to admit more semi-skilled workers and in 1926 the union was opened to unskilled workers; as a result its membership doubled in the years 1933-9, reaching a total of 390,873 in 1939. The AEU had taken the lead in campaigning (with considerable success in the 1930s) for holidays with pay for its members. It had also gained the right to negotiate for apprentices and many firms secured the 40-hour week.

During the Second World War the AEU became for a time the second largest union in Britain, more than doubling its size between 1939 and 1953; its membership stood at 825,000 by 1953. But this was later to fall back with the contraction of the engineering industry in the last phases of the war. A substantial degree of AEU expansion was among semi-skilled workers in the munitions factories, and in 1942 it was decided to admit women, which resulted in the recruitment in 1943 of 138,717 women. Another major development in wartime was the growth of a more effective federation in the engineering industry. There had been a partial federation in the industry since 1890; since 1936 it had been called the *Confederation of Shipbuilding and Engineering Unions* (see **Trade Union Federations**) to which the AEU affiliated in 1946. The war also renewed the efforts of the AEU to secure further amalgamation, and the first fruit of these efforts was the admission of the *Amalgamated Society of Glass Works' Engineers* (1944) and of the *Amalgamated Society of Vehicle Builders, Carpenters, and Mechanics* (1945).

Recent amalgamations
On July 1, 1967 the AEU joined forces with the *Amalgamated Union of Foundry Workers,* an organisation similar to the AEU. The foundry workers union was one of the oldest trade unions in Britain with the longest continuous existence. Its formation can be traced back to 1809 with the formation of the *Friendly Iron Moulders' Society* which held its first meeting at the Hand and Banner Hotel in Bolton. In 1854 the society was one of the organisations which decided not to amalgamate with the *Old Mechanics* and proceeded instead to its own series of amalgamations with other foundry societies, eventually becoming the *National Union of Foundry Workers* in 1920. Further

amalgamations took place during the Second World War, and in 1946 the *Amalgamated Union of Foundry Workers* came into existence. This was the organisation which eventually joined the AEU. But the fusion to the AEU which resulted in the two unions adopting the same name, the *Amalgamated Engineering and Foundry Workers' Union* (AEF), was a loose one as both organisations retained separate rule books.

The AUEW

1970 and 1971 saw further important amalgamations take place, such as those between the AEF and the white collar engineering union DATA *(Draughtsmen and Allied Technicians' Association)* which subsequently changed its name to TASS (Technical, Administrative, and Supervisory Section) (see **MSF**), the *Construction Engineering Union* (CEU) (an organisation whose history dates back to 1913), and the *Steel Smelters' Union,* which organised workers outside the iron and steel industry. The combined organisation became known as the *Amalgamated Union of Engineering Workers* (AUEW) and started its new life with a total membership of 1,297,000, second only to the TGWU, a position it maintained throughout the seventies.

The AUEW federation provided by rule for the President and General Secretary of the engineering section to be the corresponding officers of the AUEW. The Executive Council of the AUEW consisted of the EC of the engineering section, two representatives from the foundry section, one of whom could be its General Secretary, plus two representatives from TASS and one from the construction section. The four sections also held a combined National Conference.

The ultimate aim of the AUEW was to achieve a common rule book and a common policy but the different traditions and organisational structure of the separate unions made this difficult to achieve. National Conferences often passed resolutions supporting this sentiment but they were never translated into full amalgamation. One of the central issues which frustrated moves towards completing full amalgamation was the position of full-time TASS officials who, unlike their counterparts in the other sections, were appointed on permanent contracts. Further, TASS still retained a strong left-wing tradition whereas the AUEW National Committee (since the retirement of Hugh Scanlon) had moved steadily to the right.

In April 1980 the National Committee decided that TASS should be forced either to accept the proposed full merger or leave the federation. By the end of 1982 the situation deteriorated to such an extent that the matter had moved to the courts, finally ending in the Court of Appeal which ruled in favour of TASS whilst at the same time refusing the AUEW National Committee leave of appeal to the House of Lords. TASS thereby prevented the engineers from achieving "amalgamation by domination" and imposing on TASS minority status. Ken Gill, TASS General Secretary, accused some of the AUEW leadership of using "bullying and hectoring tactics," which discouraged other unions that might have been attracted to the AUEW.

On January 25, 1984 the four sections of the AUEW voted in favour of breaking up the four-section grouping and to replace it with a much looser two-section amalgamation. The engineering, construction, and foundry sections formed one section and TASS formed the other. With TASS excluded from the larger manual section and becoming a separate independent organisation (see **MSF**) the manual section changed its name in May 1986 reverting to its earlier title of the Amalgamated Engineering Union.

Union officials

There has been a full-time President of the union ever since its creation in 1921. The President chairs Executive Council meetings (at which he has a casting vote), deals with TUC matters, presides at the National Committee (and rules revision) and is the chief negotiating officer of the union. In this latter role his most important industrial duty is to present the annual wages and conditions claim on behalf of the Confederation of Shipbuilding Engineering Unions (CSBU) to the Engineering Employers' Federation (EEF). The President is elected by a full postal vote of all the members for a first term of office of five years and subsequent terms of five years.

Elections for the President, whose term of office runs until March 1991, were expected to have been called in September 1989 but they have now been delayed for six months. This has sparked off a row within the AEU leadership with the left claiming that the delay has been designed to allow Bill Jordan, the incumbent and right-wing candidate, an easier run at the expense of the left's leading contender Jimmy Airlie. Had the election been called for September 1989 as first planned Jimmy Airlie would have been able to run without first having to give up his seat as the executive member for Scotland. But the delay means that he must now resign his seat in order to run for President as the election for his Scottish seat coincides with the union Presidency elections.

The General Secretary post in the union has been a full-time post ever since the formation of the ASE in 1851. The incumbent is head of the internal affairs of the union, is responsible for the monthly journal and the general office staff, acts as treasurer, and, in conjunction with the President, is responsible for employers' correspondence and opening of new branches. He may attend all meetings of the EC and speak but has no vote. Like the President he is elected by a full postal ballot of the entire membership and holds office on the same basis.

There are two National Secretaries, one elected by the foundry membership and the other by the construction membership. The foundry members also elect an Assistant National Secretary who is Chairman of the foundry committee. The engineering members elect two Assistant General Secretaries who are responsible for branch correspondence, car supply, education, membership, organisation, and propaganda and political matters.

The ten Executive Council members comprise the following: seven engineering members elected from seven EC electoral divisions; two members from the foundry section (the National Secretary and the Chairman of the Foundry Committee); and the National Secretary of the construction section, elected by construction members. The two foundry members and the construction Secretary have national responsibilities in their respective autonomous sections. The seven engineering EC members are best described as the senior national industrial officers. Each executive councillor has a personal assistant allocated to him appointed by the General Secretary and is considered to be part of the technical staff and ineligible for full-time officer status. Each engineering EC member is responsible for a particular trade firm or industry, and often works with one of the seven (engineering) national organisers, who are allocated to a particular EC member, and elected from the same division.

The seven regional officers operate in the regional offices and are in use as "spare limbs", being allocated duties by the particular EC member. They are elected by engineering members in their electoral divisions. There are 27 divisional organisers and 17 assistant divisional organisers. Divisional organisers are elected by members in their organising divisions, engineering, foundry, or construction, as appropriate, whereas the assistant divisional organisers are elected by engineering members only. The lowest level of full-time official in the status hierarchy are the 120 district secretaries who are located throughout the UK and Eire.

The Table below gives a breakdown of the union's full-time officials and shows by whom they are elected.

Full-time officials	Engineering section	Foundry section	Construction section	Total
President				1
General Secretary				2
National Secretaries		1*	1*	2
EC divisions 1 - 7	7*			7
Assistant General Secretaries	2			2
Assistant National Secretary		1		1
National officers		3* (only 1 is an EC member)	1	4
National organisers	7	1		8
Regional officers	7			7
Divisional organisers	27	9	15	51
Assistant divisional organisers	17			17
District secretaries	120			120
Total	189	15	17	221

*indicates the 11 members of the union's Executive Council, along with the President. The President and General Secretary of the union are elected by all members irrespective of section.

Formally, the President of the union is the senior officer but recent events have put a strain on the authority of the present incumbent, Bill Jordan, who easily won the election in 1985 (see "Recent events").

Coverage
The AEU covers virtually every sphere of manufacturing in the country — in both public and private sectors — and a detailed coverage is too complex to give here. The union is dominant in many of the following sectors: aircraft and shipbuilding industries; scientific instruments and constructional engineering; railway workshop foundries; machine tool trades; light, medium, and heavy engineering; and the maintenance and repair of all machinery-using trades, industries, and public utilities.

The AEU has recently been party to a number of single union agreements of which the most publicised was at the Nissan car plant at Washington, Tyne and Wear. Such agreements have become increasingly common in the 1980s and are seen by some unions as a way of combating non-unionism and union derecognition. Following a recent intensive recruitment campaign union membership at the Nissan plant has now risen to more than 30 per cent in some parts of the factory. Previous estimates had indicated that union membership was as low as 7 per cent of the total work-force.

One important factor of the Nissan plant deal which inhibits a higher union membership is that there is no shop steward structure; instead, the company deals directly with full-time union officials. It is unlikely that Nissan will want to alter this arrangement. The AEU has also concluded a single union agreement with Komatsu, the earth-mover manufacturer in the north-east. Here the union does have shop stewards and union membership is close to 80 per cent. The union is also bidding for sole representation rights with Toyota, the Japanese car manufacturer, when it sets up its new plant in Derbyshire.

But single union agreements have also been a source of tension both within the AEU as well as the wider trade union movement. In the wider movement they have put strains on the TUC and its Bridlington Principles as competition between unions for members has intensified as a result of political and structural changes in the economy (see **TUC**).

In the AEU tension between the right and left wing in the union has existed for some time over the whole question regarding the efficacy of single union deals. The left is critical of them, in that they promote inter-union rivalry (as in Ford's attempt to set up a new plant in Dundee — see **TGWU**), and such deals also often tend to include provision for pendulum arbitration, the strike-substitute mechanism. Interestingly enough, even the left wing was supportive of the union's handling of the Ford Dundee affair, and at the 1988 Conference delegates refused to back a resolution attacking the union's role. Instead the motion was rejected by one of the largest majorities — 105 votes to four with six abstentions.

Organisation

The break-up of the AUEW in 1984 resulted in the foundry and construction sections adopting what is effectively the engineering rule book. Its constitution incorporates a conscious separation of executive, judicial, and legislative powers, where a policy-making national committee legislates, an elected final appeal court interprets the rules in all contentious disciplinary cases, and a separately elected executive administers the union's affairs from day to day. The present constitution of the union still retains elements inherited from the second amalgamation and elements of its structure can be traced back as far as the *Old Mechanics*.

National Committee

The National Committee is the policy-making body of the union which normally meets annually in April for two weeks and comprises 124 lay delegates. Three delegates are elected from each of the 26 engineering divisions; one additional delegate from each of the three divisions with the highest membership; the women's Annual Conference elects seven seats specifically reserved for them; 20 delegates seats are reserved for the foundry section; and 13 seats are reserved for the construction section. Throughout the best part of the eighties the NC has been right-wing dominated. In 1989 it was expected that the left would gain control of the NC but they narrowly failed to win a majority at the union's womens conference which would have virtually guaranteed them the election of seven women delegates essential to the left's bid for NC control.

The National Committee initiates policy, reviews agreements with employers, and instructs the Executive Committee for the following year. Every five years the NC also reviews and revises its rules. The AEU is almost unique in that it sets a limit on the number of conference delegates; but the National Conference lacks the authority of a major delegate conference as found in most other unions. Furthermore, the time between conferences is too long to allow the NC to cast a careful eye over the activities of the Executive Committee. Inevitably therefore, the full-time seven-member Executive strays into policy-making rather than implementing policies made for it.

There have been several conflicts between the NC and the Executive Council over the years. From time to time the NC has tried to reinforce its admitted constitutional role by approving resolutions which have included provisions for its own recall in the event of something happening or failing to happen. In 1966 a dispute between the two bodies resulted in a final appeal court ruling censuring the Executive for failing to act upon a recall motion. A notorious example, which illustrates the possible serious loss in NC powers, was an occasion in 1967 when the then right-wing President, Lord Carron, cast the massive engineers' block vote at the Labour Party and TUC Conferences in defiance of the instruction of the NC. This became known as Carron's Law, and ended with Hugh Scanlon's election as President in 1967. All Executive Council minutes are highly confidential (only decisions are reported), and thus the NC is weakened further in its policy-making role.

While it is true to say that the NC has generally been free of domination by national officials and lower level full-time officials and has sometimes acted as a check on the administration, its real role is that of providing a forum for debates on "political" issues. The NC decides the allocation of the massive block vote at the TUC and Labour Party Conferences.

District committees

In the engineering section branches are grouped into 230 districts (of which 36 are single branch districts). There are 120 full-time district secretaries, the rest are part-time lay officials. Some districts have itinerant district secretaries who are full-time officials and are responsible for a group of districts each retaining its own district committee.

District committees comprise delegates elected by the branch they represent and shop stewards, who elect one of their number for every 3,000 members annually. Additional women shop stewards are directly elected to district committees on the same basis of representation as men.

The 145 foundry branches are grouped into 14 districts and nine divisions. The construction section has no district organisation; instead, branches are grouped into six divisions.

The independence of the National Committee was at one time to be understood in the light of the high level of autonomy and wide range of functions which districts had. Rule 12 still provides that district committees negotiate with employers and regulate wages, hours of labour, terms of overtime, piecework, and general conditions affecting the interests of the trades in their respective districts. However, the power of the Executive Committee has eroded this autonomy and all district committee decisions are now subject to its approval.

Divisional committees

Divisional committees are a level higher in the union than district committees, and their main functions are to oversee the union's organisation in the districts and to provide a link between the districts and the EC and NC.

There are 27 engineering divisions which cover conveniently situated districts. Each engineering section district committee comprising 1,000 members or more sends two delegates to the divisional committee. Districts with less than 1,000 members are entitled to one delegate. Single branch districts of less than 100 members are grouped with similar branches in the area and elect one delegate for the group. Members of divisional committees must have seven years' adult membership, except women's representatives who require only three years. Construction and foundry members may send representatives to the divisional committee but they are not eligible to be elected as the committee's delegates to the NC, TUC, or Labour Party Conferences. Normally the divisional organiser acts as divisional secretary.

Each divisional committee sends delegates to the NC and elects one delegate to attend the TUC and Labour Party Conferences and, if appropriate, regional TUCs, the Welsh TUC, the Scottish TUC, and the Irish and Northern Irish TUCs. One woman delegate is elected to attend the women's Annual Conference, and two youth delegates are elected to attend the annual youth conference by each divisional committee. Delegates are also elected by divisional committees, from members employed in the particular sections of industry, to attend Trade Advisory Committees/Delegate Conferences (see "Internal union advisory committees").

Representation on divisional committees is fraught with anomalies. Smaller districts can have greater representation than those with larger memberships because a district with fewer than 1,000 members is entitled to send one delegate, whereas a district with several thousands of members is restricted to sending just two delegates.

Sectional autonomy

Following the amalgamation of the engineers, foundry workers, and construction workers with all three bodies adopting a single (essentially engineers') rule book and constitution, the smaller foundry and construction sections still retain policies autonomous for their own industries. By-laws of both sections allow delegates to be elected for their own separate National Industrial Conference (foundry section) and National Industrial Council (construction section). The foundry committee (the executive body) meets weekly to review administration matters in their section whilst the construction section National Industrial Council meets quarterly to perform the same function.

In 1983 the *British Role Turners' Society,* previously an independent trade union, amalgamated with the then AUEW. It now forms the smallest section of the union and has its own national advisory committee and branch structure.

All these bodies are under the control of the Executive Council.

Internal union advisory committees

The union has a further set of advisory committees which are intended to streamline the union's organisation in a number of industries and which serve to consider and advise the EC on problems affecting their respective industries. There are six trade advisory or standing delegate conferences within the union which cover the following sections of industry: 1. Ministry of Defence; 2. iron and steel; 3. ICI; 4. railways; 5. supervisory section; 6. UKAEA.

Advisory committees are held annually, around March/April, and usually members of the EC are allocated responsibility for them. There is also provision for the EC to convene meetings for special problems, and there are delegate conferences for the following industries: shipbuilding; Metal Box; British Nuclear Fuels; Rover; Phillips; electrical supply; Massey Ferguson; British Aerospace; paper board making.

Junior workers' Annual Conference

Open to members under 21 years of age, the Conference elects seven representatives, one from each Executive Council division, to attend the National Committee. The

Conference consists of not more than 27 delegates, one delegate from each of the engineering divisions and one from the foundry section. The Annual Conference is in effect a training ground for future officers.

Women's Annual Conference
(See "Women").

Work-place relations

The shop steward is the basis of work-place representation. Stewards are elected by members in the work-place and larger factories often elect a convenor. Shop stewards must have had 12 months' adult membership, though district committees can use their discretion, and all their appointments are subject to the approval of the district committee. Stewards must report to their district committee in writing on all matters affecting their members in the work-place. Their duties include examining and signing the contribution cards of all members, recruiting new members, and representing their members' interests to management.

Engineering shop stewards had achieved a presence for some years before the turn of the century, although the first manifestation of steward organisation did not come until the First World War, when both their numbers and powers expanded substantially, especially in engineering and munitions. The inter-war years, with mass unemployment, saw a marked decline in their numbers and influence, although they achieved a degree of partial recognition in the formal procedures in engineering.

In the late 1930s with the resurgence of demand associated with rearmament, shop stewards again achieved a level of prominence, particularly in aircraft manufacture and munitions. The Second World War gave a further boost to steward influence and a degree of organisation was achieved through the system of joint production committees in establishments associated with the war effort. The growth in informal bargaining, stemming largely from the extensive use of piece-work bargaining, and successive post-war governments pursuing a policy of full employment in the 1950s and 1960s, gave rise to much public and mass media concern about their identification with the twin problems of wage drift and unofficial strikes (particularly in the engineering industry). In Donovan's analysis of industrial relations in mid-sixties' Britain, the Royal Commission on Trade Unions and Employers' Associations, shop stewards were portrayed as forming part of the "informal system" which, because of local wage bargaining, undermined the "formal system" of national bargaining agreements and machinery.

Women

Women have been admitted into the union since 1943 and enjoy the same benefit rights as their male counterparts. There are 100,000 women in the AEU which, of a total membership of 815,072, represents just over 12 per cent. To all intents and purposes the AEU is a male-dominated union.

However, as a result of the growth in the number of single-union agreements the AEU has signed, the organisation and effective representation of women members are beginning to be important issues. The increase in single-union deals means that the union is organising all grades of workers in a plant where previously it represented mainly the male-dominated craft grades. Existing AEU structures, as the General Secretary recently revealed, "might no longer be appropriate, and branch structure would have to be examined to see if it catered for women in any meaningful way". The union would also need to provide services and education courses for women and re-examine the need for women's organisers.

There is provision under rule to convene an Annual Women's Conference consisting of "not less than 27 and not more than 54 delegates who are members of the engineering section district committess and two delegates from the foundry section". The AEU makes much of this fact in a specially produced recruitment leaflet to attract new women members. However, a resolution carried at the 1988 National Committee called on the NC "to express its grave disquiet at the fact that only two motions for the 1987 Women's Conference were debated at the 1987 National Committee. Conference feels that this indicates a lack of commitment to pursuing resolutions adopted by this Women's Conference . . . ." Furthermore, it was noted that the Executive Committee does not take women members seriously and that it must inform Conference about the work it carries out on women's issues.

Bill Jordan, the union President, announced at the 1989 Annual Women's Conference that a new post of national women's organiser might be created in response to the growing importance placed on serving the needs of women workers.

External relations
In June 1985 the AEU balloted its membership to determine whether it should retain a political fund. The result of the ballot was 238,604 (or 84 per cent) in favour and 44,399 against keeping the fund. Whilst this is a significant victory for its retention it has to be set against the low turn-out of 37 per cent. At present the annual political levy is 25p a quarter per paying member in the engineering and construction sections and 2p per week in the foundry section. Of the money raised for the political fund one-third is allocated to the district committees for local political work. The AEU is affiliated to the Labour Party and sponsors the following MPs:

R. Caborn   (Sheffield Central);
D. G. Clelland (Tynebridge);
J. Dunnachie   (Glasgow Pollok);
K. Eastman   (Manchester Blackely);
J. Evans   (St Helens North);
W. E. Garrett   (Wallsend);
G. Howarth   (Knowsley North);
R. Hughes   (Aberdeen North);
W. McKevey   (Sheffield Heeley);
S. Orme   (Salford East);
H. Walker   (Doncaster Central).

The union's group of sponsored MPs has grown significantly since the war. Until 1945 the engineers had an average of four or less MPs in each Parliament. In 1959 they still had only eight, but in 1964 the number rose to 18, but since then it has fallen to its present level of 11. The union's rules (providing one candidate for every 30,000 political levy-paying members) allow room for further growth. All candidates must have at least seven years' union membership, a provision which gives a reasonably firm guarantee that most of the union's MPs are former workers with considerable shop floor experience.

The union administers its parliamentary selection procedure in a highly centralised way. Any member of the union can offer themselves for inclusion on the AEU panel of approved parliamentary candidates. This panel is presented to the National Committee for final approval following an intensive investigation into the members' suitability to be sponsored by the union. Candidates are subjected to a series of both written and oral examinations which are conducted by the Executive Committee, existing MPs, and industrial correspondents of national newspapers. If selected membership of the panel lasts for the term time of Parliament.

In 1988 the AEU's National Committee, by a vote of 64 to 44 with seven abstentions, took the unprecedented step of stripping one of its sponsored MPs, Ron Brown, the member for Leith, of its sponsorship. This followed the much publicised mace-wielding incident in the Commons. The effect of this decision will be twofold. Firstly, he will lose the union's financial support, which under the post-war Labour Party Hastings agreement on union sponsorship of MPs, provides 80 per cent of an MP's election expenses. This amounts to between £4,000 and £5,000, plus a £600 annual retainer. Secondly, Ron Brown will lose the organisational support and resources afforded by the union.

The union is affiliated to the following organisations:
The International Metalworkers' Federation;
The European Metalworkers' Federation;
Labour Research;
Confederation of Shipbuilding and Engineering Unions;
Irish TUC;
Scottish TUC.

The AEU, until the end of 1987, was a member of Trade Unions for Labour, the co-ordinating group which raised £5 million for the Labour Party in the last general election. Announcing the decision to leave, the General Secretary, Gavin Laird, said that the AEU was now politically out of sympathy with the left-led unions that dominate the organisation and that in future, the AEU will itself decide where to place its political contributions. Ken Cure is a member of the National Executive of the Labour Party.

Policy
A key policy objective for the AEU revolves around new technology, skills, and training. AEU new technology policy adopted by the 1987 National Committee focuses on the negotiation of a national agreement which includes a training programme designed to equip AEU members for "the challenges of new technology and advanced manufacturing technology and systems.".

The AEU's Engineering 2000 programme is a series of initiatives aimed at improving training opportunities available to engineers. As part of this programme the AEU set up in May 1988 a National Skills Training Centre in Birmingham where employers were offered courses for their employees ranging from day-release to intensive full-time study in robotics, computer aided design, computer numerical control, pneumatics, and hydraulics.

The union has also undertaken a detailed study into the changing patterns and demands of skills focusing on the role of the supervisor. A report (*Advanced Manufacturing Technology: A New Challenge for Supervisors*) was published in May 1988. Drawing on the West German system of supervision ("Meister System"), the AEU report argues that this system, which places far greater responsibility on the supervisor, thereby enhancing his role and status, could be adapted to the UK context. However, it requires both a far greater degree of training than that which is provided by most employers at present as well as a reassessment of the traditional cultural assumptions about supervisors in British industry.

Earlier in 1989, as a further part of the union's concern over the lack of skills and a properly trained work-force able to cope with the demands of advanced manufacturing technologies, the AEU launched a sophisticated 10-hour training package on robotics which also includes an interactive training video which allows simulation. The cost of developing the package (£140,000) is an interesting development in its own right as it was shared equally by the union and the Department of Trade and Industry.

The AEU has also reached a novel agreement with Rowntree Macintosh, the confectionery manufacturer, to carry out a joint skills audit of maintenance work, which will eventually pave the way for a new grade of advanced and more flexible craftsman.

The aim of the survey will be to identify skill needs resulting from advanced manufacturing technologies, assess the skills of the existing work-force, and recommend future training needs.

Recent events

AEU/EETPU merger

The leaders of the AEU and the EETPU had for years been engaged in long-term discussions about a merger of the two unions but with little tangible result. However, towards the end of 1987, following continued membership decline, the two unions agreed to proceed to more serious discussions, with the EETPU insisting that talks be completed within 12 months. The formation of MSF, following the merger between the ASTMS and TASS, brought new strength to the left-wing alignment in the Labour movement, and was a spur to renewed merger talks. Further, MSF was industrially a threat to the right-led EETPU and AEU, as it would promote itself as the union for new high-tech workers, a group concerning which both the AEU and EETPU had ambitions. The AEU/EETPU merger would have created a union with over one million members, consolidating its position as the second-largest union, and provided a new focus for the right in the Labour movement.

But there were divisions in the AEU negotiating team on the merit of the merger almost from the beginning. The President, Bill Jordan, was a strong supporter of the amalgamation, whereas the General Secretary, Gavin Laird, and Executive member, John Wheatley, were deeply sceptical. Two factors appeared as the stumbling blocks in the eventual collapse of the merger. Firstly, the AEU Executive made the "democratic structure" of the union based on full-time officials, district committees, a professional executive council, a final appeal court, and a small policy-making conference, points of principle and not negotiable. The second key issue concerned the future of the General Secretary, Gavin Laird. The plans for the new union leadership allowed only for a President, who was to have been Bill Jordan, and one General Secretary, understood to be Eric Hammond, the current General Secretary of the EETPU. Given the support provided by John Wheatley to Gavin Laird, Bill Jordan was eventually outmanoeuvred and inevitably the merger talks collapsed. This collapse has resulted in a more divided AEU Executive and also weakened the position of Bill Jordan (see "Organisation").

Previously, the roles of the President and General Secretaries were clearer. The President was accountable to the AUEW constitution whereas General Secretaries were accountable only to their individual sections. Since the demise of the four sections and the foundry and construction workers amalgamating with the engineers, there is now only one General Secretary.

Whilst not formally or constitutionally an issue, in reality, the question of who leads the AEU — the President or the General Secretary — must arise. Bill Jordan was the main advocate of the protracted merger talks with the EETPU, and broke with tradition when he indicated that the union's Executive council should consider going above the National Committee's heads and ballot the membership on whether the merger talks should continue. Although this suggestion was in the end not formally proposed, it does begin to suggest that tension and frustration exist in the present leadership of the union. With the collapse of the talks the General Secretary, Gavin Laird, has asserted his office over that of the President's; whilst the power struggle is not yet over Laird does appear to be in a stronger position.

Internal power issues apart, the long-term implications of the collapsed merger talks have serious industrial relations implications. The merger would have helped to rationalise collective bargaining arrangements in the manufacturing industry, which is beleaguered by a plethora of different agreements. Further, one union would have created and legitimised a single grade of multi-skilled workers which, with the introduction of new technology, is already occurring. The collapse of the talks will probably open up rivalries between the AEU, EETPU, and MSF over the representation of these multi-skilled grades.

Reduction in the working week
A reduction in the working week has been a principal aim of the AEU and its forebears and current policy is to aim for a reduction to 35 hours a week. In 1979 the national agreement with the EEF (Engineering Employers' Federation) saw the working week cut by one hour to 39 hours. Talks began in 1983 about a further reduction but these failed to make any progress. Bill Jordan, the AEU President, and leader of the Confederation of Shipbuilding and Engineering Unions (CSEU), resurrected the talks again in 1985 and drew up plans for a cut to 37.5 hours but these proposals were rejected by the AEU at its 1987 Conference. Instead, the AEU reasserted its policy objective as the 35-hour week.

At the start of the annual negotiations for 1989 Bill Jordan proposed a compromise two-year agreement which would cut the working week in two stages to 37 hours on nationally agreed dates for the entire industry. The EEF replied that it would not contemplate a cut below 37.5 hours, and individual companies had to be left to decide when to cut hours as the reduction had to be financed by local productivity deals. Bill Jordan declared that the talks were deadlocked, and at the AEU Annual Conference in May 1989 he received unanimous support from the National Committee for a campaign in support of the union claim for a shorter working week. Unlikely to receive support for a national all-out strike, the proposal is for selective strikes and a hit list of engineering companies is being drawn up. It is likely that action will be aimed mainly at large companies with strong order books such as Rolls-Royce, GKN, British Aerospace, Ferranti, and NEI, although small component manufacturers which supply a large range of companies might also be targeted. A levy to raise a considerable fund to ensure workers at selected companies do not suffer hardship as a result of industrial action is also being planned. A strike ballot is being called and the result was expected to be declared in July 1989.

If the result were to go in favour of strike action it could mean the start of a real union offensive. However, the result of the ballot was by no means certain and EEF members were aware that in 1988, 38 per cent of their employees worked an average of 9.5 hours' overtime a week, compared with 26.6 per cent working 8.2 hours in 1981. Further, most white collar workers are still close to 37.5 hours and so have little to gain from a strike. The union threat may instead signal the demise of national bargaining in the engineering industry altogether; at the time of writing the EEF was planning a change to its constitution which would enable companies to retain membership without subscribing to national agreements. In fact this dispute could well mark the break up of the most important national pay agreement in the private sector.

Further references
J. B. Jeffreys, *The Story of the Engineers,* Lawrence & Wishart, 1945. An outstanding history of the union.

J. D. Edelstein and M. Warner, *Comparative Union Democracy,* Halstead, 1976, Transaction Books, 1979.

Richard Fletcher, "Trade Union Democracy: A case of the AUEW Rule Book", in Barret-Brown and Coates (eds.), *Trade Union Register 3,* Spokesman Books, 1973.

Irving Richter, *Political Purposes in Trade Unions,* Allen & Unwin, 1973.

R. Undy, "The Electoral Influence of the Opposition Party in the AUEW Engineering Section 1960-75", *British Journal of Industrial Relations*, 1979.

Richard Croucher, *Engineers at War*, Merlin, 1982.

Edmond Frow, Ruth Frow, and Ernie Roberts, *Democracy in the Engineering Union*, Institute for Workers' Control, Nottingham 1982.

Edmond Frow and Ruth Frow, *Engineering struggles: episodes in the story of the shop stewards' movement*, Working Class Movement Library, Manchester, 1982.

Larry James, *Power in a Trade Union*, Cambridge Studies in Management 5, Cambridge University Press, 1984. A study into the role of the district committee in the AEUW.

Keith Aitken, "Blue Book, Green Site", *Marxism Today*, December 1987.

Nigel Haworth, "Ford Unpopular, Dundee-style", *Marxism Today*, December 1987.

Eric Batstone, Stephen Gourlay, Hugo Levie, and Roy Moore, *New Technology and the Process of Labour Regulation*, Clarendon Press, 1987. (Chapter 4 has a case-study on the introduction of new technology in a small-batch engineering company.)

Peter Wickens, *The Road to Nissan — Flexibility, Quality, Teamwork*, Macmillan, 1988. (Contains an interesting chapter on how Nissan chose the AEU.)

Jacques Belanger, "Job control after reforms: a case-study in British engineering", *Industrial Relations Journal*, 18, no. 1, Spring 1987.

K. Coates and T. Topham, *Trade Unions in Britain*, third edition, Fontana, 1988.

AMMA
ASSISTANT MASTERS' AND MISTRESSES' ASSOCIATION

Non-TUC affiliated

Head Office: 7 Northumberland Place, London WC2N 5DA

Telephone: 01-930 6441

Fax: 01-930 1359

Principal officers
Joint General Secretary: Joyce Baird
Joint General Secretary: Peter Smith
Assistant General Secretary: Gerald Imison
Assistant General Secretary: Gillian Wood
Senior Assistant Secretary: Heather Gumbrell
Senior Assistant Secretary: Philip Lott
Senior Assistant Secretary: Barbara Maclean
Senior Assistant Secretary: Mark Stedman
Senior Assistant Secretary: Merly Thompson

Senior Assistant Secretary: Roland Wiles
Assistant Secretary: Steven Crane
Assistant Secretary: Sheila Dainton
Assistant Secretary: Lorna Hamilton
Assistant Secretary: Susan Johnson
Assistant Secretary: Robin Leleux
Assistant Secretary: Janet Martyn
Assistant Secretary: Alison Stanley

Union journal: Report (circulated monthly to members). AMMA also produces a wide range of publications on educational matters.

Membership
1988 Total: 126,000
1986 Total: 113,000

General

AMMA is the third largest teaching union and one of the largest unions outside the TUC. It was established in 1978 through the amalgamation of the *Assistant Masters' Association* and the *Association of Assistant Mistresses.* At the second meeting of the Assembly in October 1979, shortly after the formation of the new union and after the Executive Committee had requested branches to take a specific form of industrial action, the following resolution was debated and carried by a large majority of the membership: "That Assembly affirms that it is not opposed to industrial action but that where possible any such action shall be taken after consultation with the members of AMMA." This resolution, and the subsequent "conscience clause" which "acknowledges the right of an individual member to do as his or her personal conviction dictates", have become, not only the leading principles of the AMMA, but provide the rationale for the union's very existence.

AMMA originated in independent secondary schools, although now it has membership in every area of education. Around 15,000 members are in independent schools, but the fastest growing area of recruitment is in primary teaching. In 1984 AMMA had 11,492 members in primary schools but by May 1989 membership had risen by over 64 per cent to stand at 32,006. A good many of these new recruits were defectors from the NUT when it was involved in the prolonged period of industrial action during the mid-80s. Now that the NUT has softened its image it will be interesting to see if AMMA can sustain the recent rapid membership growth.

The only restriction to membership of AMMA applies to college principals, directors, and headteachers, as the union believes that members might be compromised in the event of an industrial dispute. The union maintains strict independence from political parties but lobbies MPs from all political persuasions. It is not a member of the TUC and makes a virtue of its independence in its recruitment and publicity literature.

Organisation

The Assembly is the supreme body of the union. Each spring an annual meeting of the Assembly is held where union policy is decided. In the period between meetings the Executive Committee conducts the business of the union and has powers to call industrial action. AMMA has no regional structure.

There are 109 branches covering each local education authority. Each branch elects a branch secretary. It is the tradition of AMMA that branches do not mandate their EC members to vote on any resolution in a particular manner. Members are free to exercise their own judgement on matters under consideration but are expected to report back to their branch and explain their actions. It is therefore open to question to what extent these representatives are really representative.

External relations
AMMA takes an active role in the following organisations: the National Foundation for Education Research; the Educational Publishers Association; and the World Confederation of Organisations of the Teaching Profession.

Conservative MP, Robert Key, is an AMMA parliamentary consultant.

Policy
On many educational matters AMMA policies differ more in degree than in fundamental purpose from the other two large teaching unions, the NUT and the NASUWT. Indeed, during the mid-80s teachers' dispute, there was more agreement between AMMA and the NUT on a number of issues, such as cover for absent teachers and salary structures, than might have been expected. At the 1989 Annual Conference, for example, the resolution which AMMA supported, calling on local authorities to monitor the effects of the law requiring schools to offer mainly Christian assemblies and religious education, would not be incompatible with the policies of the NUT or NASUWT.

The real AMMA policy distinctions, and those which enable AMMA to maintain its presence as an independent teaching union, are political. AMMA considers itself to be independent in its political affiliations and lobbies all interested MPs. Its non-membership of the TUC is also a major policy distinction. The fact that AMMA stresses that it only ever recommends a particular form of action and never instructs its members how to act, clearly had some impact with disaffected NUT and NASUWT members during the mid-80s strike period.

But unlike its sister non-TUC union, PAT, AMMA is in principle not opposed to taking strike action and has undertaken industrial action in the past and, in fact, uses strike ballots with a good deal of subtlety. For instance, in September 1988 AMMA indicated to the Secretary of State for Education, Kenneth Baker, that in return for the restoration of satisfactory pay machinery it would ballot its members on a formal undertaking not to strike during negotiations or while arbitrators were considering a binding solution; all the time AMMA insisted to the Secretary of State that it was not offering a blanket, no-strike deal.

Recent events
Towards the end of 1986 AMMA brought in City consultants to undertake an appraisal of the union's administrative and management procedures with a view to increasing their effectiveness. AMMA is keen to maintain the recruitment momentum which saw its membership increase by 40 per cent since 1985, and to ensure that union structures are able to provide the level of support necessary to sustain the aspirations of 130,000 members. The union was eager to adopt a hard-nose business approach in a bid to change the cultural context of union headquarters.

The consultants examined the union's internal administration, its membership services, management structure, and computer systems, and made their recommendations towards the end of 1988. These included:

1. The improvement of the quality of customer care, through the formation of decentralised operating groups at headquarters in order to streamline the handling of

membership casework.

2. The reduction of the number of formal standing committees and their replacement with working groups operating within set time limits and targets.

3. A speed up of membership inquiry response times by the appointment of a member's support manager.

4. An overhaul of the computer systems.

5. A staff increase, particularly in specialist service areas to keep abreast of membership demands.

AMMA has already begun to implement many of the consultants' recommendations.

Merger talks
Informal merger soundings have been made by PAT. If they were to succeed then the new organisation would become the second largest teaching union, overtaking the NASUWT and even rivalling the NUT, the largest teaching union. A rationalisation of the teaching unions has to be welcomed; teachers really need only one union.

APT
ASSOCIATION OF POLYTECHNIC TEACHERS

Non-TUC affiliated

Head Office: Caxton Chambers, 81 Albert Road, Southsea, Hampshire PO5 2SG

Telephone: 0705-818625

Principal officers
Chief Executive: Christine Cheeseman
National Chairman: Ray Powell
National Secretary: Mike Roberts

Union journal: APT Bulletin (monthly)

Membership
Total: 3,161 (January 1989)
(1983: 3,103)
(1979: 3,006)

General
Formed in 1973 following the designation of the last of the 30 polytechnics, the APT recruits lecturers and related academic staff in polytechnics and colleges of higher education, and is recognised for collective bargaining purposes. At national level policy is determined by the union's National Council, while day-to-day administration is carried out by the National Executive Committee. Locally the APT is organised according to autonomous local associations. All office holders are elected at the Annual Council meeting. The Chief Executive is appointed by the NEC and is the only full-time post.

The APT is a member of the Federation of Managerial, Professional, and General Associations. The union was involved in informal merger talks with the expelled EETPU, but these were never continued. However, PAT's closer involvement with the EETPU might make the APT rethink its position.

Until recently the APT played a minor part in negotiations, but now that polytechnics and certain colleges of higher education have corporate status the APT could see its role increased.

ASLEF
ASSOCIATED SOCIETY OF LOCOMOTIVE ENGINEERS AND FIREMEN

Head Office: 9 Arkwright Road, Hampstead, London NW3 6AB

Telephone: 01-431 0275

Principal officers
General Secretary: N. F. Milligan
General Secretary (elect): D. F. Fullick
District Secretaries: E. A. Staton
                  W. Wilkie
                  J. L. Johnson
                  N. Kirton
                  A. S. West
                  F. C. Orton-Jones
                  St J. R. Goff

Union journal: Locomotive Journal (monthly)

Membership

Current membership (1987)
Male: 20,007
Female: 27
Total: 20,034

Membership trends

	1975	1979	1981	1983	1987	change 1975-87	1983-87
Total	29,000	27,478	26,241	23,589	20,034	−31%	−15%

General
ASLEF is the smallest of the three rail unions. It has consistently sought to preserve its craft traditions and organises staff in the "line of promotion" (to footplate), i.e. traction trainees, drivers' assistants, relief drivers, and drivers. Consequently, ASLEF has

opposed British Rail and London Underground proposals for radical overhaul of working practices. Nevertheless, it has gradually made concessions, such as on flexible rostering (British Rail) and one-person-operated trains (London Underground). Negotiations over another key proposal — the introduction of the train-crew concept, involving a new flexible "trainman" grade combining the jobs of assistant driver and guard — were described by General Secretary, Neil Milligan, as "the most comprehensive, complex, and critical this century in the railway industry".

History

ASLEF reached its centenary year in 1980, having started life in February 1880 as a breakaway from the *Amalgamated Society of Railway Servants* (later to become the NUR). The first branches of ASLEF were at Sheffield, Pontypool, Neath, Liverpool, Leeds, Bradford, Tondu, and Carnforth. The following year ASLEF registered as a trade union with its head office in Leeds. By 1900 membership had reached nearly 10,000. In 1902 the union affiliated to the Labour Representation Committee.

ASLEF was involved in the first national rail strike in 1911, which only lasted for two days but nevertheless led to recognition by the railway companies. Although further rail union amalgamations took place after the 1911 strike ASLEF preferred to retain its autonomy.

The long-standing differences between the NUR and ASLEF were exacerbated in early 1924. The railway companies had presented proposals to the National Wages Board which embodied a worsening differential between locomotive drivers and other railway grades. ASLEF decided to strike and were out for nine days whilst the NUR instructed its members to work normally. Although ASLEF achieved its objective of retaining its differential, the hostility between the two unions continued up to very recent times. However, since the mid-1980s there has been a remarkable thaw, and relations between ASLEF and NUR are harmonious (see **NUR**).

Union officials

All ASLEF officials (i.e. the General Secretary, Assistant General Secretary and the seven District Secretaries) are elected for a five-year period. Only those with at least five years continuous membership of the union are eligible to stand for election.

Organisation

The supreme government of ASLEF is vested in the 46-strong Annual Assembly of Delegates which meets in May or June. Delegates are elected by ASLEF members grouped into 46 districts. Three of the delegates must be from London Underground.

In 1982 ASLEF's rules were changed to provide that the two posts of General Secretary and Assistant General Secretary be subject to re-election every five years. These changes therefore preceded the provisions of the Trade Union Act and mainly resulted from campaigning by the left in the union to make full-time officials more accountable to the union membership.

The Executive Committee is responsible for the management of the union in between Annual Assemblies. It consists of eight members (one from London Underground), elected for a three-year term of office.

Recent events

ASLEF has become increasingly pragmatic but certain branches and districts have shown their capacity and resolve to organise unofficial industrial action. In April 1988 the branch secretary at King's Cross was sacked by British Rail for being personally involved in the "unauthorised distribution of leaflets calling for an unofficial strike".

Actually, the strike call — in support of the health workers' day of action — was subsequently abandoned after BR secured an injunction.

During May 1989 very well organised unofficial strikes took place among London Underground drivers to back a claim for extra money for those operating trains without guards. One or two labour relations journalists detected in this action a perverse effect of the legislative restrictions on official strike action. Some of the organisers of the unofficial action partly blamed the decision to strike on the cumbersome negotiation procedures. The union leadership called for normal working but this had no effect. The dispute was settled when both sides accepted a package proposed by a mediation board appointed by ACAS. London Underground management had proposed major changes in working practices but the determination of the rank and file and craftiness of the leadership forced it to make significant concessions, such as abandoning plans to curtail overtime by introducing more flexible shift working and altering other work practices.

Further reference

N.McKillop, *The Lighted Flame: A History of ASLEF*, Thomas Nelson, 1950. This is the official history of ASLEF up to 1949. Whilst it contains a good account of the union's development it suffers from adopting a very uncritical perspective and is extremely biased (especially in describing the NUR - ASLEF disputes).

ASTWKT
AMALGAMATED SOCIETY OF TEXTILE WORKERS AND KINDRED TRADES

TUC affiliated

Head Office: "Foxlowe", Market Place, Leek, Staffs ST13 6AD

Telephone: 0538-382068

Principal national officers
General Secretary: Alfred Hitchmough
Organising Officer: Peter Mehars

Union journal: Textile Voice (a newsletter, issued at regular intervals to all members)

Membership

Current membership (1987)
Male: 1,155
Female: 1,683
Total: 2,838

Membership trends
1983: 3,300
1979: 6,006
1975: 5,372

General

The union organises various grades of workers in the North Staffordshire textile industry, but amalgamations have also given it membership in silk and cotton textiles as far afield as Dunfermline, Pontypridd, and Farnworth. The union is represented on the Narrow Fabrics Joint Industrial Council (JIC) and on the JIC for the Silk Industry. It also concludes a number of plant and company agreements.

History

The society originated in 1871 in the shape of a union called the *Associated Trimming Weavers' Society of Leek* which was the oldest of the unions which combined to form the Amalgamated Society in 1919. It organised certain groups of workers in the silk industry. In 1872 there was a three-week strike over demands for wage increases of 20 per cent and upwards; the *Trimming Weavers' Society* and the small trade societies played the main organising role, though the strike was largely unsuccessful.

More unions were formed in the silk industry in the Leek area and in the 1890s there were, for the first time in this industry, attempts to organise women workers in the trade unions.

In 1907 some of the various small trade societies in the Leek silk industry came together in the *Leek Textile Federation*. William Stubbs, secretary of the *Silk Twisters' Amalgamation*, and William Bromfield of the *Trimming Weavers' Society*, were nominated for Secretary; Bromfield won the vote.

Another great strike took place in the Leek silk industry in 1913, lasting two weeks and involving 4,000 workers. This time, the unions (helped by the Federation) were more united and emerged with most of their claims conceded.

In 1919 most of the Leek textile unions amalgamated to form the present Amalgamated Society of Textile Workers' and Kindred Trades. The amalgamation went ahead smoothly, although the silk twisters remained outside it, continuing alone until dissolution in 1939.

In 1918 the Joint Industrial Council for the Silk Industry was set up with the ASTWKT prominent among its constituent trade unions. The JIC acted more as a conciliation and arbitration body than as a negotiating body. This was largely because of fragmentation of bargaining: sections of the North Staffordshire textile industry came into the orbit of the Narrow Fabrics industry and, later, the hosiery industry JICs. Agreements on questions of actual wages and conditions were made (for Leek) in negotiation with the Leek Manufacturers' and Dyers' Association, and for Macclesfield with the Silk Trade Employers' Association. At an early stage the silk JIC was subdivided and in 1920 a JIC for the Leek textile industry was established. In the early 1950s the Leek silk JIC was revived as the Leek Joint Consultative Committee which emerged from an idea by Herbert Lisle (the ASTWKT General Secretary who retired in 1983).

In 1951 the society affiliated to the *Weavers' Amalgamation*, again an idea forcefully advocated by Lisle who favoured an industrial union for textiles. However, the affiliation was not a success and it was decided to withdraw on the grounds that affiliation was "costing too much".

In 1965 the *National Silk Workers' and Textile Traders' Association of Macclesfield* merged with the ASTWKT by transfer of engagements. It had been in existence since 1903 when it was the *Macclesfield Power Loom Weavers' and General Silk Workers' Association* which had not joined the federation of 1907. It brought branches from elsewhere, the main ones being in Dunfermline and Yarmouth.

Organisation

The society is governed by the Delegate Board, composed of representatives of each branch, which meets annually in May when it elects an Executive Council. The EC fixes all officers' salaries, shop stewards' fees, collectors' commission, committee fees, expenses, and determines the membership levy. These must subsequently be approved by the Delegate Board. Between Delegate Board meetings the business of the union is conducted by the Executive which has the power to call special Delegate Board meetings at any time. Any section of workers who have a grievance which may lead to a strike or a lock-out is entitled to send five representatives to state their case before the Executive Council.

All EC members are elected annually. The President, appointed annually by the Delegate Board, is not entitled to vote. In the event of a tied vote with no majority in favour or against, the motion will fail. The General Secretary is also appointed by the Delegate Board; since he too has no rights to vote, this procedure satisfies the present legal requirements.

External relations
The union is affiliated to the Labour Party.

Recent events
ASTWKT recently appointed Alf Hitchmough as General Secretary to succeed the influential Herbert Lisle. Alf Hitchmough was previously an official with the *Amalgamated Textile Workers' Union* (which merged with the *GMB* in 1986). As a condition of his acceptance to the post of General Secretary, Alf Hitchmough insisted on balloting the membership about the political fund. Following a secret ballot the union agreed to reinstate the political fund levy which had been wound down by Herbert Lisle.

The union has recently made a concerted effort to improve its effectiveness at the work-place level. As part of its campaign it has recruited more shop stewards, especially among women (who constitute the majority of the membership). All shop stewards are sent on TUC courses.

AUT
ASSOCIATION OF UNIVERSITY TEACHERS
TUC affiliated

Head Office: United House, 1 Pembridge Road, London W11 3HJ

Telephone: 01-221 4370

Fax: 01-727 6547

Principal national officers
General Secretary: Diana Warwick
Deputy General Secretary: J. R. Akker
Assistant General Secretary: A. M. Aziz
Assistant General Secretary: P. Cottrell
Assistant General Secretary: G. Talbot

Regional officers:
Scotland: D. Bleiman
North West: B. Everett
London: M. Keight
Wales and Midlands: M. Machon

Union journal: The union publishes two journals which it distributes free to all members: the *AUT Bulletin* and *AUT Woman* (termly).

Membership

Current membership (1987)
Male: 27,488
Female: 4,851
Total: 32,339

Membership trends

	1975	1979	1981	1983	1987	change 1975-87	1983-87
Men	24,187	26,248	28,895	27,647	27,488	14%	−1%
Women	4,500	4,632	5,099	4,879	4,851	8%	−1%
Total	28,687	30,880	33,994	32,526	32,339	13%	−1%

General
The AUT seeks to recruit staff in universities and equivalent institutions who are on academic or academic related salaries. The membership of the union has increased from 1,700 in 1969 to the present level of over 32,000 partly by extending its membership eligibility and partly from the general upsurge in white collar unionisation. Some 15 per cent of its members are women (which roughly reflects the percentage of women employees at academic and related levels in these institutions).

The objectives of the AUT are the advancement of university education and research, the regulation of relations between university teachers and related staff and their employers, the promotion of common action by these staff, and the safeguarding of the interests of members. The union affiliated to the TUC for the first time in 1976.

History
Founded in 1917 under the name of the *Association of University Lecturers,* the union did not include university staff in Scotland who formed their own *Scottish Association of University Teachers* in 1922 and who, although united with the main body in 1949, still have separately elected representation on the National Executive Committee. In 1919 the membership was redefined to cover all teaching staff, including lecturers, senior lecturers, readers, and professors and the name was changed to the Association of University Teachers.

Since its foundation, the AUT has extended its membership to cover academic library staff, senior administrative staff, research, and other related grades of staff. These were eventually brought into the national salary grading structure in 1974, after the national negotiating machinery for teaching grades had been established in 1970. Following a ballot of the union's membership, affiliation to the TUC took place in 1976.

Organisation
The important and primary unit of the AUT is the local association. Local associations

represent members in the individual universities, institutions, colleges, and research units up and down the country.

The governing body of the AUT is the Council which meets twice a year in May and December. Between Council meetings the daily affairs of the union and decisions on policy which cannot await a Council meeting fall within the province of the Executive Committee. The Executive Committee consists of 15 members elected by secret ballot, together with two members similarly elected by the AUT (Scotland) Council and the Honorary Secretary of the AUT (Scotland). In addition, all officers of the Association sit on the Executive Committee in a non-voting capacity. The power to call for industrial action is vested in the AUT Council or, between meetings, in the Executive Committee (rule 20). The union believes that the post of General Secretary is the Association's equivalent to that of a permanent secretary in the Civil Service; in view of legal requirements for the election of this post the union is making the necessary arrangements.

The present AUT executive does not believe that any of its current or potential actions under union rules would require it to use funds from a political fund rather than its general fund. However, union members are concerned that if any action is arbitrarily challenged under the 1984 Act, the union may be stopped in its tracks; consequently, the Representative Council has decided it needs to organise a ballot in order to agree to the setting up of a political fund.

Head Office departments are as follows: Officials; Press; Research and Information; Library; Accounts; Membership; and General Services.

The areas of responsibility of national officers are as follows:

Diana Warwick, General Secretary: national salary negotiations; relationships with government, UFC, and other national bodies; finance and public expenditure; and general matters relating to the organisation and development of AUT.

John Akker, Deputy General Secretary: conditions of service matters; contract researchers; international affairs; parliamentary liaison.

Geoffrey Talbot, Assistant General Secretary: superannuation; administrative staff; specified responsibility for certain local associations.

Adrienne Aziz, Assistant General Secretary: membership and organisation; TUC liaison; women's committee; specified responsibility for certain local associations.

Paul Cottrell, Assistant General Secretary: education and development matters; library staffs; specified responsibility for certain local associations.

Universities are autonomous institutions and as such bargain at that level. However, on pay and superannuation they have agreed to accept the outcome of national negotiations between the AUT and the Committee of Vice-Chancellors and Principals. There may well be pressure for local bargains on pay as resources are further restricted and as recruitment and retention pressures become more acute, particularly in the south-east.

Women
The AUT is particularly supportive towards its women members. It is one of the few unions to issue a separate union journal (*AUT Woman*) especially for women members. It has established a women's section, AGM and committee. Moreover (and other unions might take note), it has established a data bank on comparative terms and conditions of employment for women; its findings are being studied jointly with employers. Union and employers are also looking at ways in which the employment of women can be more representative of the population as a whole. At present women constitute 15 per cent of

the AUT, roughly comparable to the proportion employed in academic and related areas.

External relations
The AUT is not affiliated to any political party and has no sponsored MPs, although it does retain one parliamentary adviser from each of the three major parties in Parliament.

Recent events
At the beginning of 1989 the AUT became embroiled with employers in a dispute on whether they were due for a cost of living increase. In 1988 university lecturers were awarded a 23 per cent package which gave them 16 per cent from December 1986 and a further 7 per cent on 1985 pay levels. Vice-Chancellors claimed that this package was intended to cover 1989 and that the 4.5 per cent cost of living claim which the AUT had submitted was inappropriate.

The intransigence of the Vice-Chancellors led to the AUT balloting its membership on a programme of sanctions which included withdrawing co-operation from schemes for appraising the performance of university lecturers which were a key part of the 1988 pay settlement. Lecturers also voted to boycott all aspects of the university examination process. The dispute lasted for almost six months and was eventually settled on June 1 after the government made extra money available in return for agreement to move towards a more market-based method of pay determination.

The government is determined to undermine national wage bargaining by allowing local management greater discretion to award individual lecturers and professors merit payments, and by varying pay according to regional variations as well as subject scarcity.

During the recent dispute the AUT leadership demonstrated little appreciation of strategy when it first rejected an offer made by the Vice-Chancellors in March 1989, but then agreed to accept a rather similar offer nearly three months later. The lack of tactics allowed divisions and dissent to creep into a membership which,until March, had been united in its cause. This affected adversely the union's credibility with the membership.

Whilst this dispute has been settled, the fact still remains that university lecturers' pay has fallen badly behind that of other comparable professional workers. This is acknowledged by all parties. University employers have warned the government that academic staff need significant pay increases next year to avoid a damaging downward spiral in morale. There is already some evidence of a "brain drain" of academics to better paid jobs in American universities and institutes. The government, in exchange for any extra funding, is likely to demand that pay structures reflect more market-based considerations, with greater use of local bargaining. The introduction of differentials in what essentially is still a collegiate based system of employment, added to the new method of university funding with its entrepreneurial emphasis, are likely radically to alter the whole culture of university life. Can the AUT provide the necessary leadership in what are going to be turbulent times for university lecturers?

The 1988 Education Reform Act had important implications for universities. It removed the right of job tenure for academics employed after November 20, 1987, and established four university commissioners charged with reviewing the statutes and charters of every university. The government's basic aim was to challenge and effectively dilute the notion of tenure, and thereby alter the nature of the employment relationship in universities and provide employers with greater discretion over the use of staff resources.

The University of Aston sought to widen the interpretation of the Act when it attempted to make a number of tenured academic staff compulsorily redundant. The AUT pursued the case successfully to the High Court, where it was ruled that "no member of academic staff could be lawfully removed or have their contract terminated except for good causes, defined in the university's governing statutes". This has set an important precedent in defining the legal basis of tenure and could also affect the case of Hull University lecturer Edgar Page, the first lecturer to be made compulsorily redundant by any university. It is also likely to affect the deliberations of the four university commissioners who may need to take a more cautious line in implementing government proposals for reforms in the universities. (Looking beyond the confines of the academic world, the High Court ruling draws attention to the positive role which the law can play in industrial relations matters.)

Further reference
Harold Perkin, *The Key Profession*, Routledge & Kegan Paul, 1969.

BACM
BRITISH ASSOCIATION OF COLLIERY MANAGEMENT
TUC affiliated

Head Office: BACM House, 317 Nottingham Road, Old Basford, Nottingham NG7 7DP

Telephone: 0602-795819

Fax: 0602-422279

Principal national officer
General Secretary: J. Meads

Union journal: National News Letter (quarterly)

Membership
1987: 10,757
1983: 15,584
1979: 17,160

The continuing contraction in the coal industry, the privatisation of electricity supply, and the possibility of the privatisation of British Coal suggest that BACM's membership will continue to decline. However, the union itself is of the opinion that its membership will decline more slowly in the future and has devised strategies to retain membership.

General
The British Association of Colliery Management affiliated to the TUC in 1977, and represents those engaged in professional, technical, managerial, or staff duties in the mining industry or associated industries in Great Britain. It came into existence in 1947, and since then it has enjoyed good relations with all the unions in the coal-mining industry (NACODS, NUM, and UDM).

History

As early as December 1945 it was decided to form a managerial trade union in the mining industry to be known as the *Yorkshire Association of Colliery Officials and Staff* (YACOS). At the outset it was agreed that this union should cater for all non-industrial staff, from the clerk to the colliery manager, and from the supervisor to the chief engineer. Membership grew rapidly, and when branches had formed outside Yorkshire, in the East Midlands, South Wales and the North of England, it was decided to change the name to the *British Association of Colliery Officials and Staff (BACOS)*. Following the nationalisation of the coal-mining industry on January 1, 1947, BACM was formed soon afterwards in May 1947, and the BACOS membership transfered to BACM some three months later.

Union officials

Along with the General Secretary, BACM has five full-time organisers, an Assistant General Secretary, a headquarters office manager, a research officer, and clerical staff. BACM has a history of continuity; in the 35 years of its existence it has had only five presidents and the third General Secretary was appointed in 1979.

Coverage

The union caters for the needs of those engaged in the management, scientific development, and administration of the mining industry, and ancillary and associated undertakings up to British Coal Board level. Demarcation lines with other mining unions have been well established since the early 1950s. The penetration of BACM membership is very high (approximately 98 per cent) and the Association has a comprehensive conciliation agreement with British Coal for dealing with national questions relating to salaries, conditions of employment, disputes, etc. In 1985 the multilateral consultative agreement with British Coal ceased as a result of differences between BC and the NUM; however, the Association receives bilateral consultation with British Coal.

Organisation

The Annual Delegate Conference is the supreme body of government in the union. It consists of representatives from the 10 BACM branches (nine delegates per branch).

The National Executive Committee carries the business of the union between Conferences, and consists of the national officers (President, Vice-President, and Treasurer); the General Secretary; 10 branch delegates (one from each branch); and nine vocational group members, one from each of the nine vocational groups (listed below). All lay NEC members (where posts are contested) are elected by secret ballot of the relevant constituency. Only Conference delegates are eligible for nomination. The NEC appoints the General Secretary, but in the near future the Association is likely to adopt a modified version of the NEC members ballot procedure for the election of its General Secretary, with the Executive Committee endorsing its preferred candidate after formal interview. The union has accepted secret postal balloting as the only practical way to comply with current legislation.

A branch of the union is established in each area of British Coal. Members employed at headquarters (e.g. research establishments) are attached to either Headquarters North or Headquarters South branches. Other British Coal staff employed by independent organisations are attached to the branch nearest their place of employment. Where branches cover a large geographical area, sub-branches are formed. Full-time officials service each branch.

In order to ensure that each section of management is represented on the National and branch Executive Committees the membership is classified into nine vocational groups as follows:

Mining groups
1. Colliery managers and persons superior to managers.
2. Under-managers, deputy managers, and assistant managers.
3. Other mining officials not in groups 1 or 2 (e.g. mechanisation, safety and training, method study, strata control, ventilation, dust control, planning, and open-cast officials).

Other vocational groups
4. Mining, electrical, mechanical, and civil engineers.
5. Mining surveyors (including bona fide apprentices and unqualified surveyors).
6. Administrative staff, industrial relations, purchasing and stores, marketing officials.
7. Specialist sections, including architectural, coal preparation, estates, rescue, engineering drafters and tracers, and nurses.
8. Scientific, geological, coke oven chemicals, and by-product officials.
9. Finance and computer staff.

Policy
The Association is a moderate member of the TUC and in general its policies are determined with regard to what the union would call "pragmatism and common sense" in order to ensure that such policies are achievable. For years the union has argued that British Coal should pursue a policy of voluntary redundancy where jobs reduce as a result of reorganisation.

The union has indicated to British Coal that it is prepared to discuss the introduction of new technology.

Women
BACM has a small number of women members and at present there is one woman member on the National Executive Committee.

External relations
BACM has no political fund or affiliations, and its present rules do not allow it to affiliate to any political party. But it does have one parliamentary consultant — Alan McKay, MP for Penistone.

The Association has representatives on a number of TUC committees, including the TUC Energy Committee. It is a member of the Council of Managerial, Professional, and Allied Staffs (COMPAS), which includes similar TUC unions including the EMA and BALPA. In Europe BACM is represented on the ETCU Energy Industries Committee and is affiliated to FICME, Federation Internationale des Cadres des Mines which represents management staff in the coal mining industries of Western Europe.

It is an open secret that the TGWU would like to include the BACM in its newly-formed energy trade group which, if its talks with the NUM prove successful, would be a sensible move for BACM to make (see **TGWU**). However, EMA has also expressed an interest in a merger with the BACM.

BAKERS, FOOD AND ALLIED WORKERS' UNION
TUC affiliated

Head Office: Stanborough House, Great North Road, Stanborough, Welwyn Garden City, Hertfordshire AL8 7TA

Telephone: 07072-60150

Fax: 07072-61570

Principal national officers
General Secretary: Joe Marino
National President: Terry O'Neill
National Safety Officer: Nigel Bryson

Regional offices and secretaries
No. 1 Region: P. Sagoo, "Danecourt", 26 Church Hill, Walthamstow, London E17 9RY
Telephone: 01-801 0980

No. 2 Region: G. Martin, Royal Exchange Building, Room 169, Mount Stuart Square, Cardiff
Telephone: 0222-481518

No. 3 Region: J. Bryan, 4th Floor, Room 29, Grenville Buildings, 12 Cherry Street, Birmingham B2 5AR
Telephone: 021-327 2124

No. 4 Region: W. Harrison, 86 Deepdale Road, Preston, Lancashire PR1 5AR
Telephone: 061-872 6621

No. 5 Region: W. Molloy, 10 Greenside Road, Pudsey, West Yorkshire LS28 8PU
Telephone: 0532-565925

Union journal: The Food Worker (monthly)

Membership

Current membership (1987)
Male: 17,230
Female: 17,231
Total: 34,461

Membership trends

						change	
	1975	1979	1981	1983	1987	1975-87	1983-87
Men	30,906	24,481	N/A	N/A	17,230	−44%	N/A
Women	21,770	19,740	N/A	N/A	17,231	−21%	N/A
Total	52,676	44,221	40,560	37,487	34,461	−35%	−8%

General
The union deals with four national agreements, these being with the Federation of Bakers

(covering the bulk of the union's membership), the National Association of Master Bakers (small bakeries), the Plant Cake agreement, as well as the Co-op agreement. It has partial responsibility for the National Joint Industrial Council Biscuit Workers agreement. There are also members in the retail bread and flour confectionery trades.

The union has suffered a decline in membership since 1975. The decline has affected men to a greater extent than women who now, for the first time, form the majority of members. The industry itself is shifting away from large plants to smaller, more technologically advanced sites which can be operated with greater flexibility; the likelihood is that women are going to form a more significant proportion of union recruits.

In 1987 the union reported a rise in membership in the frozen foods sector and retailing in general; these are new areas which should enable the union not only to stem its declining position but perhaps expand into new ones. The union is currently reviewing its recruitment policies and has already introduced a new members' pack, increased its legal provisions, and generally revamped the range of services it offers.

The union is not experiencing any undue hostility in its role of representing workers by negotiating national agreements. Indeed recently there has been an increase in the number of agreements and talks are underway with one employer to replace the present group agreement with a national agreement. "Industrial relations" still seem to be the dominant way of managing labour in this industry.

History

Trade unionism in baking began in 1849 in the house of a Mr Hollingworth in Manchester where operative bakers met for friendly society purposes. There was then no limit to hours worked (a bill to prohibit night-working in baking had been thrown out in 1848), and a living-in system existed. A code of rules for the *Amalgamated Union of Operative Bakers of England* was drawn up in 1861, and in 1864 Thomas Hudson was elected part-time General Secretary. In the *annus mirabilis* for new unions, 1889, a bakers' strike took place in London, but with no clear result. A Whitley council called the Joint Council for Bread, Baking, and Flour Confectionery was set up in 1918 but did not survive for long.

Throughout the union's existence it has campaigned against night-work in the baking industry. In 1919 the Mackenzie committee of inquiry on night baking reported that it was objectionable on social grounds. W. Banfield who became General Secretary in 1915 worked vigorously to abandon night-work, especially after being elected to Parliament in 1932. In 1938 a private members' bill was successful and its effect was to prohibit night-work from 11p.m. to 5a.m. but it was conditional on the absence of a trade board for the industry, so the employers countered by setting up a trade board, later superseded by a wages council. By 1958 various national agreements had effectively limited night-working to those parts of the industry that were unionised.

In 1940 the union extended its activities to include biscuit workers and it has since expanded into other areas of food production.

During the 1970s the union was involved in a series of strikes in support of higher basic wage rates. Initially they achieved success, but a series of tactical miscalculations, lack of support from the TGWU who crossed picket lines and delivered flour to the bakeries, followed by hostile media coverage, led to a defeat in 1978. Following the defeat membership fell drastically by around 17,000, and in some bakeries the union lost negotiating rights altogether.

Organisation

For the purpose of government the union is divided into: an Annual Conference of

Delegates elected by the members; an Executive Council elected at Annual Conference; districts, co-ordinated by the EC, consisting of geographically grouped branches; which themselves are located within five regions.

The union is essentially a decentralised organisation, built on factory branches and local autonomy is encouraged. This autonomy is seen to hold distinct advantages for the union's present recruitment campaign in individual unorganised sites.

Shop stewards are the "recognised medium intervening with the employer on workshop grievances and on any proposed changes to existing shop practices". Rule 14.62 states that "shop stewards will avail themselves of such opportunities as may be offered by the union to increase their understanding of trade unionism in general and the wage structure and legislation affecting our trade in particular".

In any district of two or more branches there is a district board, composed of delegates from the branches, which meets quarterly. The appointment of all organising district secretaries is sanctioned by the Executive Council. Those nominated for such jobs by the branches may be required to take a test before proceeding to election by secret postal ballot.

The Executive Council co-ordinates the districts into five regions, each region being administered by a regional board of three members from and elected by each district board within the region. The regional boards also meet quarterly. In each region there is a regional officer appointed by the Executive Council of the union.

Nominations from the branches are taken for the posts of General Secretary and President, but the Executive Council still acts as a selection committee and can issue test papers and make a selection of candidates for election. Elections are by ballot postcards issued to every member and then sent to a firm of accountants appointed by the Executive Council.

The 1984 Trade Union Act seems to have made very little difference to the election of its main national paid officers; since 1925 the General Secretary and President have been elected by secret ballot.

Women
For the first time women form the majority of members in the union. It is likely that this trend will be reinforced in the future. Organisationally the union is geared to a male-oriented membership although there are signs that this is changing. The union has debated the issue of separate women's committees at Conferences but these have been rejected by women members themselves who prefer instead to use the existing union structure and machinery. Almost all women-dominated branches are run by women lay officials. Historically, of 16 EC seats one has always been reserved for a woman, but currently, six women serve as elected members. The union is aware of its female potential and presently is directing much of its resources to campaigning for such issues as screening for cervical and breast cancer. Women on maternity leave are entitled to a special subscription rate of 25p a quarter.

Policy and recent issues
Unemployed workers
Whilst the union has a special membership rate for any of its own members who become unemployed (25p a quarter), its rules preclude it from organising the unemployed.

Training
The union plays an active role in both youth and adult training initiatives and is represented on various industry training bodies and committees. It also organises its own apprentices' competition.

Ethnic minorities
The union is quite progressive in this area. Whilst figures are not available on the proportion of ethnic minorities within the union it must be a significant number, for the union produces much of its material in three different languages: Hindi, Urdu, and Punjabi. Moreover, the No. 1 Regional Officer's duties include liaison with ethnic communities. Ethnic minorities are becoming increasingly involved in the union with many becoming shop stewards and branch officials. Union policy denies membership to any person who promotes National Front propaganda and canvasses racist ideas.

New technology
The industry has experienced massive technological changes in the last five years to which the union has taken a positive stance in pressing for a shorter working week and longer holidays. Specific new technology agreements have been signed with the employers' federation.

External relations
The Bakers' Union is affiliated to CND and is regarded generally as being on the left of the Labour Party.
   The union carried out a political fund ballot and from a 62 per cent turn-out 89.7 per cent (or 19,954) voted "yes" and 10.3 per cent (or 2,237) voted "no".

Further reference
Bakers' Union: Our History 1859-1977, Bakers, Food, and Allied Workers' Union.

BALPA
BRITISH AIRLINE PILOTS' ASSOCIATION
TUC affiliated

Head Office: 81 New Road, Harlington, Hayes, Middlesex UB3 5BG

Telephone: 01-759 9331/5

Fax: 01-564 7957

Divisional office: Rooms 29/30, The Beehive, Gatwick Airport, Horley, Surrey

Principal national officers
President: Sir Alexander Glen
General Secretary: Mark Young
Deputy General Secretary: P. Smith

Union journal: The Log (circulation around 6,200)

BALPA

Membership

Current membership (1987)
Male: 3,874
Female: 26
Total: 3,900

Membership trends

	1975	1979	1981	1983	1987	change 1975-87	1983-87
Men	4,489	4,422	4,313	3,746	3,874	−14%	3%
Women	6	6	4	4	26	—	—
Total	4,495	4,428	4,317	3,750	3,900	−13%	4%

General

BALPA claims to represent over 90 per cent of all pilots in the UK civil air transport industry. It employs full-time professional staff to run the union. These include the General Secretary, a Deputy General Secretary, a technical secretary, a technical assistant, a British Airways industrial relations officer, an independent pilots industrial relations officer, and a research assistant. There is a divisional branch office at Gatwick, which is run by an assistant industrial relations officer for independent pilots. The Head Office is split into a technical department, British Airways industrial relations, independent pilots industrial relations department, and administration.

BALPA rules provide that full membership of the union is open to any person actively engaged in British commercial flying who holds a current commercial pilot's licence, a senior commercial pilot's licence, or airline transport pilot's licence or equivalent, provided that he/she does not perform managerial or executive duties with a British Civil Air Transport organisation.

Although BALPA has no formal provisions for women (who traditionally have always been a minority in the industry), women's issues which do arise are addressed through Europilote, an organisation which represents European pilots.

History

A pilot's union was formed as early as 1924, but it only lasted for a short time. BALPA itself came into being in May 1937 following unrest among the pilots of the main government-supported airline, Imperial Airways Ltd. Much of this unrest centred around the use of obsolete aircraft and the lack of new equipment (particularly for de-icing and blind flying) on the Continental routes of Imperial Airways.

An ex-pilot, W.R.D. Perkins, Conservative MP for Stroud, became Vice-President of the union in October 1937. As a result of a well-received speech in the House of Commons Robert Perkins was successful in securing the setting up of a committee of inquiry into the civil aviation industry.

One of the early problems facing BALPA was the relationship with the professional association for pilots — the Guild of Air Pilots and Air Navigators. As a result of several meetings between the Guild and BALPA an agreement was reached which provided for co-ordination between the two bodies on matters of common interest.

BALPA secured recognition from Imperial Airways in 1938 and affiliated to the TUC in 1934.

Organisation

Representation of the non-British Airways (BA) members' interests within the Association is through the Pilots Local Council of each individual company, elected annually by the local membership concerned. The chair of each PLC automatically qualifies for a seat on the Independent Councils Committee. British Airways pilots are represented by Fleet Councils which in turn have representative rights on the BA Master Council. The Chair of the National Executive Council is responsible for the day-to-day running of the Association. The Annual Delegate Conference serves as the main policy-making body of the Association.

The NEC has the power to initiate any kind of industrial action. It may decide to hold a secret ballot among the members if industrial action is to be considered, but it is not bound by the ballot result. Secret ballots are required for all elections of officials, including annual voting members of the NEC, national delegates for the annual ADC, members of PLCs and Fleet Councils, and ICC and MC members who do not automatically qualify for seats by virtue of their position, i.e. chairman. The General Secretary has always been a non-voting member of the NEC and so there is as yet no legal requirement to ballot for that position.

External relations
BALPA is not affiliated to any political party and does not support or sponsor any MPs. In addition to TUC affiliation, BALPA is a member of the International Federation of Airline Pilots' Associations. The Association maintains a close relationship with various government departments and the aviation industry generally. It is represented on standing committees at the Civil Aviation Authority, e.g. the Airworthiness Requirements Board, the Flight Time Limitations Board, and the National Aviation Security Committee, as well as being represented on international committees of the International Civil Aviation Organisation.

Main agreements and representation
BALPA has a union membership agreement with British Airways and Monarch Airways. It also has a large membership and recognition in most independent airline companies.

There is no industry-wide bargaining. Bargaining structures are entirely company-wide schemes where agreements are achieved through Head Office meetings, local pilots' panels, and various sub-committees that have both company and BALPA representation.

BALPA now also negotiates on behalf of flight engineers who are organised by NUMAST, as well as negotiating service agreements with staff associations in newer airlines (see **NUMAST**).

Recent events
The aviation industry has come out of the recession of the late 1970s and early 1980s only to be faced with a pilot shortage. BALPA is currently involved in youth training with ATITA in developing initiatives to secure an adequate supply of necessary skilled labour to maintain expansion in the industry. Further, BALPA has recently established an employment fund which can be used for training courses. At present this takes the form of converting rotary wing pilots to fixed wing pilots. Most of the larger companies are currently recruiting and several are training cadet pilots for the future.

After the decline in membership experienced in the late 1970s and early 1980s, BALPA is slowly reverting back to its former membership levels. Moreover, there are a growing number of female pilots as more women enter the profession. The union has recently set up a financial company which offers, amongst other things, pensions, mortgages, and loss of licence insurance to its members.

In March 1989 BALPA formed a recruitment agency to supply pilots and flight engineers on short-term contracts at salaries above the industry norm. This move is in response to the shortage of qualified pilots in the UK and BALPA's fear that pilots on short-term contracts were being exploited.

BALPA-TGWU (BASSA) dispute
In early 1987 British Airways was privatised; by the end of the year the company had made a successful bid to merge with British Caledonian Airways. Early 1988 saw negotiations between the company and BALPA get underway to integrate the two pilot forces as quickly and as smoothly as possible.

For some time, however, members of the British Airlines Stewards' and Stewardesses' Associaton (BASSA), the TGWU cabin crew section, had been dissatisfied with their national leadership and in January 1989 approached BALPA with a view to transfer. The trouble had been building up ever since the merger between British Airways and British Caledonian resulted in a reorganisation of the TGWU branch structure. In February BASSA broke away from the TGWU and established itself as an independent trade union under the name Cabin Crew 89. BALPA provided it with office accommodation and financial support.

The TGWU General Secretary, Ron Todd, launched a formal complaint to the TUC under Bridlington, insisting that BALPA had poached its members. BALPA claimed that had they not offered the breakaway union facilities, Cabin Crew 89 would have left the TUC structure altogether as it had also approached the EETPU. The TUC considered that BALPA was acting contrary to the interests of the trade union movement and was in breach of TUC policy. It therefore proceeded to formally discipline BALPA.

The outcome of the decision is still awaited, but should the TUC find against BALPA the decision could lead to the union's expulsion. Coming so soon after the EETPU expulsion in September 1988 a second expulsion might prove more damaging to the TUC than to BALPA (see **TUC, TGWU**).

The recent BA bid for the world's second largest airline company, United Airlines, looks like being accepted. As BA attempts to become the dominant world airline the precise implications for BALPA are unclear. Should there be any alterations to union representation arrangements it is to be hoped that they are conducted with a greater degree of finesse than the BA — British Caledonian Airways experience.

BDA
BRITISH DENTAL ASSOCIATION

Non-TUC affiliated

Head Office: 64 Wimpole Street, London W1A 8AL

Telephone: 01-935 0875

Principal national officers
Secretary: Norman H. Whitehouse, B.Ch.D.
Chairman of the Representatives Board, (principle executive committee): Alan G. Green, LDS

Union journal: The Association has two publications: the *British Dental Journal* (BDJ) is a scientific journal published twice a month. It has a large circulation of 19,000, well in excess of the Association membership, and is available to Association members and subscribers. The second, *BDA News,* is the Association newspaper, published twice a month and available to members only.

Membership(October 1988)
Men: 12,541
Women: 3,770
Students: 916
Total: 17,227

History
The Association was founded in 1880 to watch over and further the general interests of the profession. In 1952 it took over the functions of the *Incorporated Dental Society* and the *Public Dental Services Association*. In 1974 it was registered as an independent trade union.

Coverage
Only registered dental surgeons and dental students may join the Association. The membership is composed of dentists from all spheres of practice, namely general practice, hospital and community services, university teaching and research, and the armed forces.

Negotiations for dentists are conducted directly with the Department of Health; the Dental Rates Study Group determines the level of fees for treatment on behalf of general dental practitioners, while the Joint Negotiating Forum for Community Dental Services is the body which negotiates with the Central Committee for Community Dental Services (CCCDS) on behalf of all community dental staff.

The Doctors' and Dentists' Review Body (DDRB), originally formed in 1962, advises the government on the remuneration of doctors and dentists in the NHS (see **BMA**).

Organisation
The Association is based in Wimpole Street, London. It has two regional offices, one in Scotland and the other in Northern Ireland. At the regional level it is divided into 21 branches, which are further sub-divided into 120 sections.

The BDA is governed by the Representative Board whose members are elected triennially by secret ballot of the whole membership.

The Association has four main committees: (1) General Dental Services Committee (GDSC); (2) Central Committee for University Dental Teachers and Research Workers (CCUDT&RW); (3) Central Committee for Community Dental Services (CCCDS); (4) Central Committee for Hospital Dental Services (CCHDS). These committees have constitutions which entitle them to speak for all dentists in their field, whether BDA members or not. The committees negotiate centrally with the government.

Work-place activity
As a BDA member a dentist in employment in the NHS has statutory rights and protections, in the same way as members of other recognised unions. At a local level each salaried dentist also has the support of accredited representatives who can offer immediate help and advice.

External relations
The BDA is a member of the UK Inter-professional Group. The BDA does not have a political fund.

BEAMERS, TWISTERS AND DRAWERS (HAND AND MACHINE), AMALGAMATED ASSOCIATION OF

TUC affiliated

Head Office: 27 Every Street, Nelson, Lancashire BB9 7NE

Telephone: 0282-64181

Principal officer
General Secretary: Abe Edmonson

Membership

Current membership (1987)
Total: 470

Membership trends

1983: 550
1979: 1,965
1975: 955

General
Formed in 1866 and restructured into its present form in 1889 as an amalgamation of semi-autonomous district unions, it organises employees in the weaving of cotton, linen, and synthetic fibres. Its future, however, looks uncertain, as suggested by its declining membership.

BETA
BROADCASTING AND ENTERTAINMENT TRADES ALLIANCE

TUC affiliated

Head Office: 181-185 Wardour Street, London W1V 4BE

Telephone: 01-439 7585

Fax: 01-434 3974

Principal officers
General Secretary: David A. Hearn
President: Derek Cutler
Vice-President: A. Lennon
Treasurer: W. Lowes
Deputy General Secretary: P. Leach
National Industrial Officer: R. Bolton
National Industrial Officer: W. P. Bovey

Chief Accountant: E. J. Grant
Chief Administrative Officer: D. Cormack
Employment Officer: R. Edwards
Press and Publicity Officer: S. Elliott

Industrial officers
D. Beevers, Ms L. Blakeman, P. Bromley, K. Christie, Mrs C. Driver, V. Feiner, J. Fray,
B. Gascgoyne, E. Johnson, R. Johnson, I. Lindsley, B. Marsh, H. McFarlane,
G. Morrissey, B. Quinton, Ms L. Wallace

Regional offices

BETA, 2 New Road, Southampton SO2 0AA
Telephone: 0703-334763

BETA, Westminster Chambers, 3 Crosshall Street, Liverpool L1 6DQ
Telephone: 051-236 1695

BETA, Long Row Chambers, 31-33 Longrow, Nottingham NG1 2DQ
Telephone: 0602-470893

BETA, 534 Sauchiehall Street, Glasgow G2 3LX
Telephone: 041-332 4620

Union journal: BETA News (monthly, posted to all members)

Membership

Current membership (1987)
Total: 30,195
(BETA no longer makes separate male and female membership figures available.)

Membership trends *

	1975	1979	1981	1983	1987	change 1975-87	1983-87
Men	10,646	11,508	11,141	11,638	N/A	N/A	N/A
Women	3,241	3,766	4,005	4,074	N/A	N/A	N/A
Total	13,887	15,274	15,146	15,712	30,195	117%	92%

*The dramatic 117 per cent leap in membership between 1975 and 1987 is due to the fact that NATTKE, a larger union, merged with BETA in 1984.

General
BETA represents staff at all grades in the BBC and the independent television companies, and it is also the main union for independent local radio contractor's staff, and freelancers working in broadcasting. It has members employed in the audio-visual field working for such organisations as the British Council, and represents workers in film distribution and cinemas.

Following the amalgamation in 1984 with NATTKE, the union now also represents employees in theatres, film distribution, television studios, videotape manufacture, and recording, thereby strengthening its credibility in the entertainments industry.

The orderly system of national agreements which used to characterise the broadcasting industry have now been either abandoned or are under threat. The increase in single company bargaining will demand union resources which may be beyond a relatively small union such as BETA. Merger talks are taking place with the technicians' union, ACTT. Should these talks be successful, the NUJ, which also organises workers in broadcasting, has indicated that it may consider joining the new organisation. But even if these amalgamations succeed and the three unions create a new union with a total membership of around 90,000, it will still be one of the smaller unions in the TUC, with no automatic seat on the TUC General Council.

History

BETA grew from the *BBC Staff Association,* formed in 1945 from a merger of the wartime staff association, the *Association of BBC Engineers.* It became the *Association of Broadcasting Staffs* (ABS) in 1956 and affiliated to the TUC in 1963. In 1974 it became the *Association of Broadcasting and Allied Staffs* in recognition of the need to represent members working in closed circuit television and cablevision.

In February 1984 an important merger took place with the *National Association of Theatrical, Television Employees,* (NATTKE) and the two unions became known as the *Entertainment Trades Alliance* (ETA). The origins of NATTKE can be traced back to 1890 and the *UK Theatrical and Music Hall Operatives' Union,* which shortly afterwards changed its name to the *National Association of Theatrical Employees* (NATE). With the growth of the film industry, the *National Association of Cinematographer Operators* was established as an autonomous branch of NATE. In 1936 the letter "K" (denoting "and Kine") was added to the abbreviation, NATE, and in the late sixties, the second "T" (denoting television) finally produced NATTKE.

In June 1985 the ETA changed to its present name, the Broadcasting and Entertainment Trades Alliance (BETA).

Organisation

The Annual Conference is the supreme policy-making body of BETA to which branch delegates are elected on the basis of one delegate for each 100 members. In between Conferences the day-to-day business is run by the National Executive Council; representatives are elected, every two years, from the union's 10 trade divisions on the basis of one representative for each 2,000 members. The 10 divisions and the number of representatives they elect are as follows: BBC (7); ITV (4); theatre (2); film (2); cinema (2); leisure (1); IBA (1); freelance and independent (1); independent local radio (ILR) (1); management (1). In 1989 the NEC was composed of 22 members.

The trade divisions are responsible for pay and conditions, policy on professional matters of members in each division, and they also organise their own National Conference. A full-time officer is attached to each division. All members are organised into branches from which delegates are elected to geographical area committees: Scotland and Northern Ireland, the North, the Midlands, the South-West and Wales, and London and the South-East. Area committees are consultative and consider issues affecting the interest of members in the area, irrespective of trade division.

Except for the General Secretary, who is elected by a secret postal ballot every seven years, all other full-time officers are appointed by the NEC. All union ballots are secret postal ballots in line with the government's 1988 Employment Act which requires the election of union leaders. In March 1989 David Hearn, with the support of the union's NEC, was re-elected General Secretary with 5,184 votes. Other candidates were national officer Vincent Feiner (2,550 votes) and regional officer Laurie Wallace (1,650 votes).

An unusual conflict has developed following the election campaign. A complaint was made to the Electoral Reform Society, which acted as scrutineer, concerning irregularities in the pre-election literature. Vincent Feiner, the union's independent television national officer complained that his election address bulletin was taken from his briefcase and used as material in leaflets backing the General Secretary, David Hearn, who was defending his post. Although Feiner accepted the re-election of David Hearn he is still pursuing his complaint.

Policy and recent issues
In the TV-am dispute which began in November 1987 BETA members employed at TV-am refused to take industrial action in support of locked-out ACTT colleagues. At one point four BETA members were warned that they faced expulsion from the union if they covered the work of the dismissed ACTT technicians. At the official level BETA was determined to prevent any conflict developing between the two unions and instructed its members not to undertake any work normally done by technicians (see **ACTT**). BETA is holding talks with ACTT with a view to a merger. TV-am still recognises and negotiates with the other three unions in the industry, BETA, NUJ, and EETPU.

During the 1988 Annual Conference BETA voted to resist any attempt by independent television companies to undermine their joint national pay and conditions agreement negotiated with the ITV Association, the joint employers' body. In the year following the Annual Conference decision the independent television companies' joint national agreements disappeared.

Independent television
National joint bargaining was almost abandoned during negotiations in 1988, but instead, most companies agreed to reduce the scope of the agreements by adopting "core" provisions only. Two companies, Tyne Tees and Television South-West, did break with the other companies and they set up their own local agreements with the unions in 1988.

In early February 1989 independent television companies announced their decision to pull out of joint national pay bargaining. The national agreements involve BETA, NUJ and the EETPU. National joint pay bargaining has been under pressure for some time. The Monopolies and Mergers Commission inquiry into labour practices (see **ACTT**), along with the government's announcement that new franchises will primarily be awarded on commercial criteria (once very basic quality assurances have been satisfied), have contributed to these problems.

Anglia Television reached a three-year settlement with BETA and the other unions, ACTT, NUJ, and EETPU, in April 1989, covering conditions and pay which allow for much greater labour flexibility and which links pay to the retail price index. The deal allows working hours to be calculated quarterly rather than weekly to cut overtime. It was one of the first companies to negotiate since the independent TV companies pulled out of joint national bargaining earlier in the year.

Following on from the Anglia negotiations, in June 1989, ITN (Independent Television News) put forward sweeping proposals at the start of negotiations on proposed changes to working practices. These include annualised hours, performance-related pay, staff appraisals, and other new working arrangements. The existing national agreements ran out on July 1, but ITN has indicated that it would maintain existing arrangements to enable talks to proceed. Besides BETA, the ACTT, NUJ, and EETPU are also involved. The unions have put forward a joint counter-proposal, whilst at the same time accepting the principle of annualised hours. The outcome of the ITN negotiations are being watched closely by the other independent companies as they have implications for their negotiations, most of which began in July 1989.

External relations
Through the External Relations, Development, and Political sub-committee, BETA works closely with several international organisations and trade union bodies, such as the Confederation of Entertainment Unions, the Federation of Broadcasting, Film, and Theatre Unions, the National Campaign for the Arts, and SALVO, the Scottish Arts pressure group. BETA is also affiliated to the following organisations: the Campaign for Press and Broadcasting Freedom, the National Council for Civil Liberties, and the Anti-Apartheid Movement.

BETA holds a political fund and in a postal ballot held in July 1986 it recorded a 72 per cent "yes" vote, representing 7,961 votes, with a 28 per cent "no" vote (3,083 votes). The turn-out was only 30 per cent. BETA is affiliated to the Labour Party.

Recent events
Talks are still continuing between BETA and ACTT about a merger. The NUJ has indicated that it may be willing to consider joining the new organisation, or BETA alone should the talks fail.

Satellite broadcasting
Developments in satellite broadcasting pose a threat as well as opportunities for BETA. Sky Television, owned by Rupert Murdoch, has already said that it would not recognise any unions; on the other hand, British Satellite Broadcasting (BSB) has indicated that it would not consider union recognition before it had recruited 500 staff and offered them a chance to vote on whether they wanted to be members of a union or not. At the moment there are enough well trained and experienced staff to satisfy satellite companies' needs, largely because of the recognised training ground provided by the BBC. However, with the recent change in policy at the BBC (see **NUJ**), this source of able workers will probably dry up. Staff shortages may well strengthen BETA's negotiating power.

New developments in cinema
BETA represents workers employed in the cinema industry, and negotiates a national agreement covering basic pay and conditions of service with the Cinematograph Exhibitors' Association. After more than four decades of decline cinemas appear to be enjoying a revival promising new employment opportunities. The trend is towards out-of-town multi screen developments and it is envisaged that by 1994 110 new complexes will open around the country with the prospect of 5,000 new jobs. These developments offer much scope for BETA to revive its recruitment in this field, but the profile of potential members is likely to be different to the traditional usherettes, cleaners, and projectionists whom they currently represent.

The move to new up-market cinema complexes, coupled with new technology effectively deskilling the limited areas of specialist work, means that the demand for workers with managerial and marketing skills is increasing. Less skilled jobs will still exist but they are likely to result only in an increase in part-time employment. Furthermore, increased flexibility and the concept of the fixed working week are also likely to disappear. Whilst there are obvious threats to BETA's current membership profile, there are none the less opportunities to be grasped as well. That professional workers and part-time workers are more difficult to organise is undoubtedly true, but these are increasingly the sorts of workers which BETA must make provisions to recruit if it is to retain its credibility as a trade union in this sector.

At the end of 1989 BETA was involved in a dispute with the BBC over pay and conditions. BETA had made a joint submission for a 16 per cent across the board rise which BBC management had rejected, offering 7 per cent plus other allowances (see **NUJ**).

Further references

As yet there is no official history of the union, but 1990 is the centenary of the origins of NATTKE, and BETA will be bringing out a centenary publication.

Tony Hearn, "How Light is Light", *20th Broadcasting Symposium.*

BGSU
BARCLAYS GROUP STAFF UNION

Non-TUC affiliated

Head Office: Oathall House, Oathall Road, Haywards Heath, Sussex RH16 3DG

Telephone: 0444-458811

Fax: 0444-416248

Principal national officers
General Secretary: W. W. Gale
Senior Assistant General Secretary: J. S. P. Snowball
Assistant General Secretary: D. C. Nott
Assistant General Secretary: R. M. Drake
Assistant General Secretary: I. W. MacLean

Union journal: Staff Matters (monthly tabloid journal with a circulation of 45,000).

BGSU also publishes a wide range of publications for its members, office representatives, and committee members. Its *Office Representatives' Pack* is a comprehensive guide to union service, and procedures, including details of industrial relations training facilities. Numerous brochures include *Banking on Youth, Maternity and Parental Benefits, Into Retirement, Equal Opportunities, New Entrant Factfile,* and the *Part-timers Factfile.* Special newspaper editions covering such topics as pay, pensions, and job evaluation are periodically issued as circumstances require. BGSU has also produced a series of video recordings on union structure, bargaining arrangements, and facilities for members.

Membership

1988	*(1987)*
Male: 23,067	(18,900)
Female: 28,012	(16,617)
Total: 51,079	(35,517)

General

Formed in 1918 originally as a staff association BGSU is a medium-sized independently certified trade union, not affiliated to the TUC, that organises all grades of workers below Senior Director in Barclays Bank. Barclays Bank is the largest commercial bank in the United Kingdom and employs over 80,000 people. BGSU is the dominant union for nearly 64 per cent of all its employees. BIFU also recruits in the bank, but it has a much smaller membership. A major factor in BGSU's bargaining power is its high membership density throughout all grades of staff (e.g. over 70 per cent of managers are members of BGSU).

BGSU employs a total of 56 staff, of whom nine are regionally located travelling research officers who service the union's various regional/divisional committees as well as providing training to lay representatives at local level. Headquarters personnel include a member of the secretariat, who performs senior administrative functions, a communications officer, and an insurance officer.

The union's principal lay officers are the Chairman, Deputy Chairman, two Vice-Chairmen, and the Treasurer, all of whom are elected members of the Executive Committee which is BGSU's most important committee.

History

BGSU's origins were in staff consultative committees. *Barclays Bank Staff Association* (BBSA) itself was formed in 1918. Membership was automatic and free to every Barclays employee until, in 1940, membership became voluntary and subject to subscription. The *Bank Officers Guild* (BOG), which subsequently became the *National Union of Bank Employees* (NUBE) and is now the *Banking Insurance and Finance Union* (BIFU), competed with the *Staff Association* from the beginning but neither secured negotiating rights from Barclays Bank, although both were informally recognised and were given facilities on occasion to make representation to the Directors.

Barclays Bank conceded formal recognition and negotiating rights only in 1968, in which year the Joint Negotiating Council for Banking was instituted as the national negotiating body for staff employed in the London Clearing Banks. The parties to the national JNC were the Federation of London Clearing Bank Employers and the Banking Staff Council, the latter being a joint staff side body comprising the Council of Bank Staff Associations and its constituent associations, with the National Union of Bank Employees. The agreement provided for unilateral, binding arbitration rights on a limited number of specific nationally negotiable matters, and also laid down that all other employment-related matters were to be negotiated domestically at each bank. The need for the creation of a domestic procedure agreement with unilateral, binding arbitration rights led to Barclays Bank conceding equal rights to BBSA and NUBE which formed a Joint Staff Side Committee for negotiating and arbitration procedure.

At the end of 1969, which was a period of widespread bank mergers, Martins Bank Staff Association amalgamated with BBSA producing a combined membership of around 15,000 which compared with the 25,000 NUBE membership in Barclays Bank.

BBSA's representational policy was aimed at the creation of an autonomous, independent, single staff body for all Barclays Bank UK employees. Whilst merger with

NUBE was discussed agreement was never reached and in 1977 the Banking Staff Council and the Barclay's Joint Staff Side were automatically dissolved by the secession of NUBE. By that time NUBE's membership in Barclay's Bank had dropped to about 17,000, while BBSA's had steadily increased to about 35,000. In 1980 BBSA was formally retitled the Barclays Group Staff Union (BGSU).

In August 1981, following the breakdown of merger talks with BIFU, BGSU, along with the *Lloyds Bank Group Clearing Group* and the *National Westminster Staff Association,* founded the *Clearing Bank Union* (CBU), a certified independent union. The main function of the CBU was to co-ordinate national bargaining activity with the Federation of London Clearing Banks (FLCB) in respect of clerical and manual pay negotiations and other substantive issues such as hours, territorial allowances, overtime rates, holidays, and staff safety. Following the withdrawal of the Midland Bank from the Employers' Federation in 1986, and the National Westminster Bank in 1987, the resultant loss of national bargaining status and credibility led to the CBU being dissolved on April 1, 1988.

Organisation

The governing body of the BGSU is its General Committee and its supreme policy-making body is the Annual Conference of General Committee held in the spring. The General Committee consists of one elected representative from each regional committee, divisional committee and section committee together with the Executive Council.

The day-to-day running of the union is managed by the Executive Committee which is responsible for implementation of union policy. The EC is elected by full postal ballot and consists of five lay officers, 10 other lay members, and five full-time officers. The EC is responsible for the appointment of the General Secretary and the Assistant General Secretaries, although this practice will have to be reviewed in order to comply with the 1988 Employment Act.

The BGSU is organised into 23 regional committees and three divisional committees which between them cover all union members in corresponding administrative units of Barclays Bank. Their function is to consider all matters of interest to staff and pensioners of the Bank. BGSU also has a number of section committees that are exclusively concerned with particular sections of the membership as follows: appointed staff (managerial positions); Channel Islands staff; computer staff; part-time staff; technical and services staff; and pensioners.

Section committees have such executive and administrative powers and functions as are delegated to them by the EC. At General Committee, however, each section committee has only one vote whereas regional and divisional committees have one vote for every 200 (or part thereof) members. The members of the EC have speaking rights at General Committee but are not entitled to vote.

Coverage and negotiation procedure

The break-up of the FLCB, the Employers' Federation, in 1986/7 has meant the demise of national negotiations in the banking and finance industry. BGSU now negotiates directly with the Barclays Bank Group under the terms of a procedural agreement that covers all employees of the Group below Senior Director grades on United Kingdom contracts other than those on contracts with the Mercantile Credit Company and Barclays de Zoete Wedd Group (BZW).

There is a three-tier negotiating system with specialist negotiating committees determining issues exclusively related to staff covered within the Union's Selection Committee structure, and in the event of failure to agree, the issue can be referred to the General Negotiating Committee (GNC) for further consideration. The GNC is the main negotiating forum but issues remaining unresolved at that level may be referred to a Negotiating Council which also endorses the terms of any agreement reached at the other levels. In the event of a failure to agree issues may be referred to ACAS by either party, but since 1977 the bank has refused to honour this aspect of the procedure.

Women

Women members account for over 50 per cent of the total union membership. In the ten-year period from 1978-88 male membership has grown by only 22 per cent whereas women membership has grown by a massive 69 per cent. With an increasing proportion of women staff equal opportunity issues are becoming more important in union activity.

The BGSU is currently seeking recompense for loss of earnings as well as reinstatement for a former part-time female employee who was forced to retire. Earlier an industrial tribunal ruled that Barclays Bank discriminated illegally against the 60-year-old woman clerk by insisting that she had to retire because of her age. Barclays Bank policy was to allow men a choice as to whether they retired at 60 or 65.

Over 2,000 women leave Barclays Bank each year on maternity leave but fewer than 600 return to work at the end of the leave period. In an attempt to strengthen the recruitment and retention of women workers Barclays Bank recently announced its intention to extend its career breaks scheme and allow more women the right to extended leave to have families and then guarantee their jobs on return without loss of their promotion prospects. Such initiatives provide an opportunity for BGSU to formalise representation for women at the national union officer level and positively encourage women members to play a more active role in the affairs of the union and perhaps even appoint a national women's officer.

Policy

As a result of increased competitiveness and massive utilisation of information technology in finance and banking in general, BGSA has increasingly to devote more of its resources relative to the basic negotiating efforts on terms and conditions in order to keep abreast of such changes as they affect Barclays Bank. The union is striving for a greater say in decisions concerning Barclays' plans, especially those that have a direct effect on career prospects. Whilst this is being resisted by the bank, some progress is being made in extending negotiation to "non-negotiable" issues.

The union believes that, as a result of the rapid pace of development, the building of financial reserves to maintain an effective level of representation is a priority objective. BGSU's strategy is to cover budgeted representational activity out of subscriptions whilst building reserves from income generated through ancillary membership services, such as insurance facilities.

External relations

BGSU is not affiliated to any political party, has no sponsored MPs, nor does it retain any MPs as parliamentary advisers. It is not affiliated to the TUC and has never applied for affiliation.

For the time being BGSU attaches a very low priority to making formal links with any other organisation; this is a pity, for no matter what the differences are between the various unions, workers in the banking and financial sectors need only one union.

BIFU
BANKING, INSURANCE AND FINANCE UNION

TUC affiliated

Head Office: Sheffield House, 1B Amity Grove, Raynes Park, London SW20 0LG

Telephone: 01-946 9151

Fax: 01-879 3728

Principal national officers
General Secretary: Leif Mills
Assistant General Secretary (Scotland): T. Molloy
Assistant Secretary: J. Brawley
Assistant Secretary: D. Burton
Assistant Secretary: I. Cameron
Assistant Secretary: E. Sweeney
Assistant Secretary: R. O'Neil
Assistant Secretary: S. Gamble
Assistant Secretary: M. Keenan
Assistant Secretary: K. Jones
Assistant Secretary: C. More
Assistant Secretary: A. Piper
Assistant Secretary: W. Whiteman
Assistant Secretary: J. Lowe
Assistant Secretary: K. Brookes
Assistant Secretary: R. Shuttleworth
Assistant Secretary (Organisation): J. James
Assistant Secretary (Publicity): N. Howell
Research Officer: J. Robinson

BIFU also employs seven negotiating officers, and each year honorary positions of president, vice-president and general treasurer are elected at Annual Delegate Conference.

Union journal: BIFU Report (monthly, circulation around 112,000).
   BIFU also publishes a number of pamphlets and booklets which give a good guide to the union and its activities. These include: *This is BIFU,* a colourful guide to the union, designed as general recruitment literature. General modernisation of all publicity is being undertaken and indeed BIFU was the first union to advertise on radio, promoting a jobwatch helpline in London.

Membership

Current membership (1987)
Male: 76,753
Female: 89,086
Total: 165,839

Membership trends

	1975	1979	1981	1983	1987	change 1975-87	change 1983-87
Men	55,506	67,726	75,708	77,164	76,753	38%	−1%
Women	46,416	64,648	72,287	79,312	89,086	92%	12%
Total	101,922	132,374	147,995	156,476	165,839	63%	6%

General

BIFU, formerly the *National Union of Bank Employees,* organises workers at all levels in banking, insurance, finance houses, trustee savings banks and building societies. In recent years it has grown considerably and it is now the thirteenth largest union in the TUC. BIFU has a membership target of 200,000 and, at current rates of growth, this is a realistic and achievable objective.

The union offers its members discounts on continental holiday villas in an innovative move to help provide and market more services, including special financial packages. BIFU is looking into the provision of discounted mortgage and other house purchase schemes, since it has found that fewer employees than expected actually benefit from such deals offered by employers.

BIFU is continually building up its complement of full-time officials and organisers as its membership expands. Despite inter-union rivalry between various staff associations such as BGSU on the one hand, and MSF on the other, its influence is growing.

BIFU is considered to be on the right-wing of the trade union movement.

History

BIFU started life in 1946 as the *National Union of Bank Employees* (NUBE), following an amalgamation between the *Bank Officers' Guild* and the *Scottish Bankers' Association.* Both unions had their origins in the organisation of bank clerks in England and Scotland between 1917 and 1919. The union has been affiliated to the TUC since 1939, except for a short period from 1973-75 when it was expelled from the TUC for registering under the Industrial Relations Act 1971. NUBE changed its name to the *Banking Insurance and Finance Union* in 1979 to reflect its increasing diversity of membership.

Union officials

Recent years have seen a significant growth in BIFU's membership and the union has always laid great stress on continuing development. To support this growth, the union has expanded its network of officials and during the late 1970s the number of officials was doubled. The union has even employed temporary recruiters in different parts of the country, as well as seconded recruiters by agreements with certain banks.

At present, BIFU employs 16 people at assistant secretary level, eight negotiating officers, and 19 area organisers as well as over a dozen researchers and administrators. The union has a total personnel complement of over a hundred staff.

BIFU union officials come from varied backgrounds, but newly recruited staff tend to be young people (such as graduates with degrees in industrial relations or the social sciences), ex-teachers, people with experience from other unions as well as former Ruskin and Coleg Harlech students.

BIFU also makes provision for seconded officials who are appointed by the EC and seconded by agreement between the union and the particular institution. Secondees then assist the full-time officials in negotiations at the institution concerned.

Organisation

The supreme governing and decision making body in the union is the Annual Delegate Conference (ADC) held in April. Conference is made up of a voting delegate elected by each branch of the union, non-voting delegates from each area council and advisory committee, past presidents of the union, together with members of the National Executive Committee and Standing Orders Committee.

The National Executive Committee (NEC), is responsible for the general administration and government of the union between conferences. It comprises the union's president, vice-president, and general treasurer (all elected at Annual Conference), and at least one member elected by secret postal ballot by each area and/or regional council and a delegate from the various bank or financial institutional sections of the union. Including the general secretary, the NEC currently has 50 members. It has the power to appoint committees to assist in the work of the union and appoint "such officials as it shall consider necessary". It also appoints BIFU full-time officials to administer the day-to-day running of the union's affairs.

BIFU employs organisers for each of its 14 geographical areas. Each geographical area has an area or regional council, consisting of a delegate from each of the branches. The main functions of each area and/or regional council are to assist the EC in the layout of branches, to advise the EC on any regional matter on request, to ensure that membership levels are maintained by the propagation of BIFU's policies and to elect delegates to Conference.

Branch organisation in the union is generally one of the three following types.
(1) Geographic — which includes members of different status/skill from different banks;
(2) Institutional — branches containing members from one particular financial institution only;
(3) Occupational — branches containing members of a particular skill/occupation, e.g. technical and services.

The historical trend within BIFU has been to organise branches along geographical lines with a heterogeneous membership. In recent years, however, there has been a movement towards a sectionalisation of branches into more homogeneous units, for example of the occupational/institutional type. At the end of 1988, BIFU had 366 branches. The union is also creating sections which bring together staff from a single type of institution — for example insurance.

Work-place activity

The shop steward function of BIFU is provided by office representatives. BIFU's rules provide that such representatives operate "overall under the direction of and be accredited by the general secretary and/or the Executive Committee".

Women

There are almost 90,000 women in BIFU which makes it the eleventh largest TUC union for women (see **TUC**). Despite the fact that they comprise more than half the total membership of BIFU, and that since 1975 their membership has almost doubled, women are still greatly under-represented both among full-time officials and organisers, and in their number on the Executive Committee. There are 10 full-time women officials, five organisers (out of 19) and 10 Executive Committee members.

BIFU has set up a Women's Equality Working Party (which reports to the Executive Committee) and regularly sends delegates to the Women's TUC. However, there is plenty of scope for further campaigning for the rights of women both in the banking and finance industry and within the union itself. Given the fact that the percentage of women in employment in the banking, finance, building society, and insurance industry is around 50 per cent and reaches 55 per cent in the clearing banks alone, BIFU has a heavy responsibility to its female membership.

BIFU published a report entitled *Equality for Women — Proposals for Positive Action* in July 1982, pointing out that although women form the majority of workers in banking and finance, they are concentrated in the bottom clerical grades. Banks tend to rely on high staff turnover in lower grades to prevent career blockages and dissatisfaction higher up, and thus female staff rarely reached the higher level posts. The union's report recommended the development of comprehensive equal opportunities programmes in each bank or company.

Recently, however, banks have become increasingly concerned about the number of women leaving employment, often after costly investment in training by their employers. Coupled with demographic changes, which will reduce the pool of young people of working age into the 1990s, the banks have recognised the importance of retaining their existing women staff. As a result, banks have now introduced some of the most progressive personnel schemes to help their women employees. Extended maternity rights and benefits, career breaks and career counselling officers, and creche facilities are some of the more important aspects of an employment policy designed to retain as many women employees as is possible. BIFU has played an important role in ensuring that such changes which management introduce, benefit all women irrespective of age, employment status or length of service.

External relations
BIFU is not affiliated to any political party, nor to any organisations which have "party political objectives". The union's rules prevent it from affiliating to any body without the express authority of conference. Although BIFU does not sponsor MPs, it retains two parliamentary consultants, David Madel (Conservative MP for South Bedfordshire) and Jeremy Bray (Labour MP for Motherwell South). BIFU is affiliated to FIET (International Federation of Commercial, Clerical and Technical Employees) and it is the largest union within that federation. It is also affiliated to:
  Workers' Educational Association
  Workplace Nurseries' Campaign
  Women's National Cancer Control Campaign
  Labour Research Department
  Anti-Apartheid Movement.

BIFU's non-political stance means that it is unable to vote on many TUC motions at Congress because of the party-political wording of the motion — though the resolution of its 1981 Conference has now allowed the union greater flexibility. Leif Mills, General Secretary of BIFU, is a member of the TUC General Council, the TUC Special Review Body and Committee on European Strategy as well as being Chairman of its Committee for Financial Services.

BIFU is increasing its involvement in the TUC and encourages its membership to get more closely involved at Regional TUC level. This increased commitment to the TUC can be judged by the stance which the union took towards the expulsion of the EETPU in 1988. Although BIFU and EETPU were natural allies within the TUC, BIFU General Secretary Leif Mills was highly critical of the EETPU's contempt for the TUC verdict when he said that "we cannot have a situation in the TUC where any union can refuse to implement disputes committee awards or try to negotiate about them" (see **EETPU**).

Policy
BIFU is one of the few unions that has set out in written form its policy on a number of

issues. In the area of sex equality BIFu has called for financial institutions to disclose information to the union in order to monitor discriminatory practices; equalisation of pension benefits; positive discrimination in favour of women in promotions etc., if necessary by a "quota" system; and improvements in maternity leave and pay above the statutory minima.

BIFU pursues an active health and safety policy because of the special dangers that bank employees face in any bank robbery that might occur. The union has stressed that the carriage of cash should always be undertaken by trained security guards and not by clerical staff.

Recent developments in computer technology have threatened to reduce the number of staff in financial institutions as banking techniques increasingly rely on the use of on-line computer facilities for data-processing and point-of-sale banking transactions. BIFU advocates the virtues of job evaluation as a method of assessing the relative worth of jobs.

Many banks still retain a compulsory mobility clause in the contracts of employment which they issue. The union has consistently opposed such mobility clauses as it believes that staff should not be required to move home against their wishes. Apart from this, the union is concerned about the financial losses that can be incurred by employees as a result of a transfer. Whilst some progress has been made by the union in modifying the discretion of employing institutions in imposing compulsory mobility (e.g. by introducing an appeals procedure), the position is less than satisfactory. The union's long term aim remains the substitution of a wholly elective system for the filling of vacancies which would allow members greater discretion over their career patterns and replace the arbitrary exercise of managerial authority which now exists.

In its evidence to the National Consumer Council's inquiry into banking services in 1982, BIFU strongly opposed an extension of bank opening hours and a widespread return to Saturday opening. Instead, it suggested alternatives to Saturday opening such as autotellers, credit cards and cheque cards, and accused the banks of being too slow to encourage customers to use these. Nonetheless, the main clearing banks were determined to extend opening hours in response to changing consumer expectations and BIFU has now concluded an important agreement with the Midland Bank which provides overtime payment, time off in lieu and extra staff cover for Saturday opening. Lloyds Bank tried to implement a similar initiative without discussing its plans and consequently BIFU imposed an overtime ban.

In 1987, the Director General of Fair Trading asked the Monopolies and Mergers Commission to investigate the supply of credit card services in the UK. In October 1988, BIFU submitted a one-hundred-page report to the inquiry because of their direct interest in the employment of members at Barclaycard and Joint Credit Card Company.

In its report to the MMC, BIFU expressed its disappointment at the narrow terms of reference adopted by the inquiry which excluded charge cards and store credit cards. It pointed out that such cards have a wide circulation and the rates of interest charged on them are often in excess of the credit card companies and are thus also a potential source of monopoly and hence restrictive practice.

However the principal concerns of BIFU were the possible implications for employment and it stressed to the MMC that any break-up of existing arrangements would threaten jobs, particularly those of part-time workers, many of whom are young women. BIFU conducted its own detailed investigations on unemployment rates in the areas where credit cards companies organise their operations and found that there were high rates of unemployment among young people and women. BIFU also examined the possibility of staff commuting to London, as an alternative source of employment, and found that the cost would be prohibitive for many staff, particularly women who wished to work part-time or make child-care arrangements. The report concluded that alternative sources of employment for this group were very few, and that the local economies were heavily dependent on the presence of the credit card companies.

The union has responded to enormous changes in the finance sector of industry and its 1988 ADM agreed to conduct a high profile campaign with the objective of reinforcing BIFU's position as the most appropriate union for the finance sector. It has taken a positive role in initiating discussions and maintaining contact with staff associations in various arms of the industry, including the international banks — with the objective of long-term recruitment into BIFU.

Recent events
Inter-union conflict
BIFU has undergone a phase of marked expansion in membership. It is nevertheless concerned about growing competition from in-house staff unions (see **BGSU**). During 1988 it was drawn into an acrimonious inter-union dispute over union recognition at Sun Alliance and Eagle Star; first with MSF and later with SASU, the in-house staff union at Sun Alliance and Eagle Star. Both insurance companies decided to recognise BIFU in favour of staff associations. But BIFU also faces competition from unions traditionally organising in the declining manufacturing sector (such as GMB) which are looking to the service sector to help compensate for their losses in membership.

Recruitment
BIFU has launched a campaign to recruit members in the City, a hitherto traditionally non-unionised group, who, fearing redundancy resulting from the changing fortunes in the financial sector, now seeks union representation. The union's document *Sharp Practice in the City* highlights cases of unfair dismissal and outlines the assistance which BIFU can offer. Usually this takes the form of providing advice on an individual basis, since the union does not have any collective bargaining rights in this field. As a result, recruitment to the financial services branch of BIFU is now on the increase. This provides an interesting example of a trade union taking an innovative step in providing a new service for its members, while at the same time opening up opportunities for further membership recruitment. This could form the basis of a new way of representing professional workers but draws attention to the need for well resourced union organisations.

Performance-related pay
BIFU has always been opposed to performance-related pay as a matter of principle. However, in the face of its growing use by the major financial institutions, as well as support for the scheme from its members, the union has abandoned its stance of outright opposition. Instead, BIFU has recognised the need for a more sophisticated response to employer proposals if it is to retain its negotiating rights. A report reviewing the union's position on performance-related pay is in the course of preparation.

Single union agreements
In February 1989 the Midland Bank withdrew collective bargaining rights from MSF in a move to replace multi-union negotiating with single-union agreements. Such agreements are increasingly common on "greenfield sites", but the Midland is one of the first employers to make such a move to simplify its negotiating agreements. Though BIFU has gained by becoming the single union with bargaining rights, it is hoped that the decision will not increase the inter-union rivalry which already exists with MSF. In this instance, the decision has been in favour of BIFU, but it may be vulnerable if other banks decide to follow Midland's lead, especially as it has fewer members in the other three leading

clearing banks. The decision by Midland Bank also highlights the erosion of individual liberties by employers, whose decisions about union representation reflect their preferences rather than those of their employees. In the current political climate, BIFU and other unions could legitimately expose the inherent contradictions of a situation where individual choice is being restricted by the actions of employers. Employees alone should have the right to choose which union they want to represent them.

1992 and the single European market
Many organisations have been discussing the implications of 1992 and the single European market; however BIFU was the first trade union to organise a conference to consider how 1992 may affect financial institutions. The union sees considerable scope for their expansion, but is concerned about the implications for staff. BIFU has a history of assisting members in taking cases to the EC and pursuing claims, for example, for the rights of part-time workers under the Treaty of Rome.

In its discussions about the implications of the single European market, BIFU has looked closely at the various directives affecting the financial sector. Through its international union affiliation with FIET, it has been pressing for a directive which includes a commitment or clause relating to the social dimension of the proposals. It wishes to see a commitment to the protection of workers' rights, collective bargaining arrangements and trade union procedures. In his speech to the conference, Leif Mills stated "we are determined to seek to ensure that any financial institution within the Community should uphold the established patterns of trade union recognition and bargaining — and if anything extend them." This follows on from and reflects the initiatives recently taken by the TUC (see **TUC**).

Further references
B. Supple, *The Royal Exchange Assurance,* Cambridge University Press, 1970. An interesting view of white-collar work in the early post-war years.

R. Crompton and G. Jones, *White-Collar Proletariat,* Macmillan, 1984. A study of trade unionism and new technology in banking and insurance with particular focus on the role played by women.

R. Hyman and R. Price (eds), *The New Working Class? White Collar Workers and Their Organisation,* Macmillan, 1984.

A. Rajan, *New Technology and Employment in Insurance, Banking and Building Societies,* Gower, 1984.

Eric Batstone, Stephen Gourlay, Hugo Levie, and Roy Moore, *New Technology and the Process of Labour Regulation,* Clarendon Press, Oxford, 1987. Chapter 4 provides a particularly informative case study on BIFU's role in the introduction of new technology in an insurance company.

BMA
BRITISH MEDICAL ASSOCIATION

Non-TUC affiliated

Head Office: BMA House, Tavistock Square, London WC1H 9JP

Telephone: 01-387 4499

Fax: 01-383 6403

Principal officer
Secretary: Dr. I. T. Field (→ 1/11/93 ; Then Dr. J.L.T. Birley)

Union journal: British Medical Journal (redesigned in July 1988, this is the main journal publication of the BMA. It is supplemented by *BMA News Review* — a tabloid newsletter, which deals with special features or events.)

Membership

Total: 82,737 (1989)
Total: 56,000 (1979)*
*estimate

General
The BMA represents medical practitioners throughout the National Health Service and private practice. The BMA represents over 75 per cent of doctors in the medical profession, including 80 per cent of junior doctors. The BMA hopes to attract around 3,000 new members by the end of 1989 and it has prepared new recruitment literature as part of this campaign.

Through its numerous committees and scientific groupings the BMA promotes and co-ordinates the activities of the medical profession as well as negotiating and lobbying on their behalf. Over the last 10 years the BMA has expanded its trade union role; it has created 17 regional offices, each headed by a regional secretary, and introduced industrial relations officers as well as a shop steward system of work-place representation (these are known as place of work accredited representatives (POWARs)).

Proposed reforms in the NHS are a major concern at present, and the BMA is taking an active role both in defending the principles involved in the National Health Service and seeking to negotiate new contracts for general practitioners.

History
The BMA was founded in 1832 to maintain the honour and interests of the medical profession and to promote the medical and allied sciences. One of the first records of the Association is the Memorandum of Association adopted in October 1874. Throughout most of its life the Association has been a voluntary professional organisation; it only became an independent trade union with a certificate of independence in 1976. It is not a member of the TUC and has never applied to join.

Organisation
The general control and direction of the policy and affairs of the BMA are vested in a representative body which meets annually, usually in July. It comprises: (1) Chairman and Deputy Chairman of the representative body, Chairman of the Board of Science and

Education, and all Chairmen of Standing Committees; (2) all office members of the Council; (3) elected members as follows: 280 representatives of divisions; 110 general practitioners; 55 senior hospital doctors; 55 hospital doctors in training; 17 community health doctors; 12 academic medical staff; five armed forces medical staff; five occupational health staff; two from the junior members forum; two from the medical students group; nine overseas members; and six members from minority groups.

The Council administers the affairs of the Association. Between Annual Representative Meetings (ARM) it has the power to formulate and implement policies within the general framework of policies already laid down by the ARM. The Council consists of: (1) *ex-officio* members: President; Chairman and Deputy Chairman of the ARM; Chairman of Council; Treasurer; past holders of the above posts, for a period of one year after ceasing to hold office; and all Chairmen of the various committees and trusts; (2) 46 elected and voting members comprising: six from general practice; four senior hospital doctors; seven doctors in training; two from community medicine or community health; one from the armed forces; one in active practice; 17 regional representatives (one from each of the 14 NHS regions in England and one representative for Wales, Scotland, and Northern Ireland); and four members resident in the UK, Channel Islands, or Isle of Man.

Each representative is elected by secret postal ballot and holds the position for two years. The Chairman of the Council is elected by the Council from among its own members and holds office for at least three years and up to a possible maximum of five years. The Council has an Executive Committee, Finance and General Purposes Committee, and 15 standing committees.

Policy and recent events
Women
In 1988 the ARM resolved to set up a working party to review and identify the factors limiting the progress of women doctors and to recommend how gender inequality in career opportunities could be eliminated. The Council is also concerned about the implications of the proposed new contracts for general practitioners, which it considers could discourage the employment of part-time women doctors.

NHS reforms
In January 1989 the Health Secretary, Kenneth Clarke, announced the government's proposals for reform in the NHS in a White Paper, entitled *Working for Patients*. The minister stated that he aims to have the "new look" NHS in place by 1991 — a target viewed, at best, as highly optimistic by most in the medical profession.

The proposals have been roundly criticised by the BMA and other medical organisations. The fear is that the government's proposals would undermine the concept of a truly national health service which ensures a common and comprehensive standard of care throughout the country. Critics say that the emphasis would shift away from the quality of care to the cost of treatment, thereby introducing the worst commercial aspects of the US system into British medicine.

A special conference of the BMA was held in April 1989 to consider the implications of the White Paper. A composite motion summarised the views of the meeting and its main thrust was that the White Paper ignored the "critical issue of inadequate funding" of the NHS. The motion emphasised that the government's proposals would increase the proportion of the NHS budget spent on management to the detriment of patient care; fragment the NHS and destroy its comprehensive nature; lead to the formation of a two-tier health service; and not extend patient choice or put patients' needs first.

The Association has also urged all general practitioners to inform their patients about their concerns over the future of the NHS. Indeed, various campaigns are now being waged in doctors' surgeries throughout the country. A hostile reception has also been given to the proposals to give budgets to general practitioners which would allow them to buy hospital and other treatment for patients.

Contracts for general practitioners
In what has been considered a rather politically inept move, the Health Minister resolved to impose new contracts on family doctors at the same time as proposing major reforms in the Health Service. Inevitably the two issues have become linked, particularly since many of the aims of the contract negotiations are also ambitions of the White Paper.

At the special ARM in April several motions called for mass resignation from the NHS if Kenneth Clarke sought to impose the new contracts. One of the main concerns over the new contract is the proposal to increase the proportion of doctors' income determined by the number of patients on their lists, from 47 per cent to 60 per cent.

In June 1989 the BMA's medical services committee put forward a recommendation to accept changes to the proposed new contracts which it had negotiated with the Department of Health. Much to its embarrassment, members rejected the new terms, by a vote of 166 to 150. In a further ballot of general practitioners conducted by the Electoral Reform Society, the rejection of the new contracts was overwhelming — 7,075 in favour of the new contracts and 22,241 against. Despite this clear rejection by members of the BMA, the Health Secretary immediately declared his intention to proceed to implement the new contracts by April 1990.

Furthermore, he saw "no sensible basis" for continuing negotiations with the BMA leaders. Interestingly, the overwhelming vote against the proposals did serve to refute one point of view, common amongst government members: "that BMA activists had been behaving too much like trade union leaders, organising opposition that is not shared by most of their members".

Negotiators within the BMA have also been criticised for seeking to reach agreement with the Department of Health on doctors' contracts, despite the fundamental opposition of the Association to the White Paper's proposals. In the run-up to the proposed implementation date for the NHS reforms, it seems that the BMA negotiators will need to put their house in order and focus attention on the key White Paper proposals, to which it is likely to remain fundamentally opposed. In this respect the Association would be seen to be truly "working for patients" as well as for its members.

External relations
The BMA is a founder member of the Federation of Managerial, Professional, and General Associations, an umbrella organisation for certain non-TUC affiliated unions.

Further reference
Vivienne Walters, *Class Inequality and Health Care,* Croom Helm, 1980. (A particularly good account of the role played by the BMA in the creation of the National Health Service.)

CERAMIC AND ALLIED TRADES UNION

TUC affiliated

Head Office: Hillcrest House, Garth Street, Hanley, Stoke-on-Trent ST1 2AB

Telephone: 0782-272755

Principal national officers
General Secretary: Alf Clowes
Assistant General Secretary: H. Hammersley
Organiser: G. Bagnall
Organiser: J. A. Jackson
Organiser: G. Oakes

Membership

Current membership (1987)
Male: 16,266
Female: 13,691
Total: 29,957

Membership trends

1983: 28,873
1979: 44,523
1975: 44,096

General
The union was first founded in 1827 as a craft union of *Operative Potters,* later becoming
the *National Society of Male and Female Pottery Operatives,* and in 1919 the *National
Society of Pottery Workers.* In 1970 it became the Ceramic and Allied Trades Union.

At first it organised only manual pottery workers but later on workers in allied trades
throughout the industry (including white collar workers) were recruited into the union's
newly formed clerical and staff section.

The union has recently launched a recruitment campaign and, in attempting to up-date
its image, has enlisted the services of a PR company, "Frameworks". However the real
problem facing the union is perhaps not its image but the contracting nature of the
industry itself. The ceramics industry has traditionally had a high density of union
membership. But from an all-time high of around 50,000 in the late seventies,
membership slumped to 27,408 in 1982 and appears to have levelled off at around
30,000. Membership is mainly in the North Staffordshire area.

The union negotiates with the British Ceramic Manufacturers' Federation (BCMF) on
the National Joint Council for the ceramic industry (NJC) which covers directly about
27,000 process workers in some 80 firms, and most non-federated firms also follow the
same agreements. Both CATU and the BCMF have 12 representatives on the NJC. Just
recently some companies have left the employer's federation, marginally disturbing the
influence of the NJC, whose foundation dates back to 1946.

Further references

William H. Warburton, *The History of Trade Union Organisation in the North Staffordshire Potteries,* Allen & Unwin, 1931.

Frank Burchill and Richard Ross, *A History of the Potters' Union,* Ceramic and Allied Trades Union, 1977.

CMA
COMMUNICATIONS MANAGERS' ASSOCIATION

TUC affiliated

Head Office: Hughes House, Ruscombe Park, Twyford, Reading, Berkshire RG10 9JD

Telephone: 0734-342300

Fax: 0734-342087

Principal national officers
General Secretary: R. J. Cowley
Deputy General Secretary: T. L. Deegan
Assistant Secretary (Telecom): F. A. Richardson

Union journal: New Management (monthly)

Membership

Current membership (1987)
Male: 14,203
Female: 4,997
Total: 19,200

Membership trends

1983: 19,450
1979: 18,500
1976: 19,070

The figures themselves do not reveal much about the membership trends that have occurred in the union. However, CMA's membership density in the Post Office has in fact declined from around 96% in the early eighties to its present figure of approximately 90%. Much of this is a result of a major reorganisation in the Post Office which, amongst other things, has changed the way it recruits some of its professional staff particularly in finance, IT, and sales. In response to these difficulties the union, through its long-standing Organisation and Recruitment Committee, has launched a major recruitment drive. A feasibility study presently being carried out in order to examine introducing some form of job-sharing into supervisory grades, might aid this process.

General

The union is organised into branches from which an Executive Council of 18 is elected. The union's regional structure is currently under consideration and will be reviewed by its next Annual Conference. In the meantime the rules relating to Regional Councils are suspended. CMA has secured sole rights to represent senior staff within British Telecom and the Post Office. As a consequence of changes in representation in the Post Office the union had transferred to its ranks approximately 800 executive engineers from the Society of Telecom Executives (STE) who themselves withdrew from the Post Office.

Formerly called the *Post Office Management Staffs' Association,* CMA changed its name following the splitting of the Post Office into two separate organisations. The CMA works closely with other unions in BT and the Post Office and remains convinced that "given the will, a single union is achievable and workable". The union is notable for the very comprehensive and detailed Annual Report it produces, which in 1987 ran to 200 pages.

As a result of the major reorganisation that took place in the Post Office in 1986 which established separate groups for Royal Mail Letters, Royal Mail Parcels, Post Office Counters, and Girobank, along with a Corporate Services Department, CMA will for the first time have to face separate negotiations for previously commonly held terms and conditions. This structural divisiveness could be quite damaging and the CMA needs to tread with caution.

A recently negotiated Business Efficiency Agreement was concluded with the Post Office which allows for the introduction of new technology within strictly agreed circumstances. Although this is a nationally based agreement its precise terms are locally determined. CMA has produced a very comprehensive booklet in order to "demystify" the scheme and to allow its representatives to enter local negotiations on an informed basis.

Recent issues

The National Executive Council, prior to 1985, was elected by delegates at Annual Conference. As a consequence of the 1984 Trade Union Act CMA decided, without amending its rule book, to adopt broadly the procedure outlined in the Act. It believed that whilst maintaining sovereign control of its rules, it would be inappropriate for them to be amended as a result of "external pressure". Thus full postal ballots for the election of the National Executive Council are conducted under the auspices of the 1984 Act rather than the rule book. The union is reviewing the manner in which senior appointments are made. A properly constituted ballot regarding the political levy was also carried out and two-thirds of the members voted for its establishment. Despite this, the union remains unaffiliated to any political party.

External relations

The union affiliated to the TUC in 1927. Other affiliations include Amnesty International; the Postal, Telegraph, and Telephone International (PTTI); the Labour Research Department; the Trade Union Research Unit, Oxford; the Irish Confederation of Trade Unions; the Scottish TUC; the Workers' Educational Association; the United Nations Association; and the Post Office Unions' Council/British Telecom Unions' Committee.

COHSE
CONFEDERATION OF HEALTH SERVICE EMPLOYEES

TUC affiliated

Head Office: Glen House, High Street, Banstead, Surrey SM7 2LH

Telephone: 0737-3533522

Telex: 944245

Principal officers
General Secretary: Hector MacKenzie
Assistant General Secretary: Colm O'Kane
National Officer (Nurses, Equal Opportunites): Judith Carter
National Officer (Ancillary, Health and Safety): Pat McGinley
National Officer (Organisation and Membership): Keith Hickson
Finance Officer: Ann Damjanovic
Senior Specialist Officer (specialist departments including Legal, Press, Education,
Parliamentary, Editorial and International): Margaret Wheeler

Union journal and publications: COHSE publishes a monthly tabloid newspaper *(Health Services)* which is distributed free to members through the branch secretary and shop steward network. Since mid-1989 COHSE has introduced direct mail, changing the journal to a bi-monthly glossy magzine distributed to all its members by post. A monthly, eight page shop stewards' bulletin is also produced, with detailed reports on pay negotiations, new publications, and developments in equal opportunities and health safety.

The union also produces a wide range of fact-sheets, booklets, and leaflets on health and safety, including *AIDS, Hepatitis B, Violence in the Work-place, Back Injuries and Lifting;* equal opportunities *(Negotiating Equal Opportunities, Sexual Stereotyping: a Trade Union Issue,* and *Maternity Rights);* and health economics *(Trading Places — Comparing British and American Health Care Systems, Safe in Whose Hands — Making Sense of Health Care Finance).* COHSE also prepares campaign material on the health cuts, the poll tax, and staff pay and conditions.

Membership

Current membership (1987)
Male: 44,042
Female: 163,799
Total: 207,841

Membership trends

	1975	1979	1981	1983	1987	change 1975-87	1983-87
Men	43,027	48,436	50,427	48,061	44,042	2%	−8%
Women	124,173	164,494	180,282	174,808	163,799	32%	−6%
Total	167,200	212,930	230,709	222,869	207,841	24%	−7%

Regional secretaries

No. 1 (Northern):
Gill Hale, 44-46 Grosvenor Road, Jesmond, Newcastle-upon-Tyne
Telephone: 091-281 7235

No. 2 (Yorkshire and Humberside):
Terry Foster, Cemetery Road, Sharron Head, Sheffield S11 8FT
Telephone: 0742-684783

No. 3 (North-Western):
Eric Cooper, Mallinson House, Melton Street, Off Smyrna Street, Radcliffe, Greater Manchester
Telephone: 061-724 5300

No. 4 (West Midlands):
Bob Wilshaw, Dartmouth House, 67 Birmingham Road, West Bromwich
Telephone: 021-525 6100

No. 5 (North-East Thames and East Anglia):
Keith Taylor, 42-44 Sewardstone Road, Chingford, London
Telephone: 01-529 3636

No. 6 (North-West Thames and Oxford):
Ernie Brook, 112 Greyhound Lane, Streatham, London SW16
Telephone: 01-677 3622

No. 7 (South-Western):
Ty Taylor, Silverlea House, 4 Billetfield, Taunton, Somerset
Telephone: 0823-278411

No. 8 (South-East Thames):
John Jaggon, 24 Hamer Street, Gravesend
Telephone: 0474-321016

No. 9 (Scotland):
Chris Binks, 22 York Place, Perth
Telephone: 0738-31591

No. 10 (Wales):
Dave Galligan, 32 Gelliwastad Road, Pontypridd
Telephone: 0443-406418

No. 11 (Northern Ireland):
Bill Jackson, 27 Ulsterville Avenue, Lisburn Road, Belfast
Telephone: 0232-6662994

No. 12 (East Midlands):
Robert Quick, Cemetery Road, Sharron Head, Sheffield S11 8FT
Telephone: 0742-684783

No. 13 (South-West Thames and Wessex):
Ian Todd, 63 Victoria Road, Aldershot, Hants
Telephone: 0252-331602

General

COHSE is in many ways an industrial union for the NHS but it is by no means the only union representing Health Service employees. However, it is a health and social services trade union recruiting all grades of staff; other unions, with which it may compete for members, are often tied down to particular grades and spheres of influence. For example, the Royal College of Nursing and the Health Visitors' Association are restricted to particular occupations, while the general unions have some difficulty recruiting staff other than ancillary workers because they lack a "professional" image. Unfortunately for COHSE, in the past some branches (where the membership was composed mainly of nursing staff) have neglected recruiting ancillary and other grades, while in their ancillary branches, the reverse situation applied. This was a very short-sighted policy and resulted in membership being lost to other organisations, particularly NUPE.

Nearly 90 per cent of all nurses and midwives are unionised, and COHSE has the second largest membership. COHSE has 125,000 members; its four main competitors are the RCN (250,000 members), NUPE (90,000), RCM (20,622 — all midwives), and GMB (5,000). In addition the HVA, which also recruits nurses who are health visitors, has 16,000 members.

Despite considerable job losses within the NHS — not least in ancillary staff — and in contrast to other unions, COHSE's membership figures have remained remarkably buoyant. Despite some fall in overall numbers during the 1980s recruitment remains high at around 40,000 a year. The NHS campaign during 1988 increased considerably the number of new members. The ratio of men to women members remains stable, although there is a trend towards fewer ancillaries and more nurses amongst the membership.

In common with a number of other unions COHSE now offers a range of financial and other personal services to its members, as well as access to legal advice. It has also adapted to changing professional demands, as members move away from large institutions and into the community, and in many cases from the NHS to local authorities and the voluntary sector. A few members work in the private health sector and many are now employed by contract companies following the privatisation of NHS cleaning, catering, and laundry work. COHSE now negotiates with these private companies.

History

The union originated among nursing staff of mental hospitals in the early years of the century when conditions in this type of employment were very poor. Average working hours were between 84 and 90 hours a week and the starting wage of a female probationer nurse was £18 a year. Promotion to charge nurse, although rapid, only produced a wage of £45 a year. Turnover of staff was high; this, and the lack of contact between hospitals and fierce employer opposition, made trade union organisation very difficult.

There were underlying grievances. Trade unionism was probably triggered by the 1909 Asylums Superannuation Act which provided for compulsory cash deductions from wages for a statutory superannuation scheme which was less generous than the already existing optional schemes operated by many employing authorities. The grievances were strongly felt in Lancashire, and in 1909 eight nurses from Winwick Mental Asylum met to discuss grievances over pay and conditions. This led to a further meeting and the founding of the *National Asylum Workers' Union* in 1910 with George Gibson as Secretary. The NAWU affiliated to the Labour Party in 1915 and to the TUC in 1923.

In its early years the union faced severe opposition. Many of the activists were victimised but in this way the union acquired its first full-time officers. The union's first significant strike was in 1918 when nurses in Prestwich and Winwick struck against the Lancashire Asylums Board over a claim to reduce the working week to 60 hours.

The average 50-hour week was gained in 1920 by which time the membership of the union had risen to 18,000. In 1922 nurses at the Radcliffe-on-Trent Hospital struck against an attempt to increase hours to 66 and reduce wages by four shillings a week. Sixty-seven employees were dismissed for taking action and the strike was broken following an attack by police, bailiffs and blacklegs.

In 1918 another union had been founded with similar aims and interests but which was more active in general hospitals and in local authority welfare services. This was the *Poor Law Workers' Trade Union.* For a while the NAWU and the PLWTU federated but later split apart, the PLWTU becoming the *Poor Law Officers' Union* (PLOU).

In 1930 the PLOU became the *National Union of County Officers* (NUCO) and in the same year the NAWU became the *Mental Hospital and Institutional Workers' Union.* A further name change followed in 1943 when NUCO became the *Hospitals and Welfare Services Union.*

The logical merger between the two unions to form the Confederation of Health Service Employees was agreed in 1946. From its inception the union strongly supported the National Health Service but — and this comes as a surprise to many people — it has never been afraid to take a firm line in defence of its members' pay and conditions. It has fought by means of demonstrations and industrial action for improved pay for nurses in 1950, 1970, 1973, as well as more recently. The Halsbury Report of 1974 produced a large pay award for nurses and in that year COHSE's membership leapt by 20,000 — the largest percentage rise recorded that year by any TUC-affiliated union.

In 1974 COHSE was readmitted into membership of the TUC, having been suspended since 1972 for refusing to comply with the TUC policy of deregistration against the Industrial Relations Act of 1971.

During 1979 COHSE became involved in an inter-union dispute with NUPE, accusing NUPE of tactics which were designed to poach members. In the same year both unions came into conflict with the RCN, whose members had voted overwhelmingly against the principle of strike action. COHSE issued comprehensive guidelines on industrial action, which came under severe strain during the 1982 pay dispute. Joint action between NUPE, COHSE, and other Health Service unions aimed to force the government to improve on its 7.5 per cent pay offer. During the course of escalating industrial action COHSE threatened to abandon the TUC's code of conduct on Health Service disputes — resulting in its leadership being accused of insecurity and political naïvety.

Coverage

When the NHS became operative in 1948 the government had to provide means whereby all employees in hospitals and public health services could be represented and put forward views on pay and conditions. The Ministry of Health was given power to arrange a framework for negotiations and introduced Whitley Councils.

The present Whitley structure consists of a General Council and 10 functional councils, each dealing with particular groups of NHS staff. Five of these are also involved with review bodies which only recommend levels of remuneration to government. The functional councils deal with all matters relating to their structure and application as well as all detailed negotiations and bargaining.

The ten Whitley Councils and other negotiating bodies are:
1. Administrative and clerical staff (including ambulance officers and control assistants);
2. Ambulance staff;
3. Ancillary staff;
4. Scientific and professional staff (scientists, speech therapists, pharmacists, opticians, and chaplains);
5. Professional and technical "B" (works staff, laboratory staff, and technicians);
6. Doctors and dentists;
7. Nurses and midwives;

8. Professionals allied to medicine;
9. Building grades;
10. Maintenance staff.

The General Council is the connecting link, consisting of an agreed number of representatives from each of the 10 councils. Negotiations of a general, all-purpose nature take place on this Council which has no power of veto but is intended to co-ordinate.

All these Whitley Councils are composed of representatives of employers' and employees' organisations, now known as the management side and the staff side respectively. The organisations represented are those whose previous work entitles them to recognition as negotiating bodies. The number of seats each union holds varies from one Council to another but COHSE has 24 seats among seven of the 10 Whitley Councils in the NHS.

Where practicable, COHSE nominates lay members of the union on to the main negotiating committees as a back-up role to the national officers who lead the negotiations.

Organisation
All members must belong to a branch, which may be an ordinary branch, an officers' branch, or a group branch. Senior hospital employees such as administrators, nursing officers, and so on are regarded as managers by many employers but they are nevertheless employees of the Health Service and it is reasonable that they should have separate officers' branches if they so wish, but this is not obligatory and they may well stay in the ordinary branch.

For administrative purposes the country is divided into regions and all branches are allocated to one of the 13 COHSE regions. Each region has a regional office and full-time officers and staff. The regions are controlled by regional councils consisting of elected representatives of branches.

The general management and control of COHSE between each Delegate Conference is vested in the National Executive Committee consisting of the President, Vice-President, General Secretary, and the representatives elected by the regions. Much of the detailed work of the NEC is carried out by its standing committees, such as the finance and organisation committee and the parliamentary committee (of which COHSE's sponsored MPs are ex-officio members) which play an important role in the union's influence over legislation.

The Annual Delegate Conference which takes place each year in June is the supreme governing body of the union.

The General Secretary of COHSE is elected by a ballot of individual members following nominations from the branches. In March 1987 the union announced that it was to abandon its system of branch block voting for executive elections in order to comply with the 1984 Trade Union Act. NEC members, who are lay officials, are elected by a ballot of all members in their region and serve for three years. Branches conduct ballots before taking industrial action, which in COHSE's case, always includes provision for emergency cover.

A national working party on the union's structure published a consultative report in 1988, and major changes to COHSE's organisation will be considered at the union's 1989 and 1990 Conferences after full consultation.

Work-place activity
COHSE introduced a shop steward system in 1972, recognising that union stewards could relieve some of the burden of negotiation and representation carried by regional officers. Stewards also act as agents to recruit members at all the various places of work. This is an important role, given the intense inter-union competition for membership in the Health Service.

Women
Around 80 per cent of COHSE members are women and the union has strong women's

representation at officer level. Some 40 per cent of the branch secretaries are women, and a central aim of the national working party currently examining the union's organisation is to increase this proportion still further. The union has produced a wide range of publications (e.g. on maternity rights and sexual stereotyping) of specific interest to women. COHSE put forward a successful resolution to the TUC, calling for an Equal Rights Department, and to the Labour Party, calling for a Women's Minister of Cabinet status.

The union has pursued a number of successful equal rights legal cases and is involved in equal value claims, both at law and in negotiations. COHSE has an Equal Opportunities Commission run by a national officer which considers women's issues, and it is now also looking into representation amongst ethnic minorities.

Many part-time workers are women and COHSE campaigns actively for proper provision for their needs — for example, for access to continuing education and training and further employment rights.

External relations
COHSE is affiliated to the Labour Party, and in 1985 there was an 80 per cent vote in favour of retaining the political fund.

The union sponsors six Labour MPs: Michael Meacher (Oldham West); Majorie Molam (Redcar); John Walley (Stoke-on-Trent North); Allan Rogers (Rhondda) Dale Campbell-Savours (Workington); Dennis Canavan (Falkirk West).

Recent events and current policy
Training
COHSE has consistently opposed government youth training schemes, viewing them as a means of securing a cheap source of labour without providing any real training for participants. The union is concerned about the professional implications of YTS-style trainees working in hospital wards. Instead COHSE has called for the expansion of nurse training facilities, apprenticeships, and training schemes which lead to proper job opportunities.

The impending manpower crisis resulting from demographic change has strengthened COHSE's case for a widening of the entry gate for nursing — in particular, it has advocated that more older entrants must be attracted to the profession. To this end COHSE supports the provision of more "back to nursing" courses.

Nursing grades
COHSE has expressed concern about anomalies arising in the nursing regrading procedures introduced by the Health Department during 1988/89. A major problem highlighted by the union was that nurses were being placed on the wrong grades under the new clinical grading structure. Similar concerns have also been expressed by other nursing unions (see **RCN**).

Regional pay
In January 1989 the government announced proposals for limited forms of regional pay variation for both nursing and white-collar staff in the NHS. Health Service unions, including COHSE, considered that the pay differentials proposed were not only small, but would have little effect in terms of solving staff shortages.

NHS review and funding
COHSE has long expressed concern about the effects of low pay and underfunding of the NHS. A survey carried out with the Trade Union Research Unit at Ruskin College, Oxford, showed problems of low morale amongst nurses due to low pay, stress, and under-staffing. It also showed that many nurses had considered leaving the profession, citing staffing levels as one of the main problem areas.

In a day of action in March 1989 COHSE members joined NUPE in protesting against continued under-funding of the NHS and demanded that the Chancellor should spend an extra £2 billion on the service.

Possible merger
Leaders of COHSE have recently dropped their policy of outright opposition to merging with other unions. Accepting the trend towards the creation of large trade unions, the NEC is suggesting that the union should join merger talks with NUPE and NALGO. This may well be the best way forward if union representation in the Health Service is to be in any way effective.

Further references
The History of the Mental Hospital and Institutional Workers' Union from Infancy to its 21st Year, 1931, (author unknown).

Mike Carpenter, *All for One: Campaigns and Pioneers in the Making of COHSE,* COHSE publication.

Vivienne Walters, *Class Inequality and Health Care,* Croom Helm, 1980.

A. Sethi and S. Dimmock, *Industrial Relations and Health Services,* Croom Helm, 1982.

John Leopald and Phil Beaumont, "Pay bargaining and management strategy in the NHS", *Industrial Relations Journal,* 17, no. 1, 1986.

Mike Carpenter, *Working for Health — The History of COHSE,* Lawrence and Wishart, 1988.

CPSA
CIVIL AND PUBLIC SERVICES ASSOCIATION
TUC affiliated

Head Office: 160 Falcon Road, London, SW11 2LN
Telephone: 01-924 2727

Principal officers
General Secretary: John Ellis
Deputy General Secretary: John Macreadie
General Treasurer: Christine Kirk
Assistant Secretaries: Terry Adams,
Carol Bailey,
Veronica Bayne,
Frank Bonner,
Frank Campbell,
Graham Corbett,
Ralph Groves,
Geoff Lewtas,
Richard Regan,
Eddie Spence,
Brian Sturtevant,
Peter Thomason

Editor of union journal: Barry Reamsbottom

Union journal: Red Tape (circulation about 160,000)

Membership

Current membership (1987)
Male: 44,838
Female: 104,646
Total: 149,484

Membership trends

	1975	1979	1981	1983	1987	change 1975-87	1983-87
Men	70,870	63,890	65,690	55,355	44,838	−37%	−19%
Women	153,872	159,994	144,204	143,847	104,646	−32%	−27%
Total	224,742	223,884	209,894	199,202	149,484	−33%	−25%

General
The CPSA is the largest Civil Service union. It also organises staffs in the Civil Aviation Authority, BAA, research councils, and over 100 fringe bodies. Grades in membership are mainly administrative officers and assistants, typing grades, personal secretaries, and data processing staff. Numerically smaller grades represented include superintendants of typists, teleprinter operating grades, and, in certain departments such as the Department of Employment and the Courts Service, the CPSA recruits executive staff. The CPSA represents air traffic control assistants. In 1984 over 40,000 members employed in the Post Office, British Telecom, and Girobank transferred to the National Communications Union.

The CPSA is the largest union represented on the Council of Civil Service Unions, the central negotiating body for all non-industrial civil servants, with 20 of the 63 seats.

History
It is customary to date the birth of the CPSA from 1903 when the *Assistant Clerks' Association* was formed, but the powerful stimulus to purposeful organisation in the Civil Service came with the First World War and greatly expanded government activity. In the post-war years a series of amalgamations led to the formation of the *Civil Service Clerical Association* in 1922. The union was strong enough to successfully fight for the restoration of the Civil Service Arbitration Tribunal after its abolition by the government on grounds of economy in 1922.

During the 1930s there was fierce recruitment competition among the CSCA, the *Ministry of Labour Staff Association,* the *Court Officers' Association* and the *Inland Revenue Staff Association.* Only when general recruitment prospects improved in 1939 were they able partially to settle their differences by forming a loose federation called the *Civil Service Alliance* which promoted a measure of co-operation on issues affecting typing and clerical grades.

In 1973 the *Ministry of Labour Staff Association* merged with the CPSA (as it had become in 1969), followed in 1974 by the *Court Officers' Association.*

Political conflict in the CPSA has been influenced by its peculiar position of organising workers for the central state machine. Political volatility may be affected by the transient nature of some of its membership; many members are low-paid clerical workers and administrative assistants in their first jobs, and up to 15,000 claim family credit.

Organisation
The basic unit of the CPSA is the branch, of which there are about 800. The branches in a particular department are combined to form a section. There are 16 such sections:
Ministry of Defence;
Department of Health and Social Security;
Ministry of Agriculture, Fisheries, and Food;
Atomic Energy;
Customs and Excise;
Inland Revenue;
Department of Employment;
Department for National Savings;
Her Majesty's Stationery Office;
Department of the Environment;
Land Registry;
Department of Trade and Industry;
Lord Chancellor's Department;
Civil Aviation Authority Group;
BAA Group;
Home Office.

The term "group" is used in the cases of the CAA and BAA to recognise the fact that these organisations are outside the Civil Service. Each section or group has its separate annual section Conference composed of delegates from the branches.

Departmental branches assemblies
Over 10,000 members work in institutions that are considered to be too small to justify section organisation. Some of these are government departments, e.g. Education and Science. Most, however, are fringe bodies such as the British Museum or Forestry Commission.

Main conference
The sovereign governing body of the CPSA is its Annual Delegate Conference, usually referred to as "Main Conference" in order to distinguish it from the section, group, and Civil Service conferences.

National Executive Committee
This is elected by branch and work-place ballots. From 1989 postal ballots became obligatory. It is composed of the following posts: President; two Vice-Presidents; 26 elected members; General Secretary; Deputy General Secretary; General Treasurer; 13 Assistant Secretaries (including editor of *Red Tape*); and HQ Departments Assembly Negotiations Officers.

The professional full-time officers have no voting powers, although they are in all other respects full members of the Executive. The number of voting members of the NEC is therefore 28. Long before the 1984 Trade Union Act, senior full-time officials were elected by individual ballot.

Women
The CPSA has a National Women's Advisory Committee with corresponding arrangements in each section. One full-time officer is designated National Women's Officer. While the proportion of women branch officers and conference delegates has increased in recent years, it is still well below the number that would be needed to reflect

fully the fact that 70 per cent of members are women. There are only three women full-time officers.

Recent issues
Training
Early in 1989 CPSA members voted 26,619 to 16,750 against a proposed agreement that would, for the first time, have allowed the Civil Service to take YTS trainees. The leadership of the CPSA denounced the ballot. Only 32 per cent of members voted and 300 of the 750 eligible branches had not even filed voting returns.

Bargaining arrangements
There has been a seepage away from highly centralised bargaining and national agreements on a wide range of issues towards departmental and local bargaining. The CPSA has, together with the NUCPS, reached agreement with the Treasury on long-term flexible pay deals, including local pay additions in London and the South-East. As on some other issues, the CPSA's elected Deputy General Secretary, John Macreadie, a supporter of Militant, has clashed openly with the General Secretary on pay policies.

Policy and recent events
It has been suggested that internal union democracy depends on the survival of faction. By this criterion CPSA has been too democratic for its own good. Over the last two decades control of the NEC has swung from right to left and back again, at times with the Chair being held by the right, even though the left commanded a majority of the Committee. To a lesser extent, there have been publicly expressed policy differences between full-time officers. Some journalists have called the CPSA the "Beirut" of the trade unions. The feuding has led to embarrassing, highly publicised stories, such as the non-appointment of Militant supporter Kevin Roddy as head of organisation, apparently approved by the NEC but with formal ratification thwarted by the President and General Secretary. It has contributed to membership disaffection and decline and to a considerable financial deficit (though the ruinous 21-week strike of 1981 was the main cause).

Local branch politics and balloting were confused by supporters of the Militant tendency's operating under the banner of the Broad Left. The formation of Broad Left '84, a left-Labour opposition to Militant, led to the possibility of an alliance between the non-Trotskyite left and the right that took control after the NEC elections of 1988.

John Ellis, the General Secretary, had to be resilient to survive the period when he faced a Militant-dominated Executive. He continued to try to offset the wayward decisions of the Executive when CPSA members were leaving in droves in disgust at the ignominy of the shattering pay defeat of 1987 when the Executive tried to call an all-out strike but failed.

Conventional wisdom is that postal balloting has the desired effect of encouraging political moderation. Several CPSA leaders are not sure that it will have that in their union but can its outcome really be worse than what has preceded it? Is seemed to be doing the trick in elections for the Executive in 1989. After some alarm about early returns in the DHSS, the outcome was defeat and isolation for Militant, with only one remaining seat on the Executive.

Further references
E. Wigham, *From Humble Petition to Militant Action,* CPSA, 1980.

Paul Lloyd and Richard Blackwell, "Manpower economics management and industrial relations in the Civil Service", *Industrial Relations Journal,* 16, no. 4, Winter 1985.

CSMTS
CARD SETTING MACHINE TENTERS' SOCIETY

TUC affiliated

Head Office: 36 Greenton Avenue, Scholes, Cleckheaton, West Yorkshire BD19 6DT

Telephone: 0274-670022

Principal national officers
General Secretary: George Priestley
President: N. Scriven
Treasurer: B. Lord
Trustee: L. Higgins
Trustee: A. D. Warden
Trustee: D. Jollife
Executive Delegate: A. D. Warden
Executive Delegate: G. Collings

Membership

Current membership (1987)
Total: 100

Membership trends

1983: 106
1979: 130
1975: 142

General
The manufacture of card clothing is an ancient and skilled craft; the union (under rule three of its rule book) maintains a strict policy of admitting only fully apprentice-trained members. However, most carding today is done by machines, the card clothing being wrapped around rollers. The clothing itself is made in sheet form or in strips. The organisational base of the CSMTS has been undermined by the use of metallic carding. This first came into widespread use in the mid-1950s and by the 1970s it had virtually replaced flexible carding in the cotton textile industry, although the woollen industry continues to use flexible card clothing. Metallic wire carding is not made by CSMTS members, nor has the society recruited those who do make it since its manufacture has been regarded by card setting machine tenters as an engineering process not comparable with their own craft.

Collective bargaining was conducted at Employers' Federation level but with the takeover of the English Card Clothing Company by Cardo Engineering, the Employers' Federation collapsed. The union took the national agreement to the three remaining companies and had it changed to company agreements which now form the basis of bargaining in the industry; plant or company issues are discussed at joint committee level. At the time the takeover brought about a small amount of redundancy, mainly men nearing retirement age. However, apprentices are now being taken on and trained in order to replace these redundant workers thereby maintaining the current union membership.

The union is proud of the fact that it currently has no members out of work. It still maintains the same provision for any member unemployed as it did in the past; namely, that members continue on union files as full members and the union places them in a job as soon as one becomes available. Whenever a member is unemployed or working out of the trade but seeking employment within it the union stops the recruitment of apprentices until the unemployed member is taken back on.

History
The decision to establish the society was taken in 1872. Between December 1915 and May 1916 it undertook a bitter strike in pursuance of a claim for a cost of living increase. This was the longest stoppage by any group of workers during the First World War, and the terms of settlement left little room for doubt that it was a defeat for the union. The union recovered from this, and from the effects of a slump, to a peak membership of 297 in 1952. However, since then technological change has brought a falling demand for the skills of card setting machine tenters and a decline in membership, though in recent years, there has been a revival. The demand for card clothing has stabilised and training of apprentices has restarted.

Organisation
There is an Executive Council of two delegates (both now from Cleckheaton branch) with three general officers, the President, the Secretary, and the Treasurer. This meets independently of the one remaining branch and is the main policy-making body. The branch can nevertheless overthrow Executive decisions by claiming a referendum and obtaining 55 per cent of the vote. The union has now accepted that it has to have secret ballots in all areas that are covered by the 1984 Act.

The Annual General Meeting has no formal power as it has developed on an *ad hoc* basis, but it is a forum for airing grievances and debating policy.

External relations
The CSMTS is affiliated to the Labour Research Department but has no political fund.

Further reference
M. D. Spiers, *One Hundred Years of a Small Trade Union.*

DOMESTIC APPLIANCES AND GENERAL OPERATIVES, NATIONAL UNION OF
TUC affiliated

Head Office: 7-8 Imperial Buildings, (1st Floor), Corporation Street, Rotherham, South Yorkshire S60 1PB

Telephone: 0709-382820/362826

Principal national officer
General Secretary: Reg Preston

DOMESTIC APPLIANCES AND GENERAL OPERATIVES

Membership

Current membership (1987)
Male: 2,750
Women: 350
Total: 3,100

Membership trend
1983: 4,000
1979: 5,500
1975: 5,342

General
Trades represented among the membership have included, and to a diminishing extent in some cases, continue to include moulders, coremakers, fitters, grinders, glaziers, pattern makers, designers, drafters, brass finishers, filers, fettlers, bronzers, enamellers, blacksmiths, and boiler welders. Members are generally employed in the domestic appliance, kitchen range, hot water, and fender trades, or are moulders, fitters, or sheet metal workers.

History
The union was founded as the *National Union of Stove, Grate, Fender, and General Light Metal Workers* in 1890 after some of the men in the trade had joined the Knights of Labour and the representative of that society had led them in a nine-week strike which finally gained a 10 per cent pay increase. By 1934 membership had reached 6,000. Recently the union changed to its present name having previously been called the *National Union of Domestic Appliance and General Metal Workers.*

Coverage
The union is a member of the Confederation of Shipbuilding and Engineering Unions, and the Joint Committee of Light Metal Trades Unions which has national agreements with the national metal trades federation.

Organisation
There are some 25 branches mainly in Rotherham and the West Pennines, South-West Lancashire, the West Midlands, and Derby. The Executive Council is elected biennially, two from each of four districts into which the branches are grouped. When the General Secretaryship becomes vacant all branch secretaries are invited to apply. The Executive then considers all applications and a short-list is drawn up which is put to a ballot of the whole membership.

Recent events
Cumulative closures and redundancies have continued to leave the union with its lowest membership for over 50 years and a growing deficit of expenditure over income from contributions. As part of the measure to deal with these matters the union has withdrawn the post of Assistant Secretary. This leaves the General Secretary as the only full-time union officer. It is probably only a question of time before the union is forced to merge in order to maintain an adequate level of support to its members.

EETPU
ELECTRICAL, ELECTRONIC, TELECOMMUNICATIONS, AND PLUMBING UNION

Non-TUC affiliated

Head Office: Hayes Court, West Common Road, Bromley BR2 7AU

Telephone: 01-462 7755

Principal officers
General Secretary: Eric Hammond
President: Paul Gallagher
Director of Communications: John Grant
Secretary of EESA: Roy Sanderson
National Engineering Officer: Charlie MacKenzie
Head of Research: John Spellar

Union journal: Contact (monthly)

Membership

Current membership (1986)*
Male: 316,329
Female: 19,826
Total: 336,155

*The EETPU was expelled from the TUC in 1988. 1986 represents the last year the union membership figures were published in a TUC Annual Report.

Membership trends

	1975	1979	1981	1983	1986	change 1975-86	1983-86
Men	365,557	375,000	365,000	343,000	316,329	−13%	−8%
Women	54,443	45,000	30,000	22,000	19,826	−64%	−10%
Total	420,000	420,000	395,000	365,000	336,155	−20%	−8%

General
The eighth largest union in Britain, the EETPU is, as its name suggests, something of a hybrid. The Electrical Trades Union (ETU) was formerly a craft trade union which aimed to control the numbers and supply of skilled electricians by controlling apprenticeships. Historically, it possessed a membership pattern which paralleled that of the AEU. Local societies of plumbers existed before 1800 but it was not until 1865 that a national organisation, the *United Operative Plumbers' Association of Great Britain and Ireland,* was formed. The plumbers, organising mainly in construction and shipbuilding, amalgamated with the ETU in 1968.

The largest part of the membership is what is described as the engineering industry, especially electrical engineering where the skilled workers retain their grip over the bargaining units. There is a large membership in electrical contracting (all the manual workers) and the electricity supply industry. EETPU members can also be found in virtually every industrial grouping among skilled maintenance workers. The union's white collar section, the Electrical and Engineering Staff Association (EESA), recruits administrative and some technical workers in industries where traditionally it has represented manual workers.

In 1988 the EETPU was expelled from the TUC following its refusal to comply with awards made by the TUC disputes committee over its predatory actions in Orion Electric and Christian Salvesen. The union was at the centre of controversy during the 1980s and clashed repeatedly with the TUC and its affiliated unions over policy and recruitment matters, most notably in 1984 when it was close to being expelled over the use of public funds for ballots, and in 1986-7 over News International's new printing plant at Wapping.

The EETPU has been at the centre of considerable controversy over the lead it has taken in introducing single-union, no-strike deals. Its actions have forced other unions to re-examine and re-evaluate their own strategies in order to survive in the climate of declining membership and the new "enterprise culture" of 1980s' Britain. At the broader trade union organisational level the TUC was forced to set up a special review body to examine the whole question of new-style agreements and, in particular, the way in which the EETPU had acted in relation to other affiliated unions. But what perhaps started as a means of controlling the predatory actions of the EETPU turned into a much more comprehensive review of the whole organisation and purpose of the TUC, as the review body came to recognise that this really was the crux of the issue (see **TUC**). In this way the EETPU's action has been constructive.

Notwithstanding this review, the EETPU was expelled at the September 1988 Congress. Within the union there is a strong belief amongst the leadership that, in being expelled, the EETPU was the victim of a conspiracy. This colours their attitude and approach to other unions and the world at large. The EETPU is a highly bureaucratic, hierarchically structured, organisation where all "action" has to be sanctioned from the top. It is widely known that the union is loath to release information about its activities. This entry in the *Directory*, for example, did not have the benefit of any direct input from the union; officers refused to supply any details, and in the process, forfeited any chance they had to influence its content.

History

The Union was founded in 1889. Older hands among EETPU officials are fond of relating that the ETU would not have come into being as a separate organisation had it not been for the exclusive and rather self-consciously élitist attitude of the Amalgamated Society of Engineers. After repeated attempts to gain admission to the ASE, each of which was rebuffed, the electricians founded their own union. As a gesture of encouragement to the new organisation the ASE donated a copy of its rule book and it was on this that the ETU rule book was based; by then it was already 40 years old.

Between the years 1894 and 1907 no less than three consecutive ETU General Secretaries were dismissed for defalcation (the General Secretary of the plumbers was dismissed in 1907 for embezzlement and drunkenness).

By the end of the First World War developments in industry showed that the ETU's organising principles were obsolete. No changes in union organisation took place. By the end of the Second World War control of the union had largely been won by the Communist Party. In the 1950s and early 1960s a long drawn-out struggle between the controlling communists and the right wing took place, culminating in a legal battle in the High Court about alleged ballot rigging. In the case of *Byrne* v. *Foulkes* the losing candidate in the election for General Secretary alleged against 14 defendants a fraudulent conspiracy to rig the ballot. After a complex 42-day trial the Court found the case proven against five of the conspirators. The right wing then took over the leadership.

Union officials

The new Executive, elected shortly after the High Court judgement, acted rapidly to consolidate its newly-won power in the union. It sacked the Assistant General Secretary, McLennan, set aside a number of the previous Executive's rule changes, and called a new rule revision conference. In the beginning the new leadership did not have things all their own way; proposals to extend the period between Executive elections from two to five years were soundly defeated. The right wing also temporarily withdrew proposals to make membership of the Executive a full-time position, and launched instead a campaign with extensive use of the press leading up to the 1965 rule revision conference where the following changes were carried by a small majority: (1) a full-time Executive Council to be elected every five years; (2) abolition of the rank-and-file area committees; (3) power to the Executive to close branches and amalgamate others under a full-time branch officer; (4) removal of the right of appeal by branches against Executive Council decisions.

In 1962 a rank and file appeals committee had been established but in 1969 the Executive abolished it. The Executive is now both judge and prosecutor since half the Executive constitutes the disciplinary committee and the other half the appeals court. This move was thrown out by Conference but it was subsequently pushed through by means of a secret ballot of individual members who were not sufficiently appraised of the counter-arguments. Thus secret ballots may not be quite as libertarian as they seem. The same ballot was also used to dispose of the elected trustees.

Since 1969 all full-time officials have been appointed by the Executive, and Communist Party members are barred from holding any union office, including even the "office" of Conference delegate. The appointment of officials was a major sticking point which led in April 1989 to the eventual breakdown of the merger talks with the AEU. The leaders of the electricians were fearful of the consequences of allowing their officials to be subject to the same procedure as the engineers, namely, secret ballot elections by the membership. Membership of the Communist Party was debated during the union's 1989 Conference and in an attempt to appear as advocate of freedom of association and speech the leadership of the EETPU put forward a motion for the union to lift the 20-year ban on communists; not unexpectedly, Conference rejected this move.

Following the retirement of Frank Chapple, Eric Hammond was elected as EETPU General Secretary in 1983.

Organisation

Executive Council

The EETPU has a biennial Conference but it is not a governing body; decisions are noted but are not binding on the union. The full-time body of the union, responsible for making and carrying out policy, ratifying agreements, and integrating the work of the full-time officials with the national policy of the union is the 15-member Executive Council. It also has the power to participate in pay negotiations. Meetings take place monthly. All members are elected by secret postal ballot for a period of five years. The authority of the Executive Councillor in his own division does not rest on a personal basis but stems from membership of the primary continuing authority on all matters of policy and administration affecting the union — the Executive Council. The area officials are responsible to the Executive Council as a body and not to any one individual member. At the 1977 Conference a recommendation that full-time officers should be free to stand for election to the Executive was accepted; since then the influence of full-time officials in the Executive has increased.

Branches
The branch is the basic unit of organisation and there has been a determined effort in recent years to make the specialised or industrial branch the rule, rather than the exception. Consequently, it is union policy that in large industrial concentrations small branches are amalgamated on an industrial basis and have a full-time branch secretary/treasurer who may also act in local negotiations. When the branch is based on one factory or plant the union's shop stewards will belong to that branch, and are then presumed to work in close liaison with the branch secretary. The basis of EETPU policy is formal control over its membership. So long as it is able to satisfy its membership demands its position would seem to be secure.

External relations
In the political fund ballot the EETPU membership voted by 140,913 to 26,830 (a majority of 84 per cent from a turn-out of 45 per cent) to retain its fund.

In January 1989 Eric Hammond was appointed to NEDC's governing council.

Following its expulsion from the TUC the EETPU joined the Confederation of Managerial and Professional Staffs (COMPS), and in March 1989 EESA's Roy Sanderson was elected to the Chair, with PAT General Secretary, Peter Dawson, as President. Membership is drawn almost exclusively from small non-TUC affiliated unions and staff associations, most of which are to the right of the EETPU; they include: the National Association of Fire Officers; Abbey National Staff Association; the Association of Career Teachers; Granada Staff Association; the National Farmers' Union; and the Prison Service Union (see "Appendix"). Although COMPS has recently been awarded 16 places to industrial tribunals, it is doubtful that this poses a serious challenge to the TUC.

For all the EETPU's claims about gaining new members from mergers, at the time of publication only three had been registered with the Certification Officer: the *Association of British Professional Divers* (May 1989, less than 200 members); *Ministry of Defence Staff Association* (July 1989, less than 1,000 members); and *Springfields Foremans' Association* (August 1989, less than 200 members).

The EETPU has long advocated that trade unions ought to make greater use of the latest business management techniques, such as marketing and consumer research. Basic market research would have revealed that for trade unionism the "market" does not operate freely. Affiliation or non-affiliation to the TUC is a crucial determinant of recruitment and organising potential. The EETPU is finding that it is able to attract new members only from the non-affiliated segment of the "market". The essential error of the leadership of the EETPU was to view trade unionism as a simple market which through aggressive "business unionism", could be captured (see "Recent events and the EETPU in the 1990s").

Policy and expulsion from the TUC
The major problem confronting the trade union movement is that of declining union membership figures. In 1979 total TUC membership was over 12 million, but the recession in the early 1980s caused high job losses and a consequent dramatic decline in union membership, particularly in the highly unionised manufacturing sector. By 1983, while union membership continued to decline, figures revealed that not only did employment gradually begin to pick up but also that a shift was occurring in its patterns; in particular, there was a growth in the less well organised sectors and occupations, along with a trend towards part-time and self-employed work. In an attempt to arrest the decline competition between unions heightened as they launched special recruitment campaigns to woo new members.

The EETPU response involved offering employers single-union, strike-free deals. The first such deal was signed between the EETPU and Toshiba Consumer Products in 1981 and the agreement became the model for all other strike-free deals. But ultimately a more worrying aspect of EETPU strategy was the move to widen its traditional sphere of organisation. Part of this arose from the shift from electro-mechanical to electronic technology which significantly redrew traditional lines of demarcation for which there were few guidelines. But the EETPU was aggressive in its actions and deliberately sought to invade other unions' territories (most notably at Wapping, where the EETPU concluded a single-union deal with Rupert Murdoch's News International which excluded the printing unions NGA and SOGAT (see **SOGAT**)).

In its inquiry into the Wapping "fiasco" the TUC cleared the EETPU leadership from deliberately disregarding traditional areas of influence, and instead heaped the blame on the over-zealous Tom Rice, the EETPU's Fleet Street official, thus preventing any further action against the electricians. As a result of the earlier EETPU/Hitachi deal, rule 12 of the TUC had already been tightened to rule out single-union agreements which cut across other unions' existing recognition rights (in effect restricting single-union deals to green-field sites). But when the EETPU took on and beat both print unions at Wapping this was a clear signal that the union's ambitions were boundless and no union was safe from its predatory instincts. The TUC was facing a direct challenge to its authority and the action of the EETPU was inducing a state of anomie. The TUC's response was the special review body, but before it had time to present its findings to Congress further complaints were lodged with the TUC concerning two agreements, both involving the controversial strike-substitute mechanism of compulsory arbitration, signed between the EETPU and Orion Electric and Christian Salvesen.

At Orion Electric (a video recorder manufacturer in South Wales) the TGWU complained to the TUC that it was already recruiting and had some employees in membership before the company elected to deal with the EETPU following an inter-union "beauty contest". At Christian Salvesen the TGWU was the recognised union for drivers, while warehouse and cold store workers were in the TGWU, GMB, and USDAW; the three unions were trying to formulate a common approach before the EETPU signed a similar strike-free deal giving itself exclusive rights to representation. The non-union retailer Marks and Spencer denied that it was behind the deal and insisted that its contract to the distribution company Christian Salvesen was not dependent on the single-union strike-free deal.

The TUC disputes committee, after conducting its investigations in February 1988, instructed the EETPU to withdraw from both deals. The union Executive decided not to accept TUC instructions and maintained its refusal to implement the rulings despite formal requests by the TUC. After a meeting of the full General Council, the EETPU was given two weeks' notice of suspension, and on July 8 was suspended formally from the TUC. The suspension was to last until the September Congress, since only Congress has the right to expel a union.

But even before the TUC disputes committee had made its recommendation the EETPU was already touting support from other unions to create an alternative trade union centre to the TUC. A number of the smaller non-TUC unions such as PAT, UDM, APT, IOJ, and the British Union of Social Work Employees showed interest, but for the organisation to have any credibility it would have to have the support of the larger unions such as the RCN, AMMA, and NAHT, but they had all rebuffed the EETPU approach.

The action of the EETPU not to comply with the TUC instructions appears odd as it had already agreed to abide by two previous rulings in 1987 when it signed similar deals with Thorn EMI and Yuasa Batteries. Furthermore, the way it attacked and beat the two print unions at Wapping had far deeper implications for trade union organisation and unity than either the Orion or Christian Salvesen deals. The EETPU admitted that at Wapping it "did act in a way that could be interpreted as outside the spirit of the (TUC) directives", and produced a report for the TUC making extensive pledges that went beyond what was required about its future dealings at News International. Yet the EETPU refused to withdraw from the relatively minor Orion and Christian Salvesen deals although it realised that expulsion was inevitable. Admittedly, the EETPU was not asked to give anything up at Wapping as in the case of the later deals; nevertheless, the attitude which pervaded the union's responses was decidedly different — as if desiring the immortality of martyrdom.

Its action following the suspension would seem to support this view. The EETPU had decided to ballot its own membership on whether the union should comply with the TUC directive. But it is difficult to believe that it lacked the simple organisational wherewithal to ensure that the results of the ballot fell within the two-week July 7 deadline set by the TUC to comply with their suspension order. The EETPU's action had to be deliberate and calculated, designed as a show of utter contempt for the TUC.

At the EETPU's industrial conference in 1989 Eric Hammond reinforced this view when he strongly denied the charge that the union's activities were detrimental to the general interests of the TUC. Showing his defiance he said that the union would continue to support its members "even if that meant breaking every rule in the TUC book", adding that he would "turn that shaft back on the General Council itself". In July 1989 the train drivers' union ASLEF, wrote to the TUC complaining that the EETPU was "poaching" railway workers with whom it had no organisational links. It seemed that the EETPU was determined to view recruitment as a "free-for-all", aiming to grab all it could irrespective of any established custom and practice.

The outcome of the EETPU vote on whether to remain in the TUC was 128,400 votes (83.3 per cent of those voting) in favour compared with 25,680 (16.6 per cent) against. Although this was an overwhelming majority it was far from total: the turn-out was only 43 per cent. The EETPU went on to amend its constitution and included the provision that it would remain affiliated to the TUC only if it were allowed to pursue agreements it considers necessary.

On September 5, 1988 delegates voted to expel the EETPU from the TUC for refusing to accept TUC instructions to withdraw from two single-union, strike-free agreements. In his speech to Congress Norman Willis said that the electricians' union had shown no sign that it might be prepared to reconsider its rejection of the TUC disputes committee awards and that it was making demands which were unacceptable to the TUC. Only the AEU and some members of the CPSA delegation supported the EETPU in opposing the motion to expel them.

Recent events and the EETPU in the 1990s
Immediately following the expulsion of the EETPU from the TUC certain left-wingers in the union mounted a campaign for the reaffiliation of the union to the TUC. The move was also designed to persuade members not to join the breakaway, *Electrical and Plumbing Industries Union* (EPIU), which was formed at the time of expulsion. Some inter-union conflict did break out, most notably at Ford's Dagenham plant, where MSF recruited the deputy convenor and leading EETPU shop steward, George Foulkes, who had become an EPIU "recruiting agent". But although the EPIU was eventually issued with a certificate of independence by the Certification Officer, and has also applied to affiliate to the TUC, mass defections have not occurred.

Although his own members in the power-supply industry were less than enthusiastic about lending their support in the long-running dispute at GCHQ, Eric Hammond, speaking at the Labour Party Annual Conference shortly after the TUC expulsion, said that the union would consider any request from the TUC or the Civil Service unions to assist in renewed support of staff at GCHQ. The EETPU even faced preliminary legal moves taken by the Electricity Council over its planned action about GCHQ. There were some rumblings as to whether the EETPU could remain a member of the CSEU, but after debate and stout support from the AEU the union kept its seat. The whole expulsion affair seemed almost an anti-climax as calm settled over the trade union movement.

There were still many verbal exchanges between the various parties, and the EETPU reasserted its claim that there had been a cloak-and-dagger conspiracy by the TUC General Council in general, and by the TGWU, MSF, NUPE, and GMB in particular. Certainly, there might be some credibility in this line of argument; since its communist purges in the 1960s the EETPU had developed as the rallying point for all the right-wing unions. During the early Thatcher years the union had consistently clashed with the TUC and its affiliates; accusing them of being out-moded and refusing to accept the reality of the new political order. The TUC special Wembley Conference in 1982 adopted a policy of non-cooperation with government legislation. The EETPU and the AEU became involved in a subsequent row when they chose to ignore this policy and sought public funds for their union ballots. Both unions were on the brink of expulsion over the issue and relationships with the TUC became more strained.

But the conspiracy argument loses credibility when close allies on the General Council of the EETPU, such as John Lyons of EMA, writes in the union's journal that the plot against the electricians' union "carries no conviction with anyone else on the General Council"; likewise, Leif Mills of BIFU believed that the EETPU should not have refused to accept the TUC ruling adding that "we cannot have a situation in the TUC where any union can refuse to implement disputes committee awards or try to negotiate about them".

The EETPU has made overtures to a number of different unions about possible mergers in the last few months. The most important of these was the possible merger with the AEU; the EETPU leadership were particularly disappointed that there was no positive outcome. Such a merger would have stemmed the EETPU's decline in membership, brought additional security and a new political realignment for the right in the trade union movement, as well as providing a focal point for future mergers. Other unions, such as UCATT, might also have been attracted to merge. A significant advantage of the merger was that it would have allowed the EETPU an easy entry back into the TUC. The breakdown of these negotiations was a bitter blow to Eric Hammond, and his vitriolic outburst against the AEU leadership was understandable.

The EETPU leadership were faced with a dilemma when they addressed the biennial Conference in May 1989. Clearly the union had to make a decision about its future direction and the implications of particular courses of action needed to be carefully considered. The key question which the union had to address was the question of membership and how best to increase it. Two broad options now seem to present themselves.

The first option is for the union to pursue its merger ambitions with other more receptive partners which have a sufficient number of members to increase the union's critical mass, or to merge with a union which is strategically placed so as to complement the EETPU's own occupational interests. In adopting such an integrationist approach the EETPU would be recognising its industrial reality in changing from a medium-sized craft union to a general union. So far a successful non-TUC partner has not emerged and the only alternative is to approach a suitable TUC affiliate. But which?

The second option also being considered is to launch a sustained recruitment campaign in established work-places, by developing single-union no-strike deals to replace multi-union agreements. Inevitably this would bring it into direct conflict with other unions and the EETPU would find itself increasingly isolated.

However, single-union agreements may not prove to be the panacea which their proponents claim. EETPU officials have already expressed disenchantment with the agreements claiming that companies are not meeting their part of the bargain on clauses in the agreements which stipulated that there should be regular joint consultation and decision-making. Furthermore, a number of influential senior managers have expressed reservations about the philosophy underlying single-union agreements. They argue that by retaining the framework of collective bargaining such agreements frustrate moves which management would like to make towards more progressive human resource strategies inclined towards personal growth and development: the move from industrial relations to employee relations.

The broader, and single most important problem, is that if the EETPU pursues this option then it would effectively be burning its bridges with the TUC and its affiliates, and abandoning all hope of reaffiliation. Moreover, employers are concerned that other unions will regard the EETPU territory as fair recruiting ground — so they prefer to deal with a "tame" TUC affiliate. Does the EETPU have the resources and commitment to stand up to this challenge? If the TGWU/NUM/MSF and NUPE/NALGO/COHSE mergers succeed and the GMB continues its strategic development, the 350,000 EETPU members outside the TUC will find themselves effectively isolated.

The EETPU has undoubtedly introduced the TUC to new ways of presenting trade unionism, and "union image" is now a legitimate concern. By advocating single-union no-strike agreements the EETPU may appear more sophisticated and more attuned to current market philosophy, but in the final analysis the union's underlying strategy is not new: it is nothing more than the rugged individualism and sectional interest which have characterised the growth and development of British trade unions since the nineteenth century. Is a policy based on aggressive recruitment without rules, allowing each union to pursue agreements it considers necessary, the right foundation on which to build a trade union movement able to ensure its place in the twenty-first century?

Further references

G. Schaffer, *Light and Liberty: Sixty Years of the Electrical Trades Union*, 1949.

Electrical Trades Union: The Official History, 1953.

C.H. Rolph, *All Those in Favour?* (an account of the High Court action against the Electrical Trades Union and its officers), 1962.

Colin Barker, *The Power Game*, Pluto Press, 1972.

J.O. French, *Plumbers in Unity: The History of the Plumbers' Trades Union, 1865-1965*, 1965.

Olga Cannon and J.R.L. Anderson, *The Road from Wigan Pier: A Biography of Les Cannon*, Gollancz, 1973.

Patrick Wintour, "How Frank Chapple Stays on Top", *New Statesman*, July 25, 1980.

Ramsumair Singh, "Final offer arbitration in theory and practice", *Industrial Relations Journal*, 17, no. 4, 1986.

Charlie Leadbeater, "Unions go to Market", *Marxism Today*, September 1987.

Charlie Leadbeater, "Thoroughly Modern Movement", *Marxism Today*, September 1988.

Mark Hall, "An Uncertain future for unions", *Personnel Management*, September 1988.

The EETPU — General Council's Report to Congress, Trades Union Congress, 1988.

To mark the union's centenary in 1989 an EETPU officer is writing the union's history, which is expected to be published before the end of 1989.

Appendix: List of COMPS Membership

Abbey National Staff Association;
Association of Career Teachers;
Association of Hospital Engineers;
Association of Management and Professional Staffs;
Association of Managerial Electrical Executives;
Association of Professional Ambulance Personnel;
Audit Commission Staff Association;
British Aerospace (Dynamics Group) Employees Association;
British Association of Advisers and Lecturers in Physical Education (Observer Status);
NG Bailey Staff Association;
Balfour Beatty Group Staff Association;
Balfour Kilpatrick Staff Association;
BICC Staff Association;
British Transport Officers' Guild;
Electrical and Engineering Staff Association;
Federated Union of Managerial and Professional Officers;
Gas Higher Management Association;
Granada Staff Association;
Hospital Doctors Association;
Ministry of Defence Staff Association;
National Association of Fire Officers;
National Farmers' Union;
Headquarters Staff Association (Observer Status);
National Unilever Managers' Association;
Nationwide Anglia Building Society (Observer Status);
Prison Service Union;
Professional Association of Teachers;
Rolls Royce Management and Professional Staff Association;
Steel and Industrial Managers Association;
Sun Alliance Staff Union;
United Kingdom Association of Professional Engineers.

EFTU
ENGINEERING AND FASTENER TRADE UNION

(Formerly the *Screw Nut Bolt and Rivet Trade Union*)

TUC affiliated

Head Office: 434 Bearwood Road, Smethwick, Warley, West Midlands

Telephone: 021-434 3092

Principal officer
General Secretary: Bill Redmond

Membership (1987)
Male: 250
Female: 150
Total: 400

Membership trends

1975 total : 2,524
1979 total: 2,500
1983 total: 600

General
This small union was founded in 1914. All its members are employed at GKN in Birmingham where it recruits all grades of workers. Along with the General Secretary the union has three branch officials; two represent manual workers and the other represents staff. Redundancies and general cutbacks in the Midlands engineering industry have affected severely the union's membership almost to the point of extinction. The union has operated a deliberate policy of not increasing subscription rates during the last five years in the hope of attracting new members. It sends one delegate to the TUC each year. The union does not hold a political fund.

In 1989, the union adopted the name of the Engineering and Fastener Trade Union.

EIS
EDUCATIONAL INSTITUTE OF SCOTLAND
TUC affiliated

Head Office: 46 Moray Place, Edinburgh EH3 6BH

Telephone: 031-225 6244

Fax: 031-220 3151

Principal national officers
General Secretary: Jim Martin
Deputy General Secretary: Bob Beattie
Organising Secretary: Fred Forrester
Accountant: Robert Hodge, CA
Assistant Secretary: Jack Dale
Assistant Secretary: Ian McKay
Assistant Secretary: Ron Smith
Assistant Secretary: Denis Sullivan

Union journal: The Scottish Educational Journal (circulated free to all schools and colleges having members). The EIS also publishes a very useful guide, *Your Shield*, which outlines membership benefits of the union as well as explaining the nature of the Scottish education system.

Membership

Current membership (1987)
Total: 43,474

Membership trends *

	1976*	1979	1981	1983	1987	change 1976-87	1983-87
Total	45,357	48,479	46,515	45,665	43,474	−4%	−5%

*Figures for 1975 are not available as the EIS only affiliated to the TUC in July 1977.

General

The EIS is the largest teaching union in Scotland responsible for around 80 per cent of all teachers. Unlike the more fragmented union organisation in England and Wales the EIS is responsible for negotiations in all areas of education (with the sole exception of universities), including primary and secondary schools, as well as further and higher education. Amongst its members are registered teachers in prisons, educational administration, nursery schools, the educational psychologists' service and advisors' service. More recently, instructors of practical and aesthetic subjects have also become eligible for EIS membership.

Lecturers in further and higher education are organised in an autonomous national section which is formally linked with the National Association of Teachers in Further and Higher Education, its counterpart in England and Wales. Recent mergers have now made the EIS the principal union in Central Institutions (similar to polytechnics) and Colleges of Education.

The union conducts very rigorous and systematic recruitment campaigns for students and newly qualified teachers. Freshers' fairs are held at all the Colleges of Education with recruitment packs and EIS field officers in attendance. Newly qualified teachers (1,200 in 1988) are contacted prior to graduation and, if necessary, on two occasions thereafter. Lists of newly-appointed teachers are sent to EIS local secretaries who then encourage EIS school representatives to recruit these teachers.

From September 1984 to March 1986 Scottish teachers were involved in one of the most sustained campaigns in the history of Scottish education. The dispute was a watershed for Scottish teacher unions. The EIS was not a union renowned for its militancy, but with strong public support it managed to win from the Secretary of State for Scotland, George Younger (who was later replaced by Malcolm Rifkind) an independent committee of inquiry into teachers' pay and conditions of service, and management of the teaching profession in Scotland, a feat which teaching unions in England and Wales (who were involved in a similar dispute) failed to achieve.

History

The union was established in 1847 and received a Royal Charter of Incorporation from Queen Victoria in 1851. (EIS was later to change its Royal Charter so as to register as a trade union.) It is one of the oldest unions in Britain. At the time, illiteracy was widespread in Scotland. Of the inmates of Scottish prisons only one in 15 could read and write. In Paisley over 3,000 children between the ages of three and 15 were attending no school whatsoever. The Educational Institute of Scotland was founded as a professional association. In spite of denominational differences and political prejudices Scottish teachers, imbued with Christian charity, united to make themselves better teachers. They did not associate merely for mutual benefit, but to proclaim the necessity for education and to establish the value of sound learning. Therefore, in its early years the aims of the Institute were to build a programme of educational reform, to provide facilities, and to secure tenure and maintain salaries of teachers.

Since 1985 the EIS has merged with two small, but important Scottish unions, the *Association of Lecturers in Scottish Central Institutions* (ALSCI) in September 1985, and in March 1988 with the *Association of Lecturers in Colleges of Education in Scotland* (ALCES), thereby expanding its influence in the tertiary education sector.

Organisation
The Annual General (delegate) Meeting is the supreme court of the EIS, making and rescinding policy and exercising the right of approval, disapproval, or amendment of all decisions taken by subordinate bodies since the last General Meeting. The principal subordinate body is the Council of Members elected on the basis of local association constituencies and others representing special interests, which meets four times a year.

The Council has an Executive Committee and a number of other committees including an education committee and a parliamentary committee. All committees submit their minutes to the Council through the Executive Committee which meets monthly. The minutes of Executive and Council meetings and associated reports are submitted to the Annual General Meeting for approval. Of the local associations only two have full-time secretaries, these being the Glasgow Local Association and the Lanarkshire Local Association.

In an attempt to increase its responsiveness to members the Institute now has a network of five field officers distributed on a regional basis: Strathclyde has two; one for Tayside, Fife and Central, one for Grampian Highland, and Orkney/Shetland; and one for Borders, Dumfries and Galloway, Lothian and the Western Isles.

Women
Women constitute almost 64 per cent of the membership of the union. In 1984 a Women's Advisory Committee was set up to address the specific question of women's involvement in union affairs. A number of educational initiatives have been organised to encourage women's participation and the Committee was prominent in seeking changes in discriminatory practices and procedures in conditions of service and superannuation.

The EIS participates in the STUC and TUC women's events and the EIS delegation is among the largest at the STUC Women's Conference. The union has one representative elected on to the STUC Women's Committee.

External relations
The EIS held a ballot in November 1987 on the establishment of a political fund (although not linked to any party). The result was an 85 per cent "yes" vote on a 67 per cent turn-out. The political fund came into operation in September 1988.

The EIS is represented on the Women's National Commission and the STUC initiatives on "Employment and educational opportunity for women trade unionists". In this field the EIS plays a key role in Europe. The EIS participates actively in the European Trade Union Committee for Education (ETUCE) as well as the World Confederation of Organisations of the Teaching Profession. The convenor of the EIS Parliamentary Committee is a permanent member of the ETUCE Working Group on Equal Opportunities.

Policy
Since 1986 EIS has produced a major policy statement on *Multi-Cultural and Anti-*

Racist Education (1987), and has followed this with a further document, *Black Membership Recruitment and Participation*. Leaflets and posters have been produced and distributed in all schools and elsewhere. The EIS has also made special arrangements to step up recruitment of black members; ethnic monitoring of employer recruitment is systematised; and internal union publicity, administration, and training are currently being reviewed to encourage black recruitment and participation, and to monitor and review the success of the policy.

The EIS is committed to preserving the special character of the Scottish education system; towards the end of 1988 it staged a one-day strike in protest at the government's policy of attempting to "Anglicise Scottish education". Teaching in Scotland is an all-graduate profession and teachers must be registered by the General Teaching Council (GTC). There is no English equivalent.

In July 1989 the EIS rejected a government scheme to appraise teachers, describing it as an unnecessary "top-down, management-driven, bureaucratic approach". Because teaching in Scotland is an all-graduate entry profession requiring General Teaching Council registration, the EIS claims that GTC approval is sufficient proof of competence and that appraisal schemes reflect "yet another intrusion into Scotland of Kenneth Baker's Education Reform Act". The EIS rejects the crude notion of teacher performance asserting instead the vocational nature of teaching.

Further reference

David Ross, *An Unlikely Anger,* Mainstream Publications, 1986. (A very readable, EIS commissioned, book which not only records the battle for teachers' pay during the 1980s that culminated in the independent committee of inquiry, but also provides a clear account of the nature of the teaching profession in Scotland.)

EMA
ENGINEERS' AND MANAGERS' ASSOCIATION

TUC affiliated

Head Office: Station House, Fox Lane North, Chertsey, Surrey KT16 9HW

Telephone: 0932-564131

Fax: 0932-567707

Principal officers
General Secretary: John Lyons, CBE
Deputy General Secretary: D. C. Bound
SEAe General Secretary: Bob Fazakerley
National Secretary: Anne Douglas
National Research Officer: Patrick Hanson
Assistant Research Officer: T. Moulding
Journal Editor: P. Battams
Executive Assistant to the General Secretary: Glen Dobson

Union journal: EMA Newsletter (bimonthly, circulated to all members)

Membership

Current membership (1987)
Male: 40,037
Female: 352
Total: 40,389

Membership trends

	1975	1979	1981	1983	1987	change 1975-87	1983-87
Men	34,093	47,801	N/A	N/A	40,037	17%	N/A
Women	114	119	N/A	N/A	352	209%	N/A
Total	34,207	48,000	40,000	41,000	40,389	18%	−1%

General

The EMA grew out of the decision of the *Electrical Power Engineers' Association* in 1976 to recruit professional, managerial, and allied staffs outside the electricity supply industry — particularly in shipbuilding, engineering, aerospace, oil, and other industries. In doing so it encountered hostility from both TASS and ASTMS (now both MSF). In the late 1970s the EMA took legal action against the TUC and ACAS and became involved in a bitter inter-union feud. Since then relationships with the TUC have improved and the EMA now plays a positive part in influencing TUC policy and supporting its co-ordinating role. In 1985 it finally became a member of the Confederation of Shipbuilding and Engineering Unions (CSEU).

Despite optimism over growth potential in its formative years EMA membership, even at its peak, has never been more than 50,000. It has never posed an effective challenge to its principal rivals, TASS and ASTMS, now merged to form an even bigger organisation: MSF. EMA was involved in merger talks with NUMAST but talks broke down when its prospective partner decided to pursue amalgamation talks with TSSA. None the less, the EMA is still keen to pursue this option as it offers opportunities for growth. Alternative mergers are also being examined including possible amalgamation with BALPA and BACM.

History

The union was formed in January 1913 by a small group of 21 power station engineers and registered later in the same year as the *Association of Electrical Station Engineers.* The name was changed to the *Electrical Power Engineers' Association* (EPEA) in 1918. In 1942 the union affiliated to the TUC. The union was given notice of suspension from membership in 1972 for failure to comply with Congress policy of non-registration under the Industrial Relations Act, 1971. The National Executive Committee of the union decided in June 1973 to deregister in line with Congress policy and the notice of suspension was lifted.

In 1976 the Annual Delegate Conference took the decision to recruit in industries outside electricity supply. This decision to extend its recruitment base encountered severe opposition from other unions — particularly ASTMS and TASS. The TUC and the Engineering Employers' Federation (EEF) were also hostile to the move, as were the Arbitration and Conciliation Service (ACAS). Tensions built up between the EMA, the

TUC, and ACAS and lasted a number of years. In 1979 EMA took out court writs against both parties, but the matter was eventually resolved, the writs were cancelled, and EMA remained in the TUC.

Meanwhile, in January 1977, the *Association of Supervisory and Executive Engineers* (ASEE) amalgamated with the EPEA. The Engineers' and Managers' Association was formally created in April 1977, and the EPEA became the largest group within this federal organisation. In December 1977 the *Shipbuilding and Allied Industries Managers' Association* (SAIMA) transferred its engagements and likewise became a constituent group within the EMA. During 1979 the *British Aircraft Corporation Professional Pilots Staffs' Association* (BACSTAFF) and the *British Aerospace Staff Association* (BASA) both transferred their engagements to EMA and as from October 1, 1979 they were formed by the EMA into the *Aerospace Association*, an industrial group in its own right within the EMA.

Union officials

EMA's officers consist of a General Secretary, Deputy General Secretary, two group General Secretaries (SEAE and EPEA), National Secretary, ASEE Chief Executive, and national negotiating officers. The union also has a recruitment organiser, two research officers, journals editor, administration manager, and an Executive Assistant to the General Secretary.

Organisation

The supreme policy-making body of EMA is the Biennial Conference. The union is based on the principle that within the overall responsibilities of the EMA each industrial sector has its own group organisation with full industrial autonomy. Currently, EMA is composed of three industrial groups — the Electrical Power Engineers' Association (EPEA), the Association of Supervisory and Executive Engineers (ASEE), and the Shipbuilding, Engineering and Aerospace Group (SEAe). Each group has its own policy-making conference and EPEA also has its own National Executive Committee.

The General Executive Council of the EMA is elected by postal ballot and comprises 15 members, with seats allocated *pro rata* to the size of each constituent group. The GEC has the power to appoint all union officers, although to comply with current legal requirements a rule change has now been agreed to allow for the election of the General Secretary every five years.

The rules of the EMA provide that in the event of a dispute calling for strike action a secret ballot shall be taken of those members who may be required to be involved in a strike. If 60 per cent or more of those members balloted are in favour of such action the GEC may act accordingly.

Coverage

The EMA seeks to organise technical, scientific, and managerial staffs in the electricity supply industry, management staffs in the shipbuilding industry, and engineers and managers in the engineering, oil, aerospace, and other industries.

External relations

The EMA has no political fund, but it supports three Parliamentary Advisers in the House of Commons: Alf Morris (Labour MP for Manchester Wythenshawe), Roger King (Conservative MP for Birmingham Northfield), and Viscount Hanworth (Social and Liberal Democrat) in the House of Lords.

Since the decision taken at the 1981 EMA Conference the union now plays a full and active role in all major TUC matters. The EMA secured an important addition to the Bridlington Principles when they were being examined by the special review body. The TUC now recognises that the views of members have to be taken into account when "no union has an agreement to negotiate on behalf of workers who are the subject of dispute" (footnote to Principle 5 of the TUC Principles Governing Relations between Unions).

The EMA has also initiated debate about the procedures for submitting and compositing motions to Congress. The union has made important contributions to the review of the composition of the General Council (see **TUC**). It is hard to disagree with the EMA's perception that if representation rights of Section B members on the TUC General Council were to be reduced, then this would weaken the integrity and value of the TUC. The review body will report on these issues to the 1989 Congress.

The EMA continues to support the Council of Managerial, Professional, and Allied Staffs (COMPAS), which it helped to create in 1982 along with BALPA and BACM. COMPAS acts as a forum for politically unaffiliated TUC unions.

John Lyons is an elected member of the TUC General Council and chairs the TUC's Energy Committee.

Policy
The EMA's policy on nuclear power is influenced by its members who operate and maintain nuclear power stations. The union supported the major recommendations of the TUC's Nuclear Energy Review Body (NERB) which argued for the protection of the civil nuclear industry. At the 1988 Congress the EMA voted against the NALGO/NUM composite which called for the phasing out of nuclear power stations.

Skill shortage is an issue about which EMA is concerned, and it lobbies for greater support for training of engineers and engineering technicians. In this context the EMA has recognised the significance which 1992 and the free market might have, and the union has investigated the possible benefits of affiliating to various international organisations.

The union has recorded an increase in the numbers in its retired membership category (which includes many who took early retirement). The EMA has long recognised the fact of age discrimination, and in its dealings with employers has made attempts to ensure that age is not a discriminatory factor in company personnel policies.

The EMA is a member of the Electricity Supply Trade Union Council (ESTUC), an organisation of eight unions set up under the auspices of the TUC to respond to and campaign against the government's privatisation of the electricity supply industry. John Lyons, the EMA General Secretary, is the secretary of the ESTUC and has done much to shape its policies and direction. It is generally regarded as one of the most pragmatic union campaigns on privatisation; although the group remains implacably opposed to privatisation it recognises the inevitability of such a move. It has therefore aimed to achieve the best deal possible for the employees in the industry, by suggesting that, instead of the customary share issue typical of previous privatisations, it would prefer Employee Share Ownership Plans (ESOP). Such plans now have support on both the right and the left of the trade union movement; NALGO, for example, has taken a similarly pragmatic stance with regard to the privatisation of bus passenger transport (see **NALGO**).

Recent events
At the 1988 Delegate Conference the union made a major policy decision to enable it to sign single-union agreements, in order to maintain its representation in a privatised electricity industry. The EMA recognises that with new employers coming into play there is a high risk of inter-union conflict, and possibly conflict with the TUC itself. If

employers demand single-union agreements and ask for a "beauty contest", then EMA's competitors are likely to be the TGWU and EETPU. Stating his union's stance, John Lyons has said that "we will not willingly be shut out of an expanding electricity supply industry. We do not want conflict to occur, but if it does then we will have to face up to it."

Further reference
Robin Roslender, "The Engineers' and Managers' Association", *Industrial Relations Journal*, 2, 1983.

EQUITY
BRITISH ACTORS' EQUITY ASSOCIATION
TUC affiliated

Head Office: 8 Harley Street, London W1N 2AB

Telephone: 01-636 6367

Fax: 01-580 0970

Principal national officers
General Secretary: Peter Plouviez
Assistant General Secretary: Ian McGarry
Assistant Secretary (Theatre): Peter Finch
Assistant Secretary (Variety): Archie MacMillan
Assistant Secretary, Head of Administration: Malcolm Bradbury
Press and Publicity Officer: Rosie Brocklehurst

In addition, there 22 organisers based in London and the regional offices.

Union journal: Equity Journal (quarterly, posted to members)

Membership

Current membership (1987)
Male: 18,817
Female: 17,604
Total: 36,421

Membership trends

	1975	1979	1981	1983	1987	change 1975-87	change 1983-87
Men	11,790	14,665	15,851	16,765	18,817	60%	12%
Women	10,583	13,023	14,301	15,651	17,604	66%	12%
Total	22,373	27,688	30,152	32,416	36,421	63%	12%

Regional offices

Northern office
Canavon Court, 12 Blackfriars Street, Salford, Manchester M3 5BQ
Telephone: 061-832 3283

Scottish office
65 Bath Street, Glasgow G2 2BX
Telephone: 041-332 1669

Welsh office
24 Queen Street, Cardiff CF1 4BW
Telephone: 0222-397971

Variety department
31A Thayer Street, London W1M 5LH
Telephone: 01-637 9311

General
Any person who "exercises professional skill in the provision of entertainment, whether an artist, producer, stage manager, or in a similar capacity in the theatre, music hall, films, radio, television, and like media" is eligible for EQUITY membership. None the less the Executive Committee has the power to "grant any applicant temporary membership only for such period and upon payment of such entrance fee and subscription as it may deem appropriate. The election of members shall be by a majority of the Executive Committee present at any meeting".

EQUITY was one of the founders of the London Theatre Council and of the Provincial Theatre Council. It has secured minimum pay and conditions for actors throughout the professional theatre and house agreements with opera and ballet companies. Similarly, it has national agreements for the engagement of performers in television, radio, and for roles in feature films. Variety and circus artists are catered for by the Variety department and standard contracts for their engagement are agreed with the Variety and Allied Entertainments Council of Great Britain.

EQUITY has recently extended its membership base and now recruits theatre designers, directors, and choreographers.

History
Late in 1929 some members of the theatrical profession agreed that there was an urgent need for a new and strong organisation to protect the interests of the rank and file of the profession. The *Actors' Association* which had done valuable work had almost collapsed, its destruction and disintegration being due largely to the fact that it had not achieved the closed shop principle, an essential extension of collective bargaining in the theatre business.

The *Actors' Association* had become a trade union some years before 1930, and this had led to an increased membership. It had been able to establish a contract with managers for minimum wages and conditions. There was a counter-attack, however; the touring managers in particular resented the contract. A long wearisome struggle ensued resulting, after tortuous negotiations, in the realisation by the *Association* that without complete unity and 100 per cent membership it did not have the power to enforce any conditions.

Worse was to follow, for the council of the *Actors' Association* took some ill-advised and desperate measures (including strike action) to try to hold the line. Many members of the *Association*, shocked by such tactics and fearing the communist bogey, broke away to form a new Association, the *Stage Guild*. This was to be a nice, respectable, genteel body, which abhorred trade unionism and aimed to include the managers.

Unsurprisingly, it was totally ineffective on behalf of the members of the profession, and theatre managers began to flout contracts and do much as they pleased in their treatment of actors. Abuses and cases of bogus management crept back and finally provoked protest. The *Stage Guild* was swept away and a mandate gained to form an association of actors called *British Equity*. The campaign to secure contracts and full unionisation began all over again. Union supporters were asked not to perform with non-EQUITY members, thereby further jeopardising their already precarious livelihood.

Eventually EQUITY was able to obtain agreement to establish a Theatre Council. It consisted of the managers and the union and its function was to discuss problems, agree to a standard contract, and acknowledge the EQUITY Shop. Resistance to the EQUITY Shop was overcome in 1933. However, a minority of professional entertainers continued to believe that EQUITY should be more of a professional association than a union, and when EQUITY affiliated to the TUC in 1940 Godfrey Tearle, who had been President for 10 years, resigned in protest.

It has been necessary to discuss this issue in the history of EQUITY at length in order to emphasise the importance of the closed-shop principle for the well-being of EQUITY members entering the acting profession. It brought a semblance of order and balance into a profession notorious for its casual employment of actors, many of whom experience lengthy periods of unemployment. In 1970 EQUITY's "living wage" campaign succeeded in obtaining real improvements in raising minimum salaries.

In the 1950s anyone being offered professional work could obtain an EQUITY card. This remains the case today; an applicant must have proof of professional employment, and registered theatre companies are allocated annual quotas through which newcomers, both as performers or stage managers, can be recruited into the profession. More recently agreement was reached between the union and the National Council for Drama and Training, whereby drama graduates from accredited drama schools/colleges, on successful completion of their courses, join a central register for up to two years, during which time they can enter the profession on a standard approved contract. Full EQUITY membership is preceded by 30 weeks' provisional membership.

For several years until 1979, the union was troubled by a constant battle between one faction which believed that Annual and Special General Meetings should wield ultimate authority and another faction, consisting mainly of members of EQUITY Council, which said that on constitutional issues referenda should be used. According to Peter Plouviez, the General Secretary, the rules at the time gave the appearance of power to Annual and Special General Meetings and resulted in the absurd process of decisions taken at General Meetings being reversed by ballot and then considered at meetings again. Prominent in the faction favouring the powers of General Meetings were members of the Workers' Revolutionary Party, including Vanessa Redgrave.

Council was finally empowered to put rule changes to the membership in a referendum after a House of Lords' judgement in favour of Marius Goring, a member of the EQUITY Council. Subsequently, the referendum results approved the rule changes, which established an Appeals Committee to be elected by postal ballot every two years by the entire membership. If the EQUITY Council receives a petition demanding a Special General Meeting or referendum which it believes contrary to the best interests of the Association, it refers the petition to the Appeals Committee which on hearing the arguments for and against makes a final and binding decision.

The 67-member Council of EQUITY is elected biennially, by secret postal ballot of the entire membership. As well as a general list, candidates may stand in specialist and regional "boxes", reflecting the diverse elements in the entertainment and theatrical business.

Organisation

The alarm and agitation which occurred within the Council of the *Actors' Association* influenced those who drafted the rules for EQUITY. They aimed to place checks and balances on the Council of the new Association by increasing the constitutional powers and influence of Annual General Meetings and Special General Meetings which could be called on presentation to the Secretary of a written request stating the purpose of the meeting and signed by 40 members. There was an unqualified right amongst the membership to call a referendum to prevent the Council acting upon any resolution passed at an Annual or Special General Meeting, subject to the presentation of a petition to the Secretary, signed by 100 members in full benefit within 14 days of the meeting (see above for amendments to this constitution).

EQUITY has a Women's Committee elected nationally by women members; all candidates must be women. The Committee advises the EQUITY Council on women's issues. The Women's Committee recently obtained Council support for a model equal opportunities clause to be negotiated for inclusion in the union's agreements with employers, accompanied by a statement of intent to promote equal opportunities. A combination of members of the EQUITY Council and of the Women's Committee attend the annual Women's TUC.

The majority of the union's national agreements with employers contain an equal opportunities clause. In particular, EQUITY encourages integration and non-stereotypical casting; to assist employers in television, film, and theatre the union produces an Afro-Asian casting directory, which is regularly updated. A seat is reserved on EQUITY's governing body, the Council, for an Afro-Asian representative, in addition to which an Afro-Asian Artists' Committee has been created to promote the interests of ethnic minority artists and to advise the Council on issues afftecting this group of members.

EQUITY has recently made a number of new appointments in order to strengthen its provision of services to members. A Welfare Benefits Organiser has been appointed to advise and to represent members at DHSS and tax appeal tribunals, and assist with any problems they may encounter when dealing with that occupational hazard of the acting profession: registration as unemployed. A Legal Referrals Organiser, as well as a firm of solicitors, has been engaged to deal with problems arising in the performing arts, television, radio, and films.

External relations

The rules specify that EQUITY is a "non-party political and non-sectarian union". It is affiliated to the TUC, STUC, Welsh TUC, Irish Congress of Trade Unions, International Federation of Actors, the Confederation of Entertainment Unions, the Performers' Alliance (with the Musicians' Union and the Writers' Guild of Great Britain), Amnesty International, NCCL, Theatres' Advisory Council, Radio and Television Safeguards Committee, and the National Campaign for the Arts.

Policy

The creation of a fourth television channel, the growth of video tapes and discs, the development of satellite and cable television, central government insistence on "deregulation" and "liberalisation" of the air waves, have all involved EQUITY in a large number of discussions and negotiations aimed at achieving equitable payments for members' work, the safeguarding of future employment, and control over the use of recorded material. Indeed, government instructions to the BBC, following the Peacock inquiry, that a percentage of productions must be farmed out to independent producers over a given timetable, have been copied to a greater-than-usual extent by the ITV companies.

Following a meeting with television executives the Prime Minister described union agreements in television and films as "the last bastions of restrictive practices", and with this government encouragement there have been early attempts by the television companies to provide a new system for artists' repeat fees, for repeated programmes, and residual payments for overseas sales. As a result the EQUITY Council balloted the union's membership seeking to maintain this category of payments. The result in favour of maintaining these payments was the largest ever recorded in EQUITY's history; of those voting 99.32 per cent voted "yes" and a mere 0.68 per cent voted "no".

With this mandate from the members not to allow reductions in payments for repeats, EQUITY was involved (in 1988) in a series of negotiations in an attempt to reach agreement with the BBC and ITV Association, a joint employers' body, as well as the Independent Programme Producers' Association and the British Film and Television Producers' Association. EQUITY is happy to replace the residual fees with a royalties system under which repeat fees would be a percentage of the price a programme fetched when sold to a new market. This is favoured by producers because it could make it easier to sell programmes abroad and on cable and satellite networks. However, EQUITY is not prepared to accept a new deal which means actors being paid less than under the present system.

The whole business of labour practices in the film and television industry was the subject of a Monopolies and Mergers Commission inquiry under Section 79 of the 1973 Fair Trading Act (see "Recent events"). The terms of reference of the MMC inquiry were to "investigate any closed shops, formal or informal, which restricted the extent to which non-union members could perform jobs, and any minimum staffing levels". Interestingly enough, some employers' associations, most notably the ITV Association, were the staunchest defenders of the closed-shop arrangements. They maintained that formal closed-shop arrangements generally do little harm to the companies on the grounds that the labour pool within the union is big enough to allow companies a free choice of individuals, and that EQUITY represents all shades of opinion thereby avoiding harmful factional interests.

In order to raise public and political awareness on arts funding EQUITY, along with other participants in the National Campaign for the Arts, organised a national petition and urged all prospective parliamentary candidates in the 1987 general election to include a statement on the arts in their election manifestos. In conjunction with this petition a publicity campaign was organised around the slogan "I Vote for the Arts".

In 1989, as part of its campaign over the fees for repeats, EQUITY published the results of its survey which showed that although the union is growing 72 per cent of its members earn less than £10,000 per annum, and 52 per cent of those earn less than £5,000 per annum.

Recent events

The MMC inquiry, entitled *Labour Practices in TV and Film Making* (CM 66, HMSO), was published in April 1989. Whilst it found EQUITY to have restrictive agreements under the terms of the 1973 Fair Trading Act — closed-shop deals prevented employers from using non-EQUITY members — it nevertheless concluded that these agreements did not operate against the public interest. Indeed, most employers believed that such deals had benefits in that a union membership card was an effective way of maintaining professional standards.

None the less, the MMC did indicate that the problem of actors' fees for repeat programmes was a matter of some concern to employers, and EQUITY might be using its position to gain unfair advantage; unfortunately this area was outside the terms of reference of the MMC investigation.

Further references
The Stage and Television Today, weekly. Not an EQUITY publication, but usually providing some information about EQUITY and the other entertainment unions.

The prominent broadcaster, Joan Bakewell, wrote a stout defence of EQUITY's closed-shop policy in *The Sunday Times,* December 4, 1989, page C8.

P. Bassett, *Trade Unions and the Arts,* unpublished MA thesis, City University, London 1980. Includes a useful discussion on EQUITY in relation to its activities in Scotland.

The BBC broadcasted a radio play by Hugh Jenkins, former Minister for the Arts on Radio 4 on March 15, 1989. Jenkins tells the story of "British McCarthyism" and its determination, some 40 years ago, to rid EQUITY of communist influence.

FAA
FILM ARTISTES' ASSOCIATION
TUC affiliated

Head Office: 61 Marloes Road, London W8 6LE

Telephone: 01-937 4567

Principal officer
General Secretary: Michael Reynel

Membership

Current membership (1987)
Male: 1,213
Female: 977
Total: 2,320

Membership trends
1983: 3,578
1979: 2,581
1975: 1,559

General
Founded in 1932, this union caters almost entirely for crowd artistes, stand-ins, and doubles on feature films. The "glamorous" nature of film extra work is such that the union feels there are more applications for union membership than there is work for them. The union also has a special senior citizens section.

FBU
FIRE BRIGADES' UNION

TUC affiliated

Head Office: 68 Coombe Road, Kingston-upon-Thames, Surrey KT2 7AE

Telephone: 01-541 1765

Fax: 01-546 5187

Principal national officers
General Secretary: Ken Cameron
Assistant General Secretary: M. Fordham
National Officer: D. Matthews
National Officer: D. Riddell
National Officer: D. Higgins
National Officer: A. Totterdell

Union journal: Firefighter (monthly, circulation 135,000). The union has also produced a pictorial history of the FBU to mark its 50 years of existence from 1918-68: *The Fire Brigades' Union: Fifty Years of Service.*

Membership

Current membership (1987)
Male: 44,512
Female: 991
Total: 45,503

Membership trends

	1975	1979	1981	1983	1987	change 1975-87	1983-87
Men	29,700	29,700	29,700	43,105	44,512	50%	3%
Women	300	300	300	300	991	230%	230%
Total	30,000	30,000	30,000	43,405	45,503	52%	5%

General
The Fire Brigades' Union began in London in 1918. It now has in membership over 90 per cent of all uniformed personnel (full-time, and of all ranks) in the 68 local authority fire brigades in the UK. Some brigade officers (about 5,000) belong to the *National Association of Fire Officers,* although the FBU is gradually extending its dominance into the brigade officer ranks. (see "Recent events"). The FBU has a left-wing tradition and was involved in a national strike during the winter of 1977-8. Ken Cameron, the General Secretary, is a member of the General Council of the TUC. The late Terry Parry was the TUC President from 1979-80.

History
Fire brigade trade unionism began in London. The London fire-fighters were nearly always on duty; they had two hours' leave a week but otherwise were confined to quarters in small fire stations and under strict discipline. Throughout the country in the early

1900s there were fewer than 3,000 full-time professional fire-fighters; most of the large provincial fire brigades were staffed by police.

In 1913 some men in the fire brigade joined the *National Union of Corporation Workers* (later NUPE). They formed a branch and fought for recognition for fire brigade trade unionism by London County Council. This was resisted and the conflict led eventually to a ballot on strike action in 1918. Askwith, the government conciliator, was called in and devised a compromise formula whereby a fire-fighter's "representative body" (nominally not a union) would be recognised and could be accompanied by a "spokesman" who did not need to be a member of the London Fire Brigade.

There was already in existence a fire-fighter's benefit society which in 1918 registered as a friendly society calling itself the *Fireman's Trade Union*. Without rancour, and with full agreement of the *National Union of Corporation Workers*, the fire-fighters merged with this new union. One Jim Bradley, a radical Executive member of the *National Union of Corporation Workers*, was appointed for representative purposes, and in 1922, became General Secretary. The union began to expand outside London but many provincial fire brigades were still police brigades and, although improved pay and duty systems were awarded as a result of the report of the Middlebrook Committee on pay and conditions of professional fire-fighters, actually obtaining these awards from local authorities proved difficult.

In 1930 the union's name was changed to the Fire Brigades' Union. During and shortly before the war local authorities organised the *Auxiliary Fire Service*. Many members of the FBU rejected and resisted this organisation and tried to boycott the AFS, fearing that it would drag down the pay and conditions of service of regular fire-fighters. When John Horner became General Secretary (at the age of 27) he reversed this policy, forming the AFS section of the union. With nationalisation of this service to form the National Fire Service, the union was able to combine the AFS with the regular section.

However, in 1947 the fire service was reorganised and decentralised to county level and this had the effect of somewhat weakening the union. In 1952 the Ross award broke the link between fire-fighters' pay and that of the police. Whilst the principle of the 60-hour week and double shifts had been conceded in 1940 by the London County Council, the union was hectically engaged in the early 1950s in defending the newly-won two-shift duty system, as some local authorities tried to restore some kind of continuous duty.

Union officials

The FBU employs only the General Secretary, Assistant General Secretary, and the four national officers as full-time officials — all of them ex-fire-fighters. Under FBU rules national officials are elected for five years by a ballot conducted through the union's branches, with the union's chartered accountants acting as returning officers.

Coverage

As stated earlier 90 per cent of all full-time uniformed personnel in the 68 local authority fire brigades of Great Britain and Northern Ireland belong to the FBU. The union also has some part-time members in its ranks. Some brigade officers belong to the non-TUC affiliated union, the *National Association of Fire Officers*.

National pay and conditions of fire-fighters are dealt with by local authorities through the National Joint Council for Local Authority Fire Brigades. Representation on the joint national negotiating machinery has always been a sensitive issue for the FBU. Problems arise over the relative number of seats which are allocated between them and the officers' union, NAFO. The seats are allocated on the basis of proportional membership representation; the FBU is slowly gaining a greater proportion of officer members than the NAFO. In 1982 the employers revised the representation on the Joint Council following a head-count which showed that the FBU held 50 per cent of officer membership. In January 1988 the constitution of the officers' committee of the National Joint Council was changed again following a further head-count of officer membership which showed that the FBU had now over 60 per cent of all officer membership. This new constitution now gives the FBU a majority of seats over NAFO on the NJC.

Organisation

The supreme government of the union is the Annual Conference, with the general administration carried out by the Executive Council. The membership is divided into 14 regions to assist democratic administration. The Executive Council consists of one representative from each region (London has two), and there is one representative from the National Officers' Committee. These representatives are elected every four years and are eligible for re-election.

The General Secretary, Assistant General Secretary, and national officers are elected by ballots conducted through the branches with a firm of chartered accountants (named by Annual Conference) acting as returning officers. They hold office for five years and are then eligible for re-election. The President is elected in the same way but must serve at least four years on the Executive Council.

Within each fire authority there is a brigade committee composed of one delegate from each branch within the brigade's territory. To expedite union business and to strengthen brigade committees within each region there is an elected regional committee; in the case of London and Northern Ireland these committees are one and the same.

The officer's National Executive Committee advises the Executive Council on matters affecting the conditions of employment of union members who are of the rank of station officer and above, and on their organisation and recruitment. The basic units of organisation are the branches, and these are normally based in individual fire stations.

Work-place activity

There are over 120 shop stewards based at fire stations throughout the UK. Many of these are brigade secretaries or brigade chairmen.

Women

Women's membership has grown recently and accounts for around 22 per cent of FBU membership. Nearly all of them are employed as control room staff at fire stations or brigade headquarters.

Women feature very little in the affairs of the FBU although there are now a few women brigade secretaries and one woman is on the Executive Council. However, there is a section of the union which deals with the interests of control room staff, and women occupy positions as representatives in 10 out of the 14 regions of the union.

The FBU is proud of its reputation as a democratic and fair union. It has recently produced a progressive and far-reaching document — *Equal Opportunities Policy* — in order to "come to terms with and reflect the changes that are taking place in society". This document argues that the fire service has for too long been a white, male-dominated service and that women and ethnic minority groups are now under-represented. The FBU leadership believes that the racism and sexism which exist in the union — although a reflection of wider social prejudices — can no longer go unchallenged. To this end, the union has undertaken an extensive survey of employment opportunities in the fire service. It has promoted courses and workshops on equal opportunities and has changed its rule book in accordance with Resolution 96 of its Annual Conference, which overwhelmingly demanded that the union support the Commission for Racial Equality's *Code of Practice* and make a public commitment to an equal opportunities policy. At national level the Executive Council has elected an Equal Opportunities Standing Committee to develop and monitor equal opportunities throughout the union, whilst at the regional/brigade level provision has been made to elect Equal Opportunities Officials who liaise with brigade officials and the National Equal Opportunities Standing Committee. The union also proposes that all brigades be required to negotiate the union's Equal Opportunities Policy Statement and monitor and assist its progress. Other unions could learn much from this initiative.

External relations

The FBU is affiliated to the Labour Party. In 1986 the union successfully conducted a ballot over the maintenance of a political fund. Out of a very high turn-out of 87.4 per cent, 79.6 per cent (30,607) voted "yes", with only 20.4 per cent (7,652) voting "no".

The FBU has traditionally affiliated to a wide range of national and international political and libertarian pressure groups whose aims are compatible with its own policies; some of these are listed below:

Anti-apartheid movement;
Campaign for Press & Broadcasting Freedom;
1984 Campaign for Freedom;
London Hazards Centre;
War on Want;
Labour Research Department;
Socialist Health Association;
National Council for Civil Liberties;
Workers' Educational Association;
Amnesty International;
Pre-Retirement Association;
Liberation;
National Peace Council;
Anti-Nuclear Campaign;
British Bulgarian Trade Union Association;
CD Rights in Turkey;
Campaign for Labour Party Democracy;
Marx Memorial Library;
Haldane Society;
Fire Protection Society;
Britain Vietnam Association;
British Standards Institute;
Labour Common Markets Safeguards Committee;
Campaign for Nuclear Disarmament;
British Peace Assembly;
British Soviet Friendship Society;
British Safety Council;
World Disarmament;
Child Poverty Action Group;
United Nations Association;
Public Services International;
London Havana Society;
Industrial Law Society;
One World;
Red Wedge;

Justice for Mine-workers Campaign;
Disability Alliance.

The union also provides additional financial support when appeals for donations have been made by various worthy causes and organisations.

Policy
The FBU has traditionally been on the left of the labour movement. A clear guide to the criteria which govern union policies can be gleaned from the foreword to its rule book in which it states that its immediate aims are to serve the members by winning them the best possible terms and conditions of service but it recognises that this can only be brought about by struggle and as part of a working-class movement whose ultimate aim is to bring about a "socialist system of society".

Recent events
The government, by urging local authorities to review firemen's pay and conditions, is threatening the 11-year-old indexation formula whereby pay is index-linked to average earnings. The government has told the National Joint Council (NJC) of local authorities and unions that it wants to review the system of pay and conditions and introduce greater flexibility in manning arrangements. To date the NJC has resisted changes to either part-time or holiday arrangement but the government has made it clear that if the NJC does not co-operate it may be by-passed and alternative machinery brought in. In May 1989 the FBU agreed reluctantly to accept talks over pay and conditions. If radical changes to conditions of service are proposed then the FBU has already demonstrated that it is quite capable of defending itself.

Further references
Industrial Relations in the London Fire Service, Report of a Committee of Inquiry of the Advisory Conciliation and Arbitration Service, 1977.

Donald C. Pennington, "The British firemen's strike of 1977/78: an investigation of judgements in foresight and hindsight", *British Journal of Social Psychology,* XX, September 1981.

A.I.R. Swabe and Patricia Price, "Multi-unionism in the fire service", *Industrial Relations Journal,* 14, no. 4, Winter 1983.

The union is currently having its official history written and publication is expected early in 1990.

FDA
ASSOCIATION OF FIRST DIVISION CIVIL SERVANTS

TUC affiliated

Head Office: 2 Caxton Street, London SW1H 0QH

Telephone: 01-222 6242

Fax: 01-222 5926

Principal national officers
General Secretary: Elizabeth Symons
Assistant General Secretary: Robyn Dasey
Assistant General Secretary: D. Stobbs
Assistant Secretary: Jonathan Baume

Union journal: FDA News (monthly)

Membership

Current membership (1987)
Male: 7,378
Female: 1,685
Total: 9,063

Membership trends
1983: 7,503
1979: 8,368
1976: 8,281

General
The Association took its title from the category of Civil Servants it represented when first formed in 1919. It affiliated to the TUC in 1977. At the present time the FDA has in membership staff from administration trainee to permanent secretary as well as certain specialist groups in the Civil Service such as statisticians, economists, lawyers (including the newly-formed Crown Prosecution Service), museum curators, HM Inspectors of Taxes, and HM Inspectors of Schools. It also represents senior officers in the Northern Ireland Civil Service as well as having members in some other areas of the public sector: for example, the House of Commons, the British Council, and the UK Atomic Energy Authority. Branches within the FDA normally follow the departmental structure of the Civil Service and there is a high level of membership density amongst those eligible for membership. In addition to the branch structure the Association is also organised into six sections as follows: (1) HM Inspector of Schools in England and Wales; (2) HM Inspector of Schools in Scotland; (3) Legal Class; (4) Museums Class; (5) Crown Prosecution Service; (6) Northern Ireland Senior Officers. These sections are solely responsible for all professional matters concerning their members.

The FDA has close links with the *Association of HM Inspectors of Taxes* (AIT), an independent union. It has concluded a Memorandum of Understanding to enable the two organisations to act together in formulating and pursuing a common policy on matters of mutual interest. Members of the AIT have all the same rights as members of the FDA. The AIT acts independently on all matters which directly concern its members in the Inland Revenue Department but on all other issues the two unions act together. Indeed the FDA includes AIT rules within its own rule book and includes AIT membership in its figures (see "Recent Events").

Policy

The FDA is a constituent of the Council of Civil Service Unions (CCSU). It has concluded a long-term flexible pay agreement with the Treasury which establishes a pay "spine" for senior grades five to seven (i.e. principal to assistant secretary). Each grade spans a number of points with extra performance-based points awarded with departmental discretion. It is intended to allow individual departments to reward performance and meet recruitment and retention shortages in particular areas and specialist fields.

From August 1989 a form of pay comparability with the private sector is also to be introduced by the use of a pay levels survey that would "inform but not constrain" pay negotiations. The FDA is particularly keen on the comparability element because it has seen pay in the private sector board-room rising substantially over the last number of years and senior managers coming to expect a wider remuneration package including substantial non-pay elements. There is increasing pressure on senior Civil Servants to act in a more business-management way: the FDA believes that this new role should be reflected in salaries.

The FDA takes a close interest in professional issues and has campaigned for a freedom of information act and a code of ethics for Civil Servants.

In June 1988 John Ward, the former General Secretary, took the decision to resign and leave the trade union movement altogether. He had played an important role in persuading the government to revise the Armstrong memorandum which defines a code of ethics for Civil Servants. He led the negotiations which resulted in the agreement with the Treasury on pay scales for senior officials in grades five to seven, and encouraged the FDA to take a positive attitude on the Ibbs report, *The Next Steps*. The report put the case for the executive functions of the Civil Service to be moved into agencies with some independence.

Recent events

In December 1988 the AIT agreed to a transfer of engagements and from January 1989 formally became part of the FDA.

FTAT
FURNITURE, TIMBER, AND ALLIED TRADES UNION

TUC affiliated

Head Office: "Fairfields", Roe Green, Kingsbury, London NW9 0PT

Telephone: 01-204 0273

Fax: 01-204 3476

Principal officers
General Secretary: Colin Christopher
Assistant Secretary: F. Davies
Assistant Secretary: E. Goodall
Clerical and Supervisory Group Organiser: I. Rowe
Funeral Service Operatives Group Organiser: P. Hickey
Glass Processing Group Organiser: Vacant

Union journal: FTAT Record (monthly tabloid newspaper)

Current membership (1987)
Male: 41,444
Female: 5,564
Total: 47,008

Membership trends

	1975	1979	1981	1983	1987	change 1975-87	1983-87
Men	73,857	75,535	61,138	51,945	41,444	−44%	−20%
Women	10,243	9,501	7,460	6,299	5,564	−46%	−12%
Total	84,100	85,036	68,598	58,244	47,008	−44%	−19%

General
The FTAT recruits furniture workers in wood, metal, and plastic; cabinet makers; frameworkers; upholsterers; polishers; wood machinists; mattress makers; carvers and guilders; glass workers; artificial limb makers; and plywood workers. It also organises joiners and other building workers, floor coverers, shop fitters, funeral service operatives, and musical instrument makers. There is also a supervisory and clerical section.

Since 1975 FTAT membership has declined by 44 per cent, and whilst the rate of decline has slowed down the union has still suffered a 19 per cent loss of membership since 1983. These figures are greater than the trade union average, which must be of concern to the union leadership. The FTAT is proud of its independence and wishes to retain it. However, should the decline continue then a merger might have to be considered. UCATT, the building and construction union should be the obvious choice but these two unions are on opposite ends of the political spectrum, and the TGWU might be more acceptable.

History
The union was founded as the *National Amalgamated Furniture Trades Association* (NAFTA) in 1901 from the amalgamation of the *Alliance Cabinetmakers* (founded in 1868) and the *United and Operative Cabinet and Chairmakers' Society of Scotland* which was formed in 1875 from a number of local societies. In 1911 the *Amalgamated Society of French Polishers* (formed in 1853) joined NAFTA.

NAFTA ceased to exist in 1946 when it amalgamated with the *Amalgamated Union of Upholsterers* to form the *National Union of Furniture Trade Operatives* (NUFTO). The *Amalgamated Union of Upholsterers* had been founded in 1891 from a number of locally based upholstery unions, the oldest of which could be traced back to its origins in meetings in the "Upholsterers Arms" in Wardour Street, London, in 1812. In 1969 NUFTO effected an amalgamation with the *United French Polishers* and in the following year with the *Midland Glass Bevellers*.

In 1972 NUFTO amalgamated with the *Amalgamated Society of Woodcutting Machinists* to form the Furniture, Timber, and Allied Trades Union (FTAT). The *Amalgamated Society of Woodcutting Machinists* had been founded in 1866 as the *Mill Sawyers' Union of Birmingham District*. It became the *Mill Wood Cutting Machinists and Wood Turners' Society*, and finally the *Amalgamated Society of Woodcutting Machinists*, a northern craft society with its Head Office in Manchester. In 1978 the Furniture, Timber, and Allied Trades Union amalgamated with the 1,000-strong *Funeral Service Operatives' Union*. In October 1983 the small *National Society of Brushmakers and General Workers* (NSBGW), one of the oldest trade unions with the longest continuous existence in the world, and whose origins can be traced back to 1747, merged with the FTAT.

Coverage
The union has membership in and is party to agreements covering the following industries:

Furniture manufacture;
Sawmilling;
Veneer producing and plywood manufacture;
Upholstery and bedding filling materials;
Bedding and mattress manufacture;
Timber container;
Brush and broom;
Pianoforte manufacture;
Organ building;
Toys and games;
Sports goods;
Municipal passenger transport;
Funeral services;
Engineering;
Specialist vehicle building;
Artificial limb manufacture;
Shipbuilding and repair.

Organisation
The union is divided into five trade groups: woodcutting machinists group; upholstery, soft furnishing and bedding group; funeral service operatives group; flat glass and processing group; supervisory and clerical group. Most of these groups have an elected full-time trade organiser who is engaged in recruitment activities and also acts as technical advisor to a district organiser. Members in each trade group elect by branch ballot six members from within the group who form the trade group committee. Trade groups can convene a conference of delegates.

The membership of the union is further divided into branches, based on towns or areas, which are assembled into 17 districts (previously 18, but districts 16 and 17 have been combined). Each district has a district organiser elected by secret postal ballot every five years. There are 24 district organisers; four representing district 18 (Greater London and the South-East); two each in district 7 (Greater Manchester, Merseyside, and Lancashire), district 9 (Lincolnshire, Humberside, Derbyshire, Leicestershire, Nottinghamshire, and South Yorkshire), and district 10 (the West Midlands, Staffordshire, Warwickshire, Hereford and Worcester). All other districts have one organiser each.

All principal officers of the union, including the General Secretary, have, since the mid-1970s, been elected by a full postal ballot.

The supreme authority of the union is constitutionally vested in the Biennial Conference or Special Conference of Branch Delegates. Delegates to Conference are elected or appointed on the basis of one per 6,000 members. Although Conference is constitutionally the supreme authority, real control of the union rests in its elected General Executive Council (GEC) of 19 members. The GEC is elected every five years by postal ballot and administers union business. All GEC decisions are binding unless reversed by Conference or ballot. The GEC arranges in each district the establishment of a district committee which, among its other functions, promotes the strengthening of factory and shop-floor organisation and shop stewards' organisation. Only the GEC has the authority to allow a trade group to convene a conference.

Work-place activities
Shop steward organisation is highly developed in the FTAT even though their duties are not mentioned at all in the rule book.

External relations
The FTAT was one of the very first unions to hold a political fund ballot, and although its turn-out was only 30 per cent the union received a 72.5 per cent "yes" vote (11,410 votes) and a 27.5 per cent "no" vote (4,267 votes).

The FTAT is affiliated to the Labour Party and to the CND. It is generally regarded as politically inclined to the hard left.

Policy
The policies and tone of the FTAT are identifiable from the annual report presented by the General Secretary to the 1988 Conference. In it he condemns the deindustrialisation of Britain as a result of "Thatcherism" and laments the lack of investment in British industry, in training, research and development, education, housing, and the environment. He goes on to suggest that the anarchy of the "free market" approach needs to be replaced with a planned approach and adds that "we need to organise, modernise, and democratise because economics, at the end of the day, is not about profits, new technologies, market forces or declining industries. It is about people. It is about how we organise and utilise our material and human resources to create a world fit for people to live in, in comfort, dignity, fulfilment, and peace".

The FTAT must take some credit for the new regulations which became effective on March 1, 1989, with regard to the use of flame retardant foam in furniture upholstery. The FTAT began the campaign in 1968, following a polyurethane fire in a Glasgow upholstery factory where 20 of its members died.

Recent events
The 1988 Biennial Conference agreed to the election of four national secretaries (further details were not available at the time of publication).

The FTAT has negotiated a new national agreement which allows workers time off with pay for cancer screening. This agreement covers cervical and breast screening for women, and nasal cancer screening for both sexes. The incidence of nasal cancer amongst workers in the woodworking industry is about 700 in every million, and the risk is increased by inhaling wood dust. The national agreement, which came into effect in June 1989, is one of the most extensive series of changes achieved by a union for health screening.

Further references

Hew F. Read, *The Furniture Makers, A History of Trade Unionism in the Furniture Trade 1868-1972*, Malthouse, 1986.

William Kiddier, *The Old Trade Unions: From Unprinted Records of the Brushmakers,* Allen & Unwin, 1931.

FUMPO
FEDERATED UNION OF MANAGERIAL AND PROFESSIONAL OFFICERS

Non-TUC affiliated

Head Office: Terminus House, The High, Harlow, Essex CM20 1TZ

Telephone: 0279-34444 0279 434444

Fax: 0279-451176

Principal officers
General Secretary: David Davies
Deputy Geneal Secretary: Janet Winters
Assistant General Secretary (Public Relations, Journal Editor): Keith Brown
Assistant General Secretary (Industrial Relations): Brenda Playford
Finance Officer: Jenny Pearce

Union journal: Professional Officer (monthly, posted free to all members)

Membership

Current membership (1989)
Total: 10,000

General
FUMPO was formed in January 1986 as a result of a series of mergers of very small non-TUC unions which represented mainly the senior and chief officer grades in local authorities. FUMPO recruits senior management in the public sector and has representation rights on the various Whitley councils. It is a small, élitist union which takes a partisan line in its dealings with its chief rival, NALGO. Whilst industrial action is not prohibited under FUMPO rules, it is extremely unlikely that it would ever be taken, since only its National Executive Committee may authorise strike action, and then only if there is a two-thirds majority of the membership in favour. Furthermore, clause 11 of the constitution prohibits FUMPO members from giving "any support to any member who is not a member of the union (FUMPO) in the encouragement or observance of any strike or industrial action".

FUMPO welcomes the move towards greater decentralisation and "spirit of enterprise" now being introduced into the public sector, as it believes this move will enable its members to assert their position and status far more effectively. At a recent FUMPO section conference the General Secretary, David Davies, identified the union name as being "inappropriate for a body of professional and senior employees". The union is currently engaged in searching for a new name and image.

Union membership increased by around 1,500 during the 1989 NALGO dispute (see **NALGO**), and although FUMPO is keen to continue this expansion it is likely to find that recruitment is difficult as there is an upper limit to the number of potential local authority officers. Moreover, it is competing against larger, more established unions, such as NALGO. A similar problem faced the EMA when it decided to widen its recruitment base outside the electricity supply industry and encountered competition from ASTMS and TASS (now MSF). There is a current trend towards union mergers and perhaps the only real alternative for FUMPO is for it to follow suit.

GMB
GENERAL MUNICIPAL, BOILERMAKERS' AND ALLIED TRADES UNION

TUC affiliated

Head Office: Thorne House, Ruxley Ridge, Claygate, Esher, Surrey KT10 0TL

Telephone: 0372-62081

Telex: 27428

Fax: 0372-67164

Principal officers
General Secretary: John Edmonds
Boilermakers Section Secretary: Jim McFall
APEX Partnership Section: Roy Grantham

National officers
Frank Cotton, Nick Fisher, Alan Hadden,
Duncan Lapish, Donald Macgregor, Bill McGuiness,
Neil Moor, Eddie Newall, David Plant,
Sandy Scott, Rita Stephens, Donna Tovey,
David Warburton, David Williams

Union journal: GMB Journal (monthly, distributed to all members). The union also produces a large number of other publications.

Membership

Current membership (1987)
Male: 551,802
Female: 251,517
Total: 803,319

Membership trends

	1975	1979	1981	1983	1987	change 1975-87	1983-87
Men	592,073	638,484	568,533	618,918	551,802	− 7%	−11%
Women	289,283	326,352	297,281	256,269	251,517	−13%	− 2%
Total	881,356	964,836	865,814	875,187	803,319	− 9%	− 8%

Regional secretaries
London
J. Cope, 154 Brent Street, London NW4 2DP

Northern
T. Burlison, Thorne House, 77/87 West Road, Newcastle-upon-Tyne NE15 6RB

Midland and East Coast
S. Pickering, 542 Woodborough Road, Nottingham NG3 5FJ

Scottish Region
J. Morrell, 4 Park Gate, Glasgow G3 8BD

Lancashire
E. Hughes, Thorne House, 36 Station Road, Cheadle Hulme SK8 7AB

Liverpool, North Wales, and Irish
J. Wheelan, 99 Edge Road, Liverpool L7 2PE

Birmingham and West Midlands
G. Wheatley, Will Thorne House, 2 Birmingham Road, Halesowen B63 3HP

Southern
D. O. Gladwin OBE, Cooper House, 205 Hook Road, Chessington, Surrey KT9 1EP

Yorkshire and North Derbyshire
F. S. Wilkinson, Concord House, Park Lane, Leeds LS3 1NB

South-Western
I. J. Thompson, Williamson House, 17 Newport Road, Cardiff CF2 1TB

General
The GMB is the third largest union in Britain with membership in almost every sector of the economy. The union has been undergoing profound changes since its lack-lustre days in the 1960s and 1970s when it was forever overshadowed by the initiatives of its main rivals, the TGWU and the AEU. Whilst these unions are still the two largest unions in

Britain both are in some degree of difficulty, even decline, and the GMB looks to have taken the initiative at present. It is sought after by other unions wishing to find a suitable partner to amalgamate who see it as "amalgamation friendly"; in the last eight years, three important unions have amalgamated with the GMB (ASB, GLSA, APEX), and a fourth, the NUTGW, announced recently its intention to enter merger talks with the GMB, much to the chagrin of the TGWU, its more natural partner. Should these talks prove successful, the GMB would become the second largest union with about 900,000 members, overtaking the AEU and even threatening the TGWU for the pole position. The GMB believes that the pace of mergers will quicken and that by the year 2000 Britain will have four "super unions", each with more than one million members. The GMB is intent on becoming one of these four unions.

Despite the apparent losses incurred by the GMB as shown by the membership table above, the union actually recorded its first membership rise in eight years, in March 1988. A new strategy which places more emphasis on membership recruitment and organisation, especially among women, part-time workers, and in the service sector, appears to have paid off. Sectorally, membership rose in retailing, and occupationally among women and part-time workers, both of whom are targeted by the union in a special campaign.

History

The *General and Municipal Workers' Union*, the forerunner of the present GMB, was established in 1924 on the amalgamation of three unions: the *National Union of General Workers*; the *National Amalgamated Union of Labour*, and the *Municipal Employees' Association*, and was then called the *National Union of General and Municipal Workers*. The *National Union of General Workers* was originally known as the *Gasworkers and General Labourers' Union* and was formed in 1889 with Will Thorne as General Secretary. (Thorne was a militant socialist at the time and a prominent member of the Social Democratic Federation, the first British political party to be strongly influenced by Marxist ideas.) This union was in the vanguard of the so-called new unionism, and it must be noted that the nucleus of its membership — the gas stokers — were far from being unskilled and low paid workers. Its first strike resulted in a reduction from 12 to eight hours for London gas workers. This concession helped the union's rapid growth outside London. It began to organise workers in a wide variety of industries, reaching a membership of 77,000 in 1911. The name was changed to the *National Union of General and Municipal Workers* (NUGMW) in 1916. In 1921 the *National Federation of Women Workers*, led by Mary MacArthur, decided that a separate women's trade union was obsolete and amalgamated with the General Workers on the promise of a separate women's section within the union with its own national women's officer.

The *National Amalgamated Union of Labour* was also formed in 1888 on Tyneside. Its main strength was in shipbuilding, ship repairing and engineering, with some members in the newly emerging chemical industry.

The *Municipal Employees' Association* (MEA) was founded in 1894 and consisted entirely of local authority employees from all grades. In 1908 it split into two parts (see **NUPE**), one part retaining the title MEA.

The amalgamation was hastened by the slump which had caused a severe loss in union membership. The union experienced financial difficulties, expenditure over-running income from dues. Thorne remained General Secretary until 1933 when he was 76 and Clynes, who was full-time President, was 64. Of 18 full-time officers 13 were in their sixties, most having been with the amalgamation or its constituent unions since their inception. It was by now a tired administration. Worse still, thanks to the amalgamation with the *Workers' Union* and its consequently extended sphere of influence, the membership of the TGWU, the rival general union, was surging ahead.

Reorganisation was therefore proposed. Thorne retired at last and was replaced by Charles Dukes. In 1936 the Executive approved a map of reformed district organisation; the posts of full-time President and Assistant General Secretary were allowed to lapse; and compulsory retirement at 65 was passed by the union Congress. The pensioners could now be replaced by new blood in union office. Reorganisation was, however, too late to counter the vigorous recruiting drive of the National Union of Public Employees among county council manual workers and hospital staffs which had now passed into the control of the local authorities.

During the war years some women members were lost to the Engineers' Union when it relaxed its policies on dilution and opened its ranks to women, but overall membership increased to stand at 726,500 in 1943.

In 1944 an able young official named Webster (district officer, Birmingham) established a *National Trade Union Organisers' Mutual Association*, but the National Executive ruled membership was "inconsistent with the conditions of service of the union and inimical to the best interests of the organisation". He was asked to make a statement, refused, and was asked to leave.

In 1946 the union was involved in two notorious unofficial strikes in London. After protracted strikes (one in protest at victimisation of shop stewards at Cossor's factory, and another against victimisation of a union member by the Savoy Hotel management) the Executive banned three members of the London district committee from all offices in the union and dismissed the full-time officer involved in the Savoy dispute, Arthur Lewis. Later, the Executive reviewed its attitude towards shop stewards and accepted that they were a vital element in union organisation. Nevertheless, the Executive still sought to circumscribe shop steward activities. A handbook was prepared which set out their duties and responsibilities. In addition, expenditure on training and education of shop stewards was increased.

Despite this the union suffered some painful internecine conflicts between national officers, rank and file leaders, and shop stewards during the 1950s and 1960s. One battlefield was Fords of Dagenham where the NUGMW national officer for engineering, Jim Mathews, fiercely opposed unofficial action. There is little doubt that the leadership of the NUGMW throughout this period held a narrow perspective as to what shop stewards' responsibilities were excluding them from most negotiations and all pay bargaining. In 1962 Fords dismissed the 17 alleged troublemakers and the response of the NUGMW was to ballot the membership, a majority voting against strike action.

The union was by now notoriously unresponsive to rank and file demands. Membership, after recovering from the ruinous effects of the slump, reached a peak of 809,000 in 1951 but thereafter failed to increase, even declining slightly to 798,000 in 1969. To some extent this was no fault of the union since it reflected contracting employment in the gas industry, traditionally an area of strength. It also reflected however, the inflexibility of the union hierarchy in responding to work place bargaining.

Lord Cooper, who had been General Secretary since 1962, made revealing statements about the ideology of the NUGMW leadership in his evidence to the Royal Commission on Trade Unions and Employers' Associations:

> It is an elementary requirement of our basic purpose that we should do everything possible to contribute towards maximising the revenue of a firm or industry to increase the prospects of obtaining better wages and conditions. This approach is the basis of fruitful co-operation in which we have exclusive, or near-exclusive, organisation of manual workers. We consider that industrial relations would be significantly improved if more firms regarded trade unions and collective bargaining as valuable instruments in promoting the objectives of the firm to everybody's benefit.

The potential dangers of 100 per cent trade unionism without robust internal trade union democracy can well be inferred from these statements; they provide a fine example of the unitary frame of reference which presumes a harmony of interest between employer and employee.

In fact the NUGMW was not then averse to signing agreements with employers which would have the effect that unofficial strikers would be sacked with the union's approval, or expelled from the union, which would have the same result, with l00 per cent membership agreements. (This sort of agreement was made with Ilfords in 1965.)

It is well known now that during the 1960s power in trade unions was shifting relentlessly towards the shop floor and shop stewards. While the TGWU was beginning to make efforts to reform its organisation in line with these changes, the NUGMW remained intransigent (its policy was one of trying to improve communications with shop stewards by bringing them into regular contact with national and local officers) and Cooper's Canute-like stance continued. As a result the union lost members. In the 1969 strike at Fords against the company's package deal which offered improvements in pay and conditions but included penalty clauses aimed at unconstitutional action (action in breach of procedural agreements), the NUGMW refused its official support and lost 2,000 members at Halewood to the TGWU and the engineering union. It also suffered damage to its Liverpool office which was attacked during the strike.

Worse followed. The NUGMW had held what seemed to be an unbreakable relationship with the glass manufacturing firm of Pilkingtons in St Helens. For seven weeks in the spring of 1970 the workers, members of the NUGMW, came out on a strike which culminated in an attempt to form a breakaway union. The strike started at the flat drawn department of the sheetworks and spread rapidly to all the St Helens' works and the Pilkingtons factories outside St Helens. The union consistently refused to make the strike official. The confidence of its members in the union leadership drained away in the early days of the strike when it organised a ballot to discover whether its members really did support the stoppage. The results were never announced. Eventually, a second ballot organised by local clergy in St Helens secured a small majority in favour of a return to work and the strike began to crumble. The rank and file committee which led the strike had been crushed by the ballot, a £3 wage offer by the company, and the offer of a court of inquiry (from which no new conclusions materialised). The rank and file strike committee reconstituted itself as the Pilkingtons Provisional Trade Union Committee and tried to join the TGWU but this move ran foul of the Bridlington Agreement. It then tried to form its own union, the *Glass and General Workers' Union*, and for a time it seemed set to flourish, but it never achieved recognition from Pilkingtons. After being provoked into a strike over the suspension of a member, which itself resulted in 500 other members being sacked (some of whom were subsequently re-employed by the company), the new union was stifled.

The whole episode compelled a reappraisal by the NUGMW of its regional and work place organisation. It was fortunate in this respect that, although David Basnett had suffered some loss of reputation by having been the national officer concerned in the Pilkingtons dispute, he was elected to succeed Cooper as General Secretary. Basnett always had more belief than Cooper in shop steward activity and internal union democracy. Membership began to recover in the 1970s, helped by amalgamations with smaller unions such as the *National Union of Waterworks Employees* in 1972 (adding 4,000 members) and the *United Rubber, Plastic, and Allied Workers of Great Britain* in 1974 (adding 4,500). In 1975 an unusual amalgamation took place with the *Scottish Footballers' Association*, followed in 1979 by amalgamation with the Glasgow-based *Coopers' Federation*. To aid further the reorganisation and recovery process the union ceased to be known as the NUGMW and adopted the name of the General and

Municipal Workers' Union (GMWU).

The 1980s have seen this process of reorganisation and stemming of membership decline continue. The GMWU amalgamated with the *Amalgamated Society of Boilermakers, Shipwrights, Blacksmiths, and Structural Workers,* (ASB) which added 119,585 members to the newly renamed *General Municipal, Boilermakers', and Allied Trades Union* (GMBATU). The ASB is itself the product of a series of amalgamations: between the *Boilermakers' Society* (founded in 1834), and the merger in 1963 with the *Blacksmiths' Union* (founded in 1857) and the *Shipwrights' Union* (founded in 1882).

The policy of amalgamation has continued. The *Amalgamated Textile Workers' Union* (in March 1986), whilst only contributing around 20,000 members, did give the GMBATU firmer legitimacy in the textiles industry which seems in turn to have paved the way for a more important merger/amalgamation with the National Union of Tailors and Garment Workers. Talks between these two unions were only announced recently but should they succeed they could create a focal point for further amalgamations that might lead to a single grouping for all clothing and textile workers.

In a much publicised campaign the GMBATU decided to abandon its traditional "boot and braces" image and enlisted a "designer" company to produce a "more friendly" corporate identity. One consequence was that the rather clumsy GMBATU was dropped and replaced in 1987 with GMB, the name by which the union is now known (see "General").

In November 1987 the 12,000-strong *Greater London Staff Association* (GLSA) merged, and was joined in March 1989 by the *Association of Professional, Executive, Clerical, and Computer Staff* (APEX). Since 1980 APEX (the white collar union which originated as the *Clerks' Union* in 1890) was rapidly losing membership due to the sharp decline of the engineering industry, and because of the adverse effects of new technology. These two unions joined the GMB's existing white collar section, MATSA, itself too small to make any serious impact, to create the APEX Partnership, a white collar section capable of servicing workers right across the span of industries (see "Organisation").

Union officials

Successive General Secretaries
1924-1934: Will Thorne
1934-1946: Charles Duke
1946-1961: Tom Williamson
1961-1973: Jack Cooper
1973-1985: David Basnett
1985 to date: John Edmonds

Traditionally, GMB officials had a reputation for hostility towards rank and file movements and shop stewards' organisation. The implacable opposition of those such as Jim Mathews to unofficial action is legendary in the union (see "History"). This was only the most visible outward manifestation of a trade union which was very much in the hands of its officials, particularly the chief officers, over whom the lay membership had little control.

In the 1960s the union was an ossifying organisation. Another reason for this was regional autonomy. The union was divided into 10 regions (previously districts) whose regional secretaries (after the General Secretary) were the senior officers. Regional autonomy meant that communications on industrial and administrative matters from Head Office passed via the regional secretary. Head Office depended on the goodwill of the regions for information, and many decisions, especially on administrative matters, were made by the regional secretary. Until 1975 the regional secretaries dominated the Executive, which was composed of five members, along with five lay representatives from the remaining regions. Regional secretaries were able to build such a dominance within their regions that there appeared to be little control over them, from Head Office or elsewhere. This was one reason for the sluggish response to the Pilkingtons dispute.

The union had, in the past, been accused of nepotism in the appointment of officials, and there would seem to be some truth in this, although family tradition would have been closer to the mark: Lord Cooper's uncle was Lord Dukes, a previous General Secretary of the GMB; David Basnett, who retired from the post of General Secretary in 1983 (and died in January 1989), was the son of Andrew Basnett, formerly a GMB district secretary; both the father, Tom and the grandfather, Fleming, of Lancashire regional secretary Jack Eccles were full-time officers of the union; and Lord Williamson, General Secretary from 1946 to 1961, had an uncle who was a full-time officer for the Liverpool district. This list is by no means exhaustive, but too much should not be read into this family tradition. The present policy of appointing full-time officers is based on the far more professional and meritocratic approach.

Graduates are positively sought after and John Edmonds, himself a graduate of Oriel, Oxford, has had much to do with this policy. The relative lack of shop floor experience is seen by him as a small disadvantage because full-time officers perform such different roles to those of shop stewards.

Coverage
The GMB, as would be expected of a large general union, organises workers in virtually all industries. It represents virtually all grades from unskilled, semi-skilled, craft, technical, to managerial workers. The union is party to over 150 national agreements and 14 wages councils. The main sectors of its agreements are as follows: local government and the National Health Service; engineering, shipbuilding, and metal manufacturing; untilities — gas, electricity, water; food, drink, and tobacco; building materials industries; private services, hotel and catering, security, and distribution.

Organisation
Under the present constitution the union is administered according to the Core rules. The ASB (now known as BMS) and APEX have become separate sections within the GMB and the Core rules are supplemented by additional APEX rules and BMS section rules appended to the rule book. However, the Core rules override either of the supplementary section rules in the event of any conflict.

National level
The supreme authority of the GMB is vested in Congress composed of general delegates from the regions of the union and of delegates from the districts of the BMS as well as delegates from the APEX section. Delegates are elected on the following basis: one delegate from each region for every 2,000 general members; one delegate from each district for every 2,000 BMS members; and, until 1992, one delegate for every 1,600 APEX members; (thereafter, APEX becomes fully integrated into the GMB and will also elect one delegate for every 2,000 APEX members).

Central Executive Council
The day-to-day running of the union is conducted by a Central Executive Council (CEC) which is made up as follows: Group 1, three general representatives from each region; Group 2, the secretary of the BMS section plus two other representatives from the BMS section; Group 3, one woman from each region elected to a reserved seat; Group 4, one APEX representative from each region. The General Secretary is also a voting member

of the CEC.

Group 1 members are nominated by general branches in the region and elected by the general and APEX members of each region. Group 2 members are elected by the members of the BMS section only. Group 3 is elected by the members of each region. Group 4 members are nominated by APEX branches in the region and elected by all members in that region.

Full-time officials and office holders

The General Secretary is the chief officer and treasurer of the GMB and is elected every five years by secret ballot. The GMB does not have a deputy, or assistant general secretary; instead, the CEC appoints a Principal National Officer from amongst National Industrial Officers. The CEC also appoints a National APEX officer. In the BMS section, however, whilst the secretary is responsible to the CEC, he is appointed by a direct election of members of the BMS section. National Officials are elected by the whole membership of the union. Notwithstanding the BMS section, all other full-time officials, organisers, regional industrial officers, and regional secretaries are appointed directly by the General Executive Council. BMS full-time organisers are elected by members in the districts, whereas branch administrative officers are appointed by the CEC and are not subject to periodic elections.

Regional level

The GMB is divided into 10 regions. Formally, the management of regions is in the control of a regional council which must meet at least once every six months. Regional councils are made up of delegates elected every two years, one delegate for every 1,000 members up to a maximum of 130 delegates per region. No branch may have more than one representative and no branch other than an APEX branch may nominate a member as an APEX delegate. In order to protect the position of the numerically smaller BMS and APEX sections, they are entitled to one extra seat for every additional 1,000 members or two extra seats if there are 10,000 or more extra members. This ruling applies separately to both APEX and BMS.

In practice regions are run by a regional committee elected from the regional council and usually consists of around eight to 10 members, including an elected president who presides over the business of the committee, the regional secretary, and up to three trustees. Regional committees meet at least every four weeks. Apart from national or international issues, or issues which impinge directly upon other regions, regional committees have autonomy to decide whatever they consider to be in their members' best interest. Regional committees have the power to sanction a strike providing that it involves no more than 300 members.

In a recent incident, shortly before the EETPU was expelled from the TUC, a letter from the union's boilermakers' section in Manchester was circulated which was rather over-zealous with regard to membership recruitment. Addressed to all the branches in the north-western region it stated that they should make every effort to recruit EETPU members and "take them into membership without delay". It required direct intervention from the General Secretary, John Edmonds, to end this "blatant poaching" which was in clear breach of the TUC Bridlington Agreement guidelines.

Branch level

There are more than 2,600 branches in the GMB, and the tendency towards industry, company, or work-place branches rather than geographical branches, has continued. Every two years each branch elects a branch committee of at least eight members which includes a president, secretary, and an equality officer. Branch administration is in the hands of either a voluntary branch secretary who is a lay member of the union, or a "whole-time" secretary paid by commission from branch members, or a full-time branch secretary. This role, a peculiarity of the GMB, was established by the gasworkers' congress of 1912 which provided that large branches or amalgamated branches could have secretaries who would be allowed to devote their whole time to the business of the union. This system is gradually being replaced by that of branch administrative officers or district officers, who receive a salary, are in the union superannuation scheme, and do not count as lay members. It is also possible constitutionally for district officers to administer branches.

Shop stewards are elected or appointed by whichever method is deemed necessary by the membership at the work-place or in a branch, and are accountable to the regional committee. Shop stewards are for the most part also safety representatives. They are not branch officers as such.

Industrial conferences

There is provision under rule for annual national and regional conferences which are meant to increase participation of members in industrial and other issues. During 1988 the following industrial conferences were held: shipbuilding, ship repair and marine engineering; chemical; textiles; and equal rights.

Supplementary rules of the BMS section

The BMS section has its own Executive Council which is the governing body of the section, although formally it is still accountable to the CEC. The Executive Council is elected to office every six years, and comprises a secretary and six members. The secretary is elected by the whole BMS membership every six years. Rules allow for the section to hold its own annual delegate conference which decides policy for the BMS.

Supplementary rules of the APEX section

All members of the union whose employment consists mainly of managerial, supervisory, technical, professional, executive, clerical, computer, or allied work are members of the APEX section. This section came into being following the amalgamation in January 1989 of the well-known, white collar trade union APEX. The section contains not only the existing APEX members but also members of the earlier merger between the GMB and the GLSA, and also includes the existing, but rather lack-lustre GMB white collar section, MATSA.

The section organises its own delegate conference which deals with all matters of relevance to the section which are not already considered by the Congress of the union. Delegates are elected to conference by branches and those with 200 or more members are entitled to one delegate. Smaller branches are grouped, as far as possible, into 200-member groups to elect their delegate.

There is also provision for regional APEX conferences. Regional conferences are held every six months and consider and make recommendations to the union regional council on matters of interest to APEX members.

The APEX section is administered by the APEX committee which is accountable to the CEC. The committee consists of the following: (a) all APEX members of the CEC; (b) one member elected from the GLSA grouping of the APEX section; and (c) up to two members, co-opted at the committee's discretion. All committee members are subject to a reselection ballot every four years.

Work-place activity

The GMB has its own national training college where it runs a range of courses for both work-place representatives and full-time officers. The GMB is also a heavy user of trade union courses organised by the TUC education service.

The GMB is committed to improve the level and quality of work place representation available to members, and training and education are seen as integral to this process. The GMB has 25,000 shop stewards and a turn-over rate of about 6,000 per annum. In 1987 2,945 shop stewards received some form of training which, even if new stewards alone were targeted for courses, still represents a shortfall of over 50 per cent. Aware of this problem the 1988 Conference agreed to undertake a complete review of the training provision afforded by the union with a view to setting out a clear and comprehensive policy for the future.

Following a rule change at the 1988 Conference shop stewards now also take on the role of safety representatives. Health and safety have always been important issues in the GMB, and it still remains one of the very few unions to have a full-time national safety officer. The union has replaced its handbook on health and safety and issued all representatives with a new "tool-kit" in order to emphasise the practical side of a safety representative's function.

Women
Around a third of the GMB membership are women. The GMB leadership recognise that as a result of structural changes in the economy, the growth of the service industries, and the decline of manufacturing, women are increasingly going to form an important part of their membership. An imperative future consideration for the GMB, as expressed in a comment by the General Secretary, John Edmonds, is therefore how to make the union more accessible and attractive to women so as to reflect their issues and concerns more effectively. By the 1990s Edmonds estimates that the GMB will have to recruit three women for each man to make any modest growth in membership. Therefore changes in representation forms a vital strategy in the future effectiveness of the GMB (see "Policy").

Since the 1988 Conference the GMB now exercises a positive discrimination policy for Central Executive Council elections. Ten seats are now reserved exclusively for women, and with three general seats occupied by women, CEC representation is now roughly proportionate to their membership in the union. However, like any organisation, in the short-term the union still faces real difficulties in changing the balance as far as full-time officers are concerned. Nevertheless, substantially increasing women full-time officers is a longer-term objective of the GMB.

The union has had a national women's officer for some time, but in common with many unions, the post had very little union infrastructure to support the work. Aware of these structural limitations, the GMB has set about trying to offer greater support to improving representation for women members. At the branch level the GMB has introduced a branch equality officer whose major responsibility is "advancing the work of equal rights within branches". The branch equality officer represents a unique departure in the trade union movement and appears a genuine attempt to translate the various resolutions which most unions pass at conferences into some form of action. In 1988 there were 633 branch equality officers.

External relations
Following the political fund ballot conducted by the union in 1985, the results were an 89 per cent "yes" vote (or 448,426 of the membership) and an 11 per cent "no" vote (representing 17,757 of the total membership). Of the total membership 61 per cent turned out to vote. The GMB is affiliated to the Labour Party and most of its political energies are focused on it. In the run-up to the 1987 general election the union held a

series of regional conferences and workshops of GMB activists, the results of which were fed back into the Labour Party reviews.

Each region of the union has a political liaison officer who acts as contact and focus for political activity within the region. To assist its political organisation the GMB has prepared a register of all its delegates to Labour Party constituency General Committees, as well as one of all members who are local councillors. In order to promote GMB policy more effectively the union decided to publish a quarterly political bulletin: the first edition appeared in 1988. The union is also heavily involved, both nationally and regionally, in the work of TUFL (Trade Unionists For Labour), and John Edmonds is its national Vice-President.

Reflecting the union's activity in the Labour Party, the GMB parliamentary group is one of the largest of all the unions and sponsors 19 Labour MPs:

Jack Ashley	(Stoke-on-Trent)
Betty Booth	(West Bromwich West)
Nick Brown	(Newcastle East)
Tom Clark	(Monklands West)
John Cunningham	(Copeland)
Don Dixon	(Jarrow)
Pat Duffy	(Sheffield Attercliffe)
Douglas Henderson	(Newcastle North)
Gerald Kaufman	(Manchester Gorton)
Joan Lestor	(Eccles)
Austin Mitchell	(Great Grimsby)
Elliot Morley	(Glanford and Scunthorpe)
Peter Pike	(Burnley)
Giles Radice	(Durham North)
Merlyn Rees	(Morley and South East)
George Robertson	(Hamilton)
John Smith	(Monklands East)
Clive Soley	(Hammersmith)
Jack Straw	(Blackburn)

An interesting initiative which the GMB is promoting concerns sponsorship. It is encouraging its local branches and work place groups to involve themselves in sponsorship of cultural and community activities, from local festivals through to women's clinics, in order to broaden people's perceptions of trade unions, and to show that trade unions are a legitimate part of the whole community and not just some sort of "industrial service" which members can buy.

Policy
It has been noted previously that the GMB was becoming one of the most progressive unions in the trade union movement. The GMB is intent on remaining one of the largest trade unions in Britain, not simply for reasons of pride, but because size enables the union to employ more, and higher calibre, officials. The union is already pursuing a policy of recruiting graduates, recognising that "shop-floor/industrial training" is not an essential requirement of a good union official. Training full-time and lay union officials is also something which the union recognises as important in order to improve the service it can provide for its membership. Furthermore, a large union is better able to negotiate commercial discounts for outside benefits such as various insurance schemes, consumer durables, mortgages, and other loans.

The GMB invited a firm of outside consultants to perform a survey of members and potential members, who found that "non-industrial" benefits were a positive spur to joining a union. What is of interest here is not simply the result of the survey, but the very fact that the union conducted a market research exercise; to many unions this would be an anathema, but the GMB sees the benefit of employing modern business techniques to meet trade union ends.

Amalgamation with other unions is part of the union's plan for growth. Since the early 1980s the GMB has fast developed the reputation of being "amalgamation friendly", providing unions with a position of privilege during the transitional few years so that smaller unions are not overwhelmed by the larger union (see "Organisation and the APEX rules"). But amalgamations are also intended as a way of making the union structure relevant again, after its beginnings in an industrial era dominated by craft working. Coping with the demands of an ever more service-oriented economy, whose employment policies are becoming increasingly more diverse and technologically more demanding, is the objective which the GMB has set itself. The GMB is keen on amalgamations which have potential for growth and which offer new potential for recruitment rather than amalgamation for its own sake.

The GMB is a firm supporter of Neil Kinnock and the changes he has brought to the Labour Party. At the 1988 Labour Party Conference the GMB urged delegates to ignore the "prehistoric band in the party who continued to call for nationalisation of everything in the same form as in the past", and instead support policies which are responsive to consumers and express voters' aspirations for the 1990s.

The GMB also plays a leading role in shaping TUC policy. The GMB in the last few years has been keen to limit the TUC to pursuing worthwhile yet achievable objectives and direct them away from "strong on sentiment but poor on action" statements. Establishing a national data bank on health and safety at work, and developing and organising trade union education for schools and colleges using all the latest technologies and communication techniques available, are two of the specific targets which the GMB is pursuing within the TUC. Developments such as these are expensive and can only be provided effectively by a central organisation like the TUC; non-affiliated unions should want to become members because of the advantages and benefits such a body can bring. This, the GMB considers, is the way that the TUC ought to be developing in the 1990s, as campaigning, organising, and aiding recruitment, rather than making grand political statements, and all the time waiting for an easy return to the "corridors of power" (see TUC).

The union believes that the position and power of the trade union movement during the 1960s and 1970s was illusory and the gains made during that period have been largely eroded by a hostile government. Instead the GMB is turning to Europe, pointing out the strength of many of the European trade union movements whose basic rights are not dependent upon the iniquity of "free" collective bargaining. The GMB therefore advocates strong legislative support and a charter of workers' rights as the basis of future industrial relations government policy. The GMB is getting ready for the twenty-first century and is evolving a union which can respond to the challenges ahead.

Recent events
GMB and the Labour Party

The GMB demonstrated once again that it is one of the more forward-looking unions when it launched a serious attack on the outmoded method of the Labour Party's policy-making structure. A more modern structure is needed, sensitive to the needs of the media-conscious age and looking beyond the turn of the century. John Edmonds points out that the present system was designed in the 1920s and it is quite unrealistic for such a structure to have relevance today, far less for the future.

At its 1989 Annual Conference the union announced important changes to end the dominant role of the trade unions in Labour Party policy-making. John Edmonds, in a strong attack on existing decision-making procedure based on votes taken on Conference motions and amendments, said that this was "a crazy way to run a Party". Instead, the GMB suggested that a broader range of members, including MPs and union officials, regional and local government, constituency party, and socialist society members, would strengthen the Party's executive and its role.

Furthermore, Party policy ought to be reviewed constantly and updated by the executive every two years. The influence of the union's block vote was seen as hindering the Labour Party's development and the union proposed that the power of the block vote ought to be limited. The proposal was to create "two houses" representing unions and other affiliated organisations, and a constituency Party section.

Current dispute and issues
At the time of publication, the GMB was involved in the following disputes and issues:

1. At Courtaulds in Lancashire the GMB has agreed to do away with anachronistic working conditions and introduce a single grade covering a range of different workers thereby providing more flexible working arrangements.
2. At Securicor the union has negotiated an innovative deal which provides for regular health and safety screening as part of the annual pay deal.
3. In the food industry the GMB has accepted a flexible work package at Birds-Eye Walls at Grimsby and Hull, but the company has given notice that its factory at Kirkby is to close and the union is currently involved in talks over this issue.
4. In the chemical sector union members were for the first time considering holding a ballot for industrial action in support of a pay claim.
5. Along with NUPE, COHSE, and the TGWU, the GMB is fighting for an improved pay deal for ambulance workers.
6. In the public sector the GMB has established parity between white collar and blue collar jobs in a test case involving Northern Ireland Electricity. The right of a woman worker to equal pay was established under a judgement made under the Equal Pay Act 1970.

The GMB signalled an important policy shift in backing single-union agreements in a bid to move away from multi-union negotiations. Consequently, it has drawn up a model single-union agreement in an effort to increase the number of such deals for green field site plants. This may, however, bring the union too close to compulsory arbitration deals, similar to those favoured by the EETPU.

In a follow-up to its campaign to recruit more women members the GMB is to establish a youth recruitment unit to attract more members aged under 25; indeed it has been reported recently that it may even create a new section for boys and girls who deliver newspapers.

It is generally agreed that the hotel and catering industry is likely to be an important area for future union recruitment. Although the GMB has come up with new initiatives for seasonal workers, including better training and organisation of working hours, it is likely to face competition for members in this field, especially from the TGWU. The two unions have co-operated in the past but current tensions over recruitment may endanger such co-operation in the future.

Further references
H.A. Clegg, *General Union in a Changing Society,* Blackwell, 1964. The official history of the NUGMW.

153

T. Lane and K. Roberts, *Strike at Pilkingtons*, Fontana, 1971.

D. Warburton, "Trade Unions: A role in society", *NatWest Bank Review*, February 1976. A commentary on the role of trade unions by a senior GMB officer.

R. Taylor, "Officer Class", *New Society*, March 29, 1973.

E.A. and G.H. Radice, *Will Thorne: Constructive Militant*, Allen & Unwin, 1974.

Beatrix Campbell, "New Wave Unions: An Interview with John Edmonds", *Marxism Today*, September 1986.

Jackie Wills, "Identity Crisis", *Marxism Today*, April 1987.

G. Foster, "The New Face of Trade Unionism", *Management Today*, December 1987.

Charles Leadbeater, "Thoroughly Modern Movement", *Marxism Today*, September 1988.

J.E. Mortimer, *History of the Boilermakers' Society 1834-1906*, Allen & Unwin, Vol. 1, 1973.

J.E. Mortimer, *History of the Boilermakers' Society 1906-1939*, Allen & Unwin, Vol. 2, 1982.

F. Hughes, *By Hand and By Brain*, CAWU (now APEX section), 1953. The history of the Clerical and Administrative Workers' Union. An updated version is currently being written.

John Kelly and Edmund Heery, "Full-time Officers and Trade Union Recruitment", *British Journal of Industrial Relations*, XXVII, no. 2, July 1989. Offers a very good appraisal of various union recruitment strategies and suggests that, of all the major unions, the GMB possesses the best chance for organisational change and future membership growth.

GUALO
GENERAL UNION OF ASSOCIATIONS OF LOOM OVERLOOKERS

TUC affiliated

Head Office: Overlookers Institute, Jude Street, Nelson, Lancashire BB9 7HP

Telephone: 0282-64066

Principal officer
President: Ernest Macro

Membership

Current membership (1987)
Total: 1,173

Membership trends

1983: 1,327
1979: 2.410
1975: 3,183

GUALO was formed originally in 1885 and now comprises 11 autonomous associations of loom overlookers.

The union held a political fund ballot and from a very high turn-out of 92.4 per cent, 83.5 per cent (928) voted "yes" and 16.5 per cent (176) voted "no".

HCSA
HOSPITAL CONSULTANTS' AND SPECIALISTS' ASSOCIATION

TUC affiliated

Head Office: The Old Court House, London Road, Ascot, Berkshire SL5 7EN

Telephone: 0990-25052

Fax: 0990-26129

Principal officers
Chief Executive: Stephen J. Charkham
Head of Administration: W. E. Bilson
Head of Administration: F. J. Parsley

Union journal: The Consultant (quarterly). *CNS, Consultant News Service* (bimonthly)

Membership

Current membership (1987)
Male: 2,169
Female: 201
Total: 2,370

Membership trends
1979: 3,756
1983: 2,873

General
The HCSA has been in existence in one form or another since the start of the NHS. In 1969 there were about 1,000 members of the *Regional Hospital Consultants and Specialists Association* (RHCSA). Following the publication of proposals which would have altered drastically the responsibilities and work pattern of consultants, and the government's refusal to implement the recommendations of the review body, a large number of consultants, disenchanted with the BMA, left and joined the RHCSA. Membership increased rapidly and in 1974 London teaching hospital consultants were allowed to join, and the name was changed to the Hospital Consultants and Specialists Association (HCSA).

Organisation

The regional organisation of the HCSA consists of each NHS region divided on a geographical basis into counties. There are normally three county chairs per region, except for Trent, South Western, and West Midlands, where there are four. The Council is the governing body of the HCSA but all major policy decisions are made by a direct ballot of members.

The Executive Committee is formed by the national officers, i.e. the President, who chairs the Council, the Deputy President, who chairs all sub-committees (Membership and Communications; Terms and Conditions of Service; Finance), plus two Honorary Secretaries and an Honorary Treasurer. Elections to HCSA Council are held every two years by direct postal ballot. The AGM elects the national officers, and Council elects the sub-committee chair. All hold office for two years.

Policy

Relations with the BMA have never been close. The HCSA is an alternative organisation for consultants challenging the monopoly of the BMA and providing the focal point for opposition. The HCSA has made two attempts to secure recognition and negotiating rights. In 1974 the Association took its case to the Industrial Relations Court but failed on the technical question of who was the employer — the Regional Health Authorities (who hold consultants' contracts) or the DHSS and Secretary of State. A further attempt was made by application through ACAS but this was similarly unsuccessful.

Relations with other NHS unions are mainly influenced by the various TUC working parties and committees on which the HCSA is represented. It is fair to say that relationships between the HCSA and other NHS unions have improved as a consequence of this participation, though many areas of disagreement remain.

Much of HCSA activity over the last few years has been concerned with hospital staffing and career structures. It had become obvious that the majority of young doctors were choosing general practice as a first choice rather than hospital medicine. As a result there were shortages of young doctors in certain specialties. Surveys carried out by the HCSA had shown that this problem was likely to increase. The latest attempt to improve this situation was a scheme known as "Achieving a Balance" which set out to "balance" the needs of the service/training and career aspirations. In order for the scheme to work additional funds were needed to enable health authorities to implement it. Although extra funds were provided the HCSA believed that they were inadequate but that the effects of insufficient funding would not be apparent for some time.

One of the recommendations of "Achieving a Balance" was to create a new service grade, "Staff grade". The HCSA has always campaigned for such a new grade, but it believes that the salary scale was pitched too low and it fears that an opportunity has been lost. It is HCSA policy that all service grades should be amalgamated into one unified grade with entry at a point that reflects training and experience.

The HCSA has been devoting much of its time to the deteriorating financial position of the hospital service — particularly in the acute sector. The HCSA has always believed that the NHS required, not just extra funding, but also a fundamental rethink on how local hospitals are funded. The HCSA believes that the present system penalises the hospitals which increase efficiency. The HCSA does not fear the government's White Paper proposals to restructure the NHS *per se,* but it does fear that the government will simply introduce the "management changes" and inject competition into the Health Service without providing any extra resources. If the net result is only to add to hospital management staffing with no consequent improvement in patient care, then the proposals will be a failure.

HVA
HEALTH VISITORS' ASSOCIATION
TUC affiliated

Head Office: 50 Southwark Street, London SE1 1UN

Telephone: 01-378 7255

Fax: 01-407 3521

Principal officer
General Secretary: Shirley Goodwin

Union journal: The Health Visitor (monthly)

Membership

Current membership (1987)
Male: 238
Female: 16,463
Total: 16,701

Membership trends

	1975	1979	1981	1983	1987	change 1975-87	1983-87
Men	15	32	57	52	238	1,487%	358%
Women	8,588	12,083	14,132	14,832	16,463	92%	11%
Total	8,603	12,115	14,189	14,884	16,701	94%	12%

General
The HVA is the main organisation for health visitors in England, Wales, and Northern Ireland, all of whom hold the Health Visitors' Certificate. There are 120 branches. The HVA also recruits certain types of nursing staff, such as school nurses, clinic nurses, district nurses, family planning nurses, and student health visitors. All members of the Association must have a basic nursing qualification, and the HVA has always served a dual role of trade union as well as a professional body. The HVA conducted a political fund ballot in July 1988 and from a 43 per cent turn-out, 86 per cent (5,904) voted "yes" and 14 per cent (929) voted "no".

Since 1983 pay and conditions of service for members of HVA have been decided separately. Pay is the subject of a review body which was established in 1983 to advise the government on matters of remuneration for nursing staff, midwives, health visitors, and professions allied to medicine. The review body is independent and takes evidence from interested parties (see **RCN**). Conditions of service for health visitors are subject to Whitley council negotiations; the HVA has two seats on the Nursing and Midwifery Staffs Negotiating Council.

History
The Association was founded in 1896 by the first seven women sanitary inspectors, all working in London, and was called the *Women's Sanitary Inspectors' Association.* By 1906 membership had risen to 63 most of whom voted in London. In the same year

invitations to join the Association were sent out to women sanitary inspectors and health visitors working eleswhere and the first provincial centre was established in Birmingham in 1921.

In 1918 the Association chose registration as a trade union rather than as a company and has retained that status. The first General Secretary was appointed in 1923.

The three changes in the Association's name indicate the development in its membership. By 1914 so many health visitors had joined the original sanitary inspectors that the name was changed to the *Women's Sanitary Inspectors' and Health Visitors' Association.* The change to *Women Public Health Officers' Association* in 1929 was made as a result of the inclusion among the membership of other women working in public health such as school nurses, domiciliary midwives, and matrons of day nurseries. The present name was adopted in 1962 by which time health visitors constituted a large majority of the membership, although several other types of workers remain eligible and welcome to join.

IOJ
INSTITUTE OF JOURNALISTS

Non-TUC affiliated

Head Office: 2 Dock Office, Lower Road, London SE10 2XL

Telephone: 01-252 1187

Fax: 01-232 2302

Principal officer
Secretary: R. F. Farmer

Current membership (1989)
Total: 2,500

General
The IOJ was originally the organisation which recruited journalists, but following internal disagreements a split occurred which led to the formation of the NUJ. Since that time its role as organiser of journalists has reduced and the union itself hs become marginalised (see **NUJ**). Politically, it is regarded as being well to the right.

Informal merger talks were held recently with the expelled EETPU. However, the IOJ decided in the end to retain its independence (see **EETPU**).

IPMS
INSTITUTION OF PROFESSIONALS, MANAGERS, AND SPECIALISTS
(formerly the *Institute of Professional Civil Servants — IPCS*)

TUC affiliated

Head Office: 75-79 York Road, London SE1 7AQ

Telephone: 01-~~928 9951~~ 902 6600

Principal officers
General Secretary: Bill Brett
Deputy General Secretary: Tony Cooper
Assistant General Secretaries: Valerie Ellis, Jenny Thurston
Assistant Secretaries: Cliff Crook,
                 Alan Denney,
                 Ron McDowall,
                 Elizabeth Jenkins,
                 Wendi Harrison,
                 Paul Noon,
                 David Luxton,
                 John Allison,
                 Joe Duckworth,
                 John Billard,
                 Charles Harvey (Editor),
                 David Ringwood,
                 Derek Reed (research officer),
                 Monica Thompson

Union journal: State Service (monthly)

Membership

Current membership (1987)
Male: 81,893
Female: 8,927
Total: 90,820

Membership trends

	1975	1979	1981	1983	1987	change 1975-87	1983-87
Men	96,081	94,126	83,903	85,548	81,893	−15%	−4%
Women	7,421	8,016	7,510	7,542	8,927	20%	18%
Total	103,502	102,142	91,413	93,090	90,820	−12%	−2%

General
The IPCS, founded in 1919, catered for specialist grades mainly within the Civil Service, primarily scientists and technologists working in departments such as the Ministry of Defence, Department of the Environment, and the Meteorological Office. During the 1980s privatisation led to a significant number of IPCS members being employed outside the Civil Service in private companies such as BAA, Amersham International, Royal

Ordnance, Royal Dockyards (Devonport Management Ltd. and Babcock Thorn Ltd.) and British Nuclear Fuels plc. In 1982 members of the *Association of Government Supervisors and Radio Officers* entered into a merger with the IPCS. By 1989 most members belonged to one of the union's nine sectors: agriculture (scientists and advisers, such as at the Ministry of Agriculture, Fisheries, and Food); aviation (including air traffic controllers); defence; civil nuclear energy; research and regulation of the land, water, and air environment; health and safety; heritage (galleries and museums); research councils; the Scottish Office (this sector extending to the Forestry Commission and several agricultural bodies). In 1989 in a positive move to adapt to the changing pattern of its membership as a result of privatisation the union changed its name to the Institution of Professionals, Managers, and Specialists.

Organisation

The governing and policy-making body of the Institution is Conference. The Annual Conference comprises delegates elected by their branches, the National Executive Committee, the General Secretary and other employees of the Institution as determined by the NEC. The IPMS has a stated intent to elect the General Secretary by ballot of individual members, according to the requirements of the 1988 Employment Act. In line with its new name the IPMS is adopting a sectoral basis of organisation and creating a regional organisation, opening new offices in Scotland and the north of England to serve members for whom collective bargaining takes place away from London.

Women

Valerie Ellis is responsible *inter alia* for equal opportunities at a national level and there is an equal opportunities advisory committee. At work-place level an important initiative has been to encourage branches to appoint equal opportunities officers.

An issue largely contiguous is that of representation of part-time employees. IPMS recognises the need to recruit and represent contract workers and has endeavoured to develop a code of conduct governing the employment of contract workers and STAs (short term appointments), and offers an individual service to members with individual contracts. About 1,500 of the union's members have individual contracts of employment. The aim, ideally, is for terms and conditions of STAs to be no less favourable than for permanent staff in respect of pay and grading, superannuation benefits, and annual leave. STAs should not be expected to sign waiver clauses that negate their statutory rights.

Policy and recent issues
The unemployed

The Institution has a category of membership for those who cease to be in the IPMS jurisdiction as a result of unemployment, retirement, or change of job. They can retain membership as "retired members", receiving the journal and financial and insurance services, together with any grievance handling in relation to pension issues. There is a retired members' club with advisory status.

Training

The IPMS takes a close interest in apprentice training and has published the damaging effect of severe reductions in apprenticeships in government establishments in recent years against the background of justifiable concern about skill shortages. The Institution has campaigned against the curtailment of training programmes that are vital for recruitment and career development.

Ethnic minorities

The Institution is committed to campaigns against discrimination on grounds of sex, marital status, race, disability, sexual orientation, or religion.

New technologies

The IPMS welcomes new technology where it will lead to a genuine improvement in the standard of public services providing it is accompanied by reasonable benefits and safeguards. The Institution is opposed to policies that seek to use new technology as a means of achieving arbitrary cuts in jobs.

Changing collective bargaining arrangements

Privatisation has taken many IPMS members outside the Civil Service. Whether bargaining for such members takes place at company or establishment level depends on organisational strategy and structure. In February 1989 plans by the BAA, formerly the British Airports Authority, to end centralised pay bargaining as part of its strategy of devolving financial responsibility to its individual operating units was well advanced. Unions (including the IPMS) accepted the situation but there were pockets of resistance, such as among fire officers who feared that it would be easier for smaller airports to reduce staff levels and pay. In the Civil Service itself there has been a Treasury-led drive to decentralise bargaining processes under the Financial Management Initiative that seeks to devolve financial accountability.

Recent events

The IPMS pay negotiators have been obliged to sign long-term pay flexibility agreements with the government that provide for performance and regional pay variations. However, this has also been a means of partially regaining the principle of comparability by a survey of pay levels every four years — the first formal exercise in pay comparability for Civil Servants since the abolition of pay research in 1981. It is a targeted comparability in that there are higher increases for specialists in areas where comparable private sector staff are paid above levels operating in other parts of the country.

In 1988 the then IPCS, by a majority of 81 per cent of the 51 per cent turn-out, became the sixth Civil Service union and the 52nd of all unions whose members had voted to establish a political fund. By tradition and by temperament the IPMS is non-partisan and the vote did not portend affiliation to a political party, but it would enable participation in campaigns against particular government policies.

During the course of 1989 the union changed its name to the Institution of Professionals, Managers, and Specialists (IPMS) to better reflect the managerial aspirations of its membership and, perhaps at the same time, widen the union's recruitment base. The union also launched a publicity drive and policy initiatives including a regional organisation and a legal advice service for members on individual contracts.

In September 1989 the IPMS announced that it was to lead members in a planned employee buy-out of a public sector service, Crown Suppliers. The union intends to support two buy-out teams through an employee share option plan (ESOP) and has obtained financial support from the trade union bank, Unity Trust. The IPMS has recognised that innovations are necessary if the union is to prosper in the 1990s.

In a further move its leadership are also seeking greater co-operation between specialist unions and propose forming a federation of those unions which do not have political affiliations. The proposed federation would include partners such as the AUT,

EMA, NUMAST, HVA, IRSF, FDA, and STE, and within it each organisation would retain its identity but benefit from pooled resources — for example, research, publicity, computer, and legal services. With a combined membership of around 200,000, it is small in comparison with the might of the larger unions, but it could become an important alliance amongst the non-politically affiliated organisations. All unions are conscious that a proper service for their membership requires resources and that for smaller unions this is particularly difficult. In this respect the federation has to be welcomed but the IPMS's motives are as yet, far from clear. Is the federation proposal a signal to the large unions that they contemplate changes to the TUC General Council (see **TUC**)?

Further reference
J. E. Mortimer and Valerie Ellis, *A Professional Union: The Evolution of the Institution of Professional Civil Servants,* Allen & Unwin.

IRSF
INLAND REVENUE STAFF FEDERATION

TUC affiliated

Head Office: Douglas Houghton House, 231 Vauxhall Bridge Road, London SW1V 1EH

Telephone: 01-834 8254

Fax: 01-630 6258

Principal officers
General Secretary: Clive Brook
Deputy General Secretary: Jim McAuslan
Assistant Secretary: Ted Elsey
Assistant Secretary: Bill Hawkes
Assistant Secretary: Colin Sambrook
Education, Training and Campaign Officer: Doug Gowan
General Treasurer: Dave Newlyn
Regional Officer: Ron Seddon

Union journal: Assessment (monthly, free to every member)

Membership

Current membership (1987)
Male: 20,585
Female: 32,387
Total: 52,972

Membership trends

	1975	1979	1981	1983	1987	change 1975-87	1983-87
Men	26,869	24,913	22,214	21,619	20,585	−23%	−5%
Women	33,715	40,344	35,979	35,338	32,387	−4%	−8%
Total	60,584	65,257	58,193	56,957	52,972	−13%	−7%

General

In 1936 the *Association of Officers of Taxes* (AOT) absorbed two other tax officer associations, under the name of the AOT, and this federation formed the basis of what became the IRSF. The AOT (under its earlier name of the Association of Tax Clerks) affiliated to the TUC in 1911, and continual membership of the TUC has been maintained except for the 1927-45 break imposed by section 5 of the Trades Disputes and Trade Unions Act of 1927.

Although the IRSF is an independent trade union and TUC affiliate the union was for long regarded, as its title suggests, as virtually a staff association. However, during the Civil Servive pay dispute in 1981 the IRSF was pushed to the forefront of the campaign of selective strikes because of the strategic position of tax branches within the PAYE system. This has altered for good any questions regarding the status of the union.

Locally, the IRSF is open to any federation branch, subject to the consent of the Executive Committee, to affiliate with trades councils within its boundaries.

Organisation

IRSF members in each tax district, collection office, and valuation office form a local federation office. Each office is a branch of the federation. There are more than 120 branches organised on a geographical basis for each of the three sections: taxes, collection, and valuation.

Every branch holds at least three general meetings a year. The Annual meeting in the autumn elects branch officers, a committee, and a delegate to attend the next IRSF Conference, and also nominates members to stand for election of the National Executive Committee. The spring branch meeting considers motions sent from offices intended for inclusion on the Annual Conference agenda. The third is a mandating meeting held shortly before Conference to go through the Conference agenda and to mandate the delegate.

The Annual Delegate Conference is the final governing body of the federation between Conferences; the Executive Committee conducts the affairs of the federation. There are 13 seats for taxes, eight for collection, and six for valuation. The IRSF opened its first regional office in Birmingham, appointed a regional officer in 1988, and has plans to extend the regional structure of the union.

There have been tensions within the IRSF between the leadership and branches for more than 10 years. In 1978 the left had its rank and file newspaper suppressed at the Annual Delegate Conference but they staged a recovery during the 1982 Conference using the card vote of the larger branches. In response the leadership proposed a five-year restructuring plan to the 1988 Annual Delegate Conference. They suggested that the number of policy-making members, and the number of ballots, should be increased and that a more effective area/regional structure would help improve union communications. However, not surprisingly, Conference rejected these plans although it did agree to enhance the role of regional councils and re-examine branch structure.

There are also growing tensions between the IRSF and the Council for Civil Service Unions (CCSU), the central negotiating body for all non-industrial Civil Service unions.

The government's attempt to move the settlement date from the traditional April to August, and its intention to introduce local pay flexibility, and provide for an element of performance assessment would weaken the CCSU (see **NUCPS**). It is no secret that the IRSF leadership favoured this move to greater independence, but when they put these proposals to their 1988 Delegate Conference few delegates supported the changes, and on a card vote of 75 to 45 rejected the move. The card vote majority is another reflection of the left's ability to capture the larger branches and frustrate their rather moderate leadership.

External relations
In March 1986 the IRSF held a political fund ballot which produced a very high turn-out of 87 per cent of which 82 per cent (39,776) voted "yes" and 18 per cent (8,862) voted "no". By a massive majority the membership voted to establish a political fund for the first time in the history of the IRSF.

Recent events
In an attempt to deal with staff shortages in the Inland Revenue it has been proposed to ease the situation by extending the payment of Local Pay Additions (LPA) — pay supplements brought in by the Treasury last year despite opposition from the CCSU. IRSF leaders are recommending that the union lodges a claim for LPAs to be paid to all staff in the south-east. This action is bound to reopen the tensions in the CCSU which itself rejected a similar move to pay flexibility as recently as 1988. With pressure both from the government and from some of the unions within it — principally the IRSF — the CCSU may not survive much longer. The IRSF may achieve its independence from the CCSU, although in the longer term it may find this of little comfort as its isolation leaves the union increasingly more vulnerable to hostile government policy.

ISTC
IRON AND STEEL TRADES CONFEDERATION
TUC affiliated

Head Office: Swinton House, 324 Gray's Inn Road, London WC1X 8DD

Telephone: 01-837 6691

Fax: 01-278 8378

Principal national officers
General Secretary: Roy Evans
Assistant General Secretary: D.K. Brookman
National Staff Officer: H.A. Feather
National Officer: K. Clarke

Divisional offices

No. 1 division: Scotland
20 Quarry Street, Hamilton, Strathclyde ML3 7AR
Telephone: 0698-422924

No. 2 division: North-East, Cumbria, and North Yorkshire
Drinkwater House, 210-212 Marton Road, Middlesbrough, Cleveland TS4 2ET
Telephone: 0642-246040

No. 3 division: South Yorkshire, North Lincolnshire, and Derbyshire
Edgecumbe House, The Crescent, Doncaster Road, Rotherham, South Yorkshire
S65 1NL
Telephone: 0709-361541

No. 4 division: Northampton, Worcester, Stafford, Shropshire, and Warwick
Mere Green Chambers, 338 Lichfield Road, Four Oaks, Sutton Coldfield, West
Midlands B74 4BH
Telephone: 021-308 7288

Nos. 5 & 6 divisions: Wales, Gloucestershire
64 Newport Road, Cardiff, South Glamorgan CF2 1DF
Telephone: 0222-487261 & 487361

No. 7 division: North-West, North Wales, and Cheshire
56 High Street, Tarporley, Cheshire CW6 0AG
Telephone: 08293-3689

No. 8 division: London, South, and South-East England
Swinton House, 324 Gray's Inn Road, London WC1X 8DD
Telephone: 01-837 6691

Union journal: Phoenix comes out quarterly, and is the new glossy publication which
replaces *ISTC Banner* as the union journal. *Phoenix* is a very professional publication
that adopts a journal rather than the more traditional newspaper format, with extensive
use of colour printing. It has a clear layout and a useful contents page and includes,
alongside the usual journal reviews, useful facts and figures and other bargaining
information on the steel industry, a crossword, as well as a regular article written by steel
managers. Recently introduced is a separate section on the union's financial services for
members with a regular update of unit trusts. *Phoenix* has a circulation of around 11,000.

Membership

Current membership (1987)
Male: 64,011
Female: 2,989
Total: 67,000

Membership trends

	1975	1979	1981	1983	1987	change 1975-87	1983-87
Men	95,232	94,108	93,357	87,300	64,011	−33%	−27%
Women	9,253	10,167	6,818	3,706	2,989	−68%	−19%
Total	104,485	104,275	100,175	91,006	67,000	−36%	−26%

General

The ISTC is the dominant union within the British iron and steel industry and organises almost 18,000 workers, nearly all those engaged in production and ancillary work. The TGWU and the GMB have nearly 8,000 members, principally in the finishing departments of the tinplate, galvanised sheet trade, and tube-making works. The craft unions, AEU, EETPU, UCATT, and MSF have around 10,000 members and co-ordinate policy under the umbrella of the National Craftsmen's Co-ordinating Committee (NCCC). The ISTC shares recruitment of middle managers with SIMA, a section within the EETPU.

In April 1985 the ISTC finally amalgamated with the NUB (*National Union of Blast-furnacemen*) which organised blast-furnace workers in England and Wales, as well as coke workers and workers engaged at iron and limestone mines and quarries, and the last major union to retain independent status since the 1917 Confederation (see "History"). The NUB was taken into the ISTC as its Coke and Iron Section (CIS). The ISTC Executive Committee was temporarily enlarged to 24 to embrace three CIS members but reverted back to the usual 21 seats after the 1988 triennial elections (see "Organisation").

Following the 13-week strike in 1980 from January 2 until Easter (the first national strike the union was involved in since 1926), the ISTC has faced a dramatic loss of membership. Nearly 60 per cent of the membership has disappeared as a result of closures and plant rationalisation schemes.

National bargaining remains the dominant form of wage determination within the industry, although it is likely that the privatised British Steel will follow the trend of most large manufacturing concerns and move towards local sector bargaining.

History

Trade unionism in the iron and steel trades has a very long history and limited space can do only scant justice to its development. In 1863 the *North of England Ironworkers* — the first union in the trade to have a continuous existence — was formed. Up to that time there were a number of ephemeral local organisations which appeared following the repeal of the Combinations Acts in 1825. The *North of England Ironworkers* assumed a national character four years later to become the *Amalgamated Ironworkers' Association* with John Kane as General Secretary. Following a long strike called by the *North of England Ironworkers* in 1866 the Board of Conciliation and Arbitration for the North of England Iron Trade was established in 1869; it was the forerunner of the various forms of joint machinery for negotiation which became a traditional feature of the greatly extended iron and steel industry.

Following the inventions of Bessemer and Siemens the newly established steel industry produced the formation of the *British Steel Smelters' Association* in 1886, following a strike in Scotland, with John Hodge as secretary. Within a short time this union had established branches in England and Wales. Scotland was also the birthplace of the first union covering millworkers in the industry — the *Scottish Millmen's Union,* which later became the *Amalgamated Society of Iron and Steel Workers.* Whilst this union retained a predominantly Scottish flavour its organisation was later widened to include blast-furnace workers, malleable ironworkers, and finishing trades such as steel tubes, nuts, and bolts, etc.

Numerous other unions were formed from different sections of the iron and steel industry from the latter part of the nineteenth century to 1914. Such unions were generally local in character and represented specific occupations. The duplication of unions in the industry created a serious obstacle to effective organisation in the years leading up to 1914, a position accentuated by competition from the general labour union. The weakness of that position became evident as the war progressed and the government took control of the industry. In 1915 a conference was called, chaired by C. W. Bowerman, then General Secretary of the TUC, to consider the question of amalgamation. A scheme of confederation was evolved which provided for the establishment of a new union, the *British Iron and Steel and Kindred Trades Association* (termed the *Central Association*), and in addition another body, the Iron and Steel Trades Confederation, which was to be the Executive Council of the confederation consisting of representatives *pro rata* of the executives of the amalgamated unions, including the Central Association. The confederation was vested with powers of taking over the conduct of negotiations, affiliation to the TUC, legal services, benefit administration, and all the officials of the unions. The scheme was later put to each union and the following unions put the scheme to their members: the *British Steel Smelters, Mill, Iron, and Tinplate Workers* (40,000); the *Association of Iron and Steel Workers of Great Britain* (9,000); the *Amalgamated Society of Iron and Steel Workers* (10,000); the *National Steelworkers' Association Engineering and Labour League* (3,000); and the *Tin and Sheet Millmen's Association* (3,000).

The *Amalgamated Society of Iron and Steel Workers* and the *Tin and Sheet Millmen's Association* failed to carry the scheme but the other three unions went ahead and the Iron and Steel Trades Confederation came into being in 1917. The confederation scheme became so successful that complete amalgamation took place in 1921. The blast-furnace workers never put the scheme to the vote and remained outside the confederation right up until 1985, when their union, the *National Union of Blast-furnacemen,* finally agreed to merge with the ISTC.

Union officials
In 1987 the ISTC employed 17 officers in the divisions and three national officers. The decision of the 1982 Annual Delegate Conference not to elect union officials still stands and all are appointed by the Executive Council. Whilst all ISTC officials must possess a practical knowledge of the trade, the precondition of having to spend a minimum number of years in a branch office no longer applies.

Coverage
Before privatisation there were statutory duties imposed on the British Steel Corporation to negotiate terms and conditions of employment. A characteristic of the industry was the provision for joint conciliation and arbitration boards which dealt with all industrial relations matters within various sectors of the industry. As a result of privatisation the changes to bargaining arrangements are as yet unclear. In April 1988 the ISTC signed a two-year national pay agreement with British Steel (BS), which is due for renewal in 1990. Whilst the bargaining machinery is in a state of flux, what is emerging is a definite shift in emphasis from nationally negotiated percentage wage rises to locally-determined productivity payments. The 1988 pay deal was triggered locally by the signing of performance-related lump sum bonus agreements for each of the two years. National pay bargaining arrangements may not survive. At present the TUC Steel Committee, the only TUC Committee with negotiating rights, still meets British Steel on non-pay

matters.

In April 1989, due to higher than forecast inflation, British Steel was forced to renegotiate the two-year pay agreement which was signed the previous April. A "once-and-for-all" addition to local performance-related lump bonuses, which reflected BS performance since privatisation, was also agreed. Furthermore, flexible pay arrangements which might include changes to current industrial relations machinery have been signalled to the ISTC by BS management. Management are keen to ensure that new business-related arrangements are in place in time for the April 1990 agreement review. This adjustment provides a further hint as to the form that the new bargaining machinery will take.

The old structure of private sector national bargaining collapsed in the 1980s with most of that sector itself. The ISTC now bargains directly with a number of independent private companies. Several companies belong to the Engineering Employer's Federation or the Welsh Engineers' and Founder' Conciliation Board, whilst those engaged in the manufacture of special steels are members of the Engineering Employers' Sheffield Association.

Organisation

Members of the ISTC are organised in branches connected with the works in which they are employed. At a small works members may all be organised in one branch but at large intergrated works — in some caes employing several thousand workers — a number of separate branches are formed, each branch covering members employed in a specific department or process, or engaged on a particular class of work. Each branch elects annually a President, Vice-President, Secretary, works representative, and a committee, who are responsible for administering the affairs of the branch. Branches are organised into eight geographical divisions each of which has the duty of looking after the interests of the members in that division, and to maintain a good state of organisation. Supervision is provided by Head Office, which has accounts, audit, General Secretary's, and research departments.

The confederation holds an Annual Delegate Conference (ADC) which consists of works delegates appointed from the various divisions and members of the Executive Council. However, the supreme decision-making body of the confederation is the Executive Council. Tension between these two bodies surfaced in 1982 shortly after the steel strike when many members recognised their inability to influence policy decisions within the union hierarchy. The ADC passed a motion calling for future Conferences to become the supreme policy-making body of the union. Under confederation rules it is quite clear that any matter considered by conference "shall in no way be represented as or inferred to be the policy of the confederation until expressly adopted by the Executive". Since then the matter has not been directly raised.

However, during the 1988 ADC tension between delegates and the EC surfaced when a motion was put forward which urged EC members to take a more active part in Conference proceedings. Constitutionally, the position in the ISTC was that whenever individual EC members addressed Conference they merely presented a collective EC opinion and not their individual views. Roy Evans, the General Secretary, defended this practice when he suggested that the purpose of the Conference was for the EC to present its views and for members to tell the EC what they think. Delegates did not support the General Secretary and the motion was carried. It will be interesting to note if the Executive adopts this motion as ISTC policy.

Despite the privatisation of British Steel the preprivatisation arrangements for electoral purposes on the EC have not been changed, and are still broken down into three sections: section X (the old private sector), section Y (the public, previously BSC, staff and managerial sector), and sector Z (the public, previously BSC, manual sector). The next rules revision conference is planned for 1990. EC members are elected triennially after which they can stand for re-election. This practice of electing the whole EC every three years was debated during the 1988 ADC. The idea that it might be better if one-third of its members stood for election annually thereby promoting greater continuity between ECs was supported by the General Secretary, Roy Evans.

The Executive Council of the ISTC meets quarterly and is responsible for overseeing the running of the confederation, as well as appointing full-time officials and divisional officers. As the General Secretary is a non-voting member of the EC he is not subject to the legal requirement to be elected to the post by ballot. At present ISTC rules lay down that the General Secretary is appointed by the EC and holds that position until retirement. The 1990 rules revision conference may address this matter.

Work-place Activity
The ISTC is a highly centralised union with power concentrated at the top. There are around 500 branches in the union, and although on paper they enjoy some degree of autonomy in practice they are very much under the control of the full-time organisers and divisional officials. Where members are unemployed they are still allowed to be accredited delegates from the branches. The key office within the branch is that of the branch secretary.

Women
Women members of the ISTC are very much in a minority in a male-dominated union. They tend to be concentrated in three main areas: catering and canteen jobs; clerical and administrative occupations; and the technical staff sector. There is now one reserved women's seat in each divisional delegation to Conference, and recently women have been elected to the Executive Council. Unfortunately the ISTC no longer sends delegates to the Labour Women's Conference.

External relations
The ISTC is affiliated to the Labour Party both at national and local regional level. In many cases ISTC branches are affiliated to their own constituency Labour Party. The ISTC was the second union to ballot on retention of its political fund under the 1984 Act and won by a substantial majority of 6.5:1 in favour of retention despite media forecasts of a defeat. The union sponsored three Labour parliamentary candidates at the 1987 general election, but only D. Coleman (Neath) was returned. D. K. Brookman, Assistant General Secretary, is a founder of the Labour Party's National Constitutional Committee and was recently re-elected to the Committee by a huge majority, receiving nearly three million more votes than his nearest rival.

Roy Evans, the General Secretary, was President of the ECSC Consultative Committee from 1985-87, and is chairman of the Iron and Steel Department of the International Metalworkers' Federation, to which ISTC is affiliated. Although the union is no longer entitled to an automatic seat on the TUC General Council (as ISTC membership is below the 100,000 qualifying level) Roy Evans is one of its elected members.

Policy
The ISTC has consistently reaffirmed the view that it would not oppose the privatisation of the steel industry but instead would work to represent its membership irrespective of ownership.

The ISTC has suffered an enormous loss of membership since the steel strike in 1982 and, coincidentally, has adopted a less public profile to the one it had under its previous General Secretary, Bill Sirs. The 1988 ADC was almost exclusively concerned with the more traditional trade union issues, and motions on pay, bonus schemes, sick pay, and YTS dominated the proceedings. The ADC also agreed to support the approval of a statutory national minimum wage. On a wider political front motions supporting anti-apartheid were also debated and approved. Interestingly, the 1988 Delegate Conference also agreed to offer temporary membership to EETPU members who wanted to remain within the TUC.

Further references

P. Brannen, E. Batstone, D. Fatchett, and P. White, *The Worker Directors: A Sociology of Participation,* Hutchinson, 1976.

A. Pugh, *Men of Steel,* 1951.

E. Taylor, *The Better Temper,* ISTC, 1976.

J. Hodge, *From Workmen's Cottage to Windsor Castle,* 1936.

Iron and Steel Sector Working Party Progress Report, NEDC, 1980.

M. Upham, "British Steel: retrospect and prospect", *Industrial Relations Review,* July 1980. This article offers an excellent account of the events leading up to the 1980 steel strike.

F. Wilkinson, "Collective bargaining in the steel industry in the 1920s", in A. Briggs and J. Saville (eds.) *Essays in Labour History,* Croom-Helm, 1977.

Charles Doherty, *Steel and Steelworkers: the Sons of Vulcan,* Heinemann, 1982.

J. Kelly "Management Strategy and the Reform of Collective Bargaining: Cases from the British Steel Corporation", *British Journal of Industrial Relations,* XXII, no. 2, July 1984.

"Unregulated Monster in Search of Freedom", *Financial Weekly,* May 26, 1988.

MILITARY AND ORCHESTRAL MUSICAL INSTRUMENT MAKERS' TRADE SOCIETY

TUC affiliated

Head Office: 2 Whitehouse Avenue, Boreham Wood, Hertfordshire WD6 1HD

Principal officer
General Secretary: F. McKenzie

Membership

Current membership (1987)
Male: 32
Female: 9
Total: 41

Membership trends
1983: 200
1979: 226
1975:145

General
Workers employed in the trade of making instruments, workers in fields connected with military bands, and those working at established firms of military or orchestral musical instrument makers are eligible for membership.

In 1982 membership stood at 240 members, but since then membership has declined rapidly to 41 members in 1987, making it the second smallest union in the TUC. An obvious partner for a merger would be the FTAT, which also organises musical instrument makers. Although the society might find FTAT rather alien politically, the Military and Orchestral Musical Instrument Makers' Trade Society is in danger of becoming extinct unless it merges.

History
The society was formed in 1894. Until 1926 it was known as the *Military Musical Instrument Makers' Trade Society.* Up until 1945 members had to have apprenticeship papers. However, since no instruments were made between 1939 and 1945, the society had to repeal this rule so that demand for instruments could be met.

Organisation
The business of the society is carried out by a management committee called the Executive Council. The General Secretary is elected.

MSF
MANUFACTURING, SCIENCE, FINANCE
TUC affiliated

Head Office: 79 Camden Road, London NW1 9ES

Telephone: 01-267 4422

Telex: 25226

Principal officers
General Secretary: Ken Gill
Assistant General Secretary: Roger Lyons

Union journal: MSF (monthly)

Membership

Current membership (1987)
Male: 527,000
Female: 126,000
Total: 653,000

Membership trends *

	1975	1979	1981	1983	1987	change 1975-87	1983-87
Men	437,947	580,659	518,386	N/A	527,000	20%	N/A
Women	81,943	116,404	99,304	N/A	126,000	54%	N/A
Total	519,890	697,063	617,690	605,052	653,000	26%	8%

*All figures are for ASTMS and TASS combined

General

MSF was formed by the merger of the scientific and technical union ASTMS and the manufacturing white collar union TASS on January 18, 1988. The merger not only created Britain's fourth largest union and a powerful force on the left of the labour movement, but at the same time it considerably simplified bargaining arrangements in many areas and, in effect, brought in single-union arrangements.

At the time of the merger the union was run jointly by Ken Gill, former TASS General Secretary, and Clive Jenkins, former General Secretary of ASTMS. In October 1988 Clive Jenkins announced his sudden and complete retirement from the trade union world, and Ken Gill was elected unopposed as MSF General Secretary in July 1988.

MSF is presenting itself as a "new wave union" capable of representing professionals in many sectors of the economy, particularly in the "high tech" industries and occupations. But MSF is also trying to appeal to young workers and its launch was accompanied by much razzmatazz, including a video featuring the Housemartins, one of Britain's top chart groups. At one end of the spectrum the union now recruits members in Britain's growing voluntary sector as well as in the strongly contrasting group, the so-called "yuppies" in the City. Not only do these examples serve to illustrate the union's diversity of membership, but they also reflect the degree to which MSF is sensitive about the occupational and demographic changes taking place at the start of the 1990s. They also demonstrate the union's commitment to maintaining its initiative and confirming its innovative outlook.

With hindsight the merger between TASS and ASTMS seems obvious. Both were comparable in size with a strong tradition of organising professional, white collar workers. While TASS may have appeared as somewhat more to the left than ASTMS, in practice both unions had established a reputation for offering progressive policies with a high degree of professionalism. The criticism which many observers made about the MSF being dominated by the former TASS organisation does not seem to have materialised (see "Organisation").

Since its formation the following unions have merged with MSF: *United Friendly Field Management Association* (June 1988), *Imperial Supervisors' Association* (June 1988), *Church of England Children's Society Staff Association* (November 1988), and the *Imperial Group Staff Association* (March 1989).

History

As the merger to form MSF is relatively recent the histories of the two unions are outlined separately.

TASS

TASS started as the *Association of Engineering and Shipbuilding Draughtsmen* (AESD), which was formed in 1913 largely from drawing office personnel employed at John Brown's shipyard, Clydebank. By 1918 membership had risen from a few hundred to 10,911, and in the same year it affiliated to the TUC. In early 1919 it called its first strike at Holroyd's of Rochdale. By 1920 the AESD had grown to 11,920 members, and it adopted a minimum wage policy below which no AESD member would accept new employment.

In 1922 the union took into membership members of the *Tracers' Association* (an all-female union) and the AESD created a special section of membership for tracers, with provision for representation on the Executive Committee.

In the following year the union embarked on a series of strikes in order to gain recognition from employers, the largest strike taking place at English Electric and lasting for six weeks. The English Electric dispute eventually resulted in talks with the Engineering and Allied Employers' Federation (the precursor of the Engineering Employers' Federation) which led to the negotiation of a procedure agreement from March 1924.

Despite the bleak years from the General Strike until the late 1930s, membership of the AESD remained remarkably stable (8,830 in 1927, 13,903 in 1936). During that period the union pursued a policy of paying high unemployment benefits to its unemployed members so that they were not forced to accept low-paid jobs. This became more important during the 1950s and 1960s. The upturn in activity in the engineering industry towards the onset of the Second World War created a favourable climate for unions such as the AESD, and the union secured its first national wage agreement with the Shipbuilding Employers' Federation in 1941 following pressure being put on the employers by Ernest Bevin.

In the post-war years the union gradually increased its strength from 38,800 in 1945 to 57,301 in 1958. In 1961 the union changed its name to the *Draughtsmen and Allied Technicians' Association* (DATA), reflecting the growing spread of membership into new and developing technical areas within the engineering industry.

In 1964 DATA was party to a dispute which created legal history in the case of *Rookes* v. *Barnard*. Rookes was employed by BOAC in the drawing office at London airport and he had fallen out with AESD (as it was then called) in 1955. The local branch of DATA negotiated a 100 per cent membership arrangement with BOAC management and Rookes continued to refuse to join the union. The local branch then wrote to BOAC and gave notice that they would strike unless Rookes was dismissed. BOAC then lawfully terminated Rookes's contract of employment and Rookes subsequently sued the three union officers (Barnard, Fistal, and Silverthorne). The House of Lords (overturning an earlier Court of Appeal decision) held that the defendants were guilty of unlawful intimidation because they had threatened to induce a breach of contract and were therefore not protected by Section 3 of the Trade Disputes Act, 1906. This case led to the enactment of the Trade Disputes Act 1965.

On amalgamation with the *Amalgamated Union of Engineering and Foundry Workers* and the *Constructional Engineering Union* in April 1970, DATA became the *Technical and Supervisory Section of the Amalgamated Union of Engineering Workers*. A year later the union's name was changed to the AUEW (*Technical, Administrative and Supervisory Section*).

The amalgamation with the AUEW was uneasy and one of the central issues which frustrated full amalgamation, and indeed led to TASS eventually withdrawing from the AUEW, was over the position of full-time officials. Traditionally TASS appointed its officers while the engineers' officers were elected. By the early 1980s relationships between TASS and the rest of the federation deteriorated to such an extent that any discussions were mediated through other bodies, including the courts.

A first move towards TASS independence came in January 1984, when the four sections of the AUEW became a looser two-section amalgamation: the engineers, construction, and foundry workers formed one section while TASS formed the other. Subsequently, the engineering section changed its name back to AEU in 1986.

Within the looser two-section framework TASS attracted further mergers. These included the *National Union of Gold, Silver, and Allied Trades* (1981), the *National Union of Sheetmetal Workers, Coppersmiths, Heating, and Domestic Engineers* (1983), the *Association of Patternmakers and Allied Craftsmen* (1984), the *National Society of Metal Mechanics* (1985), and, a significant addition, the *Tobacco Workers' Union* in 1986.

ASTMS

The origins of ASTMS lie in the history of two unions; the *Association of Supervisory Staffs, Executives and Technicians* (ASSET), and the *Association of Scientific Workers* (AScW) which merged to become ASTMS in 1968.

ASSET started life soon after the First World War as the *National Foremen's Union*, created by supervisors in the railway workshops. There was some diversification and growth but little real progress until the Second World War and the achievement of recognition by the Engineering Employer's Federation after a long struggle. The EEF had for years held that supervisors should not be union members, but with help from the TUC, ASSET secured a procedure agreement in 1944. A barrier to the growth of the union was the insistence by the EEF that recognition would only apply where ASSET could secure a majority of a specific grade in a plant; this later became a spur to recognition.

The AScW was also campaigning for recognition by the EEF, and achieved it within months of ASSET's success. From its wartime success until 1969 ASSET's growth was restricted by the Foremen and Staff Mutual Benefit Society, an employer-backed provident society for supervisors, whose rules forbade any members to belong to a trade union. A private bill in Parliament promoted by the union secured the abolition of the offending rule, and 50,000 supervisors and other staff were at last free to join a union without sacrificing their provident benefits.

By now the union had become ASTMS following the merger in 1968 between ASSET and AScW. The merger of the unions was accomplished amicably, with the larger union — ASSET — accepting a 50/50 allocation of National Executive Committee seats between the two unions. Clive Jenkins of ASSET and John Dutton (now retired) of AScW became joint General Secretaries of the new union. Its strength at that time was less than 80,000 members: within six years it was to pass the 300,000 mark.

Much of the growth of ASTMS can be attributed to the energy and abilities of Clive Jenkins, who publicised the need for workers in traditionally non- or under-unionised sectors of employment to become union members. His own career contains links with both the founding unions of ASTMS: in 1946 he was a branch secretary and area treasurer of AScW, before becoming a full-time official of ASSET. He was appointed General Secretary of ASSET in 1961 at the age of 35.

As the union grew, attracting members from sectors where staff associations rather than independent unions had been the rule, a number of smaller unions and staff associations were merged with it. One important landmark was the merger with the *Medical Practitioners' Union* (1970).

However, whilst mergers certainly demonstrate a recruitment thrust by the union into the financial and National Health Service sectors, they cannot account for more than a small part of the union's growth. In fact two thirds of ASTMS members today have never belonged to a union or a staff association before.

Between 1970 and 1988, when ASTMS merged with TASS to form MSF, the following organisations became part of ASTMS through merger and amalgamation:

Union of Insurance Staffs (1970);
Prudential Clerical Staff Association (District Office) and
Prudential Ladies Staff Welfare Association (1970);
Medical Practitioners' Union (1970);
Royal Group Guild (1971);
Midland Bank Staff Association (1973);
Assurance Representatives' Organisation (Ireland) (1973);
Clydesdale Bank Staff Association (1974);
Guild of Hospital Pharmacists (1974);
Pearl Section (NUIW) (1974);
Forward Trust Staff Association (1975);
Kodak Senior Staff Association (1975);
London and Manchester Section (NUIW) (1975);
Midland Bank Technical Services Staff Association (1975);
Union of Speech Therapists (1975);
Health Service Chiropodists' Association (1976);
United Commercial Travellers' Association (1976);
Liverpool and Victoria Managers' Association (1976);
Group 1 Staff Association (Courtaulds) (1977);
Excess Insurance Staff Association (1977);
Managers and Overlookers' Society (1977);
Pearl Federation (1978);
Refuge Section (1979);
Reckitt and Colman Management Association (1979);
Colonial Mutual Life Assurance Society (1979);
Telephone Contract Officers Association (1980);
Australia and New Zealand Banking Group Ltd. Staff Association (1980);
Brittanic House Chief Office Staff Association (1980);
Youth Hostels Association Staff Association (1983);
Cosesa (1984);
Clerical and Secretarial Staffs Association of the University of Liverpool (1985);
Bank of New Zealand London Staff Association (1985);
Grindlays Staff Association (1985);
Sun Alliance and London Staff Association (1986).

Coverage
MSF has membership in almost every major industrial sector and company in Britain. The majority of its membership is in engineering, particularly the "high tech" aerospace, electronics, and telecommunications sectors, but there are also large pockets of members in areas such as finance, banking and insurance, health services, education, civil aviation, food and drink, shipbuilding, oil and petrochemicals, clothing, footwear and textiles, tobacco, construction, and glass manufacture. MSF also has over 30,000 members in Ireland and MSF - Ireland is the country's fourth largest union.

Organisation

At the time of merger MSF was constituted around two divisions; division A referred to the old TASS union, while ASTMS became division 1. The two unions operated under their respective rules, although a joint 50/50 National Executive Committee was formed from the start to oversee the administration of the union and steer the process of integration.

The first MSF Conference was held in camera in June 1988. High on the Conference agenda was the need to establish common boundaries between the two union organisations. Ever since the merger was announced it had been suggested that the hard left of TASS would dominate the softer left of ASTMS but the first Conference did not appear to support this claim. Two issues in particular cast doubt on this notion. First, the Conference rejected left-wing moves to include within the union's aims and objectives a commitment to public ownership, akin to the Labour Party's Clause Four. Instead, the Conference agreed to pursue policies aimed at "controlling industry in the interests of the community". Delegates, particularly from the ASTMS side of the union, argued that a commitment to traditional forms of nationalisation could affect adversely the union's image and damage MSF's recruitment plans in the less well-developed sectors and occupations of industry.

The second aspect which Conference discussed, and in which ASTMS maintained its position, concerned union branch and regional structures. Conference supported the proposal that union branches should retain 10 per cent of the subscription income they raise from their membership. This closely reflected the principle of ASTMS branches which have always had considerable independence and local autonomy in their financial affairs. ASTMS lay officials and local branches traditionally played a strong role in union decision-making and this idea has also been adopted for the MSF regional structure. Currently, decentralisation of decision-making is fashionable in business management and MSF Conference decided to follow this trend.

The two-division structure of MSF was seen as a necessary but temporary expedient. At the time of merger ASTMS was organised into 20 divisions and TASS into 11 regions. Instead, the focus for integration adopted by Conference was on the basis of 14 regions, each with its own regional council exercising a measure of control over policy and financial matters.

The second MSF Conference in May 1989 finally agreed a new rule book but it still had not been printed at the time of publication and further details were not available.

Union officials

MSF employs 24 officers at headquarters including the General Secretary, eight Assistant General Secretaries, 13 national negotiating officers, two women officers and around 170 full-time officials.

The method of appointment of officials was never in question as both TASS and ASTMS were already committed to appointments rather than selection. The appointment of officers had been a central issue which frustrated moves towards completing full amalgamation between TASS and the other three members of the AUEW.

ASTMS had for some time operated the policy of appointing high calibre graduates as union officials. Given the "high tech" image and industrial profile of a good proportion of its membership MSF is likely to retain this as its future recruitment and selection policy for future full-time officer appointments.

Women

Women constitute around 20 per cent of the total union membership and both TASS and

ASTMS had long-established traditions in catering for women members. TASS, for instance, had a seat reserved for women on the union's Executive Committee since 1922 when the union absorbed the *Tracers' Association.* ASTMS, on the other hand, achieved the highest rate of increase in women's membership of any trade union between 1968 and 1978, when its women members rose from 9,400 to 77,200, a 721 per cent increase.

Women have been specially targeted by MSF in their plans for future growth and expansion, and the union has two national officers with responsibility for women's issues. However, it is perhaps disappointing that MSF did not take the opportunity to integrate women's issues more fully into the union's operations. By creating a specific union post of "women's officer" there is a tendency for other union officials to ignore anything which is not in their remit and consequently leave women's issues to the "women's officer". Due to demographic and occupational changes in the future women will form a larger part of the labour force, particularly in the "high tech" finance and service sectors in which MSF currently recruits. In the past women have had cause to complain about limited interest in their problems as few unions actually made the necessary resources available to ensure that their issues were properly understood and represented. MSF is well placed to recruit a whole new group of women about to enter the labour market. It is hoped that they take this responsibility far more seriously than their earlier manual trade union counterparts (see "Recent events").

In the insurance sector MSF has made a number of interesting agreements which benefit women; at Norwich Union for instance, women staff are entitled to a five-year career break which, although it does not guarantee them jobs on returning, means they will be given preferential treatment in recruitment and will go back to their old grades if they are employed. Previously women who took maternity leave lost their preferential mortgage allowance, but now under the terms of the agreement they are allowed to retain it.

At a number of the larger insurance companies MSF has also made important deals which begin to remove some of the barriers between full-time and part-time workers — most of whom are women. In October 1988 the union prepared a "hit list" of companies which it considered still discriminated against part-time workers over mortgages, allowances, pensions schemes, and sick-pay benefits. This followed legal moves which MSF took regarding discriminatory practice by Norwich Union over its part-time employees. MSF had been challenging a High Court decision of July 1988 which overturned a Central Arbitration award which had supported the union's argument. MSF argued that the exclusion of part-time workers from mortgage and other schemes afforded to full-time staff was indirect sex discrimination, as the vast majority of part-timers (in the case of Norwich Union) were women. Norwich Union agreed to the union's demands out of court and MSF called off their Court of Appeal proceedings.

Ken Gill, MSF General Secretary, holds the chair of the TUC's Equal Rights committee.

External relations
MSF and the TUC
MSF, along with other left-led unions such as NALGO, TGWU, and NUPE, argues that the system of allocating membership of the General Council does not represent the spread of unions in the TUC. In particular, MSF points out that while union membership in small unions has declined, the number of seats reserved for small unions has not. It cites the case of the TUC General Council Section B, which elects representatives from three small clothing unions, NUTGW, NUHKW, and NUFLAT, noting that the skewed industrial make-up of this section is a product of the "right-wing political machine". Too often the right-wing block has diluted left-wing resolutions; an example cited by the left are the disciplinary measures taken against the EETPU.

MSF's proposals to make the General Council more representative would in effect discriminate in favour of the large unions. Numerically, this might be the correct course of action, but the TUC cannot operate according to such technical criteria — it has to take into account wider considerations. Smaller and medium-sized unions are likely to be around for the foreseeable future; consequently they must have a role in influencing the TUC's General Council, otherwise they may conclude that membership brings greater benefit to larger unions at their expense and decide to leave. EMA has already indicated its disquiet over the move to reduce small union representation.

Ken Gill, General Secretary, and Anne Gibson, National Officer, are MSF representatives on the TUC General Council. Anne Gibson is only the third woman to hold a general seat on the Council.

Policy

Almost from the beginning MSF decided that it was going to transcend the traditional insularity and chauvinism which characterised large pockets of the British trade union movement. It has adopted therefore a fairly wide-ranging perspective on current issues, analysing problems in a progressive and innovative way. One of its first important documents was *Europe 1992*, one of the best trade union assessments of the impact which the single market is likely to have in Britain. Its clear presentation of the significance of 1992 highlights the strengths as well as the weaknesses of the free market and emphasises the problems which trade unions need to be aware of and areas where they need to be particularly vigilant.

The document promotes 10 legislative and campaigning objectives which MSF believes should form the core of a trade union strategy:

1. Establishing a pan-European Industrial Sector Joint Committee bringing together trade unionists, the Commission and representatives of the principal companies operating within clearly defined industrial sectors in the Community in order to consult on matters of joint mutual interest and concern;

2. Make language training available to trade union nominees, including lay representatives, as well as appropriate time-off with pay;

3. Legislation which would allow for "best practice" on industrial democracy to be cultivated by trade unions at company level;

4. Statutory inclusion of the notion of the "public interest" in company take overs and mergers in order to take account of rights and interests of employees;

5. Harmonise European trade union rights;

6. All companies should set up with trade unions vocational training and education joint committees which would assist with technological change and avoid redundancy;

7. Joint participation in the regulation of the insurance and finance industry;

8. The adoption of the ETUC goal of a 35-hour normal basic week and the right of all workers to an occupational pension;

9. Health and safety standards should be set at the highest level, with trade unions' guaranteed involvement in their implementation and monitoring;

10. Ensure that multinational companies do not divert production and investment to countries where free trade unionism is restricted or where governments refuse to agree comparable standards to those outlined in points 1-9 above.

A significant implication of *Europe 1992* is that MSF has located its future policy objectives firmly within the wider European context. It also acknowledges that the advances which many "younger" European trade union movements have secured have stood the test of time much better than those in Britain which,with its anarchic structure, is a source of "comfort" but perhaps little else.

MSF has had several meetings with two Swedish trade unions, which between them have more than 300,000 members, to discuss a merger.

A more specific area where MSF has recognised the value of the EC dimension is its report on the hazards of VDUs, which was published in December 1988. MSF has one of the largest number of members working with VDUs: over 40 per cent of its members work in offices and the number of complaints reported to the union about muscular strain and eye problems have increased quite dramatically. The report, submitted as evidence to the House of Lords sub-committee inquiry into the use of VDUs, urged the sub-committee to endorse a draft EC directive. The directive demands that employers assume greater responsibility for the training and health implications of a VDU "work-station". Article 3 states that EC member states "shall take all necessary steps to ensure that VDU work cannot compromise the safety and health of workers", while Article 4 puts the onus on employers to "perform an analysis of work-stations in order to evaluate the safety and health risks to workers". MSF points out that there is difficulty in calculating how many people in the UK suffer from muscular complaints (known as repetitive strain injuries or RSI) as a result of working with VDUs, because the Health and Safety Executive does not collect this information.

Recent events
MSF is currently facing increased pressure from employers, particularly in the finance sector, over performance-related pay. The union has responded by issuing a policy statement to assist negotiators to deal with such demands. The statement identifies that performance pay schemes are often used as a method of bringing in supplements for grades and skills in short supply rather than rewarding performance. Moreover, the criteria used to evaluate performance are subjective and will tend to favour male over female staff.

Furthermore, the statement recognises that performance-appraisal schemes can raise standards at work, but linking assessment to pay undermines its effectiveness. In trying to run performance-related pay alongside performance-appraisal, management is likely to find conflicting and incompatible objectives which will be difficult to reconcile. MSF identifies some of these contradictions as follows:
1. Effective teamwork is likely to be replaced by competition;
2. Such schemes are likely to engender a "low trust" rather than a "high trust" response from staff as managers assume responsibility for determining merit payments;
3. Staff motivation is likely to be influenced more by pay than by professional considerations, and many staff may be unlikely to accept new challenges if the criteria for merit pay awards are perceived to be unfair.

MSF asserts in its policy statement that the provision of clarity in setting job-objectives will be achieved not by relating performance to pay, but instead, by relating performance to a properly constituted system of appraisal where the criteria for evaluation can be mutually agreed between management and the union. In this way, staff are aware of the terms of their performance appraisal.

Union derecognition
There always existed a degree of rivalry in the banking and financial sector between the former ASTMS union and BIFU, and this has continued with MSF. In 1989 the Midland

Bank announced plans to derecognise MSF, and in May of the same year the union suffered a further setback when two senior MSF Union representatives of the Midland Bank staff section Executive Committee decided to seek membership of BIFU and advised others to follow. They believed that as a result of derecognition trade union organisation would be strengthened if MSF members transferred their membership to BIFU. Before derecognition MSF claimed to have about 4,000 Midland members while BIFU had about 22,000. BIFU condemned the derecognition move by the Midland acknowledging that they, in turn, could be the victims of such a move. (BIFU has also undertaken not to breach any TUC rules.)

This move by the Midland Bank highlights the problem that, whatever the TUC may do to avoid inter-union conflict, employers themselves may precipitate it; in this instance both unions have acted constitutionally and shown respect for each other. Although MSF is forced to pursue the matter with the Midland Bank, it is difficult to see what it can achieve. As single-union bargaining becomes more fashionable, it is likely that MSF (as well as other unions) may become involved in other similar cases.

MSF is currently engaged in informal talks with the TGWU about a possible merger. If the talks were eventually to succeed the new union, with a membership of around two million would be the largest union not only in Britain but also in Europe. There are many reasons why the merger appears attractive; both unions are on the left, and if brought into one organisation its power and authority would be formidable. Against this, many MSF members and officials question whether the merger would bring any benefits, given the current disarray within the TGWU Executive (see **TGWU**).

Further references

J.E. Mortimer, *History of the Association of Engineering and Shipbuilding Draughtsmen*, AESD, London 1960. The official history of the union up to 1959 written by a former General Secretary of the Labour Party.

Hilary Wainright and Dave Elliot, *The Lucas Plan: A New Trade Unionism in the Making?*, Allison & Busby, 1982.

Olive Robinson, "Part-time employment and industrial relations developments in the EEC", *Industrial Relations Journal*, 15, no. 1, Spring 1984.

Aidan Kelly, "In support of the new working class thesis: the case of the Irish white collar worker", *Industrial Relations Journal*, 15, no. 1, Spring 1984.

Ian McLoughlin, "Engineering their future: developments in the organisation of British professional engineers", *Industrial Relations Journal*, 15, no.4, Winter 1984.

John Child and Marion Tarbuck, "The introduction of new technologies: managerial initiative and trade union responses in British banks", *Industrial Relations Journal*, 16, no.3, Autumn 1985.

George Martens, "Women at work: a case study of the insurance industry", *Industrial Relations Journal*, 16, no.4, Winter 1985.

Timothy Morris, "Trade union mergers and competition in banking", *Industrial Relations Journal*, 17, no.2, Summer 1986.

Chris Baldry and Anne Connolly, "Drawing the line: computer-aided design and the organisation of the drawing office", *New Technology, Work, and Employment*, 1, no.1, Spring 1986.

Heinz Hartmann and Michael Florian, "German trade unions and company information", *Industrial Relations Journal*, 18, no.4, Winter 1987.

Ed Snape and Greg Bamber, "Managerial and Professional Employees: Conceptualising Union Strategies and Structure", *British Journal of Industrial Relations*, XXVII, no.1, March 1989.

MU
MUSICIANS' UNION

TUC affiliated

Head Office: 60-62 Clapham Road, London SW9 0JJ

Telephone: 01-582 5566

Principal national officers
General Secretary: J.Morton
Assistant General Secretary: S. Hibbert
Assistant Secretary: J. Stoddard

Union journal: Musician (quarterly, mailed to all members)

Membership

Current membership (1987)
Male: 33,984
Female: 5,754
Total: 39,738

Membership trends

	1975	1979	1981	1983	1987	change 1975-87	1983-87
Men	32,464	36,924	35,002	33,363	33,984	5%	2%
Women	3,518	4,626	5,054	5,728	5,754	64%	0%
Total	35,982	41,550	40,056	39,091	39,738	10%	2%

General

The Musicians' Union is the second largest musicians' union in the world, second only to the American Federation of Musicians. It organises the whole of the profession including symphony orchestras, broadcasting orchestras, bands in night-clubs, bands and groups in ballrooms, rock and other groups. The union and British Actors' Equity form a *Performance Alliance* in association with the Writers' Guild of Great Britain, and the MU is also a member of the Confederation of Entertainment Unions, the Federation of Broadcasting Unions, the Federation of Theatre Unions, and the Federation of Film Unions.

The union has built up its membership from around 32,000 in 1969 to its present level of over 38,000. John Morton, General Secretary, is also President of the International Federation of Musicians.

History

The Musicians' Union was formed in 1921 as a result of an amalgamation of the *National Orchestral Union of Professional Musicians* and the *Amalgamated Musicians' Union*, both of which were formed in 1893. During the 1920s membership grew to around 20,000 but it declined substantially after the development of "talking pictures" to around 7,000 in 1940. The early problems of the union were the immigration of foreign musicians into Britain and the use of military bands and orchestras. It built up its membership to its present level by determined organisation in the post-war years.

181

Union officials

The union has a dual structure of full-time officials, some with responsibilities which relate to geograpical areas and others with responsibilities concerned with specific aspects of the union's work. At present, the union employs a General Secretary, two Assistant Secretaries and three specialists: a Music Promotion Organiser, a Session Organiser and a Music Business Adviser. The union also has eight district organisers throughout the UK.

Coverage

The union admits into membership those who "are following the profession of music in any of its branches", i.e., those engaged in performing, teaching, writing or composing music. It organises musicians in symphony orchestras, theatre orchestras, broadcasting orchestras, bands in night-clubs and ballrooms, and rock and other groups. It has a long established special section covering those engaged in arranging, composing, or copying music as well as separate sections to cover session musicians and music teachers. The union received early recognition from the BBC and it conducts regular negotiations with all major employers of musicians including the BBC, independent television companies, the Association of British Orchestras, the Theatrical Management Association, the British Resorts Association and Mecca Ltd. In addition, the union also conducts negotiations with a number of smaller independent bodies such as the Royal Opera House, Butlins Ltd, the British Film Producers' Association, and the English National Opera Company.

Organisation

The supreme authority of the union is vested in the Biennial Delegate Conference which is convened in July. The union's general management is vested in the Executive Committee which consists of 21 members elected to serve for a two-year period. The full EC meets at least four times a year. The members of the EC are elected by ballot votes from the union's nine districts. The number of representatives accorded to each district depends on member size.

There are nine district councils which meet three times a year and are formed from delegates from branches in the districts concerned, elected annually by a ballot vote of each branch in that particular district. There are around 130 branches of the MU spread throughout the UK and they normally meet monthly. Full-time officials of the MU are appointed by the Executive Committee, and the General Secretary is elected by ballot vote of the union's membership to serve until retirement, death or removal by a ballot vote of the union.

Women

Women constitute approximately 20 per cent of the membership. There are no female members on the EC. One of the eight district organisers is female.

External relations

The union is affiliated nationally to the Labour Party and a number of branches and districts are affiliated at a local level. Peter Snape, Labour MP for West Bromwich East, assists the union in parliamentary liaison. The union is also affiliated to the National Council for Civil Liberties.

The union maintains a close and effective relationship with British Actors' Equity both within the framework of the Performers Alliance which meets quarterly, and outside it as well. The joint secretaries of the Alliance are the General Secretaries of the Musicians' Union, the Writers' Guild, and Equity.

The MU has also established a joint committee with the Broadcasting and Entertainment Trades Alliance (BETA), mainly to maintain a joint strategy on developments affecting members of both unions in the BBC.

In addition, the MU is a member of the Confederation of Entertainment Unions. The confederation is the umbrella organisation for three constituent federations, the Federation of Broadcasting Unions, the Federation of Film Unions, and the Federation of Theatre Unions.

At the international level, the MU was one of the founder members of the International Federation of Musicians and maintains close links with the American Federation of Musicians.

Each year the union also sends delegates, who are selected by the National Executive Committee, to the Labour Party conference.

Policy

The Musicians' Union has always been opposed to any form of incomes policy and has consistently supported a return to free collective bargaining. It believes that members themselves should have the maximum involvement and participation in pursuing their own claims for pay and conditions and has adopted policies which reflect this belief. Total unionisation of the industry is an objective the union supports wholeheartedly.

The main policy concern of the union in recent years has been the erosion of employment opportunities for musicians arising through the use of tapes, records and, more recently, new technology in the form of synthesisers which can replace any number of musicians with one, perhaps less skilled, operator. The MU has campaigned extensively and their "Keep Music Live" sticker is well known. The union's attitude is such that it regards control over performers' rights as more important than remuneration for the use of recordings. It supported a campaign which led to an obligation being placed on commercial radio in Britain (an obligation not found in any other country), to spend a certain proportion of its receipts on musical employment. This explains the union's concern with the public use of records, with the use of live performance, and with the work of music promotion.

At the 1987 TUC, the MU submitted a motion calling on Congress to identify a strategy to improve "trade union organisation" in the face of current threats and challenges. It called on Congress to go beyond its present, defensive role of policing inter-union disputes and to adopt a more progressive attitude, helping to co-ordinate the organising efforts of unions and generally providing the means for unions to deal more effectively with the changing labour market and new employment practices. The Musicians' Union also put forward a motion on the Arts asking Congress to reaffirm its support for the publicly funded provision of arts and entertainment with full access to all sections of the community and for inclusion of the arts in the education curriculum.

A similar motion was submitted to the 1987 Labour Party conference, calling on the NEC to give a much higher priority to the arts, and for an Arts and Entertainment standing committee to be established as part of a Labour Arts Policy; such a policy is considered essential to the concern about the quality of life. This motion complements an earlier motion, submitted to the 1986 TUC, which called on Congress to reject a solely "market system" of broadcasting, and stating that privatisation of the BBC would not lead to greater consumer sovereignty but, instead, would lead to the domination of broadcasting by multinational media interests with a consequent loss of quality.

Recent events

In April 1988, the Monopolies and Merger Commission (MMC) report entitled *Labour Practices in TV and Film Making,* found that *de facto,* a closed shop existed which restricted non-union members from gaining work. Under the terms of the 1973 Fair Trading Act this amounted to a restrictive practice. The report went on to add, however, that "although there is undoubtedly scope for improvements in the arrangements between employers and the MU, the practices are not against the public interest because they cause employers relatively minor problems." The report accepted that the MU is committed to changing its agreements.

Membership of the MU is usually a guarantee to any employer that the person under contract is a musician and employers find this a useful criterion for job selection. Could the MMC have reported anything other than the fact that MU membership is not against the public interest?

NACO
NATIONAL ASSOCIATION OF CO-OPERATIVE OFFICIALS
TUC affiliated

Head Office: Saxone House, 56 Market Street, Manchester M1 1PW

Telephone: 061-834 6029

Principal national officers
General Secretary: L. W. Ewing
Assistant General Secretary: K. Yorath
Assistant Secretary: D. Williams

Union journal: NACO and the Co-operative Press Ltd jointly edit a monthly journal entitled *Co-operative Marketing and Management* which has an insert *Co-operative Official* reserved for NACO. It is distributed to all NACO members.

Membership

Current membership (1987)
Male: 4,141
Female: 282
Total: 4,423

Membership trends

	1975	1979	1981	1983	1987	change 1975-87	1983-87
Men	5,369	5,759	5,372	4,755	4,141	− 23%	−13%
Women	130	340	322	298	282	117%	− 5%
Total	5,499	6,099	5,694	5,053	4,423	− 20%	−12%

The membership trend figures reveal that the union is undergoing a gradual decline. This is as much to do with the general contraction of the co-operative movement as it is with the overall political climate. The union is attempting to arrest the situation by making itself more responsive to its membership and generally sharpening its presentation and its image.

General

NACO caters for all officials and managers employed by the co-operative movement: managerial personnel with retail, wholesale, and productive societies, and the Co-operative Insurance Society. The coverage of NACO membership extends into a wide range of industries, particularly in retailing. Membership of NACO has declined from an all-time high of 8,500 in 1966 to around half that total today. To some extent this decline was masked by the merger of the CWS with the Scottish CWS but the contraction, as well as the growing commercialisation of the co-operative movement, suggests that the union is unlikely to flourish much in the foreseeable future. Furthermore, the union faces competition for membership from the white collar section of USDAW (SATA), and MSF. In response to these pressures, NACO has re-examined its recruitment strategy. It has revamped its literature, identified its potential membership more keenly with a view to targeting it more selectively, and on the whole, has improved its communication and responsiveness to its existing membership. These measures will probably enable the union to hold its own ground.

History

NACO was formed in 1971 by an amalgamation of the former *National Union of Co-operative Officials, National Co-operative Managers' Association Ltd,* and the *Co-operative Secretaries' Association.* The *National Union of Co-operative Officials* was formed in 1917. NACO was one of the first unions to organise management at all levels.

Union officials

The only full-time officials employed by NACO are the principal officers as listed above.

Organisation

The General Council has full control of the Business of NACO. It comprises 25 members, elected by postal ballot, constituted sectionally; 17 from England and Wales, three from Scotland and one from Ireland with the remainder from CWS Ltd. Day-to-day running of the union is in the hands of the six-person Secretarial Executive which is appointed by and accountable to the General Council.

The supreme ruling body of the union is the Annual General Meeting. Members are organised into branches or Constituent Organisations comprising at least 25 persons which are geographically located and attached to a Section. There are also loose associations of craft managers (e.g. CIS managers, butchery managers, laundry managers etc). These are organised nationally to cater for sectional interest groups. There is also an appeals tribunal which serves as the ultimate appeals body to deal with matters relating to expulsion of members, refusal to admit into membership, and actions taken by NACO officials which may be considered to be contrary to the rules of the union. The rule book provides that industrial action can only be taken with the approval of the General Council by a two-thirds majority.

Women

The 265 women in NACO constitute less than 6 per cent of the total membership. There are no women on the General Council and women's affairs are not given any separate representation by the union. To a large extent this is a reflection of the fact that few women reach managerial posts in the co-operative movement.

External relations

NACO has no political fund or formal political affiliation to any party nor any sponsored MPs. However a number of NACO members are Labour and Co-operative MPs. The full-time officials of the Co-operative Party are NACO members. The union is keen to stress its "non-political" stance, despite its association with the co-operative movement.

Policy

NACO policy is largely centred around its collective bargaining function within the co-operative movement, and it has generally fostered close relations with management.

The union sponsors 10 educational conferences each year as part of a senior management development programme for the retail co-operative movement. Branches are also involved in practical training but this is generally for supervisors rather than NACO members. The General Secretary is the TUC representative on the Distributive Industrial Training Trust.

Recent events

NACO has resisted previous approaches by USDAW and others to merge. In view of its decline together with that of the co-operative movement, it might do well to reconsider this policy.

NACODS
NATIONAL ASSOCIATION OF COLLIERY OVERMEN DEPUTIES AND SHOTFIRERS

TUC affiliated

Head Office: Simpson House, 48 Nether Hall Road, Doncaster, South Yorkshire DN1 2PZ

Telephone: 0302-68015

Principal officer
General Secretary: Peter McNestry

Union journal: None

Membership

Current membership (1987)
Total: 8,835
There are no female members.

Membership trends

	1975	1979	1981	1983	1987	change 1975-87	1983-87
Total	20,589	19,146	18,575	17,079	8,835	−57%	−48%

General
NACODS organises those who have a statutory qualification as a colliery deputy. This embraces under-officials in the coal industry, i.e. "overmen, deputies, and shotfirers", and certain other officials below the grade of under-manager. NACODS members are neither part of the mining work-force nor are they a part of management. Their purpose derives from their role in enforcing the health and safety legislation which binds the industry.

Membership of the union has fluctuated in line with the levels of workers in the coal industry. In 1965 the union had a membership of 31,471. Its membership in 1987 (8,835) is its lowest ever, and with the record number of pit closures (see **NUM**) NACODS membership is certain to decline still further.

During a crucial stage in the 1984-5 miners' strike NACODS called off a planned strike after they had reached a separate agreement with the National Coal Board over procedures to handle pit closures. Many commentators, as well as their own members, believed that the terms of the agreement were not satisfactory. If NACODS had not given in to the NCB at this crucial stage of the strike, then the outcome of the whole dispute might well have been different. Indeed many would claim that the wider political implications of NACODS' capitulation to the NCB's demands played a significant role in the outcome of the 1987 general election.

In their 1986 pay agreement, NACODS gave up the right to productivity bonuses, which had been awarded to coalworkers, in return for higher basic pay, attempting thereby to identify more closely with management. NACODS' basic dilemma , whether to identify with the production workers or with management, contributed in no small measure to their own national strike in 1988 (see "Recent events").

In preparing this entry NACODS was approached, but refused to provide any information either on the union's organisation or its current activities.

History
Before 1910 when NACODS was first established as a national association, the union existed as a federation of autonomous areas under the name of the *General Federation of Firemen's, Examiners' and Deputies' Association of Great Britain*. Some area associations have been in operation for more than 100 years. The present title was adopted when the coal industry was nationalised in 1947.

Organisation
The governing body of the union is the National Conference, held annually during the last full week in June. The conference is composed of the officers, members of the National Executive Committee, and delegates. Important decisions such as acceptance or rejection of wages offers are taken at specially convened conferences.

The union rule book provides that strikes can only be called as a result of a ballot vote of the membership following a resolution of a National Conference. A two-thirds majority of those voting is required.

Political affiliation
The union is affiliated to the Labour Party and has a political fund. The result of the ballot held in 1986 was 87 per cent (representing 9,930 votes) in favour and 13 per cent (1,481 votes) against. There was a 76.2 per cent turn-out.

Recent events
Between January 1988 and March 1988, NACODS was involved in the first national

coal strike since the 1984-5 miners' strike. NACODS called a series of one-day strikes followed by an overtime ban in response to British Coal's pay offer and the imposition of new work patterns. The matter was eventually referred to the National Reference Tribunal, part of the coal industry's bargaining machinery, which awarded pit deputies a rise of 4.28 per cent. After some deliberation the award was accepted.

The TGWU, who were holding merger talks with the NUM, has also indicated that, should the two unions merge, the TGWU would be seeking to develop a more unified union structure in the coal/energy industry (see **TGWU**). With a 48 per cent decline in membership since 1983, and the prospect that decline is likely to continue for the foreseeable future, a merger with the TGWU would make sense.

Further reference

E. Heery, 'Group incentives and the mining supervisor: the effects of a payment system on first-line managers', *British Journal of Industrial Relations,* XXII, no. 3, November 1984. The article, although dated, locates the position of NACODS members in a wider power context in the coal industry before the NUM 1984-5 dispute.

NAHT
NATIONAL ASSOCIATION OF HEAD TEACHERS

Non-TUC affiliated

Head Office: 1 Heath Square, Boltro Road, Haywards Heath, West Sussex RH16 1BL

Telephone: 0444-458133

Fax: 0444-416326

Principal officers
General Secretary: David Hart
Deputy General Secretary: David Burbidge
Senior Assistant Secretary (Education): Arthur Caux
Senior Assistant Secretary (Professional Services): Eric Pilkington
Assistant Secretary: Sue Nicholson
Assistant Secretary: Gareth James
Assistant Secretary: Brian Harris
Assistant Secretary: Peter Heyller

Union journal and publicity
The NAHT produces two publications which are distributed free to all members: *NAHT Bulletin* (monthly), *Head Teachers' Review* (quarterly).

The NAHT, in conjunction with the BBC and the Industrial Society, has produced a video training package on the 1988 Education Reform Act.

Membership

Current membership (1988)
Total 34,525

General
The NAHT was formed in March 1897 at a conference in Clarendon Street School, Nottingham. It was originally titled the *National Federation of Head Teachers' Association* because local associations already existed in some of the larger cities. At the time of its formation there were 12 affiliated local associations and 1,477 members. In 1987 there were 370 local associations and over 20,000 members, which represented around an 80 per cent recruitment density.

Membership of the NAHT is restricted to head and deputy head teachers in schools mainly in the public sector although some membership is claimed in independent schools.

The NAHT is a moderate and highly professional union which enjoys its independent, non-TUC status. But it temporarily abandoned its moderation during the 1984-6 teachers' strike, when it advised its members who had kept schools open during action not to continue to do so.

Organisation
There are three distinct types of organisational units within the NAHT. The basic unit of organisation is the local association which consists of members drawn from all types of schools in a particular area. Local associations combine to form the second unit of organisation, the branch; in 1987 there were 104 branches. The third unit of representation is the confederation which is made up from branch affiliation.

The Annual Conference is the supreme policy making body of the union. Votes at the Annual Conference are made up from the local association, the branch, and the confederation. The 31-member National Council is the executive committee of the NAHT. The union is organised into 30 districts, and each district has one member on the National Council except for District 8 (Inner London) which has two.

External relations
The NAHT has no political affiliations and no political fund but it does employ parliamentary lobbyists.

It is affiliated to the German Association of Secondary Head Teachers, and has informal relations with Dutch Secondary Head Teachers, and the American National Association of Secondary School Principals.

Policy
The NAHT endorses the principal aspects of the 1988 Education Reform Act including the core curriculum and delegating managerial power to head teachers, but it is keen to ensure that the changes are not simply a cost-cutting exercise but have real benefits. As a result of the 1988 Education Reform Act, the role of head teachers has radically altered and with the establishment of the Local Management of Schools (LMS), head teachers have now taken on major responsibilities for staffing and budgetary control. They advocate that there must be proper and effective training for heads and senior teachers, sufficient administrative help, a proper balance of power between head and school governors, and an agreement over performance indicators for evaluating heads.

The 1988 Annual Conference passed a resolution which stated that head and deputy head teachers' pay should be treated separately from that of all other teachers and, furthermore, a facility for heads to have an involvement in future negotiations on the salary structure and conditions of service for teachers who work in their schools ought to be found. Widening the pay differentials in schools between teachers has its problems, but increasing the status differential between heads and "ordinary" teachers is potentially the greater problem. But the NAHT have to be careful that head teachers do not abuse their newly acquired managerial status and recognise that industrial-type management systems cannot be imported wholesale into schools.

Recent events

Towards the end of 1988 the NAHT created its own private company to provide management training for head teachers, deputies, and senior teachers most affected by the 1988 Education Reform Act. NAHT Management Development Services, the name chosen for the company, is expected to be profitable by 1991 and have a turnover of around £500,000. Although it will employ a full-time managing director, most of the other teaching/training staff are expected to be on short-term contracts. Ironically, the NAHT deplores the uncertainties of temporary assignments for its own members, and its 1988 Annual Conference demanded that a head teacher should not be subjected to act as a supply teacher.

The union has extensive archive material and 1997 is its centenary year.

Further reference

The First Fifty Years 1897-1947, Jubilee Volume, NAHT, University of London Press, 1947.

NALGO
NATIONAL AND LOCAL GOVERNMENT OFFICERS' ASSOCIATION

TUC affiliated

Head Office: 1 Mabledon Place, London WC1H 9AJ

Telephone: 01-388 2366

Fax: 01-387 6692

Principal national officers
General Secretary: John Daly
Deputy General Secretary: Alan R. Jinkinson
Assistant General Secretary (Service Conditions): Dave Prentis
Assistant General Secretary (Administration): M. Dempsey
Local Government Services Conditions Officer: Keith Sonnet
Organising Officer (Electricity Staffs): M. Jeram
Organising Officer (Gas Staffs): Dave Strizaker
Organising Officer (Health Staffs): Ada Maddocks
Organising Officer (Water/Transport): John Pitt

Organising Officer (Universities/New Towns): Alex Thompson
Research Officer: John S. Thane
Financial Officer: M. Runcie
Legal Officer: Penelope Grant
Publicity Officer: Chris Cossey
Education Officer: Regina Kibel
International Relations: L. Richards

District offices
There are 12 district offices, each headed by a district organisation officer leading a team of district officers.

Eastern
Charles Cronin, Church Lane House, Church Lane, Chelmsford, Essex CM1 1UW
Telephone: 0245-87224

East Midland
P. Artis, Pearl Assurance House, Friar Lane, Nottingham NG1 6BY
Telephone: 0602-4755756

Metropolitan
Andrew Jack, 17 Highfield Road, Golders Green, London NW11 9PF
Telephone: 01-458 9211

Southern
H. McSoley, London House, 59/65 London Street, Reading, Berkshire RG1 4PS
Telephone: 0734-596466

South Eastern
P. Wood, International House, 78 Queen's Road, Brighton BN1 3XE
Telephone: 0273-29445

South Wales
Tom Quinn, Third Floor, 1 Cathedral Road, Cardiff CF1 9SB
Telephone: 0222-398333

North Western and North Wales
Ernest Baxendale, 3/5 St John Street, Manchester M3 4DL
Telephone: 061-832 5625

North Eastern
B. Devine, Milburn House (A), Dean Street, Newcastle-upon-Tyne NE1 1LE
Telephone: 091-232 4900

South Western
Steve Johnson, NALGO House, The Crescent, Taunton, Somerset TA1 4DU
Telephone: 0823-88031

West Midlands
Sid Platt, 7th Floor, Tower Block, City Centre, 7 Hill Street, Birmingham B5 4JD
Telephone: 021-643 6084

Scottish
Charles Gallacher, Hellenic House, 87/97 Bath Street, Glasgow G2 2ER
Telephone: 041-332 0006

Yorkshire and Humberside
John Fitches, 3rd Floor, Commercial House, Wade Lane, Leeds LS2 8NJ
Telephone: 0532-449111

Union journal and publications: Public Service (monthly, circulation around 750,000). NALGO also publishes *NALGO News,* a weekly for all NALGO activists with a circulation of around 30,000. NALGO also has an extensive and varied publications record including *Beggar My Neighbour, Trade Unions and Human Rights, The Menopause Book, Caring for Muslims and their Families,* and *Food and Diet in a Multiracial Society.*

For over 60 years NALGO has been involved in home study courses and has established a reputation as a specialist in distance learning. It provides high-quality tuition material, at minimal cost, ranging from O and A level through to many professional institute courses such as Personnel Management, Public Administration, and Town Planning. A recent new development has been an arrangement with the Open College of Arts which allows NALGO members a discount on a large range of arts courses.

Membership

Current membership (1987)
Male: 384,702
Female: 374,078
Total: 758,780

Membership trends

	1975	1979	1981	1983	1987	change 1975-87	1983-87
Men	357,942	397,469	387,325	N/A	384,702	7%	N/A
Women	267,221	355,757	408,820	N/A	374,078	40%	N/A
Total	625,163	753,226	796,145	784,297	758,780	21%	−3%

General
NALGO is the largest white collar trade union in Britain and is the fourth largest union in the TUC. NALGO was originally an organisation for white collar employees of local authorities and included administrative, technical, clerical, and professional workers. When the creation of new nationalised industries and the transfer of functions to national organisations took certain services away from local government, NALGO followed its members into the new industries and authorities. Consequently it now organises workers in the National Health Service, the gas industry, electricity supply, water industry, road passenger transport, British Waterways Board, new towns, and universities.

NALGO membership covers a wide range of occupations: lawyers, accountants, engineers, architects, town planners, social workers, librarians, nurses, technicians, computer staff, administrators, telephonists, typists, and clerks. It includes low paid workers and a good number of highly paid workers. Over two-thirds of NALGO membership is located in local government.

NALGO has experienced a remarkable growth in membership in the post-war period. When the union affiliated to the TUC in 1964 it had a membership of 338,322. Between 1965 and 1982 it increased its membership at a rate of 30,000 a year; and during the 1970s it almost doubled its membership. Between 1975 and 1987, NALGO membership increased by 21 per cent, with a massive 40 per cent rise in the female membership. However, between 1983 and 1987 NALGO membership declined overall by three per cent and it was only in 1987 after five years of decline, that it registered its first modest increase.

In order to deal with the membership decline, NALGO launched a recruitment campaign in 1987 targeting branches with high levels of potential membership. Further, at the union Annual Conference in 1988, NALGO voted to end the union's traditional restriction of membership and recruit manual workers for the first time in its history. This move is an attempt to counter the loss of membership through the growth of single union deals in public services.

The restriction on recruiting manual workers has lost the union hundreds of members in the privatised bus industry. Previously, NALGO had representation on the National Bus Company NJC and joint standing committees, but privatisation created small groups of workers with different skills for whom it made sense to be represented by one union. NALGO therefore was forced to stand down and let other unions step in. However, Deputy General Secretary, Alan Jinkinson made it clear that NALGO has no intention of poaching other unions' members nor does it want to become another general union. It is likely that the privatisation of other services, like refuse collection and street cleaning, will also lead to more single union deals. The change to the membership eligibility rule will enable NALGO to avoid the situation that occurred in the bus privatisation.

NALGO is party to the staff side of the National Joint Council for Local Authorities' Administrative, Professional, Technical, and Clerical Services and also the National Joint Councils for staff grades, together with all the Whitley councils of all the public services, nationalised industries, and newly privatised industries such as gas.

In a survey carried out in 1987 by the Royal National Institute for the Deaf, NALGO was only one of two unions (BIFU was the other) which had recognised and taken steps to deal with the needs of deaf workers.

NALGO now has five representatives on the TUC General Council: the General Secretary, John Daly, and Rita Donaghy, Ada Maddocks, Norrie Steele, and Alan Jinkinson.

History

The main impetus to the foundation of NALGO came from Herbert Blain, a 26-year-old clerk in the Town Clerk's Department in Liverpool. He founded the *Liverpool Officers' Guild* in 1896 "to provide a means for social intercourse among its members and, for their improvement, advancement and recreation, also to promote a knowledge of the principles of local government". This guild became an efficiently run and effective friendly society. Blain moved to London and found that the equivalent organisation there was moribund, and he proposed the formation of a comprehensive national organisation of municipal officers. Thus it was that the National Association of Local Government Officers was set up in 1905.

NALGO started with 8,000 members, made rapid progress, and by 1914 its membership of almost 35,000 covered nearly 70 per cent of all government officers. The organisation in its early days could hardly be described as a trade union. In 1911, NALGO's first full-time General Secretary, Levi Hill wrote in the association's journal "anything savouring of trade unionism is nausea to the local government officer and his association".

During the First World War NALGO underwent a crisis in organisation and finances with the loss of most of its guild officers and members to the war effort. This crisis forced NALGO into a reorganisation which resulted in 1) a new NEC of 24 district representatives to replace the former National Council of some 200 guild representatives; 2) an annual delegate conference; 3) an organising secretary; 4) an expanded and improved journal; 5) a new subscription scale; and 6) a new statement of policy which, while still not actually mentioning salaries, set out as its main objective the creation of an "adequate and efficient local government service". The Whitley Committee Report in 1917 served to lay down the principles on which all of NALGO's negotiating structure is now based, although it was not until 1943 that the National Whitley Council for Local Government was set up and the local government "charter" adopted during 1946 laid down the first national salary scales for local government officers in England and Wales.

NALGO became a certified trade union in 1920, and by 1936 its membership had climbed back to 30,000. Shortly afterwards it absorbed the *National Poor Law Officers Association* and added a further 6,500 members to its ranks.

Immediately after the Second World War, NALGO faced the prospect of a crippling loss of members as the new Labour government set up the National Health, gas, and electricity services by removing those functions from the municipal authorities. In the event, NALGO decided to follow its members into the new services. By 1951 NALGO had 200,000 members but worked in a complex structure of negotiating bodies with an organisation still geared to its old status as a local government union. NALGO solved these organisational problems by setting up separate and largely independent bodies at each of the three levels into which the association was divided: employer-based branches, and district, and national service conditions committees. In 1952 NALGO changed its name to its present title to reflect its widening membership outside local government.

In 1961 NALGO added a strike clause to its constitution — although it was not until 1970 that it was forced into its first official strike involving 18 members of the Leeds branch in a dispute over the application of a local bonus and incentive scheme. NALGO affiliated to the TUC in 1964, some 43 years, 12 conference debates and six membership ballots after it was first suggested.

Over the years NALGO has grown as follows:

1928 — 43,602
1938 — 101,041
1948 — 170,960
1958 — 264,576
1968 — 366,951
1978 — 709,331

(See "Membership trends" for more recent developments.)

The post-war growth is a reflection not only of the growth of white collar unionisation generally, but also the growth of the public services sector. Between 1952 and 1965, total white collar staff employed in the industries NALGO organised went up by about 12 per cent — but NALGO membership increased by 57 per cent.

Today, although NALGO is still the dominant union in local government, it is not the only union organising white collar staffs in the non-governmental public services. With the decline in union membership in the eighties, competition amongst the various unions such as COHSE, NUPE, GMB, MSF, ACTSS, which also organise alongside NALGO, has increased. With this in mind, talks have begun on a possible merger with the other major local government union NUPE. COHSE has at the time of publication also indicated that it too might consider a possible merger with NALGO and NUPE which would create a union of over 1.2m members with dominant rights in local government and the Health Service.

Union officials
NALGO employs around 620 full-time officers, some 270 of whom are deployed in its 12 district offices. Each district office is headed by a district organisation officer.

Despite the large number of women members, female full-time officers are rare, with the exception of a handful of district officers (see "Women"). NALGO officials tend to come from within the union's own ranks and to have served as branch officers for a number of years. NALGO salaries for full-time officials are fairly high by trade union standards.

The union also recruits ex-students from Ruskin College and other industrial relations academic institutions such as Warwick University and the LSE. NALGO work-place activity still largely remains underdeveloped, and there is thus a high dependence on the services of district officials.

Coverage
Joint bodies upon which NALGO is represented include:

Local government staffs
National Joint Council for Administrative, Professional Technical and Clerical Services (NJC-APT&C)
National Joint Council for Administrative, Professional Technical and Clerical Services (Scottish Council)
Joint Negotiating Committee for Chief Officers of Local Authorities
Joint Negotiating Committee for Chief Officials of Local Authorities (Scotland)
Joint Negotiating Committee for the Probation Service

University staffs
Central Council for Non-Teaching Staffs
Joint Committee for Clerical and certain related Administrative Staffs
Joint Committee for Computer Operating Staffs

Education
Joint Negotiating Committee for Youth and Community Workers

Staff in new towns in England and Wales
Whitley Council for New Towns Staff

Industrial Estates Corporation and Development Agencies in England and Wales
Whitley Council for the Staffs of the Development Agencies and Development Board for Rural Wales

National Health Service
General Whitley Council, and the following functional councils:
  Administrative and Clerical Staffs Council
  Ambulance Officers Joint Negotiating Committee of Administrative and Clerical Staffs Council
  Professional and Technical Council "B"
  Nursing and Midwifery Staffs Negotiating Council
  Professions Allied to Medicine and Related Grades of Staff (PTA) Council

Electricity supply
National Joint Council (NJC)
National Joint Managerial and Higher Executive Grades Committee (NJMC)

Gas supply
British Gas National Joint Council for Gas Staffs and Senior Officers (NJC)
British Gas National Joint Council for Higher Management

Water supply
National Joint Staff Council for the Water Industry (NJSC)
Joint National Council for Chief and Senior Officers for the Water Industry (JNC)

Transport
National Joint Council for British Waterways' Salaried Staff (NJC)

NALGO also negotiates a national agreement with Passenger Transport Authorities.

(See "Recent issues and key changes to joint bodies" for developments in bargaining arrangements.)

Organisation
The government of NALGO is vested in the Annual Conference which may issue an instruction to the National Executive Council and is responsible for the direction of the general policy of NALGO.

The National Executive Council of NALGO is vested with full authority and power to manage the business of the union subject to Conference direction. The NEC is elected annually in districts by individual ballot with papers distributed through branches. The turn-out often approaches 50 per cent — high by trade union standards generally. It has the power to issue instructions to the membership to take industrial action if it considers it to be appropriate but this power can also be exercised by Conference. The current industrial action which NALGO members are pursuing (see "Recent Events"), was made by order of the NEC.

NALGO is organised into 12 districts each of which elects its own district council which is representative of the branches in each district. Each branch is a constituency for the purpose of electing members of the NEC. The Annual Conference comprises two delegates from each district council as well as representatives elected by the branches in proportion to their membership. There is also provision for the representation of sectional and professional organisations. There are 1,200 active branches within NALGO.

A distinctive feature of NALGO is the extent to which its membership participates in its government — which is based on a committee structure at all levels in the union.

Work-place activity
Despite the high level of involvement in union affairs by NALGO members compared with other unions, work-place activity has until recently been largely undeveloped. NALGO branch secretaries often deal (and have dealt) directly with the local authority, but the branch secretary comes into the particular department as an outside union representative and not as a work-place negotiator.

Following the decision of the 1977 Annual Conference to set up a "steward" system, and the NEC circular in 1978 which urged departmental representatives "to be responsible to and for a particular group of members and negotiate on behalf of this group and individuals within the group", most branches have now authorised the election of staff representatives (shop stewards). However, the 1988 rule book still gives them no formal recognition. It is apparent that NALGO leadership sees the development of work-place representatives not as a "radical upheaval" but as a "logical evolutionary development", and that the union hierarchy intends to keep a tight control on its eventual shape and form.

Women

Women constitute over 50 per cent of NALGO's membership. An equal opportunities committee sits in an advisory capacity within the union.

A report published by NALGO in 1981 entitled *Equality* concluded that women are still predominantly treated as "a secondary labour force". The survey was carried out by the Sociological Research Unit of University College, Cardiff in conjunction with NALGO Research Section. In 1988 NALGO commissioned the Trade Union Research Unit to examine the extent of low pay experienced by NALGO members. The report disclosed that 67 per cent of APT&C staff are low paid and cited evidence that many low paid are being forced to "take a second job just to make ends meet". Much publicity was given to the findings of the survey in NALGO's monthly *Public Service* (June 1989), yet the connection between low pay and gender was curiously omitted from its report.

NALGO was at the time of publication involved in a pay dispute with local authorities (see "Recent Events"), pressing for a flat rate increase of £1,200 a year or 12 per cent, whichever is greater. Part of the reason for the claim is to help low paid workers, most of whom are women: figures show that 14 per cent of male APT&C staff earn less than £150 per week, whereas 45 per cent of women fall below that figure; average pay of women APT&C staff is less than 70 per cent of their male colleagues' earnings. It is worth returning to the conclusions reached by the 1981 survey *Equality* which said that women "are less well qualified, earn less money, and are concentrated in the typing/secretarial grades. They are less likely to ask for employer-sponsored training or promotion/regrading and are less likely to get either...far from winning the battle for equality, women's position has deteriorated in the last six years". These conclusions are no less pertinent in 1989.

An industrial tribunal ruling in May 1989 could have implications for many women working in local authorities throughout the country. The tribunal ruled that a woman employed in a social services department was doing work of equal value to a man employed in a transport or engineering department who was on a higher pay scale. NALGO General Secretary, John Daly, suggested that there exists enormous potential for similar cases throughout Britain.

NALGO now sends delegates to the Women's TUC which overturns a previous NALGO ruling which stated that women are part of the mainstream labour movement and that special conferences for women are divisive. During the 1989 Women's TUC, NALGO delegates backed a motion calling on unions to secure the highest provision for women at work and to take advantage of the process of economic integration in the European Community. Further, delegates made demands for women's rights to be incorporated in a European charter.

NALGO held its first national women's conference in May 1989. Conference voted by a slender margin to allow the women's conference the right to submit motions directly to the full Conference without going to branches. However, the proposal for the chair of the National Women's Rights Committee to have a reserved seat on the NEC with full voting rights was not supported.

Ada Maddocks (national officer, health staff), a member of the TUC General Council, is to become TUC chair after Congress meets in September 1989. She is the first person from NALGO to assume the chair. Rita Donaghy, TUC General Council and NEC member, is 1989/90 NALGO President.

External relations
NALGO is the largest union within the TUC that is not affiliated to the Labour Party. However, a firm campaign is underway to alter this anomaly.

Political affiliation has always been an issue present throughout NALGO's history. NALGO did not affiliate to the TUC until 1964 on the grounds of its "association with the Labour Party". Its rules provide that no district council or branch official may affiliate to any organisation (apart from trades councils) "which is associated directly or indirectly with any particular party or organisation".

The issue of political affiliation to the Labour Party first went to a ballot of the membership in 1982. The NEC had originally voted 29 to 20, with 19 members absent, against affiliation, although the 1981 NALGO Conference voted against this position and decided to hold a ballot. In the event 49,925 members voted "yes" for affiliation, and 382,577 voted no. However, the 1988 Conference voted to ballot the union's membership on setting up a political fund, as required by the 1984 Trade Union Act. The result of the ballot was that in a 67 per cent turn-out, 393,006 members voted in favour of a fund (77.5 per cent of those voting, or 51.8 per cent of the union's total membership), with 114,645 against (22.5 per cent of those voting, 15.1 per cent of the total). After voting to create a political fund for the first time in the union's history, NALGO leaders almost immediately launched a directly political lobbying campaign for affiliation to the Labour Party.

During the 1987 general election NALGO produced a document *Make People Matter,* but the Conservative Trade Unionists organisation claimed that this was designed to persuade people not to vote Tory and obtained High Court orders which prevented NALGO campaigning on behalf of public services. The Court said that NALGO did not have a political fund which is a requirement under the 1913 Trade Union Act.

NALGO keeps in regular contact with European Community affairs through its membership on various committees, its consultant members of the European Parliament, and with the Trade Union Information Division of the Commission of the European Communities. Also, Ada Maddocks attends meetings of the Economic and Social Committee of the European Communities in her capacity as TUC representative.

NALGO maintains a large and active international relations committee which seeks to ensure that the union's views have world-wide representation wherever necessary. Some of the organisations to which NALGO is affiliated include:
Action for Benefits
Amnesty International
Anti-Apartheid Movement
CND
Campaign for Press and Broadcasting Freedom
Child Poverty Action Group
European Network for Women
Public Services International
International Transport Workers Federation
Royal Institute of International Affairs
National Museum of Labour History
War on Want
National Council for Civil Liberties
European Union of Local Authority Staff
Chile Solidarity Campaign

NALGO

Recent issues and key changes to joint bodies
Some recent issues and changes to joint bodies and industries upon which NALGO is represented include:

National Health Service
All existing Whitley Council pay bargaining arrangements in the National Health Service are under review following the government's intention to radically restructure the service and run it on business lines. Moreover, the government's restructuring scheme, whereby hospitals are in effect privatised by opting out of the NHS, fragments national pay bargaining. The Department of Health announced in November 1988 that up to 7,000 middle managers in the NHS may be removed from pay negotiating machinery as a result of the move towards performance-related pay. The proposal is that individual managers, including deputy managers of hospitals, health authority middle managers, and senior nursing officers, will be allowed to continue to have their pay based on Whitley Council rates, but will be encouraged to sign new contracts based on flexible pay scales set by the Health Department.

In March 1989, the government announced its proposal for the 110,000 workers covered by the administrative and clerical staff council. The proposal provided scope for limited pay flexibility based on performance or region, and before the end of 1989, all staff will be assimilated on to a single pay spine. A wage rise is to be given to all staff on joining the spine. At the 1989 Conference NALGO delegates agreed to accept a 9.5 per cent pay award and to go along with the restructuring exercise.

A wide-ranging report by the House of Commons' Social Services Select Committee, *Resourcing the NHS: Whitley Councils,* Volumes I and II (HMSO, March 1989), cautioned against moves to break down national pay bargaining with a shift towards local and performance-based pay systems. The report adds that introducing greater flexibility should only be allowed within a national system of pay bargaining, as local pay bargaining could lead to a wage spiral with districts outbidding one another to attract scarce resources.

Gas industry
There have been no formal changes to either the National Joint Council for Staffs and Senior Officers (NJCSSO), or the National Joint Council for Higher Management (NJCHM). However, in June 1989 British Gas announced plans to introduce performance related pay for all of its 3,800 higher managers covered by the NJCHM. NALGO policy is that this can be considered provided that any new scheme does not replace or undermine the existing status and coverage of the NJCHM agreement. NALGO is also concerned to retain a role in the process of setting targets, and rights in the event of those targets not being achieved.

The privatisation of British Gas preserved the unity of the industry which helped retain the NJC bargaining machinery. NALGO's fear is that British Gas could be fragmented once the present chairman, Sir Denis Rooke retires.

Water industry
The major issue is privatisation. NALGO has played a leading role against water privatisation. However, their efforts have not been helped by the water authorities' use of the Financial Services Act. NALGO has repeatedly asked the water authorities for information about their industry, but the authorities have used Section 47 of the Act to curb the release of information about the state of the industry prior to privatisation.

The National Joint Council for Water Service Staff came to an end in August 1989. In future NALGO will negotiate separately with the regional water authorities, or businesses, as they now refer to themselves, in the build up to privatisation.

Universities and higher education

Universities, polytechnics, and colleges of higher education are increasingly under pressure to be more "responsive" to consumer demand. Colleges operating under the PCFC umbrella are already talking in terms of a devolved, even individual college system of pay bargaining. Universities will not be able to withstand similar moves for long. NALGO's national pay bargaining status must be under threat.

Transport

As previously mentioned, NALGO has already lost formal negotiating rights in the privatised bus industry because NALGO rules did not allow it to recruit manual workers (see "General").

A key issue which is emerging in the bus industry concerns the government's intention to sell off passenger transport authority operations under the proposed Employee Share Ownership Scheme or ESOP (see "Policy"). At the time of publication there had only been two such buy-outs, but NALGO's national transport committee foresees this as being a major issue in the early 1990s.

Local government

A report produced in 1987 by LASCAB, the local authorities employers' secretariat, indicated that whilst Whitleyism, the joint national pay bargaining machinery, should continue, there ought to be greater scope for regional variation. In particular, the need for greater local discretion where national bargaining sets minimum rates, and the need to locate pay bargaining within a wider employer personnel strategy, were the two key aspects highlighted by the report.

In the area of union derecognition, the employers' commitment to the principle of collective bargaining must be welcomed; nonetheless the report does give some room for concern. Acknowledging that local government has prided itself on being a good employer the report adds that "the constant search for improved efficiency, encouragement of a more aggressive and entrepreneurial style of management...have led to a feeling that this "good employer" approach to conditions of service and industrial relations procedures can inhibit rather than assist in the effective delivery of services."

Electricity industry

The Electricity Council announced in May 1989 that it will set up a new umbrella organisation, the Electricity Association, to deal with central issues for the industry. These will include public relations, co-operation between electricity companies, and health and safety. However, details regarding pay negotiations are still not available.

NALGO is facing a recruitment crisis in the electricity supply industry. Union membership has declined dramatically in the past five years at a time when staffing levels in the industry are increasing. Over the past five years NALGO's share in the industry has declined from 85 per cent to 76 per cent with certain areas such as Southern suffering a massive drop of nearly 22 per cent. NALGO has agreed a package of measures to recruit and retain new members.

The impending electricity privatisation will pose a further threat to NALGO's negotiating position as newly privatised companies are likely to reconsider whether formal recognition of NALGO for collective bargaining purposes is appropriate.

NALGO, along with other unions, pulled out of equal opportunity talks with employers. The unions had been pressing for an improved maternity/paternity leave package. NALGO negotiators blamed the managements' "fear of doing anything to upset the future privatised employers" as causing the deadlock in the talks.

Policy

NALGO has gradually come to see itself more as a trade union than a professional organisation. It has recognised the inevitability of the need to take industrial action and, as a result of the government dismantling the public sector in the eighties, NALGO has become increasingly politicised (see "External relations").

NALGO members are often the first line of defence against public sector privatisations and dilutions and its policies have increasingly reflected these anxieties.

The government is increasingly putting pressure on public authorities to run public services more like private enterprises and a growing popular response is ESOP or employee share ownership plans, also hailed as a "popular socialism". These buy-out schemes offer employees a share in the company, job protection, and help to fend off predatory asset-strippers. Transport passenger authorities are particularly interested in ESOP because legislation is threatening to break up the large metropolitan bus services authorities and sell their off on the open market. The Yorkshire Transport Authority succumbed in 1989 to ESOP and authorities in the West Midlands and Merseyside are also investigating it. Hospitals could also be threatened by ESOP as a result of opting-out of the NHS.

NALGO takes a pragmatic stance on ESOP. Whilst recognising the fears that unions could be marginalised in an ESOP with company profits linked to employees' shares, NALGO takes the view that if privatisation is inevitable then ESOP provides a "more socially and economically acceptable way of achieving the transition from public to private ownership avoiding the worst aspects of privatisation". As one district officer suggested, if ESOP makes a small number of people millionaires "maybe that is the price we have to pay for securing jobs and retaining union involvement".

On issues such as the government's £1.5bn Employment Training Programme, NALGO, along with the TGWU, spearheaded the attack which led to the eventual TUC withdrawal from the scheme at the 1988 Congress (see **TUC**). NALGO has also played a major part in raising the "green" issue to the fore of the political arena.

However, despite these excursions into, and important contributions to, "political life", Labour Party affiliation is still a thorny unresolved question dividing the union.

Recent events

NUPE/NALGO merger

The 1989 NALGO Annual Conference endorsed an NEC interim report about a possible merger with NUPE. By rejecting a demand that NALGO should seek to assert its own constitutional and structural identity as a model for the proposed merged union, delegates have in effect told the NEC that they want the merger to take place. The interim report proposes that after intensive discussions, the two unions will produce a "white paper" which will be debated at their respective conferences in 1990. Combining the two unions would create Britain's largest union with nearly 1.5m members. Both unions have a growing female membership, often share employers, and "face identical attacks". One possible obstacle to the merger is NALGO's strong tradition of party political neutrality, while NUPE holds dear its affiliation to the Labour Party.

Should the merger take place, COHSE, which organises mainly in the Health Service, has indicated that it might also consider joining. Merging these three unions would do much to rationalise the union arrangements in the public sector. However, as a result of current privatisation of the public services and "opt-outs" from the public sector, it is increasingly likely that the outcome of the proposed merger of these public sector unions will be to create a single service union organising in the private sector rather than simply a more unified public sector structure.

General Secretary election
In July 1989 John Daly surprisingly announced his retirement as General Secretary of NALGO. The new General Secretary will be elected by all the members in a secret postal ballot, from nominations put forward by the union's councils and branches as well as the National Executive. This move to directly elect the successor to John Daly was overwhelmingly backed by delegates at the 1989 Conference against the wishes of the leadership.

The NEC wanted to introduce a "confirmatory election" system where the membership merely endorsed the NEC's candidate. This would have maintained NALGO's tradition of the General Secretary being charged with carrying out the policy decided by elected representatives. The NEC wanted minimal change to comply with the law, but conference decided on a secret ballot. As one delegate put it "we should no longer pretend that the General Secretary is simply an administrator who runs the bureaucratic machinery. He is a leader and as such, should be elected".

NALGO identity
In line with a number of the larger unions, NALGO has been seeking to improve its "corporate" image. A new logo was designed depicting three green hands "raised in a salute of affirmation" over the word NALGO. However, the 1989 Conference decided to reject it, despite already having spent £50,000. The staunchest critic of the "green hands" was Jim White, NEC member from Scotland who, at the Conference, said he spoke from a lifelong position of abhorrence to religious intolerance. Only Scotland had objected to the logo when the publicity committee discussed the logo with its districts.

First national strike
At the time of publication NALGO was involved in its first ever national strike. In a national ballot over 60 per cent of NALGO members had voted in favour of taking industrial action against a seven per cent pay offer and plans to give the 500 local authorities more flexibility in applying national agreements. NALGO's claim is for £1,200 or 12 per cent, whichever is greater.

There are two problems which have led to this dispute. Firstly, local authorities are finding it difficult to recruit certain professional staff who are in short supply, such as town planners, computer staff, accountants, environmental health officers, because public sector pay is no longer competitive. The attractive pay packages which the private sector now offer are tempting many of these workers away from public service. In 1988 some local authorities reported a 21 per cent leaving rate of staff earning £15,000 or over. As an incentive not to leave, some authorities have proposed to introduce "loyalty clauses", but this is unlikely to have any marked effect as it is directed only at existing staff. Furthermore, town halls have found it increasingly difficult to recruit the staff they need to set up and administrate the new community charge or poll tax. The second problem concerns the low paid white collar staff who, because of inflation, are simply no longer able (or prepared) to tolerate the low wages they receive.

Government cut-backs in the public sector have brought about a crisis in local government which has created resentment in the normally moderate NALGO membership. The previous edition of this directory suggested that in the past "NALGO was reluctant to back up its wage claims with industrial action"; recent events demonstrate that the face and structure of the union may be changing.

Further references

Alec Spoor, *White Collar Union — Sixty Years of NALGO,* Heinemann, 1967.

C.G.E. Neill, "NALGO and the development of occupational associations in local government", *Industrial Relations Journal,* 1979. A good account illustrating the uneasy alliance of sectional occupational interest groups within the union.

D. Volker, "NALGO affiliation to the TUC", *British Journal of Industrial Relations,* 4, no. 1, March 1966.

George Newman, *Path to Maturity: NALGO 1965-1980,* NALGO, 1982.

Nigel Nicholson et al., *Dynamics of White Collar Trade Unionism,* Academic Press, 1981.

NALHM
NATIONAL ASSOCIATION OF LICENSED
HOUSE MANAGERS

TUC affiliated

Head Office: 9 Coombe Lane, Raynes Park, London SW20 8NE

Telephone: 01-947 3080

Principal officer
General Secretary: John Madden

Union journal: Pub Manager (produced quarterly)

Membership

Current membership (1987)
Male: 8,400
Female: 4,400
Total: 12,800

Membership trends

	1975	1979	1981	1983	1987	change 1975-87	1983-87
Men	9,969	11,088	11,643	11,038	8,400	−16%	−24%
Women	2,218	5,334	6,111	5,914	4,400	98%	−26%
Total	12,187	16,422	17,754	16,952	12,800	5%	−24%

General
The union was formed in 1969, prior to which managers' interests were represented by the managers' section of the National Federation of Licensed Victuallers. It affiliated to

the TUC in September 1975 and is represented on the TUC's Hotel and Catering Industry Committee.

From 1975-7 NALHM was engaged in a long running jurisdiction dispute with the Transport and General Workers' Union over the right to recruit pub managers in the Birmingham area. Trouble chiefly centred around a pub called the Fox and Goose, blacked by the TGWU, which became known as the "pub with no beer". In the end the ruling of the TUC disputes committee under the Bridlington Principles was endorsed by Conference and the TGWU accepted the ruling.

Union membership is open to all managers and their spouses of licensed houses, off-licences, and steak bars, and the union has sole bargaining rights for licensed house managers with the major breweries. The membership of the NALHM is gradually declining and in 1987 it recorded its lowest membership figure since it affiliated to the TUC in 1975.

There are 153 branches organised into eight regions, each with a full-time officer. There is an Annual Conference in April. A regional committee composed of delegates from branches serves each region, and the regional committee appoints its representatives to serve on the National Committee. The Executive and Finance Committee consists of the national officers plus three members elected from the National Committee.

Recent events
In March 1989 the Monopolies and Mergers Commission published a major report on the brewing industry with the recommendation that the brewers should sell off a proportion of their licensed houses in order to increase competition in the industry. This recommendation might have gone some way to relieving NALHM members from the somewhat feudal ties which presently exist between them and their landlord breweries. But Lord Young, the Secretary of State for Trade and Industry, bowed to pressure from the big brewers and decided not to implement the MMC recommendation.

NAPO
NATIONAL ASSOCIATION OF PROBATION OFFICERS
TUC affiliated

Head Office: 3/4 Chivalry Road, London SW11 1HT

Telephone: 01-223 4887

Principal officers and responsibilities
General Secretary (Chief Negotiator, Officers JNC): Bill Beaumont
Assistant General Secretary (Press, Media, and Campaigning): Harry Fletcher
Assistant General Secretary (Ancillary JNC, Conditions of Service): Mike Somers
Research and Information: Pete Bowyer

Union journal: NAPO Journal (quarterly, free to all members)

Membership

Current membership (1987)
Male: 3,412
Female: 2,898
Total: 6,310

General
NAPO organises probation officers and ancillary staff connected with the probation service, as well as some social workers and probation-approved hostel workers and their supervisors. Although NAPO registered as an independent trade union in 1976, and did not join the TUC until 1984, it originated as a professional association in 1912, in response to the Probation of Offenders Act 1908.

NAPO is the sole union on the staff side of the long-standing JNC for Probation Officers. The JNC regulates pay and conditions of service for probation officers. Pay and conditions for ancillary staff are subject to a separate Ancillaries Sub-Committee, established in 1980, which also includes NALGO. But national bargaining of pay and conditions for ancillary workers is supplemented by a strong component of local pay bargaining which takes place in the 56 probation committee areas of England and Wales. In both of these national committees there is provision for either side to refer a difference to ACAS for submission to arbitration. A separate JNC for trainee probation officers was established with the Home Office in 1984.

Organisation
The supreme policy-making body of NAPO is the General Meeting, held annually, and attendance is open to all members. The National Executive Committee carries out the business of the union in between the annual meetings. The 39-member NEC consists of the officers of the union, namely the chair, the three vice-chairs and treasurer, and a representative, elected by secret ballot, from each of the union's 34 branches. There is provision for an Anti-Racism Monitoring Committee which reports to the NEC. Each branch also annually elects an anti-racism officer who liaises with the committee to ensure that union policy on racism is being carried out (see "Policy").

The officers of the union are elected annually by a national postal ballot; an amendment to the rule book was being considered at the time of publication to elect the General Secretary in a similar manner.

External relations
The union does not have a political fund but the rule book was changed by Conference in 1987 to allow a future ballot to be taken.

Policy
NAPO has a major policy stance on racism both in the probation service and in the wider social context. It has produced a manifesto for anti-racist practice which is supported by rule 17 of NAPO's constitution: "racist behaviour shall be deemed to be in breach of the objects of the Association; a member who displays such behaviour shall be liable to disciplinary action in accordance with the procedures".

The union opposed the Alton Bill to amend the Abortion Act in 1988.

Recent events
In August 1989, NAPO wrote to the Home Office to seek assurances that there were to be no major decisions taken in the next three years about the future of the probation service. NAPO is concerned that the government is contemplating wholesale reorganisation of the service as indicated in a Green Paper published in 1988. The Green Paper contained plans to introduce electronic "tagging" of offenders, the privatisation of hostels and drug abuse centres now run by the probation service, and reorganisation of the present 56 probation areas into a national service divided into large regional units. If the government were to go ahead with their proposals then NAPO is likely to lose professional influence as well as national bargaining status.

NASUWT
NATIONAL ASSOCIATION OF SCHOOLMASTERS AND UNION OF WOMEN TEACHERS

TUC affiliated

Head Office: Hillscourt, Rose Hill, Rednal, Birmingham B45 8RS

Telephone: 021-453 6150

Fax: 021-435 72224

Principal national officers
General Secretary: Fred Smithies
Deputy General Secretary and General Secretary Elect: Nigel de Gruchy
Assistant General Secretary: Bill Herron
Assistant Secretary Salaries and Conditions of Service: Frank Howard
Assistant Secretary Education: Henry Iven
Assistant Secretary Membership: Barry Gandy

Union journal and publications: Schoolmaster and Career Teacher (monthly). *School Representatives Handbook.*

Membership

Current membership (1987)
Male: 65,144
Female: 55,400
Total: 120,544

Membership trends

	1975	1979	1981	1983	1987	change 1975-87	change 1983-87
Men	65,952	81,372	N/A	72,849	65,144	−1%	−11%
Women	16,761	40,686	N/A	46,819	55,400	231%	18%
Total	82,713	122,058	119,545	119,668	120,544	46%	1%

General

NASUWT members are qualified teachers in all types of schools and colleges, excluding universities in England, Wales, Scotland, and Northern Ireland. It is the second largest teachers' union, and whilst it does have membership distributed throughout the secondary field, the largest group is among specialist teachers in secondary education. Since 1984, however, the primary sector has been the most significant area of membership growth.

The status of the teaching profession during the eighties has been steadily eroded and has recently undergone dramatic changes in terms of its collective bargaining arrangements as well as conditions of service (See **NUT**). During the drawn-out campaign of industrial action between 1984 and 1986 the NASUWT often tried to appear to be more militant than its main rival, the NUT. Rather than seeking to unite a rather fragmented profession and explore the possibility of a merger, the NASUWT is determined to maintain its independent status.

The union has now dropped the diagonal stroke between "NAS" and "UWT" and its abbreviation is simply NASUWT.

History

The NAS was formed in 1919 by men returning from the war who were disillusioned by the prospect of depressed salaries for schoolmasters and who broke away from the NUT because of hostility to its tendencies towards equal pay for women. The UWT was formed in 1965 as a totally independent union by women teachers, but through the development of mutual objectives the two associations grew together eventually leading to a merger in 1975, 10 years after the formation of the UWT.

Organisation

Members are assigned to local associations (branches) within the areas covered by their employing authorities. At present there are just over 400 local associations. Each elects its own officers to serve annually, dealing with members' problems in so far as these relate to local conditions. The local association also sends out regular information bulletins to its members, and a developing function relates to supervising the appointment of school representatives and briefing them on the handling of day-to-day problems within schools.

Local associations within the area of an education authority combine in a federation to represent their collective views, to consult and negotiate with their employers. The local associations also combine to form the 32 executive districts which elect one or more members each to serve on the National Executive. This meets once a month either as an Executive or as committees — for education, salaries and pensions, legal aid and benevolent fund, training, recruitment, and membership.

An Annual Delegate Conference is held each Easter. Delegates are appointed on a pro-rata basis by local associations and the Conference is the supreme policy-making body of the NASUWT. Between conferences, and subject to Conference decisions, the Executive is responsible for running the NASUWT.

The General Secretary is the chief negotiator at national level. There is also a Deputy

General Secretary, one Assistant General Secretary and three other assistant secretaries who are responsible for specific areas of union administration, such as finance, membership, education, salaries, pensions, and conditions of service.

At the time of publication precise details were not available of the changes under consideration by the NASUWT to its internal organisational structure which would deal with the proposed changes to collective bargaining arrangements. The introduction of local school management arising out of the Educational Reform Act is likely to increase the role of work-place negotiations.

Women

The proportion of women in the NASUWT has risen steadily over the last decade and women now make up over 45 per cent of the association's total membership.

Following a motion at the 1987 Conference, the NASUWT set up an Equal Opportunities Committee. This is made up from the standing committees of the Executive so that the work of the EOC can filter through the work of the other committees. The association has compiled a model equal opportunities policy for negotiation with the LEAs, and following a survey into the nature of sexual harassment at work, it has devised a model policy in order to deal with this issue.

Work is also in progress on drawing up a "Managed Career Breaks Scheme". The scheme is designed to guarantee that a woman will be able to return to her previous duties after having a baby. "Returners", as they are known, have become increasingly important in maintaining the level of teachers throughout the eighties. Career breaks are expected to increase in the next few years as employers will have to put even more emphasis on retaining women staff in the face of the expected downturn in young people entering the labour market thereby making recruitment more difficult.

External relations

The association is affiliated to the TUC and traditionally has been officially "non-political" and "non-sectarian". However, delegates at the 1989 Conference agreed to ballot members on whether to set up a political fund.

The NASUWT has recently established contact with other teaching unions in Europe through membership of the European Trade Union Committee for Education (ETUCE), and the IFFTU Committee for Europe (ICE), and on the international front through affiliation to the International Federation of Free Teachers' Unions (IFFTU).

Policy

The NASUWT takes a softer line than its rival, the NUT, on the government policy to introduce "licensed" teachers. The 1989 Conference agreed that the union should welcome all sorts of people who wish to become teachers and voted against both industrial action and a boycott of the training that qualified teachers will be required to give the recruits. Union rules permit the recruitment of licensed teachers. This represents a major split with the other large teachers' union, the NUT (see **NUT**).

At the 1989 Conference the NASUWT backed a call for industrial action in pursuit of a higher pay claim for the following year. The union is still keen to maintain a more militant profile in contrast to the "new realism" being advocated by the NUT. Any other line would make its commitment to independence less credible. The NASUWT agreed to meet the NUT under the auspices of the TUC only if the idea of merging the two unions was kept off the agenda.

The NASUWT is keen to develop an anti-racist policy and has already compiled an extensive background document on the subject. It has also enlisted the help of the Equal Opportunities Commission in carrying out this work.

Recent events
The NASUWT General Secretary, Fred Smithies, is due to retire in 1990. Nigel de Gruchy was elected as his replacement by 27,092 to 12,856 votes on a 37 per cent turnout. He will take over the job at Easter in 1990.

The NASUWT must take seriously the proposed announcement of merger talks between the two non-TUC unions PAT and AMMA, for if they succeed, the new organisation with around 170,000 members will push NASUWT into third place. The differences between the NASUWT and the NUT are smaller than they are with the other two unions. A merger with the NUT has to be reached if the teaching profession is not to be torn apart even further.

Further reference
R.D. Coates, *Teachers' Unions and Interest Group Politics,* Cambridge University Press, 1972.

NATFHE
NATIONAL ASSOCIATION OF TEACHERS IN FURTHER AND HIGHER EDUCATION
TUC affiliated

Head Office: 27 Britannia Street, London WC1X 9JP

Telephone: 01-837 3636

Fax: 01-837 4403

Principal officers
General Secretary: Geoff Woolf
Education Secretary: D. Batts
Assistant Secretary, Further Education: Vacancy
Assistant Secretary, Higher Education: J. Bocock
Education Officer: P. Bennett
Adult Education Officer: L. Jones
Negotiations Secretary: D. Triesman
Assistant Secretary (Negotiations): J. Munnery
Assistant Secretary (Negotiations): Vacancy
Assistant Secretary (Membership): D. Conroy
Membership Officer: N. Shah
Information Officer: P. Lanning
Journals Editor: D. Gardner
Publication Officer: D. Peart

Union journal: NATFHE Journal (monthly, sent free to all members). *Journal of Further and Higher Education* (three times a year, available on subscription).

Membership

Current membership (1987)
Male: 54,335
Female: 25,583
Total: 79,918

Membership trends

	1975	1979	1981	1983	1987	change 1975-87	1983-87
Men	47,250	50,636	16,288	52,205	54,335	15%	4%
Women	12,500	14,150	68,483	18,576	25,583	105%	38%
Total	59,750	64,786	84,771	70,781	79,918	34%	13%

General
NATFHE is the major union catering for lecturers in public sector further and higher education, the newly privatised polytechnics, and larger colleges of higher education in England and Wales. Its members work in polytechnics, colleges of higher education, institutes of education, colleges of technology, colleges of art, colleges of agriculture, colleges of further education, and adult colleges.

At national level NATFHE is recognised by the government and various local authority associations for collective bargaining purposes in pay and conditions of service, and matters of education. NATFHE occupies the majority of seats on the National Joint Council for Lecturers in Further Education in England and Wales, the formal negotiating body for the pay and conditions of service of lecturers in this sector of public education. NATFHE also has negotiating rights on the Joint Negotiating Committee for Youth and Community Workers.

It is also recognised by the Polytechnics and Colleges Employers' Forum (PCFC), the new employers' organisation set up by polytechnics and other colleges as a result of these institutions being removed from local authority control in April 1989. Negotiating machinery and NATFHE's precise role were still being discussed at the time of publication (see "Recent events").

History
On January 1, 1976, the *Association of Teachers in Colleges and Departments of Education* and the *Association of Teachers in Technical Institutions* amalgamated to form NATFHE. The ATTI had been the first teachers' union to affiliate to the TUC in 1965. NATFHE affiliated to the TUC soon after the amalgamation. More recently, in 1984, the *Association for Adult and Continuing Education* and the *Association of Teachers in Penal Establishments,* two small non-TUC unions, merged with NATFHE.

Organisation
The basic organisational unit of NATFHE is the branch, based on a single college, although a large institution such as a polytechnic may have several branches on the institution's various sites; in such a situation, the branches are linked by a co-ordinating committee. NATFHE liaison committees cover all branches in each local education authority or area.

Branches are organised into 14 regions staffed by a lay regional secretary and treasurer. Each region has a regional council on which all branches in the region are represented. There is a regional Executive Committee for each region.

The Annual Conference is NATFHE's ultimate policy-making body, normally meeting over the Spring Bank Holiday period. It consists of the National Council together with one additional member elected by each regional council for each (complete) 200 voting members of the region.

The National Council decides policy between Annual Conference. The Council consists of the President, Vice-President, ex-President, and Honorary Treasurer, who constitute the officers of the union, and the General Secretary who has no voting rights. Also included are 100 regional representatives and representatives of organisations with joint or reciprocal membership of NATFHE (e.g. EIS, NUT). Council meets at least three times a year; special meetings may be called as required.

The National Executive Committee conducts the business of the association between National Council meetings and Annual Conference. It consists of officers of the union, the General Secretary who is a non-voting member, and 35 representatives annually elected nationally from the 14 regions. Five seats are reserved exclusively for women. There are nine standing committees with representatives appointed from each region which make recommendations to the NEC and National Council, and have delegated powers to act without prior reference to the NEC. The standing committees are as follows:

Higher education
Further education
Teacher education
Art and design education
Adult and continuing education
Part-time lecturers
Race relations
Women's rights
International relations

As a result of the implementation of the Education Reform Act in April 1989 which took the polytechnics and larger colleges of higher education out of local authorities' control and allowed them to take on corporate status, NATFHE has introduced two separate sectoral bodies to reflect the split into public and private (corporate) sectors. The two sectors have been set up on an interim basis and a Structure Working Group has been organised to examine longer term arrangements (see "Recent Events").

Union officials are appointed by the NEC, with the exception of the General Secretary, who is elected by postal ballot every five years.

NATFHE organisational efficiency
In 1987 NATFHE commissioned the Industrial Relations Unit of Warwick University to undertake a study of the union's organisation and functioning. NATFHE had for some time been concerned about the impact which policy-making structures had on the work and responsibilities of Head Office and regional offices. The Warwick team were therefore asked to make recommendations on ways of improving the union's organisational efficiency and effectiveness.

The findings of the Warwick study, presented to the NEC in June 1988, suggested that there were two main sources which limited the union's policy-making process: first, the way in which the three centres of power, the National Council, Conference, and the National Executive Committee related to each other and the regions, as well as the added complication of the introduction of the separate sectoral divisions of representation for higher education (PCFC) and further education (MFHAE). The second aspect which the team suggested caused organisational inefficiency related to the work of the NEC and the proliferation of its sub-committees. Too often sub-committees failed to distinguish between day-to-day management functions and strategic issues.

On the question of Head Office and regional office systems of management, the Warwick team believed that because of the rapidly changing education environment, there was a tendency towards "crisis management" in that there was inadequate co-ordination of work, insufficient delegation of responsibility and accountability, along with poor lines of communication which contributed to a high degree of stress and low morale among staff. New administrative structures, with clearer lines of responsibility were needed, although fine-tuning of existing departments was preferred to any radical matrix-type reorganisation.

After detailed consideration, the Warwick report went on to conclude that NATFHE "should develop a more 'strategic' view of organisational change, expressed ideally in the commitment to some kind of long-term 'Review and Development Programme'". NATFHE was still considering the report at the time of publication.

External relations
As it was formed through the amalgamation of two organisations which between them covered the whole of post-school public education, NATFHE has always been an influential body in education policy-making. It is the main pressure group for promoting the interests of further education from individual college level to the Department of Education and Science. NATFHE has direct access to the Secretary of State for Education and Science and the DES consults NATFHE on major policy issues. In the House of Commons, MPs holding NATFHE membership form a sizeable group.

NATFHE takes an active role in international relations. The 1988 Conference recognised this in a rule change which raised the status of the International Relations Standing Panel to that of a Standing Committee (see "Organisation").

NATFHE recognised the significance of 1992 and the impact which the single European market could make in relation to employment and labour mobility. It could affect the role of lecturers, their professional status, as well as providing opportunities for the harmonisation of qualifications, student exchanges, and collaborative education training and research initiatives. NATFHE is a member of the European Trade Union Committee for Education and its General Secretary is on its executive board.

Other organisations to which NATFHE is affiliated include:
Amnesty International
Anti-Apartheid Movement
British Association for the Advancement of Science
British Association for Commercial and Industrial Education
British Association for Counselling
Campaign Against Berufsverbot
Campaign for Press and Broadcasting Freedom
Central Council of Physical Recreation
Chile Solidarity Campaign
Commonwealth Association for the Education of Adults
Educational Alliance
Joint Council for the Welfare of Immigrants
Maternity Alliance
National Abortion Campaign
NCCL
World Conference of Organisations of the Teaching Profession
World Disarmament Campaign
World University Service

Local branches can affiliate to any of these organisations, but they have to seek NEC approval before affiliating to any other bodies.

NATFHE sent 16 delegates to the 1988 TUC and is represented on the following committees: Women's Advisory Committee, the Arts, Entertainment and Sport Committee, and the Public Services and Local Government Committees.

NATFHE conducted a political fund ballot in 1988 and 19,437 votes supported its establishment with 5,970 against. The political fund came into operation in January 1989.

Women

Women membership has more than doubled since 1975, and has risen by 38 per cent since 1983, representing one of the fastest growing areas of recruitment for NATFHE. The union has developed a comprehensive set of policies on women's rights and education, and has a programme of positive action to encourage its women members. NATFHE is regularly represented at the TUC Women's Conference and in 1988 delegates seconded the EIS motion on International Aid and also spoke in the debate on part-time workers. Trish Leman was successful in being re-elected to the TUC Women's Advisory Committee.

Policy and Recent Events

The single biggest issue facing NATFHE is the creation of the PCFC sector by the Education Act which hived off from local authority control all polytechnics and larger colleges of higher education, affording them corporate status and effectively privatising them. NATFHE has about 17,000 members working in this sector, who were all employed by local authorities with whom NATFHE negotiated pay and conditions of service in the lecturers' NJC but, with the move to corporate status in April 1989, this body has now lost its responsibility for this section of NATFHE.

A new central body, the PCFC, the Polytechnic Central Funding Council, was created to deal with matters of policy and funding for this sector of education. Unlike the previous body NAB, which was broad-based and proceeded on the basis of consensus, membership of the PCFC is drawn from a much narrower group of representatives, dominated by staff appointed from financial and business backgrounds. Consequently, trade union influence has been seriously eroded.

The PCFC has demanded that polytechnics abandon the traditional collegiate system of management, demanding all institutions to prepare strategic plans and mission statements in order to transform the corporate sector into a more aggressive entrepreneurial, business management culture able to compete not just with each other, but also with universities.

The implications for NATFHE are that it now negotiates directly with the Polytechnics and Colleges Employers' Forum. Even before the formal vesting day, April 1, 1989, employers had made their intention to radically overhaul lecturers' contracts widely known. Employers are demanding that lecturers' contracts reflect the new competitive climate in this sector of education and are keen to gain greater local control over lecturers' pay and conditions.

The Annual Conference in 1988 had agreed that new union machinery was needed to consider pay and conditions for the new PFCF sector. Subsequently, National Council established separate meetings for the maintained sector (mainly FE lecturers) and the PFCF sector (HE lecturers). NATFHE might not survive the split.

NATFHE chief negotiating officer, David Triesman, has taken out a writ for libel against a member of the union's National Executive Committee. The polytechnic employers' side had asked Triesman to become their new chief negotiator. Triesman made it known that he had turned the offer down, and informed the General Secretary. None the less Fawzi Ibrahim, a member of the NEC, issued a press statement calling Triesman's conduct into question. Despite the approach being fairly standard practice amongst employers, Fawzi Ibrahim has clearly upset the union's chief negotiator.

In July 1989, the PCFC employers, after much tactical manoeuvring, eventually put forward their plans for lecturers' conditions which include new contracts specifying performance-related pay and greater local management input. NATFHE, whilst in principle accepting the need for new contracts, has agreed to set up working parties to look in detail at the employers' proposals. The threat to national bargaining, and new lecturer contracts, is one to which NATFHE has to respond, but on the basis of the Warwick report, can they?

NCTU
NORTHERN CARPET TRADES UNION

TUC affiliated

Head Office: 22 Claire Road, Halifax HX1 2HX

Telephone: 0422-60492

Principal national officers
General Secretary: K. Edmondson

Membership

Current membership (1987)
Male: 620
Female: 222
Total: 842

Membership trends

	1975	1979	1981	1983	1987	change 1975-87	1983-87
Men	1,706	N/A	1,362	N/A	620	−64%	N/A
Women	483	N/A	300	N/A	222	−54%	N/A
Total	2,189	2,065	1,662	1,010	842	−62%	−17%

The union now believes that the sharp reduction in membership, 62 per cent overall since 1975, has stabilised. In an attempt to rationalise its organisation the union now employs only one full-time officer, the General Secretary, and has reduced its structure from 14 to eight branches. A successful recruitment campaign in two new companies and a drive for new members already in the industry have recently been conducted. Union rules preclude the union from organising workers outside the carpet industry.

General

The union caters for all occupations within the carpet industry — preparation of yarn, design of carpets, the woven and finished product, and in some instances the retailing and fitting of carpet products. A staff branch section also caters for managerial and supervisory/administration personnel.

A national joint council negotiates a national minimum level agreement covering shop-floor workers, while company arrangements apply for the staff section.

History

The union was formed in 1892, originally covering Brussels carpet weavers only in the Halifax district. Since that date the union has changed its name on two occasions and reached its present form in the 1930s. There have been no mergers or amalgamations, although in the late seventies and early eighties the union made attempts to merge with other unions including the Scottish Carpet Workers' Union, the Power Loom Carpet Weavers' and Textile Workers' Union, the General, Municipal and Boilermakers and Allied Trade Union, as well as the National Union of Hosiery and Knitwear Workers. Despite the failure of these overtures a loose affiliation still exists with four other unions who have an interest in the carpet industry:

Scottish Carpet Workers' Union;

Power Loom Carpet Weavers' and Textile Workers' Union;

TGWU Dyers, Bleachers, and Textile Workers' Trade Group;

General, Municipal, Boilermakers and Allied Trade Union.

Organisation

The governing structure of the union is as follows: branch level, Executive Committee, and an Annual Delegate Meeting comprising representatives from each of the eight branches, this being the supreme ruling body. The General Secretary is elected by a ballot of the whole membership. At present there is no other full-time officer apart from the General Secretary but there are a few full-time convenors and some part-time officers.

Policy

The union has not held a ballot as to whether it should hold a political fund. This is in line with previous policy.

NCU
NATIONAL COMMUNICATIONS UNION

(formerly the Post Office Engineering Union: POEU)

TUC affiliated

Head Office: Greystoke House, 150 Brunswick Road, Ealing, London W5 1AW

Telephone: 01-998 2981

Telex: 916257

Fax: 01-991 1410

Principal national officers
General Secretary: Tony Young
Deputy General Secretary (Engineering Group): Vacant
Deputy General Secretary (Clerical Group): Jeannie Drake
General Treasurer: David Norman
Organiser: Brian Harper
Organiser: Simon Sapper
Education Officer: Derek Dodds
Publicity Officer: Aileen Boughen
Legal Officer: Jim Mortimer
Legal Officer: Vincent Turner
National Safety Officer: Roger Darlington

Union journal: the NCU publishes two monthly journals *The Journal* and *The Link.*

Membership

Current membership (1987)
Male: 115,989
Female: 31,825
Total: 147,814

Membership trends

						change	
	1975	*1979*	*1981*	*1983*	*1987*	*1975-87*	*1983-87*
Men	121,129	122,201	128,865	125,218	115,989	−4%	−7%
Women	3,522	3,552	3,963	4,732	31,825	796%	573%
Total	124,681	125,723	132,828	129,950	147,814	19%	14%

Union membership is almost directly linked to the rise and fall of staff employed by the British Telecom Group, the Post Office, and Girobank. The fall in membership in recent years has been largely due to management decisions to reduce staff in post levels. Although the developments in new technology will have an effect on employment over the years, this effect has not yet been seen to any significant extent. The underlying growth in all three business sectors remains buoyant.

The sharp increase in women membership resulted from the merger between the POEU and the Posts and Telecom Group of the CPSA.

General
NCU is divided into two separate groups — the clerical group and the engineering group — and organises workers primarily in the British Telecom Group, where it is the largest union, the Post Office, and Girobank PLC along the following lines:

British Telecom Group
112,600 workers, all grades below first level management, including engineering technicians, store-keepers, supplies assistants, patrolmen, drivers, motor transport technicians and allied grades, draughtsmen, photo-printers, cableship grades.

34,700 workers up to first level management, including clerical officers, clerical assistants, typists, secretaries, superintendents, data processing officers, retail grades.

Post Office
7,500 engineering workers employed in similar jobs as in BT above.
1,000 typists, secretaries, data processing officers, and superintendents.

Girobank PLC
4,700 non-managerial grades including clerical assistants, clerical officers, data processing officers, senior data processing officers, typists, and secretaries.
50 technical engineering grade workers.

In all three enterprises, NCU has sole representation rights for all listed categories of workers.

With the increasing expansion of British Telecom into new business areas, the NCU has adopted a strategy of recruitment by "following BT's work". In this context, the union has revamped the services it provides to members by emphasising existing services, such as the legal aid scheme, and introducing new services such as a membership card Countdown Scheme which gives discounts on purchases in participating stores and businesses.

History
Permanent organisation of telegraph lines workers began in 1886. However, the present union was founded in 1915 when, following the purchase of telephones by the state, the older *Engineering and Stores Association* (5,000 members) joined with the *Amalgamated Society of Telephone Employees* (11,000 members). In 1919 this organisation took the title, the Post Office Engineering Union.

The union has experienced breakaway unionism on a number of occasions. In 1911 there was dissatisfaction with union policy amongst skilled internal exchange workers — they formed the *Telephone and Telegraph Engineering Guild* which only returned to the then POEU after advisory occupational branch structures were introduced into the POEU constitution. There were further harmful breakaways in 1946 and 1949. The *Engineering Officers' (Telecommunications) Association*, (another dissident group of internal workers) was formed in 1946; and the *National Guild of Motor Engineers* was formed by motor transport workers in 1949. These two groups were persuaded to return to the fold of the POEU in 1954 only after new occupational committees were given a veto over their own business (although the NEC had the right to approve all occupational minutes).

Over the years, with the expansion of telecommunications and the coming of automatic telephone exchanges, the composition of the union changed as "indoor" workers gradually came to dominate the union at the expense of the line maintenance workers who worked out of doors. Bealey states that by 1970 56 per cent of union members were internal engineering grades and only 24 per cent were external (it is now much higher). The other 20 per cent consisted of the so-called "minority" grades.

In February 1985 the entire membership of the POEU amalgamated with the Post and Telecoms Group of the CPSA to form the National Communications Union. The dramatic increase in the scale and introduction of new technology was beginning to blur the traditional distinctions between engineering and clerical jobs. Furthermore, the splitting of the Post Office into the separate organisations, British Telecom and the Post Office, illustrated the sort of external pressures which would be put on both unions' traditional areas of work. These reasons alone would have made the merger highly desirable but following the privatisation of British Telecom in 1984, and its subsequent expansion into new business areas, the new NCU is now much better placed to take advantage of the opportunities to legitimately recruit new members through its "following BT work" policy.

Organisation

The NCU comprises two separate sections, the engineering group and the clerical group. Although there is a single National Executive Committee, each group has its own Group Executive Council which has responsibility for all matters which either or both groups do not wish to give up to the NEC. The groups, which possess their separate rule books, primarily concern themselves with specific industrial and occupational issues. Whilst most conditions of service are negotiated separately by these groups, the annual pay claim is submitted and negotiated jointly (although this does not preclude separate agreements, as in 1986).

Each group also has its own network of branches geographically based throughout the UK. There are approximately 290 engineering branches and 105 clerical branches.

The 25-member NEC controls the affairs of the union and is composed of 17 representatives elected exclusively by and from the engineering group along with six representatives elected exclusively by and from the clerical group. The national President and national Vice-President are also members of the NEC. In response to the 1984 Act, the union changed its method of election for the NEC from a branch block voting system at Annual Conference to an individual member secret ballot held primarily in the workplace.

The offices of national President and national Vice-President rotate annually between the president of the engineering group and chairman of the clerical group. The national President also chairs the NEC and presides over the main Annual Conference, the union's supreme policy-making body, held in the first full week in June every year. The Conference comprises two parts, separate engineering and clerical group conferences followed by a combined main conference.

Whilst the NCU at present retains its loose federal organisation the union is keen to move to a single integrated structure and considerable work is currently being carried out in order to bring this about.

The tendency of both the British Telecom Group and the Post Office to set up separate subsidiary companies for certain parts of their operations has forced the union to act in a similar way in the sense of establishing union organisation/consultative procedures which mirror these changes in the companies. For example, the establishment of Fulcrum Communications Ltd, British Telecom Consumer Electronics Ltd, Manx Telecom Ltd, BT (Marine) Ltd, and BT (City Consumer Products) Ltd, has meant that for the first time, important issues such as pay bargaining are now done separately through these companies rather than collectively through one single national agreement. With this shift away from national level bargaining to a decentralised company level the NCU has remodelled its district bargaining organisation in the hope of making it more responsive to the new bargaining context.

Recent issues

In January and February 1987, the union was involved in the largest strike in its history. The dispute, the first in a privatised company, was with British Telecom, and centred around a pay/productivity package linked to increased labour flexibility. After several months of negotiations the NCU held a ballot, in accordance with the 1984 Trade Union Act, to initiate industrial action. The engineering section voted by four to one to support industrial action. Further talks did not yield much progress and the union began an overtime ban to which management responded by suspending workers who refused to sign a pledge to work normally.

The NCU retaliated and authorised branches to initiate a series of twenty-four-hour stoppages in defence of suspended colleagues. A number of union members refused to accept this ruling and crossed their own picket lines which led to much bitterness and complaints resulting in temporary union suspensions. In mid-January 1987, the union declared a national all-out strike but its impact was minimised as middle management carried out emergency maintenance work. On February 16, sixteen days after the start of the national dispute, engineering staff voted, by roughly two to one, to accept a slightly improved pay and productivity package.

The union all along had insisted pay and productivity should be negotiated separately especially as BT was highly profitable and could afford the deal. But the final offer retained the link between pay and productivity and several sections of the union, particularly on the left, found it hard to forgive the ease with which the right-wing leadership, headed by the General Secretary, John Golding, conceded the dispute.

Following settlement of the dispute the NCU's disciplinary committee, inundated with complaints from local branches, proceeded with the controversial move to expel from the union members who crossed picket lines during the dispute. It was estimated that up to 2,300 engineering section members may have been expelled. Critics suggested that this merely encouraged pockets of non-unionism as expelled engineers could still continue to work at BT as there was no formal closed shop arrangement.

However, the hailed breakthrough in labour flexibility which management claimed after the dispute has proved more difficult to implement than had been envisaged. Under the agreement signed in February 1987, all districts should have completed negotiations and to have implemented the flexible working changes by the end of June 1988. However, only seven of BT's 29 districts had agreed a suitable package by the specified date. BT had insisted that negotiations to implement the changed work practices take place locally so that they could respond more effectively to customer needs in individual areas. The NCU argued that many local managers were uncertain and vague over the kind of changes they wanted and in a number of districts, local management was in direct breach of the national agreements which it had intended to implement. The question of labour flexibility was still being negotiated at the time of publication.

General Secretary
John Golding, former Labour MP for Newcastle-under-Lyme sponsored by the NCU, and a senior member of Labour's NEC, was elected to the post of General Secretary of the NCU in 1986. Politically to the right, he attracted much criticism from the left in the union. During the 1987 Conference, he narrowly survived a motion calling for his resignation over his handling of the 1987 British Telecom pay strike. When a Sunday newspaper made allegations surrounding his personal life the left saw this as their opportunity to oust him from the union.

Just prior to the 1988 Conference, the right wing of the union suffered a defeat when one of Golding's key supporters' Tony Field, lost his three-year hold on one of the key union posts, the presidency of the engineering section, to Bill Fry who had the support of the left. This time John Golding found it difficult to survive a motion presented at the 1988 Conference calling for his resignation and shortly afterwards he resigned from the post of General Secretary of the union even though he had still three years left of a five-year service contract.

Phil Holt, a militant sympathiser, was the first union member to stake a claim in public for the vacant post. He was seeking the support of the union's broad left grouping and in the last election for General Secretary, two years before against John Golding, Phil Holt came second with 18,599 votes to John Golding's 41,350. However, the broad left decided to support neither him nor the hard left candidate Bill Fry, president of the engineering section, but instead chose Tony Young, an executive member and widely regarded as an able strategist, as its candidate for the vacant post.

His main rival was Derek Bourne, who has led the union side in talks with BT over job restructuring over the past year. Derek Bourne, the favourite, had the backing of the right wing "First" group which had previously supported John Golding. In the election held in February 1989 the broad left candidate Tony Young turned out to be a convincing winner in the election for the post of the General Secretary of the NCU.

Women

NCU has now formally recognised women as a group within the union and recently established a Women's Advisory Committee. The committee will represent women and women's issues in the union. It is hoped that this move will also help attract new women members and enable existing women members to take a more active role in the union. At present the work of the committee is restricted to national level issues but consideration is being given to extending its work to the local level and make specific provisions for women's interests to be represented in branches by having a women's officer on branch committees.

Early in 1989 the NCU and BT signed an innovative agreement which allows two part-time workers to share a single job. The agreement, which covers more than 20,000 BT staff, is aimed at women workers working in the company's clerical and computer services department. So long as both parties work at least 16 hours a week they will be entitled to all the benefits enjoyed by full-time staff including maternity leave, sick pay, and pension benefits, and their promotion and staff development prospects would not be prejudiced. Very few employers have introduced such agreements and of those that do exist, most are confined to the public sector, particularly local authorities.

External relations

The NCU is affiliated to the Labour Party and was one of the first unions to hold a ballot regarding a political fund. On a 78.7 per cent turn-out, 77,183 (81 per cent) voted for and 17,757 against. In the past the old POEU leadership had considerable difficulty gaining the compliance of the membership for Labour Party affiliation. In 1947, following the repeal of the 1927 Trades Disputes Act, the union voted no to affiliation. Likewise 1958 and 1962 were frustrating times for the leadership when the question of affiliation was again rejected by the membership. It was not until 1962 that the POEU finally affiliated to the Labour Party.

This seemingly easy victory owed much to the skilful campaign carried out by the union. Although co-ordinated at national level, the campaign deliberately relied on local activists and face-to-face encounters. Specific sections and individuals within the union were identified and targeted by area organisers in order to ensure a high turn-out and a "yes" vote. Emphasis was given to local issues but located in a wider political context. The tactics of the campaign were, firstly, to establish the principle as to whether or not the union ought to have a political fund. The question of whether the NCU ought to support the Labour Party was of secondary concern and deliberately played down.

Policy

The NCU remains strongly committed to the introduction of new technology, although it does not give its support without qualification. The key questions are the uses to which technology is put. It believes that the prime purpose of communications is for people and not for profit. In its strategy document adopted by a special conference in 1984, *Making the Future Work,* the union adds that it rejects the management obsession with "efficiency" and "profitability", noting the value-laden nature of these terms, and reaffirms its belief in the necessity of the union having a wider political role and perspective.

The benefits of technological progress ought to be shared out, and reductions in the working week, which the union has a long tradition in championing, job sharing schemes, sabbaticals, paternity leave and others, are all schemes which are consistent with what the union believes as "redefining the boundaries between work and leisure". The NCU is currently engaged in talks with BT about improving maternity pay and leave as well as paternity leave. Further, the NCU, whilst tacitly accepting the need for BT to use a limited amount of sub-contractors, was seeking assurances from management that, wherever possible, the company would use direct labour.

British Telecom became a PLC on August 6, 1984, and was fully privatised in November of the same year. The union was strongly opposed to this move and in 1983, prior to the Stock Exchange flotation issue of shares, organised boycotts on share sales. The NCU also refused to make connections between the national network and Mercury, the private telephone network, but the action had eventually to be abandoned as the union faced incurring heavy damages as a result of an Appeal Court ruling following an injunction taken out by Mercury.

It is NCU policy that BT and the Post Office be recombined as one publicly owned corporation with sufficient resources to ensure that the industry is able to meet the industrial and social requirements of the nation, and that these requirements be determined in consultation with management, the unions, and consumer groups.

Recent events

Tensions between the NCU and the UCW have surfaced again over policy differences and proposed merger talks abandoned. However, informal talks are under way to create a new industrial grouping, a communications super-union involving unions from telecommunications, the media, Post Office, printing, and railways (see **UCW, SOGAT**).

Further references

Frank Bealey, *History of the POEU,* Backman & Turner, 1976.

Frank Bealey, "The political system of the Post Office Engineering Union", *British Journal of Industrial Relations,* XV, no. 3, 1977.

Shirley Lerner, *Breakaway Unions and the Small Trade Union,* Allen & Unwin, 1961. This gives a full account of the breakaway Telephone and Telegraph Engineering Guild.

E. Batstone, and S. Gourlay, *Unions, Unemployment and Innovation,* Basil Blackwell, 1986.

J. Clark et al, *The Process of Technological Change: New Technology and Social Choice in the Workplace,* Cambridge University Press, 1988.

Charles Leadbetter, "A Bad Line at BT", *Marxism Today,* March 1987. Provides a clear analysis of the 1987 BT strike.

NGA
NATIONAL GRAPHICAL ASSOCIATION (1982)

TUC affiliated

Head Office: Graphic House, 63-67 Bromham Road, Bedford MK40 2AG

Telephone: 0234-51521

Fax: 0234-270580

Principal officers
General Secretary: A.D. Dubbins
General President: J.B. Griffiths
Assistant General Secretary: J.A. Ibbotson

National officers
National Secretary (National News Officer): A. Parish
Financial Secretary: C. James
Political Officer, Industrial Officer: G. Colling
Industrial Officer (Provincial News): R.W. Tomlins
Training, Education, Research and Safety, Union Journal, Ballots: L. Willats
Industrial Officer (Company Groups): G. Jerrom
Industrial Officer (Wallcoverings, Women's Issues, and ATCA): B. Philbin
Administration (Legal): F.G. Tanner
Industrial Officer (Origination and News Agency Agreements — Members in Scotland and former SLADE Members): E. Martin
Industrial Officer (Word Processing, Photo-composition, RAGA, Agencies and Studio): C.W. Harding

Union journal: Print (monthly, circulated to each member)

Membership

Current membership (1987)
Male: 117,387
Female: 7,251
Total: 124,638

Membership trends

	1975	1979	1981	1983	1987	change 1975-87	1983-87
Men	N/A	108,340	130,154	122,557	117,387	N/A	−4%
Women	N/A	3,201	6,172	6,674	7,251	N/A	8%
Total	107,441	111,541	136,326	129,231	124,638	16%	−4%

General
From being the model craft union, the NGA has broadened its recruitment base and now caters for craft and professional workers in the printing industry. It recruits non-manual workers within the printing industry, e.g. advertising departments, lesser skilled manual

workers, white collar workers employed in art studios and advertising agencies, as well as "in plant" printers.

As a result of the radical changes brought about by the introduction of new technology the nature of printing has been transformed almost overnight. The traditional areas of work, such as compositors, stereotypers and typesetters, that the NGA so jealously guarded, were becoming redundant and the union faced a potential crisis in terms of its membership base. It was foreseeable that unless fundamental policy changes occurred the NGA faced very substantial membership losses. In fact, NGA membership has dropped by only seven per cent in the last 10 years which compares very favourably to the TUC affiliated unions' average membership decline of 19 per cent.

Perhaps no other industry has been as affected by the introduction of new technology as the printing industry; almost overnight traditional skills and printing processes were made obsolete. Traditionally, printing technology itself dictated the job and hence union demarcation: those who provided the copy were organised largely by the NUJ; those who made the printing plates, set the type and layout, organised by the NGA through strict control over the supply of labour; and the machine and press minders, largely organised by SOGAT. With the introduction of new printing technology, enabling direct input into a computer terminal, these labour demarcations became blurred resulting in inter-union rivalry as each union attempted to claim each new process for itself.

Furthermore, given that the changes also involved newspaper printing and Fleet Street, many of the problems became public property, attracting much media attention and publicity. Some of the disputes became household names, e.g. Wolverhampton Express and Star, the Kent Messenger, and Wapping (see **NUJ, SOGAT**). Mounting union hostility during the eighties, the NGA, and Fleet Street in particular, with its powerful and "mysterious" traditions, had to many come to represent the "unacceptable face of trade unionism".

The NGA has adopted a range of tactics in order to deal with potential membership decline: signing new technology agreements; direct confrontation and industrial action (since under Rule 43 work not recognised by the union could be blacked); recruitment of new groups of workers (as for instance in 1979, when the NGA amalgamated with NUWDAT which gave it a legitimate in-road to recruit the growing number of white collar workers and other technicians who operated the new computer-centred printing technology); amalgamations with other related unions (as with SLADE in 1982, which was the last remaining craft union and resulted in NGA 1982); finally, broadening the skills-base of printers by revamping the apprenticeship system, and introducing a new modular system of training in agreement with the British Printing Industries Federation.

History

The chapel as a unit of print union democracy is of great antiquity. According to J. Moxon's "Mechanick Exercises" of 1683, "Every Printing House is, by custom of time out of mind, called a chapel." Such chapels of compositors in the printing trade are the origins of the NGA and are of continuing importance in the union. However, most authorities suggest that the chapel was not fully integrated into wider union organisation of compositors until after 1840, since an early difficulty was the lack of some intermediate unity between chapel and trade society. Nevertheless, there is evidence of successful trade unionism in the enforcement of common rules governing piece-work and in efforts to control apprenticeships by London compositors by 1785.

Control of apprenticeships necessarily demanded national organisation which is precisely what the trade did not have, being organised into friendly societies on a purely local basis even after the repeal of the Combination Acts in 1825. There was an attempt to set up a *National Typographical Association* in 1845, but it collapsed in 1848.

Regional unions, in any case, became necessary to properly administer the tramping system of countering local unemployment. In 1849 the *Provincial Typographical Association* was founded, so named because the London Society of Compositors opted out. By 1890 it had dropped the "Provincial" and became the *Typographical Association* based in Manchester with a membership of 10,000. The membership of the *London Society of Compositors* had also risen — to 9,000 — and that of the *Scottish Typographical Association*, founded in 1853, stood at 3,000.

In the 1890s the trade of the compositor was assailed by technological change as the linotype machine was introduced into Britain. There was not much displacement of skilled workers since the printing industry expanded immensely, but the new machines created the new semi-skilled jobs and other unions emerged in competition with the old craft societies which were eventually forced to open their ranks to semi-skilled machine operators.

From then on there was more talk of amalgamation of the various craft societies, but the main obstacle remained the London-Provincial. Not until 1955 did any significant amalgamation take place. Then the London Society of Compositors amalgamated with the *Printing Machine Managers' Trade Society* to form the *London Typographical Society*. This amalgamated with the *Typographical Association* in 1964 to form the NGA. The amalgamation was followed by those with the *Association of Correctors of the Press* and the *National Union of Press Telegraphists* in 1965. In 1967 the *National Society of Electrotypers and Stereotypers* amalgamated with the NGA and in 1968, the *Amalgamated Society of Lithographic Printers and Auxiliaries* also decided to join ranks. In 1979 the NGA amalgamated with the small *National Union of Wallcoverings, Decorative and Allied Trades*. Finally, and after many attempts, the NGA amalgamated with the *Society of Lithographic Artists, Designers, Engravers, and Process Workers* (SLADE), and the present union, NGA (1982), officially came into being on March 29, 1982.

In June 1981 the NGA and the NUJ entered formal merger talks. This made sense to both unions since direct entry systems, whereby copy can be directly entered into computers which automatically prepare material for printing machines, were being increasingly introduced. These changes in printing technology were responsible for much inter-union friction in the industry as each union attemped to claim and gain legitimacy over the new processes. As the introduction of new processes, particularly in the provincial newspaper sector and championed by people like Eddie Shah, gathered pace, relations worsened, merger talks broke down and hostilities between the unions became more open, frequent, and bitter. The TUC, concerned about the deteriorating relationship between the two unions, intervened and arranged a series of talks which eventually produced the NGA/NUJ "Accord" in October 1985. The "Accord" provided a joint strategy to deal with direct entry from editorial departments and has largely eliminated disputes, enabling the two unions to seek a new working relationship and, perhaps, an eventual merger.

Coverage

The national system of bargaining has undergone substantial change in the 1980s. This is particularly the case in the newspaper sector where changes of ownership, relocation out of Fleet Street, and the introduction of new technology have had severe implications for the conduct of collective bargaining. With the breakdown of the Newspaper Publishers' Association (NPA) as a bargaining unit in 1986, employers in the national newspaper industry in England now negotiate separate domestic agreements with the NGA, although national arrangements still continue in Scotland where the NGA has bargaining agreements with the Scottish Daily Newspaper Society and the Society of Master Printers of Scotland.

However, outside the newspaper industry national bargaining still persists and NGA has agreements covering a wide range of issues — including pay, holiday entitlement, productivity, flexible arrangements, recruitment, and training — with the British Printing Industries Federation which covers over 2,300 member companies, representing almost three-quarters of all workers employed in this sector of the industry. National agreements also exist with the Reproduction and Graphics Association (RAGA), and Metal Packaging Manufacturers Association.

There undoubtedly has been a shift away from national bargaining to company-wide agreements although at present it is fair to say that company-wide bargaining has not deviated too far away from agreements reached nationally with the major employers' associations.

Organisation

The basis of the NGA's organisation is the chapel of which there are some 11,000; each chapel headed by a father/mother of the chapel (FOC/MOC) who is the NGA lay representative in the work-place. Each member of the NGA is also a member of a branch of which there are more than 90 throughout the United Kingdom and Ireland, most being covered by full-time branch administration.

The NGA is divided into seven regions: 1) London; 2) Northern; 3) South-Eastern; 4) Midlands and North Wales; 5) South-Western and South Wales; 6) Irish; 7) Scottish. Each is administered by a full-time regional and assistant regional secretary, together with appropriate office facilities. Each region holds an Annual Consultative Conference and receives a report from the National Councillors. A regional consultative conference cannot impose decisions on branches within its particular regional area. At national level the officers of the NGA (General Secretary, General President, Assistant General Secretary, Financial Secretary, and national officers), elected by secret ballot vote of the whole membership, are accountable to the 31-member National Council which is elected from the regions. The Irish, Scottish, and Welsh regions are entitled to one representative each; South-Western region three; Midland five; London six; and the Northern and South-Eastern regions, seven each. Each member of the National Council holds office for two years. Recently, a separate Irish industrial council and a Scottish industrial council have been constituted which deals with matters relating to their particular interests. Further, a Women's Committee, in recognition of the growing number of women joining the NGA, has also been formed which deals with all matters of interest to women. All these bodies are subordinate to the National Council.

Every two years there is an Association Delegate Meeting at which branches are represented on a basis of one delegate for every 300 members in the branch. The Delegate Meeting is the supreme policy-making body of the union.

Work-place activity

The NGA has introduced a number of changes in an attempt to reduce "chapel power". All comprehensive agreements now have to be ratified by branch committees, and branch officials are more closely involved during negotiations. But undoubtedly, the greatest impact on chapel power is the introduction of new technology and the radical restructuring of the printing industry. However, the proposed merger with SOGAT may be the last important chance which chapels have to exert their influence on union affairs. How will they use it? (see "Recent events").

Policy

The NGA nationally negotiated with the major BPIF a recruitment, training, and retraining agreement in 1985, which replaced the old apprentice system for the great bulk of the printing industry. The new system of training is modular and allows a much broader and more flexible approach ensuring relevant skills are provided for the industry. The industry reported recently that a quarter of all companies lost business because of a shortage of skilled workers. A supplementary initiative taken by NGA was to set up its own training centre, aimed at providing special high-tech skills to meet certain chronic shortages. NGA pledged £1m of its own money to carry out a feasibility study and had hoped that employers would match this figure but unfortunately companies did not support this idea, despite complaints of shortages.

Women represent a new source of union membership. In 1987 the NGA had over 8,000 female members compared with 5,000 in 1983. The NGA operates a policy of positive discrimination, and gives women precedence on all its training courses. It recently published a *Women's Handbook* which was made available to all branches and chapels. A working party of printing industry employers and unions was constituted early in 1989 to consider child care facilities. This follows a joint statement on equal opportunities agreed between the BPIF and the print unions NGA and SOGAT. This is a significant breakthrough for as yet, few private industries have adopted a nationally co-ordinated response to equal opportunities.

The NGA has recently launched a recruitment drive aimed at non-union areas of the industry. Particular areas targeted are desktop publishing where traditional publishers have stopped contracting out their printing work and are now doing it "in-house". The NGA has introduced a special "new introductory membership" category with subscription rates of £1 per week for full-time employees and 50p per week for those working less than 20 hours. The period of "introductory membership" will normally be two years but this can be varied at the discretion of the National Council

This notion of issuing a special membership status was previously used by the NGA in departing from its pre-entry closed shop practices and refusing to work with non-unionists. It created a "protective membership" category for newly organised firms which, on the payment of a smaller subscription (70 per cent reduction), entitled them to industrial protection, and the payment of strike, lock-out, and victimisation benefit.

Recruitment is a major priority for the union, and branches and chapels are increasingly being urged to adopt a keener approach and ensure that it is discussed at every opportunity. NGA regional officers have been encouraged to spend more time on recruitment and literature has been produced aimed at all categories of workers.

External relations

The NGA is affiliated to the Labour Party. The NGA has a political fund and conducted a secret ballot on whether to retain it. Out of 88,000 ballot papers returned (131,000 sent out), 68,559 voted in favour of retaining the fund, whilst only 18,931 were opposed.

Recent events

As a result of the changing pace of technological development in the printing industry, traditional demarcation lines between unions have become blurred and, increasingly, there is a move towards "integrated crews" of print workers. Ever more difficult to justify the separate unions in the print industry, the TUC advised that NGA and SOGAT bury old rivalries, complete merger negotiations, and create a new print union.

The 1988 biennial Delegate Meeting voted by a large majority to start talks between local branches on a blueprint for amalgamation. The merger also has the support of the union's General Secretary; however, there are a number of obstacles which make the merger difficult. At present, relations between the two unions are at a low ebb following a dispute over organising areas within provincial newspapers. SOGAT members are hostile to a merger partly because they would be required to reorganise their local branch structures (see **SOGAT**). But the SOGAT merger presents problems which the NGA has not faced in previous mergers; in the past it has always been the larger partner. This will not be the case with a SOGAT merger and the NGA leadership has yet to find a way of coming to terms with this.

Further references

J. Child, *Industrial Relations in the Printing Industry,* Allen Unwin, 1967.

A.E. Musson, *The Typographical Association,* Oxford University Press, 1954.

A.J.M. Sykes, "Trade union workshop organisation in the printing industry — the chapel", *Human Relations,* February, 1960.

E. Howe and H.E. Waite, *The London Society of Compositors,* Cassell, 1948.

R. Martin, *New Technology and Industrial Relations in Fleet Street,* Oxford University Press, 1981.

J. Gennard and Steve Dunn "The impact of new technology on the structure and organisation of craft unions in the printing industry", *British Journal of Industrial Relations,* March, 1983.

J. Gennard, "The NGA and the impact of new technology", *New Technology, Work and Employment,* Autumn, 1987. Both of the articles by John Gennard offer particularly good accounts of the changes in printing and the NGA's attempts to deal with the changes and the authors are indebted to them. John Gennard is the official historian of the NGA and is conducting a wider study of the union between 1948 and 1986.

NIPSA
NORTHERN IRELAND PUBLIC SERVICE ALLIANCE

Non-TUC affiliated

Head Office: Harkin House, 54 Wellington Park, Belfast BT9 6BZ

Telephone: 0232-661831

Principal national officers
General Secretary: J.McCusker
Deputy General Secretary: S. McDowell
Assistant General Secretary: L. Pimley
Assistant General Secretary: J. Henry
Assistant Secretary: J. Corey
Assistant Secretary: A. Heasley
Assistant Secretary: S. Mackell
Assistant Secretary: J. Cooper
Assistant Secretary: K. Hood

Union journal: NIPSA News is published monthly and has a circulation of around 30,000.

NIPSA

Membership

Current membership (1988)
Male: 14,700
Female: 19,100
Total: 33,800

Membership trends

	1977	1979	1982	1985	1987
Total	26,700	31,700	32,600	32,400	33,800

General
NIPSA is a non-TUC affiliated union which recruits full-time and part-time employees of all non-manual grades employed in any public service in Northern Ireland, including the Northern Ireland Civil Service, local government, health and social services, education and library service, and the housing services. It is one of the largest unions in Northern Ireland.

There are two Civil Services in Northern Ireland: the Home Civil Service, which deals with such matters as immigration, customs and excise, and the diplomatic service, and which is accountable directly to a minister(s) in London; the Northern Ireland Civil Service is part of the British Civil Service and accountable to the Secretary of State for Northern Ireland. This deals with matters such as education, health and social security, environment, and trade and industry. NIPSA has membership in both the home and the Northern Ireland Civil Services.

NIPSA is organised into two main groups: the Civil Service Group and the Public Officers Group. The Civil Service Group has a membership of 20,000, roughly 60 per cent of the total union membership, which is divided into 170 branches. It represents civil servants and the staff of public bodies employed on Civil Service terms and conditions. The group is further divided into the Northern Ireland Civil Service Association (NICSA) and the Civil Service Professional Officers Association (CSPOA). NICSA organises all the administrative, clerical, executive, and secretarial grades whilst CSPOA organises the professional, technical, and scientific grades.

Employees in education and libraries boards, the health and social services boards, the Northern Ireland Housing Executive, district councils, and a number of other public bodies are all organised in the second main NIPSA group, the Public Officers Group. This group has currently around 13,800 members or roughly 40 per cent of the total union membership.

History
In the 1950s two organisations catered for the interests of Northern Ireland civil servants: the first was the Northern Ireland Civil Service Association for clerical, executive, administrative, typing and secretarial grades; the second was the Civil Service Professional Officers Association for professional, scientific, and technical grades. During the 1960s these two organisations became closer under the umbrella of an Alliance. In 1972 a third union which organised all non-manual grades in local government and the Health Service, the Ulster Public Officers' Association, merged with the two Alliance unions to form NIPSA.

Organisation
The Annual and Special Delegate Conferences are the supreme policy-making bodies of the union. Between such conferences the management and control of the union is vested in the Alliance Council. The Alliance Council consists of the President, Vice-President, Honorary Treasurer, and 22 other elected members.

Individual members are organised into branches representing their particular interest group or location. Each branch negotiates either directly on matters of sole concern to its members or through special committees or panels based on the employing department or authority, or occupational groups. Each branch sends delegates to the Annual Conferences of its own group, and of NIPSA.

Policy
The principal aim of NIPSA is to achieve and maintain parity of pay and conditions comparable to public services in Great Britain. Over the years NIPSA has found this increasingly difficult to achieve, and pay and conditions of public servants in Northern Ireland have, as a result, been eroded. NIPSA is against privatisation and the contracting-out of public services to the private sector and supports the creation of more employment opportunities in both the public and private sectors in Northern Ireland.

An increasingly important feature of NIPSA's work over the last few years has been the implementation of comprehensive equal opportunities policies and public practices in all of the main services in Northern Ireland. To this effect, NIPSA has argued that all public service employers should set up monitoring systems embracing all dimensions of equal opportunities and that an audit of all personnel policies and practices should be carried out in all areas where problems of imbalance are identified.

Recent events
NIPSA has applied to join the TUC on a number of occasions and each time it has been turned down on the grounds that membership of the TUC would be inappropriate for a union that organises exclusively in Northern Ireland. At the time of publication NIPSA has again had its application turned down.

NLBD
NATIONAL LEAGUE OF THE BLIND AND DISABLED
TUC affiliated

Head Office: 2 Tenterden Road, London N17 8BE

Telephone: 01-808 6030

Principal officer
General Secretary: M.A. Barrett

Union journal: The Advocate (quarterly)

Membership

Current membership (1987)
Male: 2,154
Female: 729
Total: 2,883

General
Originating in 1899, when it was known as the National League of the Blind, the union took into its remit disabled workers in 1968 and amended its name to its present title. It organises mainly in sheltered industry in a range of trades such as bedding, upholstery, machine knitwear, cardboard box manufacture, light engineering, boot and shoe repair, braille printing, telephone operating, brush making, and wire work. Membership is open to any registered blind, partially sighted or seeing person.

A national survey conducted in 1987 suggested that the government should collect more accurate statistics on disabled people and employment, and that the 1944 quota system requiring employers to employ a certain number of disabled people ought to be retained and strengthened.

The NLBD held a political fund ballot and in a very high turn-out of 82.5 per cent, 90.7 per cent, (2,218) voted "yes" and 9.3 per cent, (221) voted "no".

Further reference
David Hill, "Employment of the disabled", *Industrial Relations Journal,* 16, no. 1, 1985.

NUCPS
NATIONAL UNION OF CIVIL AND PUBLIC SERVANTS
TUC affiliated

Head Office: 124/130 Southwark Street, London SE1 0TU

Telephone: 01-928 9671

Principal officers
General Secretary (Civil Service Pay): Leslie Christie
Deputy General Secretary (personnel management issues): John Sheldon
Senior Assistant General Secretary (organisation and campaigning): Eddie Reilly
National Secretary (finance and education): Mike Barke
Assistant General Secretary (equal opportunities): Judy McKnight
Assistant General Secretary (health and safety): Julian Dodds
Assistant General Secretary (general conditions): Tom Hayes

Union journal: Opinion (monthly)

Membership

Current membership (1987)
Male: 78,368
Female: 40,372
Total: 118,740

Membership trends (combined CSU and SCPS figures)

	1975	1979	1981	1983	1987	change 1975-87	1983-87
Total	146,719	154,161	144,035	133,606	118,740	−19%	−11%

General

From January 1, 1988 the Society of Civil and Public Servants merged with the Civil Service Union to create NUCPS. This increased the heterogeneity of an already diffuse membership. SCPS had represented executive officer and administrative grades. CSU represented grades such as instructional officers, stores and supervisory grades, museums and galleries staff, security staff, messengers, some customs and excise departmental grades, reprographic grades, traffic wardens, and industrial staff employed by the Metropolitan Police. Constitutionally, integration of members in the newly-formed union is by the device of organising some members in groups and the office support and specialist grades in sections.

History

In 1893 a group of young civil servants founded an organisation with the title "Association of Clerks of the Second Division, appointed under the Order in Council of 21 March 1890". In those days the only form of trade union activity available to civil servants, whether organised in staff associations or not, was the submission of petitions, the last phrase of which was "and your petitioners, as in duty bound, will ever humbly pray".

In 1918, following discussions designed to lead to the formation of a professional body for the Civil Service comparable to the British Medical Association and similar organisations, the inaugural meeting of the Society of Civil Servants was held. During its early years the society's members seem to have been uncertain whether they wanted it to be regarded primarily as a professional body, open to all salaried and established civil servants, or a staff association with a more restricted membership and more precise objectives.

The Association of Clerks of the Second Division had by 1930 become the Executive Officers' Association and the existence of two separate organisations in a basically common field of recruitment led to conflict. The two organisations therefore amalgamated to form the Society of Civil Servants (executive, directing, and analogous grades).

In 1976 Conference agreed to change the name to Society of Civil and Public Servants. SCPS affiliated to the TUC in 1978.

The CSU was established as the Government Minor and Manipulative Grades Association in 1919, becoming the Civil Service Union in 1945. The CSU rejected merger proposals from the CPSA in 1980. Following ballots of the members the CSU and SCPS merged from January 1, 1988.

Organisation

The governing body of the NUCPS that determines principles and policy is the annual

Delegate Conference. Branches are represented according to their members. Formally, between meetings of the Delegate Conference, the general management and control of the union is vested in the National Executive Council.

The NEC consists of the President, two Deputy Presidents and three Vice-Presidents (together called the "Honorary Officers") and 34 other members (called for this purpose "the Ordinary Members"). One Deputy President post, two Vice-President posts and 22 Ordinary Members' seats on the Council are occupied by members from the executive grades category of the union. One Deputy President post and 12 Ordinary Members' seats on the Council are occupied by members from the specialist and office support grades category, elected by members of that category of grades on the basis of section constituencies.

List of sections and National Executive Council seats:

Section		*NEC seats*
1.	Instructional Officers	1
2.	Communications Grades	1
3.	Museums and Galleries Grades	1
4.	Specialist Grades	1
5.	Support Grades	4
	(2 of the 4 filled by members from those grades organised by the Messenger Grades Committee, 2 from remaining grades)	
6.	Departmental and Miscellaneous Grades	2
	(1 filled by a member from those grades organised by the Traffic Wardens Grades Committee, 1 from remaining grades)	
7.	Industrial Grades	1
8.	Reprographic Grades	1

Women
The union has a National Women's Advisory Committee. Despite some progress on equal opportunities at work, women continue to occupy the lowest paid grades and there are still few employed at HEO level or above. In addition to negotiating and campaigning for improved conditions and career prospects for women at work, the NUCPS has campaigned against government policies that have particular detrimental effects on women. Policies on social security rights and payments, on maternity benefits, on rights of job-share and part-time workers, and the effects of privatisation have all been unfavourable for women workers. At the end of 1986 the Equal Opportunities Commission published *Legislating for Change,* a consultative paper reviewing the wording of the 1975 Sex Discrimination Act and the 1970 Equal Pay Act. The then SCPS, commenting on the document, emphasised the need to consolidate existing legislation; the importance of unbiased and clear working in descriptions of discrimination; that tribunal proceedings should be less cumbersome, more flexible, and should include more women on panels; and that provision for training, for childcare, and for improved communication with women about their rights was essential.

Recent issues
Training
Training issues are mainly pursued through the Council of Civil Service Unions in

negotiations with the official side. The NUCPS supports greatly expanded youth training, provided that it is quality training leading to genuine jobs, that the rate for the job is paid during training, and that there is no compulsion and full union participation.

Ethnic minorities
At the 1987 Annual Conference of SCPS the paper "Tackling Racism at Work — A Trade Union Issue" was formally adopted as society policy. The paper contains proposals to improve recruitment and career development, to develop the work of equal opportunity officers, to develop equality programmes with equality targets, and to strengthen policies against racism.

During 1987 the draft results of the 1986 Ethnic Survey in London and the South-East were circulated. SCPS, through the CCSU, asked for a number of additional tables and for some extra analysis to be included. The surveys indicate consistently that ethnic minorities in the Civil Service are concentrated in lower grades and in certain departments.

New technology
The union has pursued through CCSU a national agreement on a joint statement about union representatives; rights to information and consultation, and the continuing demand for shorter working time. A *New Technology Bulletin* has been issued on the safety of equipment. In 1987 the SCPS was involved in a consortium with CPSA, BIFU, and NALGO to produce two videos on job design, VDUs, and ergonomics that can be used as part of an education programme or at lunch-time meetings.

The union has been concerned about the lack of any nationally agreed guidelines on eyesight testing for VDU operators. Since the unilateral abandonment of the national agreement on eyesight testing for VDU operators by the official side in 1985, a wide variety of practices have become established in departments. Some offer little, if any, advice to VDU operators, whilst others encourage visits to opticians and provide special leave, and there are several departments who have decided to retain the keystone tele-binocular tests that were a feature of the national agreement.

Flexible work practices
A report on flexibility by management recommended 10 steps to radical change in work practices but had to admit that the Civil Service had actually led the private sector in developing certain work patterns: flexible hours, described as an attractive condition of service that has been helpful in retaining staff at a time of high wastage; on-call and stand-by arrangements in various functions; and "keep-in-touch" schemes for staff in temporary absence, such as maternity leave.

Policy and recent events
Since it represents executive grades of the Civil Service, the union is often in competition for members with the FDA and IRSF which may seem more attractive to members with promotion prospects. In 1987 the SCPS referred to the Council of Civil Service Unions, under an agreed procedure, the issue of poaching by the FDA. The society pursued the issue through the TUC under the Bridlington principles but the FDA would not back down.

On the pay front the NUCPS and the CPSA reached agreement with the Treasury in 1989 on flexible long-term pay deals on similar lines to other flexibility arrangements in the Civil Service. Under the 1989 agreement all scale points were increased by 4 per cent from April with further similar increases in October when new pay spines were introduced. Staff working in London received additional increases. Further adjustments to the pay spine will take place within the framework of the inter-quartile range of private sector settlements. The Council of Civil Service Unions characterised early versions of the arrangement as a "dog's breakfast". Nevertheless, while it is nothing like a return to the old "pay research" systems terminated in 1980, the unions must welcome the apparent acceptance that comparability with other groups is a significant influence on pay negotiations.

The SCPS had members affected by the ban on trade union membership at GCHQ and the union put up a long but unavailing fight against the ban.

External relations

The NUCPS is affiliated to a wide range of organisations such as Amnesty International, NHS Unlimited (an organisation that has done valuable research into the status, financing, and spread of private medical insurance and private medicine and campaigns for the strengthening of the NHS), the Howard League, and the Work-place Nurseries Campaign.

Further reference

Kathleen Edwards, *The Story of the Civil Service Union*, 1974.

NUFLAT
NATIONAL UNION OF FOOTWEAR, LEATHER, AND ALLIED TRADES

TUC affiliated

Head Office: The Grange, 108 Northampton Road, Earls Barton, Northampton NN6 0JH

Telephone: 0604-810326

Principal officers
General Secretary: G.F. Browett
Assistant General Officer: E. Mallon
General President: R.B. Stevenson
National Organiser: J. Firth
National Organiser: D.W. Richardson
National Organiser: Vacancy

Union journal: NUFLAT Journal and Report (bi-monthly, with a circulation of around 5,500. Copies are given to branches for distribution on request)

Membership

Current membership (1987)
Male: 17,556
Female: 17,509
Total: 35,065

Membership trends

	1975	1979	1981	1983	1987	change 1975-87	1983-87
Men	32,187	30,870	24,969	21,112	17,556	−45%	−17%
Women	30,268	33,874	25,103	20,785	17,509	−42%	−16%
Total	62,455	64,744	50,072	41,897	35,065	−44%	−16%

General
The union organises the vast majority of manual workers in the UK footwear manufacturing industry. It also organises, to a more limited extent, in footwear repairing and components, and since 1971, in the leather goods and glove trades. Membership in footwear manufacturing is around 90 per cent of the total labour force, and in the footwear ancillary trades it is around 5 per cent of total membership. The membership of NUFLAT has declined from 94,000 in 1940, 78,000 in 1960, 50,000 in 1980, to its present level of around 35,000. With the introduction of new technologies in some of the larger firms, and redundancies and closures, NUFLAT's membership looks like declining still further. In the early 1980s merger talks were held with NUKHW, but these have since been abandoned.

History
The *National Union of Boot and Shoe Operatives* was formed in 1874, having originally been called the *National Union of Operative Riveters and Finishers,* seceded from the *Amalgamated Cordwainers' Association* in 1873. It was primarily formed to cope with the problems arising from the trend from a hand-sewn craft industry to a machine-sewn craft, especially in relation to satisfactory payment systems. The union was launched in a time of prosperity and labour shortage, but by 1876 the boot and shoe trade was moving into the shadows of unemployment, short-time working and downward pressure on wage rates. The early years of the union up to 1889 were no more than a period of survival, with the preoccupation of the union centred on limiting and controlling the downward tendency of wage rates and coping with the problems of piece-work. Until the 1890s, development was mainly through local joint boards of conciliation and arbitration. The first National Conference of Conciliation and Arbitration was held in August 1892 in Leicester Town Hall; it considerably widened the range of bargaining to the national level.

A major clash took place in 1895, resulting in the Great Lock-out which lasted for nearly six weeks. The terms of settlement negotiated between the union and the Manufacturers' Federation were very favourable to the employers, and the scope of collective bargaining was reduced and managerial prerogative strengthened. The Great Lock-out considerably weakened the union, and it was not until 1907 that union membership began to recover from this calamity. Membership rose sharply, from about 24,000 in December 1906 to over 30,000 in December 1909, and 49,000 by 1914.

The years of the First World War considerably strengthened the union. It increased the membership to 83,000 by 1918 and in May 1919, the first Joint Industrial Council for the boot and shoe industry was established. The optimism within the industry proved to be short-lived when the post-war boom collapsed in 1920, and wage reductions took effect in 1921.

The 1920s and early 1930s proved to be a period when the union was engaged in a purely defensive struggle from a position of weakness and dependence as severe slumps began to bite into the industry. Technical change led to a reduction in staffing particularly among male workers. The decline in the number of male operatives was slightly offset by the rise in the number of female operatives, a rise due mainly to a considerable growth of fashion wear and a consequent need for more operatives in the closing departments and shoe rooms, departments almost exclusively female preserves. Superimposed on these trends were the heavy cyclical slumps of 1921-3 and 1930-3 which dramatically weakened the union. However, the union policy of moderation in return for employer acceptance of collective bargaining and encouragement of union membership enabled the union to weather the storms of the inter-war years.

The post-war years saw the union assume a role which was greatly influenced by James Crawford, who was elected General President in 1944. Crawford's solution to the problems of the inter-war years was the creation of an efficient and competitive footware industry within a healthy national economy. This policy was characterised by union co-operation in exchange for job preservation and material well-being. If productivity outstripped demand the labour force would have to decline and alternative employment be accepted. The union was committed never to return to the inter-war years of having a "surplus army" of labour attached to the industry. In the event, the labour force in footwear has declined sharply, although the Crawford philosophy has not been seriously challenged.

A series of amalgamations in 1970 between the *National Union of Boot and Shoe Operatives*, the *Amalgamated Society of Leather Workers*, the *National Union of Leather Workers and Allied Trades*, and the *National Union of Glovers and Leather Workers*, gave rise to the present day union, the *National Union of Footwear, Leather, and Allied Trades*, NUFLAT.

The late 1960s and 1970s witnessed an acceleration of the decline within an industry with an increasing incidence of redundancies, closures, short-working, and unemployment. Both the union and the employers have co-operated in lobbying the government to impose import quotas and restrictions to protect the industry from foreign competition, but have met with little success.

Coverage
NUFLAT is party to the following agreements:

The National Conference Agreement between the NUFLAT and the British Footwear Manufacturers' Federation (BFMF);
United Kingdom Fellmongers' Association;
Society of Master Saddlers;
Industrial Leather Federation;
Joint National Council for Hide and Skin Markets Trade (JIC);
Joint Central Conference, the Leather Producers' Association and NUFLAT (USDAW, TGWU, GMB) (NUFLAT chairs the union side);
National Joint Wages Board for Leathergoods and Allied Trade (NJWB);
National Standing Joint Committee for Wages and Conditions in the Glove Manufacturing Industry;
British Fur Trade Association.

Organisation

The supreme authority of the union is the biennial Conference or Special Conference of branch delegates which meets for not more than three days on the official Spring Bank Holiday. Conference delegates are elected as follows: branches with 800 members or more, one delegate for every 800 members; branches with more than 200 but less than 800, one delegate for each branch; branches with less than 200 members are grouped together on an area basis, which then elect one delegate for each group of 200 members.

The General Executive Council (GEC), which meets bi-monthly, administers all affairs and business of the union under the jurisdiction of Conference. It consists of nine elected members, together with the General President, General Secretary, and Assistant General Officer. For the election of the GEC the union is divided into areas with each area electing its own representative(s) but no branch may have more than one representative elected. The election areas and representation numbers are:

Area 1: Cumbria, Northern Ireland, Scotland (one representative);
Area 2: North-East England, North-West England, Yorkshire (one representative);
Area 3: Derbyshire, Leicestershire, Nottinghamshire, Staffordshire (two representatives);
Area 4: Northamptonshire (two representatives);
Area 5: Metropolitan, Norfolk, South-East England (one representative);
Area 6: Oxfordshire, South-West England, Wales (two representatives).

All ballots are secret and branch-based. GEC members serve for a period of two years. There is no regional structure in NUFLAT.

Union officials

NUFLAT is based on branch units with no formal regional organisation. The General President and the General Secretary are the two most senior officers in the union. The Assistant General Officer "understudies" both the President and Secretary. The only other union officers between the general officers and the branch full-time officials (BFTO) are the national organisers. All officers of the union are elected by a ballot vote of the membership (total membership in the case of the national and general officers and branch membership in the case of the BFTOs).

BFTOs are predominantly male, and have spent the majority of their working lives in the footwear or leather industry with little experience elsewhere. Nearly all BFTOs have worked within their own branch areas. In the absence of a regional structure, and with the tradition of branch autonomy, they continue to play a major role within NUFLAT.

There is a high BFTO-to-member ratio and consequently BFTOs are in close contact with events at the work-place and senior management in an industry geographically concentrated with a predominance of small, family-owned firms. This close and frequent contact with the work-place situation plays a dominant role in branch affairs and is an important contributing factor to both membership apathy and an underdeveloped shop steward system.

Work-place activity

Although NUFLAT has an extensive system of shop steward representation, work-place activity is essentially undeveloped. There are several reasons for this. Firstly, the union's commitment to the high BFTO-members ratio enables the BFTO to be in close and personal contact with events at the work-place. BFTOs are able to respond swiftly to calls because they have responsibility for such small geographical areas due to the regional concentration of employment.

In many cases work-place representatives are called shop "presidents" whose role is often limited almost invariably to the collection of dues and providing a link between the membership and BFTOs. Membership apathy is high and turn-out for branch meetings is low.

The footwear and leather trades industry is dominated by the piece-work system of payment with a great deal of standardisation and formalisation in payment systems embodied in district bargaining prices — largely the concern of BFTOs. Shop presidents rarely have much involvement in wage bargaining except in larger work-places.

Women

Women members equal that of men yet they are grossly underrepresented in the union hierarchy. There is only one female council member. Women tend to be located in the low-paid jobs in the industry, mainly in stitching or "closing" the shoes together. Cutting leather, "clicking", is the skilled, hence higher-paid job and this is dominated by men.

External relations

NUFLAT is affiliated to the Labour Party and its rules provide for the sponsoring of one parliamentary candidate. Bob Stevenson, the General President, is a member of the TUC General Council and also a member of the TUC Textile, Clothing, and Footwear Industries Committee. NUFLAT also has one other representative on this TUC committee.

The organisations to which NUFLAT is affiliated include:
International Textile, Garment, and Leather Workers Federation;
Shoe and Allied Research Association;
Workers' Educational Association;
Anti-Apartheid Movement.

NUFLAT held a political fund ballot and a high turn-out of 84 per cent resulted in 20,956 votes (77 per cent) in favour, and 5,963 votes against.

Policy and recent events

NUFLAT has long campaigned for some form of protection of the home industry against foreign competition which it sees as the main reason for the decline in employment in the industry. Through joint involvement in national, European and international levels it works for a more orderly marketing arrangement within the footwear and leather industries.

In 1980 import penetration amounted to 47 per cent but by 1988 it had risen to 65 per cent. Most of these imports are from the Far East and South America, and the pressure is most intense among makers of women's shoes. Unlike the clothing sector, which is sheltered from sudden imports by the quotas negotiated under the Multi-Fibre Arrangement, the footwear industry is wholly exposed to fluctuations in international trade. Most of the casualties have so far been concentrated among the small shoe makers but in 1988, larger manufacturers had to make lay-offs. It is these closures which are causing serious concern to NUFLAT leadership. Membership since 1983 has fallen by 17 per cent, and since 1975, by 45 per cent. NUFLAT cannot sustain these losses for long.

Throughout the 1980s the footwear industry has been examining ways of increasing its international competitiveness: the industry was the subject of a NEDO report *The Potential for Productivity Improvement in the Footwear Manufacturing Industry, 1983;* in 1987 the BFMF, the employers' federation, commissioned consultants to examine the introduction of advanced manufacturing technologies. NUFLAT contributed to both of these major surveys and supported in principle their assumptions and conclusions, namely that introducing new technologies was essential to the future of the industry.

A key issue which NUFLAT may face is the announcement in June 1989, by C. and J. Clark, one of the largest manufacturers and retailers of shoes in the UK, that it intends to close a number of its West Country factories. It has been suggested that up to 600 employees could lose their jobs. Figures released in July 1989 show that employment in the footwear industry fell by 6 per cent to 49,000 in April 1989 compared with the same months in 1988, and there were 1,700 job losses in footwear companies in the first four months of 1989. Increasing and unrestrained imports are the biggest threat to the footwear industry and these announcements lend support to NUFLAT's demands for import controls to help support the vulnerable British shoe market.

Further references
J.F.B. Goodman, E.G.A. Armstrong, J.E. Davis, and A. Wagner, *Rule Making and Industrial Peace: Industrial Relations in Footwear,* Croom Helm, 1977.

Alan Fox, *A History of the National Union of Boot and Shoe Operatives 1957-1984,* Basil Blackwell, 1958. This official history is written by a distinguished industrial relations academic.

NUHKW
NATIONAL UNION OF HOSIERY AND KNITWEAR WORKERS
TUC affiliated

Head Office: 55 New Walk, Leicester LE1 7EB

Telephone: 0533-556702

Fax: 0533-544406

Principal national officers
General Secretary: T. Kirk
General President: D.A. C. Lambert
National Officer: J. Kelly
National Officer: L. Smith

Union journal: The Hosiery and Knitwear Worker (distributed free to members, published six times a year)

Membership

Current membership (1987)
Male: 13,276
Female: 33,962
Total: 47,238

Membership trends

	1975	1979	1981	1983	1987	change 1975-87	change 1983-87
Men	18,941	19,458	15,552	15,223	13,276	−30%	−13%
Women	51,351	51,026	42,759	41,882	33,962	−34%	−19%
Total	70,292	70,484	58,311	57,105	47,238	−33%	−17%

General

NUHKW came into being in 1945 following an amalgamation of several small district unions situated in the Midlands. At that time the approximate membership of the union was 22,430, and since then the union has developed into a national organisation of just under 50,000 workers employed in factories throughout Great Britain. The membership of the NUHKW is heavily concentrated in the Midlands (Hinckley, Ilkeston, Nottingham, Leicester, Loughborough, and Mansfield) and these districts account for around 71 per cent of the total membership. As its name implies the union organises workers employed in the hosiery and knitwear industry, who are involved in the making-up process for ladies' hosiery, underwear, full-fashioned outer-wear, cut and sewn outer-wear, half-hose and socks, as well as warehousing and auxiliary jobs. The union also has a staff section (CATSA) which caters for workers such as supervisors, mechanics, warehouse workers, clerical staff, and designers.

Since 1979, when the membership reached a peak of 70,484, the NUHKW has been in steady decline as a result of the heightened competition and steady growth of foreign imports. The Multi-Fibre Arrangement (MFA) — the agreement regulating world trade in textiles — expires in 1991. All the signs are that, although it will be renewed, its terms will be less favourable to the European manufacturers than in the past. The European industry has already undergone a massive rationalisation which has greatly reduced the size of the NUHKW and the union is looking increasingly to the European Community for protection from unfair competition. The European textile industry is the most powerful in the world with a work-force of three million people but it is expected that international pressure will intensify. There is little prospect of any substantial membership increase for the union.

Perhaps the best opportunity for the union increasing its membership would be through an amalgamation. Resolutions about possible amalgamations are frequently put forward to the Annual Conference; in 1988 it was suggested that the NUHKW consider amalgamating with the NUTGW, but the NEC and Conference are keen to preserve their independent status. A merger between the NUHKW, NUTGW, and NUFLAT, all essentially single-based industrial unions, the majority of whose membership are women, and heavily reliant on piece-work methods of payment, would create a union of more than 160,000 members. Such a merger would create a stronger organisation better able to face the challenge of the 1990s.

The NUHKW has recently appointed new officials in order to assist with recruiting.

History

Trade unionism in the hosiery and knitwear industry stretches back for just over 200 years and had been the subject of numerous studies by two generations of economic historians. Before the introduction of the factory system of production, hosiery workers were usually called framework knitters, and in 1850 the hosiery industry was still largely a domestic industry. Garments were made up on a hand-driven stocking frame which stood either in the worker's own house or in a small nearby workshop.

Hosiery trade unionism in its early days was characterised by a sharp distinction between the more highly paid and usually more highly unionised workers in the large towns in the Midlands (Leicester and Nottingham in particular) and the poorly paid, usually non-unionised village workers; a fragmentation into numerous smaller societies; and a strong dependence on economic prosperity. These three characteristics were to survive long after the supersession of the hand frame by the factory system around 1880.

One of the features of the hosiery industry during the 1860s was the emergence of a conciliation board for industry, largely due to the efforts of the Nottingham manufacturer, A.J. Mundella. The board adjudicated on all disputes regarding wages, and consisted of nine hosiery workers' representatives, and was chaired by Mundella. In the last quarter of the nineteenth century the board was to become the model for institutionalised conciliation arrangements in many other industries, such as lace-making, building trades, and coal. However, Vic Allen suggests that it effectively "disarmed trade unionism at a significant period of its growth".

The 1914-18 war led to the establishment of strong employers' associations, an improvement in management/union relations, the establishment of national bargaining, and the inception of a Joint Industrial Council following the Whitley Committee recommendations in 1917.

Before the end of 1920 the post-war boom came to an end, and the hosiery industry was in the depths of a major slump. The inter-war years from 1920 to 1939 were generally a period of high unemployment, falling memberships, dwindling finances, and sagging morale. Although the number of low-cost, country factories continued to decline, new hosiery manufacturing regions began to develop in Lancashire, in London, and the Home Counties, quite outside the control of the hosiery unions, and usually paying lower wages than in the Midlands.

During the 1920s the possibility of forming a national union was scarcely considered. In 1921 the unions were approached by Andrew Conley, the secretary of the *Tailor and Garment Workers' Union,* with proposals for an amalgamation. This was rejected out of hand. The TUC attempted to promote an amalgamation in the industry in 1923, again without success.

The first serious attempt to create a national union did not come until 1935, by which time the threat from the new hosiery districts was making the traditional structure of trade unionism appear totally anachronistic. Horace Moulden, General Secretary of the *Leicester Union,* believed that the case for a national union was stronger than ever, but despite his close friendship with Jack Brewin of the *Ilkeston Union,* the talks collapsed in 1937, in the face of determined opposition from the *Hinckley Union.*

With the onset of war, the shortage of labour, the government's decision to control prices and profits in the industry, and the importance of trade union co-operation in the war effort the union were soon to find themselves in a very favourable bargaining position. The unions' most important bargaining achievement in the war years came in March 1945, with the signing of the first-ever minimum wage agreement for the industry. A second major achievement for the hosiery federation was the establishment of a *Scottish Hosiery Union* with a membership of almost 2,500.

The common fear of the recruiting intentions of the TGWU and the GMB, together with the decision of the Manufacturers' Federation in 1940 to admit firms to its membership without any obligation to observe JIC agreements, served to persuade the unions that the establishment of a national union was essential. The NUHKW came into existence on January 1, 1945, with Clifford Groocock as General Secretary.

The first priority of the NUHKW was to increase its staffing levels and to recruit hosiery workers in the new areas of the industry — in Lancashire, Yorkshire, and the Home Counties. The growth of the NUHKW outside the Midlands inevitably brought it into conflict with other unions — particularly the TGWU, GMB, and the National Union of Dyers, Bleachers, and Textile Workers. Particularly close relations existed between the Tailor and Garment Workers' Union.

As the union gradually extended its organisation outside the Midlands it faced the problem of maintaining its membership by setting up shop committees at the larger factories. The process of establishing an industrial union, representing all hosiery workers in the UK, was still far from completed in 1951.

The post-war years have seen an enormous increase in productivity in the hosiery industry, as a result of the introduction of new machinery, new methods of working, and new fibres. While the industry's net output has trebled, the number of production workers employed in the industry has fallen. The industry's total labour force (including white collar staff employees whose numbers have risen sharply) was almost exactly the same size in 1974 as in 1951. In such circumstances the union's growth levelled out, and from December 1979 to December 1980 the total work-force in the British hosiery and knitwear industry fell by 12 per cent and the union's membership dropped from over 70,000 at the end of 1979 to around 58,000 at the end of 1981. The continued decline of the British industry, and the threat from foreign competition, has continued the drop in union membership which now stands at 47,238.

Union officials
NUHKW employs two national officers, 10 district secretaries, and twelve other officers. The rule book of the union provides that full-time officials must have been members of the union for a continuous period of at least three years and be not less than 21 years of age. Whilst most NUHKW full-time officers have spent a large part of their working lives within the industry, the trend has continued of appointing younger professional officials from outside the industry.

Coverage
Around 70 per cent of the total membership of NUHKW is concentrated within the Midlands, and in many cases covers almost 100 per cent of the manual labour force. Union membership has declined at around the same rate as the decline in employment.

Historical reasons account for such a large concentration within the Midlands area, and in some areas of the country the union only exists in small pockets of membership or is non-existent as there is little or no traditional hosiery industry. Hosiery and knitwear workers in Scotland, concentrated in the Borders Region around Hawick, have traditionally been organised and formally represented by the GMB, which made significant recruiting efforts in the industry at the end of the Second World War. The GMB has its own separate agreement with the Scottish employers, negotiated through the Scottish Knitwear Trade JNC.

Several major companies have recently withdrawn from the national agreement and instead have instituted plant bargaining. These include the two largest employers in the industry, Courtaulds and Coats Viyella.

Organisation
The governing body of the NUHKW is the National Conference held every two years to formulate policy and every four years to examine all union rules. The NC comprises approximately 130 district committee members and 25 full-time officers, all of whom have voting rights.

The National Executive Committee comprises nine lay members, one from each district committee, six officers elected by National Conference plus the General President, General Secretary, and Vice-President. Proposed new rules will mean that NEC members will in future be elected by a secret ballot of the members. The union also has a formally constituted inner cabinet comprising the General President, General Secretary, Vice-President, and four lay members which has the power to act on behalf of the NEC between meetings. The major committees of the NUHKW NEC are finance, education, organising, and equal opportunities, in addition, there are a number of specialist sector committees for hose, leisure-wear, full-fashioned, and dyeing and finishing.

The union is divided into nine geographically constituted districts, of approximately 4,500 to 5,500 members per district, plus the white collar section CATSA which has approximately 4,000 members. Each district elects a committee by secret membership ballot, held every four years, which meets monthly to determine local union affairs. There are two officials and two clerical staff attached to each district.

Larger factories, employing 300 or more workers, have factory committees comprising not less than three shop stewards, whose purpose under rule is to create a liaison between management and the membership they represent. They are elected by a work-place ballot and serve for a period of two years, but are eligible to stand for re-election.

The NUHKW is currently considering a rule change in order to comply with the 1984 Trade Union Act regarding the election of its General Secretary and General President. At present, candidates are, subject to NEC scrutiny, elected by a ballot vote of the National Conference but it is hoped to change this to an election by a secret national ballot.

Work-place activity

The union has membership in around 500 factories ranging in size from a few employees to large establishments, such as Courtaulds. The hosiery and knitwear industry is characterised by a heavy reliance on piece-work, although the union's policy is to replace this method of payment by some form of basic time work plus an incentive bonus. This reliance on piece-work gives ample scope for local bargaining, particularly in the larger establishments. Wage bargaining is now almost entirely a matter for factory floor agreements, which are negotiated in conjunction with the local union officials. Such bargaining is monitored by each of the union sector committees.

Although the rule book expressly provides that factory committees "shall not make, or cause to be made, any new agreements either on working hours, conditions, or wages without the consent of the district officer of the union", in practice this is often done, and factory committees have some degree of autonomy. However, it would be misleading to overstate the extent of work-place bargaining within the union. Work-place bargaining depends for its success on the support and activism of its rank-and-file workers; as numerous resolutions to Conference calling for "improved communications" in the union amply demonstrate, an apathetic membership within the NUHKW appears to be as much the enemy of greater work-place control in the industry as is the degree of control exercised by the union's leadership.

Women

The NUHKW is predominantly a female union as women account for around 70 per cent of the membership. Despite this, men hold all the key union positions and also the skilled jobs in the industry, such as in the dyeing and finishing trade. Women's wages are consistently around 70 per cent that of men's. Of the union's 23 full-time officials only two are women; the NEC only has five of the 18 seats occupied by women, and only 42 per cent of Conference delegates are women.

In December 1986 a minimum wage for the industry was introduced which the union believes will benefit women members. Time off with pay has also been negotiated for members to take advantage of cervical smear testing and breast cancer screening. In the same year the NUHKW established an Equal Opportunities Committee to report directly to the NEC. This committee concerns itself with problems faced by women, ethnic minorities, and disabled members. The 15-member committee comprises 10 women, three ethnic members, and one who is disabled.

External relations
Despite the early involvement of the hosiery unions in the TUC and the parliamentary committee in the late nineteenth century, the NUHKW has never affiliated to the Labour Party. However, it has for the first time set up a political fund following a ballot in 1986 which saw a vote of 83 per cent (35,017) in favour (90 per cent, or 41,633 members, took part in the elections).

The NUHKW is affiliated to the International Textile, Garment, and Leather Workers' Federation.

Policy
NUHKW has consistently campaigned for the replacement of piece-work in the industry by some form of guaranteed pay plus an incentive bonus.

There is increasing concern at the growth of small, "back-street" work-places paying below national agreed rates. Reports by the Health and Safety Executive indicate that such places do not adhere to proper health and safety standards and practices. In an attempt to improve the conditions in sweat-shops NUHKW adopted a resolution during its 1988 Conference in favour of campaigning against any attempts to dilute existing health and safety legislation.

The idea of a minimum wage has traditionally been a NUHKW policy objective for quite some time and an industry minimum wage was in fact introduced in Britain in 1986. NUHKE has also campaigned for minimum labour standards on an international basis, and introduced the concept of a "social clause" or an "article of social development" which links world trade minimum labour standards. The 1988 Conference voted to campaign for wider international acceptance of the idea and to persuade GATT (General Agreement on Tariffs and Trade) to incorporate this concept into its protocols.

The knitwear and hosiery industry is characterised by low wages, and many employers are tempted to use the YTS scheme as a way of undercutting wages still further. To this effect, NUHKW's policy towards YTS schemes is quite firm and states that employee status should be guaranteed from the first day trainees commence work, and employment rights should be the same as for permanent employees. Trainees should become full employees when they have completed their training or when they achieve piece-rate earnings, whichever is the earlier. All YTS trainees should be guaranteed employment at the successful completion of their training or when they achieve piece-rate earnings.

Recent events
In a submission to the TUC Special Review Body on the future composition of the TUC General Council, MSF noted that NUJKW, NUFLAT, and NUTGW occupy three of the 11 Section B seats on the TUC General Council (see **TUC**). Many commentators have pointed out the logic of these three unions agreeing to a merger. But if the unions were to merge then they would probably only be entitled to one seat. Perhaps this is a factor contributing to the lack of urgency.

Further references
Richard Gurnham, *Hosiery Unions 1776-1976*, NUHKW, 1976. The official history of the union

sympathetically written and particularly illuminating on nineteenth-century developments and serving as a useful bibliographical guide for historical sources.

V.L. Allen, "The Origins of Industrial Conciliation and Arbitration", *International Review of Social History,* IX, 1964. A critical view of the union's participation on the conciliation boards in the nineteenth century.

CIR Report no. 76, "Mansfield Hosiery Mills Ltd". A report critical of the union's attitude towards immigrant workers.

NUIW
NATIONAL UNION OF INSURANCE WORKERS
TUC affiliated

Head Office: 27 Old Gloucester Street, London WC1N 3AF

Telephone: 01-405 6798 and 01-405 1083

Principal national officers
President: F.S. Dunlop
Treasurer: L.G. Meakins
General Secretary: R. Main

Union journal: Each of the three sections has its own journal.

Membership

Current membership (1987)
Male: 14,889
Female: 2,808
Total: 17,697

Membership trends

	1975	1979	1981	1983	1987	change 1975-87	1983-87
Men	N/A	N/A	N/A	15,785	14,889	N/A	−6%
Women	N/A	N/A	N/A	2,834	2,808	N/A	−1%
Total	25,582	20,044	19,463	18,619	17,697	−31%	−5%

General
The NUIW is a union representing the field staff of the door-to-door representatives of the industrial assurance offices. Currently there are three sections in the union, Liverpool Victoria, Prudential, and Royal London. The union is affiliated to the TUC and to the Confederation of Insurance Trade Unions.

History
The national union was formed in 1964 before which it was known as the *National*

Federation of Insurance Workers (NFIW). In 1964 there was an amalgamation of the NFIW with the *National Amalgamated Union of Life Insurance Workers* to create the present day National Union of Insurance Workers. The union was until 1985 a federation of three sections all registered as independent trade unions in their own right, but in December of that year they amalgamated into one single union. As the above membership figures show, the NUIW has incurred serious losses. Much of this has been the result of severe competition from other unions. The federated and sectionalised structure did not help matters since some of the individual sections, while autonomous, were weak, and could be easily picked off by stronger national unions. This happened in the case of the Pearl Federation Section which committed itself by ballot to joining ASTMS (now MSF) in 1978. In 1982 the 850 members of the Royal Liver and Composite Section voted four to one in a ballot to merge with the Banking and Finance Union (BIFU).

Recent developments
As part of the strategy to increase its membership and preserve its autonomy the union has recently launched a recruitment campaign by sending every potential member a professionally designed recruitment pack informing them of the benefits of union membership. Further, the union has targeted specific sectors such as Nationwide estate agencies where it hopes it can recruit and at the same time widen its potential membership base.

In order to comply with the 1984 Trade Union Act the union now elects rather than appoints its principal executive committee, the NEC, which in turn appoints the General Secretary.

External relations
The NUIW established a political fund in February 1988 following a postal ballot. There was a 51 per cent turn-out and 6,830 voted "yes" while 2,421 voted "no", a 74 per cent majority. The NUIW is not, however, affiliated to any political party.

NUJ
NATIONAL UNION OF JOURNALISTS

TUC affiliated

Head Office: Acorn House, 314-320 Gray's Inn Road, London WC1X 8DP

Telephone: 01-278 7916

Telex: 892384 LDN G

Fax: 01-837 8143

Principal national officers
General Secretary: Harry Conroy
Deputy General Secretary: Jacob Ecclestone

Assistant Secretary: Bob Norris
Assistant Secretary (Ireland): Jim Eadie
Head Office Administrator: Bernadette Newman
Editor of the *Journalist*: Tim Gopsill

National organisers
Broadcasting: John Foster
Equality: Sally Gilbert
Provincial Papers: Gary Morton
Education and Research: Gordon Parker
Magazines: Linda Rogers
National Newspaper and Agencies; Technology Officer: Mike Smith
Freelancers: Peta Van den Bergh

Regional organisers
Ireland: Patsi Dunne
North: Colin Bourne
Wales and West of England: John H. Moran
Midlands: Alison Rowe
Scotland: David Syme

Union journal: Journalist (monthly, free to members). *Equality Newsletter* is also periodically published by the NUJ.

Membership

Current membership (1987)
Male: 20,310
Female: 9,868
Total: 30,178

Membership trends

	1975	1979	1981	1983	1987	change 1975-87	1983-87
Men	22,513	23,797	24,199	22,794	20,310	−10%	−11%
Women	5,761	8,750	8,434	9,895	9,868	71%	−1%
Total	28,274	32,547	32,633	32,689	30,178	7%	−8%

General
The NUJ is the largest organisation of journalists in the world. It is a multi-media organisation embracing within its ranks members in newspapers, periodicals, book publishing, radio and television broadcasting, public relations and information services, photo-journalism, editorial design and layout, cartoonists, and self-employed freelancers. A feature of its organisation is its industrial councils, which have wide-ranging powers, particularly in terms of negotiation and recruitment organisation for each trade section of the union. It has long been a champion of press freedom and individual liberties.

In the eighties the advent of new technologies had immediate and obvious implications for the printing industry. "Wapping" and "Eddie Shah" have transcended the industrial relations realm and entered the public domain. Along with the print unions, NGA and

SOGAT, the NUJ was deeply involved in these disputes, which were often as much about inter-union rivalries as with the employers' desire to revolutionise printing (see **NGA, SOGAT**). Whilst there are still important issues unresolved in printing, these are probably more to do with actual bargaining arrangements rather than production considerations themselves (see "Coverage").

History

The NUJ was founded in 1907, following a formation conference at the Acorn Hotel in Birmingham. Before that time there had been an organisation of journalists in the larger cities and towns, and in the London suburbs where local groupings came together to form what was then popularly called "the national union". The founding manifesto, *To the Working Journalist,* originated in Manchester.

The union affiliated to the TUC in 1921 but disaffiliated in 1923 because the TUC was trying to raise money, by levy, to support the *Daily Herald*— which was the voice not only of the trade union movement at large, but also the Labour Party and therefore, in the view of the union, politically partisan. The reason for reaffiliation was the increasingly important role of the TUC in wartime.

In 1967 the wheel of history in the union's relations with the *Institute of Journalists* turned full circle. The union had started as a breakaway from the Institute. In the intervening years, notably in 1921 and 1945-8, attempts had been made to bring about a merger. New talks began in 1965, and in 1967 the dual membership "trial marriage" arrangement came into force. However, in October 1971 a special joint conference of the organisation foundered upon three issues: the matter of registration or deregistration under the Industrial Relations Act; the matter of a separate Professional Council and Conference to deal with "non-industrial" questions; and the name of the new organisation. There has been no formal or official relationship between the NUJ and IOJ since. In fact there has been much bitterness of late, particularly centred on the role of IOJ members in the NUJ disputes.

In May 1989 the NUJ reached agreement to a "transfer of engagements" with the *Irish Print Union,* however, the merger has hit legal snags. Irish law on union mergers is unclear, but because of the phrase "an Irish solution to an Irish problem", it appears that lengthy civil court proceedings will be necessary to determine whether the merger can take place.

Union officials

The NUJ employs 16 full-time officials other than the General Secretary and the Deputy Secretary. The General Secretary and Deputy General Secretary are elected every five years by a ballot of the whole membership. All other union officials are appointed by the National Executive Council.

Coverage

The NUJ is party to agreements in broadcasting and film production, including production for the cinema; broadcasting; radio and television services; printing and publishing of newspapers, national and provincial; and printing and book publishing. Freelance journalists are also included under these categories.

Recent issues

The bulk of NUJ work involves organising and recruiting workers in two industries, printing and broadcasting/film making. Both of these have been the subject of much turmoil in recent years.

Newspaper printing
As a result of new technology such as direct typesetting, the previously clear lines of union demarcation between typesetting (NGA), writing copy (NUJ), and machine operation (SOGAT), have become blurred. NUJ members now produce copy using direct typesetting on a VDU work-station which should have brought them a "natural" advantage. But technological developments have to be socially mediated and the "natural" advantage has not always worked in favour of the NUJ.

Tensions have always existed between different sections of workers and employers were often quick to exploit any divisions between the unions. In early 1985 Portsmouth and Sunderland Newspapers signed the first editorial direct entry agreement in the provincial press. Amongst other things the agreement allowed NGA members to be redeployed into the editorial department without having to transfer union membership. Traditionally, the NUJ organised editorial work and so naturally opposed the agreement arguing that the NUJ had sole representation rights in editorial departments. Consequently, the NUJ called its members out on strike. Although NUJ members supported the strike call, NGA members crossed picket lines and the dispute eventually collapsed. In effect, the NUJ failed to force the company to withdraw NGA rights in the key editorial area.

This dispute led to much resentment and bitterness between the two unions. In the end the TUC, concerned about the deteriorating relations between the NUJ and NGA, invited Lord McCarthy to act as mediator. As a result the two unions signed a "Joint Accord" in October 1985 which provided the unions with the basis of a working relationship and brought an end to the disputes over the introduction of direct entry work (see **NGA**).

But the "natural" advantage to NUJ members of the introduction of direct typesetting is also being undermined in other ways. In January 1987 the NUJ decided to withdraw from national pay bargaining with the Newspaper Society (NS), the employers' organisation for local and regional newspapers. This followed pressure from the NS which claimed that an employer in financial difficulty was not necessarily bound to implement any agreement reached between the NUJ and the NS. The NUJ believed that its members would do better under local bargaining if newspaper owners were in difficulty. Unfortunately, the NUJ decision to withdraw from national pay bargaining has to some extent backfired because some employers are now questioning the need for NUJ recognition at all.

Many provincial employers are simply beginning to ignore the NUJ and a good number of members are now being confronted with new contracts which stipulate that salaries will no longer be negotiated with the union. The *Belfast Telegraph,* and newspapers owned by the Thompson Regional Newspapers (TRN) group are among those initiating the changes, while another provincial publisher, Celtic Newspapers Group, has offered journalists new contracts which in effect would end NUJ recognition.

In 1989 the league table of companies where deunionisation has taken place includes: Thomson Regional Newspapers (Reading, Cardiff, Blackburn, Middlesborough, Chester, Aberdeen, Belfast, Merthyr Tydfil, Newcastle); Westminster Press (Swindon, Basildon, and Brighton); Northcliffe Newspapers (Exeter, Plymouth, Gloucester, Grimsby, Scunthorpe, Tunbridge Wells, Swansea); East Midlands and Allied Newspapers (Stamford, Southampton, Kent Messenger Group, Lincoln, Hitchen, Barnsley).

Book publishing
There are also tensions within the book publishing industry which run parallel with the changes which have taken place in the newspaper and television industries. Although

union organisation in the publishing industry has never had the impact that it did in either newspapers or television, company level collective bargaining was quite well developed. Industrial relations in the publishing industry were considered for a long time to be conducted in a "civilised manner", with publishing companies being largely family-run businesses with strong paternalistic traditions.

Since the mid-eighties, however, publishing companies have become the subject of take-overs by large conglomerate organisations and many formerly independent companies have been reduced to mere "profit centres". Increased competitiveness and wider international markets are driving companies to cut costs and erode conditions of employment, resulting in a growing trend towards non-unionism in book publishing. In companies such as Penguin, Octopus, Marshall Cavendish and William Collins NUJ agreements are threatened.

Broadcasting

Finally, similar problems are being experienced in broadcasting although the players are different. The BBC and the independent television companies are the employers, and the technicians' union ACTT; BETA who organise studio and clerical staff; EETPU electricians; and NUJ journalists; the unions. Changes to bargaining arrangements and working practices are still being worked out (see "Recent events"; **BETA, ACTT**).

A number of companies have already pulled out of national bargaining arrangements such as Tyne Tees and TSW. The long-running dispute at TV-am, which resulted in open hostility between the NUJ and ACTT over the NUJ's refusal not to support ACTT members' action, bears some comparison to disputes in the newspaper industry (see **ACTT**).

Organisation

In common with the print unions, the NUJ rule book provides for the establishment of chapels wherever there are three or more members in an office or organisation. Each chapel reports to a branch and is obliged to report any dispute in which it is involved to the branch and the NEC. The chair of the area council must also be informed. Each chapel annually elects a father or mother as the chapel's representative on all matters affecting members' conditions of employment, and each chapel meets monthly. Usually, editors are not allowed to stand for office as FOC/MOCs. Chapels also elect a clerk to keep their records, and an equality officer, to promote equality issues through in-house negotiations. Equality officers are a recent addition to NUJ rules, and with proper integration into the union structure they could make an important contribution to the union's ability to recruit women members (see "Women").

Chapels are subject to the branch which is almost invariably based on a geographical location. There are 163 branches throughout the UK, as well as Paris, Ireland, Brussels, and Geneva. In London, because of the concentration of members belonging to particular trade sectors of journalism, some branches exist exclusively on a sector basis (freelance, evening papers, magazine, news agencies etc.). Federated chapels are formed wherever a company employing NUJ members is part of a group of companies in which other NUJ members are employed.

The union is divided into geographical units called area councils which are a forum for branch representatives on a wider basis. Area councils have several functions and responsibilities, but principally act as clearing houses for regional problems and as centres for the exchange of ideas and consideration of issues. They also have a role to play in disputes and in conciliation where domestic complaints arise.

Another feature of the NUJ structure is the tier of industrial councils which have wide-ranging powers, particularly in negotiating pay and conditions. Industrial councils exist for each of the following sectors of membership: England, Wales, Northern Ireland, Western Europe: journalists in broadcasting, freelance, magazines and books, national newspapers and agencies, provincial newspapers, public relations and information. The members of industrial councils are elected by members of branches in the appropriate industrial sector. They have autonomy to determine their own policy within the confines of general union policy but they can be overruled by the NEC. The freelance industrial council appoints from its number a member to serve, with full voting rights, upon each of the other industrial councils. A representative of the equality council is also a member of all industrial councils to monitor the progress of equality in each sector council.

The supreme administrative body of the NUJ is the National Executive Committee (NEC). The NEC is elected annually from the membership of the union, voting on an industrial sector basis for nominees within each sector. The NEC consists of national officers (President, Vice-President, General Treasurer) and as many others as are elected by the members in industrial sectors on the basis of one NEC member for each 1,500 members in the sector. The General Secretary and Deputy General Secretary are members of the NEC and all committees, but do not vote. The NEC also elects from its own number specialist committees which are specified under union rules. These are: General purposes; Finance; Recruitment and organisation; Employment; Development; Education; International.

An equality council and race relations working party are new features of NUJ structure. The equality council consists of 14 members, seven are elected annually from branch nominations, and one representative from each of the union's seven industrial councils. Its purpose is to promote and monitor equality within the union organisation, campaign against sexism in the media, and encourage equality groups at chapel and branch level. The race relations working party consists of seven members, five of whom are elected annually at the Annual Delegate Meeting, and two are NEC appointments. Its purpose is to monitor racial issues within the union and the media in general.

There is also an ethics council which aims to improve and maintain ethical standards both within the union and as widely as possible through promotion of the NUJ's code of conduct by which journalists maintain their impartiality and professional status.

The Annual Delegate Meeting decides union policy each year. Branches elect delegates in proportion to size (e.g. one delegate for the first 50 members, and up to a maximum of 12 delegates for branches with membership exceeding 1,050). The ADM is usually held in mid-April, and elects the President, Vice-President, and General Treasurer. Polling is held at the ADM for a variety of committees: appeals, standing orders, and structure working party. The ADM also elects the union's delegates to the TUC, the Women's TUC, and the Congress of the International Federation of Journalists, and a poll is held to set up an emergency committee of four NEC members and the three national officers; this committee has powers to deal with matters as if it were the NEC itself.

Over the past 25 years there have been five serious sets of proposals for structural reform in the NUJ. These have all been rejected by the succeeding ADM. The most recent plans were put to the 1989 ADM as a package of proposals which centred on reforming the branch system. It was argued that branches, which constitutionally provide delegates to all bodies, are unrepresentative. Instead, the plans recommended that branches should be formed by chapels electing "branch delegates" thereby encouraging chapels to exercise power. Conference found the proposals unacceptable and referred them back to the working party for a further report to the 1990 ADM.

Women

There are four women full-time officials and six women on the NEC. Women form approximately one-third of the total NUJ membership. In the early eighties the NUJ supported efforts made by some of its members to further the case of women's equality in union affairs. The NUJ set up an Equality Working Party (EWP) to survey the extent of women's participation in union affairs. The EWP also produced some very good literature, and in 1982 the Annual Conference agreed to replace the EWP with a formally constituted and elected Equality Council (EQ) to pursue working for women's issues (see "Organisation").

Equality Newsletter is produced by the Equality Council and is its official bulletin. The EQ is also preparing three new leaflets on AIDS, rape reporting, and homelessness. The EQ holds annual conferences. The work of the EQ also includes holding workshops on issues such as sexual harassment at work, childcare and flexible working hours, women in Europe, and tackling racism. However, progress of the EQ is hampered by the fact that it is not properly integrated into the industrial sectors of the union which inevitably limits its effectiveness.

The 1989 NUJ presidency, for the first time in its history, is filled by two women on a job-share basis. Under rule all elected voluntary posts within the union are open to job-sharing in that two candidates may stand jointly for election to one post and, if elected, they share the workload between them. Should one of the partners resign, then the other must also give up the post.

External relations

The NUJ is non-political and does not have a political fund. It operates on the basis of maintaining contacts with politicians of all parties. There are several MPs who are NUJ members including Michael Foot, Brian Wilson, Chris Mullin, and Bruce Grocott. Max Madden, also a member, organises meetings of Labour MPs from time to time. Teddy Taylor is the only Conservative NUJ member who takes any active interest in union matters.

The NUJ was involved in lobbying Parliament over the Copyright, Design, and Patents Bill, which sought to strip staff journalists on newspapers and magazines of copyright protection. Despite the union's efforts the Bill was passed almost unaltered. However, on the European front, the NUJ is represented on the Copyright Working Party of the International Federation of Journalists which is examining copyright provisions of EC broadcasting draft directives. The working party has also made a detailed submission on a consultative EC white paper on copyright and the challenge of new technology. On EC matters the NUJ has established useful contact with a number of MEPs including Labour members Les Huckfield, Alex Falconer, Ken Collins, and Michael Elliot. Further, Barbara Castle MEP was awarded life membership of the NUJ.

The NUJ has been making strong representations to secure the release of John McCarthy, an NUJ member, taken hostage in Beirut in April 1986. It is working with the Trade Union Friends of Palestine, and in 1989 a small delegation met up with Yasser Arafat, the PLO leader, to enlist his support in freeing John McCarthy. Friends of John McCarthy, an organisation set up to campaign for his release, was given a free office in the union's Head Office.

NUJ maintains strong links with journalists throughout the world in its attempt to preserve press freedoms. During 1988 it sent representatives to Moscow as guests of the Union of Soviet Journalists to further the intentions of *glasnost* and *perestroika* and promote greater European dialogue.

Policy

The NUJ is concerned about the increase in censorship in the last number of years. At the 1987 TUC it moved an emergency resolution expressing its anger that basic freedoms of speech, information, and publishing were being severely restricted by the government's "Spycatcher" case. The motion went on to state that "the failure of newspaper and broadcasting editors to resist government pressure demonstrates the extent to which freedom of speech has been eroded".

The NUJ continues to fight for the basic freedom of expression and in 1989 it became involved in a legal battle to declare the Home Secretary's ban on the verbatim broadcasting of representatives of Republican and Loyalist organisations in Northern Ireland unlawful. The NUJ is committed to take the case right through the English courts to the European Court, where there is considered to be a better chance of success under Article 10 of the European Convention on Human Rights, which guarantees freedom of expression and information. BETA, the broadcasting union, has agreed to meet 10 per cent of the court costs.

Recent events
Direct inputting: NUJ/NGA
A recent issue which again is causing difficulties between the NUJ and the NGA concerns direct inputting in magazine publishing. As in provincial newspapers, there is provision in the 1985 "Joint Accord" between the two unions on the allocation of this work. But management has refused to negotiate with the NGA on the allocation and details of the work preferring instead to sub-contract it elsewhere. The NGA's ability to mount an effective campaign is hampered by the fact that its members work for contract printers and not for the publishers who are introducing the new changes.

In a bid to prevent the work disappearing from magazine publishing houses altogether, the NUJ announced in June 1988 a major shift in the union's policy on the introduction of new technology in magazine publication. Chapels were given the go-ahead to negotiate agreements with publishers over the introduction of direct inputting and page make-up.

The divisions which have surfaced between the NGA and the NUJ raise an important issue for all inter-union dispute procedures, including the recent TUC Special Review Body code of practice covering the Bridlington Principles (see **TUC**). No matter what sophisticated methods trade unions devise to resolve their differences employers can simply choose to ignore them. Indeed, creating instability between unions seems to be a deliberate tactic by magazine publishers to introduce new working practices with the eventual objective of achieving a de-unionised work-place. A solution which ensures trade union presence in magazine publishing is more important than which union actually represents those workers. This makes merger talks all the more poignant.

NUJ merger
Since 1988 relationships between the media unions, ACTT, BETA, NGA, and the NUJ have steadily improved. Regular meetings take place between general secretaries and presidents and the NUJ has signalled its willingness to begin early merger discussions with an amalgamated ACTT/BETA. However if the ACTT/BETA amalgamation does not succeed then the NUJ has indicated that it is likely to seek amalgamation discussions with BETA alone (see **BETA**). The NUJ is keen to be part of a single media union, which is being mooted by Alan Tuffin, the General Secretary of the UCW (see **UCW**).

Disputes
At the time of publication the NUJ was involved in a number of disputes and negotiations.

— BBC dispute
NUJ members at the BBC are in 1989 involved in industrial action, in a bid to get the

BBC to revise its pay offer. The union has called lightning strikes and disrupted TV programme schedules. The NUJ is acting in joint accord with BETA, and the two unions have made a joint submission seeking a 16 per cent pay rise. The BBC is offering a 7 per cent rise in basic pay and other allowances, plus a £200 lump sum for most staff. Talks at ACAS have so far failed to find a solution, although a compromise suggestion by the unions, to consolidate the £200 lump sum payment, was rejected by BBC management. Union attitudes hardened when reports emerged that the BBC had recruited Peter Sissons, the ITN news presenter, offering him a £500,000 three-year contract.

Behind the dispute, and the hard line taken by BBC management, is the government's attempt to get "value for money" from the BBC by indexing the licence fee to the rise in the retail price index. This, BBC management claims, limits any room they have for manoeuvre as they have been forced to draw up plans to deal with the fall in income. One of the measures adopted by BBC management involves reducing staff costs by 1 per cent a year up to 1993.

The BBC has traditionally been a secure employer, and whilst pay has always lagged behind in the public sector corporation the almost guaranteed security, and the more "gentlemanly-like" working environment, has largely off-set the lure of the extra income which could be earned in the private sector. The new BBC staffing policy obviously has implications for long-term security, and the problem has been further exacerbated recently because pay differentials between the BBC and the independent sector have now widened considerably, pushing staff loyalty to the limits. Balance sheet management may have some short-term benefits but the undisputed world-wide reputation of the BBC could not have been established without staff commitment and loyalty.

To rub salt into the wound, earlier in 1989, senior management at the BBC was awarded improved pay and conditions of up to £20,000 per annum, as well as company cars and bonus payments.

— Independent TV sector

ITN, the independent television news company, has put forward sweeping proposals at the start of negotiations on proposed changes to working practices. These include annualised hours, performance-related pay, staff appraisals, and other new working arrangements. The existing national agreements expired on 1 July, but ITN indicated that it will maintain existing arrangements to enable talks to proceed. Besides the NUJ other unions — ACTT, BETA, and EETPU — are also involved. The unions have put forward a joint counter-proposal, whilst at the same time accepting the principle of annualised hours.

The outcome of ITN negotiations will be closely watched by the other independent companies since this will have implications for their own members (see **BETA**).

If the changes in printing dominated the eighties, then perhaps broadcasting will become the issue for the nineties. Whilst many unions and groups of workers have either fought their battles over technological changes, or are still preparing for them, the NUJ is aware that it may face a "repeat performance" since it also organises in broadcasting. But the experience gained during the turmoil in the printing industry looks like being put to good use. The NUJ is working much more closely with the other unions involved in broadcasting, namely ACTT, EETPU, and BETA. It has developed an especially good relationship with BETA, submitting a joint pay proposal to the BBC, and its desire to open merger talks with BETA has to be considered as a wise move.

Further references

P. Beharrel and G. Philo (eds.), *Trade Unions and the Media*, 1977.

F.J. Mansfield, *Gentlemen, the Press: Chronicles of a Crusade,* (official history of the NUJ), W.H. Allen, 1943.

C.J. Bundock, *The NUJ: A Jubilee History 1907-57,* Oxford University Press.

Denis MacShane, *Using the Media*, Pluto Press, 1979.

NULMW
NATIONAL UNION OF LOCK AND METAL WORKERS

TUC affiliated

Head Office: Bellamy House, Wilkes Street, Willenhall WV13 2BS

Telephone: 0902-366651/2

Principal national officers
General Secretary: M.C. Bradley
Assistant General Secretary: D.R. Thomas
National Officer: L.W. Wells

Membership

Current membership
Male: 2,533
Female: 2,707
Total: 5,240

General
Formed on March 9, 1889, the union has membership throughout the lock industry which is located mainly in the West Midlands and particularly in the Willenhall area. There are two sections: (a) hourly-paid operatives, and (b) clerical, technical, and supervisory staff. The main negotiating machinery is the Joint Industrial Council for the Lock, Latch, and Key Industry, and the National Union is the sole representative of employed persons. The British Lock Manufacturers' Association represents employers.

The union suffered a severe loss of members when the industry was plunged into recession early in the eighties. Recent general rises in living standards, accompanied by a heightened desire for household security have revived the industry as well as the union. Security is now a growth area. New companies are setting up in business and existing companies have also increased employment. Membership in 1987 increased by eight per cent and the union is confident that the rise can be sustained. Last year a vigorous recruitment campaign among twilight shift workers brought 65 new members into the union.

Organisation

The industry is so highly localised that no branch organisation as such is considered necessary. Indeed, the Annual Conference is open to all members and is held in the local church hall. There are shop stewards and an elected lay executive of 18 including the President. Women, who now constitute the majority of the union membership, hold seven Executive Council seats.

Recent events

In November 1987, NULMW elected Bradley as its new General Secretary. He is keen to improve the service to existing members, and new benefits, similar to those associated with larger unions, were introduced. They include a financial counselling scheme, personal loans, and discount travel. The union is eager to promote a modern and progressive image. For the first time in its history the union voted in 1987 to establish a political fund. From a very high turnout of 87 per cent, 3,751 voted "yes" and only 592 voted "no".

On March 31 1988, the Spring Trapmakers Society was officially dissolved. The Society was for all practical purposes part of the NULMW.

Further reference

Brian Stenner, *The Lock and Metal Workers,* Malthouse, 1989.

NUM
NATIONAL UNION OF MINEWORKERS

TUC affiliated

Head Office: Holly Street, Sheffield

Telephone: 0742-766900

Fax: 0742-766400

Principal officers
President: Arthur Scargill
General Secretary: Peter Heathfield

Union journal: The Miner (monthly, distributed free to all members). A number of areas and branches also produce their own journals and regular broadsheets.

Membership

Current membership (1987)
Male: 87,000
Female: 4,000
Total: 91,000

Membership trends

	1975	1979	1981	1983	1987	change 1975-87	1983-87
Total	261,871	253,142	249,711	208,051	91,000	−65%	−56%

General

There can be no doubt that the most signal event of the 1980s for the NUM was the strike of 1984-5 from which the union emerged unbowed but in tatters. High oil prices in the 1970s had helped the union to bargain wages up but had also postponed the day of reckoning for pits that were becoming exhausted. By 1984 British Coal had a much broader definition of "uneconomic" pits and was looking for closures. The government had studiously avoided any confrontation with the NUM but — with coal stocks at high levels — judged the time right to "take on" the miners. Arthur Scargill predicted correctly that the closure of Cortonwood Colliery would be the first of many and gave instructions for a strike on an area and colliery basis.

Each area was mandated by area ballot to call a strike against closures. The idea was that this would avoid the need for a national ballot of the entire membership. This was probably justified in that the management had previously introduced productivity agreements on a pit-by-pit basis but, of course, in social conflict the justice of the situation is often irrelevant and in this case the absence of the ballot proved to be the feet of clay of the strike leadership. Heavily financially supported by business contacts, via David Hart, some disaffected miners were able to obtain a judgement from the courts that calling the strike official was in breach of the union's rules. In spite of protests that the union would not be "constitutionalised out of action", this was crucial because it helped in the formation of the breakaway union and lost the legitimacy of the strike.

The winter was mild and Britain's bill for importing foreign supplies of oil and coal soared by over 40 per cent to more than £10 billion. Some government ministers were on record as saying that it was a worthwhile "investment" to defeat the NUM. Policing was heavy to stop the flying pickets, so successful during previous coal strikes in the 1970s, and there were many arrests and fines for public order offences. The NUM tried to protect its funds from the courts but to no avail in the face of sequestration orders.

In March 1985, in a proud show of defiance, the miners at Maerdy marched back to work with bands playing. They had been defeated and knew that their pit would soon be closed. Many other collieries did not survive the strike and subsequently nearly 100 were closed with almost 100,000 job losses. NUM membership fell below 100,000, losing its automatic seat on the TUC General Council, and by 1989 was down to about a third of its pre-strike level. Partly as a result, proposals are well advanced for a merger with the Transport and General Workers Union, with the enthusiastic approval of Arthur Scargill.

History

Coal-mining tended to develop in areas isolated from the large towns where other industries were located, and miners were socially isolated from the mainstream of early industrial society. To this isolation was usually added a cleavage between masters and men which was sharper than in other industries. The working of coal was closely bound up with the ownership of land so that the relationship between owners and men resembled that of lord and serf. (In Scotland miners were serfs until 1799. In the English coalfields serfdom had largely been replaced by long engagements — e.g. the yearly bond — by 1700.)

The feudal division was soon overlaid by a capitalist one. The prospects for miners setting up as independent masters were remote on account of the cost of sinking a new colliery. Isolation and class division, together with a highly co-operative pattern of work and life, developed in the mining community a strong sense of solidarity and interdependence. For a long time, however, the miners were too depressed a group of workers to find expression in trade union organisation. Miners were the first group of workers, outside the ranks of the skilled crafts-workers, to attempt trade union action.

Widespread strikes in Northumberland and Durham in 1740, 1765, and 1810 suggest the existence then of some temporary form of trade union organisation. The repeal of the Combination Acts in 1824 was followed a few years later by the formation of some local unions of miners, of which the best known was that led by Thomas Hepburn on the Tyne.

Local efforts at organisation were followed by the creation at Wakefield in 1824 of the first national union, *The Miners' Association of Great Britain and Ireland.* Greatly weakened by the long strike of 1844 in Durham, it failed to survive the economic crisis of 1847-8. Despite efforts to rebuild the association, trade unionism in the coalfields was almost non-existent by 1855.

Revival stemmed from the agitation of Alexander Macdonald for the redress of miners' grievances by legal action, e.g. the right to appoint checkweighers, improved safety laws, shorter working days, employers' liability for accidents, and reform of master and servant law. Some local associations were formed (e.g. in South Yorkshire) in 1858 and in 1863 the *Miners' National Union* was launched at a conference in Leeds.

Macdonald's union did not favour strike action, although it encouraged the development of collective bargaining. The more militant districts, led by Lancashire, formed the rival *Amalgamated Association of Miners* in 1869.

During the boom of 1871-3 miners' wages were relatively high and the inter-union rivalry had little effect as collective bargaining gradually developed. Macdonald and Thomas Burt, both miners, became the first trade unionists to be elected as MPs. In the trade depression of 1875-9 wages were cut substantially and the *Amalgamated Association* was wound up. The National Union had survived as an effective organisation only in Northumberland and Durham and collective bargaining was retained only by acceptance of sliding scale agreements whereby wages followed coal prices rapidly downwards.

In many districts the men resorted to a policy of "ca' canny" in an attempt to halt the fall in prices. Yorkshire adopted such a policy in 1881, accompanied by opposition to the sliding scale and demands for an increase in wages. Lancashire, the Midlands, and Scotland started a new federation along similar lines. In 1888 a conference of the new sliding scale areas set up the *Miners' Federation of Great Britain* with a policy of a living wage, irrespective of prices, and a legal eight-hour day. Northumberland and Durham remained in the national union in opposition to the legal eight-hour day. When the eight-hour bill finally became law in 1908, they too adhered to the Federation.

By 1914 a demand for the nationalisation of the mines was being made by the Federation and this policy was put before the Sankey Commission in 1919. Half the members of the Commission and the chair reported in favour of nationalisation but the government took no action. After 1920 the coal industry suffered stationary or declining demand and falling prices. The return to the gold standard worsened coal's competitive position and the coal-owners imposed wage cuts. This brought a depressive period of embittered industrial relations, culminating in the Great Lock-out and the General Strike of 1926. In the 1930s there were no national stoppages but unemployment was high, output did not regain its former levels, and the work-force continued to fall. Despite the recommendations of several commissions and inquiries little was done by way of reorganisation or fresh ideas.

The industrial defeats of the 1920s and the obvious disadvantages of the disunity between districts produced a demand for reorganisation by 1927 and discussion continued during the 1930s. The government took control of the mines in 1942 and on January 1, 1947 the industry passed into public ownership.

The *Miners' Federation of Great Britain* had been composed of about 40 separate unions and the Federation had already prepared for the advent of nationalisation by altering its constitution in 1945 to become the National Union of Mineworkers, following the Nottingham conference in 1944.

Organisation and officials

The removal of the Head Office from London to Yorkshire reflected and was intended to entrench the dominance of the Yorkshire area in the NUM. During the 1970s it could plausibly be argued that some of the less important mining areas were over-represented on the NEC but this was certainly not the case at the time of the 1984-5 strike. The defection of some Nottingham miners and other groups into the breakaway UDM and the continued contraction of the industry has left the Yorkshire area in unassailable control.

In the grim aftermath of the strike defeat there was some opposition to Scargill but those of his opponents who had not decamped were divided. After first disowning his casting vote in order to avoid the necessity for re-election under the 1984 Trade Union Act, Scargill moved against the "new realists" to reassert his authority by submitting himself for re-election in 1988. His election opponent was John Walsh, a North Yorkshire NUM official. Although Walsh won the backing of more NUM areas — 10 to Mr Scargill's nine — the big areas, and especially Yorkshire, mainly went Scargill's way. The vote of the Yorkshire area was crucial since the sheer number of votes for Mr Scargill swamped Mr Walsh's gains elsewhere. Essentially, Scargill had nothing to show for his strategies but he had been right about the closure programme, never disowned the rank and file when others vacillated and, consequently, most of them returned his loyalty. However, as a plebiscite on the policies he had pursued, Mr Scargill's majority was down considerably from when he first became President in 1981. If the union had not split apart as a result of the strike it is possible to conjecture that he would have lost. In any case, his victory was a pyrrhic one in a union that is now small, dwindling, and ready to merge with the Transport and General Workers Union.

Women

Whilst the NUM is obviously in a male-dominated industry, every effort has been made to represent women members who work in canteens, colliery offices, and area offices and to encourage their involvement in the union.

External relations

The NUM has extensive international affiliations and has taken a special interest in the struggles of Bolivian and South African miners. The union continues to sponsor a substantial number of MPs:

L. Cuncliffe (Leigh)
A. Eadie (Midlothian)
G. Buckley (Hemsworth)
J. Thompson (Wensbeck)
K. Baron (Rother Valley)
E. Illsley (Barnsley Central)
R. Campbell (Blyth Valley)
J. Hood (Clydesdale)
J. Cummings (Easington)

M. Redmond (Don Valley)
T. Petchett   (Barnsley East)
D. Skinner   (Bolsover)

The pattern of NUM sponsorship has changed substantially over the years. In the past, primary stress was laid on the candidate's social origins, record of union service, and local standing. Such candidates typically tended to be from a nonconformist background with only elementary education, were in their late 40s or 50s, and had entered the mining industry at an early age. Nowadays the NUM is putting forward younger candidates and appears to have waived its ban on younger NUM officials. The union's traditional vitality and high membership participation always ensures that the mining lodges produce a large number of capable candidates.

During 1979-80, a new branch of the local Labour Party was established at Scargill's NUM headquarters and miners have been encouraged to join their ward branches. As a result, the Yorkshire NUM gained control of Barnsley CLP and secured a position from which it can dictate the choice of Barnsley Labour candidates.

Recent events
The recent history of the NUM is dominated by the 1984-5 strike in which the union was effectively broken. During the strike much government propaganda was devoted to justifying the pit closure program. The conventional wisdom was that if British Coal ended high cost production the economy would benefit from a smaller but economically viable industry that would not require government subsidy. But British Coal cannot feasibly respond to competitive pressures by cost-cutting and productivity increases. Lower wages and more efficiency will not close the cost differential between deep-mined British coal and strip-mined South African or Australian coal. The free market approach means that British deep coal-mining will be rationalised and production concentrated at the Selby complex, Ashfordby, Hawkhurst Moor (Coventry), and, possibly, Margam. Yet, under the privatisation of electricity, nuclear power — certain to be more costly — is to be guaranteed a 20 per cent share of electricity supply, paid for by a surcharge on consumers. The NUM, led by Scargill, fought almost to its death against the closure strategy and had little choice but to do so. Its stand may yet be vindicated — after it has vanished.

Further references
There is a voluminous literature on industrial relations in coal-mining. This mainly stems from the unique place that the miners occupy in the history of the British labour movement but has been augmented by the extensive output of commentaries on the 1984-5 strike.

R.P. Arnot, *The Miners: A History of the Miners' Federation of Great Britain, 1889-1910,* Allen & Unwin, 1949.

R.P. Arnot, *The Miners: The Years of Struggle,* Allen & Unwin, 1953.

R.P. Arnot, *The Miners: One Union, One Industry,* Allen & Unwin, 1979.

R.P. Arnot, *The Miners in Crisis and War,* Allen & Unwin, 1961.

R.P. Arnot, *The South Wales Miners* (2 vols.) Allen & Unwin, 1967 and 1975.

H. Francis & D. Smith, *The Fed: A History of the South Wales Miners in the Twentieth Century,* Lawrence & Wishart.

B.J. McCormick, *Industrial Relations in the Coal Industry,* Macmillan 1979.

M. Pitt, *The World on our Backs,* Lawrence & Wishart, 1979.

M. Adeney & J. Lloyd, *The Miners' Strike 1984-85; Loss without Limit,* Routledge & Kegan Paul, 1986.

H. Beynon (ed.), *Digging Deeper: Issues in the Miners' Strike,* Verso, 1985.

J. & R. Winterton, *The 1984-85 Miners' Strike in Yorkshire,* Manchester University Press, 1986.

D. Douglass & J. Krieger, *A Miner's Life,* Routledge & Kegan Paul, 1983.

NUMAST
NATIONAL UNION OF MARINE AVIATION AND SHIPPING TRANSPORT OFFICERS

(Formerly, the Merchant Navy and Airline Officers' Association: MNAOA)

TUC affiliated

Head Office: Oceanair House, 750-760 High Road, Leytonstone, London E11 3BB

Telephone: 01-989 6677

Telex: 892648 NUMAST G

Fax: 01-530 1015

International Cables and Telemessages: UNIDECKENG LONDON E11

Principal officers: Head Office
General Secretary: E. Nevin
Deputy General Secretary: P.J. Newman
Assistant General Secretary: P.G. McEwan
Assistant General Secretary: B.D. Orrell
Executive Officer: J. Bromley
National Secretary: G.W. Wilson
Assistant National Officer: W. Harrison
Industrial Officer: M. Bourne
District Organiser: G. Gurman
District Organiser: M. Howard
Legal Officer: M. Rogers
Editor & Publicity: A. Linington
Data Processing: V. Carthy

Northern Office: Nautilus House, Mariner's Park, Wallasey, Merseyside L45 7PH

Telephone: 051-639 8454

Fax: 051-691 1921.

Officers
Assistant General Secretary: D.R. Bond
Regional Secretary: L. Attwood
Regional Secretary: R.S. Elliott
District Organiser: B. Parker

Civil Aviation Office: c/o BALPA, 81 New Road, Harlington, Middlesex UB3 5BG

Telephone: 01-759 9331

Union Journal and publications: The Telegraph (monthly, circulated in bulk to ships, and sent free of charge to all members). The journal received praise from the TUC's union journal competition as "a serious paper, full of facts and useful information".

Besides *The Telegraph*, NUMAST publishes a number of other pamphlets and booklets including: *Guidelines for NUMAST Safety Representatives, Employment Advice on Foreign Flag, Ill-health: Personal Pension Plan*, and a glossy, laminated folder, *NUMAST publicity and educational materials.*

Membership

Current membership (1987)
Male: 20,882
Female: 319
Total: 21,201

Membership trends

	1975	1979	1981	1983	1987	change 1975-87	1983-87
Men	29,900	34,650	30,295	24,138	20,882	−30%	−13%
Women	150	400	165	230	319	113%	39%
Total	30,050	35,050	30,460	24,368	21,201	−29%	−13%

General
NUMAST recruits mainly officers in the UK Merchant Navy as follows: navigating officers (including masters); engineering officers; deck cadets; engineering cadets; pursers; catering and medical officers; radio officers; and associated shore staff. Civil aviation officers are also recruited, and although they are formally NUMAST members, NUMAST has an agreement with the pilots' union BALPA, whereby BALPA actually represents them on site.

NUMAST has put together an attractive package of commercial services including unit trusts, mortgages, life assurance, and personal loans as well as a special credit card administered by a bank but carrying the NUMAST logo.

History
There are two strands to the development of NUMAST: officers and telegraphists. Officers' unionisation can be traced back to 1887 with the formation of the *Marine Engineers' Association,* which amalgamated in 1956 with the *Navigators and Engineer Officers' Union* (NEOU) (itself formed in 1936), which gave rise to the *Merchant Navy and Airline Officers' Association* (MNAOA). The origins of the first telegraphists' union dates back to 1912, with the *Association of Wireless Telegraphists.* It amalgamated with the *Cable Telegraphists' Union* in 1921 under the title, *Association of Wireless and Cable*

Telegraphists. In 1938 it changed its name to *Radio Officers' Union,* and in 1967 to *Radio and Electronic Officers' Union* (REOU). In June 1985, the MNAOA and REOU amalgamated under the name of National Union of Marine Aviation and Shipping Transport Officers (NUMAST).

Organisation
The supreme ruling body of NUMAST is the Biennial General Meeting. The day-to-day management of the union is carried out by a 44-member Council, four of whom, the General Secretary, Deputy General Secretary, Assistant General Secretary, and the Executive Officer, are all ex-officio members. Following rule changes in 1987 Council is now subject to a rolling postal ballot system of election where half the positions are vacated every two years.

The work of the Council is divided into a number of national advisory committees: establishment committee; resolutions committee; safety and welfare committee; communications working party; electronics working party; national air committee; national ferries committee; MMSAA committee of management; and national radio officers/inspectors and technical employees committee. Full Council meets once a month.

NUMAST has limited branch organisation on account of the world-wide distribution of membership. Instead, a system of liaison officers and correspondence operates. Liaison officers are mainly concentrated in the short sea trades and perform similar functions to those of shore-based shop stewards. Correspondents have a more restricted role in assisting the flow of information between ship and shore.

NUMAST is keen to expand membership involvement in its affairs. It sends lay committee members as well as elected liaison officers on external TUC shop stewards courses, and regards the exposure which NUMAST members gain to other union cultures as invaluable.

Coverage
NUMAST negotiates agreements with the British Shipping Federation (BSF), which represents the majority of shipping companies (fishing vessels and tugs notwithstanding). These negotiations, which cover around 7,000 NUMAST members, are conducted through the National Maritime Board (NMB) and cover four categories: shipmasters; navigating officers; engineering officers; and radio officers. NUMAST has sole representation rights for these categories of workers.

The present government has, in recent years, encouraged the break up of central (NMB) bargaining. During the 1988 negotiations the following employers announced that, as from 1989, they wished to dissociate themselves from NMB negotiations: Esso, Mobil, Cunard Line, Cunard Ellerman, Sealink, and Furness Withy (see **NUS**).

NUMAST also has representation rights on the National Joint Council for Civil Air Transport (NJCCAT) where it negotiates terms and conditions of employment for engineering officers.

External relations
"Non party political" is current NUMAST policy. However, it recognises that campaigns against such government policies as civil aviation and maritime safety, and sea dumping of toxic wastes, could be declared "political", under the 1984 Trade Union Act, and as the union does not have a properly constituted political fund, undoubtedly legal proceedings would have detrimental consequences. Therefore, following the 1989 Biennial Conference, Council is to consider "how or when to commence any prelude to the sequence of balloting which would have to occur for a political fund to be

established". NUMAST might thus have to modify its "non-political" policy.

NUMAST is affiliated for research and industrial purposes to:

International Transport Workers' Federation;
Flight Engineers International Association;
Committee of Transport Workers' Union in the EEC;
Noise Abatement Society;
Industrial Society;
Campaign for Press and Broadcasting Freedom;
Trade Union Labour and Democratic History Society;
Amnesty International;
Flight Safety Committee;
Workers' Educational Association;
Income Data Services Ltd;
Anti-Apartheid Movement;
Ruskin College Trade Union Research Unit.

The General Secretary, Eric Nevin, is a member of the TUC General Council and serves on the Education and Training Committee, Trade Union Education Committee, Social Insurance and Industrial Welfare Committee, Nuclear Energy Review Body, and the Transport Industries Committee. He also represents the TUC on the Health and Safety Executive's Advisory Committee on Toxic Substances.

NUMAST takes an active interest in education and training and is involved with a number of bodies such as BTEC and SCOTVEC, validating courses for various officers' certificates or "tickets". In 1987 NUMAST secured a position on the executive committee of Ruskin College, Oxford.

Policy
A major concern for NUMAST is its declining membership. In the Council's report to its 1989 Biennial Conference it suggests that the cause can be attributed to a number of "Western world" governments who in recent years have implemented "political philosophy in a more extreme way than in earlier more pragmatic times". The decline of the UK registered merchant fleet is seen as the major reason for NUMAST's problems and the union has made representations to parliamentary committees, ministers, and MPs, regarding the strategic economic and defence implications for the state. The lobbying by NUMAST seems to some extent to have paid off. In a report *Defence Committee, Ninth Report, The Availability of Merchant Shipping for Defence Purposes,* HMSO, July 24, 1989, this very problem is highlighted and it urges the government to increase support to the merchant fleet.

International maritime and air safety are also important areas of interest which NUMAST pursues with a good degree of vigour. In particular, noise control, car deck fumes control, and prevention of pollution from ships are issues which NUMAST is addressing.

Relations with other unions
NUMAST has an agreement with the pilots' union BALPA regarding negotiating and representing NUMAST flight engineer members. The contract is to be renewed in October 1989 and whilst NUMAST members are happy with this arrangement there does seem to be some tension between the two unions which may cause problems in the renewal negotiations. This is because NUMAST subscriptions are much lower than those of BALPA.

The 1987 Biennial Conference decided to begin discussions with the Engineers' and Managers' Association, EMA, with a view to establishing a common structure between the two unions. But these talks have been suspended as NUMAST has entered into serious discussion with TSSA, the railway white collar union. Although there have been a number of difficulties over friendly benefits and other welfare issues, these are not seen as major obstacles. TSSA's political fund might be more difficult to resolve, but nonetheless, in the light of NUMAST's increasing excursions into the "political arena" (see "External relations"), this too may not prove unsurmountable. Should the merger between TSSA and NUMAST take place then it is not inconceivable that EMA might be tempted to join them.

Relationships with NUS suffered a set back as a result of the dispute between the NUS and P&O European Ferries (Dover). NUMAST members were responsible for manning the ferries and carrying out many of the duties normally performed by NUS members. This did lead to a good deal of bad feeling both at the formal union level as well as at the personal, ships' company level.

NUPE
NATIONAL UNION OF PUBLIC EMPLOYEES

TUC affiliated

Head Office: Civic House, 20 Grand Depot Road, Woolwich, London SE18 6SF

Telephone: 01-854 2244

Fax: 01-316 7770

Principal national officers
General Secretary: Rodney Bickerstaffe
Deputy General Secretary: Tom Sawyer
Assistant General Secretary: Ron Keating
National Secretary: Bob Jones
National Secretary: Alistair Macrae
National Secretary: Allan Taylor
Treasurer: Richard Humphrey
National Officer: Gary Cooper
National Officer: Roger Poole
National Officer: Harry Barker
Women's Officer: Maureen O'Hara
Equal Rights Officer: Gloria Mills
Press Officer: Lyn Bryan
Journal Editor: Duncan Milligan

Divisional offices

Northern: S. King, Southend, Fernwood Road, Jesmond, Newcastle-upon-Tyne NE2 1TH

North West: A. Martin, Civic House, 131 Katherine Street, Ashton-under-Lyne, Lancs OL6 7DE

Yorkshire and Humberside: R. French, Blackgates House, Bradford Road, Tingley, Wakefield WF3 1SD

Scotland: R. Curran, Douglas House, Belford House, Edinburgh EH4 3UQ

West Midlands: J. Dempsey, Civic House, 101 Sutton New Road, Erdington, Birmingham B23 6RE

Northern Ireland: I.M. McCormack, 523 Antrim Road, Belfast BT15 3BS

Southern & Eastern: S. Hilliard, Garland Hill House, Sandy Lane, St Paul's Cray, Orpington BR5 3SZ

Greater London: C. Humphreys, Civic House, Aberdeen Terrace, Blackheath, London SE3 0QY

South Western: F. Huff, 853 Fishponds Road, Fishponds, Bristol BS16 2LG

Wales: D. Gregory, 158-159 St Helens Road, Swansea SA1 4DG

East Midlands: N. Wright, 6 Sherwood Rise, Nottingham NG7 6JS

Union journal: NUPE Journal (ten issues a year, circulation 160,000, mailed direct to branch secretaries for distribution by shop stewards).

NUPE also jointly publishes with NALGO a journal entitled *Privatisation News,* and was planning a further joint venture with other unions in the Health Service including the TGWU, COHSE, and NALGO, entitled *Privatisation and the Health Service.*

Membership

Current membership (1987)
Male: 216,977
Female: 433,953
Total: 650,930

Membership trends

	1975	1979	1981	1983	1987	change 1975-87	change 1983-87
Men	201,847	230,590	234,666	229,682	216,977	7%	−6%
Women	382,638	461,180	469,332	459,364	433,953	13%	−6%
Total	584,485	691,770	703,998	689,046	650,930	11%	−6%

General
NUPE is Britain's fifth largest union. It probably has more women members than any other British trade union, almost 74 per cent of its total membership being female. There are 13 women members on the 26-strong Executive Council, and 18 women area officers employed by the union. Five seats on the Executive Council are reserved for women (see

"Organisation"). There is one woman divisional officer and one woman assistant divisional officer.

About 50 per cent of NUPE membership are employed by local authorities, of whom about four-fifths are manual workers. The National Health Service employs about a third of NUPE members, most of whom are ancillary workers, the other being nurses, midwives, and ambulance workers. Around 5 per cent of the membership are employed by universities (mainly porters, cleaning, and kitchen staff), while water authorities employ about 4 per cent.

NUPE is represented on all the national joint councils for local authority workers, the Whitley Council for National Health Service employees, the national joint councils for the water service, and the national councils for university non-teaching staffs.

History

NUPE originated in 1888 with the formation of the *London County Council Employees' Protection Society,* under the presidency of Albin Taylor, an employee at the engine workshop of the LCC's sewage plant. Branches were formed in many parts of the country and the more appropriate title of *Municipal Employees' Association* was adopted in 1894. In 1908, as a result of what were largely personal differences of opinion, the MEA split into two parts. One part, with Albin Taylor as General Secretary, adopted the title of the *National Union of Corporation Workers,* whilst the other part retained the title MEA but subsequently merged with other unions in 1923 to form what is now the *General, Municipal, Boilermakers, and Allied Trades Union.*

In 1925 Taylor retired and was replaced as General Secretary by Jack Willis, a builder's leader and Mayor of Bermondsey, described by Professor B.C. Roberts in his book *The Trades Union Congress, 1863-1921,* as a "well known advocate of militant industrial unionism". In 1928 the NUCW changed its name to the National Union of Public Employees, to better pursue its aim of being the one union for public sector workers.

Throughout much of its life NUPE has faced severe competition from the GMB and the TGWU but its growth record forced these unions to be more circumspect and show greater flexibility in their dealings with the union. Twenty times Bryn Roberts' attempts to gain election to the TUC General Council were defeated by their block vote, but eventually in 1963 Sidney Hill secured a seat on the General Council.

The most remarkable aspect of NUPE's history is its substantial growth in membership. Over the years it has grown as follows:

1928 11,500
1938   40,200
1948 140,000
1958 200,000
1968 256,000
1978 693,097
1988 658,827

General Secretaries
1902-25 Albin Taylor
1925-33 Jack Willis
1933-62 Bryn Roberts
1962-67 Sydney Hill
1968-82 Alan Fisher
1982-   Rodney Bickerstaffe

This rapid growth reflects the growth of the public services sector. In 1948 there were 1.8 million people employed in education, local government, and health. By 1974 this number had risen to 3.9 million. However, union recruitment has not been that easy. Not only has there traditionally been a rapid turnover of staff and a predominance of women part-time workers, but also the public services sector has been characterised by a dispersion of work-groups. Added to this, the fact that there have always been large pockets of non-unionists in the public service sector has meant that competition between NUPE and its rivals has been sharp because non-unionists are not covered by the Bridlington Agreement (see **TUC**).

In the early years NUPE survived primarily because of its historic dominance in London, sustained by close political links with the various Councils. But its real growth came after 1929 following reorganisation of local government which gave the County Councils responsibility for trunk roads, higher education, and for some aspects of health. With the assumption of these new responsibilities County Councils employed more staff, and hence it was possible for NUPE to recruit previously unorganised rural workers throughout the 1930s. Thus NUPE's inter-war growth can be explained in part by the way in which County Councils (and smaller Urban District Councils) took on new functions and workers. Each independent employer followed different terms and conditions with a multiplicity of unions. It was more usual for an employing authority to be faced with a single union or none at all. It was only when amalgamations began that competition between unions grew in real earnest. Given the increased scope for inter-union competition in the 1930s, NUPE grew largely at the expense of GMB. The GMB's leadership was ageing and had lost its drive. Another factor was the way in which NUPE energetically took up every grievance. With little or no local bargaining over pay union competition centred around the ability of each union to take up grievances in order to increase membership.

NUPE's success in recruitment continued in the post-war era. Whilst the TGWU and the GMB were secure in their dominance of the regional negotiating structure in various sectors, NUPE had to orchestrate a campaign to redress this balance at national level. Bryn Roberts' campaign for a system of national negotiations in the public services had been repeatedly defeated in the TUC (as had his demand for the reorganisation of the trade unions along industrial lines). During the war a National Whitley Council for road workers was set up, and later the Local Authority Whitley Council for non-trading services began to influence wage bargaining. In 1948 the Whitley system was reorganised in the National Health Service with central control over wages and conditions. NUPE's membership in the rural areas benefited as their wages and conditions were increased in line with the rest of the country.

NUPE's membership increased substantially in the late 1960s and during the 1970s. Following the introduction of incentive payment schemes, as recommended by the National Board for Prices and Incomes in 1967, NUPE instigated a shop steward system to enable the union to cope more effectively with developments in work-place organisation in the public services. Much of NUPE's growth in the late 1970s can be attributed to the changes effected by the union to take account of the upsurge in militancy at work-place level.

In 1974 NUPE commissioned a report by a study team from the University of Warwick — *Organisation and Change in the National Union of Public Employees*. The central tenet of the report was that there was a need to integrate work-place organisation within the union at local level in order to improve work-place and branch democracy. The report was written from a perspective which stressed internal union democracy as an objective over and above other union aims. Its effect was to increase the openness of the union and the involvement and accountability of its full-time officers to the rank and file membership.

The consequent reorganisation within NUPE meant that national officers came under sustained pressure from the Executive Council and from the various national committees covering industrial groupings of membership — local government, health services, water services, and universities. They responded by generating expectations about pay and conditions, and union services such as education and training, which might be impossible to achieve in the short term. Both these effects were apparent during the "winter of discontent", a strike of public sector manual workers in the first three months of 1979.

The industrial action taken early in 1979 was the most widespread action of the low-paid for many years. It affected caretakers, nurses, hospital ancillary workers, grave-diggers, highway maintenance workers, ambulance personnel, university porters, and water workers. Local branches in NUPE were left to decide which sections of workers to call out on strike within cash limits set by the overall strike pay available in each area. There was little effective co-ordination between NUPE and the other public sector unions involved (GMB, TGWU, COHSE) despite the fact that the local authority workers' claim had been delayed to enable joint action to be taken. During the scattered and uncoordinated strike actions, the union leadership of all four unions failed to formulate a national strategy and local tactics to suit such a struggle. There was a great deal of bitterness and rivalry between the various unions involved in the dispute, both at local and national level. Both COHSE and GMB believed that NUPE was putting forward unduly militant claims and demands in order to attract and recruit more members. One GMB national officer bitterly expressed concern about NUPE's free-wheeling tactics during the dispute.

The dispute was eventually settled by the government who agreed to set up a commission if the unions agreed to accept its findings. The Clegg Commission, which reported in August 1979, rejected most of NUPE's submissions in favour of those of the employers. The report was a bitter pill for NUPE to swallow and its leadership had to settle for a fairly modest increase in the face of much hostility from the membership. The strike had raised expectations among the membership of eradicating low pay. In the event the Clegg Commission awarded the lowest increases to the low-paid, almost all of whom were part-time women workers. At NUPE's 1980 Conference, demands for an £85 minimum wage and a 35-hour-week were rejected, Alan Fisher, the then General Secretary, considering them "unrealistic for the November 1980 pay round".

Union officials
During the 1930s NUPE gained a reputation for taking up every grievance by its staff of young, energetic, and often idealistic officers. The officer became the main means whereby the often scattered membership was able to air its grievances, the main focal point of trade union activity, and was often expected to attend every branch meeting.

It used to be union policy to appoint its officers from outside the union, but in the last 10 years the union has concentrated on recruiting from its own ranks.

Coverage
Joint bodies upon which NUPE is represented include:

Local government
National Joint Council for Local Authorities' Services (Manual Workers);
National Joint Council for Local Authorities' Administrative, Professional, Technical, and Clerical Services;
Provincial Joint Council for Local Authorities' Services (Manual Workers);

Provincial Joint Council for Local Authorities' Administrative, Professional, Technical, and Clerical Services;

National Health Service
General Council of the Whitley Council for NHS employees and the following functional councils:
Ancillary Staffs' Council;
Nurses and Midwives' Staffs' Council;
Administrative and Clerical Staffs' Council;
Ambulancemen's Council;
Professional and Technical Staffs' Council;

Water services
National Joint Industrial Committee for the Water Industry;
National Joint Staff Council for the Water Industry;

Non-teaching staffs
Joint Committee for Technical Staffs (Universities);
Joint Committee for Manual and Ancillary Staffs.

Organisation
The supreme government of NUPE is vested in the National Conference which is convened annually in the month of May. The National Conference consists of direct delegates from each branch of 250 members or more and indirectly elected delegates from smaller branches (elected on an area basis).

The union's general management is vested in the 26-member Executive Council which is elected by a full individual postal ballot of all members once every two years. There are 21 general seats and five seats open to women only. It is a lay executive with members remaining in their usual employment. In practice the senior member who has not previously been President is also elected. Full-time officials are not allowed to stand as candidates for the Executive Council.

The EC meetings are held at weekends at least every six weeks and EC committees are held every four weeks in the period between EC meetings. There are four committees: development, economic, finance, and organisation. The EC is responsible for the general management and policies of the union and is attended by senior officers without voting rights.

There are four National Committees (NC) which report directly to the Executive Council. The Local Government National Committee and the Health Service National Committee comprise 21 representatives elected by branch ballot, one vote for every 50 members, and drawn from each of the union's 21 areas. The Water Service National Committee and the Universities National Committee comprise 11 representatives elected by branch ballot and drawn from each of the union's 11 divisions. The National Committees, which meet quarterly, deal with the special and distinct service interests of the members within the service covered by the committee, and apply and develop the policy of the union in respect of that service. They also consider any matters which may be referred to it by Area Committee, Executive Council, or National Conference, consider reports from other related National Committees, and are themselves consulted with regard to wage negotiations and major conditions of service. A national officer acts as secretary to the committee but has no power to vote.

NUPE also has a number of National Advisory Committees (NAC) which advise the EC on all matters related to the special occupational interests of the members within that section or group. They are: (a) Ambulance National Advisory Committee; (b) Craftsmen's National Advisory Committee; (c) Nurses' National Advisory Committee; (d) Nursery Nurses' National Advisory Committee; (e) School Meals' National Advisory Committee. Recently, to reflect and deal with current membership and policy issues, three new NAC's have been constituted: a Women's NAC, a Race NAC, and a Health and Safety NAC. These new NACs also advise the EC and cover matters relating to women, ethnic minority membership and equal opportunities, and health and safety respectively.

Membership for all the NACs is drawn from each of the union's 11 divisions, which in turn have their own Divisional Advisory Committee (DAC). A national officer acts as secretary to the committee, but without the power to vote, and ensures regular liaison throughout the committee structure as well as working closely with other senior officers.

Branches
There are more than 1,600 branches of the union throughout the UK which are usually district-based to cover all NUPE members employed by a single employing authority. In some cases, however, branches are based on a single occupation within a particular employing authority.

District committees
The union integrates its branches and shop steward representatives at the place of work by a system of district committees. These consist of branch secretaries, branch chairman/woman, and union stewards of all branches within a geographical area covered by a local authority or National Health Service district. Water services and university lay officials attend the local authority district committee.

Area committees
Each district committee sends delegates to the area committees for its respective service. There are normally two local government, two health service, one water, and one university area committee within each of the 11 geographical divisions of the union. Area committees deal with all industrial relations matters pertaining to the relevant service aspect in the area.

Divisional councils
There are 11 geographical divisions (eight for England and one each for Scotland, Wales, and Northern Ireland), each with its own divisional council consisting of representatives drawn from the area committees within the division, plus two women members elected by the divisional conference.

There are 11 full-time divisional officers, each with overall responsibility for one of the geographical divisions. They act as secretaries of divisional council without voting rights.

Divisional conferences
These meet annually and consist of delegates from each district committee within the division, plus the divisional council. The divisional conference receives reports from divisional council, relevant area committees, the EC, divisional officers, and delegates from any section within the division.

Work-place activity
There are around 23,000 NUPE shop stewards elected by work-place groups. NUPE is unusual in that its leadership has attempted to reconstruct the union in order to integrate

shop stewards into its official procedures. Shop stewards were introduced into the union on a large scale only after the National Board for Prices and Incomes recommended the introduction of incentive schemes in 1967. Shop steward organisations in the local authorities and hospitals were still being built up in 1973 when NUPE commissioned the Warwick report *(Organisation and Change in the National Union of Public Employees)* which was delivered in 1974. The report recommended that, where possible, branch structure should reflect the then new local government and health service reorganisation and boundaries. Shop stewards within each district were to form a district committee, and in the case of districts with several branches, both the branch secretaries and shop stewards were to sit on the district committee with the branch secretaries as senior stewards. A link with the higher levels of the union was to be provided by the election of representatives from the district committees to the area committees and divisional councils. These changes certainly represent an attempt to improve internal union democracy, particularly at work-place level. During the "winter of discontent" in 1978/9 NUPE shop stewards did exercise their democratic rights and run the dispute, albeit largely uncoordinated. But perhaps more recent changes to union structure, such as the introduction of the National Women's Advisory Committee and the Race National Advisory Committee, provide better indicators of effective union work-place representation (see also "Policy").

Women

Women constitute 74 per cent of total NUPE membership. As the membership figures reveal, the proportion of women has in fact increased. Nearly all women NUPE members are concentrated in education (cleaners and school meals staff), local government (home helps or workers in residential homes etc.), and amongst hospital ancillary staff in the National Health Service.

Internal NUPE surveys carried out in the early 1980s showed that women were less active in the running of the union than men. In response NUPE has made a number of changes to its structure which have led to increased activity by its half a million women members. Branches are encouraged to elect Women's Liaison Officers; a number have also set up Branch Equality Committees. NUPE has set up a Women's National Advisory Committee, Divisional Advisory Committees, and appointed a National Women's Officer. There are five places reserved for women on the EC and in 1987, for the first time, a majority of the Executive were women. These changes have all played their part in promoting women's issues at every level of the union and developing important policy changes.

The policy of "equal value principles" is now central to all pay negotiations. Towards the end of 1988 NUPE published guidance to MPs as part of a campaign for new legislation. The aim was to allow claims by women on the basis that men would be paid more for a job performed by women if they were employed to do it, even if no men were actually so employed. NUPE is presently backing an equal value case in which the work of women hospital night domestics is being compared to that of groundsmen and male porters.

A substantial number of women members of NUPE are part-time workers — particularly in education, local government, and the National Health Service (50 per cent). NUPE has produced a number of publications specifically for part-time workers. These include a booklet on part-time work, leaflets on maternity rights, and handbooks for workers on social security, employment rights, and terms and conditions.

In 1988, as part of an effort to give higher priority to issues affecting women, NUPE launched an health advice package. The pack of 17 booklets offers advice on a range of issues including stress, abortion, cervical cancer screening, and sexual harassment and is distributed to union branches.

Only seven out of 150 full-time officers' positions are filled by women.

External relations
NUPE is affiliated to the Labour Party and is one of its largest financial supporters. In 1985, in line with the 1984 Trade Union Act, NUPE held a ballot which overwhelmingly backed the retention of the political fund. Unlike many political levy ballots, NUPE, at least in several regions, explicitly campaigned for the Labour Party link. NUPE has also increased the number of MPs it sponsors. These are:

David Blunkett	(Sheffield Brightside)
David Clark	(South Shields)
Jeremy Corbyn	(Islington East)
Ron Davies	(Caerphilly)
David Hinchliffe	(Wakefield)
Henry McLeish	(Fife Central)
Alice Mahon	(Halifax)
Tom Pendry	(Stalybridge and Hyde)
Clare Short	(Birmingham Ladywood)
Keith Vaz	(Leicester East)

Recent issues
The big challenge facing NUPE is the government's attack on the public service sector. Perhaps surprisingly NUPE membership in total has remained stable over recent years. But in each of the major sectors in which the union organises workers, namely, local authorities, the National Health Service, the water services, and the universities sector, the government has proposed radical changes which are bound to have a fundamental impact on the way NUPE both organises and represents its members.

The extension of compulsory competitive tendering and the new rules for tendering are likely to bring about wide-ranging changes in the working practices of local authority manual workers. Competitive tendering is already forcing local authorities to consider incentive bonus schemes, profit sharing, performance appraisal, hours of work, and self-supervision for manual workers. But its extension will also hasten the introduction of demarcation changes, different working methods, work time flexibility, and more effective managerial control of sickness and other absences from work. Such changes will mean that authorities will have to put out to tender a range of services including refuse collection and leisure service management.

Even if local authorities maintain services in-house there will be changes in working practices to improve flexibility and productivity. Of most immediate concern will be the harmonisation of working conditions between manual and white collar workers in order to improve utilisation of both labour and capital. At the 1988 Annual Conference the NUPE executive sought the views of its members on a possible merger with NALGO, the local government white collar union. The executive, aware of the threats posed by the far-reaching government changes, are keen on such a merger which they believe could occur within the next five years. Links between the two unions have been growing rapidly in recent years, with liaison increasing on a range of subjects including training, equal opportunities, and privatisation. Bringing out a joint journal is already being seriously considered.

Early in 1989 the government issued its proposals for radical changes in the National Health Service. Whilst they stopped short of the wholesale privatisation of the National

Health Service, they nevertheless propose a system of internal markets for health services in order to introduce a sense of competition. Further, hospitals will be allowed totally to opt out of the National Health Service. The privatisation of some of the services (for example, auxiliary nurses' work) is already being considered. The national system for wage bargaining, the Whitley Councils, are also under threat. Employers are keen to introduce greater regional and local pay variations by giving managers more discretion in pay determination.

The implications for workers in the NHS will be similar to those in local authorities. On its own NUPE is unlikely to be very successful in its attempts to represent its membership effectively. Whilst the proposed merger with NALGO is to be welcomed, what is really required is a "super-union" which can organise and co-ordinate right across the whole of the Health Service. For instance, manual workers alone are represented by four separate unions: TGWU, GMB, COHSE, and NUPE. Union representation in the NHS is too fragmented. NUPE in 1988 tried to set up merger talks with COHSE but these were rejected by COHSE members (see "Recent events").

It is already known that the government plans to privatise the Water Authorities. The Water Employers' Association has already given notice of the termination of national bargaining arrangements to take effect from September 1989. With the tight financial constraints placed on universities as well as the promotion of greater enterprise in the raising and managing of resources, university manual workers, whom NUPE presently organises, will also face similar pressures of demarcation, flexibility, and the introduction of local level pay bargaining. The future for NUPE looks challenging (see "Recent events").

Policy

NUPE has traditionally championed the cause of the low-paid. In the May 1988 Annual Conference Rodney Bickerstaffe "revealed" the governments' plans to abolish Wages Councils. Although at the time the government denied this it did cause them much embarrassment. More recent events have proved that NUPE was right in its claim. The government's view now is that "the time has come for the Councils to be abolished and that more flexible individualised systems of pay in line with market conditions should be developed".

Tackling racism is a priority for NUPE and they are one of the more progressive unions in this field. In 1985 the union published a major report on race equality and then set up a Race National Advisory Committee. In 1986 a new Equal Rights department headed by a national Equal Rights Officer with special responsibilities for race, lesbian and gay, and disability issues was created. Equality within NUPE is becoming a key area for action, including training for officials in handling race discrimination cases, ethnic monitoring, setting up divisional race advisory committees, and translating literature into languages other than English. Campaigns have also been started on sickle cell disorder, reform of immigration and nationality law, and equal opportunities in public services for black workers and service users.

NUPE represents over 70 per cent of all ambulance staff in the National Health Service. For some time NUPE has maintained that ambulance training needs to reflect the needs of a technologically and culturally different society from the one in which the existing structure was developed. It conducted its own survey within the ambulance service which suggested that training has been a low priority and present arrangements for promotion are too haphazard. In its attempt to raise the profile of the ambulance workers and enhance their professional standing NUPE published a document (*Training for a Better Service: A New Strategy for Ambulance Training*, 1988), which proposed a radical overhaul of ambulance training capable of taking it into the next century. It recommended that new entrant training for qualified ambulance personnel should be extended from six weeks to two years and reflect more closely the tasks expected of different grades of staff. Further, it recommended that selection procedures should be reorganised to give greater representation to women and ethnic minorities.

NUPE is faced with privatisation programmes in the Health Service, water services, and in local authorities which are leading to increased casualisation and flexible working arrangements. Increasingly NUPE is developing strategies based on the recognition that nearly two-thirds of its members work part-time. Control over working time and defence against arbitrary reductions in working hours are therefore central concerns. Integral to this approach is the campaign for a wide range of child care and other support.

NUPE was one of the leading unions in the campaign against acceptance of the government's new Employment Training scheme (ET). The union sees training as an equal opportunities issue and aims to expand provision at work to widen access to training, particularly for women, part-time workers, and black workers. ET was judged a poor quality scheme which did not pay the rate for the job or guarantee high quality training and did not meet any of the equal opportunity criteria. Instead of participating in ET the union urged branches to negotiate alternative training for unemployed people. Whatever the weaknesses of ET, participation in it does allow some influence at national level. But to advocate the extension of local bargaining when the union is facing major challenges to its very bargaining status appears misplaced.

There has always been great rivalry between the unions in the National Health Service, and NUPE has been portrayed as being unduly militant in order to attract and recruit more members. In the past this may have been true. In the 1979 strike NUPE was seen as aggressive in its tactics but it did increase its membership. More recently, in the nurses' grading dispute in 1987/8 (see **RCN**) there was much greater co-operation between the TUC-affiliated unions. However, there were still significant differences between the TUC-affiliated unions and the RCN.

Since 1928 it has been NUPE policy to work towards the creation of one union for all public service employees. Although talks have taken place in the past with COHSE, most recently in 1988 when overtures were again made, it appears that NALGO might emerge as the most likely contender for amalgamation. This would certainly make sense, particularly in the local government sector where both unions between them would form the largest union. Amalgamation of the two unions would enable them to remain in the top five largest unions in the country. This amalgamation would also place the new union in a strong position to take advantage of any European initiatives. It is a pity that the unions representing in the Health Service must remain fragmented, particularly at a time when the NHS faces the biggest challenge to its existence since its creation in 1948.

Recent events

NUPE has recently made a joint submission with TGWU and the GMB for a substantial flat-rate pay increase. Although negotiations are not due to begin until September 1989 the unions have indicated that they would not be prepared to settle below the current 8.3 per cent rate of inflation. Whilst the flat-rate increase will benefit the low-paid, if it disadvantages local authorities facing competitive tendering then the unions can expect to face even greater resistance from employers. At the time of publication the employers were already in dispute with NALGO over a 7 per cent offer made to local authority white collar workers, so NUPE's joint submission is unlikely to make easy progress.

The talks on the proposed merger between NUPE and NALGO are still continuing and a merger is expected in the early 1990s. COHSE has indicated that it would be prepared to enter discussions if the merger goes ahead. A unified union of around 1.5 million members in the public services and the NHS has to be welcomed.

In May 1989 Thames Water Authority made the first independent pay offer since it opted out of national pay bargaining arrangements. All other water authorities are due to bargain separately on pay and conditions from 1990 in the run-up to water privatisation. One of the main reasons Thames gave for opting out of national wage bargaining was that it was being constrained by the national agreement from paying more. NUPE, along with GMB and TGWU which also represent water workers, has urged its members to reject the offer which is below a national deal agreed earlier and have issued ballot papers calling for industrial action.

Further references

W.W. Craik, *Bryn Roberts and NUPE,* Allen & Unwin, 1955.

Sydney Fryer, A. Fairclough, and T.B. Manson, "Facilities for female shop stewards: collective agreements and the Employment Protection Act", *British Journal of Industrial Relations,* 1978.

John Suddaby, "The public sector strike in Camden: Winter '79", *New Left Review,* August 1979. A view of the 1979 strike from an activist, which shows the effectiveness of militancy by NUPE at work-place level.

Organisation and Change in the National Union of Public Employees, NUPE, 1974. The official report submitted to the union by a study team from the University of Warwick.

John Leopold and Phil Beaumont, "Pay bargaining and management strategy in the NHS", *Industrial Relations Journal,* 17, no. 1, 1986.

David Sapsford, "Local authority employment creation initiatives: who gets the jobs?", *Industrial Relations Journal,* 17, no. 3, 1986.

Ian Kessler, "Shop Stewards in Local Government", *British Journal of Industrial Relations,* XXIV, no. 3, November 1986.

NUR
NATIONAL UNION OF RAILWAYMEN

TUC affiliated

Head Office: Unity House, Euston Road, London NW1 2BL

Telephone: 01-387 4771

Principal officers
General Secretary: J. Knapp
Senior Assistant General Secretary: A. Dodds
Assistant General Secretaries: V. Hince, G. Petchey

Union journal: Transport Review (fortnightly)

Membership

Current membership (1987)
Male: 111,635
Female: 5,959
Total: 117,594

Membership trends

	1975	1979	1981	1983	1987	change 1975-87	1983-87
Men	175,035	170,497	N/A	135,343	111,635	−36%	−18%
Women	5,394	9,503	N/A	7,875	5,959	10%	−24%
Total	180,429	180,000	160,000	143,218	117,594	−35%	−18%

General
The largest of the three rail unions, although its membership has continued to decline (over 180,000 in 1975), the NUR still exerts considerable influence in trade union affairs. The NUR and its precursor, the *Amalgamated Society of Railway Servants,* occupy a special place in the history of British trade unionism, especially in connection with the Taff Vale case and the Osborne judgement, and in having played an important role in the events leading to the foundation of the Labour Party.

The NUR supports industrial unionism and has fought tenaciously to retain the principle of national industry-wide collective bargaining. Industrial unionism might be thought to put the NUR at odds with ASLEF, the craft union, but since 1983 the NUR has built a relationship with ASLEF that is the most cordial between the two in living memory. All important industrial issues of mutual interest are now discussed between them at the Rail Federation Council. A measure of the accord is that it is now normal for the NUR and ASLEF to submit a joint pay claim. During the 1989 dispute about pay and the principle of national bargaining they kept close counsel until the NUR executive, whose trust in management had been considerably eroded, declined the terms that ASLEF and TSSA had accepted. Nevertheless, it is difficult to control rivalry, and the acceptance by the NUR guards to bring about the ending of the demarcation between themselves and drivers (introducing a new flexible "train-man" grade, combining the existing jobs of assistant driver and guard) leaves the NUR vulnerable to poaching.

History
In 1871 the *Amalgamated Society of Railway Servants* was formed in Leeds and quickly grew to 17,000 members. The early 1880s to 1913 was a significant formative period in the labour and trade union movement and ASRS was prominent. The trade union movement suffered two blows from the courts in the Taff Vale case and the Osborne judgement — both against the ASRS. The Taff Vale case arose from a strike on the Taff Vale railway in South Wales, following the alleged victimisation of a signalman who had led a movement for a pay rise. Although the strike itself lasted only 11 days the litigation reached the House of Lords where a decision of profound importance was made: that trade union funds were liable for damages inflicted by their officials. The total costs arising from the case, for which the ASRS was made liable, amounted to £42,000, an enormous sum in those days. Legislation giving trade unions immunity from such actions for damages was passed in the Trade Disputes Act of 1906 but this area of immunity was very much narrowed by legislation in the 1980s.

The Osborne judgement followed an ASRS decision of 1903 to introduce a compulsory political levy of one shilling per member per year to augment Labour Party funds. W. V. Osborne, secretary of the Walthamstow branch of the union, brought an injunction to restrain the ASRS from contributing to the upkeep of the Labour Party — a restraint eventually confirmed by the Court of Appeal. Union leaders reacted angrily and at the 1910 Trades Union Congress a resolution calling for legislation to reverse the Osborne judgement was carried overwhelmingly. In 1913 this was effected with the Trade Union Act.

The first national rail strike took place in 1911, largely as a result of management's refusal to renegotiate the terms of arbitration originally agreed in 1907. The strike lasted for just two days. A Royal Commission was set up to examine the operation of the railway conciliation boards, and, following its report later in the year, a new scheme was introduced. After many years of insisting on almost military discipline from their employees, the railway companies conceded recognition of the rail unions, whose membership then grew rapidly.

The most important outcome of the 1911 strike was the amalgamation of the ASRS with the *United Pointsmen's and Signalmen's Society* (UPSS), formed in 1880, and the *General Railway Workers' Union* (GRWU), formed in 1890, to form the National Union of Railwaymen on March 29, 1913. The Executive Committees of these three unions, together with that of ASLEF, had met during and after the strike. At a "fusion of forces" conference in Manchester in 1911 the main principles of an amalgamation scheme were agreed, but ASLEF later withdrew when its executive disagreed with the terms of the amalgamation. At its inception the NUR had nearly 180,000 members, of whom 23,158 had belonged to the GRWU and 4,100 to the UPSS. Membership quickly increased to a total of 273,000 by 1914.

After the Second World War the railways declined. Despite nationalisation and attempts to develop a sensible, integrated transport system, competition from road haulage, buses and — most of all — from private motor vehicles (temporarily advantaged by cheap petrol) cast the railways in a poor light. Employment fell and, with it, NUR membership — from 254,687 in 1965 to 180,000 in 1978. Most of this reduction came with the Beeching cuts that severely mutilated the rail network. By 1987 membership had fallen below 120,000, overwhelmingly as a result of job losses in the industries in which the NUR organises, rather than de-unionisation. Naturally, however, it is more difficult to keep members in sectors that always were hard to unionise but where public ownership helped the union, e.g. the former British transport hotels.

Organisation

The NUR traditionally has been highly centralised. Its organisational structure has in this sense followed from its precept of industrial unionism. However, the working model no longer conforms with reality. The NUR may have retained members in the sectors that have been privatised — for example, in the National Freight Corporation, Sealink and various bus companies — but the industrial relations in those enterprises are managed at company level. London Underground is a separate bargaining unit (about 9,000 NUR members), so there remained in 1989 centralised national collective bargaining with British Rail for about 70,000 NUR members. However, BR wanted to reform bargaining structures following the reorganisation of the previously monolithic British Railways Board into five "business units" — Intercity, Network South-East, provincial passenger services, freight, and parcels. In November 1988 the management therefore announced its intention to dismantle the negotiating machinery and set up five bargaining units covering operations staff, civil engineers, signals staff, mechanical and electrical engineers, and services staff.

The NUR was suspicious of these proposals and, together with a claim for a substantial pay increase, they were a major factor in the dispute of 1989 when the union used one-day strikes. All the same, the NUR executive had, long before, accepted that internal reform of its own organisation was inevitable. To this effect, in 1987 it had commissioned a study by the Industrial Relations Unit at Warwick University which reported in 1988.

The report confirmed that the NUR remained one of the most centralised of British trade unions, with the Annual Meeting of 77 delegates, the Executive Committee, and the General Secretary holding virtually complete power. On the basis of a detailed survey the report noted: "We have been struck by the intensity of the criticism expressed to us about Unity House (Head Office). In the union outside there is widespread cynicism and dissatisfaction... activists and branch officers alike repeatedly complain that information on national developments is slow and inadequate, that communications are often couched in obscure jargon and that individual cases and queries become buried in bureaucracy."

Exceptionally among British unions, the NUR has a full-time executive equivalent in size to the total number of national and divisional officers. The Warwick report suggested that, in view of privatisation and changed bargaining structures, there was not sufficient work at Head Office to justify the continuous presence there of 21 executive members. Apart from the few who sit on the key sub-committees, it was a full-time body without a full-time job to do. The report therefore proposed its deployment in the regions on perhaps two days a week.

The response to calls for organisational reform of the NUR graphically illustrates the strengths and weaknesses of trade union democracy. Within the executive there is some support for decentralisation as a way of maintaining closer links with the membership and specialised grades in an increasingly fragmented sector. This is despite the self-effacement required for a union executive to reform itself. However, from some numerically important rail branches there is considerable rank and file opposition to BR's proposed dismantling of national pay bargaining. Yet internal decentralisation must be, to some extent, a de facto recognition of decentralised bargaining structures. This pressure is accentuated because the NUR executive in 1989 did not reflect the regional balance of its membership, so that areas outside London and the south-east were over-represented.

The Warwick report further commented: "Unless ordinary members can be won back to an identification with the union and unless the tensions between Unity House and the other levels of the union can be eased, then any reform in the intermediate structures of branch and district will be largely futile."

The NUR has begun to offer a wide range of financial services as a way of halting the fall in membership and to promote recruitment. New benefits arranged through Unity Trust, the trade union bank, include low-cost mortgages, personal loans, and insurance. The NUR is also offering holiday discounts, special terms for domestic building work, and lump sum compensation for members who have been downgraded by employers because of ill-health.

Women
The union is male-dominated but the National Executive has instructed district committees to set up women's advisory committees and, following this, the 1986 AGM instructed the National Executive to set up a national women's advisory committee.

Recent issues
Decentralisation of collective bargaining
Privatisation has frequently led to the fragmentation of bargaining, as in the cases of the

National Freight Corporation, buses, ferries, and hotels. In addition, BR announced its intention to decentralise bargaining. Together with pay, this was an issue in the 1989 dispute.

Changed Work Practices

In a ballot organised by the NUR in 1988, rail guards voted by 3,701 to 3,317 to accept changes proposed by BR. These included the introduction of a flexible "train-man" grade, combining the jobs of assistant driver and guard. BR has also proposed a three-day working week with shifts of 13 hours for some track maintenance staff, but while the NUR is willing to negotiate about this its negotiators are wary. The NUR is increasingly concerned at the growing pressure within BR for wider use of part-time staff, not objecting to part-time working as such but to the replacement of one full-time job by a part-time job or use of part-time working as a means of casualising the work-force.

External relations

The NUR sponsors the following MPs:

P.C. Snape	(West Bromwich East)
R. Cook	(Edinburgh Central)
T. Dalyell	(West Lothian)
D. Anderson	(Swansea)
J. Marek	(Wrexham)
G.P. Dunwoody	(Crewe & Nantwich)
F. Dobson	(Holborn & St Pancras)
D. Dewar	(Glasgow Garscadden)

Recent events

For the NUR 1989 was dominated by the dispute with British Rail over pay and the management's proposals to decentralise collective bargaining. In November 1988 BR gave notice of its intention to end the 80-year-old bargaining machinery. BR informed the NUR that it intended to impose a package of pay-related measures, including regional allowances and performance-related bonuses for technicians in the south-east, without waiting for union approval. The BR personnel director declared in May 1989 that if agreement on the bargaining changes had not been reached by the implementation date in November, it would be very difficult to stop management creating whatever arrangements it wanted.

The NUR responded to the imposed pay package by balloting members for approval for a series of one-day strikes. A majority was secured but BR tried for an injunction to ban the first strike on the grounds that some 32 NUR members did not receive ballot papers. This action was thrown out of court. Next, two disgruntled members were financially assisted by the 1984 legislative creation, the CROTUM (Commissioner for the Rights Of Trade Union Members), to seek an injunction on similar lines but this action was also refused.

The strikes therefore went ahead. At first management took a hard line and the government, though formally not intervening, volubly looked forward to a rerun of the Scargill/NUM defeat. However, the leading union negotiator's conduct was beyond reproach and BR was out-generalled and outmanoeuvred by the NUR despite, or perhaps because of, its obsolete organisation. The ballot gave the strikes legitimacy and, for most people, money wage increases were trailing well behind price inflation. The Clapham rail disaster had brought alarming revelations of underinvestment, undermanning, and dangerously high levels of dependence on overtime working.

Further references

P.S. Bagwell, *The National Union of Railwaymen 1913-1963*, NUR, 1963.

P.S. Bagwell, *The Railwaymen*, 2 vols, Allen & Unwin, 1963 and 1982.

J.D.M. Bell, *Industrial Unionism: A Critical Analysis*, McNaughton & Gowenlock, 1949.

F. McKenna, *The Railway Workers, 1840-1970*, Faber, 1980.

P.S. Bagwell, *End of the Line? The Fate of British Railways under Thatcher*, Verso 1984.

A. Ferner, "Political Constraints and Management Strategies: The case of working practices in British Rail", *British Journal of Industrial Relations*, 23, no. 1, 1985.

NUS
NATIONAL UNION OF SEAMEN

TUC affiliated

Head Office: Maritime House, Old Town, Clapham, London SW4 0JP

Telephone: 01-622 5581

Telex: 8814611

Fax: 01-738 8636

Principal national officers
General Secretary: S. McCluskie
Acting Deputy General Secretary: P.A. McGregor

Union journal: The Seaman (monthly circulation around 15,000).
The NUS achieved the unique feat of winning the award for the best trade union newspaper in both the 1986 and 1987 Annual Trade Union Journals Competition run by the TUC. In addition the union won the best publicity category in the 1987 competition for the booklet *Disaster at Zebrugge: the Crew's Story*. The NUS has now won more awards for its publications than any other union since the TUC's annual competition was first launched in 1977.

Membership

Current membership (1987)
Male: 19,986
Female: 997
Total: 20,963

Membership trends

	1975	1979	1981	1983	1987	change 1975-87	1983-87
Men	44,000	45,654	33,832	24,163	19,986	−55%	−17%
Women	300	1,392	1,106	837	977	226%	17%
Total	44,300	47,046	34,938	25,000	20,963	−53%	−16%

General

The National Union of Seamen is one of Britain's long-established unions, although of late it has witnessed a severe decline in membership due to changes in ship technology and the continuing decline in the UK shipping industry in general; since 1975 it has lost more than half its membership. It is the sole organisation representing UK ratings employed in the UK shipping industry. Because of the reduced number of UK-registered ships, the majority of the union's members are now employed on ships trading to European countries.

The General Secretary, Sam McCluskie, is Treasurer of the Labour Party and as such is a member of the Party's National Executive Committee.

History

Seafarers were among the first of Britain's workers to recognise the value and importance of trade unionism, and around the beginning of the nineteenth century sailors' friendly societies were set up in several ports, particularly along the north-east coast. The first national organisation of which there appears to be any record seems to have been formed before the middle of the nineteenth century, noted by the Webbs in their standard work on British trade unionism. The organisation was only a loose federation of practically autonomous port unions, the most prominent of which was the *North of England Sailors and Seagoing Firemen's Friendly Association,* formed at Sunderland in 1879, and known generally as the *Sunderland Seamen's Union.*

Among the members of this association was a deck-hand named James Havelock Wilson. In 1887 Wilson set up the *National Amalgamated Sailors' and Firemen's Union of Great Britain and Ireland.* The new union, with 500 members, made its first appearance at the TUC in 1888. By the following year membership had increased dramatically to 65,000, with branches in nearly 60 ports. As a response to the growing influence of the union the owners set up the Shipping Federation in 1890. In 1893, after a bitter strike at Hull which spread to national level, the *National Amalgamated Union* went into voluntary liquidation following a costly libel suit. Wilson, by then the MP for Middlesbrough, set up a new union, this time named the *National Sailors' and Firemen's Union.* The newly-formed union agitated for legislative reform, and by 1910 improvements in the Merchant Shipping Acts had been secured together with the extension of the Workmen's Compensation Acts to seafarers.

The union put forward its claim for the establishment of a national wages board in 1911, as part of a charter for seafarers formulated simultaneously in seven maritime countries by the International Committee of Seafarers' Unions. Following its rejection the seafarers' union in five countries declared a strike, which was supported by dockers and road transport workers. The principal storm centres of the strike were in the Bristol Channel and in Liverpool. Despite a long and bitter struggle, in which police harassment and the use of blacklegs were rife, the union secured informal recognition, although they did not achieve their aim of the establishment of a national negotiating wage board.

With the outbreak of the First World War the union turned its attention to securing provision for its members and their families who were victims of enemy action at sea. In

1916, following disruptions caused by seafarers going on strike, the government issued an invitation to the union to discuss the possibility of a national wage, the supply of seafarers, and the regulation of the employment of "Chinese and other natives". Following a series of meetings the National Maritime Board was established to jointly regulate the supply of seafarers and to regulate terms and conditions for various categories of seafarers.

In the early 1920s there was a recrudescence of strike activity. Firstly, there was severe depression following a boom, and falling money wages caused unrest. Secondly, there was bitter inter-union and intra-union strife, for reasons only partly economic.

Unofficial action became a major phenomenon in the shipbuilding industry; the most prominent aspect was opposition to the leadership of the NUS. At that time the top priority of Wilson was harmony with the ship owners in order to maintain the National Maritime Board and the closed shop for seafarers, to which end he sacrificed all else. That the unofficial rank and file action was not more frequent or widespread is attributable to the need to be in favour with the union in order to obtain a berth. As Henry Pelling observed in *The History of British Trade Unionism,* the NUS in Wilson's final years "seemed to have become little more than a 'company union'". The NUS was the only TUC-affiliated union to oppose the General Strike in 1926, and funded a right-wing miners' breakaway union (the Miners' Industrial (non-political) Union). The NUS was expelled from the TUC in 1928. Following Wilson's death in the spring of 1929 the NUS was reaffiliated into TUC membership later in the year.

Havelock Wilson was replaced by W.R. Spence, and relations with other unions and the rank and file of the NUS improved. Between 1929 and 1932 the total world tonnage laid up as a result of the Great Depression increased fourfold. In 1930 Spence reported to the union that 20,000 seafarers were out of work and six million tons of shipping were lying idle in world ports. When business recovered Spence pursued an energetic policy which, with the forceful support of Ernest Bevin, secured substantial gains without strike action being taken.

An important development in 1937 was the establishment of a system of joint supply of labour, operated by the National Maritime Board (NMB) in conjunction with the Board of Trade. Considerable progress was also made towards the raising of standards of crew accommodation. Comfort was made a specific requirement for the first time, and sleeping quarters, mess rooms, hospital arrangements, ventilation, and proper provision for recreation were all embodied in new regulations emanating from the Board of Trade.

During the Second World War, the merchant navy suffered heavy losses particularly with the increased use of U-boats. The NUS claim that their losses of life (30,000 men) represented a higher proportion of casualties than in the armed forces. A number of substantial improvements were made by the NUS during wartime, especially with the establishment of the merchant navy pool, which facilitated continuous employment for seafarers.

In 1955 the NUS was involved in a nine-week strike which, although confined to two ports and liner shipping, was to resuscitate rank and file grievances over the merchant shipping acts, and the lack of union representation on board. Common to all these complaints was a fierce resentment directed against the union leadership over the distance between national and local officials on the one hand and the rank and file on the other, and for its complacency and half-heartedness in pursuing union claims.

It was immediately after the 1960 unofficial strike that the National Seamen's Reform Movement came into being. This was formed as a "ginger" movement, concerned with changing its policy and direction to one of greater militancy and increased democratic control.

The 1966 seamen's strike was a milestone in the history of the union. Not only was it directed at the shipowners, but it also took place at a time when the Labour government was attempting to operate a strict incomes policy. Bill Hogarth, the General Secretary of the union, centred the NUS claim on a reduction of hours from 56 to 40 a week and a £60 per month wage for seamen. The strike lasted for 47 days and was concluded with much dissension among union members. However, during the course of the strike the reform of merchant shipping legislation as it affected seamen was made a major dispute issue by the union. During the strike Harold Wilson made his famous statement in the House of Commons about a "tightly-knit group of politically motivated men" who were out to "take over" the NUS leadership for the Communist Party. (One of the men named by Wilson, Jim Slater, later became General Secretary of the union.) However, the Pearson Court of Inquiry set the tone for further changes in the working conditions of seafarers. The Court of Inquiry's report laid the foundation for subsequent changes in the merchant shipping acts. The union particularly welcomed the improvements made in on-board disciplinary arrangements and the introduction of the legal right of seamen to strike whilst their ships were berthed in UK ports.

Union officials

The rules of the NUS provide that applicants for union office must have had five years' sea service and must not have reached the age of 45 years, except in "special and extraordinary circumstances". Branch officials are appointed by the General Secretary, subject to confirmation by the Executive Council following three months' probationary employment.

The union maintains 19 branch offices in the British Isles and one in Barbados, 17 of which are staffed by full-time officers. Most ferry ports have lay member committees, the officers of which deal directly with their immediate employers.

Coverage

The union recruits its members among seafarers employed by UK registered shipping companies as well as by some companies based in Crown Dependencies and Overseas Dependencies. Agreements reached at the industry's negotiating forum, the National Maritime Board, establish minimum terms and conditions which are observed by those employers who are party to the Board's decisions.

The union is party to agreements with 42 companies (covering some 3,000 members) in the offshore gas and oil sector. It is also a member of the inter-union British Seafarers Joint Council. The NUS has recently begun organising offshore catering companies and has successfully negotiated a number of sole recognition agreements.

With the emergence of company level bargaining in the mid 1960s, union agreements with individual companies were based on the premise that the terms offered would be superior to those determined at national level. In the late 1980s, however, agreements based on inferior terms were from time to time accepted as an alternative to the labour market being opened up to non-union labour and all that that implies. In summary it can be said that the fragmentation of the wage-bargaining system is still continuing, so generating its own uncertainties about the continued functioning of the National Maritime Board and the application of its many agreements to British seafarers.

Organisation

The supreme ruling body of the union is the Biennial General Meeting, to which delegates are elected in proportion to the size of the branch. Branches with 100 — 1,500 members are entitled to send one delegate, 1,501 — 2,500 two, 2,501 — 3,500 three delegates, with an extra delegate for each additional 1,000 members thereafter.

The Executive Council is elected every three years by ballot of the whole membership; it comprises 13 members and acts as the negotiating body of the union in a National

Maritime Board context. Deputy National Secretaries and National Secretaries are elected by secret ballot of the entire membership. Under current rules they are elected for life. The positions of the General Secretary, Deputy General Secretary, and Chairman of the Executive Council are the subject of re-election every five years as required by the Trade Union Act 1984.

The union has a ballot procedure on annual wage negotiations.

Work-place activity

The unofficial strike of 1960 and the 1966 strike have resulted in the creation of the concept of "shop steward at sea" in the form of "shipboard liaison representatives". The NUS rule book provides that such liaison representatives cannot sanction the withdrawal of labour or any other form of industrial action without the consent of an executive officer (i.e. the General Secretary, Assistant General Secretary/Treasurer or National Secretary). The 1982 Biennial General Meeting agreed to set up shipboard branches in a radical extension of its shore-based organisation. The concept of the shipboard branch did not generate the expected degree of response and to all intents and purposes it can at best be described as dormant. In the context of the union's rules only executive officers have the authority to sanction a withdrawal of labour from any ship while it is safely berthed in the UK. In any dispute likely to affect the majority of the membership the Executive Council is obliged to take a vote of all members at home, who are able and willing to vote, before a strike can be called. In the 1981 pay dispute this procedure was avoided by recourse to selective strikes.

Women

The number of women members in the union has remained at around the 4 per cent mark throughout the eighties. Nearly all are employed as stewards and catering staff on ferries and passenger ships.

External relations

The NUS is affiliated to the Labour Party. There is one sponsored MP, John Prescott (East Hull), who is a member of the Shadow Cabinet and Transport Spokesman. When Prescott stood for the post of Deputy Leader of the Labour Party in 1988 he was not supported by the NUS as they chose instead to vote for Roy Hattersley. The union has a political fund, and in a vote there was a 86.5 per cent vote in favour of retention although the turn-out was only 34 per cent.

The union continues to be affiliated to the International Transport Workers' Federation, and Sam McCluskie is a member of the maritime policy and seafarers' section committee.

The NUS has representation on the TUC's oil advisory committee.

Policy and recent events

The NUS has consistently campaigned, in conjunction with the International Transport Workers' Federation (ITF) to which it is affiliated, against the flying of "flags of convenience" by shipping companies, on the grounds that such companies use such flags as a means of staffing ships with cheap labour.

The ITF won an important legal victory in 1980 in its campaign to drive from the seas ships flying "flags of convenience". The Court of Appeal decided that any dispute arising from actions taken by the ITF to further that "ultimate objective" was a trade dispute and covered by the immunities from court action afforded by the 1974 Trade Union and Labour Relations Act. However, subsequent Conservative anti-union legislation has made such industrial action liable in tort.

The 1978 Merchant Shipping Act overturned a 140-year rule which allowed ships' masters to fine seafarers. Instead, shore-based tribunals made up of equal numbers of employer and union representatives now deal with cases of misconduct. The union is also a signatory party to the Code of Conduct for seafarers which became operative on 1 January, 1979.

In December 1987 a strike of members employed by the Isle of Man Steampacket Company over dismissals and changes in working conditions led to the national ferry port strike of January-February 1988. The dispute was settled through the medium of ACAS, the Arbitration, Conciliation, and Advisory Service. A number of jobs were lost but the terms and conditions set out in the agreement with the company remained largely unaltered.

A similar dispute arose with members employed by P&O European Ferries Dover, who went on strike on 3 February, 1988. In this case the company sought to impose about 360 redundancies plus drastic changes in terms and conditions. The company was intent on making changes irrespective of union and employee wishes and stubbornly refused to negotiate. Ultimately, because of breaches of various injunctions, the union's assets were sequestrated and placed in the hands of an accountant appointed by the High Court. This was because the union would not dissociate itself from what the court called illegal mass picketing. As a result the union lost control of its funds and its properties. The sequestration order was finally lifted on 15 August, 1988 and normal union business was resumed. The union lost over £1.9m out of assets totalling some £2.6m. The P&O dispute eventually ended on 9 June, 1989, as a result of a ballot conducted among its remaining participants.

This was a very long drawn out dispute which almost saw the demise of the union itself and left much of its membership divided and embittered. The NUS had little choice in entering the dispute as this was forced onto them by the actions of the employers, P&O. But it took the NUS leadership a long time to realise that the dispute was not being carried out in Dover, but instead was being conducted in the courts in London. Traditional tactics were no longer effective against employers determined to use new Tory laws to establish their "rights to manage".

In March 1989, following a decision in support of amalgamation taken at the 1988 Biennial General Meeting, a membership ballot came out strongly in favour of the union amalgamating with the National Union of Railwaymen, in preference to remaining an independent organisation or, as seemed most likely, merging with the Transport and General Workers' Union.

The election for the post of Deputy General Secretary had to be postponed towards the end of 1988 because of a discrepancy in the issuing of ballot forms. 17,754 ballot papers were dispatched by Unity Balloting Services, a subsidiary of the trade union bank Unity Trust, whereas the NUS believed that only 16,834 should have been issued. New ballot forms have been issued and the result of the election is expected in September 1989. There are three candidates standing: Tony McGuire, the acting Deputy General Secretary is the favourite; Bob Raynor, Harwich branch secretary, and John Wood, the P&O strike leader, hopes to capture the support of the militant left.

Joint pay bargaining

The National Maritime Board has been the negotiating arm of the Merchant Navy Establishment (the recruiting pool which covers more than 20,000 officers and ratings) since 1947. It has been operated jointly by employers belonging to the General Council of British Shipping, the NUS, and the officers' union, NUMAST. Towards the end of 1988 three major shipping companies, Sealink, Cunard, and Furness Withy, announced their intention to withdraw from pay negotiations conducted by the NMB. Sealink, one of the two British ferry companies employing nearly 3,000 officers and ratings, has stated that it finds "totally unacceptable" a situation in which the deep-sea sector of the industry continues to influence and regulate pay settlements which are not necessarily related to the ferry sector.

Sealink, the largest unionised of the three companies, has however stated that it still wishes to remain a member of the NMB, and it would not follow P&O European Ferries in no longer negotiating with the NUS and NUMAST. Instead of the national wage agreement it wishes to negotiate with unions on a company basis and would not pursue "different levels of productivity payment at different locations".

The effects of the threat to the status of the national wage bargaining machinery are uncertain. Serious breaches in the agreement on national bargaining were signalled in 1981 when the Shipping Council expelled Canadian Pacific for breaking ranks during the 1981 seamen's strike. Thereafter Cunard sought separate deals for its employees on the QE2. There has also been a growing number of shipping companies who have registered (and reregistered) their vessels under non-British flags and employed crews on terms and conditions outside the NMB agreement.

At present about 40 of the 60 British-registered shipping companies negotiate through the NMB. While dismantling the NMB may not be viable in the short term, it would be most unlikely if major reforms in the traditional structure did not occur in the more medium to longer term.

Further references

J. Havelock Wilson, *My Stormy Voyage through Life,* Vol. 1 (Vol. 2 never published), Co-operative Press, 1925.

Basil Mogeridge, "Militancy and inter-union rivalries in British shipping, 1911-1929", *International Review of Social Science,* 6, no. 3, 1961.

S. G. Sturmey, *British Shipping and World Competition,* University of London, The Athlone Press, 1926.

L. Hemingway, *Conflict and Democracy,* Oxford, Clarendon Press, 1978. Chapter 4 contains an account of the conflict between the National Seamen's Reform Movement and the leadership of the NUS from 1960 to 1974.

J. McConville, *The Shipping Industry in the UK,* International Institute for Labour Studies.

Tony Wailey, "The Seamen's Strike, Liverpool 1966", *History Workshop,* May 1978.

J. Kitchen, *The Employment of Merchant Seamen,* Croom Helm, 1980.

Charles Leadbeater, "McCluskie's Last Stand", *Marxism Today,* June 1988.

Arthur Marsh and Vicky Ryan are currently writing the official history of the NUS.

NUT
NATIONAL UNION OF TEACHERS

TUC affiliated

Head Office: Hamilton House, Mabledon Place, London WC1H 9BD

Telephone: 01-388 6191

Fax: 01-387 8458

Principal national officers
General Secretary: Fred Jarvis
General Secretary Designate: Doug McAvoy
Assistant Secretary (Education): A. Evans
Assistant Secretary (Salaries): G. B. Fawcett
Assistant Secretary (Accounts): A. G. Wills
Assistant Secretary (Membership): A. Jarman
Assistant Secretary (Organisation): D. MacFarlane
Assistant Secretary (Regions): R. P. Boland
Assistant Secretary (Solicitor): C. Clayton

Union journal: The Teacher (posted weekly to every school, £15 per year's individual subscription. In addition, the union publishes many specialist books and pamphlets concerned with education, union benefits, legal aid, conditions of service, and entitlements. The *NUT Education Review,* a comprehensive account of education policies and development throughout England and Wales, is published twice yearly, £3.00 for members).

Membership

Current membership (1987)
Male: 53,488
Female: 124,806
Total: 178,294

Membership trends

	1975	1979	1981	1983	1987	change 1975-87	1983-87
Men	69,961	92,000	N/A	59,462	53,488	−24%	−10%
Women	211,894	156,896	N/A	151,037	124,806	−41%	−17%
Total	281,855	248,896	224,090	210,499	178,294	−37%	−15%

General
The NUT is the largest of the six teaching unions and is open to all teachers who are recognised as qualified according to rule. Recently there have been significant changes regarding the pay, working conditions, and collective bargaining machinery for teachers. The Burnham Committees, which were set up in 1965 for pay negotiations, have been scrapped and replaced by a new, but temporary, advisory committee.

Concern over the low level of teachers' pay has been a problem for the union almost since the Houghton pay review in 1974. Discontent over pay began to translate itself into direct industrial action during the early 1980s, fuelled by a government determined to keep a tight reign on public sector spending — each 1 per cent on teachers' pay adds £75m to public spending. The government was also keen to introduce certain reforms to pay structure and conditions of service, such as merit payments. However, under the terms of reference of the Burnham Committees discussions on changes in conditions of service were outside its remit: Burnham was able to negotiate only on matters of pay.

In 1984 the NUT withdrew from talks with employers over a proposal to reform teachers' pay, and because of its outright majority on the union side of Burnham the joint working party on pay reform was abandoned. Instead, the NUT put forward a claim for a minimum increase of £1,200. Following the breakdown of these negotiations, and after conducting membership ballots, the NUT, along with the other main teaching unions, NASUWT, AMMA, and EIS, began industrial action including snap one-day strikes. In addition, members worked to rule and refused to cover for absent colleagues, to undertake lunch-time supervision, and evening and weekend "voluntary" duties. Many local authorities supported the teachers' dispute, although one, the Conservative-controlled authority of Solihull, did manage to win a High Court injunction and union action there had to be abandoned.

By 1985 industrial action had escalated to the pitch of indiscriminate "guerrilla" strikes, and even the moderate National Association of Head Teachers advised its members who had kept schools open during action not to continue to do so.

Performance-related pay and a "radical new approach" to pay were formally proposed by the employers but unanimously rejected by all the unions. In an effort to break the consensus which appeared to exist between the unions, the NUT was stripped of its outright majority on Burnham. Whilst agreement was eventually reached with some of the smaller teaching unions, the opposition of the two largest unions, the NUT and NASUWT, effectively made the agreement inoperative.

Continued government frustration at its inability to resolve the pay dispute, plus its increasing desire to ensure that an element of performance-related pay should be introduced, led to the government announcement that it would abolish Burnham and replace it with an interim advisory committee reporting directly to the Secretary of State for Education. In February 1988 the Teachers' Pay and Conditions Act received its royal assent, and thereby removed the right of teachers' unions to negotiate pay and conditions. This action prompted a new wave of strikes in schools and even the non-TUC affiliated union, AMMA, held a strike ballot, the first in its history.

By March 1987 the government had formulated final pay increases for teachers and for conditions of service which would become part of contracts of employment. The main element of the proposals was an average salary increase of 16.4 per cent to be paid in two instalments. In addition a single "teachers' basic scale" was created, and "incentive allowances" based on additional responsibility, outstanding classroom performance, or for posts which were difficult to fill because of skill shortages, were introduced. Further, "professional duties" were more precisely defined specifying the subordination of teachers to the head teacher, making it more difficult for teachers to withdraw their goodwill on future occasions. The previously so-called "voluntary duties" such as cover for absent colleagues and lunch-time supervision, which had become such effective industrial weapons, were also formally defined and admitted as part of normal teachers' duties. Finally, under the direction of their heads, teachers were obliged to work for a specified 1,265 hours a year.

After winning the General Election in 1987 wider and more radical reforms to education were introduced by the government. The 1988 Education Reform Act, master-minded by Kenneth Baker who replaced Sir Keith Joseph as Secretary of State for Education, laid down the framework for the national curriculum. He also proposed decentralisation of decision-making to schools, giving greater control to parents over their children's schooling and new rights for schools to become independent of local authorities.

Whilst the intense industrial action between 1984 and 1986 eventually resulted in a 16.4 per cent pay rise, public support for continued union action was waning. Moreover, the NUT itself has suffered a loss of over 40,000 members in the past five years, many defecting to the no-strike union PAT (see **PAT** "Membership"). This massive loss of membership has become a major issue for the NUT and is an important reason for the union adopting "new realism". Master-minded by the General Secretary designate Doug McAvoy, it is perhaps best typified by the change in the union logo from a hand carrying a torch, which to some suggested a "strident, aggressive, and uncaring union" to its new "softer" symbol of an outstretched hand. The idea of the outstretched hand reflects the direction which McAvoy wishes to pursue; the reforms may be seen as providing opportunities for teachers to regain some of their lost status while at the same time promoting professional and educational issues above those of the narrower "workerist" matters of pay and conditions. The left would prefer to retain the more traditional strategies based on industrial militancy to the stealth advocated by the McAvoy reforms.

History

Before 1870 there were already a number of teachers' associations. They were localised, small, and possessed little influence, and were, in most instances, connected with particular religious denominations. In 1870 the passage of the Education Act, the growing interest in popular education, and general discontent of teachers with their conditions led to a conference of representatives of various local teachers' associations being held in London. They formed the *National Union of Elementary Teachers*. The aim of the union was "to unite together, by means of local associations, public elementary teachers...in order to provide machinery by means of which teachers may give expression to their opinions...and also take united action in any matter affecting their interests". In those days there was little or no provision for a teacher or his dependants against sickness, old age, or premature death. The union made provision for establishing friendly benefits for such purposes.

Out of an organisation of some 400 elementary teachers in 1870 there has grown a comprehensive organisation for the teaching profession which serves members in all types of schools and further education establishments.

The union affiliated to the TUC in 1970, one year after the NASUWT.

Organisation

The machinery of the union is simple in design. It consists of local associations covering England and Wales, linked together to form county or metropolitan divisions. The supreme authority of the union is the Annual Conference which meets at Easter and consists of representatives of the local associations and the county/metropolitan divisions. Between conferences the affairs of the union are managed by the Executive which consists of 37 members elected biennially and the five officers (not officials) of the union — President, Senior Vice-President, Junior Vice-President, ex-President and Treasurer. These officers are elected biennially in a postal ballot with the counting of votes administered by the Electoral Reform Society.

The 1988 Annual Conference agreed that as a result of present and future developments in education, including the 1988 Education Reform Act, there was a need to greatly enhance the provision of services to members at local level. It proposed far-reaching changes to the union's regional structure, to increase the number of staff in each regional office from four to 10, and to create a new post of Regional Secretary. Such changes would allow regions to exercise much greater discretion in all union and industrial relations affairs.

Women
Women account for over 70 per cent of the total membership of the NUT, but in terms of the number of full-time officials women are disproportionately represented.

There is an active Equal Opportunities Committee which is concerned with three main areas which were identified in the union's 1984 Memorandum of Equal Opportunities. These are career development for women, the involvement of women in the union, and sex discrimination in schools. The committee was concerned to examine the implications of the Education Reform Act in relation to the effect on the position of women teachers and on equal opportunities work in the curriculum.

The union also runs a number of training courses which aim to assist participants to develop clear and realistic plans to promote gender issues at local level. The NUT publishes a number of booklets: *Equality, Women — What Does the NUT Offer You?*, *Towards Equality for Girls and Boys: Guidelines on Countering Sexism in Schools.*

In a novel development the NUT has agreed to send representatives to sit on a joint *ad hoc* working party with the construction industry UCATT to look into the question of why so few girls enter the building industry.

Towards the end of 1988 the NUT signed an agreement with the Kent local authority which guarantees women the right to a career break lasting up to seven years. This is one of the longest career breaks ever negotiated and will ensure that women teachers' promotion prospects are not damaged by time away from work to bring up children. In return, women will be expected to keep up to date with the latest teaching developments and devote a minimum of 10 days a year to this involvement.

External relations
The General Secretary, Fred Jarvis, was President of the 1978 TUC and acted as chairman of the General Council and its inner cabinet, the Finance and General Purposes Committee for the year 1986/7. He was the first teachers' representative to have held that post. He is due to retire in September 1989.

The NUT pursues an active policy of developing international contacts and regularly sends delegates to Central America, Africa, USSR, Israel, and Sweden.

Policy
City Technical College
NUT policy towards the business-sponsored City Technical College (CTC) is unclear. On the one hand the 1989 Conference passed a motion advising teachers not to work at CTCs, but Conference only narrowly defeated a call for tougher action which would have committed the union to backing industrial action against the colleges. However, Fred Jarvis stressed that the union would try to represent those members who ignored union advice by working at the colleges.

School discipline
The document, *Inquiry into Discipline in Schools,* was a NUT submission to an inquiry by the Department of Education and Science into discipline in schools. In it the NUT supported the claim that problems had increased and that discipline had deteriorated in recent years. It blamed wider social trends such as unemployment, and the poor quality of inner-city life, and suggested that increasing schools' resources, enhancing teacher training and in-service education could improve the situation. The NUT also called for a tougher line to be taken with difficult pupils and greater prosecution of offenders.

Race equality

The NUT has welcomed the government's attempt to monitor the racial composition of teachers with a view to increasing the number of teachers from ethnic minority backgrounds. The NUT has always had a progressive attitude towards race equality and is one of the few unions which was singled out for its positive stance in a survey conducted by the Labour Research Department.

Teacher shortages

Government plans to tackle the shortage of teachers were unveiled in June 1989; the key proposal was its scheme for "articled teachers". Under the scheme, graduates, although formally attached to a teacher training college, would complete at least four-fifths of their training at a school jointly supervised by the school and college. The Postgraduate Certificate of Education would normally take an articled teacher two years to complete.

The union is opposed to the government's plans for an easier route into the teaching profession, whereby mature entrants would receive on-the-job training at a school instead of spending a year at a teacher training college. The 1989 Annual Conference delegates were almost unanimous in their support for teachers taking industrial action against people who make a mid-career move into teaching without formal training.

Concern over the shortage of teachers has been expressed by all the teaching unions. The Commons Education Select Committee in its July 1989 report strongly criticised the government for its attitude towards teachers' pay, and its optimism regarding shortages. The Committee proposed that a substantial increase in public expenditure on education was necessary for "future prosperity and well-being". A similar line of criticism was also put forward by Her Majesty's Inspectors. Teaching will have to compete fiercely with other, better paid jobs for the dwindling supply of graduates in the early 1990s as a result of demographic changes. However the shortage of teachers will also come at a time when much of the new national curriculum is due to come on stream and the school rolls resume their long upward climb.

The need to deal with the problem of the shortage of teachers forms a central part of the union's strategy in pushing the NUT towards accepting the notion of "new realism". It believes the government has miscalculated its answer to teacher shortages and that eventually it will have to recognise that extra resources must be injected into education. By shedding its militant, confrontational image the NUT is hoping to win the moral ground and rise above the politics of the situation by concentrating on professional issues such as improving educational standards and training, which can then be translated into improved pay and conditions for teachers. Whether the adoption of "new realism" by the NUT will solve the severe loss of membership and restore the union's credibility remains to be seen (see "Recent events").

Recent events

Following much pressure from all six teaching unions about the future of pay negotiations, in July 1989 the Education Secretary outlined three options for restoring collective bargaining rights in time for the 1991 pay settlement. First, a return to a forum of employers and unions, while allowing the government to exercise some control over costs, pay structure, and job conditions through built-in safeguards. Second, to turn the present temporary advisory body into a permanent review body, which might be given a clear remit but linked with a no-strike agreement. Third, a national framework but with greater decentralised bargaining, allowing local authorities and the new grant-maintained schools to opt out.

At the time of publication the non-TUC union PAT announced that it was having exploratory talks about the possibility of a merger with the other non-TUC union

AMMA. If the merger proved successful then the new union would become the second largest teaching union with a membership almost the size of the NUT. This raises the prospect of the teaching unions becoming even more divided unless the NUT can take the initiative and work seriously towards bringing about one union representing all teachers before the end of the century.

Further references

W. Roy, "Membership participation in the NUT", *British Journal of Industrial Relations,* 2, no. 2, 1964, pp.189-208.

C. J. Margerison and C. K. Elliot, "A predictive study in teacher militancy", *British Journal of Industrial Relations,* 8, no. 3, 1970, pp.408-17.

W. Roy, *The Teachers' Union,* Teachers' Publishing Company, 1968.

R. Bourne and B. MacArthur, *The Struggle for Education 1870-1970,* Teachers' Publishing Company, 1970.

R. Seifert, "Some Aspects of Factional Opposition: Rank and File and the National Union of Teachers 1967-82", *British Journal of Industrial Relations,* 22, no. 3, November 1984, pp.372-90.

NUTGW
NATIONAL UNION OF TAILORS AND GARMENT WORKERS

TUC affiliated

Head Office: 16 Charles Square, London N1 6NP

Telephone: 01-251 9406

Fax: 01-608 0666

Principal national officers
General Secretary: Alec Smith
Deputy General Secretary: Anne Spencer

Divisional offices/officers

North East
G. Bowen, 18 Norfolk Street, Sunderland, Tyne and Wear

North West
M. Marston, 409 Wilmslow Road, Manchester M20 9NB

Western
J. Hawkins, 14 North Road, Cardiff CF1 3DY

Yorkshire & Humberside
H. North, Circle House, 29 Lady Lane, Leeds LS2 7LS

London & Midlands
C. Tindley, 1A Headlands, Kettering, Northants

Scottish
F. Dickinson, Albany Chambers, 534 Sauchiehall Street, Glasgow G2 3LX

Irish
M. Dummigan, 44 Elmwood Avenue, Belfast, Northern Ireland BT9 6BB

The Union has a further eight offices around the country.

Union journal: The *Garment Worker* (published monthly)

Membership

Current membership (1987)
Male: 6,893
Female: 69,975
Total: 76,868

Membership trends

	1975	*1979*	*1981*	*1983*	*1987*	*change 1975-87*	*1983-87*
Men	13,359	11,198	7,825	7,589	6,893	−48%	−9%
Women	96,070	106,164	73,936	68,541	69,975	−27%	2%
Total	109,429	117,362	81,761	76,130	76,868	−30%	1%

General

The NUTGW is the largest union in the clothing and textile industries, with over 90 per cent of its membership being women. In 1979 the clothing industry employed 320,000 people but has since lost over 110,000 jobs in the UK. In 1988 it employed around 210,000 people. Most of the job losses were concentrated in the larger factories and in tailored outer-wear where the union has the highest level of organisation. Membership has now stabilised and since 1987 the union has experienced a slight increase. Special recruitment efforts have been made in recent years targeted at the sweat-shops of East London and the West Midlands. In addition, efforts are being made to recruit more part-time workers into the union. A large proportion of the union's membership is employed in wages council sectors.

History

In the very early days, a tailor made an entire garment with his own hands. In London the best hand-made garments were made by what is known as the retail bespoke or the West End trade. Division of labour began when work was parcelled out to apprentices. Later, the journeyman who worked at home employed his wife or daughter to help him with his tasks. By the middle of the nineteenth century it was common for a journeyman, a wage earner who worked for a master contractor, to employ one or two "kippers", that is, female tailors. The invention of the treadle sewing machine made further inroads into the hand-craft trade when it became customary to make parts of the garment by machine.

In the early and middle nineteenth century Scandinavian and German tailors entered the London clothing industry and brought with them new skills in ladies' tailoring. The middle of the nineteenth century also witnessed the growth of "sweated labour". Some of the master tailors set up premises in the East End of London and hired a small number of workers. The wages of the female homeworkers, often dockers' wives, were exceedingly low. In Leeds, the other large centre of the industry, there was no cheap supply of female labour, and thus the self-contained "factory" was more common. Home-working, or the domestic putting-out system, therefore grew in London but not in Leeds.

The immigration of Russian and Polish Jews into Britain in the 1880s and 1890s brought further innovations into the industry, which led to homeworkers themselves hiring their family and relatives and setting up shop with still more subdivision of tasks to rationalise and increase their production. The "subdivisional" system of production became the exclusive province of the Jewish subcontractor who combined a high degree of division of labour with relatively high wages. At the same time "sweating" amongst the East End female homeworkers was so severe that it led to the Trade Board Act of 1909 — the forerunner of the wages council system. The Trade Board Act was immediately applied to the ready-made and bespoke tailoring trades. The Act raised the wages of the female workers, but it scarcely affected the Jewish tailors — whose wages were generally above the legal minimum. The Act led to the drawing together of competing unions and to the formation of employers' associations.

Trade union organisation in tailoring had existed long before the Trade Board Act. London journeymen tailors were among the first craftworkers to form trade unions. Organisation centred around local trade clubs and public houses. In 1833 the London tailors formed the *First Grand Lodge of Operative Tailors* which joined the *Grand National Consolidated Trade Union* inspired by Robert Owen. After the general strike in 1836, which was a total failure, the organisation folded.

In 1866 an amalgamation of many small societies with a membership of about 2,000 formed the *Amalgamated Society of Tailors*. Until the First World War, the union confined its activities to recruiting skilled handicraft tailors, and was conservative and pacific in its politics. Such conservatism led to a breakaway union being formed from its London West End branch in the form of the *London Society of Tailors and Tailoresses*.

The immigrant Jewish tailors from Russia and Poland formed trade unions during the last quarter of the nineteenth century — particularly in London. However, these unions were tiny and fragmented, and lacked any degree of permanence or stability. Anti-alien sentiment in England reached a peak towards the end of the nineteenth century, and this served to unite the Jewish unions. The *United Ladies' Tailors' and Mantle Makers' Union* was a result of such unification when it was formed in 1901. This union had a continuous existence until 1939, when it amalgamated with the NUTGW.

The multiplicity and fragmentation of unions within the clothing industry continued until 1916, fuelled as it was by rivalry between Leeds and London, and anti-alien sentiment against the Jewish unions. Finally, in 1916 the *Clothing Operatives* and the *Amalgamated Jewish Tailors* — both with headquarters in Leeds — merged with the *London Society of Tailors,* the *London and Provincial Cutters* and the *London Tailors', Machinists' and Pressers' Union.* Thus the *United Garment Workers'* was formed, the first clothing union to succeed in uniting the Jewish with the English workers, and cutters with low-paid factory women. In 1920 this amalgamation was followd by the addition of the *Scottish Operative Tailors' and Tailoresses* and the industrial union was retitled the *Tailors' and Garment Workers' Union.*

In 1932 the NUTGW assumed its present title when the *Amalgamated Society of Tailors* merged with the *Tailors' and Garments Workers' Union.* The *United Ladies' Tailors and Mantle Makers' Union* merged with the NUTGW in 1939.

The NUTGW remained unchanged until 1982 when in October of that year it merged with the two small felt hatters' unions, the *Amalgamated Society of Journeymen Felt*

Hatters and Allied Workers and the *Amalgamated Felt Hat Trimmers', Woolformers' and Allied Workers' Association.*

Union officials

The NUTGW now employs only seven divisional officers and 30 area officers. The former regions of London, Southern, Eastern, and Midlands have been combined into one London and Midland division which operates from the Kettering offices. All full-time officers are appointed by the Executive Board; the exceptions are the General Secretary and Assistant General Secretary who are elected by a ballot of the membership. Divisional officers co-ordinate all the work in their division and are responsible to the Executive Board.

Initially, full-time officials in the industry tended to have a long background within the clothing industry, with an age range of between 30-45 years of age. During the seventies there was a tendency for younger, full-time officials to be appointed from outside the union — usually graduates from Ruskin College, Oxford, or the LSE. More recently, in 1987/8, the NUTGW, eager to serve its large female membership, appointed women as its last three trainee full-time officers. The clothing industry is characterised by a low level of work-place bargaining, and full-time officials tend to be fully stretched with a high degree of membership dependence. Aware of this fact the NUTGW launched its *Shop Stewards Action Pack* in 1987 in an attempt to place more responsibility on shop stewards for recruiting and dealing with members' more immediate problems. The action pack, which included a series of leaflets on union services and rights, was commended by the Trade Unions Journals Competition for its clarity of style and presentation.

Coverage

A large proportion of the NUTGW membership is employed in the wages council sector. There is current concern over the government's attack on wages councils which is likely to remove 2.5 million workers (or around 11 per cent of the total work-force) from wage council protection. The NUTGW is fighting a campaign to prevent what it sees as the return to the "Victorian sweat-shops". This is particularly disillusioning for the union which was instrumental in rationalising the clothing industries wages councils and bargaining machinery in the early 1980s. The NUTGW still places major emphasis on the annual wage negotiations with the British Clothing Industry Association, which represents most of the major employers in the clothing industry. Details of this agreement normally form the basis of an agreed submission to the Clothing Manufacturers' Wages Council, which eventually covers the whole industry.

Membership (Dec. 1987) *Division*		*% of total*
North East	12,236	15.9
North West	10,022	13.0
Western	9,627	12.5
Yorkshire & Humberside	14,228	18.5
London & Midlands	8,205	10.7
Scottish	12,507	16.3
Irish	10,043	13.1
Total	76,868	100.0

Organisation

The supreme policy-making body in the union is the General Conference, which meets every two years. Delegates to the General Conference are elected from the 300 or so branches. The 1985 Conference made important rule changes which gave members opportunities for participation in union affairs as well as increasing the number of delegates for larger branches.

The union's general management is vested in the Executive Board which reflects the changing patterns within the clothing industry. The Executive Board has now been reduced to 14 lay members plus the General Secretary (in a non-voting capacity). The lay members are elected by a secret postal ballot, conducted in 1988 by the Electoral Reform Society, to serve for two years. At the end of their period they are eligible to stand for re-election.

The Executive Board meets at least quarterly and is responsible for the union's finances and property. The EB also appoints full-time officials and has the power to sanction official strikes. Both the General Secretary and the Deputy General Secretary are elected by a secret postal ballot of the whole membership. Alec Smith was re-elected in 1988 as General Secretary having significantly increased his support in the union. He received the nomination of 81 per cent of branches whereas in 1978 he was able to secure only 60 per cent branch support.

The NUTGW has a system of divisional councils which are composed of the Executive Board members representing or residing in the division, the full-time officers serving in the division, and a number of rank and file representatives.

A recent study, *The Finances of British Trade Unions 1975-85,* conducted by Paul Willman and Timothy Morris on behalf of the Department of Employment, indicated that despite the fall in union membership the financial position of the NUTGW appeared to be secure. In particular, attention was drawn to the union's earnings from investments.

Work-place activity

The union, despite having suffered a membership decline, has increased the number of its shop stewards. It now has approximately 3,300 shop stewards (or 23 members to every one shop steward). This figure compares quite favourably to the 1982 ratio of 37 members to every shop steward. Part of the increase in the number of shop stewards is perhaps due to the study carried out by Boraston, Clegg, and Rimmer *(Work-place and Union),* which noted that the clothing industry is characterised by a large number of small establishments which made effective trade union organisation very difficult. Too many branches did not have a worthwhile service.

Major steps have been undertaken recently to secure greater membership participation and union effectiveness in the work-place. The union devotes a considerable amount of its resources to shop steward training, mainly on TUC courses. General courses in basic shop steward practice and procedure as well as more specialised courses in work study and piece-work bargaining are attended by most NUTGW shop stewards. Each shop steward also receives the union's new *Shop Stewards' Action Pack.* The centre of union activity is now the factory where union meetings are normally held during working hours. This is aimed at overcoming the inconvenience of attending evening meetings experienced by many members. Most branches have been reformed to become representative forums for shop stewards. The attempt to increase membership participation seems to be working. The 1988/9 Executive Board elections registered a record number of votes.

Women

Women constitute over 90 per cent of the NUTGW membership, the highest proportion of all TUC-affiliated unions with the exception of the Health Visitors' Association. For too long women played only a marginal role in the formal affairs of the union. In the early eighties only 7 per cent of the Executive Board were women. This situation is now altering. A number of changes have been initiated in order to improve women's ability to take part in running and shaping the policies of the union. Rescheduling evening meetings has undoubtedly helped. In the latest Executive Board elections 11 of the 14 members elected were women. Women also formed over 80 per cent of delegates to the last Conference.

The areas of the clothing industry where the proportion of women is highest are in the manufacture of lingerie, hats, caps, dresses, and shirts which are particularly poorly paid. Wage rates in sectors such as outer-wear and rain-wear, where more men are employed, are significantly higher. Moreover, the most highly paid occupations within the clothing industry are largely the preserve of men. These are the "aristocrats" of the industry who negotiate a "log" or task. The structure of the clothing industry means that the chances of promotion are slim for women workers; although some women do become supervisors, they are seldom considered for managerial posts. It is commonly the case that factory grades consist only of machinists and managers.

Policy
The NUTGW ranks thirteenth in the top twenty trade unions in terms of female membership, and with 91 per cent of the total membership being female the union has the highest density of women members relative to men in the trade union movement. Given this high proportion of women one would expect that women's issues would receive a high degree of priority in its policies. The union has a long tradition of promoting women's issues. In the 1977 Trades Union Congress the union moved a resolution calling for amendments to the Equal Pay Act to give effect to the International Labour Office formula of equal pay for work of equal value. In the 1979 TUC the union moved a resolution stating that a first principle concerning the working life of all must be their health, safety, and welfare, and called for discussions to be initiated with the Health and Safety Commission with a view to extending the protection afforded to women on night-work and shift-work and to those other categories of women at present without such protective legislation.

This concern for women's issues is still an important feature of the union. In the 1987 TUC the NUTGW supported Congress in its condemnation of the 1986 Social Security Act (SERPS) change to Statutory Sick Pay Schemes with its attendant loss of Family Credit in low-pay industries. At the same Congress the union also secured acceptance of an amendment on campaigning to include specific reference to the involvement of women in trade union activities. At the 1988 TUC the NUTGW supported the call for Congress to fight for the introduction of new laws to tackle inequalities suffered by women. In October 1987 the union started its own vigorous campaign for home-workers and was successful in securing formal recognition of home-workers in Wages Council Orders and persuading the government to make better provision for home-workers. The long campaign which the union has fought to make cancer screening facilities available to all union members has paid off. A mobile screening unit now operates throughout the clothing industry. The union also campaigns against the introduction of VAT on children's clothing.

The clothing industry traditionally has always had a concentration of workers from ethnic minorities. A recent initiative which the union is pursuing concerns the large concentration of ethnic minority workers in East London and the Midlands. Two special exercises are begin carried out in these areas. In East London a Greek-speaking worker was appointed to recruit among the Cypriot community, and in the West Midlands a Punjabi officer was appointed for a two-year period to work in that area.

Recent events
The NUTGW has expressed interest in the possibility of a merger with the GMB.

Further references
Margaret Steward and Leslie Hunter, *The Needle is Threaded*, Heinemann/Newman Nearne, 1964. A historical account of unions in the clothing industry.

Shirley W. Lerner, *Breakaway Unions and the Small Trade Union*, Allen & Unwin, 1961. A fascinating account of the rivalries of the many unions in the clothing industry leading up to the formation of the NUTGW in 1939.

Boraston, Clegg, and Rimmer, *Workplace and Union*, 1975. This book, which is essentially a study of work-place industrial relations in a number of unions, has a small section devoted to the NUTGW.

For a fuller account of the position of women in the clothing industry, *Women at Work,* Tavistock, 1977, provides an excellent picture. It exposes the appalling treatment of women home-workers in the garment industry by unscrupulous employers. Although slightly dated it is still worth reading.

PAT
PROFESSIONAL ASSOCIATION OF TEACHERS
Non-TUC affiliated

Head Office: 99 Friar Gate, Derby DE1 1EZ

Telephone: 0332-372337

Principal national officers
General Secretary: Peter Dawson OBE
Deputy General Secretary: David Jones
Assistant General Secretary: John R. Andrews
Assistant General Secretary: Geoffrey Gospel
Assistant General Secretary: Miss J. M. Miller

Union journal: The *Professional Teacher* is published termly in February, May and September and has a circulation of around 43,000. It is directly sent to all members as well as all Chief Education Officers, libraries, and the national press.

Membership (1989)
Total membership is around 43,000, although the union would not provide exact figures (see "General").

General
The PAT was formed in 1970 by two teachers tired of what they saw as union militancy as typified by strike action. The union today is still bound by the no-strike clause of its constitution. For most of the seventies the majority of the established teaching unions did not take PAT very seriously but two factors have altered this position. The first was an

upsurge in teachers joining PAT during the 1985/6 teachers' strike when the association's membership increased by more than a third to reach 40,000. Many teachers at the time opposed the tactics of the mainstream unions, NUT and NASUWT, and defected to PAT (see **NUT**). The second reason was that PAT was admitted to the Burnham pay negotiating machinery (now abolished), a forum from which it was excluded during the seventies, thereby providing PAT with a similar status to the other teaching unions.

PAT is the very model of a modern Thatcherite union, with its zippy, publicity-oriented machinery, its no-strike clause, its independent political stance, and hostility to TUC membership. It is also a highly secretive organisation, tightly controlled from the centre; the lack of current membership figures in this entry is a case in point. It has sought the support of the EETPU for a number of years, and PAT openly welcomed the EETPU's expulsion from the TUC as a golden opportunity to forge a new alliance of organisations committed to pragmatic policies. (For its part the EETPU has been more cautious in discussing an alternative TUC — see **EETPU**.)

PAT is a strong supporter of current education reforms, breaking with the almost blanket opposition found elsewhere in the education world. It is particularly keen on the extension of parental choice, although it does have reservations about certain aspects of the government's proposals such as the new national system of testing schoolchildren.

Whilst membership is open to the whole of the teaching profession, including the tertiary sector, most of its members are drawn from the primary and secondary sectors.

Organisation

The governing body of the union is the National Council and its subsidiary group, the Finance and General Purposes Committee. The National Council has three major committees: the Education Committee, Professional Services Committee, and Legal and Parliamentary Committee; and three sector committees: Tertiary Education Committee, Scottish Executive Committee, and Wales Committee. The union holds an Annual Conference, usually at the end of July, but this is not a decision-making body and all policy is formulated by Council on recommendations of its committees.

National officers are elected by postal ballot of all members whilst council members are elected by regional ballot. The main unit of organisation is the federation of which there is one in each local education authority throughout the UK; attached to each federation are branches based on membership numbers. Every school with PAT members has a representative who receives a special monthly newsletter from Head Office. PAT has a network of honorary-appointed Field Officers who are trained to assist members in difficulty at local level.

The union has a separate office in Edinburgh with a Secretary for Scotland. Wales, whilst it does not have separate premises, does have a Welsh Secretary.

Policy

PAT is politically independent and to the right wing of the trade union movement. It believes that teachers should work beyond their contract, must be morally upright outside work, and never take industrial action. Earlier in 1989 the union launched a document entitled *Professional Code for Teachers,* in which it spelt out a range of actions it considers incompatible with professional teachers — including refusing to teach, set and mark exams, or meet parents. The 16-page code insisted that teachers must place the interests of pupils above everything else, that they should give time to activities outside the timetable, provide cover for absent colleagues, dress appropriately, and remain neutral when teaching controversial subjects.

The association is convinced that the teaching profession is riddled with ideologically motivated teachers committed to a revolutionary notion of society. It believes that may current teachers and trainers should consider seeking alternative forms of employment.

PAT is a strong supporter of CTCs (City Technical Colleges) and sees this government initiative as a way of extending its influence at the expense of other unions in the teaching profession. PAT made overtures to one of the CTCs, Nottingham, offering a single-union, no-strike agreement, but for the time being Nottingham CTC has ruled this out.

Recent events

PAT recently announced that it would be seeking merger talks with its fellow non-TUC union AMMA. If successful, the new organisation would be the second largest teaching union with a membership of around 170,000. To have this large a teaching union not affiliated to the TUC, might prove very useful to the Secretary of State for Education tactically in getting through difficult education reforms, but the question remains as to whether the teaching profession will be any better off with the merger (see **AMMA**).

Further references

Professional Code for Teachers, Professional Association of Teachers, 1989.

The Training of Teachers, Professional Code for Teachers, 1988.

PHYSIOTHERAPY, CHARTERED SOCIETY OF

Non-TUC affiliated

Head Office: 14 Bedford Row, London WC1R 4ED

Telephone: 01-242 1941

Fax: 01-831 4509

Principal officers
Secretary: Toby Simon
Director of Professional Affairs: Penelope Robinson
Director of Industrial Relations: Phil Gray
Director of Education: Alan Walker
Director of Public Relations: Stuart Skyte
Journal Editor: Jill Whitehouse
Director of Finance and Administration: Jim Banbury

Union journal: Physiotherapy (monthly, free to members). The union also publishes its *Annual Report* each May.

Membership

Current membership (1989)
Total: 24,000
Total: 20,500 (1983)

General

The Chartered Society of Physiotherapy represents Britain's chartered physiotherapists, most of whom work in the National Health Service. The remainder work in private practice, private hospitals, occupational health, sports clubs and clinics, special schools, and voluntary organisations.

The society combines the roles of professional body, educational institution, and trade union. It has been a recognised negotiating body for physiotherapists, holding four seats on the Whitley Councils for the NHS, and it is the eighth largest trade union in the NHS.

History

The Society, originally called the *Society of Trained Masseuses,* was founded in 1894 by four nurses who practised massage. The First World War created a big demand for masseuses, and as a result the Society received a Royal Charter in 1920 in recognition of its work. Originally membership was restricted to women, but men were admitted in 1920. Following several mergers and name changes the society adopted its present name in 1942. In 1976 the Society received its independent status from the Certification Officer and became a trade union.

Organisation

The Society's governing body is its Council which has 39 elected and eight co-opted members. The elected members represent physiotherapy teachers and lecturers (4), private practitioners (4), NHS employees (8), others (4), students (2), and board representation (17).

There are functional standing committees covering professional practice, industrial relations, the journal, education and international affairs; a policy and resources committee; and several sub-committees.

The society is organised into 76 branches and each branch is attached to one of the 17 boards which equate with Regional Health Authorities. There are 650 shop stewards and 700 safety representatives.

POA
PRISON OFFICERS' ASSOCIATION

TUC affiliated

Head Office: Cronin House, 245 Church Street, Edmonton, London N9 9HW

Telephone: 01-803 0255

Fax: 01-803 1716

Principal national officers
General Secretary: D. Evans
Deputy General Secretary: J. Hall
Assistant Secretary: J. Sutcliffe
Assistant Secretary: P. Ryder

Finance Officer: T. Jarman
Research Officer: P. Sullivan

Union journal: Gatelodge (bi-monthly, circulated to all members). In 1989 Conference decided to make greater use of *Gatelodge Extra,* a fortnightly feature, circulated to all members which deals with single or limited items of importance.

There are three other modes used by the POA to communicate information to its membership: *Telephone Mailbox,* an electronic mail system which publicises meetings and other topical information; *POA circulars,* used for NEC decisions, instructions, and agreements; and finally, *Action Updates,* which were originally introduced to allow assistant secretaries to pass on information to the membership, are gradually being phased out and replaced by *Gatelodge Extra.*

Apart from *Action Updates,* the General Secretary has direct editorial responsibility for all of POA's publications, which partly explains way *Action Updates* are being phased out (see "Policy and recent events").

Membership

Current membership (1987)
Male: 22,802
Female: 1,556
Total: 24,358

Membership trends

	1975	1979	1981	1983	1987	change 1975-87	1983-87
Men	18,699	19,157	19,762	21,137	22,802	22%	8%
Women	1,029	1,312	1,527	1,683	1,556	51%	−8%
Total	19,728	20,469	21,289	22,820	24,358	23%	7%

General

The Prison Officers' Association is the officially recognised association for all members of the prison officer grade in England, Wales, and Northern Ireland, and nursing officers and ancillary staff of the Broadmoor, Rampton, and Moss Side special hospitals in England.

The departmental Whitley Council was created after the POA came into being. The staff side comprises nominees of the association, while on the official side are representatives of the Home Office (Prison Department) (HOPD). Since 1986 the HOPD has been restructured and the POA is itself having to alter its structure in order, as noted in its 1988 annual report, to "deal with the highly efficient and formidable bureaucracy, whose sophisticated network of communications and staff resources dwarf those of the POA".

Fresh Start (see "Policy and recent events") has totally altered the conditions of service for prison officers, and with its emphasis on decentralised bargaining it seriously threatens to undermine national arrangements. The POA had already made provisions to create regional structures in order to support the national organisation, but because of the growth of local level bargaining, the newly created regional structures are challenging the national union structure. It is a matter which the POA still has to resolve.

The Royal College of Nurses has indicated that it would like to attract prison nurses currently organised by the POA. The RCN, not being a TUC affiliate, is not bound to observe the Bridlington Principles and can poach freely.

History
In 1919 there was a strike among members of the police force. At the time some police and prison officers were organised in a body known as the *Police and Prison Officers' Union*. The strike did not affect very many prison officers, although some 70 who did take strike action were sacked at Wormwood Scrubs.

The major consequence of the strike was the withdrawal from the police of the right of freedom of organisation through the Police Act of 1919. Although not specifically mentioned in that legislation, similar restrictions were imposed on prison officers by administrative action, and so-called "representative boards" were introduced into the prisons. These boards were part of the administrative machine, being financed and controlled by the authorities; there was no appeal against the decision of the Home Office (Prison Commissioners) in England, the Prison Department in Scotland, and the Prison Branch of the Ministry of Home Affairs in Northern Ireland. Pay was bad, hours were long, and overtime payments were meagre.

Nevertheless, some officers battled on for independent trade unionism. In 1938 they demanded the right of appeal to independent arbitration against the refusal of the authorities to improve working conditions, and also demanded to be assisted in presentation of their case by persons not employed by nor under the control of the authorities. The concession of this demand was followed in 1939 by the official recognition of the Prison Officers' Association.

Organisation
The organisation of the association is national and local. The management of the POA is vested in the Annual Conference, the National Executive Committee, and the officers. The NEC consists of 10 elected members: the Chairman, elected for a period of five years; two Vice-Chairmen, elected for a four-year period, one election being held every two years; the Finance Officer, elected for a period of five years; and six branch nominated members, elected for a period of five years, two elected each year. The officers of the union are the General Secretary, two Assistant General Secretaries, and a Research Officer. A Deputy General Secretary works in the Northern Ireland office. All elections take place at Annual Conference. Rule changes are, at the time of publication, being contemplated but are not expected until 1990.

Policy and recent events
Fresh Start
In an attempt to bring some order into an increasingly disordered pattern at work in which 30 per cent of prison officers' pay came from overtime, the Home Office introduced the Fresh Start scheme. This was accepted by the POA membership in a ballot in May 1987. But Fresh Start was not only intended to bring stability to prison officers' working contracts, it was also introduced to achieve a 15 per cent cost saving by altering rotas, and to reduce the working week from an average of 56 hours — including 16 hours of overtime — to 48 hours.

Since its introduction Fresh Start has been bedevilled by a series of local disputes as some prison governors sought to implement local manning reviews in a fairly heavy-handed manner. These disputes escalated and led the POA into a two-year battle with the government over the implementation of Fresh Start. Prison officers in Holloway, Wandsworth, Norwich, Isle of Wight, Parkhurst, and Hull were among those involved in industrial action.

The dispute at Wandsworth was particularly notable. The governor tried to enforce local manning levels without any agreement, and for the first time since 1919 police officers had to take over security from the striking prison officers. This led to cries from back-bench Conservative MPs to remove the POA members' right to strike, and the Chairman of the all-party Home Affairs Select Committee, John Wheeler, called on the Home Office to cease recognition of the POA and de-unionise the prison service.

The fundamental reasons for the dispute are due to the state of overcrowding in British prisons, the growth in the prison population, chronic understaffing, which in the prison context can put staff in danger, and the rather poor management skills exhibited by some prison governors.

After two years the dispute was brought to an end in February 1989 following a deal between the Home Office and the POA which agreed that new rotas would not be implemented until the established disputes procedure had been followed. However, the failure of Fresh Start to provide a new beginning, coupled with the chronic problems of Britain's prisons would suggest that the end of the dispute is far from settled. Furthermore, surveys have found that only about 10 per cent savings are being realised. The POA, although regarded by many affiliated TUC unions with a good deal of suspicion for its right wing attitudes, is probably one of the most militant unions in protecting members' interests, and it is perhaps not unfair to speculate that the truce worked out with the HOPD in February 1989 is only temporary.

The Home Office is caught in a dilemma in that any measures use to reduce overcrowding and modernise prisons, thereby lowering staff tensions, are offset by the rising prison population, which since 1985 has risen by around 50 per cent. This rise is further exacerbated by the fact that since 1972 the number of offenders incarcerated has risen from 12.9 per cent in 1977 to 18.2 per cent in 1987. The government response to the growing problem in prisons, of which the POA dispute is symptomatic, is towards privatisation of the service rather than increasing public spending.

Privatisation might provide the government with a more permanent solution for weakening the POA, because privately-run prisons are likely to set up their own bargaining arrangements and may not recognise the POA. To this end the rival breakaway union, the Prison Officers' Union, set up by five sacked former POA officials (see "Prison Service Union"), might serve the private sector needs. But a privatised prison sector remains a rather distant vision, and the rival union may not survive. For the time being the POA remains a force to be reckoned with.

The Prison Service Union

In March 1987 five senior full-time officials of the POA, including the Deputy General Secretary and four Assistant General Secretaries, were sacked by the union for taking strike action over a pay dispute. The dismissals were backed by a card vote of about 13,000 to 10,000 members in favour of the sacking. The sacked officials, who were members of APEX, were seeking pay rises under a disputed formula between APEX and POA.

Whilst APEX managed to achieve some recompense for the sacked officials through industrial tribunals, the question of reinstatement was not resolved. Consequently, the five officials launched a new prison officers' union in February 1989, the Prison Service Union (PSU), to rival the POA. In typical breakaway fashion (see **UDM**), the PSU hopes to be a more democratic union, more regionally oriented, and is willing to agree a no-strike deal in exchange for binding arbitration. The five officials' claim that the power of the POA is too heavily concentrated on the NEC, has some justification, but by the same token the Fresh Start dispute was essentially initiated from "below" and therefore not under the control of the POA leadership.

Although the PSU has sought recognition from the Home Office it has made little progress so far. However appealing a rival union organisation is to employers who, in the short term, can derive considerable publicity by playing the "red" card, in the longer term the problems facing the underfunded prison service require much more substantial, structural changes; that, however, is not to underestimate the role that the PSU could play as part of long-term plans.

POWER LOOM CARPET WEAVERS' AND TEXTILE WORKERS' UNION

TUC affiliated

Head Office: Carpet Weavers' Hall, Callows Lane, Kidderminster, Worcestershire DY10 2JG

Telephone: 0562-823192

Principal national officers
General Secretary: Brian Moule
Assistant and Financial Secretary: Ronald White

Membership

Current membership (1987)
Male: 1,700
Female: 1,500
Total: 3,200

Membership trends

						change	
	1975	1979	1981	1983	1987	1975-87	1983-87
Men	3,260	4,015	2,311	1,750	1,700	−48%	−3%
Women	2,120	2,008	1,575	1,450	1,500	−29%	3%
Total	5,380	6,023	3,886	3,200	3,200	−41%	0%

General
"Guardians of our rights we stand,
Heart with heart, and hand in hand;
We succour brethren in distress,
And help the wrong'd to get redress."

Despite the quaintness of the union motto, which it proudly displays on the front of its rule book, the Power Loom Carpet Weavers' and Textile Workers' Union is in fact a small but progressive union with a high membership density particularly in the Kidderminster area. It caters for all occupations within the carpet and textile industries, from raw material preparation to sales and fitting. It also recruits all grades of white collar workers.

The union is in loose affiliation with the following unions, which have membership in the carpet industry, to form the National Association of Carpet Trade Unions:

306

POWER LOOM CARPET WEAVERS' AND TEXTILE WORKERS' UNION

TGWU Dyers, Bleachers, and Textile Workers' National Trade Group;
General, Municipal, Boilermakers, and Allied Trade Union;
Northern Carpet Trade Union;
Scottish Carpet Workers' Union.

Together they form the union side in the National Joint Council for the Carpet Industry. There is also a Scottish, Northern, and Kidderminster Joint Council for negotiations. Outside these two bodies the union is free to negotiate terms and conditions at company level. "On top" deals are encouraged at local and plant level.

The Power Loom Carpet Weavers' and Textile Workers' Association has members at Axminster (Devon), Wilton, Romsey, Warwick, Stourport, and Aberdare, besides the main Kidderminster membership.

History

The union was formed in 1866, although there are sound historical indications of a trade society for carpet weavers existing in Kidderminster in 1817. It is an example of a union whose establishment followed a permanent association of employers. The *Power Loom Carpet Manufacturers' Association* was formed in 1864, and among its aims were: "the prevention of strikes and disagreements, the control of labour supply, the protection of the trade in matters connected with wages and the employment of work people, as well as the consideration of all subjects connected with the trade".

In 1917 the union opened its membership to textile workers, many of whom were women, who were employed in the carpet industry but were not weavers. This strengthened the union and increased its flexibility and capacity for change. In recent years adaptability has more than ever been necessary in an industry subject to technological changes and to changes in the pattern of demand (woven carpets face strong competition from tufted carpets).

So far industry and union have adapted well to being furnishers of comfort and colour for the many, rather than providing a luxury for the few. Despite the economic recession of the eighties union membership has survived remarkably well, with its officers not expecting any real membership recruitment difficulties.

Organisation

The union is governed by an Executive Committee consisting of 11 qualified voting members, including the President and Vice-President. The Executive also includes the non-voting General Secretary and full-time officials also without voting rights. Two places on the Executive are specifically reserved for women. All Executive posts are elected by balloting all members prior to the Annual Delegate Policy Conference. Ordinary Executive members are elected on a three-year cycle, the President and the General Secretary for a period of five years.

Recent events

The political fund ballot held in 1985 produced 2,242 "yes" votes and 697 "no" votes, representing a 75.3 per cent majority for its retention. The turn-out was a high 88.7 per cent.

The union attempted recently, but without success, to organise the unemployed. Existing members who become unemployed do, however, retain full membership status for up to one year.

Further reference

Arthur Marsh, *The Carpet Weavers,* Malthouse,1989.

RCM
ROYAL COLLEGE OF MIDWIVES

Non-TUC affiliated

Head Office: 15 Mansfield Street, London W1M 0BE

Telephone: 01-580 6523 & 01-637 8823

Fax: 01-436 3951

Principal officer
General Secretary: R. M. Ashton

Regional offices and officers
RCM Scottish Board: S. Davidson, Secretary Treasurer, 37 Frederick Street, Edinburgh
EH2 1EP
Telephone: 031-225 1633

RCM Northern Ireland Board: G. Hamilton, Professional Officer, Friends Provident
Building, 58 Howard Street, Belfast BT1 6PU
Telephone: 0232-241531

RCM Welsh Board: E. R. Jenkins, Professional Officer, Suite 4 Floor 3, Alexandra
House, 1 Alexandra Road, Swansea
Telephone: 0792-50082

Union journal: Midwives' Chronicle (monthly)

Membership
Total: 30,358 (1988)
Total: 27,385 (1987)
Total: 25,845 (1986)

General
The RCM restricts its recruitment to midwives and related staff and is both a trade union
and a professional organisation. As a professional body the RCM dates back to 1881
when it was known as the *Midwives' Institute*; it has always sought to advance the art and
science of midwifery and to maintain high professional standards. It takes a keen interest
in international midwifery and sends representatives all over the world, particularly to the
Commonwealth. As the sole professional body representing midwives the RCM is
consulted by and has elected representatives on two statutory bodies, the United
Kingdom Central Council and National Boards.

The RCM only became an independent trade union in 1976 and more than three-
quarters of all practising midwives are members. It is rapidly developing its trade union
role, and the nine industrial relations officers now form the largest single group of staff
within RCM headquarters. The RCM has one seat on the General Whitley Council and
three seats on the Nursing and Midwifery Staffs Negotiating Councils, bodies which deal
solely with conditions of service. Since 1983 pay is dealt with separately by the review
body for nursing staff, midwives, health visitors, and professions allied to medicine to
which the RCM makes a submission. Membership has risen by 20 per cent since 1986 but

the RCM is concerned about the high level of staff shortages in the NHS. In line with many other unions the RCM now offers a series of discount packages such as insurance and car purchase to its members.

Organisation
Although the RCM holds an Annual General Meeting, the Council of the RCM is required constitutionally to take responsibility for the total work of the College. The work of the Council is carried out largely through its six standing committees: finance, editorial, ethical, RCM/Royal College of Obstetricians, education, and benevolent fund. The RCM is also organised into the English, Northern Ireland, Scottish, and Welsh boards, each of which supports local branches.

Policy and recent events
The RCM has always held a no-strike policy which distinguishes it from the other trade unions such as COHSE and NUPE which also organise midwives. This policy was reaffirmed in a membership ballot towards the end of 1988 which was carried out in response to the implementation of the clinical grading review earlier in the year (see **RCN**). However, only a month after the ballot, on November 15, 1988, the RCM called its first ever day of action over the gradings issue. Further days of action were held subsequently although the RCM leadership has indicated that the no-strike policy is unlikely to be reviewed in the foreseeable future. The concern over gradings, pay, and conditions, and the acute staff shortages in midwifery are key issues which confront the RCM; within the context of the increased commercialisation of the NHS and hospital opting-out, the RCM is likely to experience increased role-conflict between its professional and trade union interests.

External relations
The RCM has representation on the International Confederation of Midwives and the EEC Midwives' Liaison Committee as well as having observer status on the BMA/EEC Committee. It has no political fund and is not affiliated to the TUC.

RCN
ROYAL COLLEGE OF NURSES
Head Office: 20 Cavendish Square, London W1M 0AB

Telephone: 01-409 3333

Principal officers
General Secretary: Christine Hancock
Labour Relations Director: Val Cowie
Deputy Labour Relations Director: Tony Nicholson

Union journal: Lampada Newspaper (six times a year to all members); *Nursing Standard* magazine, produced weekly by Scutari Projects, the RCN publishing company, (circulation over 60,000); *Newsline Bulletin*: circulated to key members, stewards, and branch officials fortnightly.

Membership
1975: 84,393
1988: 281,075

General
The RCN is a registered trade union but it also a professional body and, as such, has been exempted from the requirement under the 1988 Employment Act that its General Secretary seek periodic re-election. However, a motion that the General Secretary should seek periodic re-election has been debated at the Annual Congress of the College. The College has a royal charter that sets out its main objectives as follows.
(a) to promote the science and art of nursing and the better education and training of nurses and their efficiency in the profession of nursing;
(b) to promote the advance of nursing as a profession in all or any of its branches;
(c) to promote the professional standing and interests of members of the nursing profession;
(d) to promote through the medium of international agencies and otherwise the foregoing purposes in other countries as well as in the United Kingdom;
(e) to assist nurses who, by reason of adversity, ill health, or otherwise, are in need of assistance of any nature;
(f) to institute and conduct examinations and to grant certificates to those who satisfy the requirements laid down by the Council of the College.

The College has an unswerving policy commitment to the NHS. It believes that a comprehensive system of health care should be the right of every individual and available on the basis of need, free at the point of delivery, and financed from taxation. The RCN has opposed the precipitate and unproven radical changes in the NHS on which the government embarked in 1988.

Probably the most controversial rule of the RCN is on industrial action (rule 12 of the College rules). Strictly speaking, it is not a no-strike rule and states: "Neither the Council nor any Official of the College nor any membership entity of the College shall be empowered to initiate or be a party to the withdrawal of service of members of the College in furtherance of an industrial dispute unless or until the policy of the College in respect of industrial action by nurses is changed by the College in General Meeting. A resolution passed by a two-thirds majority shall be required to change the policy by ballot of all members. Alternatively, the College in General Meeting may empower the Council to take a decision in respect of limited industrial action if circumstances should be such as to warrant such action. Again a two-thirds majority of members present or voting by proxy at a General Meeting shall be required to authorise the Council." Rule 12 is therefore College policy. The RCN does not sign "no-strike" deals with employers. The policy on industrial action could be changed at a few weeks' notice and has in fact been the subject of ballots in 1979, 1982, and 1988. On the last occasion 107,492 members, or 79 per cent of those voting, decided to uphold the policy, with 27,736 against. The RCN leaders talk of a pact with the public and it has resulted in the RCN being a strong bargaining body. However, the RCN is against "no-strike" measures being imposed by legislation in the public services.

Affilation to the TUC, which would also require a two-thirds majority, has been debated at General Meetings and was rejected in a membership ballot in 1982. However, RCN leaders rebuffed an approach from the EETPU to join it in an alternative organisation in 1988.

History
The College was founded in 1916, incorporated by royal charter in 1928, and certified as

an independent trade union in 1977. When the negotiating machinery of the NHS was set up it took the form of Whitley councils. The RCN has continued to be represented on the general Whitley council and on the nursing and midwifery staffs negotiating council, but a significant change was the detachment of nurses' pay onto a pay review body, separate from other NHS grades in the early 1980s.

Organisation

The governing body of the RCN is the Council — 25 members elected by secret postal ballot. There are "constituencies" in that 14 elected members comprise the English section, two each for Wales, Scotland, and Northern Ireland, and two elected members for the student section. Nominations for the election of members of Council are made by RCN branches within the relevant electoral division that the Council member will represent. The President and Deputy President are elected by the membership of the College as a whole, the nominating bodies being the RCN branches and those membership entities operating at national level as determined by the Council. These elections are separate but concurrent.

The RCN Congress meets annually and considers a wide range of topics put forward by membership entities, for example, in 1988 a call for affiliation to the TUC was debated. Congress is the main debating body of the RCN but it is not sovereign and its decisions are advisory to the Council. The voting membership of Congress is drawn from the branches on the basis of one representative per 1,000 members or part thereof and other membership entities in a formula agreed at the meeting in Glasgow in 1987, following consultation with the membership. Individual RCN members may attend as non-voting members. The Congress receives recommendations, resolutions, and matters for discussion from Council, the national boards, branches, associations, societies, forums, the Committee on Economic and Social Policy, and from the RCN's General Secretary and Director of Education.

A reformed regional organisation was introduced in 1984, increasing the number of offices to serve the membership. There are 14 regional offices, corresponding to the regional health authorities. Each office has a senior officer accountable to the Deputy General Secretary for all College services, both trade union and professional, within the region.

Men were admitted into membership for the first time in 1960. In 1988 the Congress voted to move towards admitting auxillary staff and support worker grades in order to sustain the growth of the union.

Finance

The RCN is well off financially as a result of relatively high subscription rates and so has considerable resources to fund its campaigns. Some diminution in its income occurred due to the poor initial results of Scutari Projects, the RCN's own publishing company, but this investment is expected to pay off in the long run.

Recent issues

Training

The clinical grading structure introduced in September 1988 established a new career ladder for nurses. At first there were protests by nurses who felt that they were wrongly graded (see "Recent events"). The Project 2,000 nurse training reforms from October 1989 raise training standards and abolish the split between enrolled nurses and registered nurses. The new registered nurse is a "knowledgeable doer", able to marshall information, make an assessment of clinical need, devise a plan of care, and implement it. Professional bodies want nurses to do less supervision and more active care. Nurse helpers, given better training than auxillaries have received, and able to obtain qualifications for the first time, work under the direction of nurses. The RCN is likely to open its ranks to such people. The nursing "entry gate" will be widened by allowing nurse helpers who gain qualifications to enter nurse training, making it easier for enrolled nurses to convert to registered status, and attracting a wider range of applicants. Nursing students will be supervised and taught wholly by qualified teachers, rather than being used as "pairs of hands" on wards under the control of Health Service managers.

Employment and recruitment problems
A survey conducted for the RCN by the Institute for Manpower Studies stated that authorities must concentrate on attracting former nurses. Those who have left nursing to have children are more likely to be attracted back by flexible hours and crèche facilities than by higher pay. Of those who had left the NHS for other jobs, including nursing in the private sector, more thought that staffing levels were more important than pay.

Pay flexibility and regional pay
The RCN Congress in 1989 criticised and voted against government proposals for regional pay variations and discretionary special payments on the grounds that they would create labour market instability and pay spirals and exacerbate staff discrepancies between regions.

Recent events
Before the pay increases that were incorporated into the transfer of nursing staff on to the new clinical grading structure in 1988 there was considerable dissatisfaction over pay. This was shown by difficulties for some regions in retaining nurses and by evidence from a survey published in December 1987 that stated that about 20 per cent of nurses had an additional job, mostly working extra hours for their own authority through a nursing agency.

In February 1988 discontent about pay, understaffing, persistent under-funding of their pay awards and of the NHS, and the consequent run-down state of many NHS facilities led to a week of protests. Unlike COHSE and NUPE members and in accordance with rule, RCN members did not strike but campaigned vigorously and attracted favourable publicity.

The award of the pay increase attached to regrading from the pay review body was not the end of the story; it was soon calculated that the government had seriously underestimated the cost of the new grading structure and had underfunded it. The RCN therefore found itself with the sort of task that its pressure group tactics can engage in successfully — to make it less uncomfortable for government ministers to secure the funding than to forget about it. In addition, many nurses were dissatisfied with their grades. The RCN had to restrain members from taking any form of industrial action that might result in their doing less for their patients than normally.

During the regrading disputes inter-union conflict, mainly between the RCN and COHSE and focusing on the former's no-strike policy, burst forth. Recriminations and abuse about members leaving the RCN in droves and then about desertions from COHSE to the RCN were the order of the day. Doubts among RCN traditionalists about the appropriateness of admitting unqualified nursing staff into membership may have been increased by the pattern of industrial action over regrading. Hector MacKenzie, General Secretary of COHSE, was quoted as saying that, unlike the RCN, his union was not prepared to mislead members into believing that if they trusted in health authority managers and the government all would be well.

The government sought to exploit this potential disunity by agreeing to meet leaders of the RCN and shunning requests for meetings from TUC-affiliated unions. MacKenzie of COHSE criticised the resultant agreement about informal appeals on the new gradings between the RCN and Kenneth Clarke, the Health Secretary, on the grounds that appeals ought to be controlled by the negotiating council. In a report in February 1989 the nurses' pay review body was highly critical of the way that the government and Health Service managers introduced the revised clinical grading structure. Apparently, some of the problems of implementation might have been avoided if health authority managers had been better prepared and equipped to communicate the purpose and implications of the new structure to staff.

ROSSENDALE UNION OF BOOT, SHOE, AND SLIPPER OPERATIVES

TUC affiliated

Head Office: 7 Tenterfield Street, Waterfoot, Rossendale, Lancashire BB4 7BA

Telephone: 0762-215657

Principal national officers
General Secretary: Michael Murray
President: D. Broxton

Union journal: At one time the union did publish a journal called *Unity,* but this has not been published for some years.

Current membership (1987)
Male: 1,605
Female: 2,852
Total: 4,457

Membership trends
1983: 4,191
1979: 5,818

General
The union was formed in 1895 and throughout its 94-year history has retained its independence from its larger sister union, NUFLAT. However this was as much to do with the employers, the Lancashire Footwear Manufacturers' Association (LMFA) with whom it bargained, as any other reason. Since the LFMA employers' federation was wound up in 1987 it is difficult to see how this small union can survive. It makes sense to merge with NUFLAT. There are two full-time officials.

Organisation
The supreme policy-making body of the union is the General Meeting of all members held in March and September each year. The union is managed by an Executive

Committee which is representative of the various departments in the trade, and six areas: Rossendale, Burnley, Blackburn, Fylde, Chorley and St Helens, and Bury. The union maintains a work-place representative system and provides each one with a well-written handbook.

External relations
The union balloted its membership regarding the political fund, and from a 40 per cent turn-out 77.5 per cent, or 1,244, voted "yes" with 22.5 per cent, or 358, voting "no".

Further references
For a more detailed account of the role of the Rossendale union in the footwear industry see:

J. F. B. Goodman et al, *Rule Making and Industrial Peace,* Croom Helm, 1977.

Alan Fox, *The History of the National Union of Boot and Shoe Operatives,* Basil Blackwell, 1958.

SCALEMAKERS
NATIONAL UNION OF SCALEMAKERS
TUC affiliated

Head Office: 1st Floor, Queensway House, 57 Livery Street, Birmingham B3 1HA

Telephone: 021-236 8998

Principal officer
General Secretary: Arthur Smith

Membership

Current membership (1987)
Male: 866
Female: 69
Total: 935

Membership trends

	1975	1979	1981	1983	1987	change 1975-87	1983-87
Men	1,833	1,866	1,251	1,182	866	−53%	−27%
Women	59	71	49	28	69	17%	146%
Total	1,892	1,937	1,300	1,210	935	−51%	23%

General
Membership is composed of weighing and testing machine fitters (electrical, electronic, and mechanical), sectional workers, and all other workers employed in the weighing, testing, and counting machine industries and affiliated trades. Essentially the union is a

craft trade union and membership is widely spread throughout the UK. Since 1975 the union has lost over half of its membership with half of that loss coming between 1983 and 1987. Recently there has been a move away from national bargaining and the union has created a domestic level negotiating committee to deal with such matters.

During the union's political fund ballot, 460 voted "yes" and 135 voted "no", representing a winning majority of 77 per cent from a 54 per cent turn-out.

History
In 1909 the *Amalgamated Society of Scale Beam and Weighing Machine Makers* was formed as a result of a strike at Messrs Hodgson and Stead. The word "amalgamated" had no real significance but was the fashion in those days and looked important. In 1923 the name was changed to the *Society of Scale Beam and Weighing Machinists,* and in 1930 to the *National Union of Scalemakers.* The change of name resulted from a split in the union, the London branch separating from the rest following wage reductions and a large defalcation in the funds. The separate parts of the union were brought together by the TUC to make a fresh amalgamation in 1928. In 1930 the union opened its ranks to all workers in the industry, although to this day it remains primarily a craft union.

Organisation
The union is divided into branches and is governed by an Executive Council, composed of a General President, Vice-President, and General and Financial Secretary nominated by any branch and elected by postal ballot of the whole membership, and four members elected by ballot vote of the delegates at the Annual Conference each May.

SCOTTISH UNION OF POWER LOOM OVERLOOKERS
TUC affiliated

Head Office: 3 Napier Terrace, Dundee DD2 2SL

Telephone: 0382-612196

Principal officer
General Secretary: J. Reilly

Membership (1987)
Total: 60

Membership trends
1983: 100
1979: 200
1975: 350

SHEFFIELD WOOL SHEAR WORKERS' UNION

TUC affiliated

Head Office: 50 Bankfield Road, Malin Bridge, Sheffield S6 4RD

Principal officer
General Secretary: R. Cutler

Current membership (1987)
Male: 14
Female: 3
Total: 17

General
This union has the distinction of being the smallest union affiliated to the TUC. The entire membership works in one factory making sheep shears of high quality in much the same way since the company was founded in 1730. The Wool Shear Workers' Union was formed in 1890 and at that time there were workers in other factories, although the numbers have never risen above a few hundred. The union does not send a delegate to TUC conferences.

Further reference
The Guardian, August 24, 1979.

SHUTTLEMAKERS, SOCIETY OF

TUC affiliated

Head Office: 211 Burnley Road, Colne, Lancashire BB8 8JD

Principal officer
President: Leslie Illingworth
(There are no full-time officers)

Membership
1987: 41
1983: 67
1979: 110
1975: 129

General
The union was formed in 1891. After the Second World War membership increased to 600 — about 90 per cent of all shuttlemakers in the country. The union has been affiliated to the TUC and the GFTU (General Federation of Trade Unions) for over 50 years. The introduction of the shuttleless loom and the loss of the Indian markets has brought a gradual decline in this area of employment.

SOGAT
SOCIETY OF GRAPHICAL AND ALLIED TRADES '82

TUC affiliated

Head Office: SOGAT House, 274/288 London Road, Hadleigh, Benfleet, Essex SS7 2DE

Telephone: 0702-554111

Fax: 0702-559737

Telex: 0702-265871

Principal national officers
General Secretary: Brenda Dean
General President: D. G. Sergeant
Organising Secretary: J. Mitchell
General Officer: E. R. Chard
General Officer: E. O'Brien
General Officer: F. Smith
General Officer: R. Gillespie
General Officer: G. Beattie
Financial Secretary: D. Washington

Union journal: SOGAT Journal (monthly, circulation 55,000, distributed mainly through branches and chapels). The journal, which has been revamped and comes out in colour, was a "very close contender" for first place in the 1987 TUC Trade Union Journals Competition. SOGAT also produces a range of very fine pamphlets and other material which it distributes periodically to its members. For example, the union commissioned Lord McCarthy to write a booklet explaining the 1987 Employment Bill.

Membership

Current membership (1987)
Male: 137,037
Female: 56,801
Total: 193,838

Membership trends

	1975	1979	1981	1983	1987	change 1975-87	1983-87
Men	128,181	136,251	161,267	147,864	137,037	7%	−7%
Women	67,341	69,533	75,393	65,741	56,801	−16%	−14%
Total	195,522	205,784	236,660	213,605	193,838	−1%	−9%

General
SOGAT is the largest of the print unions and has membership among art, technical, administrative, executive, sales, clerical, and process workers in the paper, cardboard, newsprint, packaging and printing industries, and in newspaper production and distribution. From organising essentially semi-skilled workers SOGAT increasingly sees

itself as the general print union open to all grades and types of workers. In an effort to attract new recruits it has gone to a great deal of effort to present itself as a fresh union geared to the needs of the future.

All its booklets, journals, and general publicity have been very effectively revamped (see "Union Journal"). SOGAT conducted a survey amongst its members which showed that around three-quarters of the membership receive no financial service from the union. In an attempt to remedy this SOGAT has issued a plastic KeyCard which gives members access to free and comprehensive financial advice on mortgages, insurance, and pensions, simply by telephoning and quoting the card number.

SOGAT has also produced a recruitment pack available to all officials and issued to all new members which contains information concerning the services the union provides and advice on how to use the union to greatest effect. Indeed, the last Biennial Delegate Council, in 1988, made a rule change (rule 19) which emphasised that the priority of all organisers is to campaign in areas where there is no existing union organisation.

History
SOGAT

SOGAT '82 is the result of a merger in 1982 between two of the largest unions in the print industry, SOGAT and NATSOPA.

SOGAT itself is the result of a complex series of amalgamations. Probably the main amalgamation ensuring future growth was that of the *Printers' Warehousemen, Paper Mill Workers and Vellum and Parchment Makers* to form the *National Union of Bookbinders and Machine Rulers*. The printing and paper workers' union had started to recruit women · who worked as assistants to the skilled bookbinders, since the bookbinders, a craft society type of union, had made no effort to recruit women. This caused intense conflict between the two unions. Remarkably, they were able to resolve it by amalgamation, which produced the trade section governing structure of SOGAT. This was necessary in order to convince the bookbinders that their craft would be effectively safeguarded within the amalgamation.

Until 1966 SOGAT was known as the *National Union of Printing, Bookbinding, and Paper Workers*. In that year an amalgamation was initiated with the *National Society of Operative Printers and Assistants*. When amalgamation was terminated in 1972 the *National Union of Printing, Bookbinding, and Paper Workers* was reconstructed as the *Society of Graphical and Allied Trades*. This name continued after amalgamation with the *Scottish Graphical Association* in 1975.

NATSOPA

While craftworkers in the printing industry were, by the late nineteenth century, well organised into craft societies such as the *London Society of Compositors*, child-workers, women, and labourers were mainly unorganised and often worked in deplorable conditions for miserable wages. In fact the labourers' work was demanding in nerve, strength, skill, and experience, while conditions in the underground machine rooms were crowded, dark, noisy, and unhealthy. In 1899 the wages paid for 55 hours of such work were 12 to 14 shillings.

At this time many new unions were springing up. A strike occurred amongst printers' labourers at the firm of Spottiswoodes for a £1 minimum weekly wage. Labourers in other firms struck for this and many employers began to accede to the demand. The next step was the formation of a *Printers' Labourers' Union* which emulated the older craft societies in printing by basing itself on the chapel system.

The main area of recruitment at first was not the casual "unskilled" labourers, but numerous assistants who worked in the pressrooms of printing firms, especially those who worked on the rotary machines used in newspaper printing. These men were not "labourers" so the title of the union was changed to the *Operative Printers' Assistants' Society*. Later, when the society extended its membership and activities beyond London, the word "National" was added. A very critical change of title was made in 1912, by the insertion of "and" between the words "Printers" and "Assistants", signifying the union's claim to recruit craftsworkers.

NATSOPA frequently came into conflict with the craft unions which were hostile to what they considered to be territorial encroachments by the new union. These disputes were exacerbated after 1920 when craft societies decided to open membership to non-craft workers. Nevertheless, NATSOPA continued to grow and reached 18,000 members in 1939.

In 1952 NATSOPA was involved in a notorious dispute with the anti-union firm of D. C. Thompson but it failed to enforce its claim that the firm should reinstate NATSOPA members whom it had sacked.

Recent history

In 1966 the two unions NATSOPA and the forerunner of SOGAT (the *National Union of Printing, Bookbinding and Paper Workers)* did merge, but rule book problems followed and they were to "divorce" but amalgamate again in 1982 as SOGAT '82.

Even in 1982 the narrowness of the ballot result in NATSOPA, with 16,000 for and 13,000 against merger, reflected the antipathy felt by NATSOPA members whose more developed system of democracy they were reluctant to lose. NATSOPA had a strong tradition of balloting members, its executive was composed of lay members and its national officers submitted themselves for re-election every three years. These issues have only recently been resolved through the publication of the new rule book in October 1988.

Organisation

The government of SOGAT is the Biennial Delegate Council (BDC) which meets during May or June. Each branch with a working membership of not less than 100 is entitled to one delegate; a second delegate is allowed to branches with 700 working members; and thereafter there is an additional delegate for each 500 members. The National Executive Committee is responsible for the management of the affairs of the union. The NEC is made up of 36 representatives elected according to the following regional area entitlement:

Area	*NEC members*
1. London	8
2. Home Counties	6
3. South West and South Wales	3
4. Yorkshire	2
5. Midland	3
6. East Anglia	1
7. North Western, North Wales	5
8. Northern	1
9. Scottish	4
10. Irish	1
11. ATAES Branch	2

No more than two representatives can be elected from any one branch and no more than one member from any one chapel may be eligible for election so long as another chapel in the same group is unrepresented.

The branches are the centre of the union structure. Branches consist of the following officials: Chairman, Secretary, Treasurer, Auditors, and Committee Health and Safety Advisor. They are able to spend up to 40 per cent of their total general fund for local management expenses. In order to achieve the widest representation of members branches have the power to act in whatever way is (constitutionally) necessary in order to meet the needs of their own locality. In addition they govern the election of members to the branch committee, branch delegates to district council meetings, delegates to BDC local trades' councils and any other local bodies.

There are currently 76 branches (44 of which are full-time) employing 94 officers and 133 staff. Between them they service 150,616 working members who are employed in 5,412 chapels. The 32 part-time branches cover 10,703 working members who are employed in 304 chapels. In an attempt to develop a more rational and efficient branch structure SOGAT is urging branches, particularly part-time ones, to consider or participate in merger discussions.

The General Secretary, Brenda Dean, was recently re-elected to the post in a secret ballot. She won 76.1 per cent of the vote which drew a 40 per cent turn-out.

Work-place activity
As in other print unions, work-place activity is undertaken in chapels. Every firm where two or more members of a branch are employed constitutes the basis for a chapel, which is empowered to appoint a father of the chapel (FOC) who serves for a period of at least one year. Every member who fails to join a chapel can be fined up to £100 and be liable to expulsion from the union. Every chapel forms its own fund drawn from members' subscriptions, and draws up its own rules for the conduct of chapel business which are submitted to branches for approval.

Formally, the duties of an FOC are to preside over all chapel meetings, maintain the principles of the union, deal with grievances, and collect subscriptions. In reality FOCs, especially in the larger chapels, have enjoyed considerable autonomy, and exerted a far greater degree of control over such matters as manning and discipline than most other unions. SOGAT's new rule book (1988) is attempting to shift the emphasis away from chapels and instead promote branches in a bid to integrate chapels more fully into the union structure. Chapel autonomy on local level bargaining has been further curtailed by the new rules, and they must now inform and seek consent from the NEC (through their branch structures) for any local negotiations concerning wages and working conditions before agreements can be implemented.

Women
Women form some 30 per cent of the total working membership of SOGAT. Significantly, recruitment statistics published by the union indicate that women constituted more than 36 per cent of all new recruits. SOGAT is keen to ensure that its organisation is able to represent women and their issues effectively and consequently has undertaken a number of initiatives to meet this end.

The 1984 BDC invited a research team from the Polytechnic of North London to prepare a research project into the role of women in the union. The results of the research, *Women in SOGAT '82*, were presented to the NEC in October 1985 making the following main points: there is substantial under-representation of women in proportion to the union's female membership at all decision-making levels; at work, pay differentials between men and women are worsening; SOGAT rules constitute a barrier to women reaching positions of influence within the union; there already exists substantial support for women at local levels but it needs positive encouragement from national SOGAT level. The 1986 BDC noted the findings of the report and stressed its independent status.

Since the publication of the report women's issues have undoubtedly received a higher profile. The 1986 BDC decided that positive discrimination for women should be recommended at every level of the union and that the NEC ought to regularly monitor the situation and to this end set up a "positive action sub-committee". National and local agreements on a number of issues such as cancer screening, maternity/paternity leave, sexual harassment, and equal pay and opportunities have been negotiated. However, special measures to encourage women to take an active role in the union affairs and the appointment of an organiser for women members were turned down at the 1988 BDC. At the same time, further rule changes regarding the setting up of a National Women's Advisory Committee (as is the practice in many other unions) was also voted down.

Since 1945 there have only been four female organisers, there are now none. On the 36-member NEC there are only three women. The number of women delegates at the 1988 BDC was only 40, or around 9 per cent of the total. Of the 43 full-time branches comprising 98 full-time officers, only five are women. Facts such as these, all gleaned from a recent report (*Equality*), would suggest that there are problems inherent in the structure of the union constitution which need to be addressed in order to encourage women to play a more active role in the union.

External relations
Brenda Dean is a member of the TUC General Council and a member of the National Economic Development Organisation's council. SOGAT is affiliated to the Labour Party; it sponsors two Labour MPs: Bob Litherland (Greater Manchester), and Ron Leighton (Newham North East). SOGAT was the first union to hold a ballot over the political levy and received a 78 per cent vote in favour of its retention.

Each year SOGAT publishes an *International Report*, which details its various affiliations, donations, and foreign delegations. It is affiliated to:

Amnesty International;
Anti-Apartheid;
CND;
Chile Solidarity Campaign;
FIET;
Irish Congress of Trade Unions;
ICEF;
Liberation '87;
National Peace Council;
South African Congress of Trade Unions;
War on Want.

Policy
Between January 1986 and February 1987 SOGAT was involved in the most serious and devastating dispute in its entire history. News International issued notice to terminate the collective agreements with all unions representing some 5,500 Fleet Street workers, and its intention to move its entire printing operations to a new, purpose-built site at Wapping. News International also wanted to have only one union representing its entire work-force and sought to reach agreement with the EETPU (see **EETPU**). A year-long bloody and bitter dispute followed which was conducted both in the streets and on mass picket lines as well as in the High Court. After a series of court injunctions, writs, fines for contempt of court (which SOGAT had eventually to purge), sequestration of assets, and the almost total demise of SOGAT, the dispute was finally called off on February 5, 1987.

News International agreed to make their cash compensation available until March 10.

As a result of the strike perhaps the most pressing objective for SOGAT, apart from restoring its financial position, is to avoid such a damaging dispute again. The dispute, initiated as a result of technological advances in the printing industry which cut across traditional lines of union demarcation, has highlighted the need for a rationalisation of the unions representing printworkers in order to make them more responsive and representative.

SOGAT and the NGA have been urged to reach a merger by their respective delegate conferences as well as the TUC. Recently the merged plans have run into trouble and a split has appeared regarding branch structure. It would be a sign of weakness if the leadership of both unions allowed the talks to falter at this advanced stage of the proceedings as most other aspects of the merger have already been agreed, including the size and role of the merged union's Conference, and procedures for electing its President and General Secretary.

Should the talks fail then SOGAT has already indicated that it is likely to explore the possibility of creating a super communications union comprising the NCU, UCW, NUJ, BETA, and ACTT, with a total membership of around 700,000 making it one of the largest TUC affiliates.

Recent events

As part of their annual pay negotiations with the British Printing Industry Federation, SOGAT recently signed a deal which commits all signatories to set up joint working parties to consider the implications of 1992 on employment and industrial matters and the implications of the single market. The deal is the first made under a five-year plan for industrial relations, and with regard to wages is unusual as it sets actual rather than minimum rates which would appear to fly in the face of the current trend towards local bargaining.

SOGAT recently took the unusual step of paying for a four-page advertisement supplement in the *UK Press Gazette,* the journalists' trade magazine, in order to proclaim the union's faith and commitment to technological change. In it SOGAT put forward the idea that the benefits of technological change should be shared by management, employees, and the consumer. Perhaps the next stage should be to place similar adverts in the national popular press where everybody can read about SOGAT.

Further references

C. J. Bundock, *The National Union of Printing, Bookbinding and Paperworkers,* Oxford University Press, 1959.

J. Child, *Industrial Relations in the British Printing Industry,* Allen & Unwin, 1967.

P. Routledge, "The dispute at Times Newspapers Limited: a view from inside", *Industrial Relations Journal,* 1980.

Abolition and After: Paper Box Wages Council, Labour Studies Group, Department of Applied Economics, University of Cambridge, for the Department of Employment, 1980.

R. Martin, *New Technology and Industrial Relations in Fleet Street,* Oxford University Press, 1981.

L. Melvern, *The End of the Street,* Methuen, 1986.

Mike Power and Helen Hague, "A tale of Wapping Woe", *Marxism Today,* March 1987.

SPOA
SCOTTISH PRISON OFFICERS' ASSOCIATION
TUC affiliated

Head Office: 21 Calder Road, Saughton, Edinburgh EH11 3PF
Telephone: 031-443 8105
Fax: 031-444 0657

Principal national officers
General Secretary: J. B. Renton MBE
Deputy General Secretary: W. Goodall

Current membership (1987)
Male: 3,026
Female: 229
Total: 3,255

General
Formed as an independent association in 1971, before which it was a branch of the Prison Officers' Association, the Scottish Prison Officers' Association affiliated to the TUC on January 1, 1980. It works closely with the POA, although the Scottish prison service is administered by the Scottish Office.

SSTA
SCOTTISH SECONDARY TEACHERS' ASSOCIATION
STUC affiliated

Head Office: 15 Dundas Street, Edinburgh EH3 6QG

Telephone: 031-55919/0605

Principal national officers
President: T. Wallace
Vice-President: G. M. T. Sturrock
Past President: D. C. Halliday
General Secretary: Alex A. Stanley
General Treasurer: J. R. McKelvie

Union journal: The Bulletin is issued to all members about six times a year. SSTA has recently begun to publish the *Secondary Teacher,* a quarterly publication, copies of which are sent to all Scottish secondary schools.

Membership

Current membership (1987)
Total: 7,214

The union does not keep separate membership figures for male/female members but indicates that there is a 45:55 per cent split.

According to union sources 10 years ago membership was only a few hundred more than in 1987. For three years it grew and in 1980 stood at just over 8,000 but then it fell again, and in 1983 it was again 7,000. Since that time the union has recorded a slight increase despite an 11 per cent reduction in the number of secondary teachers employed in Scotland over the last five years. As a proportion of Scottish secondary teachers, SSTA organised around 30 per cent of all Scottish secondary teachers in 1975, 26 per cent in 1983, and 29 per cent in 1987. The SSTA is confident that its membership density will continue to grow.

General

Formally constituted on January 1, 1946 as a separate union, the history of the SSTA can be traced back to 1917 when, as the *Secondary Education Association* (SEA), it agreed to amalgamate with the then predominantly female, non-graduate, primary teachers' organisation, the *Educational Institute of Scotland*, the dominant teaching union in Scotland. An ill-conceived constitution led to persistent feuding over union policy and the male, graduate entry, secondary teachers section felt threatened by the much larger female section. Following a number of attempts to overcome these difficulties the secondary teachers organised their own conference, and in May 1945 held their first Annual General Congress which led directly to the formation and constitution of SSTA in 1946.

SSTA organises registered teachers engaged in post-primary schools in Scotland. It has representation on the Scottish Joint Negotiating Committee for Teaching Staff in School Education as well as on the General Teaching Council for Scotland. The union believes that reasonable salary differentials based on qualifications and sector of employment should be preserved and this forms one of its major policy differences with its rival, the EIS.

The SSTA, along with the other teaching unions, took industrial action during the 1984-6 pay dispute which resulted in the Secretary of State for Scotland granting an independent pay review. A major policy difference between the SSTA and its major rival, the EIS, centres on the method of pay determination; the SSTA would like to see a permanent pay review body formally set up whereas the EIS is for a return to negotiations (see **EIS**).

In Scottish terms SSTA is a medium-sized union and has been affiliated to the STUC since 1980. The union does not maintain a political fund. Whilst affiliation to the TUC has never formally been discussed, in principle there would be no objection. SSTA is currently contemplating involving itself in the European Secondary Teachers' Movement.

The only full-time post in the union is that of the General Secretary who is elected by a full postal ballot of all the membership. The supreme authority of the union is the Congress which is held in the spring of each year. Between Congress the affairs of the union are run by Council which meets four times a year. Membership of the Council is drawn from the union's 13 regions, which broadly correspond with local government areas, who each elect three representatives to serve for a period of two years. Each region is run by an Executive Committee which meets five times a year. At the local level the membership is served by a school representative.

SSTA provides a number of business-type services for its members including a discount card, and unit trust linked savings plan.

STE
SOCIETY OF TELECOM EXECUTIVES

(formerly *Society of Post Office Engineers: SPOE*)

TUC affiliated

Head Office: Arthur Willet House, 1 Park Road, Teddington, Middlesex TW11 0AR

Telephone: 01-943 5181

Telex: 927162 STE G

Fax: 01-943 2532

Principal national officers
General Secretary: S. Petch
Deputy General Secretary: H. Marchant
Assistant Secretary: B. Marshall
Assistant Secretary: B. McGowan
Assistant Secretary: L. Baker
Assistant Secretary: A. Askew

Union journal: The Review (monthly, circulation about 28,000)

Membership

Current membership (1987)
Male: 25,615
Female: 3,219
Total: 28,834

Membership trends

	1975	1979	1981	1983	1987	change 1975-87	1983-87
Men	21,491	21,522	23,356	22,275	25,615	19%	15%
Women	1,110	1,945	1,109	730	3,219	190%	341%
Total	22,601	23,467	24,465	23,005	28,834	28%	25%

General
The union organises middle managerial and professional staff mostly in the British Telecom Group. Despite what the union claims is an attempt by BT to de-unionise top management, the STE recently made some useful inroads among senior managers and now represents around 400 of BT's 900 senior managers. But BT's decision to expand its middle management structure has also played a part in the union's successful recruitment campaign. All pay bargaining is conducted at national level but with BT policy of increasingly reorganising its areas of business into subsidiaries it will be difficult for the STE to retain the present status of national bargaining.

In an attempt to make its management more suited to the needs of the private sector BT has introduced a merit pay scheme which is meant to supplement, but not replace, standard national pay negotiations. In response the STE called a special conference and after some strong opposition gave the scheme formal acceptance. The union, however, remains sceptical about performance-related pay, its General Secretary commenting that "you will get people working in favour of their targets rather than in favour of their colleagues".

History

The main predecessor of the STE was the *Society of Post Office Engineering Inspectors* which was founded in 1912. Following amalgamation in 1947 with the *Society of Chief Inspectors,* the name was changed to the *Society of Telecommunications Engineers.* In 1969 a further amalgamation with the *Telecommunications Traffic Association* resulted in another name change to the *Society of Post Office Engineers* (SPOE). In 1972, SPOE amalgamated with the *Association of Post Office Executives,* and in 1975 the *Telecommunications Sales Superintendents Association* joined by a transfer of engagements. As a result of hiving off of telecom activity from the Post Office in 1982 senior staff in British Telecom, who were members of the SCPS, were transferred to the SPOE. Likewise, SPOE transferred its own Post Office membership to the CMA. Following the rationalisation of union representation among the three unions, the SPOE changed its name to the Society of Telecom Executives (STE).

Organisation

There is an Annual Delegate Conference which is the supreme ruling body of the union. The Executive Council consists of 12 members elected annually plus an elected President. In order to comply with the 1984 Trade Union Act all elections previously carried out by Conference have been changed to full balloting of the membership. Full-time officials are appointed by the Executive Council. The General Secretary is not an elected post. In 1986 the STE created the post of National Officer.

Women

The steep rise in women members is due to the transfer of members from the Society of Civil and Public Servants into the STE in 1982 (see "Membership trends" and "History"). Aware of this, the union conducted a survey in 1987/8 to determine issues of special concern to women members. The survey found widespread discrimination at BT where women constitute about 30 per cent of the total work-force but with less than 15 per cent in management grades. As a result of the survey BT has now introduced a career break scheme to encourage women to remain in employment (see **NCU**).

External relations

The STE political fund was first established just before the 1984 Trade Union Act became operative.

Recent events

In its drive to weaken the power of the STE, BT is extending the merit payment awards first negotiated in 1987. They are now keen to introduce personal contracts, which would include a company car, medical insurance, and telephone allowance, to all their middle managers thereby effectively removing any pay structure for management and inevitably weakening the influence of the STE. As a result, and in opposition to these plans, union membership among senior BT staff has taken a dramatic jump by 17 per cent since January 1989.

TGWU
TRANSPORT AND GENERAL WORKERS' UNION

TUC affiliated

Head Office: Transport House, Smith Square, Westminster, London SW1P 3JB

Telephone: 01-828 7788

Telex: 919009

Fax: 01-630 5861

Principal national officers
General Secretary: Ron Todd
Deputy Geneal Secretary: Bill Morris
Assistant General Secretary: Eddie Haigh
Administrative Officer: Ray Collins

Trade group and departmental national officers
Docks and waterways: J. Connolly (National Secretary)
Passenger services: C. Twort (National Secretary), G. Stevenson (National Secretary Designate)
Road transport, commercial: J. Ashwell (National Secretary), G. Oram (National Officer)
Civil air transport: G. Ryde (National Secretary)
Public services: J. Dromey (National Secretary), D. Bryan (National Officer)
Vehicle building and automotive: M. Murphy (National Secretary), J. Adams (National Secretary Designate)
Power and engineering: F. Howell (National Secretary), J. Mowatt (National Officer)
General workers: P. Evans (National Secretary), B. Cox (Liaison National Officer)
Textile: P. Booth (National Secretary)
Chemical, rubber manufacturing, and oil refining: F. Higgs (National Secretary)
Food, drink, and tobacco: R. Harrison (National Secretary), W. Northcliffe (National Officer)
Agriculture and allied workers: B. Leathwood (National Secretary)
Building construction and civil engineering (including building crafts): G. P. Henderson (National Secretary)
Administrative, clerical, technical, and supervisory: A. C. Sullivan (National Secretary), T. Lyle (National Officer)
Legal: A. C. Blyghton (Legal Secretary)
Research and education: R. Scott (National Secretary), F. Cosgrove (Director of Studies)
Women: M. Prosser (National Secretary)
Publications: C. Kaufman

Regional Secretaries
Region 1 (London and Home Counties)
K. Reids, "Woodberry", 218 Green Lanes, London N4 2HB. *Telephone:* 01-800 4281. *Fax:* 01-809 6501

Region 2 (Southern)
J. Ashman, 67/75 London Road, Southampton SO9 5HH. *Telephone:* 0703 637373. *Fax:* 0703 6332108

Region 3 (South-West)
J. Joynson, Transport House, Victoria Street, Bristol BS1 6AY. *Telephone:* 0272 230555. *Fax:* 0272 230560

Region 4 (Wales)
G. Wright, 1 Cathedral Road, Cardiff CF1 9SD. *Telephone:* 0222 394521. *Fax:* 0222 390684

Region 5 (Midlands)
J. Hunt, 9/17 Victoria Street, West Bromwich B70 8HX. *Telephone:* 021-553 6051. *Fax:* 021-553 7846

Region 6 (North-West)
R. Owens, Transport House, 1 Crescent, Salford M5 4PR. *Telephone:* 061-736 1407. *Fax:* 061-737 5299

Region 7 (Scotland)
D. Shoat, 290 Bath Street, Glasgow G2 4LD. *Telephone:* 041-332 7321. *Fax:* 041-332 6157

Region 8 (Northern)
J. Mills, Transport House, John Dobson Street, Newcastle-upon-Tyne NE1 8TW. *Telephone: 091 2328951. Fax:* 091 2618825

Region 9 (Yorkshire)
M. Davey, 22 Blenheim Terrace, Leeds LS2 9HF. *Telephone:* 0532 451587. *Fax:* 0532 420637

Region 10 (Humber and East Coast)
M. Snow, Bevin House, George Street, Hull HU1 3DB. *Telephone:* 0482 24167. *Fax:* 0482 214774

Region 11 (Ireland)
J. Freeman, Transport House, 102 High Street, Belfast BT1 2DL. *Telephone:* 0232-232381. *Fax:* 0232-240133

Union journal and publications: The union produces four regular publications: the *T&G Record,* free to members, a monthly tabloid newspaper sent to branches for distribution by shop stewards and branch officers. This is the main journal for the whole union. *The Landworker,* monthly, formerly the journal of the NUAAW. *Highway,* quarterly for commercial road transport drivers; formerly the journal of the *Scottish Commercial Motormen's Union* which amalgamated with the TGWU in 1971. *ACTTS Magazine,* bimonthly journal for non-manual members.

All journals are now published from Transport House; the editor-in-chief is Chris Kaufman.

Under the Link-Up recruitment campaign, the union also publishes a fine set of booklets covering a wide range of issues including the law, equal opportunities, health, and safety at work. A further interesting development is a series of pocket size booklets, *AMMO,* providing useful information on a wide range of issues such as the jobs crisis, the poll tax, 1992, and the NHS.

Education

Your Union at Work is an important union provision designed for individual study at home as well as bringing members together in "study circles" at the work-place.

In 1984 the TGWU, in conjunction with the University of Surrey, developed the Distance Learning course for those members who have completed the range of union and TUC courses and who cannot take up full-time education but wish to pursue their studies at home. The one-year course provides a deeper understanding of economic and political issues. The union provides bursaries for members studying at Ruskin College, Northern College, Newbattle Abbey, and Coleg Harlech. Support is also provided on courses at Gwent College of Higher Education and Middlesex Polytechnic.

Membership

Current membership (1987)
Male: 1,125,927
Female: 222,785
Total: 1,348,712

Membership trends

	1975	1979	1981	1983	1987	change 1975-87	1983-87
Men	1,566,583	1,743,512	1,438,445	1,320,678	1,125,927	−28%	−15%
Women	289,582	342,769	257,373	226,765	222,785	−23%	− 2%
Total	1,856,165	2,086,281	1,695,818	1,547,443	1,348,712	−27%	−13%

General

The TGWU is Britain's largest union. It is a general union, open to all types of workers, but in sectors such as oil refining, flour milling, and the docks it approximates to an industrial union, but has to share the field with other unions. It is almost the only union for road transport drivers across the whole range of industries (about 20,000, however, are members of the United Road Transport Union). The TGWU is also characteristically "general" in having membership among production workers in most manufacturing industries, while also often having membership among clerical and administrative staff in some of those industries. In recent years it has recruited among such diverse groups of employees as garage mechanics, stable lads and girls, bookmakers, and hotel staff. The union has strongly promoted plant and work-place bargaining by shop stewards and is consequently party to many plant agreements, in addition to the many company and national (industry-wide) agreements to which it is signatory.

During the 1980s the TGWU faced a continual decline in membership and its current figure of around 1.3m members matches the membership figure for 1962. Whilst virtually all TUC trade unions have suffered membership losses during the 1980s (see TUC), the rate of decline for the TGWU has exceeded that of other unions. Between 1979 and 1986 total TUC membership loss was 21 per cent; the TGWU in the same period lost over 31 per cent. But even more worrying for the TGWU is that a number of the larger unions are reporting (slight) membership growth, whereas the TGWU is still losing members. Encouragingly though, the rate of decline appears to have slowed down quite considerably:

1985: 1,434,005
1986: 1,377,944
1987: 1,348,712

The union may in fact report its first gain when figures are published at the 1989 TUC Congress.

In its attempt to arrest the drastic membership decline the TGWU has produced two important strategic documents which form the basis of a sustained and concerted recruitment campaign: Link-Up, introduced in 1987 and revamped in 1989, forms the core of the union's recruitment strategy, while the policy document *Forwards T&G* lays the ground to take the union into the next century (see "Recent events").

History

In March 1920 the *Dock, Wharf, Riverside and General Workers' Union,* whose main source of membership was London, took the initiative in organising a discussion with the shipping staffs on the need for amalgamation. Unity of purpose was achieved and organisational details were elaborated. These were preliminaries. The first real step towards the creation of the TGWU came when a delegation from the other main dockers' union, the *National Union of Dock, Riverside, and General Workers,* based in Liverpool and led by James Sexton, agreed to join forces in forming a new union.

There was now an excellent chance of carrying other smaller unions with them. So it was agreed to appoint Ernest Bevin of the DWRGWU as provisional secretary and Harry Gosling (a member of neither union but president of the Transport Workers' Federation) as provisional chairperson of an amalgamation committee which then decided on a list of other unions, all connected with the docks industry, whom they would invite to their next meeting.

There were 59 delegates present, representing 13 unions, when the conference amalgamation opened at Anderton's Hotel on Fleet Street on August 18, 1920. From the London area came the *National Union of Dock, Wharves and Shipping Staffs* (6,500 members), *Amalgamated Stevedores Labour Protection League* (5,500 members), *South Side Labour Protection League* (2,500 members), *National Union of Ships' Clerks and Grain Weighers* (East Ham Union) (732 members), *Amalgamated Society of Watermen, Lightermen and Bargemen* (Harry Gosling's union) (7,000 members), and the *Dock, Wharf, Riverside, and General Workers' Union* (Tillet and Bevin) (120,000 members).

From Cardiff came delegates from the *Cardiff Coal Trimmers* (1,600 members) and from Swansea delegates from the *National Amalgamated Labourers' Union.* Glasgow was represented by delegates from the *Scottish Union of Dockers* (11,000 members), Liverpool by Sexton's union and by the *Liverpool Clerks and Mersey Watermen* and Newcastle by the *North of England Trimmers' and Teamers' Association.*

There had been many such proposed amalgamation schemes previously among these unions but all had foundered. Now Bevin played a master stroke by putting forward proposals on the organisation of the new union which enabled amalgamation to occur and provided a lasting constitutional framework. It was necessary to leave each sectional industrial group — the dockers, road transport, and clerical staff — the autonomy to deal with their own affairs but it was also necessary to prevent autonomy undermining unity which was, after all, the point of amalgamation. Indeed, the Webbs had suggested, in their classic work, *Industrial Democracy,* that is was virtually impossible to combine workers of different occupations in a stable amalgamation. For example, dockers would be certain to argue that they alone should determine issues affecting their own trade, without interference from carters or clerks. This difficulty was met by the creation of trade groups in which members in similar trades and occupations would be grouped together. However, as a check on sectionalism, it was proposed to set up a territorial grouping of members on a geographical basis. Like a hoop around a barrel, there would be a National Executive representative of both national trade groups and geographical areas which would have control over finances, strike action, and general policy.

At a further meeting it was decided to invite the road transport unions into the amalgamation, their leaders were pleased to accept, their members having just suffered wage cuts as a result of the slump.

In the subsequent ballot of the members of the various unions on the amalgamation, only three unions voted against or failed to obtain enough votes to satisfy legal requirements — the London stevedores, the Scottish dockers and the Cardiff coal trimmers. On January 1, 1922 the Transport and General Workers' Union came into legal existence with Ernest Bevin as General Secretary. It consisted initially of 300,000 members, most of them dockworkers, transport workers on trams or buses or lorry and cart drivers. The original trade groups in 1922 were docks, waterways, administrative, clerical and supervisory, road transport-passenger, road transport-commercial, and general workers. That it was an amalgamation which had penetration into these areas suggests potential expansion but at its outset the TGWU was primarily a dockers' union with the general workers' section as a relatively minor residual grouping. In fact, there was nothing certain about the growth pattern of the TGWU for it was born into the slump and in six of its first 10 years, including the first two, it lost members. In 1923 it faced internal revolt in the unofficial strike against wage cuts of London dockers. The unofficial committee was supported by the *Amalgmated Stevedores Labour Protection League* which had stayed outside the TGWU amalgamation and now encouraged disaffected TGWU members to join it. The attempt to organise a larger breakaway was not a success and the strike collapsed. The feud between the TGWU and the stevedores continued, however, flaring up again in the 1950s' dock strikes.

Further rank and file opposition in the docks trade group came from the Glasgow dockers who had been belatedly taken into the TGWU, under protest, as part of the Scottish Union of Dock Labourers. From 1929 they set up an Anti-Registration League (registration of dockworkers was a prerequisite for the effective decasualisation of dock work) and then seceded to form the autonomous Scottish TGWU.

The second most important area of TGWU membership after the docks was road passenger transport, and among the most militant industrial groups in the country during the 1930s was the London bus section of the TGWU. The industry was still profitable, as yet facing negligible competition from private cars, and the workers suffered little from the effects of the slump, average earnings remaining comparatively high. They were a compact body of employees, displaying strong solidarity and possessing a tradition of industrial democracy. They had been a difficult group to integrate into the TGWU amalgamation. Being dissatisfied with the national passenger transport trade group, they pressed for and were conceded a greater measure of self-determination through an elected Central London Area Bus Committee which enjoyed the functions of a national trade group committee with its own full-time officer and the right of direct access to the Executive Council. A rank and file movement took control of the Central Bus Committee and, although ultimately out-manoeuvred by Bevin, agitated strongly and caused him a great deal of trouble. At the 1937 Biennial Delegate Conference the Executive Council submitted recommendations based on an enquiry into activities of members of the Central Bus Section. As a result the rules of the union were amended to strengthen the right of expulsion. A section of the rank and file movement carried out a threat to form a breakaway union and established the National Passenger Workers' Union in 1938. This breakaway survived another eight years but had no success in shifting the loyalty of most London bus workers away from the TGWU, largely because the TGWU achieved an agreement with London Transport which conferred exclusive bargaining rights and a closed shop.

The TGWU quite rapidly became less of a union of transport workers and more of a general workers' union. In 1929 it amalgamated with the *Workers' Union,* thereby gaining membership of some 100,000 workers in a variety of trades, particularly engineering, doubling the size of the existing general workers' trade group and extending its industrial coverage. (This amalgamation was also the origin of the TGWU's membership in agriculture.) Previously, in 1926, the power workers' trade group had been established following amalgamation with the *National Union of Enginemen, Firemen, Motormen, and Mechanics.* A further territorial region was established following the accession of the *North Wales Quarrymen's Union* into the TGWU (although it retained some autonomy and separate affiliation to the TUC). Another early amalgamation was with the London-based *United Order of General Labourers.*

In the 1920 amalgamation scheme provision had been made for five trade groups and for sub-sections for numerically important trades within three of the groups. The docks' group had a sub-section for coal shipping; the general workers' group had one for metal and chemical trades; and the road transport group had sub-sections for the passenger and commercial transport workers. As groups expanded it was union policy to sub-divide them into trade union sections as a step toward group status. In 1922, for instance, road transport-passenger and road transport-commercial became full trade groups. A group was able to have its own trade machinery and specialist officers at all levels. The general workers' trade group was used as a residual category and a step towards the formation of new national trade groups, first for metals, engineering, and chemicals and then for building in 1938, following amalgamation with the *"Altogether" Builders' and Labourers' Society.* Workers in agriculture, the fishing industry, government and public services, and flourmilling had their own sections.

Sections had only a specialist national official and a national trade committee and at other levels had to use composite trade group officials. The right to establish trade groups rested with the Biennial Delegate Conference and each time it met there were a number of claimants to trade group status but very few were conceded.

There were only three years between 1922 and 1940 during which an amalgamation did not take place (see "Appendix"). Just prior to the General Strike, negotiations were being held to bring together the TGWU, the National Union of General and Municipal Workers, the Electrical Trades' Union and six smaller unions. Negotiations lapsed because of the General Strike and were never properly renewed. In the 1930s the TGWU withdrew its claim to organise the nursing profession and the catering industry, leaving these fields of recruitment to other unions. Bevin had also meticulously steered it away from extending its interests to seafarers when pressed to form an alternative to Havelock Wilson's National Union of Seamen, which had become a company union working hand-in-glove with the employers in the Shipping Federation. Instead, Bevin established a close working relationship with Spence, the new General Secretary who took over when Wilson died in 1929. This is not to say that the TGWU leadership was averse to widening its spheres of influence. For example, to the indignation of an outraged Jockey Club, it did take up membership of stable lads and girls after an enthusiastic meeting at Newmarket.

Although the TGWU had always had a nucleus of membership in the road haulage industry among its carter members, it proved difficult to extend membership among the multitude of small employing units. However, in 1938 the Road Haulage Wages Act replaced voluntary regulations of wages and conditions by statutory regulation by central and area wages boards. The union had pursued this measure which would not detract from its authority — indeed its effective enforcement depended largely on the vigilance of the union — while it increased union coverage since its jurisdiction extended to C-licence holders operating vehicles for the transport of their own produce.

In 1928 Transport House in Smith Square was opened.

1939-45

The most important change of the war years was that Ernest Bevin became Minister of Labour, Arthur Deakin became Acting General Secretary of the union. His rise coincided with the increase in the power and influence of trade unions; they had friends in the government and increased their size and strength as a result of the high level of employment. Membership of the TGWU increased from less than 700,000 in 1939 to over 1.2 million in 1946.

1945 to date

Deakin was elected General Secretary in 1945 receiving 58 per cent of the 347,523 votes cast. An important constitutional change was made when the 1945 Biennial Delegate Conference passed a motion barring members of the Communist Party from holding any office in the union, either as lay members or as full-time officials. At present under Schedule 1 (2) of the rules of the TGWU, membership of an organisation which "in the opinion of the General Executive Council is contrary, detrimental, inconsistent, or injurious to the policy and purpose of the union will render the member liable to be declared ineligible to hold any office within the Union either as a lay-member or as a permanent or full-time officer, or such other penalties as in the opinion of the General Executive Council shall seem just".

In collective bargaining the most significant reform of the immediate post-war years achieved by the union was partial decasualisation of port employment under the National Dock Labour Scheme of 1947, which was really a continuation of various wartime schemes in that it provided for local dock labour boards under joint union-management control and guaranteed pay. Despite this, some said because of it, in their improved social and economic position and with increased bargaining power, the dockers engaged in strike action after the war on an unprecedented scale. The strikes were invariably against union advice and in contravention of agreements and negotiating procedures. Such activity culminated in the decision of a group of Hull dockers to secede from the TGWU and join the London-based National Amalgamated Stevedores and Dockers in 1954. They were followed by some other disgruntled dockers in Birkenhead, Liverpool, and Manchester. Since this was an infringement of the Bridlington agreement on inter-union relations the NASD was suspended from the TUC, but when the NASD decided to return the new recruits many refused to go.

There continued to be demands for separate trade groups from many trades among the TGWU membership but Deakin and the General Executive Council were reluctant to increase the number of trade groups, an excess of which they believed would hamper efficient organisation. However, it was necessary to form a chemical workers' section to meet the challenge of competition for members from the Chemical Workers' Union. This section became a full trade group in 1954.

Deakin died in 1954, being replaced by the former Deputy General Secretary, Tiffin. Frank Cousins was appointed Deputy General Secretary under Tiffin and was then elected General Secretary by a big majority in 1956 after Tiffin's death.

Cousins had made his reputation in the union as a critic of the centralised type of administration developed by Bevin and continued by Deakin. Well suited to a slowly growing new amalgamation in an economy devastated by slump, these policies were inappropriate to the full employment economy of post-war Britain in which bargaining power at work-place level had increased strongly. Deakin's restricted conception of the role of shop stewards and insistence on the negotiating role of full-time officers were likewise inappropriate. Cousins showed more sympathy and understanding with shop stewards but there was no recasting of union organisation.

When Cousins retired Jack Jones, who had been vigorously propounding reforms to make TGWU organisation more attuned to the realities of work-place power, was elected to succeed him in 1969. During the 1960s change had been taking place, mainly in acceptance of local and plant bargaining, but it was *ad hoc,* piecemeal, and untidy. Now, change towards work-place negotiation by shop stewards and reference back of settlements to members was specifically encouraged and given direction by the General Secretary. The decentralisation of collective bargaining levels in the TGWU took five main forms:

(1) Movement from national (usually industry-wide) level negotiations to lower (usually work-place) level bargaining. This was true of the docks, engineering, and of bargaining relationships with large companies which had withdrawn from employers' associations or from industry-level Joint Industrial Councils (JICs), e.g. Dunlop.

(2) Increases in the scope and content of lower level and particularly work-place bargaining such that bargaining at these levels more closely determined actual pay and conditions. The vogue for productivity bargaining greatly accelerated this change.

(3) An increase in lay representation on national, regional, and company negotiating bodies where representation of full-time officers was reduced to provide seats for shop stewards who were, in this way and others, brought more fully into the official machinery of government of the TGWU.

(4) Reference back procedures were introduced or extended.

(5) District committees were developed to overcome trade group fragmentation.

Union officials

To implement these changes Jack Jones established many more district committees and appointed more district officials throughout the union. They were appointed with the express objective of encouraging work-place organisation and autonomy by assisting shop stewards to negotiate for themselves. One of the conseqences of this change was some decline in the authority of trade group organisation.

There was a quite drastic removal of some of the "old school" full-time officials who did not accept such changes as reference back to members. For instance, Kealey, the union negotiator at Fords, resigned under pressure in 1969 after failing to comply with a Delegate Conference decision and was replaced by Moss Evans, who eventually went on to become General Secretary, while at least one other national trade group secretary decided that resignation was now advisable.

Jones was in favour of co-operation on pay policy with the Labour government, being one of the architects of the "social contract". But then at his last union Conference in 1977 he lost an appeal for another year of co-operation with Labour. The domination of the TGWU by its General Secretary had been weakened, as Moss Evans, who succeeded Jack Jones as General Secretary, discovered, and this process has continued to create problems for the present incumbent, Ron Todd.

1970 to the present

The union continued to grow, both through fresh recruitment and through further amalgamations, reaching over two million members. Of particular significance was the 1972 merger with the *National Union of Vehicle Builders,* establishing a new vehicle building and automotive trade group in the union and strengthening its power in the motor industry. In chemicals its strength increased through the accession of the *Process and General Workers' Union* and, particularly in the drug and fine chemical section of the industry, the belated amalgamation with the *Chemical Workers' Union,* led by Bob Edwards — like Jack Jones, a Spanish Civil War veteran. Earlier, the mergers with the *National Association of Operative Plasterers* and with the *Scottish Tilers and Cement Workers* had established TGWU more firmly in the building industry. Its strength in transport was extended by the amalgamation with the *Scottish Commercial Motormen's Union* and in the docks by the amalgamations with the *Watermen, Lightermen, Tugmen, and Bargemen's Union*, the *Scottish TGWU* (mainly Glasgow dockers), and the *Iron, Steel, and Wood Barge Builders' and Helpers' Association*. More attention began to be directed towards recruitment and effective representation of clerical and administrative membership, but this continued to be a weak point for the TGWU, despite impressive gains in membership.

In the early 1980s the TGWU, in common with smaller unions, was faced with a continual decline in membership in the face of trifling improvements in trade and employment following the resolute and draconian monetarism of the government's deflationary economic policies. The trade groups worst affected were passenger and commercial services, construction, food, drink, and tobacco, chemicals, and general workers. Over this period the decline in membership was 10 per cent, leaving 1.7 million members.

In 1982 the *National Union of Agricultural and Allied Workers* amalgamated bringing 70,000 members, along with the 37,000 members of the *National Union of Dyers, Bleachers, and Textile Workers*. A further 1,000 members arrived from the old "blue" union of dock workers, the *National Amalgamated Stevedores and Dockers*, historically a tenacious rival of the official TGWU policies in London, Hull, Manchester, and Liverpool, but no longer financially viable.

The size and strength of the TGWU were built through mergers and amalgamations, but in the 1980s the union no longer appears to be "merger friendly"; although six more unions have amalgamated since 1982 (see "Appendix"), none of them contributed much to the TGWU's membership figures, nor have they provided the TGWU with a sector that could be the basis for future membership expansion. In this the TGWU has given way to its rival, the GMB, which has consciously sought mergers for their strategic significance and has deliberately made itself attractive to other unions (see **GMB**). Although the TGWU is currently conducting merger talks with the NUM, it is the proposed merger with MSF, which holds real hope for the future of the TGWU (see "Recent events").

Coverage
The wide membership coverage of the TGWU is well enough reflected in its trade groups to need little further elaboration, which would in any case entail listing a huge array of negotiating bodies at industry-wide or national, company plant, and work-place level.

Organisation
Every member of the TGWU is attached to a branch. It is union policy that each member joins with colleagues to elect a work-place representative, usually, although not invariably, called a shop steward. While the branch remains an important administrative unit for the union at the grass roots and an important channel of communication (exclusively so for nominations and election), increasingly its functions and machinery as well as its officers are supplemented and strengthened by that of work-place representatives and shop stewards.

Large-scale production and the spread of "scientific management" combined to increase the responsibilities of shop stewards. Rule 11 of the TGWU rule book states:

> For the purpose of representing the membership on matters affecting their employment, a shop steward or equivalent representative shall be elected by the membership in a defined working area or at a branch meeting by a show of hands or ballot as may from time to time be determined.

Shop stewards shall receive the fullest support and protection from the union, and immediate inquiry shall be undertaken by the appropriate trade group or district committees into every case of dismissal of a shop steward with a view to preventing victimisation, either open or concealed.

Since these changes, which were initiated by Jack Jones, the TGWU has been known as the shop stewards' union. When shop stewards were dismissed at Tilbury docks during the 1989 dockers' dispute over the abolition of the National Docks Labour Scheme, Ron Todd was constitutionally bound to defend them although to the public at large it perhaps appeared as a "knee-jerk" reaction (see "Recent events").

Regional and district committees

There are 11 territorial divisions or regions. District committees have been widely established in most regions; some unite branches within a district on a community basis irrespective of industry, and others co-ordinate branches in particular industries, such as automotive trades, oil trades, or ACTSS (Administrative, Clerical, Technical and Supervisory Staff) membership. The rapid growth of the district committee system reflects the development of plant bargaining, resulting in the negotiation of hundreds of agreements on wages, conditions, and procedures. This necessitates co-ordination within each district.

The regional committee is the ruling body for each region and is a direct link with the General Executive Council. It consists of representatives (who hold office for two years) elected by or from the district or regional trade group committees or by electoral conference within the region. These committees function mainly to supervise and co-ordinate regional union activity. The regions exercise considerable autonomy, though recently this has been the cause of some concern to the union leadership, who are attempting to promote more cohesion and unity within the union. Without such unity the TGWU is unlikely to maintain its position as Britain's largest union nor hope to regain its reputation as its most influential and respected union during the 1990s.

National trade group or section committee

TGWU membership[1] by trade group or section committee

Trade groups and Section committees	Membership 1980	Membership 1986	Membership 1988
Docks, waterways, fishing, and other maritime services	45,000	28,000	26,000
Passenger services	129,000	98,000	92,560
Road transport (commercial)	208,000	144,000	135,000
Civil air transport		36,000	37,000
Public services	189,000[2]	100,000	135,000
Vehicle building and automotive	169,000	100,000	97,000
Power and engineering	241,000	147,000	135,000
General workers'	238,000	125,000	126,000
Textile	37,000[3]	50,000	49,000

Chemical, oil refining, and rubber manufacturing	125,000	100,000	126,000
Food, drink, and tobacco	209,000	143,000	132,000
Agriculture and allied workers	73,000	50,000	41,000
Building, construction, and civil engineering group & building craft section	350,000[4]	50,000	54,000
Administrative, clerical, technical, & supervisory staff (ACTSS)	151,100	100,000	97,000

[1] All figures are approximate and may not be strictly comparable
[2] Includes figures for civil transport
[3] Includes figures for dyers and bleachers
[4] Likely to be an over-estimate

Biennial Delegate Conference

The Biennial Delegate Conference is the supreme policy-making authority within the union. Each branch is entitled to elect, by a show of hands or by ballot, one delegate. Regional trade groups also elect, by ballot vote, one delegate for every 1,000 members. The General Executive Council can be represented by up to three members who can take part in debates but are not allowed to vote.

Rules revision conference

The 1949 Biennial Delegate Conference established the rules revision conference as the sole authority of the union to make, amend, or revoke the rules or constitution of the union. This body meets only every six years, though special rules conferences can be convened. An interesting feature of this body is that its basis of representation is different from that of the policy-making Conference; the delegates are elected on a territorial basis of approximately one per 10,000 members, therefore reducing the trade bias in the drawing up of new rules. The idea is that rules are for the whole union and not to benefit any particular section. It is a matter for speculation whether the rules revision conference, or the BDC which created it, is the supreme constitutional authority.

A special recalled rules revision conference was held in November 1988 which agreed to rule changes for the periodic elections of the General Secretary, Deputy General Secretary, and Assistant General Secretary. This was necessary to comply with the 1988 Employment Act which requires postal balloting for elections. But Conference decided to take advantage of the transitional arrangements provided under the legislation and agreed that Ron Todd would not have to stand for re-election before his retirement in 1992. The Deputy General Secretary and Assistant General Secretary will be subject to election within the terms of the Act.

General Executive Council

The 39-strong General Executive Council is the governing body of the union responsible for the general administration and management of the union, subject to the policy laid down by the BDC to which it reports. The TGWU is rare in that it nominates lay GEC members to sit on the TUC General Council.

In the GEC are merged the dual structures of the union, the trade and territorial organisation. There are 25 territorial representatives elected by ballot of the membership in the regions concerned. Each of the 14 trade groups has one representative, nominated by and elected from branch members who are members of the particular trade group. Members of the GEC are all lay members with at least two years of financial membership, and hold office for two years although they are eligible to stand for re-election. Meetings are held quarterly, special sessions being convened by the General Secretary when necessary.

Until 1981 the right dominated the GEC; but although the left (composed of the old-style Communist Party and the Tribunite left) was in a minority it was relatively united. Since then the left has gained ascendancy in the GEC and now dominates it by a majority of 21-18. But the old-style left has given way to the hard and ultra-left, and the deep mistrust and disunity has left the TGWU without any clear purpose or strategy.

Finance and general purposes committee
The GEC elects a finance and general purposes committee which meets monthly or as convened by the General Secretary. It is concerned with finance, properties, and investments of the union, stoppages of work, the authorisation of strike pay, emergency problems, and other matters referred to it by the GEC. Although the left has won control of the GEC the right still controls this important "inner cabinet" committee and has used its majority on a number of occasions to frustrate the left-led leadership. A notable case was during the appointment of the south-west regional secretary in 1986, when the committee twice refused to appoint any candidate. The incident was only resolved when the General Secretary pulled the appointment away from them and put it before the full GEC.

Full-time and permanent officers
All officers of the union must have worked in one of the industries covered by the union including the General Secretary, Executive officers including the Deputy General Secretary, Assistant General Secretary, Executive Finance Secretary, administrative officer, national secretaries and officer, regional secretaries, regional and district officers, trustees, delegates to constitutional committees, and branch officers.

The General Secretary, Deputy General Secretary, and Assistant General Secretary are elected according to the requirements of the 1988 Employment Act. There was a good deal of controversy when Ron Todd was elected General Secretary in 1985 which led to a rerun following a public row with accusations of ballot-rigging. Although the 1988 Employment Act requires union General Secretaries and some other national officials to seek re-election every five years in a postal ballot, Ron Todd was advised that he need not stand for re-election because he was elected before October 1985, the cut-off period stipulated in the Act. Instead, he will hold office until he retires in 1992 and thereby provide the TGWU with a long period of much needed stability.

All other officials are appointed by the GEC and hold office "during the pleasure of the union" which normally means until retirement. But the TGWU is rare in having (particularly under Jack Jones) fixed the retirement of several full-time officials. In Region 10 they even retired the regional secretary.

The General Secretary is responsible to the GEC for all aspects of policy and administration and is the voice of the GEC at the BDC and outside the union. The Deputy General Secretary shares many of these duties. Recently he has been instrumental in "Link-Up", the union's important recruitment campaign and in trying to lead the union into new but difficult areas, such as dealing with a fragmented labour market and "flexible work patterns".

Women
In December 1987 women's membership stood at 222,785, which on the 1986 figures represents only a very small reduction and could even be source of satisfaction. But the 1988 figure of 213,723 represents a 10,000 fall in women's membership since the

224,506 recorded in 1986, and this has to be a cause for concern. This is especially true in view of the fact that the TGWU has run special campaigns to encourage women to become members, and also that women represent an increasingly important source of future union membership growth. One small piece of comfort perhaps might be that the relative proportion of women to men remains roughly the same, hovering around the 20 per cent mark.

In 1986 the GEC decided that the work of the Women's Advisory Committee (WAC) should be more closely "dovetailed into the mainstream work of the union" and proposed that the "WAC report directly to the regional committee". Following the 1987 BDC the union also established an Equal Opportunities Working Party with representatives from each region. Whilst bureaucratic integration is necessary women's issues are still seen as marginal to the "mainstream work" *(sic)* of the union, and a cultural rather than structural transformation is required before this situation is altered.

The TGWU has promoted a number of campaigns, for example against breast and cervical cancer and repetitive strain injury. These campaigns involved close liaison with the parliamentary group, and Maria Fyfe, a union-sponsored MP with many years of trade union experience, has been appointed to the Labour front benches to work on women's matters.

External relations

The union affiliates 1.25m of its members to the Labour Party, the largest single union affiliation, and its biggest financial contribitor (amounting to almost £1m in 1988). Eddie Haigh, the Assistant General Secretary, is a member of the National Executive Committee of the Labour Party and he also chairs the Organisation Committee and Regional Liaison Committee. Bill Morris is a member of the Conference Arrangements Committee and Ron Todd is an auditor.

The union maintains a parliamentary group of 33 sponsored MPs:

Graham Allen	(Nottingham North)
Tony Banks	(Newham North)
Margaret Beckett	(Derby South)
Syd Bidwell	(Ealing Southall)
Tony Blair	(Sedgefield)
Gordon Brown	(Dunfermline East)
Norman Buchan	(Paisley South)
Ann Clwyd	(Cynon Valley)
Stan Crowther	(Rotherham)
Maria Fyfe	(Glasgow Maryhill)
George Galloway	(Glasgow Hillhead)
Norman Goodman	(Greenock and Port Glasgow)
Harriet Harman	(Peckham)
Roy Hughes	(Newport East)
Adam Ingram	(East Kilbride)
Barry Jones	(Alyn and Deeside)
Neil Kinnock	(Islwyn)
Terry Lewis	(Worsley)
Eddie Loyden	(Liverpool Garston)
Ian McCartney	(Makerfield)
Kevin McNamara	(Hull North)
Max Madden	(Bradford West)
David Marshall	(Glasgow Shettleston)
Eric Martlew	(Bradford West)

Paul Murphy	(Torfaen)
Gordon Oakes	(Halton)
Bob Parry	(Liverpool Riverside)
Joyce Quin	(Gateshead East)
John Reid	(Motherwell North)
Allan Roberts	(Bootle)
Joan Ruddock	(Lewisham Deptford)
Peter Shore	(Bethnal Green and Stepney)
Gavin Strang	(Edinburgh East)

The TGWU and the Labour Party

Controversy and contradiction seem to surround the TGWU's current relationship with the Labour Party. Following the third successive general election defeat in 1987 the Labour Party set up a two-year policy review aimed at modernising both its policies and method of organisation. The TGWU is well represented both on the Party's National Executive Committee and the policy review group. During the 1988 Labour Party Conference interim review documents were submitted and approved by delegates, including the TGWU. But at the same time as backing the interim reports and providing a show of unity, Ron Todd made his controversial speech on unilateralism which immediately cast doubt on the sincerity of the union's commitment to unity and appeared to scupper the Party's search for policies on which it could win a general election.

The TGWU threw its support behind the Kinnock/Hattersley ticket for the leadership election only at the last minute, and while support for Kinnock was never really in doubt, the union seriously considered backing John Prescott for the post of deputy leader of the Labour Party. In preparation for the 1989 Labour Party Conference consideration was given to transforming the union block vote. It is an open secret that the Labour leadership would like to see "union power" considerably diminished. However, the TGWU proposes only marginal changes to the block vote reform, reducing the unions' share from the present 90 per cent to 70 per cent. What are the main reasons for these controversies and why does the TGWU seem unconcerned about returning a Labour government?

The reasons are partly historical, based on sentimentality over past influence in the Labour Party. In the post-war years the union benefited from both Ernest Bevin and Frank Cousins (former TGWU General Secretaries) being members of the Cabinet. Jack Jones, though not achieving such office, nevertheless exerted considerable influence over the Labour Party both in and out of power during the 1970s. His involvement in the Labour-union pact, the Social Contract, made him a key figure. During the Labour Party's years in opposition in the 1980s the TGWU's influence has declined. Despite being the biggest contributor to Labour Party funds the union feels that it is no longer calling the tune in shaping Labour Party policies. Other unions are in the ascendancy, notably the GMB, with their support for the "new realism" advocated by the Party leadership. In many ways the TGWU represents the "old guard" opposing Neil Kinnock's ambitions for *"perestroika"*. Its 39-member GEC is dominated by the left which is reluctant to accept the shift to a more market-oriented culture. Its determination to maintain this stance, exemplified by its stubborn support for unilateralism, seems to rise above all other considerations.

The TGWU and the TUC

Unlike the GMB the TGWU was never keen on the move in 1982 to alter the composition of the TUC General Council from trade groupings to "automacity". The old system of trade groupings greatly enhanced the TGWU's power in the TUC — voting for each trade group was done by all TUC affiliates and the TGWU was famous (or infamous) for its dealings and patronage. When Congress agreed to change the system of General Council representation from one organised around occupational trade groupings to one known as "automacity", it carried with it a provision for review after five years; in the meantime the special review body, as part of its wide-ranging remit, has examined the composition of the General Council, and its recommendations are to be considered at the 1989 Congress.

The TGWU and other large, left-led unions such as MSF, NALGO, and NUPE, will probably argue against the recommendations on the basis that the system of allocating membership to the General Council does not represent the spread of unions and that while union membership in small unions has declined the number of seats reserved for small unions has not.

As the largest union the TGWU jealously guards its independence and is sensitive about the way in which its influence is being steadily eroded. At the same time, the TGWU is going to be reluctant to underwrite extra TUC services which are likely to emerge from the special review body recommendations when it can provide them itself more cheaply (see **TUC**).

Recent events
The 1989 BDC reaffirmed its "opposition to anti-trade union legislation" but voted to change TGWU policy and accept government funding for conducting postal ballots. In the next four years the union faces four postal ballots which are likely to cost over £4m.

Earlier in 1989 the union agreed to set up race equality committees and the three largest regions, London, Midlands, and the North-West, are piloting the scheme before it is established in all the regions. A national race equality officer is likely to be appointed if the scheme proves successful.

The 1989 BDC also saw the formal launch of the important policy document *Forwards T&G* which set out the union's strategy to take it into the next century. The tactics proposed are an attempt both to widen and increase the union's membership. The document covers equal opportunities, political initiatives, health and safety, branch activity, co-ordination between trade groups, communications, training, relations with other unions, international links, trades councils, new management techniques, and organisation structures. To what extent this document is able to revive the TGWU remains to be seen.

Apart from developments concerning the Labour Party and the TUC, other recent events of significance are more clearly understood in relation to trade groups.

Docks and waterways
The dominant issue has been the abolition of the National Dock Labour scheme (NDLB scheme) announced by the government on April 6, 1989. Under this scheme only registered dockers could work in specified ports and the union had extensive negotiating powers in respect of working practices. Both government and employers saw the NDLB scheme as one of the last bastions of restrictive practice which denied management flexibility to ports within the scheme and limited opportunities to make the ports responsive to market forces.

The Dock Labour scheme was formed in 1947 by the Attlee government and has a special place in the history of the TGWU. In 1951 employment in ports covered by the scheme had reached a peak of 82,000 but by 1979 this had fallen to 27,000. Accelerated decline during the 1980s reduced employment by two-thirds to stand at 9,400 in 1989. Though small in size the dockers are an integral part of the history of the TGWU and the British trade union movement in general, and there is still much emotional attachment to them.

Since the National Dock Labour scheme was created by an act of Parliament, only the government could abolish it. This created difficulties for the TGWU when the proposal to abolish the scheme was announced. As it was the government's initiative the TGWU became involved in complex legal proceedings to test what, if any, action it could legitimately take. The TGWU leadership were mindful of the lessons of previous disputes, for example those involving the NUM, SOGAT and NUS, which suffered sequestration and virtual bankruptcy by ignoring the various legal hurdles. The leadership dealt with the legal procedures skilfully. Moreover, they successfully restrained dock leaders who were keen to move without delay into national strike action.

The TGWU pursued the case through the High Court, Court of Appeal, and up to the House of Lords, and were successful in establishing that the strike was a lawful trade dispute rather than a political protest. Thus, publicly, the TGWU threw all its support behind the dockers; privately however, Ron Todd must have had reservations about jeopardising the £76m assets of the TGWU's 1.2m members for the sake of 9,400 dockers.

By the time the protracted legal proceedings had been resolved strike action was called only shortly before the abolition came into effect. This meant that dockers had only limited time to take legitimate action while the NDLS was still in place; thereafter they would be officially in breach of contract, liable to dismissal and in danger of losing their entitlement to the special government compensation scheme. Initially, support for the dispute was fairly strong; however, as employers started to put increasing pressure on dockers a slow drift back to work began. The dispute took a sudden twist when employers at Tilbury dismissed TGWU stewards, and the union leadership, aware that the dispute was beginning to disintegrate, tried to turn it into a strike over union recognition in British ports. A series of national conferences were convened to try to maintain support but in the end there was considerable disarray amongst members and the strike crumbled. Liverpool dockers, the most militant of the groups, held out a while longer but even they recognised the futility of prolonging the action and decided to march back to work united with dignity intact.

In the final analysis the TGWU has demonstrated an astuteness and awareness of strategy in dealing with the increasingly legalistic nature of British industrial relations as well as establishing an important legal precedent. None the less the union has been forced to relinquish its legally established national negotiating rights in the face of the joint determination of government and employers to bring in more flexible local working arrangements. The future of this trade group must be in doubt following the reduction in its membership.

Passenger services

The government strategy of deregulating passenger transport has thrown the whole industry into a state of flux; along with the ensuing sell-offs and take-overs, these factors have brought about the end of national pay bargaining procedures which have been replaced by new company bargaining structures.

The passenger services trade group held its first National Industrial Conference in April 1989 and discussed its response to deregulation and its impact on TGWU members and the travelling public. The TUC's passenger charter, launched in August 1988, which called for a more reliable, convenient, and modern service, was endorsed strongly by the group. Taxi drivers and the coaching sector were identified under the union's Link-Up campaign for special attention.

Road transport (commercial)

There has been a strong growth in the road haulage industry but the trade group has continued to see a decline in its membership, which in 1988 was down to 135,109, a decrease of over 8,000 on 1986. Part of the membership decline is due to the growth of contract hire at the expense of company-own distribution departments. This has had the effect of reducing national and large-scale company bargaining and leaving a more fragmented and difficult sector to organise.

The group has produced a charter as part of its Link-Up campaign to stem the membership decline. The campaign issues of the charter include promoting union facilities and benefits, stressing items such as terms and conditions of employment, health and safety, and rest and refreshment facilities.

Civil air transport
Two issues currently dominate the activities of this section. The acquisition of British Caledonian by British Airways created difficulties for the civil air transport section in terms of harmonising structures, agreements, and operating arrangements. Dissatisfaction with the way the TGWU was handling the negotiations resulted in the defection of 4,000 cabin staff to create the breakaway union Cabin Crew 89. The TGWU has complained to the TUC disputes committee claiming that the airline pilots' union, BALPA, by offering financial assistance and administrative aid to the breakaway group, was in breach of TUC rules. If the TUC were in fact to find in the TGWU's favour, BALPA could follow the EETPU and be expelled by Congress.

National negotiating machinery has been disbanded and replaced by local level bargaining with individual airport companies. The airlines have followed a similar pattern and BA is now proposing to decentralise its bargaining machinery as well as introducing regional pay and procedural arrangements. This could substantially weaken the ability of the union to negotiate effectively in the future.

In a further development at BA the TGWU called a strike in August 1989 in support of an air-stewardess who was dismissed in January 1989 for alleged irregularities in the conduct of an in-flight bar. The TGWU has demanded reinstatement and BA management has asked for written assurances that cabin staff would work normally. The dispute was on-going at the time of publication, but it would seem that following the formation of Cabin Crew 89 the TGWU felt some degree of culpability and had to make its presence felt.

Public services
Pay and conditions and privatisation were the dominant issues for the public services trade group. Despite a long and bitter dispute against privatisation of the Royal Ordinance factories and Royal Naval Dockyards, both were eventually sold off and new bargaining machinery introduced.

The third term of the Conservative government's office has seen the public sector targeted for dismantling and an attack on national bargaining. The trade group has demonstrated a good deal of initiative by taking a strategic approach to these threats. Whilst recognising the challenge to national bargaining the trade group has developed a sanguine line on the inevitability of greater local bargaining yet stresses the opportunities which this provides. Much of the TGWU's strength in the 1960s and 1970s was dependent on its structure which positively encouraged local shop steward bargaining; the trade group has attempted to build on this tradition while locating it within a more modern strategic organisational structure. New recruiting material has been produced, and the trade group committee was regularly briefed on the problems and opportunities confronting the group. There is a high degree of co-ordination and co-operation both with other trade groups and with other unions (see **NALGO, NUPE**).

Vehicle building and automotive

Since 1980 the membership of the vehicle building trade group, which in the post-war era was the backbone of the TGWU, has decreased by over 43 per cent, and in 1988 stood at just over 97,000. During the early 1980s the vehicle industry suffered some of the biggest casualties in the bid to rationalise productive capacity. But in the last few years the industry has benefited from the consumer boom and sales have reached record levels. The UK car market in 1988 was the third biggest in Europe and displayed an annual growth rate which was double the European average.

However, union membership has not kept pace with the increase in optimism in the vehicle industry. This has been due partly to the introduction of new technologies and a further streamlining in the "scientific" production processes, which have made the industry less labour intensive. However, new plants have opened up, mainly by the Japanese, and the TGWU could have expected to have gained new membership, for example at Nissan in Washington, Toyota in Derbyshire, and more recently at the new Honda/Rover plant in Swindon. Instead, the union lost out to rival unions (notably the AEU) when the new investors chose single-union representation often by running "beauty contests".

A case in point was when Ford announced that it was going to open a new plant in Dundee yet at the same time announced that it had already agreed to single-union representation with the AEU. The TGWU successfully protested against this decision on the grounds that it already represented the majority of Ford workers and that the proposed Dundee plant was therefore not really a greenfield site (see **TUC**). Ford withdrew the offer to build the new plant at Dundee and the TGWU recorded this as a victory. There is no doubt that the AEU violated the "Blue Book" Agreements and the TGWU was correct in its condemnation of the action of both Ford and the AEU, but the fact remains that Dundee lost not only the plant but also the multiplier effect that it would have had on its local economy. To see a public relations disaster as a victory is perverse.

But competition in the 1990s for vehicle building is likely to increase as over-capacity and the effects of the 1992 single market take effect, combined with the dampening down of consumer spending. Some existing employers are already beginning to see the new car manufacturers as having a distinct competitive advantage over the established multi-union plants. How will the TGWU respond to employer demands for single-union representation at Longbridge or Dagenham?

Power and engineering

This trade group's membership has declined by nearly 13,000 since 1986. It consists of engineering industry manual workers, British Steel, electrical cable-making, iron and steel, light metals, electricity, gas, and electricity supply. Privatisation of public sector services and demands for greater labour flexibility are the key issues concerning this trade group.

General workers

The general workers trade group has recorded a slight membership increase on the 1986 figure, which went against the trend for the union as a whole. In 1986 the membership was 124,765 while in 1988 it had increased to 126,319. The trade group organises workers in building materials, sawmilling, roadstone quarrying, packaging, paper, fibre and glass, furniture, and agency staff. The trade group has produced a detailed report to the GEC on its planned recruitment campaign. Targeted areas include contract cleaners, agency staff, sawmilling, retail distribution, and roadstone quarrying. The *Sheffield Sawmakers' Protection Society* joined this trade group when it merged with the TGWU (see "Appendix"). The group won an important single agreement with Manpower PLC, the "temp" staff agency.

Textile
The membership figure for the textile trade group of 49,275 represents a slight increase on that of 1986. The textile industry is facing severe foreign competition leading to many factory closures and redundancies. Although the group lobbied during the GATT negotiations for the need to maintain an effective regulatory system for international trade in textiles and the clothing industry, the fact remains that the UK industry itself is undergoing a long-term decline due to lack of investment in both technology and manpower, and is too fragmented to compete with cheaper foreign competition, mainly from the Far East. This is echoed in a recent NEDO report, *Making the Most of Manufacturing in the Knitting and Clothing Industries* (NEDO Books, August 1989). However, the announcement that the National Union of Tailor and Garment Workers is seeking merger talks with the GMB has come as a shock as most commentators would have seen the TGWU as the more natural partner. The reasons why the TGWU appears less "merger friendly" have to be carefully examined.

Chemical, rubber manufactuirng, and oil refining
The plastics materials industry has suffered a massive deterioration in the balance of trade within the European Community. The British chemicals industry as a whole is widely acknowledged to have made dramatic improvements in productivity with relatively low labour costs. But the government policy of letting the market decide has encouraged a rise in imports from the EC where greater protection is afforded to companies at the expense of the unprotected UK industry. The trade group has campaigned extensively and has written both to the Secretary of State for Trade and Industry and the Secretary of State for Energy, but without much success.

Food, drink, and tobacco
There have been some important single-union agreements which have affected this sector of the TGWU. Christian Salvesen (Warrington) recognised the EETPU for drivers and warehousemen; Coca Cola/Schweppes gave preference to the AEU; Christian Salvesen (Neasden) signed a single-union deal with the GMB. Major retailers such as Asda, Safeway, and Tesco have also favoured either USDAW or the GMB over the TGWU. There is perhaps little doubt that some of the companies with which the union negotiates in this trade group have attempted to weaken the importance of the TGWU. But for the trade group national secretary to explain these developments in terms of a conspiracy theory, although convenient, denies any real examination or understanding of the root causes of these deals.

Agriculture and allied workers
The agricultural and allied workers trade group has recently been integrated into mainstream TGWU activity. There has occurred a process of rationalisation of branches and administration which, while saving on union costs, has weakened local contact, a hallmark of the old *National Union of Agricultural and Allied Workers*. The trade group still issues its own journal, the *Landworker,* but it is now edited and published at Transport House. If the trade group is to maintain effective representation then close servicing is essential for a dispersed, rural membership. Administrative cost-cutting should not be treated as the measure of effective trade unionism.

The agriculture industry has the second worst safety record among British industry — only construction is worse. The fact that the trade group claims that there are no safety representatives nor ways of involving the membership in their own safety points to the need for the union itself to supply greater resources for this issue.

The advent of 1992 and the Channel Tunnel may well prove to have a deleterious effect on the UK horticulture and poultry industries as cheap food comes flooding in from the Continent (listeria and salmonella outbreaks notwithstanding).

One possible challenge for the future which might benefit the trade group is the change in land-use policy announced earlier in 1989 in response to over-production of food within the EC. British farming has become one of the most efficient in Europe through large-scale investment paid for by government subsidy. The shift in government policy along with the rise of the "organic food" culture are likely to lead to an expansion of employment opportunities for the industry.

Building, construction, and civil engineering
The TGWU has been consistent in campaigning for more public investment and stability in the construction industry. Skill shortages, particularly in the south-east, were the subject of a House of Commons Select Committee to which the TGWU gave evidence. One area of concern is the increasing use of self-employed labour — the "lump" which tends to be non-unionised. UCATT, the other major union organising workers in the building and construction industry, recently changed its rule and agreed to recruit lump workers (see **UCATT**).

In January 1988 the *National Union of Asphalt Workers* voted to merge with the TGWU and became a member of this trade section.

Administrative, clerical, technical, and supervisory staff
The ACTSS white collar section has for a long time been the poor relation amongst the trade groups of the TGWU. ACTSS organises clerical workers mainly in the manufacturing sector and suffered large membership losses during the early 1980s. But the announcement in May 1989 that the TGWU was to have talks concerning a merger with the newly-created MSF has placed the ACTSS at the centre of the union's future strategy. As ACTSS acknowledges, it is the main white collar section of the TGWU and represents one of the few areas where there is strong potential for union growth. Without a strong base in the hi-tech services sector the TGWU is unlikely to maintain its present position as Britain's largest union. The GMB recognised the strategic importance of having a strong representation in this sector and seized the initiative when in early 1989 it merged with APEX, a union with a tradition of white collar representation.

The TGWU has limited options if it wishes seriously to develop this sector of representation. The TGWU could decide to pursue a long-term policy of building membership in the service sector, but perhaps its relative inexperience coupled with the fact that other unions have a more established tradition in this area mitigates against this course of action. The alternative is to adopt what has been the very essence of TGWU growth, that is, to pursue a merger with the MSF. A TGWU merger with the MSF would create a powerful manufacturing union of around 1.9m members with representation in most sectors of the economy. The merger would also create a strong left-wing grouping within the wider labour movement.

Energy trade group: TGWU/NUM merger
The TGWU has announced plans to create a new energy trade group centred around the NUM and merger talks are being held at the time of publication. The union views this move as being an important part of its future development strategy and has also indicated that it would like to include the pit deputies union, NACODS, and the colliery managers union, BACM, in the near future; perhaps in time the UDM might also be brought in. There is a lot of sense in a new energy section embracing all the miners.

Although the NUM is financially rather embarrassed and still owes the TGWU millions of pounds, initial reaction from TGWU members to the merger plans has been favourable but reservations have been expressed about Arthur Scargill. If all merger talks, including those with the MSF, prove to be successful then by the early 1990s the TGWU would have two million members, making it by far the largest union in Britain and Europe. Undoubtedly, the move would strengthen the left in the labour movement; whether this proves to be effective, remains to be seen.

Further references

V. L Allen, *Trade Union Leadership,* Longmans Green, 1957. The most comprehensive study of the TGWU and the problems of amalgamation and integration and of the leadership of Bevin and Deakin between its formation and 1955. We are grateful to Mr Allen, for permission to draw extensively on the book for the historical section.

A. Bullock, *The Life and Times of Ernest Bevin, Vol. I: Trade Union Leader 1881-1940,* Heinemann, 1960. Hardly dispassionate but shows Bevin's vital role in the development of the TGWU.

G. Goodman, *The Awkward Warrior,* Davis-Poynter, 1980. A biography of Frank Cousins.

F. E. Gannett and B. F. Catherwood, *Industrial and Labour Relations in Great Britain,* P. King & Son 1939, pp.152-202. A chapter on the Transport and General Workers' Union, written by TGWU staff.

R. Undy, "The devolution of bargaining levels and responsibilities in the Transport and General Workers' Union 1965-75", *Industrial Relations Journal,* 9, no. 3.

D. Wilson, *Dockers,* Fontana/Collins, 1972.

J. Lovell, *Stevedores and Dockers,* Macmillan, 1969.

H. A. Clegg, *Industrial Relations in London Transport,* Blackwell, 1950.

Industrial Relations in the Coaching Industry, Advisory Conciliation and Arbitration Service Report no. 16, 1978. Interesting case studies of an industry where union organisation is not well developed.

Angela Tuckett, *The Scottish Carter,* Allen & Unwin, 1967. A history of the Scottish Commerical Motormen's Union which amalgamated with the TGWU in 1971. Alex Kitson was the General Secretary of this union.

R. Hyman, *The Workers' Union,* Clarendon Press, 1971. This union amalgamated with the TGWU in 1929, greatly augmenting its scope and membership.

M. Stephens, *Ernest Bevin: Unskilled Labourer and World Statesman,* Transport and General Workers' Union, 1981.

Phillip Bassett, "Brothers at Arms", *Marxism Today,* December 1986.

Beatrix Campbell, "Link-Up the Left", *Marxism Today,* June 1989.

John Kelly and Edmund Heery, "Full-time Officers and Trade Union Recruitment", *British Journal of Industrial Relations,* XXVII, no. 2, July 1989.

Ken Coates and Tony Topham are currently engaged in writing the official history of the TGWU which will be published in 1990 by Cambridge University Press.

Appendix

List of amalgamated unions

1922

Amalgamated Society of Watermen, Lightermen, and Bargemen

Amalgamated Carters, Lorrymen, and Motormen's Union

Amalgamated Association of Carters and Motormen

Associated Horsemen's Union

Dock, Wharf, Riverside, and General Workers' Union

Labour Protection League

National Amalgamated Labourers' Union

National Union of Docks, Wharves, and Shipping Staffs

National Union of Ship's Clerks, Grain Weighers, and Coalmeters

National Union of Vehicle Workers

National Amalgamated Coal Workers' Union

National Union of Dock, Riverside, and General Workers

National Union of British Fishermen

North of England Trimmers' and Teemers' Association

North of Scotland Horse and Motormen's Association

United Vehicle Workers

Belfast Breadservers' Association

Greenock Sugar Porters' Association

1923

Dundee Jute and Flax Stowers' Association

North Wales Craftsmen and General Workers' Union

North Wales Quarrymen's Union

Scottish Union of Dock Labourers

1924

United Order of General Labourers

1925

Association of Coastwise Masters, Mates and Engineers

1926

Weaver Watermen's Association

Irish Mental Hospital Workers' Union

National Amalgamated Union of Enginemen, Firemen, Motormen, Mechanics, and Electrical Workers (formed 1889)

1928

Cumberland Enginemen, Boilermen, and Electrical Workers' Union (formed 1890)

1929

Workers' Union (formed 1890)

1930

Belfast Operative Bakers' Union

Northern Ireland Textile Workers' Union

London Co-operative Mutuality Club Collectors' Association

1933

National Union of Co-operative Insurance Society Employees

Portadown Textile Workers' Union

Scottish Farm Servants' Union

1934

"Altogether" Builders', Labourers', and Constructional Workers' Society

Scottish Busmen's Union

1935

National Winding and General Engineers' Society

1936

Electricity Supply Staff Association (Dublin)

Halifax and District Carters' and Motormen's Association

1937

Power Loom Tenters' Trade Union of Ireland

Belfast Journeymen Butchers' Association

Scottish Seafisher's Union

1938
Humber Amalgamated Steam Trawlers'
Engineers' and Firemen's Union
Imperial War Graves Commission Staff
Association

1939
Port of London Deal Porters' Union
North of England Engineers' and
Firemen's Amalgamation

1940
National Glass Workers' Trade Protection
Association
Radcliffe and District Enginemen and
Boilermen's Provident Society
National Glass Bottle Makers' Society

1942
Liverpool Pilots' Association

1943
Manchester Ship Canal Pilots'
Association

1944
Grangemouth Pilots' Association

1945
Leith and Granton Pilots
Dundee Pilots
Methil Pilots

1946
Government Civil Employees'
Association

1947
Liverpool and District Carters' and
Motormen's Union

1951
Lurgan Hemmers', Veiners', and General
Workers' Union
United Cut Nail Makers of Great Britain
Protection Society

1961
Scottish Textile Workers' Union

1963
Gibraltar Confederation of Labour and
the Gibraltar Apprentices and Ex-
Apprentices Union, Gibraltar Labour
Trades Union

1965
North of Ireland Operative Butchers' and
Allied Workers Association

1966
United Fishermen's Union

1967
Cardiff, Penarth, and Barry Coal
Trimmers' Union

1968
Scottish Slaters, Tilers, Roofers, and
Cement Workers' Society
National Association of Operative
Plasterers (est. 1860)

1969
Amalgamated Society of Foremen
Lightermen of River Thames
Irish Union of Hairdressers and Allied
Workers
Port of Liverpool Staff Association
Process and General Workers' Union

1970
Sheffield Amalgamated Union of File
Trades

1971
Scottish Commercial Motormen's Union
(formed 1898)
Watermen, Lightermen, Tugmen, and
Bargemen's Union
Chemical Workers Union

1972
National Union of Vehicle Builders (est.
1884, previously United Kingdom
Society of Coach Makers)
Scottish Transport and General Workers'
Union (Docks)

1973
Iron, Steel, and Wood Barge Builders and
Helpers' Association

1974
Union of Bookmakers' Employees
Union of Kodak Workers

1975
File Grinders' Society

1976
Grimsby Steam and Diesel Fishing
Vessels Engineers' and Firemen's
Union

1978
National Association of Youth Hostel
Wardens
Staff Associations for Royal Automobile
Club Employees

1979
Association of Licensed Aircraft
Engineers

1982
National Union of Agricultural and
Allied Workers
National Union of Dyers, Bleachers, and
Textile Workers
National Amalgamated Stevedores and
Dockers
National Union of Co-operative
Insurance Society Employees

1984
Burnley, Nelson and Rossendale Distict
Textile Workers' Union
The Northern Textile Workers' Union
The Sheffield Sawmakers' Protection
Society

1986
United Kingdom Pilots' Association
(Marine)

1987
National Union of Asphalt Workers
National Tile, Faience, and Mosaic Fixers'
Society

TSSA
TRANSPORT SALARIED STAFFS' ASSOCIATION

Head Office: Walkden House, 10 Melton Street, Euston, London NW1 2EJ

Telephone: 01-387 2101

Principal officers
General Secretary: R. A. Rosser JP
Assistant General Secretary: V. N. Birnie
Finance and Education Secretary; W. I. Etherington
Scottish Secretary: R. S. King (based at Glasgow)
Irish Secretary: D. Casey (based at Dublin)

Divisional secretaries
BR Eastern & Anglia regions: C. A. Cullen
LM region, Manchester Ship Canal: D. C. Burn
BR Eng. Ltd., BRB HQ & Lynx Express: D. Cameron
Western region, BR Property Board, and Travellers-Fare: I. Byiers
Southern region and Sealink: W. Frew
Headquarters office: J. L. Richardson
LRT and LCBS: J. L. Juby
Organising Officer: V. A. Zaiger
Head of national negotiating dept: J. Munday
Editor, *TSSA Journal:* J. Cobley

Union journal: TSSA Journal (monthly, free to all members)

Membership (1987)
Male: 30,735
Female: 10,245
Total: 40,980

Membership trends

	1975	1979	1981	1983	1987	change 1975-87	1983-87
Men	56,595	52,573	N/A	39,980	30,735	−46%	−23%
Women	17,697	17,000	N/A	13,541	10,245	−42%	−24%
Total	74,292	69,573	64,361	53,521	40,980	−45%	−23%

General
The TSSA is one of the oldest established white collar unions in Britain. Its membership includes salaried employees of railways, docks, the travel trade, hotels, road haulage, freight forwarding, bus, canals, shipping companies, and London Regional Transport. The TSSA has membership in Eire.

History
The TSSA came into existence in May 1897 at Sheffield as the *National Association of General Railway Clerks*. The first Delegate Conference was held at Nottingham in 1898 when the name was changed to the *Railway Clerks' Association*.

The first full-time General Secretary was appointed in 1902. Railway managements were hostile, but despite persecution and victimisation the union survived, affiliating to the TUC in 1903.

In 1906 the General Secretary died in tragic circumstances. A young goods agent, A. G. Walkden, accepted the post at a substantial cut in salary and guided the RCA for the next 30 years. By 1914 the RCA had 233 branches and a total membership of 29,394. So far the railway managements had refused to recognise or receive representations from the RCA and its only contact with management had been indirectly through deputations and round-robins. In 1919 the RCA secured recognition, backed by a membership of 84,337 and the threat of strike action. Full machinery for negotiation and consultation was drawn up and agreements reached on the basic terms and conditions of employment in 1921.

During the inter-war years the RCA was affected by the amalgamation of the old railway companies, the General Strike of 1926, the election of railway workers to Parliament, the establishment of superannuation funds, and the foundation of the London Passenger Transport Board. (For greater detail on the history of railway unions see **NUR**.)

After 1945 inland transport was transferred to state ownership and TSSA membership grew in the newly-formed national undertakings. In 1950, to meet the changing face of the union and to reflect its increasing involvement outside the railways, the name was changed to the Transport Salaried Staffs' Association.

Union officials

The General Secretary is elected by postal ballot of all members and reports to the 16-strong Executive Committee. Divisional officers are allocated responsibilities on a geographical and/ or company basis.

Organisation

The supreme governing body of the union is the Annual Delegate Conference. Programmes and policies ratified by majority vote of the delegates from the branches set the framework for what the union's leaders will seek to accomplish for members. Every branch has the right to be represented at Conference and to submit motions on matters of concern to members. Every fifth year rules revisions are considered and additional motions relating to union rules are allowed.

Branches are grouped into 16 divisions and constituent branches are represented by delegates on the basis of numerical strength. The object of a divisional council is to organise its division and ensure that branches are working efficiently, for example, that organising work is being carried out and that there is no serious build-up of arrears of members' contributions. Divisional council meetings are held not less than twice and no more than three times a year.

The Executive Committee manages and administers the union's affairs in line with the rules and policies decided at Annual Conference. It consists of 16 members elected by individual secret ballot of members within each divisional council area. Executive members are elected for a three-year term of office after which they are eligible for re-election providing they have not then served for a consecutive period of six years. After that period they cannot serve again until a further three years have elapsed. There is also a President and a Treasurer — ex-officio members of the Executive Committee but with full voting rights. They are elected annually by individual secret ballot of the members.

Women

Around a quarter of TSSA members are women. There are two women on the Executive Committee.

External relations

The TSSA has a long tradition of involvement in the labour movement. It sponsors two MPs: J. Home Robertson and A. Williams. In addition, candidates for the Dail Eireann are sponsored. Apart from affiliation to the TUC, TSSA is affiliated to the Scottish TUC, the Irish Congress of Trade Unions, and the International Transport Workers' Federation. In 1988 political fund income was £65,731 and expenditure £45,766. TSSA is affiliated to the Labour Party, and General Secretary, Richard Rosser, has been a member of the Labour Party National Executive Committee. The union is also affiliated to the Fabian Society, Amnesty International, Transport 2000, the Socialist Health Association, the National Council for Civil Liberties, and the Anti-Apatheid Movement.

Recent events

The TSSA had has to address the problem of a considerable decline in membership. In 1988, for the eleventh year in succession, a fall in membership was recorded. Since 1979 membership has declined by over 40 per cent. Primarily this has resulted from job losses in its traditional strongholds of British Rail, London Regional Transport, and British Rail Engineering. However, the privatisation of transport undertakings and consequent changes in the management attitude to dealing with a white collar union, even to the extent of withdrawal of recognition, has been a factor. In 1987 the number whose membership lapsed was over 5,000. No single common factor could be identified for these lapses but complaints continued to be received from individual union members that they "never hear from the union". In 1988 there were strong indications that less than 40 per cent of new salaried staff entrants into British Rail had been recruited into memberhip by branches. The question of poor attendance at branch meetings and the shortage of members willing to put themselves forward as branch officers was raised by several branches as part of an exercise to examine the reasons for apathy towards TSSA.

A new financial package negotiated with Unity Financial Services, offering the membership personal bank accounts, personal loans, insurance facilities, and mortgage assistance on favourable terms was launched in October 1988. Also included in the package to all members was a discounted holiday offer.

Relations with other unions, such as the NUR, have sometimes been delicate. As a result of a TUC disputes committee award in 1987 the NUR agreed to release a number of clerical staff members who were seeking transfer to the TSSA. The TSSA has a spheres of influence agreement with the TGWU, and under its terms some clerical staff in garages and garage-based assistant operating managers in London Buses wanted to transfer to TSSA in 1988. Following local and national meetings between the unions some transfers were agreed.

In 1988 the TSSA was forced to accept the end of collective pay bargaining for middle managers in British Rail, after the members concerned had voted not to oppose individual contracts based on performance-related pay. The TSSA tried to rally members' support to oppose the new pay system when British Rail attempted to implement the individual contracts without further negotiation. However, in a ballot of 6,500 middle managers, only 38 per cent opposed the scheme. Actually, a majority of the members affected had already signed the new contracts without waiting for the ballot result.

The TSSA was involved in industrial action in 1989 after negotiations about a national pay increase for British Rail employees were deadlocked (see **NUR**). The TSSA joined the other rail unions in pointing out that British Rail had tried to ignore the union referral of the pay dispute to the Railway Staff National Tribunal by its tactic of imposing a "final" pay offer of 7 per cent — significantly below the prevailing rate of inflation — after having announced record profits of £304 million.

Further references

Christine Edwards and Edmund Heery, "Recession in the Public Sector: Industrial Relations in Freightliner 1981-1985", *British Journal of Industrial Relations*, XXVII, no. 1, March 1989.

Patrick Dawson, "Intelligent knowledge-based systems (IKBS): organisational implications", *New Technology, Work and Employment*, 3, no. 1, Spring 1988.

UCATT
UNION OF CONSTRUCTION, ALLIED TRADES, AND TECHNICIANS

TUC affiliated

Head Office: UCATT House, 177 Abbeville Road, Clapham, London SW4 9RL

Telephone: 01-622 2442/2362

Fax: 01-720 4081

Principal national officers
General Secretary: A. Williams
Assistant General Secretary: J. Hardman
National Officer: B. Birdsell
National Officer: A. Black
National Officer: L. Eaton
National Officer: T. Graves
National Officer: A. Verdeilles

Executive Council
George Brumwell (Chairman), Jack Henry, Charles Kelly, Jack Rogers, Brian Veal

UCATT regional offices and officials

Scotland
Vacancy, 6 Fitzroy Place, Glasgow G3 7RL
Telephone: 041-221 4893

Yorkshire
P. Corby, Winwaed House, 64/66 Cross Gate Road, Leeds 15
Telephone: 0532-640211

Midlands
L. Irwin, Gough Street, off Suffolk Street, Birmingham B1 1HN
Telephone: 021-643 4151

North
E. J. Ablett (acting), 8 Red Rose Terrace, Chester-le-Street, Co. Durham DH3 3LN
Telephone: 0385-881746

North-West
A. Lowe, 137 Dickenson Road, Rusholme, Manchester M14 5HZ
Telephone: 061-224 3391

Eastern
D. Hardy, 119 Newmarket Road, Cambridge CB5 8HA
Telephone: 0223-67691

London
L. Eaton, 94 London Road, Crayford, Kent DA1 4BT
Telephone: 0322-57627

South
A. Woods, 5 Hemstead Road, Southampton, Hampshire
Telephone: 0703-227634

South-West
R. E. Heal, 217 St Johns Lane, Bedminster, Bristol BS3 5AS
Telephone: 0272-667649

South Wales
G. Rowden, 199 Newport Road, Cardiff, Glamorgan
Telephone: 0222-31841

Northern Ireland
T. Smith, 79/81 May Street, Belfast BT1 3JL
Telephone: 0232-22366

Republic of Ireland
R. P. Rice, 56 Parnell Square West, Dublin
Telephone: 0001-744626

Union journal: Viewpoint (monthly). Recently the journal has been improved and now includes full colour printing. The shop stewards' *Bulletin* remains a quarterly publication but special editions for Scotland and the Republic of Ireland have been added. The union is currently preparing a *Safe Sites* campaign pack in response to the recent increase in accidents in the building industry. Literature for the self-employed, policy and recruitment, training, equality, and women is also being prepared.

Membership

Current membership (1987)
Male: 253,087
Female: 2,796
Total: 255,883

Membership trends

	1975	1979	1981	1983	1987	change 1975-87	1983-87
Men	272,466	346,015	273,519	258,237	253,087	−7%	−2%
Women	2,320	1,762	1,732	1,763	2,796	21%	59%
Total	274,786	347,777	275,251	260,000	255,883	−7%	−2%

General
UCATT is now the eighth largest union within the TUC and has members in shipbuilding and repair, steel, engineering, furniture making, local authorities, and the National Health Service. The main concentration of UCATT membership, however, is in the private sector of the building industry — approximately 70 per cent of its membership. Within the building industry UCATT seeks to organise all types of workers, i.e.

woodworkers, bricklayers, painters, plasterers, labourers, etc. Membership of the union increased from 262,600 in 1971 to a peak of 347,777 in 1980, thereafter it declined rapidly as the recession hit the construction industry, and in 1985 reached its lowest-ever figure of 248,963. Since then, however, the construction industry has picked up and after some intensive recruitment campaigns UCATT has managed to record a membership growth to its present level of 265,894. Interestingly enough the growth in women membership has, in percentage terms, been rather spectacular, recording a rise of 68 per cent in the period 1983-1987.

The union now actively recruits self-employed operatives which represents a dramatic turn-around in union policy. The number of self-employed operatives has risen substantially in the last five years and now amounts to over half a million potential recruits, a sizeable figure which UCATT cannot afford to ignore (see "Policy").

In line with other unions UCATT is conscious of the services it provides to its membership, and in November 1986 launched its Money Savers scheme to promote and co-ordinate its services. The scheme is in two parts: Financial Services — which cover aspects such as life assurance, motor and other insurance, mortgages and unit trusts; and Discount Services — where UCATT uses its purchasing power to negotiate discounts which it passes on to its membership. These include holidays, motor cars, an accountancy service, and permanent health insurance.

History

The first recorded attempts to combine, following the collapse of the medieval guild system, resulted in 1800 in the *Friendly Society of Carpenters and Joiners*, which met at the Running Horse in London. Few records remain of unionism throughout the period of the Combination Acts, but it is certainly true that this period heralded the birth of the unions of bricklayers and masons.

Following the repeal of the Combination Acts in 1824 there occurred a sudden expansion of union activity which, except in the case of the carpenters' union, was thwarted by the ensuing depression of 1825. The *Operative Stonemasons' Society* was created in 1831 and became one of the strongest unions in the country.

The *Operative Stonemasons' Society*, along with Robert Owen, supplied the inspiration for the *Great Operative Builders' Union*, the first attempt at a general union for all building trade workers. This federal body, despite its large size (40,000 members), did not survive long. At its birth in 1832 hopes were high, but by 1834 the "Document" had effectively killed off the union, along with its contemporary, the GNCTU. The *Operative Stonemasons' Society* managed to continue, however, and by 1846 had won considerable victories against the "Document".

Until 1860 only the masons managed to retain an effective organisation. After the "Great Lock-out" of 1859 and 1860 trade unionism flourished once more, with further significant victories over the "Document". The *Amalgamated Society of Carpenters and Joiners* was founded with Robert Applegarth becoming its secretary in 1862; and the *Operative Bricklayers' Society*, under the direction of Edwin Coulson the London painter, formed the *Amalgamated Association of Operative Painters*.

The Trade Union Act of 1871 served to provide a more congenial climate for trade unionism, and the building unions slowly prospered and increased in membership. After the boom of the 1890s, the old unionism of the building trades' workers came under severe pressure, only punctuated by the First World War. Between the wars the building trades federated amongst themselves. The masons joined the builders to become the *Amalgamated Union of Building Trade Workers*, and the two existing unions of carpenters and joiners became the *Amalgamated Society of Woodworkers*. The painters and decorators also reforged old alliances at this time.

Since 1945 the benefits of rationalisation and co-operation have become increasingly evident within the building trades, although the divisions between craft and non-craft still surface occasionally. The eventual formation of UCATT came about largely because in the 1950s and 1960s all three major unions — woodworkers, painters, and bricklayers — had been finding it difficult to stem a decline in membership. The number of workers unionised in building and civil engineering declined as a proportion of the labour force from 45 per cent in 1948 to around 30 per cent in the late 1960s. Financial difficulties, coupled with the growing practice of labour-only sub-contracting, fostered an alliance between the *Amalgamated Society of Woodworkers*, craftsworkers, and the painters and bricklayers, albeit as junior partners under AWS rules.

Traditionally, the AWS had been an exclusive craft union with an elitist style of leadership. As technological change reduced the number of craft woodworkers and brought into the AWS a growing number of less skilled members, financial and constitutional changes were brought in by the leadership which served further to enhance the remoteness of the union from its members. The leadership of the newly-created UCATT set about organising the union into 12 regions, administered by 12 regional secretaries appointed by the Executive Council. The Executive Council also exercised control over the number of organisers in each region. These regional organisers were elected by the membership in each region for a period of five years and, if they were subsequently re-elected, they were confirmed in office until retirement. The district management committees, which met monthly, were replaced by regional councils of elected lay members which met every six months. The Annual Delegate Conference was replaced by biennial conferences at national level and alternating biennial conferences at regional level.

These measures served to strengthen the control of the union by the Executive Council at the expense of the activists. George Smith, who was elected General Secretary of the AWS in 1959, proceeded with the programme of rationalisation and centralised administration was carried out at the same time. He was instrumental in using the AWS as a centre-piece for mergers and forging a new union with a regional structure and centralised administration. On January 1, 1970 the *Amalgamated Society of Painters and Decorators* (ASPD) and the *Association of Building Technicians* (ABT) transferred their engagements to the AWS, and in December of that year the *Amalgamated Union of Building Trade Workers* (AUBTW) also agreed to transfer its engagements. UCATT therefore came into existence on July 1, 1971 with 262,600 members.

Whilst rationalisation and centralised administration gave UCATT financial viability they also emphasised the remoteness of Head Office from union members, the seeming irrelevance of national negotiations, and a feeling amongst many members that the union was becoming undemocratic and unresponsive to the membership. The Building Workers' Charter Group was set up in April 1970 as a means of democratising the union, largely as a response to the reforms by activists.

The Building Workers' Charter Group organised *ad hoc* joint branch committees in large towns, often with the assistance of regional organisers. At the 1974 National Delegate Conference the leadership were defeated on their policy on wages, the Shrewsbury pickets, and structure. The pressure brought to bear on national negotiations was so intense in 1972 that the wages demands of the Charter Group culminated in the longest national strike since 1924, which depended on its success on flying pickets and *ad hoc* site action committees. The subsequent rules revision in 1975 resulted in a number of reforms which gave the site activists some satisfaction — such as the election of officials at all levels; larger regional councils with more frequent meetings, a form of district organisation within regions based on shop stewards and branches, and the concession that regional committees could declare strikes official, subject to Executive Council approval.

Further organisational changes were made at the union's sexennial meeting of the rules revision committee, which produced a new rule book in September 1982 which has sought to sever the AWS links (see "Organisation").

Sir George Smith's tragic death in late 1978 led to the election of Les Wood, the Assistant General Secretary, as the new General Secretary of UCATT who held the post until his retirement in November 1985. Albert Williams, who was previously chairman of the Executive Committee, is now the elected General Secretary of UCATT.

Union officials

Despite their relatively large number (12 regional officers in 1988) UCATT officials have to spend a great deal of time servicing the existing membership rather than recruiting new members. This dependence of the membership on the services of officials is reinforced by the hostility of many building employers to trade unionists. The building industry is characterised by a large number of very small employers, many of whom operate blacklists of militant trade unionists, and allegations by site stewards that the Economic League supplies employers with photographs of "militants" are common. The job of the officials is made no easier because not only do they face the active hostility to trade unionism by employers, but they also have to battle against individualistic attitudes and the long traditions of self-employment amongst workers in the building industry. The older ex-AWS officers are declining in numbers and UCATT increasingly recruits from ex-activists. All regional officers have to stand for re-election, by voting in branches, every five years (see "Organisation").

Coverage

UCATT holds the secretaryship of the union sides in the following bargaining machinery: the National Joint Council for the Building Industry; the National Joint Council for the Exhibition Industry; the Works Services Trades Joint Council for the Department of the Environment and Transport; Scottish Decorators' Federation; the Department of Trade and Industry Joint Industrial Council; the National Joint Council for the Monumental Masonry Industry; the Joint Council for the Building and Civil Engineering Industry (Northern Ireland); and the Joint Negotiating Committee for Local Authorities' Services (Building and Civil Engineering). UCATT is also a party to a large number of agreements in the building industry, furniture making, and the timber container industry.

UCATT has major representation rights on the National Joint Council for the Building Industry (NJCBI) as well as on the Civil Engineering Construction Conciliation Board (CECCB). This NJC covers the three large employers' associations — the Building Employers' Confederation (BEC), the National Federation of Roofing Contractors (NFRC), and the Federation of Civil Engineering Contractors (FCEC). In addition, UCATT negotiates with the 20,000 medium and smaller-sized building firms who are members of the Federation of Master Builders (FMB) on the Building and Allied Trades Joint Industrial Council (BATJIC).

Organisation

The present organisation of UCATT is based on the decisions of the 32-strong rules revision committee which met in 1982. These rules change marked the final stage in a gradual process which saw the union move away from its inherited AWS structure based on separate trades of woodworking, bricklaying, and plastering and decorating.

The main effects of the rules revision were to divide the union into five divisions, which are based on 12 geographical regions, and to eliminate representation by trade on all bodies of the union. The five divisions and their respective regions are:

Division One: Northern and Scottish regions;

Division Two: North-West and South Wales regions;

Division Three: Yorkshire and Midlands regions;

Division Four: London, Northern Ireland, and the Republic of Ireland regions;

Division Five: South-West, Southern, and Eastern regions.

The Executive Council now comprises five members who are each elected from a division, to serve for a five-year period, by a full postal ballot. The switch to regional representation on the Executive was also extended to the General Council of the union. The General Council was extended from 11 to 12 members — one for each region. The regional council committees have been abolished and the influence and size of regional councils, which used to comprise up to 25 members, have been diminished under the new UCATT rules. Instead, regional councils are now made up of between five and nine members each, and UCATT has introduced regional industrial advisory committees which bring together lay members covered by particular agreements for consultation and discussion. The special 1985 rules revision committee agreed to move from voting in branches to individual secret postal ballots.

With the old trade divisions eliminated UCATT now has a highly centralised structure which is able to give quicker, more effective, and more direct consultation with the membership. It can also speed up decision-making during pay negotiations or industrial action. UCATT has a separate disciplinary procedure for members and officials, and equality of opportunity for both men and women is formally written into the rule book.

UCATT's policy-making body is the Biennial National Conference, with the union's policy between conferences being administered by the Executive Council and the General Secretary. The (regionalised) General Council is elected by a postal ballot and carries out a general overseeing role over the affairs of the union, including hearing of appeals, examining the accounts of the Executive Council, and acting as trustee. The General Council also has the power to relieve the Executive Council of its duties in extreme circumstances, subject to the ratification of the membership.

UCATT's 12 regions are administered from a regional office and staffed by officials, elected by branch votes. Each region has a regional council of between five and nine members which is elected by the membership in that area on a three-year basis. Regional secretaries and other full-time officials are elected to serve for a five-year period. Each region must set up a shop stewards organisation to facilitate communication in the maintenance of union activity throughout the region, and which is under the jurisdiction of the regional council. UCATT's rules also provide for the establishment of strike committees in the event of an industrial dispute in a particular locality.

Work-place activity
Work-place organisation in building is particularly difficult. As each stage in construction is complete the worker knows that he has to seek work elsewhere. The image of the tough, independent, individualistic worker is largely correct, and in such an environment any kind of work-place organisation is difficult to achieve. Younger workers, particularly, change jobs frequently; the jobs done by UCATT members are not in large work units; and the union appears remote from workers. In such circumstances where a site does become fully organised, particularly on the long-life sites, the stewards tend to be very politically aware as they tend to be the people who are prepared to put their heads on the chopping block in an uncertain industry. Workers who have both an ideology of struggle and organising skills are inevitably in the forefront of site organisation and provide the

leftist opposition to what they see as domination of the site activists by the union leadership. The reality of work-place organisation difficulties was summarised by one worker who said "When the job finishes you have to start all over again to organise. I haven't been on a site yet where you didn't have to battle". The leftism of the active building worker arises from insecurity and constant battles to organise.

The construction of the Channel Tunnel illustrates well the different approaches to work-place activity. There are two separate locations involved: the Isle of Grain, set on the Thames estuary; and Shakespeare Cliff, Dover. The Isle of Grain has more in common with a traditional factory assembly line than a building site. Here 400 operatives are employed in temporary metal clad hangars either producing segments for the tunnel or loading the finished product on to trucks. Each factory has six lines, each manned by "stations" of 15 men, along which the segments move through four stages of production; one segment being completed every 10 minutes. High turn-over (over 70 per cent), numerous stoppages, and aggressive confrontation, characterise industrial relations.

The Shakespeare site is recognisable as a construction site and employs 2,000 workers. In it there is a fully equipped leisure complex and workers go through an induction course at a nearby training centre where management and UCATT full-time officials give courses on safety and try to instill an *esprit de corps*. As a result, labour turn-over is less than 1 per cent, absenteeism is almost a non-issue, and the emphasis of UCATT shop stewards is towards amiable local negotiations.

Women

The construction industry is traditionally a male preserve. Whilst men dominate the union, both in terms of numbers and union politics, the number of women members is growing at a very strong rate. In the 12-year period 1975-1987, women membership increased by 27 per cent compared to a 3 per cent decline in male membership over the same period. But in the last five years the figures are even more impressive; women membership increased by 68 per cent compared to the 2 per cent rise recorded for male membership figures.

Growth figures such as these have not gone unnoticed at UCATT Head Office and a number of initiatives have been developed to take advantage of this trend. At national level the union created in 1983 a special Employment of Women Working Party, and since then three regional advisory committees have been established while other regions are encouraged to do likewise.

The 1988 sexennial rule revision decided that from 1989 women membership will be be represented at both the annual TUC and Labour Party Conferences for the first time in the union's history.

A very interesting development took place in March 1988, when the EC issued a code of practice to help victims of work-place sexual harassment and abuse. The code of practice states that UCATT representatives have a duty at all times to represent the victim of sexual harassment recognising that the perpetrator is often also a UCATT member. The code of practice goes on to add that representatives have a duty to "ensure that the harassor and not the victim is transferred; make the victim aware of their right to take the case to an industrial tribunal under the Sex Discrimination Act; and attempt to resolve the matter between the parties at the lowest stage".

At the beginning of 1989 UCATT launched a drive to boost equal opportunities for women. The union's EC has set up a working party to examine ways in which both the union as well as the construction industry can be made more attractive to women. The EC has also asked all branches to make equal opportunities a regular item for discussion at their meetings.

External relations

UCATT is affiliated to the Labour Party and sponsors one MP, Eric Heffer (Liverpool Walton), but for a union with over a quarter of a million members it really should have more. The UCATT 1988 Biennial Conference did not support Eric Heffer when he stood for Deputy Leadership of the Labour Party, but instead pledged its support to Neil Kinnock and Roy Hattersley.

In September 1985 UCATT launched a strong campaign, under the slogan "Your Union Your Voice — Let's Keep It That Way!", to retain its political fund, and in March 1986 a full postal ballot was conducted. The result of the ballot was 56,733 for its retention and only 5,295 against, a 95 per cent majority.

The General Secretary of UCATT, Albert Williams, is currently President of the European Federation of Building and Woodworkers. He was elected unanimously. The Federation brings together unions in all 12 EEC countries which together cover over two-and-a-half million workers.

Policy

The biggest single policy change since the union was created in 1971 was the decision taken by the 1988 Biennial Conference, by a 62 to 49 majority, to end the union's long-standing opposition to self-employed or "lump" labour. Prior to this historic decision the union had been carrying out a series of consultation exercises. In February 1987 UCATT launched its *Employment in the Construction Industry — A UCATT Charter for Change*, a policy document on the abuse of self-employment in the construction industry. The issues covered were:

(1) the impact of Health and Safety and Training;
(2) the advantages of self-employment to construction workers;
(3) details of agreements with employers;
(4) the problem of "cowboy" contractors;
(5) the loss of jobs in the construction industry, the growth of self-employment, the abuse of the 714 certificate, and the 30 per cent systems.

This radical shift in policy is the union's response to a declining membership in the early part of the 1980s, and a rapid growth in self-employment during the expansion of the building industry in recent years. Traditionally, public sector building, or direct works departments of local authorities, has been the main recruiting ground for the union. With the decline of public sector building together with the ending of contract compliance and tendering of services under the Local Government Act, the union had to respond if it was to survive as a viable independent trade union into the 1990s. Despite considerable opposition from the left UCATT felt it had no alternative but to end its hostility towards the self-employed and begin recruiting them. Up until 1982 250,000 714 self-employed certificates had been issued by the Inland Revenue, but between 1982 and 1987 400,000 714s were issued making a total of over 600,000 self-employed workers engaged in the construction industry; in areas such as the south-east virtually all construction workers were self-employed.

The vast majority of these workers are not represented by any union and UCATT believes that it is possible to recruit 100,000 of them in the next two years. Rule 26 of the national agreement states that employers will "take all appropriate steps in an endeavour to ensure that all building trades operatives are in the direct employment of the company or its sub-contractors and, in either case, are employed at the rates of wages and under conditions laid down by the Council". Negotiations are currently taking place with the Building Employers' Confederation to amend this clause so as to include self-employed workers in the national agreements, but talks are still at a very early stage.

The Money Savers scheme, which UCATT launched in November 1986 to promote and co-ordinate its services to the membership, was augmented in March 1989 when a new accountancy service, aimed at attracting the self-employed, was introduced.

UCATT still supports public building, and in 1987 a motion to the TUC called on Congress to support DLOs (local authority direct labour organisations), oppose the Local Government Bill which places restrictions on DLOs, and to continue to support public investment in housing and construction in response to community needs. UCATT put forward the idea of the construction industry as a "divided industry — private, prestige projects booming but savage cut-backs in public sector housing and construction". A further motion called on Congress to initiate a campaign in opposition to the Local Authority Bill, and UCATT launched its campaign pamphlet "Strictly Private".

UCATT also gave major support to the Action for Homes and Jobs Petition which was an attempt to draw attention to the continuing areas of housing need and highlight the scope for job-creation and training if investment is put into tackling the problems of housing and inner-city decay. The petition was launched in July 1987 and included tenants' groups, trade unions, local authorities, and MPs.

The 1988 National Delegate Conference ignored the advice of its Executive Council and backed a call for the next Labour government to take the construction industry into public ownership. Conference also strongly argued against any mergers with other unions and for preserving the identity of UCATT. The EETPU and the AEU were both considered for possible merger talks for the formation of a single, large union for skilled workers. This proposal still has a good deal of credibility and is worthy of future consideration, especially as union density is being increasingly concentrated into a smaller number of large trade unions.

During the 1988 TUC, UCATT did not support the TUC boycott of the government's Employment Training Scheme (ETS). UCATT has been a stout defender of the Construction Industry Training Board (CITB) scheme since it meets all the criteria and safeguards laid down by Congress to ensure quality of training. Indeed, the two leading unions which led the campaign to pull out of ETS, the TGWU and NALGO, both conceded that they would not object to UCATT remaining involved in the CITB scheme.

UCATT support for ETS was reaffirmed during the 1988 Labour Party Conference where it put forward a motion, which was eventually defeated, calling on the Labour Party to criticise but not boycott the scheme. The nub of the UCATT argument is that "ETS is a political initiative taken by the government to wrong-foot the TUC and the Labour Party. By boycotting ETS, the government can blame and portray (them) as being the people who are unconstructive and negative in stopping the unemployed from getting training, which would then leave the unemployed unrepresented, without a voice, and at the mercy of the private sector schemes". UCATT has negotiated, through the CITB, a scheme for 6,000 ETS trainees which meets all TUC safeguards.

In January 1987 UCATT pioneered an interesting agreement binding on all contractors involved in the building of the International Conference Centre in Birmingham. Amongst other things it demands that 30 per cent of labour be drawn from deprived areas of Birmingham, and that 10 per cent of the total intake be apprentices. In 1989 a similar agreement was negotiated in the London Docklands site of Canary Wharf, but with the addition of an equal opportunities clause and a 39-hour week.

Drink has always played a part in the portrayal of the macho image in the building industry, but recently it has been recognised by UCATT as a growing problem, and the union has taken a progressive stance by pressing employers to introduce alcohol policies to help employees with drink-related problems which affect their work.

Recent events

UCATT must be very concerned by the withdrawal of the Electrical Contractors' Association from the CITB, effectively reducing the number of apprentices in training by almost a quarter. UCATT plays a significant role on the CITB, the largest training organisation in the country, and at the 1988 TUC was one of the few unions to support the government's Employment Training initiative.

Further references

S. Higginbottom, *Our Society's History*, AWS, 1939.

T. J. Connelly, *The Woodworkers, 1860-1960*, AWS, 1960.

W. S. Hilton, *Foes to Tyranny: A History of the Amalgamated Union of Building Trade Workers*, AUBTW, 1963.

W. S. Hilton, *Industrial Relations in Construction*, Pergamon Press, 1968.

J. England, "How UCATT revised its rules: an anatomy of organisational change", *British Journal of Industrial Relations*, 1979.

T. Austin, "The 'lump' in the construction industry", Theo Nichols (ed.), *Capital and Labour*, Fontana, 1980.

L. Wood, *A Union to Build: The Story of UCATT*, Lawrence & Wishart, 1979.

R. Price, *Masters, Unions, and Men: Work Control in Building and the Rise of Labour 1830-1914*, Cambridge University Press, 1980.

J. D'Arcy, *Contract Journal*, June 1982.

Stephen Frenkel and Graeme Martin, "Managing labour on a large construction site", *Industrial Relations Journal*, 17, no. 2, 1986.

UCW
UNION OF COMMUNICATION WORKERS

TUC affiliated

Head Office: House Crescent Lane, Clapham, London SW4 9RN

Telephone: 01-622 9977 [150 The Broadway Wimbledon SW19 1RX 0181 971 7200 (2.98)]

Telex: 913585

Fax: 01-720 6853

Principal national officers
General Secretary: Allan Tuffin
Deputy General Secretary: Tony Clarke
Assistant Secretary (Counter and Clerical Services): E. W. Dudley
Assistant Secretary (Telecoms): P. Dwyer

Assistant Secretary (Legal & Medical): P. Grace
Assistant Secretary (Posts): A. A. Johnson
Assistant Secretary (Posts): H. J. Jones
Assistant Secretary (Telecoms): M. Morritt
Assistant Secretary (Telecoms): J. E. Stone
Organising Secretary: D. G. Hodgson
General Treasurer: Vacant
Editor: J. Jacques

Union journal: The Post (normally, 12 issues a year, with a circulation of 71,000). The UCW also produces a *Branch Officials Bulletin* (BOB) and a *Special Branch Circular* (SBC) to inform branches regularly of union affairs. In addition the UCW produces a series of information handbooks on a variety of subjects for its members.

The latest external publications are: (1) the Submission to the House of Commons Select Committee on Trade and Industry's Report on Postal Business Reorganisation, July 1986; and (2) the Submission to the House of Commons Select Committee on Trade and Industry's Report on The Post Office, December 1987.

Membership

Current membership (1987)
Male: 149,334
Female: 48,424
Total: 197,758

Membership trends

	1975	1979	1981	1983	1987	change 1975-87	1983-87
Men	143,807	152,589	N/A	147,320	149,334	4%	1%
Women	41,193	50,863	N/A	49,106	48,424	18%	−1%
Total	185,000	203,452	202,160	196,426	197,758	7%	1%

General

The UCW is the largest union organising all hourly-paid grades of workers in the Post Office. The UCW also has some members in British Telecom and the Girobank. In the Post Office employment is set to rise due to the expansion of services and volume of work; however, the union's membership in BT looks likely to decline as the introduction of more sophisticated technology makes existing jobs obsolete.

The UCW, in common with most other large unions, has introduced a members' induction package which includes such items as discounts for mortgages, insurance schemes, and legal advice.

After a series of major industrial disputes (see "Recent events") the UCW is examining ways of restructuring union representation. Too often local issues were being referred upwards to national level where they escalated, when in fact they could have been dealt with at the local level. The UCW inherited its structure from the old UPW which developed in response to the demands of the Civil Service. As the Post Office becomes more sensitive to market considerations, so the union must also adapt to make itself more effective in representing its members' grievances and aspirations in the new working environment. In the Post Office the shift away from national bargaining to regional and local negotiations, and the creation of three separate operating units —

Counter Services, Post, and Parcels — will place different demands on the union.

The UCW is affiliated to the TUC and the Labour Party. Its General Secretary is a member of the TUC General Council and its Deputy General Secretary is a member of the Labour Party's National Executive Committee.

History

The Union of Communication Workers was formerly known as the *Union of Post Office Workers,* and this union was formed in 1921 as a result of successive mergers of the following organisations:

	Year of Origin
Fawcett Association	1890
Postal and Telegraph Clerks' Association	1913
Postmen's Federation	1891
Adult Messengers' Association	
Bagmen's Association Central	
London's Postmen's Association	1906
London Postal Porters' Association	1902
Tracers' Association	1892
Tube Staff Association	1903

Many of the traditions and the style of the UCW have come from the organisations which operated with the minimum of full-time officials and took major decisions at conferences or even, as in the case of the *Fawcett Association,* at mass meetings of members. As a result of having the longest experience of working in the public sector Post Office trade union leaders have traditionally thought in terms of greater democracy in state-owned industries. The people who set up the UPW amalgamation in 1920 were guild socialists who held a broad conception of trade unionism. For example, support for a form of joint control in the Post Office has a long history within the union. Even before the amalgamation in 1920, the *Postal and Telegraph Clerks' Association* had committed itself to a policy of "joint control" of the Post Office between the authorities and the employees, and in 1919 the delegates who attended the amalgamation conference made the demand for joint control one of its objectives. This objective has survived to the present day, in that Rule 2 of the UCW states "to pursue joint consultation with management in order to secure the greatest possible measure of effective participation by the union in all decisions affecting the working lives of its members".

Post Office trade unions were originally recognised by employers in 1906, and their main method of improving their conditions was to put pressure on MPs. It was only during the First World War, when the arbitration court was set up and the Whitley council machinery designed, that a regular method of bargaining was developed.

The General Strike of 1926 resulted in the passing of the Trade Disputes Act 1927, which forced the UPW to disaffiliate from both the TUC and the Labour Party. In 1931 a deputation from union headquarters met the then Postmaster-General, Clement Attlee. As a result the rights of the union's branch secretaries were recognised and defined.

Until very recent times the UPW was part of a minority in the labour movement which opposed the setting-up of public corporations. The 1946 UPW Annual Conference chair criticised the "child-like faith that public utility boards will provide responsible administration". The UPW rejoined the TUC and reaffiliated to the Labour Party in 1946, following the repeal of the 1927 Trade Disputes Act.

At the Annual Conference in 1969 there was a full-scale debate about workers' control in the Post Office, a debate occasioned by the plan, subsequently implemented, to turn the Post Office into a public corporation. The real issue debated was whether or not the union should demand 50 per cent representation on the board immediately or refuse to participate until assured a majority of seats. The second alternative was carried. Post Office workers lost their status as Civil Servants and the UPW withdrew from the national Whitley council. The unions in the Post Office saw this as an opportunity to rationalise the structure of trade unionism in the Post Office, and formed the Council of Post Office Unions. This organisation was wound up in December 1981.

The union is not known for its militancy but in its recent history it has been involved in a number of disputes. In 1962 there was a month-long work-to-rule; in July 1964 there was a one-day strike of postal workers followed by an overtime ban; and in 1969 there was a ten-day strike by overseas telegraph operators. But it was the strike of 1971 which is the most notable.

In 1971 the UPW called a strike of all grades in support of a pay claim. At the end of seven weeks the union recommended a return to work, not having agreed any pay rise, while a Court Of Inquiry was sitting to look into the dispute. The final settlement, based on the Court of Inquiry Report, was much closer to the employers offer than to the union demand. The whole episode has been regarded as a heavy defeat both within and outside the union. Thousands of members had suffered hardship and the union was heavily in debt, apparently for nothing, since the agreed pay rises might easily have been obtained without a strike.

During 1976-7 when the UPW was involved in industrial action over apartheid in South Africa as well as in support of the workers' demand for union recognition at Grunwick, a series of injunctions were awarded which were designed to stop the planned action. As a result of the legal battles the existing Post Office legislation was interpreted in such a way as to cast doubt on the legality of the UPW taking industrial action. Prior to this the union view was that it could take strike action and had done so, notably in 1971.

On January 1, 1978 an experiment in industrial democracy was launched within the Post Office. Under the experiment the Post Office Board at national level consisted of 19 members, of which seven were trade union nominees (two of whom were UPW nominees). The experiment also provided for similar arrangements at regional and area level. The Labour government grandly claimed that this two-year experiment represented the beginning of "socialisation of public ownership". Sir Keith Joseph killed the experiment by refusing — in the face of union enthusiasm — to reappoint the union nominees to the Board in December 1979. Joseph made this decision within two days of receiving an interim, but lengthy, Warwick University report which had been commissioned by the Post Office. The Warwick team of Eric Batstone, Anthony Ferner, and Michael Terry asserted that:

> It is clear that issues with industrial relations, particularly negotiating, implications are now often handled outside the main Board. Where major industrial relations questions are discussed at the Board the account is clearly incomplete. We have come across instances where union nominees appear to be completely unaware that major strategic issues are being dealt with outside the Board. Key Board members appear to play an active role behind the scenes on many issues and rarely are union nominees included in this.

This experience of boardroom manoeuvres provided the UCW with a salutary lesson for its naive belief that worker participations at Board level would lead to genuine participation in the formulation of policy in the Post Office (see "Recent events").

In 1981, following the passing of the Telecommunications Act, which led to the break-up of the Post Office into two businesses (Posts and Telecommunications), the UPW changed its name to the Union of Communication Workers, by which it is presently known.

Coverage
The union represents a number of occupational categories in the Post Office businesses and British Telecom. The Post Office businesses include Letter, Parcels, and Counters. In addition there are about 200 members in Girobank PLC. There are also members represented at the National Television Licence Records Office (NTVLRO) in Bristol. Grades represented in the Post Office, Girobank, and NTVLRO are: postal cadet; postman/woman; postman/woman higher grade; cleaner; catering; doorkeeper; lift operator; postal assistant; and postal officer. Grades represented in British Telecom are: telephonist; operator; senior operator; telegraphist; radio officer; general assistant; cleaner; and catering grades.

All negotiations regarding pay and conditions of service are negotiated nationally with the individual Post Office businesses, British Telecom and its subsidiaries, and Girobank PLC. The negotiations range from pay rates and annual leave entitlement to an agreement on facilities for local officials to perform their union duties.

Organisation
The striking feature of the UCW is its high degree of centralisation. The sovereign authority of the union is the Annual Conference, held for six days each May, at which the union's policy is decided. Branches are represented by about 1,550 delegates, the number of delegates per branch being determined according to size of membership.

There are 980 branches of the union in Post Office and BT areas. These may be organised as single-grade branches, multi-grade (e.g. indoor grades) branches, or amalgamated branches, i.e. where all grades in an area are represented by the same branch. The decision as to the type of branch organisation is a local one. The branch deal with purely local matters, conducting negotiations through local managers.

Branches are graded geographically into 25 district councils, the officers of which — with one exception — act in an organising and advisory role, that is, they have no direct representative capacity. The exception is the London district council, whose officers have the right of direct representation to the directors of the London postal and telecommunications regions.

Branch officials are elected annually by the branch membership. Their work is voluntary and they remain PO and BT employees. Similarly, district council officers are elected by the branches in the district councils. They also remain PO and BT employees.

The Executive Council manages the affairs of the union between Annual Conferences. It consists of 35 members, and meets once a month on the last Thursday of each month for a whole day. Twenty-two members of the Executive Council are elected annually by Conference and are eligible for re-election each year. They remain PO and BT employees during their terms of office. The remaining 13 members of the EC are elected by the membership.

As a result of the Post Office split into two separate businesses of posts and telecommunications (which has since been privatised and turned into a separate private company), the UCW agreed at a special conference in 1981 to set up two autonomous groups: posts and telecoms. The two groups are headed by autonomous management committees: PGMC (the Postal Group Management Committee) and TGMC (the Telecommunications Group Management Committee). They consist of 15 PO and seven BT members and have responsibility for pay and conditions of service issues. The PGMC further divides into a Counter Section, a Clerical Section Committee and Postal Section Committee. The PGMC and TGMC committees are composed of national officers and

Executive Council members who are elected by the annual EC elections and periodic national officer elections as a result of individual member ballots.

There are 13 national elected officers of the UCW: the General Secretary, Deputy General Secretary, eight assistant secretaries, general treasurer, organising secretary, and the editor of *The Post*. At the UCW headquarters there are eight departments: General Secretary's, telecommunications, counter and clerical, posts, legal and medical, general treasurer's, organising, and editorial.

The UCW is a centralised union and it acknowledges that to some extent the recent break-out of industrial action (see "Recent events") is partly a result of the lack of flexibility in the union organisation. A recent article by the General Secretary, Alan Tuffin, indicated the "need to strengthen local union organisation and increase the expertise of local officials to respond more effectively to change and take on additional responsibilities".

Women

Women membership has increased and now accounts for around a third of the UCW membership (see "Membership trends"). There are five women on the Executive Council, and of the eight assistant secretaries two are women. Women members tend to be predominantly telephonists nearly all of whom are employed on day-shift working. Until the Sex Discrimination Act was enacted in 1975 there were no women night telephonists, although there are a small number now.

External relations

The ballot held in 1985 regarding the political fund produced 102,564 votes (75.5 per cent) in favour of its retention with only 33,337 votes (24.5 per cent) against. The turn-out was a high 69.4 per cent.

The UCW is affiliated to the Labour Party. Following a rule change the UCW now sends the General Secretary, Deputy General Secretary, one national officer, three members of the Executive Council, plus four ordinary members to the Labour Party Conference. The union sponsors two Labour MPs: Bryan Gould (Dagenham) and Harry Ewing (Falkirk East).

Internationally the UCW is affiliated to the Postal Telegraph and Telephone International (PTTI) based in Geneva.

Policy

A document brought out in 1988, *Beyond Social Ownership,* continues the long UCW tradition of emphasising industrial democracy. The document was intended to contribute to the debate on the Labour Party policy review, and argued that an aggressive strategy of nationalisation as the socialist way forward into the 1990s is "economically simplistic and highly problematic". The UCW believes that more imaginative responses are required to entice a whole generation of voters brought up as consumers and unaware of the old-style "principles".

In the 1988 Labour Party leadership elections the UCW supported Neil Kinnock and Roy Hattersley, as it did in 1983. Politically, the union is on the centre-right.

The UCW takes a pragmatic view of Employee Share Ownership Schemes (ESOP), which some commentators have suggested as an alternative to full privatisation of sections of the Post Office. If the union can retain influence and maintain decent conditions then ESOP must be preferable to other more risky forms of privatisation (see **NALGO**). The parcel section looks the most vulnerable to privatisation.

At the 1988 TUC the UCW submitted a motion "to defend and advance members' interests in an economic environment dominated by multinational companies and international financial companies". The motion was part of a larger campaign by the UCW to alert workers to 1992 and the need for greater European-wide bargaining. Like the GMB, the UCW believes that in many instances European legislation provides far greater protection on issues such as health and safety, information disclosure, and equal pay, than that which is achieved under British-style collective bargaining arrangements.

Recent events

The UCW is fast gaining a reputation for militancy. Until the 1980s, apart from the fateful 1971 strike and Grunwick (see "History"), the union had undertaken only minor excursions into industrial action. The reorganisation and imposition of stricter business criteria on the Post Office during the later part of the 1980s have altered the character of the union for good.

Towards the end of 1987 the union was involved in a dispute over a shorter working week. The 1987 UCW Annual Conference passed a resolution calling for industrial action if the Post Office did not respond to its claim for a shorter working week. The union had demanded a three-hour cut in the 43-hour, six-day week. The last cut in the working week was in 1965. The dispute was finally settled just before the start of the busy Christmas period, the union agreeing to accept a cut of one-and-a-half hours, although some sections of the union (mainly in London) threatened unofficial action in defiance of the union settlement.

Signs of deteriorating industrial relations between the UCW and Post Office management were evident. The UCW claimed the management were using "team briefing" sessions to encourage anti-union feeling and ruled that members should refuse to attend. Management resorted to a court injunction, successfully preventing the union instruction. The resort to the High Court may have provided management with a legal victory but it would hardly do much to encourage participative discussion in team briefings.

August and September 1988 saw another national strike lending further testimony to deteriorating industrial relations in the Post Office and to the new-found militancy of the UCW. The dispute was triggered by management who broke the national agreement and unilaterally imposed regional pay supplements in an attempt to deal with staff shortages and recruiting problems, particularly in London and the south-east. The dispute was finally settled by a negotiated agreement allowing for local recruitment supplements in London and the south-east. Although a number of provincial cities were against the settlement the UCW recognised the problems faced by the Post Office, and through the strike asserted its rights to "change by agreement".

Finally, counter staff, who had not been involved in a national strike since 1971, also threatened national industrial action towards the end of September 1988. This was in response to Post Office management's plans to downgrade 250 Crown Post Offices to sub-Post Offices. Although a series of lightning strikes did take place counter staff ignored a union instruction to stage a one-day strike in December 1988, and support for the dispute fizzled out with no clear result.

To simply conclude that the spate of industrial action in the Post Office is due to the new-found militancy of the UCW would be naive and mistaken. The seeds for the disruption in the Post Office since 1987 were sown in 1981 when the Post Office was split into separate services and the two sections (post and telecommunications) cannot be viewed in isolation (see NCU). At the time of separation both sections inherited the Civil Service industrial relations structure and machinery. The demands made on the Post Office to operate more like a business required quite different human resource strategies from those which they inherited from the days of public utility. An overhaul of existing industrial relations machinery was inevitable. Moves to a more decentralised, market responsive service, with greater emphasis on core labour flexibility, less overtime, and more flexibility at peak times achieved by greater use of casual and part-time staff, are being sought actively by the Post Office. Splitting the Post Office into three separate and autonomous operating units, letters, parcels, and counter services, is going to demand different staffing criteria from each of the units. This is the challenge which the UCW must meet in the 1990s.

UCW/SOGAT merger

The UCW has always favoured a single union for Post Office and Telecom workers. Talks between the UCW and NCU, which represents the majority of BT workers, seemed to be making steady progress, but following political differences at the 1988 Labour Party Conference the talks have been abandoned.

Instead, the UCW has now entered merger talks with SOGAT and the two unions are looking to create a much more ambitious super-union embracing communication workers in the media, the Post Office, telecoms, and the railways: this would include the NGA, ACTT, BETA, NUR, ASLEF, STE, NUJ, CMA, and the NCU. With a combined total membership of around one million members the super-union would expect to be one of the four or five unions dominating the TUC in the 1990s. With falling union membership, rapidly changing technologies, economic changes demanding new working practices with greater labour flexibility, and decentralised bargaining, the idea behind a single union under a new "communications" grouping must be viewed as a positive response.

For the best part of the 1980s trade unions have been on the defensive, fighting to preserve a trade union structure designed for a different industrial era. The idea of taking the initiative, breaking down established patterns of organisation in favour of new exigencies has to be lauded. Old established traditions and patterns of organisation will not guarantee trade unions' continued relevance into the twenty-first century; new forms of worker expression have to be found.

At the time of publication the UCW is again threatening industrial action over a 7 per cent pay offer. The union is concerned that after four months of talks Post Office management has offered the 15,000 counter workers a deal below the level of inflation and below the 8 per cent plus settlements awarded to such groups as railway workers, local government officers, and other public sector workers during the "summer of strife" in 1989. Management has refused a union request for binding arbitration.

The union has to be certain of avoiding a repetition of the situation earlier in the year when industrial action over the down-grading of 250 Crown Post Offices petered out. Should the union decide to ballot its counter workers then it has to ensure that it receives very strong support, otherwise its credibility will be seriously undermined and the calls from Tory back-benchers to introduce a "no-strike clause" in the Post Office might be politically attractive to the government, which is currently trailing behind Labour in the national opinion polls.

Further references

Alan Clinton, *The Post Office Workers; A Trade Union History,* Allen & Unwin, 1983.

Michael Corby, *The Postal Business: A Study in Public Sector Management,* Kogan Page, 1979.

"Post Office and Productivity", *New Statesman,* February 8, 1980.

Michael Moran, *The Union of Post Office Workers,* Macmillan, 1974.

New Technology, The Post Office and the Union of Post Office Workers, Science Policy Research Unit, University of Sussex, 1980.

Alan Tuffin, "Fighting tomorrow's battles today", *The Guardian,* August 7, 1989.

UDM
UNION OF DEMOCRATIC MINEWORKERS
Non-TUC affiliated

Head Office: Miners' Offices, Berry Hill Lane, Mansfield, Notts NG18 4JU

Telephone: 0623-26094/5/6

Fax: 0623-642300

Principal officers
General Secretary: Roy Lynk
National Secretary: John Liptrott
Finance Officer: David Prendergast

Membership

Current membership (1988)
Total: 28,000 (estimate)

General
The UDM was formed in 1985, following profound differences between the national leadership of the NUM and the Nottingham area during the miners' strike in 1984-85 (see **NUM**). The Nottinghamshire miners refused to support the national strike, and led by Roy Lynk, with a good deal of encouragement from senior coal managers, Tory MPs, and other interested parties, they left the NUM. The Nottinghamshire coalfields have always been productive and this provided security to the breakaway union.

But the initial optimism which surrounded the UDM's formation has given way to the same sorts of problems now facing most unions today, namely recruitment. The union regularly sends recruiters to the Yorkshire coalfields and elsewhere, and it is too early for the recently signed single-union deals at Ashfordby and Margam to have any significant impact on membership, as they do not begin production until the 1990s (see "Policy and recent events"). The UDM is keen to preserve its independence, and recently postponed merger talks with the EETPU.

A major aim behind the formation of the union was to enhance internal union democracy. The leaders of the breakaway UDM group argued that Arthur Scargill had dominated the NUM membership and that the union had lost its democratic traditions. But there are signs that internal tensions are developing in the UDM over the leadership style of its General Secretary, Roy Lynk. Further similarities between the NUM and the UDM are emerging; the small South Derbyshire UDM is concerned at the dominance of the much larger Nottingham section. The pressures created by the privatisation of the electricity supply industry have intensified the competitive drive of British Coal managers who will be forced to compete with cheaper foreign imports of coal and other fuels. British Coal's production strategy is to concentrate on a small number of highly capital-intensive super-pits, which will necessitate the acceleration of pit closures and demand flexible work patterns with round-the-clock production. During its first few years the union enjoyed a "special relationship" with British Coal, but this has now ended and the UDM is finding that the glamour of being the "breakaway union" is no longer much use at the hard edge of coal production in the 1990s.

Organisation

Details of UDM organisation are partial and rely on secondary sources. A standard questionnaire was sent to the union's General Secretary, Roy Lynk, who replied that the union was not interested in participating as it felt that "some of the questions are too searching".

The union is organised into three sections; two mining sections, Nottingham and South Derbyshire; and the newly created National Federation of Employees (NFE), which recruits clerical workers. The NFE was set up in 1988 as part of the union's drive to increase its membership base, and is particularly aimed at non-miners who want a "non-political form of unionism".

External relations

Following the expulsion of the EETPU from the TUC it was thought that the UDM and the EETPU would initially form a political alliance which would act as a focal point for the right-wing non-TUC affiliated unions and other groups, and which would eventually lead to a full-scale merger. Despite extensive talks this has not come about, and in May 1989 talks between the UDM and the EETPU were called off.

On several occasions the UDM has applied to join the TUC but each time it has been refused membership.

The UDM has a political fund which was approved by the Certification Officer on August 25, 1988. Unfortunately, the union would not release details of the ballot results.

Policy and recent events

Until its 1988 Conference in Weymouth union policy was to oppose the privatisation of the coal industry. At the Conference Roy Lynk said that he had a mandate to pursue the interests of the union's membership as a whole. He thus suggested that the UDM should consider the possibility of becoming involved in worker buy-outs and Employee Share Ownership Schemes (ESOP). Cecil Parkinson, Secretary of State for Energy, also addressed UDM delegates at the Weymouth Conference and supported the speech made by Roy Lynk about the share ownership issue.

Since the Conference Roy Lynk had made it known that the UDM is planning an employee buy-out of up to 30 UDM-controlled pits from British Coal. Institutions in the City are keen to support UDM plans following their endorsement by the Prime Minister, Margaret Thatcher. Nottinghamshire contains several key marginal seats and the Tories believe that by encouraging wider share ownership, they will improve their chances of winning the next general election.

In May 1989 the UDM signed an agreement with British Coal giving it sole negotiating rights at the proposed Margam pit in South Wales which is due to start production in 1993. Earlier in the year the union also signed a similar single-union agreement covering the Ashfordby colliery in Leicestershire where production is expected to begin in 1991. These agreements give the UDM exclusive negotiating rights for 10 years from the start of production at both pits. The agreements commit the union to six-day, flexible working patterns which the NUM were resisting, and the move is bound to intensify conflict between the two unions.

URTU
UNITED ROAD TRANSPORT UNION

TUC affiliated

Head Office: 76 High Lane, Chorlton-cum-Hardy, Manchester M21 1FD

Telephone: 061-881 6245/6

Fax: 061-862 9127

Principal national officers
General Secretary: Frank Griffin
Assistant General Secretary: A. T. Hughes
President: A. Jewsbury

Union journal and publications: Wheels (bi-monthly). This union newspaper is distributed widely throughout the road haulage industry. URTU has also prepared a *Café Accommodation Handbook* which is compiled by the membership, giving a lorry driver's guide to overnight accommodation and eating facilities. The handbook also contains useful sections on road traffic and EEC regulations etc.

Membership

Current membership (1987)
Male: 18,971
Female: 1,574
Total: 20,545

Membership trends

	1975	1979	1981	1983	1987	change 1975-87	1983-87
Men	22,050	24,519	25,700	20,328	18,971	−14%	− 7%
Women	450	2,500	700	2,300	1,574	250%	−32%
Total	22,500	27,019	26,400	22,628	20,545	− 9%	− 9%

Union membership has declined by 9 per cent since 1983 and the union has responded by offering members a wider service, including free legal aid for all matters including civil and domestic actions. Improved death benefits, a national dental plan, and a compensation scheme for loss of driving licence, are further examples of the union's increased attempts to extend the service it provides to existing members. Full union benefits are available to unemployed members by paying a nominal 1p per week. This is a practice many other unions already adopt but it is questionable whether this initiative will stem membership decline.

Women members, although still a very small proportion of total members, have in fact increased. This is mainly in the distribution area which employs women as ancillary workers.

General
URTU organises road haulage drivers, although its rule book also provides for the organisation of "their assistants and production workers as well as service industries". Its

members work in road haulage, international haulage, food and drink industries, and for some local authorities. The union has recently widened its scope to become more actively involved in the recruitment of workers in the distribution industry. Given the size and area of organisation the union is an obvious target for a merger, but it has shown remarkable resilience in surviving in the face of competition. URTU has no political affiliations and is not represented on the General Council of the TUC.

History
URTU has its origins in the *United Carters' Association* which was formed in 1890. In 1891 this body became the *United Carters' Association of England.* The union changed its name to the *United Carters and Motormen's Association of England* in 1912, and to the *United Road Transport Workers' Association of England* in 1926. It adopted its present title in 1964.

Union organisation
URTU employs two divisional officers and 13 regional officers, apart from the General Secretary and Assistant General Secretary. All full-time officials, apart from the President and General Secretary, are appointed by the Executive Committee. The post of General Secretary, previously appointed at the Triennial Delegate Conference, is now to be elected on a postal ballot for a five-year period. URTU officers must have had at least 12 months' membership of the union at the time of application, and all have spent a large part of their working life within the industry. URTU claims that it has more officers per unit of membership than any other union. The average number of members serviced by an officer in URTU is 1,800, compared with an overall TUC average of 5,000-6,000.

The supreme policy-making body in URTU is the Triennial Delegate Meeting, which lasts for one day, and consists of the President, General Secretary, and delegates elected by the membership on the basis of one delegate for every 400 members. The day-to-day management of the union is carried out by the Executive Committee, which consists of the President, General Secretary, and not more than three representatives from each division. Four representatives in addition to the chairman form a quorum with power to act. EC members are elected for a three-year term of office. The EC meets once a month.

The union is divided into two trade groups, one for road haulage and commercial activities and one for bakery, food, and drink. Trade group conferences are held. URTU is also organised into sections which comprise a number of members employed in each work group. Where possible, branches may be set up upon the request of a majority of the section within a geographical area as defined by the EC.

Work-place activity
Road haulage drivers spend nearly all their working time on the road, and so membership participation is low in section/branch meetings and union elections. Secret balloting of members has been a widespread practice in the union.

Women
Its women membership, although small, has grown in the last few years. The union has sought to encourage women and now provides a sickness payment scheme to ensure full benefit payment during pregnancy.

Despite the rise in women members and the union's apparent interest in encouraging their membership and activity within the union, URTU appears to have no specific policy on women members. Apart from changes in the sickness payment scheme to enable pregnant women to draw full benefit (up to £80 in any three-year period) the union still has no full-time women officers and the EC is composed solely of men.

External relations
URTU is not affiliated to the Labour Party nor any other political party and has not held a ballot on the question of the political levy. It is affiliated to the International Transport Federation, the International Union of Food Workers, and the European Committees of Transport Workers and Food Allied Workers. The union is also represented on the TUC transport industries committee, the Distributive Industry Training Board, the Food, Drink, and Tobacco Training Board, and the Road Transport Industry Training Board.

Policy
Historically the union has been a supporter of single-union agreements. It has also entered into arbitration agreements but is critical of pendulum arbitration arrangements. URTU has traditionally never relied on closed shop agreements, although it does have some agreements where it has sole representation. The union is currently addressing the implications for effective representation of the shift from national bargaining to regional and local level company bargaining. Through its representation rights on various training bodies URTU is actively encouraging the extension of training not only to the unemployed, but also to employed members.

The union has always sought to cultivate the image of the "Lorry Drivers' Union" and has guarded its independence jealously over the years. It has long been a supporter of increasing the movement of haulage by road rather than rail or other forms of transport. The current concern with the general increase in road traffic could find the union under pressure, especially if a more co-ordinated transport policy is adopted.

The union has been committed since 1979 to a policy of opposition to any racialist organisation but there does not appear to have been any real initiatives to enact and develop this position.

As traditionally lorry drivers rely on long hours of work to maintain their income URTU opposes any move in the reduction in the working week.

URTU is losing membership despite the measures it has adopted; in the long term a sensible course of action has to be a merger with a larger union.

USDAW
UNION OF SHOP, DISTRIBUTION, AND ALLIED WORKERS

TUC affiliated

Head Office: 188 Wilmslow Road, Fallowfield, Manchester M14 6LJ

Telephone: 061-224 2804 & 061-225 8081

Fax: 061-257 2566

Principal officers
General Secretary: Garfield Davies
Deputy General Secretary: John Flood
Administrative and Executive Officer: Geoff Walker
Central Treasurer: John Youd
President: Syd Tierney

National officers
W. J. Conners
P. Gaffney
M. Gordon
G. Martin
F. Murphy
T. F. Sullivan

Departmental heads
Administrative Services Officer: V. Lowe, MIS
Audit Officer: N. Robertson
Education Officer: C. J. Thorne, MA
Finance Department: K. Ashworth
Legal Officer: A. C. Heywood, LLB
Productivity Services Officer: M. Leahy
Public Relations Officer: P. H. Jones
Research and Political Officer: Diana Jeuda, BA
Women's Officer: Bernadette Hillon

Union offices
USDAW is divided into eight divisions. A divisional officer, his deputy, and a team of area organisers, of which the union employs 125 nationally, are located at the following USDAW offices:

South Wales and Western Division
B. T. Ropke, Walter Padley House, 40 Charles Street, Cardiff CF1 4RN
Telephone: 0223-25626

Eastern Division
T. Osborne, 2 High Street, West Alley, Hitchin, Herts
Telephone: 0462-54564

Midlands Division
J. Toogood, 10 Pershore Street, Birmingham B5 4HT
Telephone: 021-622 2995

North-Western Division
W. R. Smith, 145 Edge Lane, Liverpool L7 2PG
Telephone: 051-263 7521

Manchester Division
J.C. Callahan, 13 Warwick Road, Old Trafford, Manchester M16 0QX
Telephone: 061-872 3527

North-Eastern Division
T. Jacques, Concord House, Park Lane, Leeds LS3 1EJ
Telephone: 0532-441881

Scottish Division
P. McCormick, "Muirfield", 342 Albert Drive, Glasgow G41 5PG
Telephone: 041-427 1121

Southern Division
R. A. Hammond, "Ruskin House", 23 Coombe Road, Croydon CR0 1BD
Telephone: 01-688 4800

There are 25 other USDAW offices throughout the eight divisions.

Union journal: USDAW produces a monthly journal, *Dawn,* with a circulation of around 110,000 which is distributed in bulk to the membership via shop stewards. This is a change from previous practice when the journal was distributed through branch secretaries, and represents an acknowledgement of the value to the membership, as well as the union, of face-to-face contact with shop stewards.

The union also publishes material on a range of industrial and political topics including: sexual harassment; maternity rights; pensions; violent crime; training; AIDS; health and safety.

Membership

Current membership (1987)
Male: 150,329
Female: 236,878
Total: 387,207

Membership trends

	1975	1979	1981	1983	1987	change 1975-87	1983-87
Men	153,653	179,732	N/A	159,275	150,329	−2%	−6%
Women	223,649	290,285	N/A	244,171	236,878	6%	−3%
Total	377,302	470,017	437,864	403,446	387,207	3%	−4%

General

USDAW is the seventh largest union in Britain. It came into being on January 1, 1947, upon the amalgamation of the *National Union of Distributive and Allied Workers* (NUDAW) and the *National Amalgamated Union of Shop Assistants, Warehousemen, and Clerks* (NAUSAWC). USDAW membership is organised accordingly: retail co-op; retail services; CWS (wholesale), private retail distribution and trade; industrial sector; optical; hairdressing; credit collection and others; and white collar workers, through SATA.

Recently USDAW recruited a quarter of the 4,000 employees employed by Harrods, the London department store.

Around 60 per cent of the union's membership is female, although there are only three women members on the 16-strong Executive Council, and the union has no female national or divisional officers. However, the union does have two women occupying senior departmental positions: the Women's Officer and the Research and Political Officer.

At the end of 1985 Bill Whatley retired and Garfield Davies became USDAW General Secretary. Garfield Davies was previously a national officer with responsibilities in the retail co-operative movement milk and meat trades. In his election brief he portrayed himself as the "campaigning General Secretary", and when he took his (automatic) seat on the TUC General Council he was greeted as a person who could provide new initiatives and spirit to the TUC.

USDAW membership peaked in 1979 at 470,017 and declined sharply throughout the 1980s to a low of 381,984 at the end of 1986. In 1987 USDAW recorded a rise of 5,223 members to 387,207 (an increase of 1.37 per cent). Although the rise was small it was the first membership rise recorded by one of the TUC's larger affiliated unions and does represent a change in the eight-year downward trend. In fact, during 1987 108,444 new members were actually enrolled, but because of high levels of labour turn-over in the retailing sector USDAW has to recruit at least 100,000 new members each year simply to maintain current membership levels. Retailing is now considered to be the fastest-growing area of employment in Britain as well as one of the fastest-growing areas of trade unionism.

In 1986 the union's ADM, under the banner "The Campaigning Union — Ready to Take Action" made recruitment the priority for the union in the forthcoming year. A novel recruitment campaign was launched shortly after the ADM which featured a campaign bus which toured the major cities with "Don't miss the bus — join USDAW" emblazoned on it. The following ADM reaffirmed the priority given to recruitment when Syd Tierney, the union President, called on delegates to concentrate on recruitment rather than on other issues like Sunday trading.

In September 1987 USDAW put out a new recruitment pack specifically designed for lay-recruiters, such as shop stewards and branch chairmen. This represented a break with the past, as recruitment was previously carried out by the full-time officials of the union. This was the initiative of a special Campaigning Recruitment Committee set up to consider and put forward new recruitment tactics in the light of the major transformation affecting the retailing industry. The new campaign was later formalised as "Reach Out".

"Reach Out" is the latest, and most ambitious, campaign of USDAW's recruitment strategy. It was publicly launched by Garfield Davies in January 1989, with the aim of identifying, educating, communicating, and servicing members, and was to target companies where a nucleus of members already existed. At its launch Davies reaffirmed the priority of recruitment over other issues. Visits to supermarkets and the new retailing complexes are planned in the hope of reaching out to part-time workers. It is intended to use the 1989 ADM as a key part of the campaign strategy.

As part of USDAW's "Reach Out" campaign the union has computerised membership registrations at Head Office, and has issued to every member a new style of personalised plastic membership card, containing the member's name, branch number, and membership number. The new cards will eventually enable USDAW to assemble a package of financial services for members, offering discounts on such items as holidays, insurance, and other purchases. USDAW hopes to introduce such a service towards the end of 1989.

In a further move to standardise and modernise their visual and public image, USDAW has introduced a new logo with the motto "Unity is Strength" and has also commissioned a new union banner.

History

USDAW was formed by the amalgamation of the *National Union of Distributive and Allied Workers* (NUDAW) and the *National Amalgamated Union of Shop Assistants, Warehousemen, and Clerks* (NAUSAWC) in 1947. Both these unions grew out of smaller local unions which gradually increased in size and scope and merged with one another. NUDAW and its forerunners concentrated their main organisation efforts on workers in co-operative employment. In 1921, following an amalgamation between the *Amalgamated Union of Co-operative Employees* and *Warehouse and General Workers' Union*, NUDAW came into being with a membership of 105,000. By contrast, NAUSAWC and its forerunners organised the private retailing and wholesaling sector, by the recruitment of shop assistants and, later, warehouse workers and clerks into the union. By 1920, following the absorption of the National Association of Grocers' Assistants, the membership had grown to 86,000. Following further amalgamations NAUSAWC (108,781) and NUDAW (267,497) merged together in 1947 to create USDAW.

The latest addition to the union was the Scottish bakers' section which was formed from the transfer of engagements of the *Scottish Union of Bakers and Allied Workers* to USDAW in January 1978.

Union officials
USDAW employs 104 area organisers spread throughout the eight divisions as well as nine regional officers, eight divisional officers, and eight deputy divisional officers. These posts are all appointed by the Executive Council. The union is comparatively well staffed by full-time officials in relation to its membership size, and it also employs some 134 administrative personnel at its headquarters in Manchester.

There are obvious reasons why USDAW should employ so many staff. Every year the union has to recruit well over 100,000 new members in order simply to maintain its total membership size. For example, in 1987 the union recruited 108,444 new members but the total net increase was only 5,223 over the previous 12 months. With such a high turn-over of members it is important that the administrative machinery of the union is run efficiently. Another reason is the high dependence by the rank and file on the services of the full-time officials — particularly area organisers — as work-place bargaining at local level is weak (see "Workplace activity").

There is a very strong tradition in USDAW of appointing officers from within the union. Nearly all officers have at some time or another been branch secretaries or work-place activists, who are then "promoted" to the level of area organiser. This career structure, with so many interests at stake serves to act as an impediment to organisational change. For example, a former General Secretary, Lord Allen, who retired in 1979, served as an official since 1946 and had been an USDAW member for 46 years. In recent years, and in common with some other unions, there has been a tendency for area organisers to be appointed from outside the union, either from other unions or from Ruskin College, Oxford.

USDAW operates an extensive education and training scheme which enables it to produce its own "home-grown" officials. Priority is given to the training of work-place representatives at schools which are attended by about 900 people each year. Some 1,000 people enrol annually for the union's home study course, and each year preparatory courses are provided for those members who wish to develop the necessary knowledge and skills to occupy full-time positions within the union.

The office of President of USDAW is a lay office, but it can be held by a full-time official. Such an official retains a normal job and carries out the role as President as well. The current President is Syd Tierney who has retained the post for 12 years. He was until his recent retirement a full-time official, and also a national officer. Generally speaking USDAW Presidents are either MPs or full-time officers, although the post of President is intended as a lay position. In April 1987 Tierney was re-elected President of USDAW for the sixth term. The post comes up for re-election every two years, and Audrey Wise (MP for Preston) is to challenge Syd Tierney for the Presidency in elections in 1989. Audrey Wise, an USDAW-sponsored MP, is being supported by the union's broad left group. The election of the President is now conducted by a full postal ballot of the entire membership.

Coverage

Roughly 200,000 of USDAW's membership are employed either by the Co-operative Wholesale Society or by the retail co-operative societies. The co-operative sector membership (as a proportion of total membership) is declining rapidly as the union recruits new members in the retail trade outside the co-operative sector. This historical dependence on the co-operative sector accounts for the union's headquarters being sited in Manchester (some 23 per cent of the total membership of the union is located in the Manchester or North-Western divisions).

USDAW has always believed in trying to organise and represent all employees of a single co-operative society, company, or single site of a company. Where the number of maintenance or other craftsmen is small the union specifically represents them as well as production, warehousing, transport, sales, catering, administration, supervisory, or managerial grades. The majority of members work in retailing and wholesale distribution, but considerable numbers are engaged in food manufacturing, chemical process industries, or service trades such as catering, laundries, and hairdressing. The union organises shop managers as well as sales assistants, factory or warehouse supervisors, along with operatives, drivers, clerks, insurance workers, butchers at abattoirs, milkmen/women, in addition to meat packers and dairy process workers.

About a quarter of USDAW's membership is made up of part-time workers. The union has a Part-Time Workers' Charter listing improvements in collective bargaining and legal protection aimed at improving the position of part-time workers.

USDAW is represented on six wages councils, often alongside other unions, and thus is responsible for representing pockets of low paid workers in various sectors. USDAW is party to agreements covering various classes of workers in the following trades or industries:

Retail Co-operative Society;
Co-operative Wholesale Society Ltd;
Retail distributive trades;
Multiple wines and spirits;
Multiple tailoring;
Mail order;
Hairdressing;
Credit trade;
Retail meat trade;
Wholesale meat and kindred trades;
Bacon curing industry;
Milk industry;
Catering;
Baking trade;
Flour milling;
Seed crushing, compound, and provender;
Aerated waters;
Laundry trade;
Dental technicians;
Gelatine and glue;
Soap, candle, and edible fats;
Glass containers;
Road haulage;
Co-operative Retail Services Ltd;
Co-operative Insurance Society;

Multiple footwear;
Retail multiple furnishing;
Drapery and department stores;
Pools industry;
Check trade;
Retail pharmacy;
Multiple meat trade;
Hide and skin;
Wholesale grocery provisions;
Milk Marketing Board;
NAAFI;
Biscuit industry;
Food manufacturing;
Cocoa, chocolate, and confectionery;
Brewing industry;
Ophthalmic optical industry;
Chemical and allied industries;
Surgical dressings;
Rubber manufacturing;
Boot and shoe repairing.

USDAW is also party to a number of multiple agreements in which it is the single union recognised for bargaining purposes. These agreements cover all employees below senior management level. A number of factory and warehouse agreements are also single-union agreements. A further recent development is that compulsory arbitration is provided for in some local agreements; such a provision is made after the workers have already joined the union, and if they wish, they have the right to reject it.

A major development in company bargaining occurred towards the end of 1988. Tesco, the large supermarket chain, announced its withdrawal from the Multiple Food Retailers' Employers' Agreement (MFREA) which covers some 87,000 workers. Instead, Tesco will now negotiate directly with USDAW. Tesco members already had their own national committee for joint consultation and this will now take on a negotiating role as well. Tesco accounted for some 45,000 of the workers covered by the MFREA agreement.

The significance of the Tesco initiative is that from April 1989 the 10 largest supermarket companies in the MFREA will negotiate separately with USDAW. This will bring an end to national industry-wide bargaining for pay and conditions such as holiday and sick pay entitlement, although negotiations will probably still cover grading structures and other matters of mutual concern. USDAW's 1987 Conference in fact urged the union to move to separate negotiations because of increasing mergers, and the decline in the number of employers in the MFREA meant that there was now perhaps less need for USDAW to organise industry-wide bargaining.

Organisation
The supreme policy-making body of the union is the Annual Delegate Meeting (ADM), which meets for a period of four days usually towards the end of April. The union's general management is vested in the 16-member Executive Council which is now elected by a full postal ballot of the entire membership every two years. The next elections are due in 1989.

Branches

There are more than 1,200 branches of the union throughout the UK. The majority of the union's branches are organised either on a single employer or trade basis. Most branches are composed of members from the same employer (e.g. Kellogg's Ltd in Manchester) or of members working in one particular trade (e.g. multiple tailoring).

USDAW's official handout stresses that "The branch structure of USDAW is designed so that members are grouped together where they have similar interests". Only in districts or towns where there are too few members to organise branches in this way are there mixed branches comprising members from a number of trades or employers.

In fact, USDAW has many branches which cover huge areas and in which members work for many employers. Such branches are not conducive to the development of trade union consciousness or any sense of group identity. In such branches, which are generally described as area or holding branches, it is impossible to have any sense of common employer or geographical identity, nor is it possible for members to acquaint themselves with other USDAW members in the same town, and it is almost impossible to effect links with trades councils and other bodies.

One example of such an area or holding branch is Birmingham dry goods. It draws its 1,400 members from an area covering Stafford, Worcester, Coventry, and Dudley. Most of its members work in retail trades such as newsagents, furniture, British Home Stores, Sketchley Dry Cleaners, Allied Carpets, etc. Within this huge area there are other members of USDAW who are placed in other branches. This kind of branch strengthens the power of the union hierarchy, since members are entirely dependent on USDAW full-time officials whose deployment is controlled by divisional officers and not the membership. If USDAW is to retain its relevance to retail workers in a time of enormous developments in retailing, then a more imaginative and less centralised organisational structure may be necessary.

There are no rules in the USDAW rule book about the frequency of branch meetings. Most union business is conducted by branch committees, assuming there is one. The rule book still only allows the Executive Council and President to be elected by secret postal ballot. All other elections, including the recent re-election of the General Secretary, take place at branch meetings which members have to attend in order to register their vote.

Divisional councils

Divisional councils are based upon the eight divisions of the union throughout the country. Each divisional council is composed of 10 elected members. The divisional council usually meets once a month, together with the divisional officer. Divisional officers not only oversee the union's activities within the divisions but also negotiate local agreements on wages and conditions for members who are covered by national agreement.

Executive Council

The Executive Council comprises the union's President, General Secretary, and 16 Executive councillors (two from each of the eight divisions) who are elected every two years by full postal ballot of the entire membership. The election of the General Secretary is as yet unchanged, but it is being considered. Full-time officials of the union are eligible to stand for EC office, although the EC has traditionally been composed of an overwhelming majority of lay members. The Executive Council meets monthly.

Annual Delegate Meeting

Every USDAW branch is entitled to elect one delegate to attend and vote at the ADM. Branches with a membership of over 500 are entitled to one further delegate for every additional 500 members. The voting strength of a branch delegate is equal to the total number of members of the branch the delegate represents. The ADM usually takes place in early spring.

Federations

Federations within USDAW are groupings of union branches in a locality or region. Branches elect representatives to attend federation meetings. which are usually held once a quarter. There are some 33 federations in USDAW, and their function is to stimulate the exchange of views between rank and file members and to arrange social and educational activities.

Trade conferences

Trade conferences have been held in USDAW since 1950. They are arranged annually or biennially for each of the trades or industries in which the union has substantial membership and where some form of negotiating machinery exists in which the union plays a substantial part. Each branch with the relevant trade interest elects its delegates to the appropriate national trade conference.

It used to be the practice that certain sections of the union, such as the retail co-operative trade and the retail private trades, convened divisional trade conferences prior to the full national trade conference but this practice has now been abandoned. Although there was some objection to this, the union claims that it was forced to wind up divisional trade conferences because of poor attendances. Further, USDAW claims that the role of divisional trade conferences has been superseded by the new divisional campaigning activities which are seen as playing a vital role in the union's new recruitment campaign (see "Policy").

In recent years the trade machinery has been adapted to provide for occasional conferences of delegates representing the union's membership in some of the large and widely-spread national companies (e.g. John Lewis department stores).

All trade conferences are consultative and advisory and their decisions are subject to endorsement by the union's Executive Council.

USDAW also makes special provision for certain sections of membership, particularly the Co-operative Insurance Society agents, Supervisory, Administrative, and Technical Association (SATA), and the members of the former Scottish Bakers' Union.

In 1986 USDAW ran its first national youth Conference specifically to represent active members under the age of 26. Delegates are elected to the Conference on the basis of five from each of the union's divisions. National youth conferences are convened annually, and the 1987 Conference considered ways in which young people could be made to play a more prominent part in the affairs of the union. Among the many suggestions delegates called for a more imaginative union journal which reflected present-day youth culture.

Headquarters

To aid the Executive Council and its officers USDAW headquarters maintains several departments. These are: audit, administration, public relations, education and training, finance (including records and benefits), legal, productivity services, research and politics, and women's issues.

Work-place activity

There are provisions in USDAW rules to elect shop stewards by work-groups. The rules provide that shop stewards are responsible at all times to the branch committee and serve for a period of two years. Shop stewards must be 18 years of age or over, and have been a member of USDAW for at least 12 months. The 1987 ADM amended the rule that prospective shop stewards had to have attended at least 50 per cent of branch meetings in the last 12 months, and now there is no such attendance requirement.

Work-place bargaining is not very well developed in the trades or industries in which USDAW is represented largely due to the continued importance of national bargaining, particularly in retail distribution and the milk industry. Local bargaining is significant, however, in food and the chemical industries and in many areas of warehousing. The lay membership of USDAW is generally disorganised, and has a high degree of dependence on the servicing of full-time officials. Given the fact that there is an annual membership turn-over within the union of around 36 per cent full-time officials are kept busy, and work-place activity is minimal compared to other large unions, although this is now being changed. USDAW recently introduced a sophisticated training pack for its shop stewards, involving a "first aid" self-learning kit using video-tape technology which can be used at home or in the work-place.

Women

USDAW has a high percentage of women members (around 60 per cent). In 1982 the Executive Council submitted a document to its Annual Delegate Meeting entitled "Women in USDAW". The document tended to address itself to women in trade unions generally and said little about USDAW itself. Recognising this, the EC set up a working party to consider the question of women and USDAW more carefully. The outcome of this initiative was that USDAW now has a National Women's Committee and a network of divisional women's committees which carry out a dual function of encouraging women members to play a prominent role in the affairs of USDAW as well as raising issues which are of special interest to them, either for campaigns, or for negotiators to take up. The National Committee now has its own Women's Officer who acts as its secretary. Recently USDAW has produced booklets on sexual harassment, equal pay, cancer screening, and maternity rights.

USDAW has campaigned for equal pay for work of equal value, the extension of maternity leave and adequate state benefits, strengthening sex discrimination legislation, and improved child care facilities. Women's issues are also, wherever possible, incorporated into its agreements with employers. Certainly since 1982, USDAW has adopted a higher profile towards women, who form the majority of its membership. However, the union still does not have enough female officers in relation to the proportion of the female membership. A recent report produced for USDAW found that 58 per cent of women members believed there was too much jargon at branch meetings, 56 per cent thought they were dominated by cliques, and more than 40 per cent thought they were irrelevant.

USDAW has recently signed an agreement with the Co-operative Retail Society which offers personal alarms and guarantees of minimum staff levels to employees working in the evenings. The union has been worried about the problem of staff, particularly women, being attacked by members of the public. The risk of attack is especially high when the premises involved are licensed. Under the national agreement with the Co-operative Retail Society, a new grade of assistant to the manager at each store has been created so that one person will be responsible for security at all times. There are never to be fewer than two staff. The company has also agreed to look at lighting levels outside stores. Training for women retail staff in how to protect themselves against attack, and the provision of attack alarms, have generally become more common.

It has become common practice in most retailing establishments to make retail assistants wear their names on identity badges. But this practice is a source of complaint amongst many USDAW women members who believe that it is open to abuse and in fact increases the risk of sexual harassment.

External relations

USDAW is affiliated to the Labour Party, and Garfield Davies, as part of his election campaign profile for the post of General Secretary, made increasing the role of USDAW in the Labour Party an election issue. Prior to his election as General Secretary USDAW had only two sponsored Labour MPs. This was seen to be a gross under-representation for such a large union. USDAW has redressed this imbalance and now sponsors 10 Labour MPs, including a number of important front-bench spokesmen and shadow cabinet members:

Robin Corbett (Birmingham, Erdington);
Derek Foster (Bishop Auckland);
Bryan Gould (Dagenham);
Tommy Graham (Renfrew West and Inverclyde);
Roy Hattersley (Birmingham, Sparkbrook);
David Lambie (Cunninghame South);
Ray Powell (Ogmore);
Ted Rowlands (Merthyr Tydfil);
Andrew Smith (Oxford East);
Audrey Wise (Preston).

The 1988 ADM supported Neil Kinnock and Roy Hattersley for the leadership of the Labour Party by seven votes to one in preference to Tony Benn and Eric Heffer. USDAW supported the Labour Party leadership in expelling the Militant Tendency in 1986. In the 1987 general election USDAW was a member of Trade Unions for Labour (TUFL) and campaigned under the slogan "eight million people on the bread line". USDAW is generally seen to be on the right of the party.

The General Secretary of USDAW, Garfield Davies, replaced his predecessor Bill Whatley on the TUC General Council in January 1986. He is a member of the TUC General Council and sits on the Economic and Employment Policy Committee, and chairs the Distribution and Food Industry Committee. He also served on the special TUC review body.

One of the first priorities of the newly-appointed General Secretary was to ballot the membership regarding USDAW's political fund. In accordance with the requirements of the Trade Union Act 1984 USDAW held a ballot in November 1985 and overwhelmingly decided (by a majority of seven to one) to retain its political levy. The exact results were 88 per cent in favour of retention of the political fund (representing 134,592 votes), with 11.65 per cent (4,968 votes) against. Although in monetary terms USDAW has almost doubled the size of its political fund from £172,000 in 1977, to £316,000 in 1985, in relation to other unions it has, in the same time period, fallen from having the seventh to the ninth largest union political fund.

Since October 1986 USDAW has increased its representation on the TUC General Council; Bernadette Hillon, the union's national Women's Officer, has become USDAW's second representative. Bernadette Hillon is a member of the Social Insurance, Industrial Welfare, Education, Equal Rights, and the Women's and the Media Working Group Committees.

In October 1988 Sadshivrao Deshmukh, an USDAW convenor at Selfridges department store in London, was appointed for three years to serve on the TUC Race Relations Advisory Committee.

Policy

USDAW has put forward and supported several resolutions at Trade Union Congresses.

It has consistently supported motions relating to the problem of low paid workers. Garfield Davies opened up the debate at the 1987 TUC on employment rights and legal protection, focusing on the problems experienced by low paid workers. USDAW's support of the motion at the 1988 TUC calling for legal opposition to the Poll Tax was based largely on the inequitable effect of the Poll Tax on the low paid.

USDAW was party to a joint venture (with the GMB and NUPE) in commissioning Cambridge economists Peter Brosnan and Frank Wilkinson, to produce a survey into low pay (*Cheap Labour: Britain's False Economy,* October 1987, Low Pay Unit, London). One of the chief findings of the study was the evidence supporting the introduction of a minimum wage of £2.40 per hour and suggesting that, contrary to government wisdom, this would create an extra 10,000 new jobs.

USDAW has recently mounted an extensive campaign in defence of wages councils, which was given heavy coverage in the February 1989 issue of its journal, *Dawn.* The government has indicated that it wishes to abolish the councils in an attempt to free the labour market and promote greater industrial efficiency. USDAW maintains that wage council rates have risen no faster, and in many cases more slowly, than average basic earnings and that the system is poorly enforced, with one in four employers consistently underpaying. With this level of underpayment USDAW argues that many employers would pay less than current legal rates if they could, and calls instead, for an increase in the number of wage council inspectors. USDAW reports that the removal of young people from wages council protection provoked numerous unsolicited inquiries from people wishing to join the union.

Continuing with USDAW's fight against low pay, the union has launched a campaign called "Claim It" which is aimed at encouraging members who might be eligible for family credit and/or housing benefit, to claim their rights. A survey conducted by USDAW during the 1988 ADM identified as many as 149,000 USDAW members who might be eligible to claim these benefits. "Claim It" leaflets have been circulated to all branches which have been encouraged to ensure that their constituent members are aware of their rights, and to provide their members with help in order to claim their full entitlements.

USDAW has always been opposed to the thorny question of Sunday trading. In 1985, when the issue was debated in Parliament, USDAW earmarked £100,000 to publicise the union's opposition to Sunday trading. Housewives and shop-workers were deliberately targeted and advertisements were placed in women's magazines such as *Woman's Own* and *True Romance,* as part of a clever advertising campaign mounted by USDAW. Whilst USDAW played its part in a coalition of interest groups which successfully defeated the proposal to amend the 1950 Shops Act and allow Sunday trading, all parties involved recognise the vexed nature of the problem and that the issue of Sunday trading is bound to re-emerge.

Large shopping complexes on green-field sites geared to the needs of the motorist, are changing for ever the way in which people shop. Within an increasingly leisure-oriented society shopping itself is now being seen as a leisure activity. Also, increasingly flexible patterns of employment as well as the significant rise in the number of women who work, are bringing about major changes in shopping patterns.

The consumer boom of the 1980s would seem to indicate that people enjoy the activity of being consumers. In all spheres of life, whether it be the NHS, education, the arts, and even unions, the "consumer perspective" is gaining ascendance. Instead of relying on the purely defensive posture of outright hostility to Sunday trading, USDAW might well take this opportunity to seize the initiative in an attempt to win the moral ground (at present occupied by the Tory right), and influence the debate about the way in which retailing, and particularly Sunday trading, should develop. Such a progressive stance would do much to lift the public image of trade unionism and USDAW would gain support and influence amongst a much wider section of society.

However, USDAW's response to the retailing revolution was to consider a paper on retailing in the 1990s, prepared by the union's Executive Committee and presented to the 1988 ADM. The paper argued that the new developments, whilst they can bring certain gains such as a safe and comfortable working environment and improved work facilities, nevertheless posed a series of problems to the union. The development of complex shift systems and part-time working would all make trade union organisation difficult.

But organising under conditions of adversity is what trade unions have always had to do. The fact that some workers might actually want to choose non-standard working hours and that probably most of the part-time workers are likely to be women, a section which has been specially targeted in the union's recent recruitment campaign, appears not to have been properly considered.

Nor have the results of a recent survey carried out by USDAW been fully understood. The survey argues that there is little evidence to suggest that part-time workers are inherently less disposed to join unions. The survey found that the most common reason cited by part-time workers for not joining a union was simply that they had not been asked. The second most common reason was that it was not worth joining a union because of limited working hours.

The 1988 ADM reaffirmed its opposition to Sunday trading and called for a more rigid enforcement of legal restrictions under the 1950 Shops Act. In September 1988 in response to the ADM USDAW launched a new campaign, "Shop Watch", which set up teams of USDAW members to monitor any changes taking place in retailing. The purpose of the teams is to influence new shopping developments before plans are finalised and to take steps to prevent shops from opening illegally on Sundays. USDAW has issued a campaign pack which provides advice on trading laws and the planning process. Check-lists for local contacts, model resolutions for Labour Party and trades councils, and standard letters for reporting breaches of the shopping laws have also been included in the pack. Such policies are unlikely to win a great deal of public sympathy and USDAW must seek more imaginative ways of protecting its members, while at the same time supporting the move towards greater flexibility in shopping patterns.

USDAW was one of the first unions to condemn the government's Job Training Scheme (JTS) which was discussed at the 1987 TUC. However, USDAW is a strong supporter of the Youth Training Scheme (YTS) and produced a special YTS pack to assist shop stewards to monitor the scheme. USDAW has been successful in a number of instances, particularly for those undertaking a second year's training, in obtaining top-ups, in the form of employee status and the rate for the job. Agreements were negotiated, for example, with Foster Brothers, Sainsburys, Empire Stores, and the Milk Marketing Board, all of which bettered the minimum statutory provisions.

When the 1988 TUC debated the government's Employment Training Scheme (ETS), USDAW supported remaining within the Scheme. At first it voted in favour of conditional support, and then voted for the compromise of two-year involvement. USDAW believes that in order to afford some protection to trainees it should give qualified support to ETS, but the union is committeed to reviewing its position if the undertaking (that ETS will operate on an entirely voluntary basis) is broken. The union played an active role in the distributive and the catering industrial training boards (both now abolished) and would like to see them restored. USDAW believes that these bodies performed a valuable strategic role in the planning and co-ordination of training which has now become fragmented and inadequate.

USDAW has been a strong campaigner against apartheid in South Africa and supported the 1988 TUC call for sanctions. USDAW has also taken a number of initiatives itself. Amongst others, it has withdrawn all its investments from firms who are trading in South Africa. It has contacted all major retailing companies in the UK urging them not to purchase or stock South African goods. A "Central Support Fund for South African Trade Unionists" has been established to enable USDAW to give financial backing to the victims of apartheid, and to this end a voluntary levy of all its membership to donate one hour's pay to the fund was organised. The policy adopted by the 1987 TUC in support of South African trade unionists, and which called for a levy of all trade union members, was in fact moved by USDAW.

Other key policies which USDAW supports include the closing of all nuclear power stations, and the strengthening of health and safety legislation, particularly in seeking ways of establishing suitable minimum standards for protective clothing, and in relation to the health hazards of VDUs. USDAW has many members who work with the latest Electronic Point of Sale systems (EPOS). USDAW has recently adopted a "green" dimension and is pressing the government to protect the environment by banning dangerous pesticides and chemicals as well as calling for legislation to reduce or ban the use of the chemical group Chlorofluorocarbons in aerosols to protect the ozone layer. USDAW supported a motion put forward by COHSE to improve the care afforded to AIDS sufferers, and itself has published *USDAW and AIDS*.

USDAW does not appear to have any specific policies regarding 1992, but its position is perhaps best reflected in a speech given by the General Secretary, Garfield Davies, in his address on behalf of Euro-FIET (the European section of the International Federation of Commercial, Clerical, Professional, and Technical Employees), at the centenary conference of the UGT (the Spanish equivalent of the TUC). His speech made it quite clear that 1992 should be viewed not just from an economic viewpoint alone but that social criteria had to be realised before the European initiative could be judged a success. He singled out the guarantee of social and employment rights along with the extension of trade union freedoms. Further aspects were the extension of industrial democracy, and social policies to reduce social inequality and to redress regional unemployment and imbalance.

The union set up a working party which examined new technology in retailing, in mail order, and in manufacturing industries. A new technology pack was produced as a guide for negotiators, shop stewards, and safety representatives, to help them cope with the introduction of new technology at a particular work-place. An extensive training programme has been carried out. New technology agreements are signed regularly with employers, and where necessary the union's own Productivity Services Department and Health and Safety Officer give technical assistance to deal with practical problems and opportunities for sharing the benefits of new technology.

In line with the TUC and other unions USDAW has set up a race relations committee. The union is proud of the fact that half of its committee members are black. One of the first tasks of the committee was to produce a Black Workers' Charter, and the committee is currently addressing how it can attract more black members to take on responsibilities within the union and stand for elected office. The committee is also examining ways of bringing problems of racial discrimination out into the open and encourage black members to bring their specific problems to the union's attention. The union's education officer is the co-ordinating official of this committee and a programme of racial equality training is being developed.

In practice much of USDAW's ethnic minority membership is concentrated in factories and warehouses where black members frequently serve as branch officers and shop stewards. Although in retailing (apart from ethnic family businesses), the proportion of black workers is generally below their proportions in the local community, a number of black branch officers have been elected and they, like their colleagues in industrial branches, are playing an increasing role in divisional and national activities.

Recent events

The union's 1989 Annual Conference expressed concern about schemes which could lead to employers taking disciplinary action as a result of problems over the implementation of customer care schemes which are becoming common amongst the major retailers. Delegates also passed resolutions urging standard working patterns to be maintained, although there were calls from women workers to be given the right to take unpaid leave in school holidays. Currently, retail workers are facing mounting pressure from employers to accept split shift systems, annualised hours, and greater use of flexible and temporary workers. In expressing blanket opposition to these pressures from employers USDAW is failing to appreciate that some of these changes would actually benefit women workers.

Further references

Sir William Richardson, *A Union of Many Trades: The History of USDAW,* USDAW 1979. The official history of USDAW.

Eric Batstone, Stephen Gourlay, Hugo Levie, Roy Moore, *New Technology and the Process of Labour Regulation,* Clarendon Press, 1987. (Chapter 2 provides a interesting case-study of USDAW's involvement in the introduction of new technology at a chemical plant.)

S.L. Smith, "How Much Change in Store: The Impact of New Technologies on Managers and Staffs in Retail Distribution", in D. Knights and H. Willmott (eds.), *New Technology and the Labour Process,* Macmillan, 1987.

WRITERS' GUILD OF GREAT BRITAIN

TUC affiliated

Head Office: 430 Edgware Road, London W2 1EH

Telephone: 01-706 8074

Fax: 01-706 3414

Principal national officers
General Secretary: Walter J. Jeffrey
President: Maureen Duffy

Union journal: The Writers' Newsletter (sent to every member 10 times per annum)

Membership

Current membership (1987)
Male: 1,030
Female: 521
Total: 1,551

Membership trend
Total 1983: 1,349
Total 1979: 1,623
Total 1975: 1,233

General

The Guild is the trade union of practising writers of all disciplines except journalism, and its members are self-employed. The Guild has collective agreements with the major employers in television, film, radio, publishing, and theatre, including the BBC, the British Film and Television Producers' Association, the Independent Programme Producers' Association, the Royal Shakespeare Company, the National Theatre Company, the English Stage Company, as well as a number of leading publishers. All agreements are negotiated nationally but are not all industry-wide. The Guild has for some time had a close working relationship with both the Musicians' Union and the actors' Equity, and is keen to establish closer contacts with the NUJ.

History

The Guild came into existence in 1959 when the *Screenwriters' Guild* joined forces with television and radio writers. It has steadily increased its membership and its sphere of activity, opening its doors to book writers in 1974.

Organisation

The General Secretary is the only full-time officer and there are no branch or regional offices. Entrusted with the government of the Guild is the Executive Council which meets monthly. It is composed of 30 members: the chair and two deputies, an honorary treasurer, five regional chairs and 21 councillors, 15 of whom have full membership credits on film, television, or radio and six of whom have full membership credits in books, stage plays, or other published works. All members of the EC are elected by postal ballot. There are regional committees representing Scotland, Wales, the North, and West of England.

External relations

The Guild has no political affiliations; indeed this is expressly precluded by its constitution.

Recent events

The Guild has recently signed an agreement with the British Film and Television Producers' Association and the Independent Programme Producers' Association, which for the first time provides an industrial agreement covering both independent television productions as well as independent film productions.

WWU
WIRE WORKERS' UNION

(Formerly the *Amalgamated Society of Wire Drawers and Kindred Workers*)

TUC affiliated

Head Office: Prospect House, Alma Street, Sheffield S3 8SA

Telephone: 0742-21674

Principal national officers
General Secretary: Matt Ardron
General Treasurer: M. Thornton
National Organiser: E.B. Lynch

Union journal: None

Membership

Current membership (1987)
Male: 4,736
Female: 367
Total: 5,103

Membership trends
1983: 5,183
1979: 9,770
1975: 10,399

General
The union, previously known as the *Amalgamated Society of Wire Drawers and Kindred Workers,* changed its name in January 1986 to the Wire Workers' Union. It seeks to organise employees in the wire and wire rope industries as well as those employed by wire goods manufacturers. The membership of the union is centred mainly in the areas of Sheffield, Manchester, Birmingham, Warrington, Halifax, Ambergate, Cardiff, the North-East, as well as Scotland. National collective bargaining is conducted in the Wire and Wire Rope Industries JIC on which the union has five representatives, compared to one each for the TGWU and GMB.

History
The society from which the present union directly arose was founded in 1840 as a craft trade union for wire workers. An amalgamation with the *Fine Wire Drawers* took place in 1910, and in the early 1920s the society changed from being a craft trade union to an industrial union covering employees engaged in the manufacturing and processing of wire; in some cases extending from the manufacture of wire rods to the finished product made from wire.

Organisation
The supreme ruling body of the union is the Executive Council, composed of 15 members elected from the districts and branches of the union. The EC elects the President and Vice-President. The General Secretary of the union is elected for a term of

office laid down by the EC. There is an Annual Delegate Meeting of the union which convenes in June, although it serves only as a forum where issues affecting the society can be raised. Only the EC has the authority to declare official industrial action.

External relations
The union is not affiliated to any political party.

YAPLO
YORKSHIRE ASSOCIATION OF POWER LOOM OVERLOOKERS

TUC affiliated

Head Office: 20 Hallfield Road, Bradford BD1 3RQ

Telephone: 0274-727966

Principal officer
General Secretary: Tony Barrow

Membership

Current membership (1987)
Total: 561

Membership trends
1983: 643
1979: 1,130
1975: 1,377

CONFEDERATIONS OF UNIONS

General
General Federation of Trade Unions
Central House, Upper Woburn Place, London WC1H 0HY
Telephone: 01-387 2578, 388 0852, 388 9760

Peter Potts (General Secretary)
David Lambert (Chair of Management Committee)

Carpet and Textiles
National Affiliation of Carpet Trade Unions
Carpet Weavers' Hall, Callowes Lane, Kidderminster, Worcester DY10 2JG
Telephone: 0562 823192

Brian Moule (Secretary)

Northern Counties Textile Trades Federation
2A New Brown Street, Nelson, Lancashire BB9 7NY
Telephone: 0282 64613

Harry Howorth (Secretary)

Civil Service
Council of Civil Service Unions
58 Rochester Row, London SW1P 3JU
Telephone: 01-834 8393

Peter Jones (Secretary)

Engineering and Shipbuilding
Confederation of Shipbuilding and Engineering Unions
140-142 Walworth Road, London SE17 1JW
Telephone: 01-703 2215

Alex Ferry MBE (General Secretary)
Jack McNaught (Executive Officer)

Entertainment and Broadcasting
Confederation of Entertainment Unions
60-62 Clapham Road, London SW9 0JJ
Telephone: 01-582 5566

Alan Sapper (President)
John Morton (Secretary)

Federation of Broadcasting Unions
181-185 Wardour Street, London W1V 3AA
Telephone: 01-439 7585

John Morton (Chair)
Paddy Leech (Secretary)

Federation of Film Unions
111 Wardour Street, London W1V 4AY
Telephone: 01-437 8506

Tony Hearn (President)
Alan Sapper (Secretary)

Federation of Theatre Unions
181-185 Wardour Street, London W1V 3AA
Telephone: 01-439 7585

Peter Plouviez (Chair)
Tony Hearn (Secretary)

Furniture
National Federation of Furniture Trade Unions
"Fairfields", Roe Green, Kingsbury, London NW9 0PT
Telephone: 01-204 0273

Colin Christopher (General Secretary)

Insurance and Banking
Confederation of Insurance Trade Unions
27 Old Gloucester Street, London WC1N 3AS
Telephone: 01-405 6798

Ken Rose (Chair)
Bob Main (Secretary)

Post Office
Post Office Unions' Council
(Post Office and National Giro Bank)
Room 213, Alder House, 1 Aldersgate Street, London EC1A 1AL
Telephone: 01-606 6486

John Griffiths (Secretary)

Telecommunications
British Telecommunications Union Committee
(British Telecommunications)
14-15 Bridgewater Square, London EC2Y 8BS
Telephone: 01-628 4914

Alan Chamberlain (Secretary)

INDEX

This index includes names of all trade unions in the directory, including confederations of unions, both in full and by acronym, together with the names of the principal office holder(s) in each union.